PHILOSOPHIES
OF ART AND BEAUTY

Philosophies
of
ART and BEAUTY

SELECTED READINGS IN AESTHETICS
FROM PLATO TO HEIDEGGER

Edited by
ALBERT HOFSTADTER
and
RICHARD KUHNS

The University of Chicago Press

In this edition a later, revised translation, by Albert Hofstadter, of Heidegger's essay "The Origin of the Work of Art" has been substituted for the translation used in the original edition.

The University of Chicago Press, Chicago 60637
The University of Chicago Press, Ltd., London

Published 1964. Phoenix Edition 1976
Printed in the United States of America
International Standard Book Number: 0-226-34812-1

ACKNOWLEDGMENTS

The editors wish to thank the following for permission to reprint material included in this anthology:

CAMBRIDGE UNIVERSITY PRESS—for selection from *Second Characters*, by the Earl of Shaftesbury, edited by Benjamin Rand.

COSMOPOLITAN SCIENCE AND ART SERVICE CO., INC., and THE EXECUTORS OF THE ESTATE OF DR. LUDWIG SCHOPP—for selection from *De Ordine*, by St. Augustine, translated by Robert P. Russell.

ENCYCLOPÆDIA BRITANNICA—for "Aesthetics," by Benedetto Croce.

THE EXECUTORS OF THE ESTATE OF C. K. OGDEN and W. F. JACKSON KNIGHT—for selection from De Musica, by St. Augustine, translated by W. F. Jackson Knight.

FABER AND FABER LTD.—for selection from *The Enneads*, by Plotinus, translated by Stephen MacKenna.

HARPER & ROW, PUBLISHERS, INC.—for Albert Hofstadter's translation of Martin Heidegger's "The Origin of the Work of Art," originally published in Heidegger's *Poetry, Language, Thought*, © 1971 by Harper & Row.

G. P. PUTNAM'S SONS—For selection from *Art as Experience*, by John Dewey. Copyright, 1934, by John Dewey. Published by Minton, Balch & Co.

RANDOM HOUSE, INC.—for selection from *The Birth of Tragedy*, by Friedrich Nietzsche, translated by Clifton P. Fadiman, in *The Philosophy of Nietzsche*. Copyright, 1927, and renewed, 1954, by Random House, Inc.

UNIVERSITY OF MISSOURI PRESS—for selection from *Commentary on Plato's "Symposium,"* by Marsilio Ficino, translated by Sears Reynolds Jayne.

THE CLARENDON PRESS, OXFORD—for selections from *Aristotle's Works*, edited by W. D. Ross—and for selections from *The Works of Plato*, translated by Benjamin Jowett.

PREFACE

The philosophy of art constitutes one of the recurrent concerns of Western philosophy. Nevertheless, what a philosopher has to say about art, the way he uses art in his exploration of the human situation, the lessons he draws from art in learning about reality—all this is often neglected for the more traditional topics of metaphysics and epistemology. In order to illustrate the relevance of art to philosophy, as well as of philosophy to art, we have brought together the writings of a number of philosophers. In every case we have let them speak at length, for philosophies of art cannot be stated briefly. They draw their strength not only from philosophical inquiry, but also from research into the arts themselves.

The demands of space made by each writer have limited the number that could be included. Yet we have, we believe, for all our selectiveness, included the best. Obviously some inclusions and exclusions are a function of our personal preferences and tastes; that is unavoidable. Because we have not tried to be chronologically complete or systematically thorough there are chronological gaps, such as that between Augustine and Ficino, and there are positions unrepresented, such as those of Thomas Aquinas, Marx, Freud, and Jung. The gaps occur because there are periods in Western thought in which the philosophy of art was of little interest to philosophers. The omission of certain positions is harder to justify, but we found as we examined the literature that there are some positions without able defenders. There are other positions which, to be represented, would have to be synthesized out of bits and fragments. We have taken it as a principle that where sustained argument could be found it was preferable to aphorisms and vague, incomplete statement. The psychological writings, though fruitful, do not present a truly philosophical position.

It may also seem surprising that no French philosopher is included. We considered Batteux, Boileau, Dubos, Diderot, Alain, Bergson, Sartre, and others. But in every case we concluded that what we found was not a philosophy of art, in the fullest sense, but either criticism, or theory of taste, or at most fragments of a philosophy. The philosophers we have chosen are thinkers who have taken the problems of art and beauty as central to the elaboration of their philosophies. Together they show us the power and insight of which philosophy of art is capable. We have tried to present them in as full a form as a collection of this kind permits. Though we have been forced to omit passages within all except one or two of the essays, the abridgments are in the service of clarity, and do not, we believe, exclude anything of importance for an understanding of the thought.

Our principle of selection, then, is simply greatness: these writings present the most profound and fruitful philosophies of art in the Western tradition.

CONTENTS

5-24
45-51
57-77
80-96
126-138
139-170

Contents / xi

INTRODUCTION

This anthology begins with Plato and concludes with Heidegger, a span of some 2,200 years. That it should begin with the most notorious inquiry into art of the classical world and end with a well-known contemporary existentialist would suggest that all of Western thought on art and beauty is included here. But it will be immediately evident, on consulting the table of contents, that the inclusions are few, and that the names, while mostly familiar, are but a small selection from a much larger company. While the philosophy of art and beauty is as old as philosophy and as new as the present, it has not always been a dominant philosophical interest. It comes to the forefront of philosophical thought, and then recedes, only to be brought forth once more as the leading theme. Through this collection we can see how it has been developed and transformed through the years, how it reflects the temper of an age and provides leading ideas for artists, critics, and the society that nurtures art. For philosophies of art and beauty are as various as the philosophies of human conduct, politics, science, history, and ultimate reality that have been the chief work of the human mind throughout our history.

Beyond our natural desire to understand the human activity of the making and enjoyment of art, there is a profound motive and primitive need behind philosophies of art. A powerful analogy immediately comes to men when they think about themselves and the universe they inhabit: the maker of the universe and the object he makes are like the human maker and his artifact. The order and harmony of the cosmos are like the beauty of art. Somehow man participates in the ordering of the universe in his power to make and to respond to art objects. Thus, early philosophies of art and beauty are intermixed with cosmological inquiries and it is only relatively late in the development of philosophy that the philosophy of art can be thought of as distinct from ontology and theology. The greatest philosophies of art, then, are part of broader inquiries into man and nature.

To a reader familiar with writings in aesthetics and the philosophy of art our selections may appear strangely overweighted in the direction of idealism and the high German metaphysics of the late eighteenth and early nineteenth centuries. There is good reason for this: our selections have to do with aesthetics as a branch of philosophy, not with criticism or the principles of criticism. In a philosophy of art, or in philosophical aesthetics, more generally speaking, beauty and art are understood in terms of essential philosophical ideas, while philosophy itself is taken to be at least in part constituted by aesthetic reflection. Thus the great philosophies of art have interpreted beauty and art in metaphysical terms as a natural expression of the belief that philosophy is born in the aspiration toward and understanding of the beautiful. As Croce has said, "from this character of aesthetics it follows that its history cannot be separated from that of philosophy at large, from which aesthetics receives light and guidance, and gives back light and guidance in its turn." However, not all philosophers and not all forms of philosophy give equal weight to aesthetics and the philosophy of art; hence the historically spotty and discontinuous character of the selections. For reasons that may become apparent, certain periods (for example, the eighteenth and nineteenth centuries) placed philosophy of art at the center of philosophical speculation.

The interest in the philosophy of beauty and art goes back to the very beginning of philosophy in Greece. Because of the tendency in classical Greek thought to interpret reality in terms drawn from life and human purposes, the genesis of objects through human or divine agents, as well as through natural processes, receives close attention. The metaphysical categories of both Plato and Aristotle were anchored in the realm of social reality, but the Platonic separation of the social and the ideal opened the way for the ultimately mystical speculations of Neoplatonism. There, too, the concept of beauty, as well as the associated concept of art, was of the first importance. In the philosophy of Plotinus beauty is given its most exalted transcendent development, while in Augustine it becomes the property of God's creation: Plotinian emanations are transformed into God's divine harmonies. Reality now is found to lie in the domain of mind and mind's ultimate activities and objects. Consequently, since art represents one of the deepest and most characteristic acts of the spirit, and since beauty represents one of its most deeply desired objects, it is natural to expect aesthetic considerations to play a central role in the thought of these late classical and early medieval philosophers.

With the development of medieval philosophy the aesthetic motivation is undiminished, but the analogies and problems shift from the constructive and metaphysical to the logical and theological. The essential ideas now are concerned with religious problems and the question of art becomes subsidiary, i.e., the artistic is chiefly an adornment for the temple of God. The beautiful retains its central position, but no longer in relation to art. Beauty now becomes a sign of God's handiwork. Thus both the Platonistic mysticism of Bonaventura and the Aristotelian realism of Aquinas are enclosed within the framework of theology: beauty is the mark (or achievement) of the well made, whether it be a universe or a candelabra, and the well made is an imitation of an idea in the mind of the Creator. Thus one of the central questions, raised by St. Augustine's uncertainty about the classical literary and philosophical contribution to the culture of our world, is finally resolved in showing that a justification can be given for human art and the human longing for the beautiful. That the answer was not always so reasonably given is shockingly demonstrated in the iconoclastic controversy. But in the West we have well learned the answer Aquinas worked out: all that man creates as art is valuable so long as it symbolizes truth, but truth can be gained through what pleases in sight because the beautiful inspires love and the aspiration of love is, if guided by faith, toward the truth. While the concept of faith has changed since Aquinas wrote, the assumption that art and truth are intimately related has remained. But Aquinas still treats the philosophy of art as essentially a theological issue.

This suppression of the philosophy of art and aesthetics for religious (theological) ends was lifted only by degrees. The first step toward the readmission of philosophical aesthetics to the central concern of philosophers was taken by the critical theories of the Renaissance. Only after the techniques of art making and the standards of decorum were explored, the rules laid down, and the purposes of artists articulated, could philosophers reassert the value of philosophical aesthetics as a way of exploring reality. And undoubtedly the revitalizing force of Platonic ideas helped to liberate art. The Renaissance sees a revival of Platonic (Platonistic) philosophizing about beauty which connects this period, especially in Italy, with the Plotinian and Augustinian of a far earlier time. Ficino's translations of the dialogues of Plato and the *Enneads* of Plotinus did much to make the scholarly world aware of how much Christian theology had deviated from classical philosophy. The aim of art is beauty; and beauty is itself a value of harmonious proportion, brought down from the cosmos to art. "Beauty," Alberti writes, "is a kind of harmony and concord of all the parts to form a whole which is constructed according to a fixed number, and a certain relation and order, as symmetry, the highest and most perfect law of nature, demands." But this kind of Neoplatonism had really been exhausted as a source for serious philosophical work. A philosophy of art and beauty requires a firm anchor in the energies of the organic realm. It is Shaftesbury, in England, who first joins traditional Neoplatonism to an organic and vitalistic interpretation of reality. It is probably no exaggeration to attribute to Shaftesbury the origin of all modern philosophies of art.

The curious historical contingency in the influence of Shaftesbury's work is that it realizes itself in Germany, but not in England. In England Shaftesbury's sense of beauty or aesthetic-sense theory was taken up by Francis Hutcheson, among others, without the philosophical Platonism; and the result is that aesthetics ceases to be a fundamental philosophical discipline for Hutcheson and for the English in general. This dissipation of philosophical aesthetics is most clearly seen in David Hume who, profoundly influenced by Hutcheson, is able to write only as a critic of criticism, not as a philosopher of art. In England the interest in aesthetics evolves toward a form of analytical, psychological theorizing about art. The attempt is made to determine lawful connections between the characteristics of aesthetic objects and human psychological dispositions. Consequently, English theorizing, as in the writing of Addison, Hutcheson, Hogarth, Gerard, Burke, Kames, and Alison, leads to a psychology of the aesthetic rather than to a philosophy of art. This development is of special interest to the more recent concern with aesthetic phenomenology. The only deviation from this tradition in England is found in the work of Collingwood, who derives his philosophy from Croce.

On the Continent, especially in Germany, Shaftesbury's writings had a profound effect. Shaftesbury's Neoplatonism, together with the Leibnizian interpretation of the universe in vitalistic and spiritualistic terms, provided the historical preconditions for the growth in Germany of aesthetics as a fundamental philosophical discipline.

In Germany the placing of art in the very center of philosophical concerns does not occur immediately. For Baumgarten, who wrote the first systematic treatise on aesthetics and indeed coined the term "aesthetics" from the Greek *aisthesis*, the study of aesthetics forms a lower-level counterpart to logic. It is in the writing of Kant that aesthetics first becomes in a certain way the central philosophical discipline. In his Introduction to *The Critique of Judgment* (not reproduced here) Kant makes it clear that the aesthetic doctrine of the "critique of aesthetical judgment" is meant to bridge the gap between, and thereby form into a whole, the disparate parts of philosophy given in *The Critique of Pure Reason* and *The Critique of Practical Reason*. Aesthetics becomes the bridge uniting theoretical and practical philosophy.

While the main drive of Kant's arguments is toward the clarification of beauty, genius, judgment, the sublime, the classification of the arts, and related problems, there is a recurrent hint that the beauty of nature and the beauty of art are expressive of an underlying spiritual reality. (See, e.g., par. 59, *Critique of Aesthetical Judgment*, below, page 339). It is in our experience of beauty that the congruence of nature and the moral will is realized for us, to such an extent that it becomes a meaningful postulate of reason to assert that man as a moral being inhabits a universe compatible with his spiritual longings.

This prepares the way for German absolute idealism in which reality is identified as mental or spiritual in essence, and in which aesthetics emerges clearly either as the supreme phase of philosophy or as a component of the supreme phase in Schelling's so-called aesthetic idealism. Here aesthetics is explicitly and exultantly treated as the keystone of the arch of philosophy, and art is viewed as the organon or peculiar instrument of the highest philosophical thinking. For Hegel, who learned much and borrowed heavily from Schelling, art becomes one of the three phases of Absolute Spirit, the first or immediate stage in which spirit ultimately achieves its own self-consciousness. From there spirit realizes itself in religion and philosophy. This celebration of art as revelatory of a spiritual reality and as itself the high point of human creative energy had a profound effect on what we call Romanticism. Indeed, Romanticism in art is the counterpart of absolute idealism in philosophy, and in it can be discovered, more directly than we realize, the setting of our own artistic values—but not of our own philosophy which has, at least in the Anglo-Saxon countries, become realistic, naturalistic, positivistic. Consequently, in England and the United States art has received a far lower rating from philosophy, and no longer provides material for central philosophical speculation. This diminished philosophical significance is due to the fact that naturalism demands that thought about art be subjected to the limitations of scientific method and verification. Political naturalism (such as socialist realism) demands that art become subject to a social critique. Positivism tends to see art as valuable only insofar as it is instrumental, utilitarian or expressive of noncognitive needs. Art therefore ceases to be revelatory of reality; consequently it loses philosophical dignity. One form of naturalism, however, that does try to do justice to the claims of the human spirit, philosophically speaking, is that of men like Dewey, Santayana and Whitehead. Recent critical naturalism of this kind does not argue, as idealism did, that reality as a whole is ultimately spiritual, but sees art as one of the loftiest strata of the human spirit, which itself stands at the height of reality. Modern naturalism of this kind has thus resuscitated the artistic, giving it special philosophical status.

There was a later development in German philosophy which also gave a central place to art, namely the voluntarism of Schopenhauer and Nietzsche. What they had to offer was never fully exploited in the United States and England, but has been developed in Germany, in the philosophy of life of Dilthey and more recently in the existentialism of Heidegger. For Heidegger human existence is both the introduction and the key to the study of ontology in general. Consequently, art is for him one of the main avenues to the nature of being. Art is one of the ways in which truth is revealed, a Heideggerian view that parallels Schelling's view into the fact that art is one of the keys to philosophical understanding.

The immediate philosophic scene reveals a number of fresh and possibly significant contributions to the philosophy of art. Analytic philosophy, a dominant philosophical mode in England and the United States, has begun to recognize aesthetic judgment and the aesthetic uses of language as important linguistic phenomena. Without aspiring to a complete philosophy of art—indeed, analytic philosophy rejects "philosophies of" as conscious aims of philosophic method—this recent movement recognizes the aesthetic use of language as demanding the same careful analysis that has been accorded the scientific and ethical uses of language. Whether this will culminate in a philosophy of art it is too early to say.

Analytic philosophers have drawn considerably from the formalist analyses of language that were common in the field of Slavic linguistics, from the New Critics in the United States and England, and from logicians whose interest lay in the syntactic structure of language. But none of these streams of thought has grown to the size and power that would make a philosophy of art possible.

Another contemporary development that has much to contribute toward a philosophy of art is psychoanalysis in both its Freudian and Jungian forms. Here there are accounts of how symbols are formed and how they function, of the psychology of creativity, and of the psychological mechanisms whereby art is produced and responded to.

Philosophy has yet to make use of the rich material that psychoanalysis offers. The psychoanalytic theory of art cannot come into its own, philosophically, until philosophy fully exploits the psychoanalytic notions of art and artist.

Both analytic philosophy and psychoanalysis fail to consider art in its cultural-historical development. For this we must turn to the academic discipline of art history on the one hand, and the inheritors of the Hegelian tradition on the other. Marxist and socio-economic critiques of art are no longer interested in art as a spiritual manifestation in Hegel's sense, but they are interested in art as a manifestation of ideology. Art expresses the dominant class interests of the period in which it is produced. Marxist analyses of art are therefore directed toward the interpretation of art objects, and the molding of art production to accord with the social beliefs of a ruling group. On matters of interpretation (itself a problem of major philosophical import) Marxist philosophy of art raises the same question of method raised by the psychoanalytic and the art-historical: how is one mode of interpretation to be justified as against another? Here the discipline of art history, initially uncommitted on matters of principles of interpretation, has a great deal to offer philosophies of art. Art history tries to relate art products to the culture as an expression and manifestation of its fundamental aspirations and interpretations of experience. Yet since Hegel's philosophy of art there has been little realized in this rich field. Starts have been made by Dilthey, Mannheim, Riegl, Panofsky, etc., but no philosophy of art history has yet emerged. Perhaps our age, so eclectic and piecemeal in its approach to problems of cultural interpretation, is not the one in which to look for a complete philosophical system. In any case, we can today look forward to renewed efforts to develop a philosophical aesthetics, to use art to throw light on philosophical problems, and to conceive philosophy as a way of understanding the nature of art and its place in human life.

PHILOSOPHIES
OF ART AND BEAUTY

PLATO

Plato, the greatest literary artist among philosophers, is the founder of philosophical aesthetics. In his dialogues the central problems of philosophy of art are set out, explored, and resolved according to a metaphysics that has had the most profound influence on Western thought. Plato's writings are not systematic, and there is much in them that is tentative and suggestive, yet they are full of wonderful insights, and when taken as a whole, a clear philosophy of beauty and art emerges from them.

The selections here emphasize four themes: 1) the generic idea of art, techne, whose principle is measure; 2) the special concept of imitative art, mimesis, its aim and its deficiencies; 3) the concept of poetic inspiration, enthusiasm, or madness, or mania, as a necessary condition for poetic creativity; 4) the concept of erotic madness and its connection with the vision of Beauty. The extent to which these themes can be integrated is a conclusion the reader must draw for himself.

1) Art, conceived generally as techne, presupposes a knowing and a making: knowing the end to be aimed at and the best means for achieving the end. When a maker commands his art he can judge the excellence of his product according to his insight into proportion and measure. Fundamentally, then, the

artist must, if he is to work well, know the nature of Measure (metron, Philebus 64 e). Basic to any one art is the art of measure without which there can be no art at all. For to know the proper length of a speech, the proper proportion of a painting, the proper distribution of functions in a society, the proper organization of language in a poem, is to command the art of measurement. Measure for Plato embraces the principles of the good and the beautiful, and in our terms the principle of taste as well.

2) Among the arts, the highest is that of the divine maker (the Demiurgos) who composed the universe as an imitation of Ideas or unchanging Forms. Like him, the statesman, most exalted of human makers, envisages the human community according to the Ideas of justice, the good, courage, temperance, and the beautiful. Within the state the various arts are practiced likewise as imitations of an external order of existence but the literary artist or the plastic artist, unlike the Demiurgos and the statesman, may fail to know the ultimate reality and instead present the mere appearance of perceivable nature. Therefore his art comes under the critical purview of the ruling statesman who exercises his legislative art in controlling the production and use of what we today would call the fine arts. While Plato distrusts the writer of dramas and would deny him a chorus, he sees an important role for the other literary arts as long as they are controlled by the vision of education which the philosopher possesses. There must be true imitation (eikastike) and not false imitation (phantastike) as Plato says in the Sophist. The determination of what is fit and what is unfit imitation depends upon the moral ends of the polis.

3) Yet there is something in imitative art that is different from, and not reducible to, techne. The poet is inspired, a winged, holy thing, filled with the power of the divine, hence mad in a noble way far above ordinary knowledge and consciousness. It is this possession which enables him to achieve the authentically artistic that is more than techne. Conscious, rational intellect cannot reduce this to a rule, nor can the man who commands techne raise himself to the genuinely poetic without divine assistance. (Cf., Phaedrus 245; Ion, 533-5.)

4) This poetic madness is but one of four types of madness: prophetic, initiatory, poetic, and erotic (Phaedrus 244 and 265 ff.). Such madness relates men to the gods and to the beauty of the eternal realm they inhabit. The vision of the beautiful described in the Symposium is possible only through the erotic longing of the lover, who is driven by the needs of his soul to contemplate the unchanging form of beauty. Poetic madness relates the poet to his muse, erotic madness relates the individual to his special divinity with its special form of beauty. But there is also, Plato implies by his picture of Socrates, a philosophic madness without which the philosopher could never produce his special kind of imitation, the city of his vision, represented in the Republic. *In short, all making is a kind of imitation; all that the gods or men may create is the re-presentation of a vision in a material medium. Only the man who understands the fundamental principle of measure can judge which imitations are worthy, which debased. The arts of literature and painting are therefore properly subordinate to a generic principle of judgment, and the needs of the human community control the divine inspirations of art.*

THE ARTS AND MEASURE

A fundamental principle which defines art is "measure," by which Plato means the determination of appropriate relationships through knowledge of proportion and of the mean.

FROM *Statesman*
(283ᵇ-285ᵇ)

Stranger. Let us begin by considering the whole nature of excess and defect, and then we shall have a rational ground on which we may praise or blame too much length or too much shortness in discussions of this kind.

Young Socrates. Let us do so.

Str. The points on which I think that we ought to dwell are the following:—

Y. Soc. What?

Str. Length and shortness, excess and defect; with all of these the art of measurement is conversant.

Y. Soc. Yes.

Str. And the art of measurement has to be divided into two parts, with a view to our present purpose.

Y. Soc. Where would you make the division?

Str. As thus: I would make two parts, one having regard to the relativity of greatness and smallness to each other; and there is another, without which the existence of production would be impossible.

Y. Soc. What do you mean?

Str. Do you not think that it is only natural for the greater to be called greater with reference to the less alone, and the less less with reference to the greater alone?

Y. Soc. Yes.

Str. Well, but is there not also something exceeding and exceeded by the principle of the mean, both in speech and action, and is not this a reality, and the chief mark of difference between good and bad men?

Y. Soc. Plainly.

Str. Then we must suppose that the great and small exist and are discerned in both these ways, and not, as we were saying before, only relatively to one another, but there must also be another comparison of them with the mean or ideal standard; would you like to hear the reason why?

Y. Soc. Certainly.

284   *Str.* If we assume the greater to exist only in relation to the less, there will never be any comparison of either with the mean.

Y. Soc. True.

Str. And would not this doctrine be the ruin of all the arts and their creations; would not the art of the Statesman and the aforesaid art of weaving disappear? For all these arts are on the watch against excess and defect, not as unrealities, but as real evils, which occasion a difficulty in action; and the excellence of beauty of every work of art is due to this observance of measure.

Y. Soc. Certainly.

Str. But if the science of the Statesman disappears, the search for the royal science will be impossible.

Y. Soc. Very true.

Str. Well, then, as in the case of the Sophist we extorted the inference that not-being had an existence, because here was the point at which the argument eluded our grasp, so in this we must endeavour to show that the greater and less are not only to be measured with one another, but also have to do with the production of the mean; for if this is not admitted, neither a statesman nor any other man of action can be an undisputed master of his science.

Y. Soc. Yes, we must certainly do again what we did then.

Str. But this, Socrates, is a greater work than the other, of which we only too well remember the length. I think, however, that we may fairly assume something of this sort:—

Y. Soc. What?

Str. That we shall some day require this notion of a mean with a view to the demonstration of absolute truth; meanwhile, the argument that the very existence of the arts must be held to depend on the possibility of measuring more or less, not only with one another, but also with a view to the attainment of the mean, seems to afford a grand support and satisfactory proof of the doctrine which we are maintaining; for if there are arts, there is a standard of measure, and if there is a standard of measure, there are arts; but if either is wanting, there is neither.

Y. Soc. True; and what is the next step?

Str. The next step clearly is to divide the art of measurement into two parts, as we have said already, and to place in the one part all the arts which measure number, length, depth, breadth, swiftness with their opposites; and to have another part in which they are measured with the mean, and the fit, and the opportune, and the due, and with all those words, in short, which denote a mean or standard removed from the extremes.

Y. Soc. Here are two vast divisions, embracing two very different spheres.

Str. There are many accomplished men, Socrates, who say, believing themselves to speak wisely, that the art of measurement is universal, and has to do with all things. And this means what we are now saying; for all things which come within the province of art do certainly in some sense partake of measure. But these persons, because they are not accustomed to distinguish classes according to real forms, jumble together two widely different things, relation to one another, and to a standard, under the idea that they are the same, and also fall into the converse error of dividing other things not according to their real parts. Whereas the right way is, if a man has first seen the unity of things, to go on with the enquiry and not desist until he has found all the differences contained in it which form distinct classes; nor again should he be able to rest contented with the manifold diversities which are seen in a multitude of things until he has comprehended all of them that have any affinity within the bounds of one similarity and embraced them within the reality of a single kind. But we have said enough on this head, and also of excess and defect; we have only to bear

285

in mind that two divisions of the art of measurement have been discovered which are concerned with them, and not forget what they are.

. . . . .

IMITATIVE ART
Definition and Criticism

The famous passages in *The Republic* on art are addressed to the definition of imitation, its meaning and its inadequacy as a criterion. In the *Sophist* two kinds of imitation are distinguished. Two passages from the *Laws* help us to understand the competition between the poet and the philosopher, which Plato sees as an inevitable part of the confusion about imitation.

FROM *The Republic*
(376d-402c, with omissions; 595a-608b, with omissions)

BOOK II

(*Socrates, narrating his discussion with Adeimantus first and then Glaucon*)

Come then, and let us pass a leisure hour in story-telling, and our story shall be the education of our heroes.

By all means.

And what shall be their education? Can we find a better than the traditional sort?—and this has two divisions, gymnastic for the body, and music for the soul.

True.

Shall we begin education with music, and go on to gymnastic afterwards?

By all means.

And when you speak of music, do you include literature or not?

I do.

And literature may be either true or false?

Yes.

And the young should be trained in both kinds, and we begin 377
with the false?

I do not understand your meaning, he said.

You know, I said, that we begin by telling children stories which,
though not wholly destitute of truth, are in the main fictitious; and
these stories are told them when they are not of an age to learn
gymnastics.

Very true.

That was my meaning when I said that we must teach music
before gymnastics.

Quite right, he said.

You know also that the beginning is the most important part of
any work, especially in the case of a young and tender thing; for
that is the time at which the character is being formed and the desired impression is more readily taken.

Quite true.

And shall we just carelessly allow children to hear any casual
tales which may be devised by casual persons, and to receive into
their minds ideas for the most part the very opposite of those which
we should wish them to have when they are grown up?

We cannot.

Then the first thing will be to establish a censorship of the writers of fiction, and let the censors receive any tale of fiction which is
good, and reject the bad; and we will desire mothers and nurses to
tell their children the authorised ones only. Let them fashion the
mind with such tales, even more fondly than they mould the body
with their hands; but most of those which are now in use must be
discarded.

Of what tales are you speaking? he said.

You may find a model of the lesser in the greater, I said; for
they are necessarily of the same type, and there is the same spirit
in both of them.

Very likely, he replied; but I do not as yet know what you would
term the greater.

Those, I said, which are narrated by Homer and Hesiod, and the
rest of the poets, who have ever been the great story-tellers of mankind.

But which stories do you mean, he said; and what fault do you
find with them?

A fault which is most serious, I said; the fault of telling a lie,
and, what is more, a bad lie.

But when is this fault committed?

Whenever an erroneous representation is made of the nature of gods and heroes,—as when a painter paints a portrait not having the shadow of a likeness to the original.

Yes, he said, that sort of thing is certainly very blameable; but what are the stories which you mean?

First of all, I said, there was that greatest of all lies, in high places, which the poet told about Uranus, and which was a bad lie too,—I mean what Hesiod says that Uranus did, and how Cronus retaliated on him. The doings of Cronus, and the sufferings which in turn his son inflicted upon him, even if they were true, ought certainly not to be lightly told to young and thoughtless persons; if possible, they had better be buried in silence. But if there is an absolute necessity for their mention, a chosen few might hear them in a mystery, and they should sacrifice not a common [Eleusinian] pig, but some huge and unprocurable victim; and then the number of the hearers will be very few indeed.

Why, yes, said he, those stories are extremely objectionable.

Yes, Adeimantus, they are stories not to be repeated in our State; the young man should not be told that in committing the worst of crimes he is far from doing anything outrageous; and that even if he chastises his father when he does wrong, in whatever manner, he will only be following the example of the first and greatest among the gods.

I entirely agree with you, he said; in my opinion those stories are quite unfit to be repeated.

Neither, if we mean our future guardians to regard the habit of quarrelling among themselves as of all things the basest, should any word be said to them of the wars in heaven, and of the plots and fightings of the gods against one another, for they are not true. No, we shall never mention the battles of the giants, or let them be embroidered on garments; and we shall be silent about the innumerable other quarrels of gods and heroes with their friends and relatives. If they would only believe us we would tell them that quarrelling is unholy, and that never up to this time has there been any quarrel between citizens; this is what old men and old woman should begin by telling children; and when they grow up, the poets also should be told to compose for them in a similar spirit. But the narrative of Hephaestus binding Here his mother, or how on another occasion Zeus sent him flying for taking her part when she was being beaten, and all the battles of the gods in

Homer—these tales must not be admitted into our State, whether they are supposed to have an allegorical meaning or not. For a young person cannot judge what is allegorical and what is literal; anything that he receives into his mind at that age is likely to become indelible and unalterable; and therefore it is most important that the tales which the young first hear should be models of virtuous thoughts.

There you are right, he replied; but if any one asks where are such models to be found and of what tales are you speaking—how shall we answer him?

I said to him, You and I, Adeimantus, at this moment are not **379** poets, but founders of a State: now the founders of a State ought to know the general forms in which poets should cast their tales, and the limits which must be observed by them, but to make the tales is not their business.

Very true, he said; but what are these forms of theology which you mean?

Something of this kind, I replied:—God is always to be represented as he truly is, whatever be the sort of poetry, epic, lyric or tragic, in which the representation is given.

Right.

And is he not truly good? and must he not be represented as such?

Certainly.

And no good thing is hurtful?

No, indeed.

And that which is not hurtful hurts not?

Certainly not.

And that which hurts not does no evil?

No.

And can that which does no evil be a cause of evil?

Impossible.

And the good is advantageous?

Yes.

And therefore the cause of well-being?

Yes.

It follows therefore that the good is not the cause of all things, but of the good only?

Assuredly.

Then God, if he be good, is not the author of all things, as the many assert, but he is the cause of a few things only, and not of most things that occur to men. For few are the goods of human life, and many are the evils, and the good is to be attributed to God alone; of the evils the causes are to be sought elsewhere, and not in him.

That appears to me to be most true, he said.

Then we must not listen to Homer or to any other poet who is guilty of the folly of saying that two casks

> 'Lie at the threshold of Zeus, full of lots, one of good, the other of evil lots,'

and that he to whom Zeus gives a mixture of the two

> 'Sometimes meets with evil fortune, at other times with good;'

but that he to whom is given the cup of unmingled ill,

> 'Him wild hunger drives o'er the beauteous earth.'

And again—

> 'Zeus, who is the dispenser of good and evil to us.'

And if any one asserts that the violation of oaths and treaties, which was really the work of Pandarus, was brought about by Athene and Zeus, or that the strife and contention of the gods was instigated by Themis and Zeus, he shall not have our approval; neither will we allow our young men to hear the words of Aeschylus, that

380
> 'God plants guilt among men when he desires utterly to destroy a house.'

And if a poet writes of the sufferings of Niobe—the subject of the tragedy in which these iambic verses occur—or of the house of Pelops, or of the Trojan war or on any similar theme, either we must not permit him to say that these are the works of God, or if they are of God, he must devise some explanation of them such as we are seeking; he must say that God did what was just and right, and they were the better for being punished; but that those who are punished are miserable, and that God is the author of their misery—the poet is not to be permitted to say; though he may say that the wicked are miserable because they require to be punished, and are benefited by receiving punishment from God; but that God being good is the author of evil to any one is to be strenuously denied, and not to be said or sung or heard in verse or prose by any one whether old or young in any well-ordered common-wealth. Such a fiction is suicidal, ruinous, impious.

I agree with you, he replied, and am ready to give my assent to the law.

Let this then be one of our rules and principles concerning the gods, to which our poets and reciters will be expected to conform —that God is not the author of all things, but of good only.

. . . . .

And what do you think of a second principle? Shall I ask you whether God is a magician, and of a nature to appear insidiously now in one shape, and now in another—sometimes himself chang-ing and passing into many forms, sometimes deceiving us with the semblance of such transformations; or is he one and the same im-mutably fixed in his own proper image?

. . . . .

Well, but can you imagine that God will be willing to lie, whether in word or deed, or to put forth a phantom of himself?

I cannot say, he replied.

Do you not know, I said, that the true lie, if such an expression may be allowed, is hated of gods and men?

What do you mean? he said.

I mean that no one is willingly deceived in that which is the truest and highest part of himself, or about the truest and highest matters; there, above all, he is most afraid of a lie having posses-sion of him.

Still, he said, I do not comprehend you.

The reason is, I replied, that you attribute some profound mean-ing to my words; but I am only saying that deception, or being de-ceived or uninformed about the highest realities in the highest part of themselves, which is the soul, and in that part of them to have and to hold the lie, is what mankind least like;—that, I say, is what they utterly detest.

There is nothing more hateful to them.

And, as I was just now remarking, this ignorance in the soul of him who is deceived may be called the true lie; for the lie in words is only a kind of imitation and shadowy image of a previous affec-tion of the soul, not pure unadulterated falsehood. Am I not right?

Perfectly right.

The true lie is hated not only by the gods, but also by men?

382

Yes.

Whereas the lie in words is in certain cases useful and not hateful; in dealing with enemies—that would be an instance; or again, when those whom we call our friends in a fit of madness or illusion are going to do some harm, then it is useful and is a sort of medicine or preventive; also in the tales of mythology, of which we were just now speaking—because we do not know the truth about ancient times, we make falsehood as much like truth as we can, and so turn it to account.

Very true, he said.

But can any of these reasons apply to God? Can we suppose that he is ignorant of antiquity, and therefore has recourse to invention?

That would be ridiculous, he said.

Then the lying poet has no place in our idea of God?

I should say not.

Or perhaps he may tell a lie because he is afraid of enemies?

That is inconceivable.

But he may have friends who are senseless or mad?

But no mad or senseless person can be a friend of God.

Then no motive can be imagined why God should lie?

None whatever.

Then the superhuman and divine is absolutely incapable of falsehood?

Yes.

Then is God perfectly simple and true both in word and deed; he changes not; he deceives not, either by sign or word, by dream or waking vision.

383 Your thoughts, he said, are the reflection of my own.

You agree with me then, I said, that this is the second type or form in which we should write and speak about divine things. The gods are not magicians who transform themselves, neither do they deceive mankind in any way.

· · · · ·

BOOK III

Such then, I said, are our principles of theology—some tales are to
386 be told, and others are not to be told to our disciples from their youth upwards, if we mean them to honour the gods and their parents, and to value friendship with one another.

Yes; and I think that our principles are right, he said.

But if they are to be courageous, must they not learn other lessons besides these, and lessons of such a kind as will take away the fear of death? Can any man be courageous who has the fear of death in him?

Certainly not, he said.

And can he be fearless of death, or will he choose death in battle rather than defeat and slavery, who believes the world below to be real and terrible?

Impossible.

Then we must assume a control over the narrators of this class of tales as well as over the others, and beg them not simply to revile, but rather to commend the world below, intimating to them that their descriptions are untrue, and will do harm to our future warriors.

That will be our duty, he said.

. . . . .

Also we shall have to reject all the terrible and appalling names which describe the world below—Cocytus and Styx, ghosts under the earth, and sapless shades, and any similar words of which the very mention causes a shudder to pass through the inmost soul of him who hears them. I do not say that these horrible stories may not have a use of some kind; but there is a danger that the nerves of our guardians may be rendered too excitable and effeminate by them.

There is a real danger, he said.

Then we must have no more of them.

True.

Another and a nobler strain must be composed and sung by us.

Clearly.

And shall we proceed to get rid of the weepings and wailings of famous men?

They will go with the rest.

But shall we be right in getting rid of them? Reflect: our principle is that the good man will not consider death terrible to any other good man who is his comrade.

Yes; that is our principle.

And therefore he will not sorrow for his departed friend as though he had suffered anything terrible?

He will not.

Such an one, as we further maintain, is sufficient for himself and his own happiness, and therefore is least in need of other men.

True, he said.

And for this reason the loss of a son or brother, or the deprivation of fortune, is to him of all men least terrible.

Assuredly.

And therefore he will be least likely to lament, and will bear with the greatest equanimity any misfortune of this sort which may befall him.

Yes, he will feel such a misfortune far less than another.

Then we shall be right in getting rid of the lamentations of famous men, and making them over to women (and not even to 388 women who are good for anything), or to men of a baser sort, that those who are being educated by us to be the defenders of their country may scorn to do the like.

· · · · ·

For if, my sweet Adeimantus, our youth seriously listen to such unworthy representations of the gods, instead of laughing at them as they ought, hardly will any of them deem that he himself, being but a man, can be dishonoured by similar actions; neither will he rebuke any inclination which may arise in his mind to say and do the like. And instead of having any shame or self-control, he will be always whining and lamenting on slight occasions.

Yes, he said, that is most true.

Yes, I replied; but that surely is what ought not to be, as the argument has just proved to us; and by that proof we must abide until it is disproved by a better.

It ought not to be.

Neither ought our guardians to be given to laughter. For a fit of laughter which has been indulged to excess almost always produces a violent reaction.

So I believe.

Then persons of worth, even if only mortal men, must not be represented as overcome by laughter, and still less must such a representation of the gods be allowed.

389 Still less of the gods, as you say, he replied.

Then we shall not suffer such an expression to be used about the gods as that of Homer when he describes how

'Inextinguishable laughter arose among the blessed gods,
when they saw Hephaestus bustling about the mansion.'

On your views, we must not admit them.

On my views, if you like to father them on me; that we must not admit them is certain.

Again, truth should be highly valued; if, as we were saying, a lie is useless to the gods, and useful only as a medicine to men, then the use of such medicines should be restricted to physicians; private individuals have no business with them.

Clearly not, he said.

Then if any one at all is to have the privilege of lying, the rulers of the State should be the persons; and they, in their dealings either with enemies or with their own citizens, may be allowed to lie for the public good. But nobody else should meddle with anything of the kind; and although the rulers have this privilege, for a private man to lie to them in return is to be deemed a more heinous fault than for the patient or the pupil of a gymnasium not to speak the truth about his own bodily illnesses to the physician or to the trainer, or for a sailor not to tell the captain what is happening about the ship and the rest of the crew, and how things are going with himself or his fellow sailors.

. . . . .

But now that we are determining what classes of subjects are or 392 are not to be spoken of, let us see whether any have been omitted by us. The manner in which gods and demigods and heroes and the world below should be treated has been already laid down.

Very true.

And what shall we say about men? That is clearly the remaining portion of our subject.

Clearly so.

But we are not in a condition to answer this question at present, my friend.

Why not?

Because, if I am not mistaken, we shall have to say that about men poets and story-tellers are guilty of making the gravest misstatements when they tell us that wicked men are often happy, and the good miserable; and that injustice is profitable when undetected, but that justice is a man's own loss and another's gain— these things we shall forbid them to utter, and command them to sing and say the opposite.

To be sure we shall, he replied.

But if you admit that I am right in this, then I shall maintain that you have implied the principle for which we have been all along contending.

I grant the truth of your inference.

That such things are or are not to be said about men is a question which we cannot determine until we have discovered what justice is, and how naturally advantageous to the possessor, whether he seems to be just or not.

Most true, he said.

Enough of the subjects of poetry: let us now speak of the style; and when this has been considered, both matter and manner will have been completely treated.

I do not understand what you mean, said Adeimantus.

Then I must make you understand; and perhaps I may be more intelligible if I put the matter in this way. You are aware, I suppose, that all mythology and poetry is a narration of events, either past, present, or to come?

Certainly, he replied.

And narration may be either simple narration, or imitation, or a union of the two?

That again, he said, I do not quite understand.

I fear that I must be a ridiculous teacher when I have so much difficulty in making myself apprehended. Like a bad speaker, therefore, I will not take the whole of the subject, but will break a piece off in illustration of my meaning. You know the first lines of 393 the Iliad, in which the poet says that Chryses prayed Agamemnon to release his daughter, and that Agamemnon flew into a passion with him; whereupon Chryses, failing of his object, invoked the anger of the God against the Achaeans. Now as far as these lines,

> 'And he prayed all the Greeks, but especially the two sons
> of Atreus, the chiefs of the people,'

the poet is speaking in his own person; he never leads us to suppose that he is any one else. But in what follows he takes the person of Chryses, and then he does all that he can to make us believe that the speaker is not Homer, but the aged priest himself. And in this double form he has cast the entire narrative of the events which occurred at Troy and in Ithaca and throughout the Odyssey.

Yes.

And a narrative it remains both in the speeches which the poet recites from time to time and in the intermediate passages?

Quite true.

But when the poet speaks in the person of another, may we not say that he assimilates his style to that of the person who, as he informs you, is going to speak?

Certainly.

And this assimiliation of himself to another, either by the use of voice or gesture, is the imitation of the person whose character he assumes?

Of course.

Then in this case the narrative of the poet may be said to proceed by way of imitation?

Very true.

Or, if the poet everywhere appears and never conceals himself, then again the imitation is dropped, and his poetry becomes simple narration. However, in order that I may make my meaning quite clear, and that you may no more say, 'I don't understand,' I will show how the change might be effected. If Homer had said, "The priest came, having his daughter's ransom in his hands, supplicating the Achaeans, and above all the kings;' and then if, instead of speaking in the person of Chryses, he had continued in his own person, the words would have been, not imitation, but simple narration.

. . . . .

. . . Poetry and mythology are, in some cases, wholly imitative—instances of this are supplied by tragedy and comedy; there is likewise the opposite style, in which the poet is the only speaker—of this the dithyramb affords the best example; and the combination of both is found in epic, and in several other styles of poetry. Do I take you with me?

Yes, he said; I see now what you meant.

I will ask you to remember also what I began by saying, that we had done with the subject and might proceed to the style.

Yes, I remember.

In saying this, I intended to imply that we must come to an understanding about the mimetic art,—whether the poets, in narrating their stories, are to be allowed by us to imitate, and if so whether in whole or in part, and if the latter, in what parts; or should all imitation be prohibited?

You mean, I suspect, to ask whether tragedy and comedy shall be admitted into our State?

Yes, I said; but there may be more than this in question: I really do not know as yet, but whither the argument may blow, thither we go.

And go we will, he said.

Then, Adeimantus, let me ask you whether our guardians ought to be imitators; or rather, has not this question been decided by the rule already laid down that one man can only do one thing well, and not many; and that if he attempt many, he will altogether fail of gaining much reputation in any?

Certainly.

And this is equally true of imitation; no one man can imitate many things as well as he would imitate a single one?

He cannot.

395   Then the same person will hardly be able to play a serious part in life, and at the same time to be an imitator and imitate many other parts as well; for even when two species of imitation are nearly allied, the same persons cannot succeed in both, as, for example, the writers of tragedy and comedy—did you not just now call them imitations?

Yes, I did; and you are right in thinking that the same persons cannot succeed in both.

Any more than they can be rhapsodists and actors at once?

True.

Neither are comic and tragic actors the same; yet all these things are but imitations.

They are so.

And human nature, Adeimantus, appears to have been coined into yet smaller pieces, and to be as incapable of imitating many things well, as of performing well the actions of which the imitations are copies.

Quite true, he replied.

If then we adhere to our original notion and bear in mind that our guardians, setting aside every other business, are to dedicate themselves wholly to the maintenance of freedom in the State, making this their craft, and engaging in no work which does not bear on this end, they ought not to practise or imitate anything else; if they imitate at all, they should imitate from youth upward only those characters which are suitable to their profession—the courageous, temperate, holy, free, and the like; but they should not depict or be skilful at imitating any kind of illiberality or baseness, lest from imitation they should come to be what they imitate. Did you never observe how imitations, beginning in early youth and continuing far into life, at length grow into habits and become a second nature, affecting body, voice, and mind?

Yes, certainly, he said.

Then, I said, we will not allow those for whom we profess a care and of whom we say that they ought to be good men, to imitate a woman, whether young or old, quarrelling with her husband, or striving and vaunting against the gods in conceit of her happiness, or when she is in affliction, or sorrow, or weeping; and certainly not one who is in sickness, love, or labour.

Very right, he said.

Neither must they represent slaves, male or female, performing the offices of slaves?

They must not.

And surely not bad men, whether cowards or any others, who do the reverse of what we have just been prescribing, who scold or mock or revile one another in drink or out of drink, or who in any other manner sin against themselves and their neighbours in word or deed, as the manner of such is. Neither should they be trained 396 to imitate the action or speech of men or women who are mad or bad; for madness, like vice, is to be known but not to be practised or imitated.

Very true, he replied.

Neither may they imitate smiths or other artificers, or oarsmen, or boatswains, or the like?

How can they, he said, when they are not allowed to apply their minds to the callings of any of these?

Nor may they imitate the neighing of horses, the bellowing of bulls, the murmur of rivers and roll of the ocean, thunder, and all that sort of thing?

Nay, he said, if madness be forbidden, neither may they copy the behaviour of madmen.

You mean, I said, if I understand you aright, that there is one sort of narrative style which may be employed by a truly good man when he has anything to say, and that another sort will be used by a man of an opposite character and education.

And which are these two sorts? he asked.

Suppose, I answered, that a just and good man in the course of a narration comes on some saying or action of another good man,—I should imagine that he will like to personate him, and will not be ashamed of this sort of imitation: he will be most ready to play the part of the good man when he is acting firmly and wisely; in a less degree when he is overtaken by illness or love or drink, or has met with any other disaster. But when he comes to a character which is unworthy of him, he will not make a study of that; he will disdain such a person, and will assume his likeness, if at all, for a moment only when he is performing some good action; at other times he will be ashamed to play a part which he has never practised, nor will he like to fashion and frame himself after the baser models; he feels the employment of such an art, unless in jest, to be beneath him, and his mind revolts at it.

So I should expect, he replied.

Then he will adopt a mode of narration such as we have illustrated out of Homer, that is to say, his style will be both imitative and narrative; but there will be very little of the former, and a great deal of the latter. Do you agree?

Certainly, he said; that is the model which such a speaker must
397 necessarily take.

But there is another sort of character who will narrate anything, and, the worse he is, the more unscrupulous he will be; nothing will be too bad for him: and he will be ready to imitate anything, not as a joke, but in right good earnest, and before a large company. As I was just now saying, he will attempt to represent the roll of thunder, the noise of wind and hail, or the creaking of wheels, and pulleys, and the various sounds of flutes, pipes, trumpets, and all sorts of instruments: he will bark like a dog, bleat like a sheep, or crow like a cock; his entire art will consist in imitation of voice and gesture, and there will be very little narration.

That, he said, will be his mode of speaking.

These, then, are the two kinds of style?

Yes.

And you would agree with me in saying that one of them is simple and has but slight changes; and if the harmony and rhythm are also chosen for their simplicity, the result is that the speaker, if he speaks correctly, is always pretty much the same in style, and he will keep within the limits of a single harmony (for the changes are not great), and in like manner he will make use of nearly the same rhythm?

That is quite true, he said.

Whereas the other requires all sorts of harmonies and all sorts of rhythms, if the music and the style are to correspond, because the style has all sorts of changes.

That is also perfectly true, he replied.

And do not the two styles, or the mixture of the two, comprehend all poetry, and every form of expression in words? No one can say anything except in one or other of them or in both together.

They include all, he said.

And shall we receive into our State all the three styles, or one only of the two unmixed styles? or would you include the mixed?

I should prefer only to admit the pure imitator of virtue.

Yes, I said, Adeimantus; but the mixed style is also very charming: and indeed the pantomimic, which is the opposite of the one chosen by you, is the most popular style with children and their attendants, and with the world in general.

I do not deny it.

But I suppose you would argue that such a style is unsuitable to our State, in which human nature is not twofold or manifold, for one man plays one part only?

Yes; quite unsuitable.

And this is the reason why in our State, and in our State only, we shall find a shoemaker to be a shoemaker and not a pilot also, and a husbandman to be a husbandman and not a dicast also, and a soldier a soldier and not a trader also, and the same throughout?

True, he said.

And therefore when any one of these pantomimic gentlemen, 398 who are so clever that they can imitate anything, comes to us, and makes a proposal to exhibit himself and his poetry, we will fall down and worship him as a sweet and holy and wonderful being; but we must also inform him that in our State such as he are not permitted to exist; the law will not allow them. And so when we have anointed him with myrrh, and set a garland of wool upon his head, we shall send him away to another city. For we mean to employ for our souls' health the rougher and severer poet or storyteller, who will imitate the style of the virtuous only, and will follow those models which we prescribed at first when we began the education of our soldiers.

We certainly will, he said, if we have the power.

Then now, my friend, I said, that part of music or literary education which relates to the story or myth may be considered to be finished; for the matter and manner have both been discussed.

I think so too, he said.

Next in order will follow melody and song.

That is obvious.

Every one can see already what we ought to say about them, if we are to be consistent with ourselves.

I fear, said Glaucon, laughing, that the word 'every one' hardly includes me, for I cannot at the moment say what they should be; though I may guess.

At any rate you can tell that a song or ode has three parts—the words, the melody, and the rhythm; that degree of knowledge I may presuppose?

Yes, he said; so much as that you may.

And as for the words, there will surely be no difference between words which are and which are not set to music; both will conform to the same laws, and these have been already determined by us?

Yes.

And the melody and rhythm will depend upon the words?

Certainly.

We were saying, when we spoke of the subject-matter, that we had no need of lamentations and strains of sorrow?

True.

And which are the harmonies expressive of sorrow? You are musical, and can tell me.

The harmonies which you mean are the mixed or tenor Lydian, and the full-toned or bass Lydian, and such like.

These then, I said, must be banished; even to women who have a character to maintain they are of no use, and much less to men.

Certainly.

In the next place, drunkenness and softness and indolence are utterly unbecoming the character of our guardians.

Utterly unbecoming.

And which are the soft or drinking harmonies?

399   The Ionian, he replied, and the Lydian; they are termed 'relaxed.'

Well, and are these of any military use?

Quite the reverse, he replied; and if so the Dorian and the Phrygian are the only ones which you have left.

I answered: Of the harmonies I know nothing, but I want to have one warlike, to sound the note or accent which a brave man utters in the hour of danger and stern resolve, or when his cause is failing, and he is going to wounds or death or is overtaken by some other evil, and at every such crisis meets the blows of fortune with firm step and a determination to endure; and another to be used by him in times of peace and freedom of action, when there is no pressure of necessity, and he is seeking to persuade God by prayer, or man by instruction and admonition, or on the other hand, when he is expressing his willingness to yield to persuasion or entreaty or admonition, and which represents him when by prudent conduct he has attained his end, not carried away by his success, but acting moderately and wisely under the circumstances, and acquiescing in the event. These two harmonies I ask you to leave; the strain of necessity and the strain of freedom, the strain of the unfortunate and the strain of the fortunate, the strain of courage, and the strain of temperance; these, I say, leave.

And these, he replied, are the Dorian and Phrygian harmonies of which I was just now speaking.

Then, I said, if these and these only are to be used in our songs and melodies, we shall not want multiplicity of notes or a panharmonic scale?

I suppose not.

Then we shall not maintain the artificers of lyres with three corners and complex scales, or the makers of any other many-stringed curiously-harmonised instruments?

Certainly not.

But what do you say to flute-makers and flute-players? Would you admit them into our State when you reflect that in this composite use of harmony the flute is worse than all the stringed instruments put together; even the panharmonic music is only an imitation of the flute?

Clearly not.

There remain then only the lyre and the harp for use in the city, and the shepherds may have a pipe in the country.

That is surely the conclusion to be drawn from the argument.

The preferring of Apollo and his instruments to Marsyas and his instruments is not at all strange, I said.

Not at all, he replied.

And so, by the dog of Egypt, we have been unconsciously purging the State, which not long ago we termed luxurious.

And we have done wisely, he replied.

Then let us now finish the purgation, I said. Next in order to harmonies, rhythms will naturally follow, and they should be subject to the same rules, for we ought not to seek out complex systems of metre, or metres of every kind, but rather to discover what rhythms are the expressions of a courageous and harmonious life; and when we have found them, we shall adapt the foot and the melody to words having a like spirit, not the words to the foot and melody. To say what these rhythms are will be your duty—you must teach me them, as you have already taught me the harmonies.

But, indeed, he replied, I cannot tell you. I only know that there are some three principles of rhythm out of which metrical systems are framed, just as in sounds there are four notes out of which all the harmonies are composed; that is an observation which I have made. But of what sort of lives they are severally the imitations I am unable to say.

Then, I said, we must take Damon into our counsels; and he will tell us what rhythms are expressive of meanness, or insolence, or fury, or other unworthiness, and what are to be reserved for the expression of opposite feelings. And I think that I have an indistinct recollection of his mentioning a complex Cretic rhythm; also a dactylic or heroic, and he arranged them in some manner which I do not quite understand, making the rhythms equal in the rise and fall of the foot, long and short alternating; and, unless I am mistaken, he spoke of an iambic as well as of a trochaic rhythm, and assigned to them short and long quantities.[1] Also in some cases he appeared to praise or censure the movement of the foot quite as much as the rhythm; or perhaps a combination of the two; for I am not certain what he meant. These matters, however, as I was saying, had better be referred to Damon himself, for the analysis of the subject would be difficult, you know?

Rather so, I should say.

But there is no difficulty in seeing that grace or the absence of grace is an effect of good or bad rhythm.

None at all.

And also that good and bad rhythm naturally assimilate to a good and bad style; and that harmony and discord in like manner follow style; for our principle is that rhythm and harmony are regulated by the words, and not the words by them.

---

[1] Socrates expresses himself carelessly in accordance with his assumed ignorance of the details of the subject. In the first part of the sentence he appears to be speaking of paeonic rhythms which are in the ratio of 3/2; in the second part, of dactylic and anapaestic rhythms, which are in the ratio of 1/1; in the last clause, of iambic and trochaic rhythms, which are in the ratio of 1/2 or 2/1.

Just so, he said, they should follow the words.

And will not the words and the character of the style depend on the temper of the soul?

Yes.

And everything else on the style?

Yes.

Then beauty of style and harmony and grace and good rhythm depend on simplicity,—I mean the true simplicity of a rightly and nobly ordered mind and character, not that other simplicity which is only an euphemism for folly?

Very true, he replied.

And if our youth are to do their work in life, must they not make these graces and harmonies their perpetual aim?

They must.

And surely the art of the painter and every other creative and 401 constructive art are full of them,—weaving, embroidery, architecture, and every kind of manufacture; also nature, animal and vegetable,—in all of them there is grace or the absence of grace. And ugliness and discord and inharmonious motion are nearly allied to ill words and ill nature, as grace and harmony are the twin sisters of goodness and virtue and bear their likeness.

That is quite true, he said.

But shall our superintendence go no further, and are the poets only to be required by us to express the image of the good in their works, on pain, if they do anything else, of expulsion from our State? Or is the same control to be extended to other artists, and are they also to be prohibited from exhibiting the opposite forms of vice and intemperance and meanness and indecency in sculpture and building and the other creative arts; and is he who cannot conform to this rule of ours to be prevented from practising his art in our State, lest the taste of our citizens be corrupted by him? We would not have our guardians grow up amid images of moral deformity, as in some noxious pasture, and there browse and feed upon many a baneful herb and flower day by day, little by little, until they silently gather a festering mass of corruption in their own soul. Let our artists rather be those who are gifted to discern the true nature of the beautiful and graceful; then will our youth dwell in a land of health, amid fair sights and sounds, and receive the good in everything; and beauty, the effluence of fair works, shall flow into the eye and ear, like a health-giving breeze from a purer region, and insensibly draw the soul from earliest years into likeness and sympathy with the beauty of reason.

There can be no nobler training than that, he replied.

And therefore, I said, Glaucon, musical training is a more potent instrument than any other, because rhythm and harmony find their way into the inward places of the soul, on which they mightily fasten, imparting grace, and making the soul of him who is rightly educated graceful, or of him who is ill-educated ungraceful; and also because he who has received this true education of the inner being will most shrewdly perceive omissions or faults in art and nature, and with a true taste, while he praises and rejoices over and receives into his soul the good, and becomes noble and good, he will justly blame and hate the bad, now in the days of his youth, even before he is able to know the reason why; and when reason comes he will recognise and salute the friend with whom his education has made him long familiar.

Yes, he said, I quite agree with you in thinking that our youth should be trained in music and on the grounds which you mention.

Just as in learning to read, I said, we were satisfied when we knew the letters of the alphabet, which are very few, in all their recurring sizes and combinations; not slighting them as unimportant whether they occupy a space large or small, but everywhere eager to make them out; and not thinking ourselves perfect in the art of reading until we recognise them wherever they are found:

True—

Or, as we recognise the reflection of letters in the water, or in a mirror, only when we know the letters themselves; the same art and study giving us the knowledge of both:

Exactly—

Even so, as I maintain, neither we nor our guardians, whom we have to educate, can ever become musical until we and they know the essential forms, in all their combinations, and can recognise them and their images wherever they are found, not slighting them either in small things or great, but believing them all to be within the sphere of one art and study.

Most assuredly.

And when a beautiful soul harmonises with a beautiful form, and the two are cast in one mould, that will be the fairest of sights to him who has an eye to see it?

The fairest indeed.

And the fairest is also the loveliest?

That may be assumed.

And the man who has the spirit of harmony will be most in love with the loveliest; but he will not love him who is of an inharmonious soul?

That is true, he replied, if the deficiency be in his soul; but if there be any merely bodily defect in another he will be patient of it, and will love all the same.

I perceive, I said, that you have or have had experiences of this sort, and I agree. But let me ask you another question: Has excess of pleasure any affinity to temperance?

How can that be? he replied; pleasure deprives a man of the use of his faculties quite as much as pain.

Or any affinity to virtue in general?

None whatever.   403

Any affinity to wantonness and intemperance?

Yes, the greatest.

And is there any greater or keener pleasure than that of sensual love?

No, nor a madder.

Whereas true love is a love of beauty and order—temperate and harmonious?

Quite true, he said.

Then no intemperance or madness should be allowed to approach true love?

Certainly not.

Then mad or intemperate pleasure must never be allowed to come near the lover and his beloved; neither of them can have any part in it if their love is of the right sort?

No, indeed, Socrates, it must never come near them.

Then I suppose that in the city which we are founding you would make a law to the effect that a friend should use no other familiarity to his love than a father would use to his son, and then only for a noble purpose, and he must first have the other's consent; and this rule is to limit him in all his intercourse, and he is never to be seen going further, or, if he exceeds, he is to be deemed guilty of coarseness and bad taste.

I quite agree, he said.

Thus much of music, which makes a fair ending; for what should be the end of music if not the love of beauty?

I agree, he said.

· · · · ·

BOOK X

595 Of the many excellences which I perceive in the order of our State, there is none which upon reflection pleases me better than the rule about poetry.

To what do you refer?

To the rejection of imitative poetry, which certainly ought not to be received; as I see far more clearly now that the parts of the soul have been distinguished.

What do you mean?

Speaking in confidence, for I should not like to have my words repeated to the tragedians and the rest of the imitative tribe—but I do not mind saying to you, that all poetical imitations are ruinous to the understanding of the hearers, and that the knowledge of their true nature is the only antidote to them.

Explain the purport of your remark.

Well, I will tell you, although I have always from my earliest youth had an awe and love of Homer, which even now makes the words falter on my lips, for he is the great captain and teacher of the whole of that charming tragic company; but a man is not to be reverenced more than the truth, and therefore I will speak out.

Very good, he said.

Listen to me then, or rather, answer me.

Put your question.

Can you tell me what imitation is? for I really do not know.

A likely thing, then, that I should know.

596 Why not? for the duller eye may often see a thing sooner than the keener.

Very true, he said; but in your presence, even if I had any faint notion, I could not muster courage to utter it. Will you enquire yourself?

Well then, shall we begin the enquiry in our usual manner: Whenever a number of individuals have a common name, we assume them to have also a corresponding idea or form:—do you understand me?

I do.

Let us take any common instance; there are beds and tables in the world—plenty of them, are there not?

Yes.

But there are only two ideas or forms of them—one the idea of a bed, the other of a table.

True.

And the maker of either of them makes a bed or he makes a table for our use, in accordance with the idea—that is our way of speaking in this and similar instances—but no artificer makes the ideas themselves: how could he?

Impossible.

And there is another artist,—I should like to know what you would say of him.

Who is he?

One who is the maker of all the works of all other workmen.

What an extraordinary man!

Wait a little, and there will be more reason for your saying so. For this is he who is able to make not only vessels of every kind, but plants and animals, himself and all other things—the earth and heaven, and the things which are in heaven or under the earth; he makes the gods also.

He must be a wizard and no mistake.

Oh! you are incredulous, are you? Do you mean that there is no such maker or creator, or that in one sense there might be a maker of all these things but in another not? Do you see that there is a way in which you could make them all yourself?

What way?

An easy way enough; or rather, there are many ways in which the feat might be quickly and easily accomplished, none quicker than that of turning a mirror round and round—you would soon enough make the sun and the heavens, and the earth and yourself, and other animals and plants, and all the other things of which we were just now speaking, in the mirror.

Yes, he said; but they would be appearances only.

Very good, I said, you are coming to the point now. And the painter too is, as I conceive, just such another—a creator of appearances, is he not?

Of course.

But then I suppose you will say that what he creates is untrue. And yet there is a sense in which the painter also creates a bed?

Yes, he said, but not a real bed.

And what of the maker of the bed? were you not saying that he 597 too makes, not the idea which, according to our view, is the essence of the bed, but only a particular bed?

Yes, I did.

Then if he does not make that which exists he cannot make true existence, but only some semblance of existence; and if any one were to say that the work of the maker of the bed, or of any other workman, has real existence, he could hardly be supposed to be speaking the truth.

At any rate, he replied, philosophers would say that he was not speaking the truth.

No wonder, then, that his work too is an indistinct expression of truth.

No wonder.

Suppose now that by the light of the examples just offered we enquire who this imitator is?

If you please.

Well then, here are three beds: one existing in nature, which is made by God, as I think that we may say—for no one else can be the maker?

No.

There is another which is the work of the carpenter?

Yes.

And the work of the painter is a third?

Yes.

Beds, then, are of three kinds, and there are three artists who superintend them: God, the maker of the bed, and the painter?

Yes, there are three of them.

God, whether from choice or from necessity, made one bed in nature and one only; two or more such ideal beds neither ever have been nor ever will be made by God.

Why is that?

Because even if He had made but two, a third would still appear behind them which both of them would have for their idea, and that would be the ideal bed and not the two others.

Very true, he said.

God knew this, and He desired to be the real maker of a real bed, not a particular maker of a particular bed; and therefore He created a bed which is essentially and by nature one only.

So we believe.

Shall we, then, speak of Him as the natural author or maker of the bed?

Yes, he replied; inasmuch as by the natural process of creation He is the author of this and of all other things.

And what shall we say of the carpenter—is not he also the maker of the bed?

Yes.

But would you call the painter a creator and maker?

Certainly not.

Yet if he is not the maker, what is he in relation to the bed?

I think, he said, that we may fairly designate him as the imitator of that which the others make.

Good, I said; then you call him who is third in the descent from nature an imitator?

Certainly, he said.

And the tragic poet is an imitator, and therefore, like all other imitators, he is thrice removed from the king and from the truth?

That appears to be so.

Then about the imitator we are agreed. And what about the painter?—I would like to know whether he may be thought to imitate that which originally exists in nature, or only the creations of artists? 598

The latter.

As they are or as they appear? you have still to determine this.

What do you mean?

I mean, that you may look at a bed from different points of view, obliquely or directly or from any other point of view, and the bed will appear different, but there is no difference in reality. And the same of all things.

Yes, he said, the difference is only apparent.

Now let me ask you another question: Which is the art of painting designed to be—an imitation of things as they are, or as they appear—of appearance or of reality?

Of appearance.

Then the imitator, I said, is a long way off the truth, and can do all things because he lightly touches on a small part of them, and that part an image. For example: A painter will paint a cobbler, carpenter, or any other artist, though he knows nothing of their arts; and, if he is a good artist, he may deceive children or simple persons, when he shows them his picture of a carpenter from a distance, and they will fancy that they are looking at a real carpenter.

Certainly.

And whenever any one informs us that he has found a man who knows all the arts, and all things else that anybody knows, and every single thing with a higher degree of accuracy than any other man—whoever tells us this, I think that we can only imagine him to be a simple creature who is likely to have been deceived by some wizard or actor whom he met, and whom he thought all-knowing, because he himself was unable to analyse the nature of knowledge and ignorance and imitation.

Most true.

And so, when we hear persons saying that the tragedians, and Homer, who is at their head, know all the arts and all things human, virtue as well as vice, and divine things too, for that the good poet cannot compose well unless he knows his subject, and that he who has not this knowledge can never be a poet, we ought to consider whether here also there may not be a similar illusion. Perhaps they may have come across imitators and been deceived by them; they may not have remembered when they saw their works that these were but imitations thrice removed from the truth, and could easily be made without any knowledge of the truth, because they are appearances only and not realities? Or, after all, they may be in the right, and poets do really know the things about which they seem to the many to speak so well?

The question, he said, should by all means be considered.

Now do you suppose that if a person were able to make the original as well as the image, he would seriously devote himself to the image-making branch? Would he allow imitation to be the ruling principle of his life, as if he had nothing higher in him?

I should say not.

The real artist, who knew what he was imitating, would be interested in realities and not in imitations; and would desire to leave as memorials of himself works many and fair; and, instead of being the author of encomiums, he would prefer to be the theme of them.

Yes, he said, that would be to him a source of much greater honour and profit.

Then, I said, we must put a question to Homer; not about medicine, or any of the arts to which his poems only incidentally refer: we are not going to ask him, or any other poet, whether he has cured patients like Asclepius, or left behind him a school of medicine such as the Asclepiads were, or whether he only talks about medicine and other arts at second-hand; but we have a right to know respecting military tactics, politics, education, which are the chiefest and noblest subjects of his poems, and we may fairly ask him about them. 'Friend Homer,' then we say to him, 'if you are only in the second remove from truth in what you say of virtue, and not in the third—not an image maker or imitator—and if you are able to discern what pursuits make men better or worse in private or public life, tell us what State was ever better governed by your help? The good order of Lacedaemon is due to Lycurgus, and many other cities great and small have been similarly benefited by others; but who says that you have been a good legislator to them and have done them any good? Italy and Sicily boast of Charondas, and there is Solon who is renowned among us; but what city has anything to say about you?' Is there any city which he might name?

I think not, said Glaucon; not even the Homerids themselves pretend that he was a legislator.

Well, but is there any war on record which was carried on successfully by him, or aided by his counsels, when he was alive? 600

There is not.

Or is there any invention of his, applicable to the arts or to human life, such as Thales the Milesian or Anacharsis the Scythian, and other ingenious men have conceived, which is attributed to him?

There is absolutely nothing of the kind.

But, if Homer never did any public service, was he privately a guide or teacher of any? Had he in his lifetime friends who loved to associate with him, and who handed down to posterity an Homeric way of life, such as was established by Pythagoras who was so greatly beloved for his wisdom, and whose followers are to this day quite celebrated for the order which was named after him?

Nothing of the kind is recorded of him. For surely, Socrates, Creophylus, the companion of Homer, that child of flesh, whose name always makes us laugh, might be more justly ridiculed for his stupidity, if, as is said, Homer was greatly neglected by him and others in his own day when he was alive?

Yes, I replied, that is the tradition. But can you imagine, Glaucon, that if Homer had really been able to educate and improve mankind—if he had possessed knowledge and not been a mere imitator—can you imagine, I say, that he would not have had many followers, and been honoured and loved by them? Protagoras of Abdera, and Prodicus of Ceos, and a host of others, have only to whisper to their contemporaries: 'You will never be able to manage either your own house or your own State until you appoint us to be your ministers of education'—and this ingenious device of theirs has such an effect in making men love them that their companions all but carry them about on their shoulders. And is it conceivable that the contemporaries of Homer, or again of Hesiod, would have allowed either of them to go about as rhapsodists, if they had really been able to make mankind virtuous? Would they not have been as unwilling to part with them as with gold, and have compelled them to stay at home with them? Or, if the master would not stay, then the disciples would have followed him about everywhere, until they had got education enough?

Yes, Socrates, that, I think, is quite true.

Then must we not infer that all these poetical individuals, beginning with Homer, are only imitators; they copy images of virtue and the like, but the truth they never reach? The poet is like a painter who, as we have already observed, will make a likeness of a cobbler though he understands nothing of cobbling; and his picture is good enough for those who know no more than he does, and judge only by colours and figures.

Quite so.

In like manner the poet with his words and phrases may be said to lay on the colours of the several arts, himself understanding their nature only enough to imitate them; and other people, who are as ignorant as he is, and judge only from his words, imagine that if he speaks of cobbling, or of military tactics, or of anything else, in metre and harmony and rhythm, he speaks very well—such is the sweet influence which melody and rhythm by nature have. And I think that you must have observed again and again what a poor appearance the tales of poets make when stripped of the colours which music puts upon them, and recited in simple prose.

Yes, he said.

They are like faces which were never really beautiful, but only blooming; and now the bloom of youth has passed away from them?

Exactly.

Here is another point: The imitator or maker of the image knows nothing of true existence; he knows appearances only. Am I not right?

Yes.

Then let us have a clear understanding, and not be satisfied with half an explanation.

Proceed.

Of the painter we say that he will paint reins, and he will paint a bit?

Yes.

And the worker in leather and brass will make them?

Certainly.

But does the painter know the right form of the bit and reins? Nay, hardly even the workers in brass and leather who make them; only the horseman who knows how to use them—he knows their right form.

Most true.

And may we not say the same of all things?

What?

That there are three arts which are concerned with all things: one which uses, another which makes, a third which imitates them?

Yes.

And the excellence or beauty or truth of every structure, animate or inanimate, and of every action of man, is relative to the use for which nature or the artist has intended them.

True.

Then the user of them must have the greatest experience of them, and he must indicate to the maker the good or bad qualities which develop themselves in use; for example, the flute-player will tell the flute-maker which of his flutes is satisfactory to the performer; he will tell him how he ought to make them, and the other will attend to his instructions?

Of course.

The one knows and therefore speaks with authority about the goodness and badness of flutes, while the other, confiding in him, will do what he is told by him?

True.

The instrument is the same, but about the excellence or badness of it the maker will only attain to a correct belief; and this he will gain from him who knows, by talking to him and being compelled to hear what he has to say, whereas the user will have knowl- 602 edge?

True.

But will the imitator have either? Will he know from use whether or no his drawing is correct or beautiful? or will he have right opinion from being compelled to associate with another who knows and gives him instructions about what he should draw?

Neither.

Then he will no more have true opinion than he will have knowledge about the goodness or badness of his imitations?

I suppose not.

The imitative artist will be in a brilliant state of intelligence about his own creations?

Nay, very much the reverse.

And still he will go on imitating without knowing what makes a thing good or bad, and may be expected therefore to imitate only that which appears to be good to the ignorant multitude?

Just so.

Thus far then we are pretty well agreed that the imitator has no knowledge worth mentioning of what he imitates. Imitation is only a kind of play or sport, and the tragic poets, whether they write in Iambic or in Heroic verse, are imitators in the highest degree?

Very true.

And now tell me, I conjure you, has not imitation been shown by us to be concerned with that which is thrice removed from the truth?

Certainly.

And what is the faculty in man to which imitation is addressed?

What do you mean?

I will explain: The body which is large when seen near, appears small when seen at a distance?

True.

And the same object appears straight when looked at out of the water, and crooked when in the water; and the concave becomes convex, owing to the illusion about colours to which the sight is liable. Thus every sort of confusion is revealed within us; and this is that weakness of the human mind on which the art of conjuring and of deceiving by light and shadow and other ingenious devices imposes, having an effect upon us like magic.

True.

And the arts of measuring and numbering and weighing come to the rescue of the human understanding—there is the beauty of them—and the apparent greater or less, or more or heavier, no longer have the mastery over us, but give way before calculation and measure and weight?

Most true.

And this, surely, must be the work of the calculating and rational principle in the soul?

To be sure.

And when this principle measures and certifies that some things are equal, or that some are greater or less than others, there occurs an apparent contradiction?

True.

But were we not saying that such a contradiction is impossible—the same faculty cannot have contrary opinions at the same time about the same thing? 603

Very true.

Then that part of the soul which has an opinion contrary to measure is not the same with that which has an opinion in accordance with measure?

True.

And the better part of the soul is likely to be that which trusts to measure and calculation?

Certainly.

And that which is opposed to them is one of the inferior principles of the soul?

No doubt.

This was the conclusion at which I was seeking to arrive when I said that painting or drawing, and imitation in general, when doing their own proper work, are far removed from truth, and the companions and friends and associates of a principle within us which is equally removed from reason, and that they have no true or healthy aim.

Exactly.

The imitative art is an inferior who marries an inferior, and has inferior offspring.

Very true.

And is this confined to the sight only, or does it extend to the hearing also, relating in fact to what we term poetry?

Probably the same would be true of poetry.

Do not rely, I said, on a probability derived from the analogy of painting; but let us examine further and see whether the faculty with which poetical imitation is concerned is good or bad.

By all means.

We may state the question thus:—Imitation imitates the actions of men, whether voluntary or involuntary, on which, as they imagine, a good or bad result has ensued, and they rejoice or sorrow accordingly. Is there anything more?

No, there is nothing else.

But in all this variety of circumstances is the man at unity with himself—or rather, as in the instance of sight there was confusion and opposition in his opinions about the same things, so here also is there not strife and inconsistency in his life? Though I need hardly raise the question again, for I remember that all this has been already admitted; and the soul has been acknowledged by us to be full of these and ten thousand similar oppositions occurring at the same moment?

And we were right, he said.

Yes, I said, thus far we were right; but there was an omission which must now be supplied.

What was the omission?

Were we not saying that a good man, who has the misfortune to lose his son or anything else which is most dear to him, will bear the loss with more equanimity than another?

Yes.

But will he have no sorrow, or shall we say that although he cannot help sorrowing, he will moderate his sorrow?

The latter, he said, is the truer statement.

604   Tell me: will he be more likely to struggle and hold out against his sorrow when he is seen by his equals, or when he is alone?

It will make a great difference whether he is seen or not.

When he is by himself he will not mind saying or doing many things which he would be ashamed of any one hearing or seeing him do?

True.

There is a principle of law and reason in him which bids him resist, as well as a feeling of his misfortune which is forcing him to indulge his sorrow?

True.

But when a man is drawn in two opposite directions, to and from the same object, this, as we affirm, necessarily implies two distinct principles in him?

Certainly.

One of them is ready to follow the guidance of the law?

How do you mean?

The law would say that to be patient under suffering is best, and that we should not give way to impatience, as there is no knowing whether such things are good or evil; and nothing is gained by impatience; also, because no human thing is of serious importance, and grief stands in the way of that which at the moment is most required.

What is most required? he asked.

That we should take counsel about what has happened, and when the dice have been thrown order our affairs in the way which reason deems best; not, like children who have had a fall, keeping hold of the part struck and wasting time in setting up a howl, but always accustoming the soul forthwith to apply a remedy, raising up that which is sickly and fallen, banishing the cry of sorrow by the healing art.

Yes, he said, that is the true way of meeting the attacks of fortune.

Yes, I said; and the higher principle is ready to follow this suggestion of reason?

Clearly.

And the other principle, which inclines us to recollection of our troubles and to lamentation, and can never have enough of them, we may call irrational, useless, and cowardly?

Indeed, we may.

And does not the latter—I mean the rebellious principle—furnish a great variety of materials for imitation? Whereas the wise and calm temperament, being always nearly equable, is not easy to imitate or to appreciate when imitated, especially at a public festival when a promiscuous crowd is assembled in a theatre. For the feeling represented is one to which they are strangers.

Certainly.

Then the imitative poet who aims at being popular is not by nature made, nor is his art intended, to please or to affect the rational principle in the soul; but he will prefer the passionate and fitful temper, which is easily imitated? 605

Clearly.

And now we may fairly take him and place him by the side of the painter, for he is like him in two ways: first, inasmuch as his creations have an inferior degree of truth—in this, I say, he is like him; and he is also like him in being concerned with an inferior part of the soul; and therefore we shall be right in refusing to admit him into a well-ordered State, because he awakens and nourishes and strengthens the feelings and impairs the reason. As in a city when the evil are permitted to have authority and the good are put out of the way, so in the soul of man, as we maintain, the imitative poet implants an evil constitution, for he indulges the irrational nature which has no discernment of greater and less, but thinks the same thing at one time great and at another small—he is a manufacturer of images and is very far removed from the truth.

Exactly.

But we have not yet brought forward the heaviest count in our accusation:—the power which poetry has of harming even the good (and there are very few who are not harmed), is surely an awful thing?

Yes, certainly, if the effect is what you say.

Hear and judge: The best of us, as I conceive, when we listen to a passage of Homer, or one of the tragedians in which he represents some pitiful hero who is drawling out his sorrows in a long oration, or weeping, and smiting his breast—the best of us, you know, delight in giving way to sympathy, and are in raptures at the excellence of the poet who stirs our feelings most.

Yes, of course I know.

But when any sorrow of our own happens to us, then you may observe that we pride ourselves on the opposite quality—we would fain be quiet and patient; this is the manly part, and the other which delighted us in the recitation is now deemed to be the part of a woman.

Very true, he said.

Now can we be right in praising and admiring another who is doing that which any one of us would abominate and be ashamed of in his own person?

No, he said, that is certainly not reasonable.

Nay, I said, quite reasonable from one point of view.

What point of view?

If you consider, I said, that when in misfortune we feel a natural hunger and desire to relieve our sorrow by weeping and lamentation, and that this feeling which is kept under control in our own calamities is satisfied and delighted by the poets;—the better nature in each of us, not having been sufficiently trained by reason or habit, allows the sympathetic element to break loose because the sorrow is another's; and the spectator fancies that there can be no disgrace to himself in praising and pitying any one who comes telling him what a good man he is, and making a fuss about his troubles; he thinks that the pleasure is a gain, and why should he be supercilious and lose this and the poem too? Few persons ever reflect, as I should imagine, that from the evil of other men something of evil is communicated to themselves. And so the feeling of sorrow which has gathered strength at the sight of the misfortunes of others is with difficulty repressed in our own.

How very true!

And does not the same hold also of the ridiculous? There are jests which you would be ashamed to make yourself, and yet on the comic stage, or indeed in private, when you hear them, you are greatly amused by them, and are not at all disgusted at their unseemliness;—the case of pity is repeated;—there is a principle in human nature which is disposed to raise a laugh, and this which you once restrained by reason, because you were afraid of being thought a buffoon, is now let out again; and having stimulated the risible faculty at the theatre, you are betrayed unconsciously to yourself into playing the comic poet at home.

Quite true, he said.

And the same may be said of lust and anger and all the other affections, of desire and pain and pleasure, which are held to be inseparable from every action—in all of them poetry feeds and waters the passions instead of drying them up; she lets them rule, although they ought to be controlled, if mankind are ever to increase in happiness and virtue.

I cannot deny it.

Therefore, Glaucon, I said, whenever you meet with any of the eulogists of Homer declaring that he has been the educator of Hellas, and that he is profitable for education and for the ordering of human things, and that you should take him up again and again 607 and get to know him and regulate your whole life according to him, we may love and honour those who say these things—they are excellent people, as far as their lights extend; and we are ready to acknowledge that Homer is the greatest of poets and first of tragedy writers; but we must remain firm in our conviction that hymns to the gods and praises of famous men are the only poetry which ought to be admitted into our State. For if you go beyond this and allow the honeyed muse to enter, either in epic or lyric verse, not law and the reason of mankind, which by common consent have ever been deemed best, but pleasure and pain will be the rulers in our State.

That is most true, he said.

And now since we have reverted to the subject of poetry, let this our defence serve to show the reasonableness of our former judgment in sending away out of our State an art having the tendencies which we have described; for reason constrained us. But that she may not impute to us any harshness or want of politeness, let us tell her that there is an ancient quarrel between philosophy and poetry; of which there are many proofs, such as the saying of 'the yelping hound howling at her lord,' or of one 'mighty in the vain talk of fools,' and 'the mob of sages circumventing Zeus,' and the 'subtle thinkers who are beggars after all'; and there are innumerable other signs of ancient enmity between them. Notwithstanding this, let us assure our sweet friend and the sister arts of imitation, that if she will only prove her title to exist in a well-ordered State we shall be delighted to receive her—we are very conscious of her charms; but we may not on that account betray the truth. I dare say, Glaucon, that you are as much charmed by her as I am, especially when she appears in Homer?

Yes, indeed, I am greatly charmed.

Shall I propose, then, that she be allowed to return from exile, but upon this condition only—that she make a defence of herself in lyrical or some other metre?

Certainly.

And we may further grant to those of her defenders who are lovers of poetry and yet not poets the permission to speak in prose on her behalf: let them show not only that she is pleasant but also useful to States and to human life, and we will listen in a kindly spirit; for if this can be proved we shall surely be the gainers—I mean, if there is a use in poetry as well as a delight?

Certainly, he said, we shall be the gainers.

If her defence fails, then, my dear friend, like other persons who are enamoured of something, but put a restraint upon themselves when they think their desires are opposed to their interests, so too must we after the manner of lovers give her up, though not without a struggle. We too are inspired by that love of poetry which the 608 education of noble States has implanted in us, and therefore we would have her appear at her best and truest; but so long as she is unable to make good her defence, this argument of ours shall be a charm to us, which we will repeat to ourselves while we listen to her strains; that we may not fall away into the childish love of her which captivates the many. At all events we are well aware that poetry being such as we have described is not to be regarded seriously as attaining to the truth; and he who listens to her, fearing for the safety of the city which is within him, should be on his guard against her seductions and make our words his law.

Yes, he said, I quite agree with you.

Yes, I said, my dear Glaucon, for great is the issue at stake, greater than appears, whether a man is to be good or bad. And what will any one be profited if under the influence of honour or money or power, aye, or under the excitement of poetry, he neglect justice and virtue?

. . . . .

FROM *Sophist*
(264ᵈ-267ᵈ)

Stranger. We divided image-making into two sorts; the one likeness-making, the other imaginative or phantastic.

Theaetetus. True.

Str. And we said that we were uncertain in which we should place the Sophist.

Theaet. We did say so.

Str. And our heads began to go round more and more when it was asserted that there is no such thing as an image or idol or appearance, because in no manner or time or place can there ever be such a thing as falsehood.

Theaet. True.

Str. And now, since there has been shown to be false speech and false opinion, there may be imitations of real existences, and out of this condition of the mind an art of deception may arise.

Theaet. Quite possible.

Str. And we have already admitted, in what preceded, that the Sophist was lurking in one of the divisions of the likeness-making art?

Theaet. Yes.

Str. Let us, then, renew the attempt, and in dividing any class, always take the part to the right, holding fast to that which holds the Sophist, until we have stripped him of all his common properties, and reached his difference or peculiar. Then we may exhibit him in his true nature, first to ourselves and then to kindred dialectical spirits. 265

Theaet. Very good.

Str. You may remember that all art was originally divided by us into creative and acquisitive.

Theaet. Yes.

Str. And the Sophist was flitting before us in the acquisitive class, in the subdivisions of hunting, contests, merchandize, and the like.

Theaet. Very true.

Str. But now that the imitative art has enclosed him, it is clear that we must begin by dividing the art of creation; for imitation is a kind of creation—of images, however, as we affirm, and not of real things.

Theat. Quite true.

Str. In the first place, there are two kinds of creation.

Theaet. What are they?

Str. One of them is human and the other divine.

Theaet. I do not follow.

Str. Every power, as you may remember our saying originally, which causes things to exist, not previously existing, was defined by us as creative.

Theaet. I remember.

Str. Looking, now, at the world and all the animals and plants, at things which grow upon the earth from seeds and roots, as well as at inanimate substances which are formed within the earth, fusile or non-fusile, shall we say that they come into existence—not having existed previously—by the creation of God, or shall we agree with vulgar opinion about them?

Theaet. What is it?

Str. The opinion that nature brings them into being from some spontaneous and unintelligent cause. Or shall we say that they are created by a divine reason and a knowledge which comes from God?

Theaet. I dare say that, owing to my youth, I may often waver in my view, but now when I look at you and see that you incline to refer them to God, I defer to your authority.

Str. Nobly said, Theaetetus, and if I thought that you were one of those who would hereafter change your mind, I would have gently argued with you, and forced you to assent; but as I perceive that you will come of yourself and without any argument of mine, to that belief which, as you say, attracts you, I will not forestall the work of time. Let me suppose, then, that things which are said to be made by nature are the work of divine art, and that things which are made by man out of these are work of human art. And so there are two kinds of making and production, the one human and the other divine.

Theaet. True.

Str. Then, now, subdivide each of the two sections which we have already.

Theaet. How do you mean?

Str. I mean to say that you should make a vertical division of production or invention, as you have already made a lateral one. 266

Theaet. I have done so.

Str. Then, now, there are in all four parts or segments—two of them have reference to us and are human, and two of them have reference to the gods and are divine.

Theaet. True.

Str. And, again, in the division which was supposed to be made in the other way, one part in each subdivision is the making of the things themselves, but the two remaining parts may be called the making of likenesses; and so the productive art is again divided into two parts.

Theaet. Tell me the divisions once more.

Str. I suppose that we, and the other animals, and the elements out of which things are made—fire, water, and the like—are known by us to be each and all the creation and work of God.

Theaet. True.

Str. And there are images of them, which are not them, but which correspond to them; and these are also the creation of a wonderful skill.

Theaet. What are they?

Str. The appearances which spring up of themselves in sleep or by day, such as a shadow when darkness arises in a fire, or the reflection which is produced when the light in bright and smooth objects meets on their surface with an external light, and creates a perception the opposite of our ordinary sight.

Theaet. Yes; and the images as well as the creation are equally the work of a divine hand.

Str. And what shall we say of human art? Do we not make one house by the art of building, and another by the art of drawing, which is a sort of dream created by man for those who are awake?

Theaet. Quite true.

Str. And other products of human creation are also twofold and go in pairs; there is the thing, with which the art of making the thing is concerned, and the image, with which imitation is concerned.

Theaet. Now I begin to understand, and am ready to acknowledge that there are two kinds of production, and each of them twofold; in the lateral division there is both a divine and a human production; in the vertical there are realities and a creation of a kind of similitudes.

Str. And let us not forget that of the imitative class the one part was to have been likeness-making, and the other phantastic, if it could be shown that falsehood is a reality and belongs to the class of real being.

Theaet. Yes.

Str. And this appeared to be the case; and therefore now, without hesitation, we shall number the different kinds as two.

Theaet. True.

267 *Str.* Then, now, let us again divide the phantastic art.

Theaet. Where shall we make the division?

Str. There is one kind which is produced by an instrument, and another in which the creator of the appearance is himself the instrument.

Theaet. What do you mean?

Str. When any one makes himself appear like another in his figure or his voice, imitation is the name for this part of the phantastic art.

Theaet. Yes.

Str. Let this, then, be named the art of mimicry, and this the province assigned to it; as for the other division, we are weary and will give that up, leaving to some one else the duty of making the class and giving it a suitable name.

Theaet. Let us do as you say—assign a sphere to the one and leave the other.

Str. There is a further distinction, Theaetetus, which is worthy of our consideration, and for a reason which I will tell you.

Theaet. Let me hear.

Str. There are some who imitate, knowing what they imitate, and some who do not know. And what line of distinction can there possibly be greater than that which divides ignorance from knowledge?

Theaet. There can be no greater.

Str. Was not the sort of imitation of which we spoke just now the imitation of those who know? For he who would imitate you would surely know you and your figure?

Theaet. Naturally.

Str. And what would you say of the figure or form of justice or of virtue in general? Are we not well aware that many, having no knowledge of either, but only a sort of opinion, do their best to show that this opinion is really entertained by them, by expressing it, as far as they can, in word and deed?

Theaet. Yes, that is very common.

Str. And do they always fail in their attempt to be thought just, when they are not? Or is not the very opposite true?

Theaet. The very opposite.

Str. Such a one, then, should be described as an imitator—to be distinguished from the other, as he who is ignorant is distinguished from him who knows?

Theaet. True.

Str. Can we find a suitable name for each of them? This is clearly not an easy task; for among the ancients there was some confusion of ideas, which prevented them from attempting to divide genera into species; wherefore there is no great abundance of names. Yet, for the sake of distinctness, I will make bold to call the imitation which coexists with opinion, the imitation of appearance—that which coexists with science, a scientific or learned imitation.

· · · · ·

FROM *Laws*
(667ᵇ-669ᵃ; 816ᶜ-817ᵈ)

BOOK II

Athenian Stranger. When things have an accompanying charm, either the best thing in them is this very charm, or there is some rightness or utility possessed by them;—for example, I should say that eating and drinking, and the use of food in general, have an accompanying charm which we call pleasure; but that this rightness and utility is just the healthfulness of the things served up to us, which is their true rightness.

Cleinias. Just so.

Ath. Thus, too, I should say that learning has a certain accompanying charm which is the pleasure; but that the right and the profitable, the good and the noble, are qualities which the truth gives to it.

Cle. Exactly.

Ath. And so in the imitative arts,—if they succeed in making likenesses, and are accompanied by pleasure, may not their works be said to have a charm?

Cle. Yes.

Ath. But equal proportions, whether of quality or quantity, and not pleasure, speaking generally, would give them truth or rightness.

Cle. Yes.

Ath. Then that only can be rightly judged by the standard of pleasure, which makes or furnishes no utility or truth or likeness, nor on the other hand is productive of any hurtful quality, but exists solely for the sake of the accompanying charm; and the term 'pleasure' is most appropriately applied to it when these other qualities are absent.

Cle. You are speaking of harmless pleasure, are you not?

Ath. Yes; and this I term amusement, when doing neither harm nor good in any degree worth speaking of.

Cle. Very true.

Ath. Then, if such be our principles, we must assert that imitation is not to be judged of by pleasure and false opinion; and this is true of all equality, for the equal is not equal or the symmetrical symmetrical, because somebody thinks or likes something, but they are to be judged of by the standard of truth, and by no other whatever.

Cle. Quite true.

668 *Ath.* Do we not regard all music as representative and imitative?

Cle. Certainly.

Ath. Then, when any one says that music is to be judged of by pleasure, his doctrine cannot be admitted; and if there be any music of which pleasure is the criterion, such music is not to be sought out or deemed to have any real excellence, but only that other kind of music which is an imitation of the good.

Cle. Very true.

Ath. And those who seek for the best kind of song and music ought not to seek for that which is pleasant, but for that which is true; and the truth of imitation consists, as we were saying, in rendering the thing imitated according to quantity and quality.

Cle. Certainly.

Ath. And every one will admit that musical compositions are all imitative and representative. Will not poets and spectators and actors all agree in this?

Cle. They will.

Ath. Surely then he who would judge correctly must know what each composition is; for if he does not know what is the character and meaning of the piece, and what it represents, he will never discern whether the intention is true or false.

Cle. Certainly not.

Ath. And will he who does not know what is true be able to distinguish what is good and bad? My statement is not very clear; but perhaps you will understand me better if I put the matter in another way.

Cle. How?

Ath. There are ten thousand likenesses of objects of sight?

Cle. Yes.

Ath. And can he who does not know what the exact object is which is imitated, ever know whether the resemblance is truthfully executed? I mean, for example, whether a statue has the proportions of a body, and the true situation of the parts; what those proportions are, and how the parts fit into one another in due order; also their colours and conformations, or whether this is all confused in the execution: do you think that any one can know about this, who does not know what the animal is which has been imitated?

Cle. Impossible.

Ath. But even if we know that the thing pictured or sculptured is a man, who has received at the hand of the artist all his proper parts and colours and shapes, must we not also know whether the work is beautiful or in any respect deficient in beauty? 669

Cle. If this were not required, Stranger, we should all of us be judges of beauty.

Ath. Very true; and may we not say that in everything imitated, whether in drawing, music, or any other art, he who is to be a competent judge must possess three things;—he must know, in the first place, of what the imitation is; secondly, he must know that it is true; and thirdly, that it has been well executed in words and melodies and rhythms?

. . . . .

BOOK VII

Athenian Stranger. I have described the dances which are appropriate to noble bodies and generous souls. But it is necessary also to consider and know uncomely persons and thoughts, and those which are intended to produce laughter in comedy, and have a comic character in respect of style, song, and dance, and of the imitations which these afford. For serious things cannot be understood without laughable things, nor opposites at all without opposites, if a man is really to have intelligence of either; but he cannot carry out both in action, if he is to have any degree of virtue. And for this very reason he should learn them both, in order that he may not in ignorance do or say anything which is ridiculous and out of place—he should command slaves and hired strangers to imitate such things, but he should never take any serious interest in them himself, nor should any freeman or freewoman be discovered taking pains to learn them; and there should always be some element of novelty in the imitation. Let these then be laid down, 817 both in law and in our discourse, as the regulations of laughable amusements which are generally called comedy. And, if any of the serious poets, as they are termed, who write tragedy, come to us and say—'O strangers, may we go to your city and country or may we not, and shall we bring with us our poetry—what is your will about these matters?'—how shall we answer the divine men? I think that our answer should be as follows:—Best of strangers, we will say to them, we also according to our ability are tragic poets, and our tragedy is the best and noblest; for our whole state is an imitation of the best and noblest life, which we affirm to be indeed the very truth of tragedy. You are poets and we are poets, both makers of the same strains, rivals and antagonists in the noblest of dramas, which true law can alone perfect, as our hope is. Do not then suppose that we shall all in a moment allow you to erect your stage in the agora, or introduce the fair voices of your actors, speaking above our own, and permit you to harangue our women and children, and the common people, about our institutions, in language other than our own, and very often the opposite of our own. For a state would be mad which gave you this licence, until the magistrates had determined whether your poetry might be recited, and was fit for publication or not. Wherefore, O ye sons and scions of the softer Muses, first of all show your songs to the magistrates, and let them compare them with our own, and if they are the same or better we will give you a chorus; but if not, then, my friends, we cannot. Let these, then, be the customs ordained by law about all dances and the teaching of them, and let matters relating to slaves be separated from those relating to masters, if you do not object.

· · · · ·

ARTISTIC INSPIRATION

In the *Ion* and the *Phaedrus* Plato explains what the source
of artistic creativity is.

FROM *Ion*
(532ᵇ-536ᵇ)

Ion. Why then, Socrates, do I lose attention and go to sleep and
have absolutely no ideas of the least value, when any one speaks of
any other poet; but when Homer is mentioned, I wake up at once
and am all attention and have plenty to say?

Socrates. The reason, my friend, is obvious. No one can fail to
see that you speak of Homer without any art or knowledge. If you
were able to speak of him by rules of art, you would have been
able to speak of all other poets; for poetry is a whole.

Ion. Yes.

Soc. And when any one acquires any other art as a whole, the
same may be said of them. Would you like me to explain my meaning, Ion?

Ion. Yes, indeed, Socrates; I very much wish that you would: for
I love to hear you wise men talk.

Soc. O that we were wise, Ion, and that you could truly call us
so; but you rhapsodes and actors, and the poets whose verses you
sing, are wise; whereas I am a common man, who only speak the
truth. For consider what a very commonplace and trivial thing is
this which I have said—a thing which any man might say: that
when a man has acquired a knowledge of a whole art, the enquiry
into good and bad is one and the same. Let us consider this matter;
is not the art of painting a whole?

Ion. Yes.

Soc. And there are and have been many painters good and bad?

Ion. Yes.

Soc. And did you ever know any one who was skilful in pointing out the excellences and defects of Polygnotus the son of Aglao-
phon, but incapable of criticizing other painters; and when the 533
work of any other painter was produced, went to sleep and was at a
loss, and had no ideas; but when he had to give his opinion about

Polygnotus, or whoever the painter might be, and about him only, woke up and was attentive and had plenty to say?

Ion. No indeed, I have never known such a person.

Soc. Or did you ever know of any one in sculpture, who was skilful in expounding the merits of Daedalus the son of Metion, or of Epeius the son of Panopeus, or of Theodorus the Samian, or of any individual sculptor; but when the works of sculptors in general were produced, was at a loss and went to sleep and had nothing to say?

Ion. No indeed; no more than the other.

Soc. And if I am not mistaken, you never met with any one among flute-players or harp-players or singers to the harp or rhapsodes who was able to discourse of Olympus or Thamyras or Orpheus, or Phemius the rhapsode of Ithaca, but was at a loss when he came to speak of Ion of Ephesus, and had no notion of his merits or defects?

Ion. I cannot deny what you say, Socrates. Nevertheless I am conscious in my own self, and the world agrees with me in thinking that I do speak better and have more to say about Homer than any other man. But I do not speak equally well about others—tell me the reason of this.

Soc. I perceive, Ion; and I will proceed to explain to you what I imagine to be the reason of this. The gift which you possess of speaking excellently about Homer is not an art, but, as I was just saying, an inspiration; there is a divinity moving you, like that contained in the stone which Euripides calls a magnet, but which is commonly known as the stone of Heraclea. This stone not only attracts iron rings, but also imparts to them a similar power of attracting other rings; and sometimes you may see a number of pieces of iron and rings suspended from one another so as to form quite a long chain: and all of them derive their power of suspension from the original stone. In like manner the Muse first of all inspires men herself; and from these inspired persons a chain of other persons is suspended, who take the inspiration. For all good poets, epic as well as lyric, compose their beautiful poems not by art, but because they are inspired and possessed. And as the Corybantian revellers when they dance are not in their right mind, so the lyric poets are not in their right mind when they are composing their beautiful strains: but when falling under the power of music and metre they are inspired and possessed; like Bacchic maidens who draw milk and honey from the rivers when they are under the influence of Dionysus but not when they are in their right mind. And the soul of the lyric poet does the same, as they themselves say; for they tell us that they bring songs from honeyed fountains, culling them out of the gardens and dells of the Muses; they, like the bees, winging their way from flower to flower. And this is true. For the poet is a light and winged and holy thing, and there is no invention in him until he has been inspired and is out of his senses, and the mind is no longer in him: when he has not attained to this state, he is powerless and is unable to utter his oracles. Many are the noble words in which poets speak concerning the actions of men; but like yourself when speaking about Homer, they do not speak of them by any rules of art: they are simply inspired to utter that to which the Muse impels them, and that only; and when inspired, one of them will make dithyrambs, another hymns of praise, another choral strains, another epic or iambic verses—and he who is good at one is not good at any other kind of verse: for not by art does the poet sing, but by power divine. Had he learned by rules of art, he would have known how to speak not of one theme only, but of all; and therefore God takes away the minds of poets, and uses them as his ministers, as he also uses diviners and holy prophets, in order that we who hear them may know them to be speaking not of themselves who utter these priceless words in a state of unconsciousness, but that God himself is the speaker, and that through them he is conversing with us. And Tynnichus the Chalcidian affords a striking instance of what I am saying: he wrote nothing that any one would care to remember but the famous paean which is in every one's mouth, one of the finest poems ever written, simply an invention of the Muses, as he himself says. For in this way the God would seem to indicate to us and not allow us to doubt that these beautiful poems are not human, or the work of man, but divine and the work of God; and that the poets are only the interpreters of the Gods by whom they are severally possessed. Was not this the lesson which the God intended to teach when by the mouth of the worst of poets he sang the best of songs? Am I 535 not right, Ion?

Ion. Yes, indeed, Socrates, I feel that you are; for your words touch my soul, and I am persuaded that good poets by a divine inspiration interpret the things of the Gods to us.

Soc. And you rhapsodists are the interpreters of the poets?

Ion. There again you are right.

Soc. Then you are the interpreters of interpreters?

Ion. Precisely.

Soc. I wish you would frankly tell me, Ion, what I am going to ask of you: When you produce the greatest effect upon the audience in the recitation of some striking passage, such as the apparition of Odysseus leaping forth on the floor, recognized by the suitors and casting his arrows at his feet, or the description of Achilles rushing at Hector, or the sorrows of Andromache, Hecuba, or Priam,—are you in your right mind? Are you not carried out of yourself, and does not your soul in an ecstasy seem to be among the persons or places of which you are speaking, whether they are in Ithaca or in Troy or whatever may be the scene of the poem?

Ion. That proof strikes home to me, Socrates. For I must frankly confess that at the tale of pity my eyes are filled with tears, and when I speak of horrors, my hair stands on end and my heart throbs.

Soc. Well, Ion, and what are we to say of a man who at a sacrifice or festival, when he is dressed in holiday attire, and has golden crowns upon his head, of which nobody has robbed him, appears weeping or panic-stricken in the presence of more than twenty thousand friendly faces, when there is no one despoiling or wronging him;—is he in his right mind or is he not?

Ion. No indeed, Socrates, I must say that, strictly speaking, he is not in his right mind.

Soc. And are you aware that you produce similar effects on most spectators?

Ion. Only too well; for I look down upon them from the stage, and behold the various emotions of pity, wonder, sternness, stamped upon their countenances when I am speaking: and I am obliged to give my very best attention to them; for if I make them cry I myself shall laugh, and if I make them laugh I myself shall cry when the time of payment arrives.

Soc. Do you know that the spectator is the last of the rings which, as I am saying, receive the power of the original magnet from one another? The rhapsode like yourself and the actor are intermediate links, and the poet himself is the first of them. Through all these the God sways the souls of men in any direction which he pleases, and makes one man hang down from another. Thus there is a vast chain of dancers and masters and undermasters of choruses, who are suspended, as if from the stone, at the side of the rings which hang down from the Muse. And every poet has some Muse from whom he is suspended, and by whom he is said to be possessed, which is nearly the same thing; for he is taken hold of. And from these first rings, which are the poets, depend others, some deriving their inspiration from Orpheus, others from Musaeus; but the greater number are possessed and held by Homer. Of whom, Ion, you are one, and are possessed by Homer; and when any one repeats the words of another poet you go to sleep, and know not what to say; but when any one recites a strain of Homer you wake up in a moment, and your soul leaps within you, and you have plenty to say; for not by art or knowledge about Homer do you say what you say, but by divine inspiration and by possession; just as the Corybantian revellers too have a quick perception of that strain only which is appropriated to the God by whom they are possessed, and have plenty of dances and words for that, but take no heed of any other. And you, Ion, when the name of Homer is mentioned have plenty to say, and have nothing to say of others. You ask, 'Why is this?' The answer is that you praise Homer not by art but by divine inspiration.

. . . . .

FROM *Phaedrus*
(246ᵃ-256ᵈ)

Socrates. Of the nature of the soul, though her true form be ever a theme of large and more than mortal discourse, let me speak briefly, and in a figure. And let the figure be composite—a pair of winged horses and a charioteer. Now the winged horses and the charioteers of the gods are all of them noble and of noble descent, but those of other races are mixed; the human charioteer drives his in a pair; and one of them is noble and of noble breed, and the other is ignoble and of ignoble breed; and the driving of them of necessity gives a great deal of trouble to him. I will endeavour to explain to you in what way the mortal differs from the immortal creature. The soul in her totality has the care of inanimate being everywhere, and traverses the whole heaven in divers forms appearing:—when perfect and fully winged she soars upward, and orders the whole world; whereas the imperfect soul, losing her wings and drooping in her flight at last settles on the solid ground—there, finding a home, she receives an earthly frame which appears to be self-moved, but is really moved by her power; and this composition of soul and body is called a living and mortal creature. For immortal no such union can be reasonably believed to be; although fancy, not having seen nor surely known the nature of God may imagine an immortal creature having both a body and also a soul which are united throughout all time. Let that, however, be as God wills, and be spoken of acceptably to him. And now let us ask the reason why the soul loses her wings!

The wing is the corporeal element which is most akin to the divine, and which by nature tends to soar aloft and carry that which gravitates downwards into the upper region, which is the habitation of the gods. The divine is beauty, wisdom, goodness, and the like; and by these the wing of the soul is nourished, and grows apace; but when fed upon evil and foulness and the opposite of good, wastes and falls away. Zeus, the mighty lord, holding the reins of a winged chariot, leads the way in heaven, ordering all and taking care of all; and there follows him the array of gods and demi-gods, marshalled in eleven bands; Hestia alone abides at home in the house of heaven; of the rest they who are reckoned among the princely twelve march in their appointed order. They see many blessed sights in the inner heaven, and there are many ways to and fro, along which the blessed gods are passing, every one doing his own work; he may follow who will and can, for jealousy has no place in the celestial choir. But when they go to banquet and festival, then they move up the steep to the top of the vault of heaven. The chariots of the gods in even poise, obeying the rein, glide rapidly; but the others labour, for the vicious steed goes heavily, weighing down the charioteer to the earth when his steed has not been thoroughly trained:—and this is the hour of agony and extremest conflict for the soul. For the immortals, when they are at the end of their course, go forth and stand upon the outside of heaven, and the revolution of the spheres carries them round, and they behold the things beyond. But of the heaven which is above the heavens, what earthly poet ever did or ever will sing worthily? It is such as I will describe; for I must dare to speak the truth, when truth is my theme. There abides the very being with which true knowledge is concerned; the colourless, formless, intangible essence, visible only to mind, the pilot of the soul. The divine intelligence, being nurtured upon mind and pure knowledge, and the intelligence of every soul which is capable of receiving the food proper to it, rejoices at beholding reality, and once more gazing upon truth, is replenished and made glad, until the revolution of the worlds brings her round again to the same place. In the revolution she beholds justice, and temperance, and knowledge abso-

247

lute, not in the form of generation or of relation, which men call existence, but knowledge absolute in existence absolute; and beholding the other true existences in like manner, and feasting upon them, she passes down into the interior of the heavens and returns home; and there the charioteer putting up his horses at the stall, gives them ambrosia to eat and nectar to drink.

Such is the life of the gods; but of other souls, that which follows God best and is likest to him lifts the head of the charioteer into the outer world, and is carried round in the revolution, troubled indeed by the steeds, and with difficulty beholding true being; while another only rises and falls, and sees, and again fails to see by reason of the unruliness of the steeds. The rest of the souls are also longing after the upper world and they all follow, but not being strong enough they are carried round below the surface, plunging, treading on one another, each striving to be first; and there is confusion and perspiration and the extremity of effort; and many of them are lamed or have their wings broken through the ill-driving of the charioteers; and all of them after a fruitless toil, not having attained to the mysteries of true being, go away, and feed upon opinion. The reason why the souls exhibit this exceeding eagerness to behold the plain of truth is that pasturage is found there, which is suited to the highest part of the soul; and the wing on which the soul soars is nourished with this. And there is a law of Destiny, that the soul which attains any vision of truth in company with a god is preserved from harm until the next period, and if attaining always is always unharmed. But when she is unable to follow, and fails to behold the truth, and through some ill-hap sinks beneath the double load of forgetfulness and vice, and her wings fall from her and she drops to the ground, then the law ordains that this soul shall at her first birth pass, not into any other animal, but only into man; and the soul which has seen most of truth shall come to the birth as a philosopher, or artist, or some musical and loving nature; that which has seen truth in the second degree shall be some righteous king or warrior chief; the soul which is of the third class shall be a politician, or economist, or trader; the fourth shall be a lover of gymnastic toils, or a physician; the fifth shall lead the life of a prophet or hierophant; to the sixth the character of a poet or some other imitative artist will be assigned; to the seventh the life of an artisan or husbandman; to the eighth that of a sophist or demagogue; to the ninth that of a tyrant;—all these are states of probation, in which he who does righteously improves, and he who does unrighteously, deteriorates his lot.

249 Ten thousand years must elapse before the soul of each one can return to the place from whence she came, for she cannot grow her wings in less; only the soul of a philosopher, guileless and true, or the soul of a lover, who is not devoid of philosophy, may acquire wings in the third of the recurring periods of a thousand years; he is distinguished from the ordinary good man who gains wings in three thousand years:—and they who choose this life three times in succession have wings given them, and go away at the end of three thousand years. But the others receive judgment when they have completed their first life, and after the judgment they go, some of them to the houses of correction which are under the earth, and are punished; others to some place in heaven whither they are lightly borne by justice, and there they live in a manner worthy of the life which they led here when in the form of men. And at the end of the first thousand years the good souls and also the evil souls both come to draw lots and choose their second life, and they may take any which they please. The soul of a man may pass into the life of a beast, or from the beast return again into the man. But the soul which has never seen the truth will not pass into the human form. For a man must have intelligence of universals, and be able to proceed from the many particulars of sense to one conception of reason;—this is the recollection of those things which our soul once saw while following God—when regardless of that which we now call being she raised her head up towards the true being. And therefore the mind of the philosopher alone has wings; and this is just, for he is always, according to the measure of his abilities, clinging in recollection to those things in which God abides, and in beholding which He is what He is. And he who employs aright these memories is ever being initiated into perfect mysteries and alone becomes truly perfect. But, as he forgets earthly interests and is rapt in the divine, the vulgar deem him mad, and rebuke him; they do not see that he is inspired.

Thus far I have been speaking of the fourth and last kind of madness, which is imputed to him who, when he sees the beauty of earth, is transported with the recollection of the true beauty; he would like to fly away, but he cannot; he is like a bird fluttering and looking upward and careless of the world below; and he is therefore thought to be mad. And I have shown this of all inspirations to be the noblest and highest and the offspring of the highest to him who has or shares in it, and that he who loves the beautiful is called a lover because he partakes of it. For, as has been already said, every soul of man has in the way of nature beheld true being; this was the condition of her passing into the form of man. But all souls do not easily recall the things of the other world; they may have seen them for a short time only, or they may have been unfortunate in their earthly lot, and, having had their hearts turned to unrighteousness through some corrupting influence, they may have lost the memory of the holy things which once they saw. Few only retain an adequate remembrance of them; and they, when they behold here any image of that other world, are rapt in amazement; but they are ignorant of what this rapture means, because they do not clearly perceive. For there is no light of justice or temperance or any of the higher ideas which are precious to souls in the earthly copies of them: they are seen through a glass dimly; and there are few who, going to the images, behold in them the realities, and these only with difficulty. There was a time when with the rest of the happy band they saw beauty shining in brightness, —we philosophers following in the train of Zeus, others in company with other gods; and then we beheld the beatific vision and were initiated into a mystery which may be truly called most blessed, celebrated by us in our state of innocence, before we had any experience of evils to come, when we were admitted to the sight of apparitions innocent and simple and calm and happy, which we beheld shining in pure light, pure ourselves and not yet enshrined in that living tomb which we carry about, now that we are imprisoned in the body, like an oyster in his shell. Let me linger over the memory of scenes which have passed away.

But of beauty, I repeat again that we saw her there shining in company with the celestial forms; and coming to earth we find her here too, shining in clearness through the clearest aperture of sense. For sight is the most piercing of our bodily senses; though not by that is wisdom seen; her loveliness would have been transporting if there had been a visible image of her, and the other ideas, if they had visible counterparts, would be equally lovely. But this is the privilege of beauty, that being the loveliest she is also the most palpable to sight. Now he who is not newly initiated or who has become corrupted, does not easily rise out of this world to the sight of true beauty in the other; he looks only at her earthly namesake, and instead of being awed at the sight of her, he is given over to pleasure, and like a brutish beast he rushes on to enjoy and beget;

he consorts with wantonness, and is not afraid or ashamed of pursuing pleasure in violation of nature. But he whose initiation is recent, and who has been the spectator of many glories in the other world, is amazed when he sees any one having a god-like face or form, which is the expression of divine beauty; and at first a shudder runs through him, and again the old awe steals over him; then looking upon the face of his beloved as of a god he reverences him, and if he were not afraid of being thought a downright madman, he would sacrifice to his beloved as to the image of a god; then while he gazes on him there is a sort of reaction, and the shudder passes into an unusual heat and perspiration; for, as he receives the effluence of beauty through the eyes, the wing moistens and he warms. And as he warms, the parts out of which the wing grew, and which had been hitherto closed and rigid, and had prevented the wing from shooting forth, are melted, and as nourishment streams upon him, the lower end of the wings begins to swell and grow from the root upwards; and the growth extends under the whole soul—for once the whole was winged. During this process the whole soul is all in a state of ebullition and effervescence, —which may be compared to the irritation and uneasiness in the gums at the time of cutting teeth,—bubbles up, and has a feeling of uneasiness and tickling; but when in like manner the soul is beginning to grow wings, the beauty of the beloved meets her eye and she receives the sensible warm motion of particles which flow towards her, therefore called emotion (ἵμερος), and is refreshed and warmed by them, and then she ceases from her pain with joy. But when she is parted from her beloved and her moisture fails, then the orifices of the passage out of which the wing shoots dry up and close, and intercept the germ of the wing; which, being shut up with the emotion, throbbing as with the pulsations of an artery, pricks the aperture which is nearest, until at length the entire soul is pierced and maddened and pained, and at the recollection of beauty is again delighted. And from both of them together the soul is oppressed at the strangeness of her condition, and is in a great strait and excitement, and in her madness can neither sleep by night nor abide in her place by day. And wherever she thinks that she will behold the beautiful one, thither in her desire she runs. And when she has seen him, and bathed herself in the waters of beauty, her constraint is loosened, and she is refreshed, and has no 252 more pangs and pains; and this is the sweetest of all pleasures at the time, and is the reason why the soul of the lover will never for-

sake his beautiful one, whom he esteems above all; he has forgotten mother and brethren and companions, and he thinks nothing
of the neglect and loss of his property; the rules and proprieties of
life, on which he formerly prided himself, he now despises, and is
ready to sleep like a servant, wherever he is allowed, as near as he
can to his desired one, who is the object of his worship, and the
physician who can alone assuage the greatness of his pain. And this
state, my dear imaginary youth to whom I am talking, is by men
called love, and among the gods has a name at which you, in your
simplicity, may be inclined to mock; there are two lines in the
apocryphal writings of Homer in which the name occurs. One of
them is rather outrageous, and not altogether metrical. They are
as follows:—

> 'Mortals call him fluttering love,
> But the immortals call him winged one,
> Because the growing of wings is a necessity to him.'

You may believe this, but not unless you like. At any rate the loves
of lovers and their causes are such as I have described.

Now the lover who is taken to be the attendant of Zeus is better
able to bear the winged god, and can endure a heavier burden;
but the attendants and companions of Ares, when under the influence of love, if they fancy that they have been at all wronged, are
ready to kill and put an end to themselves and their beloved. And
he who follows in the train of any other god, while he is unspoiled
and the impression lasts, honours and imitates him, as far as he is
able; and after the manner of his god he behaves in his intercourse
with his beloved and with the rest of the world during the first
period of his earthly existence. Every one chooses his love from the
ranks of beauty according to his character, and this he makes his
god, and fashions and adorns as a sort of image which he is to fall
down and worship. The followers of Zeus desire that their beloved
should have a soul like him; and therefore they seek out some one
of a philosophical and imperial nature, and when they have found
him and loved him, they do all they can to confirm such a nature
in him, and if they have no experience of such a disposition hitherto, they learn of any one who can teach them, and themselves
follow in the same way. And they have the less difficulty in finding
the nature of their own god in themselves, because they have 253
been compelled to gaze intensely on him; their recollection clings
to him, and they become possessed of him, and receive from him

their character and disposition, so far as man can participate in God. The qualities of their god they attribute to the beloved, wherefore they love him all the more, and if, like the Bacchic Nymphs, they draw inspiration from Zeus, they pour out their own fountain upon him, wanting to make him as like as possible to their own god. But those who are the followers of Herè seek a royal love, and when they have found him they do just the same with him; and in like manner the followers of Apollo, and of every other god walking in the ways of their god, seek a love who is to be made like him whom they serve, and when they have found him, they themselves imitate their god, and persuade their love to do the same, and educate him into the manner and nature of the god as far as they each can; for no feelings of envy or jealousy are entertained by them towards their beloved, but they do their utmost to create in him the greatest likeness of themselves and of the god whom they honour. Thus fair and blissful to the beloved is the desire of the inspired lover, and the initiation of which I speak into the mysteries of true love, if he be captured by the lover and their purpose is effected. Now the beloved is taken captive in the following manner:—

As I said at the beginning of this tale, I divided each soul into three—two horses and a charioteer; and one of the horses was good and the other bad: the division may remain, but I have not yet explained in what the goodness or badness of either consists, and to that I will proceed. The right-hand horse is upright and cleanly made; he has a lofty neck and an aquiline nose; his colour is white, and his eyes dark; he is a lover of honour and modesty and temperance, and the follower of true glory; he needs no touch of the whip, but is guided by word and admonition only. The other is a crooked lumbering animal, put together anyhow; he has a short thick neck; he is flat-faced and of a dark colour, with grey eyes and blood-red complexion; the mate of insolence and pride, shag-eared and deaf, hardly yielding to whip and spur. Now when the charioteer beholds the vision of love, and has his whole soul warmed through sense, and is full of the prickings and ticklings of desire, 254 the obedient steed, then as always under the government of shame, refrains from leaping on the beloved; but the other, heedless of the pricks and of the blows of the whip, plunges and runs away, giving all manner of trouble to his companion and the charioteer, whom he forces to approach the beloved and to remember the joys of love. They at first indignantly oppose him and will not be urged on to do terrible and unlawful deeds; but at last, when he persists in plaguing them, they yield and agree to do as he bids them. And now they are at the spot and behold the flashing beauty of the beloved; which when the charioteer sees, his memory is carried to the true beauty, whom he beholds in company with Modesty like an image placed upon a holy pedestal. He sees her, but he is afraid and falls backwards in adoration, and by his fall is compelled to pull back the reins with such violence as to bring both the steeds on their haunches, the one willing and unresisting, the unruly one very unwilling; and when they have gone back a little, the one is overcome with shame and wonder, and his whole soul is bathed in perspiration; the other, when the pain is over which the bridle and the fall had given him, having with difficulty taken breath, is full of wrath and reproaches, which he heaps upon the charioteer and his fellow-steed, for want of courage and manhood, declaring that they have been false to their agreement and guilty of desertion. Again they refuse, and again he urges them on, and will scarce yield to their prayer that he would wait until another time. When the appointed hour comes, they make as if they had forgotten, and he reminds them, fighting and neighing and dragging them on, until at length he, on the same thoughts intent, forces them to draw near again. And when they are near he stoops his head and puts up his tail, and takes the bit in his teeth and pulls shamelessly. Then the charioteer is worse off than ever; he falls back like a racer at the barrier, and with a still more violent wrench drags the bit out of the teeth of the wild steed and covers his abusive tongue and jaws with blood, and forces his legs and haunches to the ground and punishes him sorely. And when this has happened several times and the villain has ceased from his wanton way, he is tamed and humbled, and follows the will of the charioteer, and when he sees the beautiful one he is ready to die of fear. And from that time forward the soul of the lover follows the beloved in modesty and holy fear.

And so the beloved who, like a god, has received every true and loyal service from his lover, not in pretence but in reality, being also himself of a nature friendly to his admirer, if in former days he has blushed to own his passion and turned away his lover, because his youthful companions or others slanderously told him that he would be disgraced, now as years advance, at the appointed age and time, is led to receive him into communion. For fate which has ordained that there shall be no friendship among the evil has also ordained that there shall ever be friendship among the good. And

255

the beloved when he has received him into communion and intimacy, is quite amazed at the good-will of the lover; he recognises
that the inspired friend is worth all other friends or kinsmen; they
have nothing of friendship in them worthy to be compared with
his. And when his feeling continues and he is nearer to him and
embraces him, in gymnastic exercises and at other times of meeting, then the fountain of that stream, which Zeus when he was in
love with Ganymede named Desire, overflows upon the lover, and
some enters into his soul, and some when he is filled flows out
again; and as a breeze or an echo rebounds from the smooth rocks
and returns whence it came, so does the stream of beauty, passing
through the eyes which are the windows of the soul, come back
to the beautiful one; there arriving and quickening the passages of
the wings, watering them and inclining them to grow, and filling
the soul of the beloved also with love. And thus he loves, but he
knows not what; he does not understand and cannot explain his
own state; he appears to have caught the infection of blindness
from another; the lover is his mirror in whom he is beholding himself, but he is not aware of this. When he is with the lover, both
cease from their pain, but when he is away then he longs as he is
longed for, and has love's image, love for love (Anteros) lodging
in his breast, which he calls and believes to be not love but friendship only, and his desire is as the desire of the other, but weaker; he
wants to see him, touch him, kiss, embrace him, and probably not
long afterwards his desire is accomplished. When they meet, the
256 wanton steed of the lover has a word to say to the charioteer; he
would like to have a little pleasure in return for many pains, but
the wanton steed of the beloved says not a word, for he is bursting
with passion which he understands not;—he throws his arms round
the lover and embraces him as his dearest friend; and, when they
are side by side, he is not in a state in which he can refuse the lover
anything, if he ask him; although his fellow-steed and the charioteer oppose him with the arguments of shame and reason. After
this their happiness depends upon their self-control; if the better
elements of mind which lead to order and philosophy prevail, then
they pass their life here in happiness and harmony—masters of
themselves and orderly—enslaving the vicious and emancipating
the virtuous elements of the soul; and when the end comes, they
are light and winged for flight, having conquered in one of the
three heavenly or truly Olympian victories; nor can human discipline or divine inspiration confer any greater blessing on man than

this. If, on the other hand, they leave philosophy and lead the lower life of ambition, then probably, after wine or in some other careless hour, the two wanton animals take the two souls when off their guard and bring them together, and they accomplish that desire of their hearts which to the many is bliss; and this having once enjoyed they continue to enjoy, yet rarely because they have not the approval of the whole soul. They too are dear, but not so dear to one another as the others, either at the time of their love or afterwards. They consider that they have given and taken from each other the most sacred pledges, and they may not break them and fall into enmity. At last they pass out of the body, unwinged, but eager to soar, and thus obtain no mean reward of love and madness. For those who have once begun the heavenward pilgrimage may not go down again to darkness and the journey beneath the earth, but they live in light always; happy companions in their pilgrimage, and when the time comes at which they receive their wings they have the same plumage because of their love.

Thus great are the heavenly blessings which the friendship of a lover will confer upon you, my youth. Whereas the attachment of the non-lover, which is alloyed with a worldly prudence and has worldly and niggardly ways of doling out benefits, will breed in your soul those vulgar qualities which the populace applaud, will send you bowling round the earth during a period of nine thousand years, and leave you a fool in the world below.

And thus, dear Eros, I have made and paid my recantation, as well and as fairly as I could; more especially in the matter of the poetical figures which I was compelled to use, because Phaedrus would have them. And now forgive the past and accept the present, and be gracious and merciful to me, and do not in thine anger deprive me of sight, or take from me the art of love which thou hast given me, but grant that I may be yet more esteemed in the eyes of the fair. And if Phaedrus or I myself said anything rude in our first speeches, blame Lysias, who is the father of the brat, and let us have no more of his progeny; bid him study philosophy, like his brother Polemarchus; and then his lover Phaedrus will no longer halt between two opinions, but will dedicate himself wholly to love and to philosophical discourses.

. . . . .

THE LOVE OF BEAUTY

The *Symposium* presents Plato's philosophy of beauty, a vision that has been a source of inspiration to all Western philosophy.

FROM *Symposium*
201ᶜ-212ᵃ

Socrates. And now, taking my leave of you, I will rehearse a tale of love which I heard from Diotima of Mantineia, a woman wise in this and in many other kinds of knowledge, who in the days of old, when the Athenians offered sacrifice before the coming of the plague, delayed the disease ten years. She was my instructress in the art of love, and I shall repeat to you what she said to me, beginning with the admissions made by Agathon, which are nearly if not quite the same which I made to the wise woman when she questioned me: I think that this will be the easiest way, and I shall take both parts myself as well as I can. As you, Agathon, suggested, I must speak first of the being and nature of Love, and then of his works. First I said to her in nearly the same words which he used to me, that Love was a mighty god, and likewise fair; and she proved to me as I proved to him that, by my own showing, Love was neither fair nor good. 'What do you mean, Diotima,' I said, 'is love then evil and foul?' 'Hush,' she cried; 'must that be foul which 202 is not fair?' 'Certainly,' I said. 'And is that which is not wise, ignorant? do you not see that there is a mean between wisdom and ignorance?' 'And what may that be?' I said. 'Right opinion,' she replied; 'which, as you know, being incapable of giving a reason, is not knowledge (for how can knowledge be devoid of reason? nor again, ignorance, for neither can ignorance attain the truth), but is clearly something which is a mean between ignorance and wisdom.' 'Quite true,' I replied. 'Do not then insist,' she said, 'that what is not fair is of necessity foul, or what is not good evil; or infer that because love is not fair and good he is therefore foul and evil; for he is in a mean between them.' 'Well,' I said, 'Love is surely admitted by all to be a great god.' 'By those who know or by those who do not know?' 'By all.' 'And how, Socrates,' she said with a smile, 'can Love be acknowledged to be a great god by those who say that he is not a god at all?' 'And who are they?' I said. 'You and I are two of them,' she replied. 'How can that be?' I said. 'It is quite intelligible,' she replied; 'for you yourself would acknowledge that the gods are happy and fair—of course you would— would you dare to say that any god was not?' 'Certainly not,' I replied. 'And you mean by the happy, those who are the possessors of things good or fair?' 'Yes.' 'And you admitted that Love, because he was in want, desires those good and fair things of which he is in want?' 'Yes, I did.' 'But how can he be a god who has no portion in what is either good or fair?' 'Impossible.' 'Then you see that you also deny the divinity of Love.'

'What then is Love?' I asked; 'Is he mortal?' 'No.' 'What then?' 'As in the former instance, he is neither mortal nor immortal, but in a mean between the two.' 'What is he, Diotima?' 'He is a great spirit (δαίμων), and like all spirits he is intermediate between the divine and the mortal.' 'And what,' I said, 'is his power?' 'He interprets,' she replied, 'between gods and men, conveying and taking across to the gods the prayers and sacrifices of men, and to men the commands and replies of the gods; he is the mediator who spans the chasm which divides them, and therefore in him all is bound together, and through him the arts of the prophet and the priest, their sacrifices and mysteries and charms, and all prophecy and incantation, find their way. For God mingles not with man; but through Love all the intercourse and converse of god with man, whether awake or asleep, is carried on. The wisdom which understands this is spiritual; all other wisdom, such as that of arts and handicrafts, is mean and vulgar. Now these spirits or intermediate powers are many and diverse, and one of them is Love.' 'And who,' I said, 'was his father, and who his mother?' 'The tale,' she said, 'will take time; nevertheless I will tell you. On the birthday of Aphrodite there was a feast of the gods, at which the god Poros or Plenty, who is the son of Metis or Discretion, was one of the guests. When the feast was over, Penia or Poverty, as the manner is on such occasions, came about the doors to beg. Now Plenty, who was the worse for nectar (there was no wine in those days), went into the garden of Zeus and fell into a heavy sleep; and Poverty considering her own straitened circumstances, plotted to have a child by him, and accordingly she lay down at his side and conceived Love, who partly because he is naturally a lover of the beautiful, and because Aphrodite is herself beautiful, and also because he was born on her birthday, is her follower and attendant.

And as his parentage is, so also are his fortunes. In the first place he is always poor, and anything but tender and fair, as the many imagine him; and he is rough and squalid, and has no shoes, nor a house to dwell in; on the bare earth exposed he lies under the open heaven, in the streets, or at the doors of houses, taking his rest; and like his mother he is always in distress. Like his father too, whom he also partly resembles, he is always plotting against the fair and good; he is bold, enterprising, strong, a mighty hunter, always weaving some intrigue or other, keen in the pursuit of wisdom, fertile in resources; a philosopher at all times, terrible as an enchanter, sorcerer, sophist. He is by nature neither mortal nor immortal, but alive and flourishing at one moment when he is in plenty, and dead at another moment, and again alive by reason of his father's nature. But that which is always flowing in is always flowing out, and so he is never in want and never in wealth; and, further, he is in a mean between ignorance and knowledge. The truth of the matter is this: No god is a philosopher or seeker after wisdom, for he is wise already; nor does any man who is wise seek after wis-

204 dom. Neither do the ignorant seek after wisdom. For herein is the evil of ignorance, that he who is neither good nor wise is nevertheless satisfied with himself: he has no desire for that of which he feels no want.' 'But who then, Diotima,' I said, 'are the lovers of wisdom, if they are neither the wise nor the foolish?' 'A child may answer that question,' she replied; 'they are those who are in a mean between the two; Love is one of them. For wisdom is a most beautiful thing, and Love is of the beautiful; and therefore Love is also a philosopher or lover of wisdom, and being a lover of wisdom is in a mean between the wise and the ignorant. And of this too his birth is the cause; for his father is wealthy and wise, and his mother poor and foolish. Such, my dear Socrates, is the nature of the spirit Love. The error in your conception of him was very natural, and as I imagine from what you say, has arisen out of a confusion of love and the beloved, which made you think that love was all beautiful. For the beloved is the truly beautiful, and delicate, and perfect, and blessed; but the principle of love is of another nature, and is such as I have described.'

I said: 'O thou stranger woman, thou sayest well; but, assuming Love to be such as you say, what is the use of him to men?' 'That, Socrates,' she replied, 'I will attempt to unfold: of his nature and birth I have already spoken; and you acknowledge that love is of the beautiful. But some one will say: Of the beautiful in what, So-

crates and Diotima?—or rather let me put the question more clearly, and ask: When a man loves the beautiful, what does he desire?'
I answered her 'That the beautiful may be his.' 'Still,' she said, 'the
answer suggests a further question: What is given by the possession
of beauty?' 'To what you have asked,' I replied, 'I have no answer
ready.' 'Then,' she said, 'let me put the word "good" in the place
of the beautiful, and repeat the question once more: If he who
loves loves the good, what is it then that he loves?' 'The possession
of the good,' I said. 'And what does he gain who possesses the
good?' 'Happiness,' I replied; 'there is less difficulty in answering
that question.' 'Yes,' she said, 'the happy are made happy by the   205
acquisition of good things. Nor is there any need to ask why a man
desires happiness; the answer is already final.' 'You are right,' I
said. 'And is this wish and this desire common to all? and do all
men always desire their own good, or only some men?—what say
you?' 'All men,' I replied; 'the desire is common to all.' 'Why,
then,' she rejoined, 'are not all men, Socrates, said to love, but
only some of them? whereas you say that all men are always loving
the same things.' 'I myself wonder,' I said, 'why this is.' 'There is
nothing to wonder at,' she replied; 'the reason is that one part of
love is separated off and receives the name of the whole, but the
other parts have other names.' 'Give an illustration,' I said. She
answered me as follows: 'There is poetry, which, as you know, is
complex and manifold. All creation or passage of non-being into
being is poetry or making, and the processes of all art are creative;
and the masters of arts are all poets or makers.' 'Very true.' 'Still,'
she said, 'you know that they are not called poets, but have other
names; only that portion of the art which is separated off from the
rest, and is concerned with music and metre, is termed poetry, and
they who possess poetry in this sense of the word are called poets.'
'Very true,' I said. 'And the same holds of love. For you may say
generally that all desire of good and happiness is only the great and
subtle power of love; but they who are drawn towards him by any
other path, whether the path of money-making or gymnastics or
philosophy, are not called lovers—the name of the whole is appropriated to those whose affection takes one form only—they alone
are said to love, or to be lovers.' 'I dare say,' I replied, 'that you are
right.' 'Yes,' she added, 'and you hear people say that lovers are
seeking for their other half; but I say that they are seeking neither
for the half of themselves, nor for the whole, unless the half or the
whole be also a good. And they will cut off their own hands and

feet and cast them away, if they are evil; for they love not what is their own, unless perchance there be some one who calls what belongs to him the good, and what belongs to another the evil. For there is nothing which men love but the good. Is there anything?' 'Certainly, I should say, that there is nothing.' 'Then,' she said, 'the simple truth is, that men love the good.' 'Yes,' I said. 'To which must be added that they love the possession of the good?' 'Yes, that must be added.' 'And not only the possession, but the everlasting possession of the good?' 'That must be added too.' 'Then love,' she said, 'may be described generally as the love of the everlasting possession of the good?' 'That is most true.'

'Then if this be the nature of love, can you tell me further,' she said, 'what is the manner of the pursuit? what are they doing who show all this eagerness and heat which is called love? and what is the object which they have in view? Answer me.' 'Nay, Diotima,' I replied, 'if I had known, I should not have wondered at your wisdom, neither should I have come to learn from you about this very matter.' 'Well,' she said, 'I will teach you:—The object which they have in view is birth in beauty, whether of body or soul.' 'I do not understand you,' I said; 'the oracle requires an explanation.' 'I will make my meaning clearer,' she replied. 'I mean to say, that all men are bringing to the birth in their bodies and in their souls. There is a certain age at which human nature is desirous of procreation —procreation which must be in beauty and not in deformity; and this procreation is the union of man and woman, and is a divine thing; for conception and generation are an immortal principle in the mortal creature, and in the inharmonious they can never be. But the deformed is always inharmonious with the divine, and the beautiful harmonious. Beauty, then, is the destiny or goddess of parturition who presides at birth, and therefore, when approaching beauty, the conceiving power is propitious, and diffusive, and benign, and begets and bears fruit: at the sight of ugliness she frowns and contracts and has a sense of pain, and turns away, and shrivels up, and not without a pang refrains from conception. And this is the reason why, when the hour of conception arrives, and the teeming nature is full, there is such a flutter and ecstasy about beauty whose approach is the alleviation of the pain of travail. For love, Socrates, is not, as you imagine, the love of the beautiful only.' 'What then?' 'The love of generation and of birth in beauty.' 'Yes,' I said. 'Yes, indeed,' she replied. 'But why of generation?' 'Because to the mortal creature, generation is a sort of eternity and immortality,' she replied; 'and if, as has been already admitted, love is of the everlasting possession of the good, all men will necessarily desire immortality together with good: Wherefore love is of 207 immortality.'

All this she taught me at various times when she spoke of love. And I remember her once saying to me, 'What is the cause, Socrates, of love, and the attendant desire? See you not how all animals, birds, as well as beasts, in their desire of procreation, are in agony when they take the infection of love, which begins with the desire of union; whereto is added the care of offspring, on whose behalf the weakest are ready to battle against the strongest even to the uttermost, and to die for them, and will let themselves be tormented with hunger or suffer anything in order to maintain their young. Man may be supposed to act thus from reason; but why should animals have these passionate feelings? Can you tell me why?' Again I replied that I did not know. She said to me: 'And do you expect ever to become a master in the art of love, if you do not know this?' 'But I have told you already, Diotima, that my ignorance is the reason why I come to you; for I am conscious that I want a teacher; tell me then the cause of this and of the other mysteries of love.' 'Marvel not,' she said, 'if you believe that love is of the immortal, as we have several times acknowledged; for here again, and on the same principle too, the mortal nature is seeking as far as is possible to be everlasting and immortal: and this is only to be attained by generation, because generation always leaves behind a new existence in the place of the old. Nay even in the life of the same individual there is succession and not absolute unity: a man is called the same, and yet in the short interval which elapses between youth and age, and in which every animal is said to have life and identity, he is undergoing a perpetual process of loss and reparation—hair, flesh, bones, blood, and the whole body are always changing. Which is true not only of the body, but also of the soul, whose habits, tempers, opinions, desires, pleasures, pains, fears, never remain the same in any one of us, but are always coming and going; and equally true of knowledge, and what is still more surprising to us mortals, not only do the sciences in general 208 spring up and decay, so that in respect of them we are never the same; but each of them individually experiences a like change. For what is implied in the word "recollection," but the departure of knowledge, which is ever being forgotten, and is renewed and preserved by recollection, and appears to be the same although in reality new, according to that law of succession by which all mortal things are preserved, not absolutely the same, but by substitution, the old worn-out mortality leaving another new and similar existence behind—unlike the divine, which is always the same and not another? And in this way, Socrates, the mortal body, or mortal anything, partakes of immortality; but the immortal in another way. Marvel not then at the love which all men have of their offspring; for that universal love and interest is for the sake of immortality.'

I was astonished at her words, and said: 'Is this really true, O thou wise Diotima?' And she answered with all the authority of an accomplished sophist: 'Of that, Socrates, you may be assured;—think only of the ambition of men, and you will wonder at the senselessness of their ways, unless you consider how they are stirred by the love of an immortality of fame. They are ready to run all risks greater far than they would have run for their children, and to spend money and undergo any sort of toil, and even to die, for the sake of leaving behind them a name which shall be eternal. Do you imagine that Alcestis would have died to save Admetus, or Achilles to avenge Patroclus, or your own Codrus in order to preserve the kingdom for his sons, if they had not imagined that the memory of their virtues, which still survives among us, would be immortal? Nay,' she said, 'I am persuaded that all men do all things, and the better they are the more they do them, in hope of the glorious fame of immortal virtue; for they desire the immortal.

"Those who are pregnant in the body only, betake themselves to women and beget children—this is the character of their love; their offspring, as they hope, will preserve their memory and give them the blessedness and immortality which they desire in the future. But souls which are pregnant—for there certainly are men who are more creative in their souls than in their bodies—conceive that which is proper for the soul to conceive or contain. And what are these conceptions?—wisdom and virtue in general. And such creators are poets and all artists who are deserving of the name inventor. But the greatest and fairest sort of wisdom by far is that which is concerned with the ordering of states and families, and which is called temperance and justice. And he who in youth has the seed of these implanted in him and is himself inspired, when he comes to maturity desires to beget and generate. He wanders about seeking beauty that he may beget offspring—for in deformity he will beget nothing—and naturally embraces the beautiful rather than the deformed body; above all when he finds a fair and noble and well-nurtured soul, he embraces the two in one person, and to such an one he is full of speech about virtue and the nature and pursuits of a good man; and he tries to educate him; and at the touch of the beautiful which is ever present to his memory, even when absent, he brings forth that which he had conceived long before, and in company with him tends that which he brings forth; and they are married by a far nearer tie and have a closer friendship than those who beget mortal children, for the children who are their common offspring are fairer and more immortal. Who, when he thinks of Homer and Hesiod and other great poets, would not rather have their children than ordinary human ones? Who would not emulate them in the creation of children such as theirs, which have preserved their memory and given them everlasting glory? Or who would not have such children as Lycurgus left behind him to be the saviours, not only of Lacedaemon, but of Hellas, as one may say? There is Solon, too, who is the revered father of Athenian laws; and many others there are in many other places, both among Hellenes and barbarians, who have given to the world many noble works, and have been the parents of virtue of every kind; and many temples have been raised in their honour for the sake of children such as theirs; which were never raised in honour of any one, for the sake of his mortal children.

'These are the lesser mysteries of love, into which even you, Socrates, may enter; to the greater and more hidden ones which are 210 the crown of these, and to which, if you pursue them in a right spirit, they will lead, I know not whether you will be able to attain. But I will do my utmost to inform you, and do you follow if you can. For he who would proceed aright in this matter should begin in youth to visit beautiful forms; and first, if he be guided by his instructor aright, to love one such form only—out of that he should create fair thoughts; and soon he will of himself perceive that the beauty of one form is akin to the beauty of another; and then if beauty of form in general is his pursuit, how foolish would he be not to recognize that the beauty in every form is one and the same! And when he perceives this he will abate his violent love of the one, which he will despise and deem a small thing, and will become a lover of all beautiful forms; in the next stage he will consider that the beauty of the mind is more honourable than the beauty of the outward form. So that if a virtuous soul have but a little comeliness, he will be content to love and tend him, and will search out and bring to the birth thoughts which may improve the young, until he is compelled to contemplate and see the beauty of institutions and laws, and to understand that the beauty of them all is of one family, and that personal beauty is a trifle; and after laws and institutions he will go on to the sciences, that he may see their beauty, being not like a servant in love with the beauty of one youth or man or institution, himself a slave mean and narrow-minded, but drawing towards and contemplating the vast sea of beauty, he will create many fair and noble thoughts and notions in boundless love of wisdom; until on that shore he grows and waxes strong, and at last the vision is revealed to him of a single science, which is the science of beauty everywhere. To this I will proceed; please to give me your very best attention:

211 'He who has been instructed thus far in the things of love, and who has learned to see the beautiful in due order and succession, when he comes toward the end will suddenly perceive a nature of wondrous beauty (and this, Socrates, is the final cause of all our former toils)—a nature which in the first place is everlasting, not growing and decaying, or waxing and waning; secondly, not fair in one point of view and foul in another, or at one time or in one relation or at one place fair, at another time or in another relation or at another place foul, as if fair to some and foul to others, or in the likeness of a face or hands or any other part of the bodily frame, or in any form of speech or knowledge, or existing in any other being, as for example, in an animal, or in heaven, or in earth, or in any other place; but beauty absolute, separate, simple, and everlasting, which without diminution and without increase, or any change, is imparted to the ever-growing and perishing beauties of all other things. He who from these ascending under the influence of true love, begins to perceive that beauty, is not far from the end. And the true order of going, or being led by another, to the things of love, is to begin from the beauties of earth and mount upwards for the sake of that other beauty, using these as steps only, and from one going on to two, and from two to all fair forms, and from fair forms to fair practices, and from fair practices to fair notions, until from fair notions he arrives at the notion of absolute beauty, and at last knows what the essence of beauty is. This, my dear Socrates,' said the stranger of Mantineia, 'is that life above all others which man should live, in the contemplation of beauty absolute; a beauty which if you once beheld, you would see not to be after the measure of gold, and garments, and fair boys and youths, whose pres-

ence now entrances you; and you and many a one would be content to live seeing them only and conversing with them without meat or drink, if that were possible—you only want to look at them and to be with them. But what if man had eyes to see the true beauty—the divine beauty, I mean, pure and clear and unalloyed, not clogged with the pollutions of mortality and all the colours and vanities of human life—thither looking, and holding converse with the true beauty simple and divine? Remember how 212 in that communion only, beholding beauty with the eye of the mind, he will be enabled to bring forth, not images of beauty, but realities (for he has hold not of an image but of a reality), and bringing forth and nourishing true virtue to become the friend of God and be immortal, if mortal man may. Would that be an ignoble life?'

• • • • •

ARISTOTLE

Aristotle's philosophy of art is known through the Poetics, without doubt the most influential single work on art. Yet the Poetics gives by itself an incomplete picture of Aristotle's thought, for he has much to say about the definition of art, art and nature, beauty, and artistic goodness throughout his writing. It is only when we take all this into account that we can see what his philosophy of art is. In the total picture the Poetics appears as essentially a work on one kind of techne (the imitative sort) with little to say on many problems essential to Aristotle's position.

Aristotle's philosophy of art is therefore presented through a number of passages culled from many books, and arranged in accordance with central problems. The first section, "What is Art," distinguishes art from nature and from acting. Art is a capacity to make, concerned with contriving the coming-into-being of ends determined by reason. In artistic making—as Section II, "Nature and Art," shows—the envisioned end determines the appropriate means for its realization. Section III, "Standard of Artistic Goodness," is concerned with the determination of excellence in techne. The well-made artistic work has a perfection of form and a sureness of method which guarantees that it will be a satisfactory whole in itself and efficacious in its work. This implies, as

Section IV, "Beauty," points out, that the elements in its composition exhibit symmetry, harmony, and definiteness.

All these conditions for techne are assumed in the discussion of imitative art which constitutes the Poetics, a treatise which centers upon one kind of imitative art, poetry, and within that, tragic drama. Many of the statements about tragic drama are amplified elsewhere in Aristotle's writing, e.g., in the Rhetoric, where pity and fear are described, and in the Politics, where catharsis is illustrated. Important material from the Nicomachean Ethics has not been included because of its generality, but the reader is advised to read Book III in connection with the conception of action and tragic flaw (hamartia). Section VI, "Theory of Music," presents a brief, enlightening statement about the uses and powers of music, and also serves to point out how Aristotle differs from Plato in his evaluation of art.

While Plato insists that artistic imitation, especially tragedy, feeds the passions and misleads the seeker after truth, Aristotle answers that the arts in general are valuable because they repair the deficiencies in nature, and that tragic drama in particular is justifiable because of the moral contribution it makes. Tragedy is a means of gaining knowledge, through its presentation of philosophic truths, and is a way of coping with the enthusiastic states common to all men. Although Aristotle, like Plato, is interested in madness (see especially, Poetics, Chapter 17; On Dreams, I, 1 and II, 2; Problems, XXX, 1), he depreciates the importance of beauty and erotic love which figure so centrally in Plato's discussion of the arts. The rejection of Plato's metaphysical idealism accounts for Aristotle's treatment of beauty as a property of the art work or natural object and for his emphasis upon the moral benefits of tragedy as against the inspired search for the Beautiful which Plato sees as the proper end of art.

On the other hand Aristotle follows Plato on many points. He agrees that art is a kind of techne, that there is a measure and mean appropriate to the exercise of techne, and that the most important human arts, such as music, painting, sculpture, literature, are imitative of human souls, bodies, and actions. If the Poetics is considered as in part an answer to Plato's criticism of the imitative arts, then it is clear that Aristotle regards Plato's condemnation as inappropriate, for the imitative arts are human instruments of learning, and their effects upon the spectator beneficial. Aristotle's justification of this answer is found throughout his writings, but is perhaps most skillfully realized in those parts of the Poetics which lay down the conditions for the well-made plot and the creation of character. In addition, Aristotle has an *historical and anthropological interest that leads him to justify the imitative art of tragedy as the natural later development of a human religious activity. Tragedy has found, now, its proper form and realized its nature.*

WHAT IS ART?

FROM *Metaphysics*
(1070ª 4-1070ª 30; 1046ª 5-1046ᵇ 28 with omissions)

BOOK XII

1070ª   . . . Each substance comes into being out of something that
 5 shares its name. (Natural objects and other things both rank as
substances.) For things come into being either by art or by nature
 or by luck or by spontaneity. Now art is a principle of movement in
something other than the thing moved, nature is a principle in the
thing itself (for man begets man), and the other causes are priva-
tions of these two.

 There are three kinds of substance—the matter, which is a 'this'
 10 in appearance (for all things that are characterized by contact
 19 and not by organic unity are matter and substratum, e.g. fire, flesh,
head; for these are all matter, and the last matter is the matter of
 11 that which is in the full sense substance); the nature, which is a
'this' or positive state towards which movement takes place; and
again, thirdly, the particular substance which is composed of these
two, e.g. Socrates or Callias. Now in some cases the 'this' does not
exist apart from the composite substance, e.g. the form of house
 15 does not so exist, unless the art of building exists apart (nor is
there generation and destruction of these forms, but it is in
another way that the house apart from its matter, and health, and
all ideals of art, exist and do not exist); but if the 'this' exists apart
from the concrete thing, it is only in the case of natural objects.
And so Plato was not far wrong when he said that there are as
many Forms as there are kinds of natural object (if there *are*
 21 Forms distinct from the things of this earth). The moving causes
exist as things preceding the effects, but causes in the sense of
definitions are simultaneous with their effects. For when a man is
healthy, then health also exists; and the shape of a bronze sphere

exists at the same time as the bronze sphere. (But we must exam- 25
ine whether any form also survives afterwards. For in some cases
there is nothing to prevent this; e.g. the soul may be of this sort—
not all soul but the reason; for presumably it is impossible that *all*
soul should survive.) Evidently then there is no necessity, on this
ground at least, for the existence of the Ideas. For man is begotten
by man, a given man by an individual father; and similarly in the 30
arts; for the medical art is the formal cause of health.

. . . . .

BOOK IX

. . . We have pointed out elsewhere[1] that 'potency' and the 1046ª
word 'can' have several senses. Of these we may neglect all the po- 5
tencies that are so called by an equivocation. For some are called
so by analogy, as in geometry we say one thing is or is not a 'power'
of another by virtue of the presence or absence of some relation between them. But all potencies that conform to the same type are
originative sources of some kind, and are called potencies in refer- 10
ence to one primary kind of potency, which is an originative source
of change in another thing or in the thing itself *qua* other.

. . . . .

. . . In a sense the potency of acting and of being acted on is
one (for a thing may be 'capable' either because it can itself be 20
acted on or because something else can be acted on by it), but in
a sense the potencies are different. For the one is in the thing
acted on; it is because it contains a certain originative source, and
because even the matter is an originative source, that the thing
acted on is acted on, and one thing by one, another by another;
for that which is oily can be burnt, and that which yields in a 25
particular way can be crushed; and similarly in all other cases. But
the other potency is in the agent, e.g. heat and the art of building
are present, one in that which can produce heat and the other in
the man who can build.

. . . . .

2 Since some such originative sources are present in soulless
things, and others in things possessed of soul, and in soul, and in
the rational part of the soul, clearly some potencies will be non- 1046ᵇ

---

[1] Cf. v. 12.

rational and some will be accompanied by a rational formula. This is why all arts, i.e. all productive forms of knowledge, are potencies; they are originative sources of change in another thing or in the artist himself considered as other.

5 And each of those which are accompanied by a rational formula is alike capable of contrary effects, but one non-rational power produces one effect; e.g. the hot is capable only of heating, but the medical art can produce both disease and health. The reason is that science is a rational formula, and the same rational formula explains a thing and its privation, only not in the same way; and in 10 a sense it applies to both, but in a sense it applies rather to the positive fact. Therefore such sciences must deal with contraries, but with one in virtue of their own nature and with the other not in virtue of their nature; for the rational formula applies to one object in virtue of that object's nature, and to the other, in a sense, accidentally. For it is by denial and removal that it exhibits the con- 15 trary; for the contrary is the primary privation, and this is the removal of the positive term. Now since contraries do not occur in the same thing, but science is a potency which depends on the possession of a rational formula, and the soul possesses an originative source of movement; therefore, while the wholesome produces 20 only health and the calorific only heat and the frigorific only cold, the scientific man produces both the contrary effects. For the rational formula is one which applies to both, though not in the same way, and it is in a soul which possesses an originative source of movement; so that the soul will start both processes from the same originative source, having linked them up with the same thing. And so the things whose potency is according to a rational formula act contrariwise to the things whose potency is non-rational; for the products of the former are included under one originative source, the rational formula.

25 It is obvious also that the potency of merely doing a thing or having it done to one is implied in that of doing it or having it done *well*, but the latter is not always implied in the former: for he who does a thing well must also do it, but he who does it merely need not also do it well.

FROM *Nicomachean Ethics*
(1140ᵃ 1-1140ᵃ 24)

BOOK VII

4 In the variable are included both things made and things 1140ᵃ
done; making and acting are different (for their nature we treat
even the discussions outside our school as reliable); so that the
reasoned state of capacity to act is different from the reasoned 5
state of capacity to make. Hence too they are not included one in
the other; for neither is acting making nor is making acting. Now
since architecture is an art and is essentially a reasoned state of
capacity to make, and there is neither any art that is not such a
state nor any such state that is not an art, *art* is identical with a 10
state of capacity to make, involving a true course of reasoning. All
art is concerned with coming into being, i.e. with contriving and
considering how something may come into being which is capable
of either being or not being, and whose origin is in the maker and
not in the thing made; for art is concerned neither with things that
are, or come into being, by necessity, nor with things that do so in
accordance with nature (since these have their origin in them- 15
selves). Making and acting being different, art must be a matter of
making, not of acting. And in a sense chance and art are concerned with the same objects; as Agathon says, 'art loves chance
and chance loves art'. Art, then, as has been said, is a state con- 20
cerned with making, involving a true course of reasoning, and lack
of art on the contrary is a state concerned with making, involving
a false course of reasoning; both are concerned with the variable.

COMING-TO-BE AND
ARTISTIC PRODUCTION
Nature and Art

FROM *Parts of Animals*
(639ᵇ 12-640ᵃ 29)

BOOK I

639ᵇ   . . . The causes concerned in the generation of the works of nature are, as we see, more than one. There is the final cause and
there is the motor cause. Now we must decide which of these two
causes comes first, which second. Plainly, however, that cause is the
15 first which we call the final one. For this is the Reason, and the
Reason forms the starting-point, alike in the works of art and in
works of nature. For consider how the physician or how the builder
sets about his work. He starts by forming for himself a definite picture, in the one case perceptible to mind, in the other to sense, of
his end—the physician of health, the builder of a house—and this
he holds forward as the reason and explanation of each subsequent
20 step that he takes, and of his acting in this or that way as the case
may be. Now in the works of nature the good end and the final
cause is still more dominant than in works of art such as these, nor
is necessity a factor with the same significance in them all; though
almost all writers, while they try to refer their origin to this cause,
do so without distinguishing the various senses in which the term
necessity is used. For there is absolute necessity, manifested in
25 eternal phenomena; and there is hypothetical necessity, manifested
in everything that is generated by nature as in everything that is
produced by art, be it a house or what it may. For if a house or
other such final object is to be realized, it is necessary that such
and such material shall exist; and it is necessary that first this and
then that shall be produced, and first this and then that set in
30 motion, and so on in continuous succession, until the end and
final result is reached, for the sake of which each prior thing
is produced and exists. As with these productions of art, so
also is it with the productions of nature. The mode of necessity,

however, and the mode of ratiocination are different in natural 640ᶜ
science from what they are in the theoretical sciences; of which we
have spoken elsewhere. For in the latter the starting-point is that
which is; in the former that which is to be. For it is that which is 5
yet to be—health, let us say, or a man—that, owing to its being of
such and such characters, necessitates the pre-existence or previous
production of this and that antecedent; and not this or that antecedent which, because it exists or has been generated, makes it necessary that health or a man is in, or shall come into, existence.
Nor is it possible to trace back the series of necessary antecedents
to a starting-point, of which you can say that, existing itself from
eternity, it has determined their existence as its consequent. These
however, again, are matters that have been dealt with in another 10
treatise. There too it was stated in what cases absolute and hypothetical necessity exist; in what cases also the proposition expressing hypothetical necessity is simply convertible, and what cause it
is that determines this convertibility.

Another matter which must not be passed over without consideration is, whether the proper subject of our exposition is that
with which the ancient writers concerned themselves, namely, what
is the process of formation of each animal; or whether it is not
rather, what are the characters of a given creature when formed.
For there is no small difference between these two views. The best
course appears to be that we should follow the method already
mentioned, and begin with the phenomena presented by each 15
group of animals, and, when this is done, proceed afterwards to
state the causes of those phenomena, and to deal with their evolution. For elsewhere, as for instance in house building, this is the
true sequence. The plan of the house, or the house, has this and
that form; and because it has this and that form, therefore is its
construction carried out in this or that manner. For the process of
evolution is for the sake of the thing finally evolved, and not this
for the sake of the process. Empedocles, then, was in error when he
said that many of the characters presented by animals were merely
the results of incidental occurrences during their development; for 20
instance, that the backbone was divided as it is into vertebrae, because it happened to be broken owing to the contorted position of
the foetus in the womb. In so saying he overlooked the fact that
propagation implies a creative seed endowed with certain formative properties. Secondly, he neglected another fact, namely, that
the parent animal pre-exists, not only in idea, but actually in time. 25

For man is generated from man; and thus it is the possession of certain characters by the parent that determines the development of like characters in the child. The same statement holds good also for the operations of art, and even for those which are apparently spontaneous. For the same result as is produced by art may occur spontaneously. Spontaneity, for instance, may bring about the res-
30 toration of health. The products of art, however, require the pre-existence of an efficient cause homogeneous with themselves, such as the statuary's art, which must necessarily precede the statue; for this cannot possibly be produced spontaneously. Art indeed consists in the conception of the result to be produced before its realization in the material. As with spontaneity, so with chance; for this also produces the same result as art, and by the same process.

· · · · ·

FROM *Physics*

(198^b 10-200^b 9)

BOOK II

198^b 8 We must explain then (1) that Nature belongs to the class of causes which act for the sake of something; (2) about the necessary and its place in physical problems, for all writers ascribe things to this cause, arguing that since the hot and the cold, &c., are of such and such a kind, therefore certain things *necessarily* are and
15 come to be—and if they mention any other cause (one his 'friendship and strife', another his 'mind'), it is only to touch on it, and then good-bye to it.

A difficulty presents itself: why should not nature work, not for the sake of something, nor because it is better so, but just as the sky rains, not in order to make the corn grow, but of necessity?
20 What is drawn up must cool, and what has been cooled must become water and descend, the result of this being that the corn grows. Similarly, if a man's crop is spoiled on the threshing-floor, the rain did not fall for the sake of this—in order that the crop might be spoiled—but that result just followed. Why then should it not be the same with the parts in nature, e.g. that our teeth
25 should come up *of necessity*—the front teeth sh .rp, fitted for tearing, the molars broad and useful for grinding down the food—since they did not arise for this end, but it was merely a coincident result; and so with all other parts in which we suppose that there is

purpose? Wherever then all the parts came about just what they 30 would have been if they had come to be for an end, such things survived, being organized spontaneously in a fitting way; whereas those which grew otherwise perished and continue to perish, as Empedocles says his 'man-faced ox-progeny' did.

Such are the arguments (and others of the kind) which may cause difficulty on this point. Yet it is impossible that this should be the true view. For teeth and all other natural things either in- 35 variably or normally come about in a given way; but of not one of the results of chance or spontaneity is this true. We do not ascribe to chance or mere coincidence the frequency of rain in winter, but 199ᵃ frequent rain in summer we do; nor heat in the dog-days, but only if we have it in winter. If then, it is agreed that things are either the result of coincidence or for an end, and these cannot be the re- sult of coincidence or spontaneity, it follows that they must be for 5 an end; and that such things are all due to nature even the cham- pions of the theory which is before us would agree. Therefore ac- tion for an end is present in things which come to be and are by nature.

Further, where a series has a completion, all the preceding steps are for the sake of that. Now surely as in intelligent action, so in 10 nature; and as in nature, so it is in each action, if nothing inter- feres. Now intelligent action is for the sake of an end; therefore the nature of things also is so. Thus if a house, e.g., had been a thing made by nature, it would have been made in the same way as it is now by art; and if things made by nature were made also by art, they would come to be in the same way as by nature. Each step 15 then in the series is for the sake of the next; and generally art partly completes what nature cannot bring to a finish, and partly imitates her. If, therefore, artificial products are for the sake of an end, so clearly also are natural products. The relation of the later to the earlier terms of the series is the same in both.

This is most obvious in the animals other than man: they make 20 things neither by art nor after inquiry or deliberation. Wherefore people discuss whether it is by intelligence or by some other faculty that these creatures work,—spiders, ants, and the like. By gradual advance in this direction we come to see clearly that in plants too that is produced which is conducive to the end—leaves, e.g. grow to 25 provide shade for the fruit. If then it is both by nature and for an end that the swallow makes its nest and the spider its web, and plants grow leaves for the sake of the fruit and send their roots

down (not up) for the sake of nourishment, it is plain that this
30 kind of cause is operative in things which come to be and are by nature. And since 'nature' means two things, the matter and the
form, of which the latter is the end, and since all the rest is for the
sake of the end, the form must be the cause in the sense of 'that for
the sake of which'.

Now mistakes come to pass even in the operations of art: the
grammarian makes a mistake in writing and the doctor pours out
35 the wrong dose. Hence clearly mistakes are possible in the operations
199b of nature also. If then in art there are cases in which what is
rightly produced serves a purpose, and if where mistakes occur
there was a purpose in what was attempted, only it was not attained, so must it be also in natural products, and monstrosities will
5 be failures in the purposive effort. Thus in the original combinations the 'ox-progeny' if they failed to reach a determinate end
must have arisen through the corruption of some principle corresponding to what is now the seed.

Further, seed must have come into being first, and not straightway the animals: the words 'whole-natured first . . .' must have
meant seed.

Again, in plants too we find the relation of means to end,
10 though the degree of organization is less. Were there then in plants
also 'olive-headed vine-progeny', like the 'man-headed ox-progeny',
or not? An absurd suggestion; yet there must have been, if there
were such things among animals.

Moreover, among the seeds anything must have come to be at
random. But the person who asserts this entirely does away with
15 'nature' and what exists 'by nature'. For those things are natural
which, by a continuous movement originated from an internal
principle, arrive at some completion: the same completion is not
reached from every principle; nor any chance completion, but always the tendency in each is towards the same end, if there is no
impediment.

The end and the means towards it may come about by chance.
20 We say, for instance, that a stranger has come by chance, paid the
ransom, and gone away, when he does so as if he had come for
that purpose, though it was not for that that he came. This is incidental, for chance is an incidental cause, as I remarked before. But
when an event takes place always or for the most part, it is not inci-
25 dental or by chance. In natural products the sequence is invariable,
if there is no impediment.

It is absurd to suppose that purpose is not present because we do not observe the agent deliberating. Art does not deliberate. If the ship-building art were in the wood, it would produce the same results *by nature*. If, therefore, purpose is present in art, it is present also in nature. The best illustration is a doctor doctoring him- 30 self: nature is like that.

It is plain then that nature is a cause, a cause that operates for a purpose.

9   As regards what is 'of necessity', we must ask whether the ne- cessity is 'hypothetical', or 'simple' as well. The current view 35 places what is of necessity in the process of production, just as if 200ᵃ one were to suppose that the wall of a house necessarily comes to be because what is heavy is naturally carried downwards and what is light to the top, wherefore the stones and foundations take the lowest place, with earth above because it is lighter, and wood at the top of all as being the lightest. Whereas, though the wall does not 5 come to be *without* these, it is not *due* to these, except as its material cause: it comes to be for the sake of sheltering and guard- ing certain things. Similarly in all other things which involve pro- duction for an end; the product cannot come to be without things which have a necessary nature, but it is not due to these (except 10 as its material); it comes to be for an end. For instance, why is a saw such as it is? To effect so-and-so and for the sake of so-and-so. This end, however, cannot be realized unless the saw is made of iron. It is, therefore, necessary for it to be of iron, *if* we are to have a saw and perform the operation of sawing. What is necessary then, is necessary *on a hypothesis*; it is not a result necessarily deter- mined by antecedents. Necessity is in the matter, while 'that for the sake of which' is in the definition.

Necessity in mathematics is in a way similar to necessity in 15 things which come to be through the operation of nature. Since a straight line is what it is, it is necessary that the angles of a triangle should equal two right angles. But not conversely; though if the angles are *not* equal to two right angles, then the straight line is not what it is either. But in things which come to be for an end, the reverse is true. If the end is to exist or does exist, that also which 20 precedes it will exist or does exist; otherwise just as there, if the conclusion is not true, the premiss will not be true, so here the end or 'that for the sake of which' will not exist. For this too is it- self a starting-point, but of the reasoning, not of the action; while

in mathematics the starting-point is the starting point of the rea-
25 soning only, as there is no action. If then there is to be a house,
such-and-such things must be made or be there already or exist, or
generally the matter relative to the end, bricks and stones if it is a
house. But the end is not due to these except as the matter, nor
will it come to exist because of them. Yet if they do not exist at
all, neither will the house, or the saw—the former in the absence
of stones, the latter in the absence of iron—just as in the other case
the premisses will not be true, if the angles of the triangle are not
equal to two right angles.

30   The necessary in nature, then, is plainly what we call by the
name of matter, and the changes in it. Both causes must be
stated by the physicist, but especially the end; for that is the cause
of the matter, not *vice versa*; and the end is 'that for the sake of
35 which', and the beginning starts from the definition or essence; as
200ᵇ in artificial products, since a house is of such-and-such a kind,
certain things must *necessarily* come to be or be there already, or
since health is this, these things must necessarily come to be or be
there already. Similarly if man is this, then these; if these, then
5   those. Perhaps the necessary is present also in the definition. For if
one defines the operation of sawing as being a certain kind of
dividing, then this cannot come about unless the saw has teeth of
a certain kind; and these cannot be unless it is of iron. For in the
definition too there are some parts that are, as it were, its matter.

FROM *Metaphysics*
(1032ᵃ 12-1032ᵃ 30; 1034ᵃ 8-1034ᵇ 7)

BOOK VII

1032ᵃ 7 Of things that come to be, some come to be by nature, some
by art, some spontaneously. Now everything that comes to be
comes to be by the agency of something and from something and
comes to be something. And the something which I say it comes
to be may be found in any category; it may come to be either a
'this' or of some size or of some quality or somewhere.

15   Now natural comings to be are the comings to be of those things
which come to be by nature; and that out of which they come to
be is what we call matter; and that by which they come to be is
something which exists naturally; and the something which they
come to be is a man or a plant or one of the things of this kind,

which we say are substances if anything is—all things produced 20
either by nature or by art have matter; for each of them is capable
both of being and of not being, and this capacity is the matter in
each—and, in general, both that from which they are produced is
nature, and the type according to which they are produced is nature (for that which is produced, e.g. a plant or an animal, has a
nature), and so is that by which they are produced—the so-called
'formal' nature, which is specifically the same (though this is in 25
another individual); for man begets man.

Thus, then, are natural products produced; all other productions
are called 'makings'. And all makings proceed either from art or
from a faculty or from thought. Some of them happen also spontaneously or by luck just as natural products sometimes do; for 30
there also the same things sometimes are produced without seed as
well as from seed. Concerning these cases, then, we must inquire
later, but from art proceed the things of which the form is in the
soul of the artist. (By form I mean the essence of each thing and 1032ᵇ
its primary substance.) For even contraries have in a sense the
same form; for the substance of a privation is the opposite substance, e.g. health is the substance of disease (for disease is the ab- 5
sence of health); and health is the formula in the soul or the
knowledge of it. The healthy subject is produced as the result of
the following train of thought:—since *this* is health, if the subject is to be healthy *this* must first be present, e.g. a uniform state
of body, and if this is to be present, there must be heat; and the
physician goes on thinking thus until he reduces the matter to a
final something which he himself can produce. Then the process
from this point onward, i.e. the process towards health, is called a 10
'making'. Therefore it follows that in a sense health comes from
health and house from house, that with matter from that without
matter; for the medical art and the building art are the form of
health and of the house, and when I speak of substance without
matter I mean the essence.

Of the productions or processes one part is called thinking and 15
the other making—that which proceeds from the starting-point and
the form is thinking, and that which proceeds from the final step of
the thinking is making. And each of the other, intermediate, things
is produced in the same way. I mean, for instance, if the subject is
to be healthy his bodily state must be made uniform. What then
does being made uniform imply? This or that. And this depends
on his being made warm. What does this imply? Something else. 20

And this something is present potentially; and what is present potentially is already in the physician's power.

The active principle then and the starting-point for the process of becoming healthy is, if it happens by art, the form in the soul, and if spontaneously, it is that, whatever it is, which starts the making, for the man who makes by art, as in healing the starting-point is perhaps the production of warmth (and this the physician produces by rubbing). Warmth in the body, then, is either a part of health or is followed (either directly or through several intermediate steps) by something similar which is a part of health; and this, viz. that which produces the part of health, is the limiting-point—and so too with a house (the stones are the limiting-point here) and in all other cases.

. . . . .

1034ᵃ 9 The question might be raised, why some things are produced spontaneously as well as by art, e.g. health, while others are not, e.g. a house. The reason is that in some cases the matter which governs the production in the making and producing of any work of art, and in which a part of the product is present—some matter is such as to be set in motion by itself and some is not of this nature, and of the former kind some can move itself in the particular way required, while other matter is incapable of this; for many things can be set in motion by themselves but not in some particular way, e.g. that of dancing. The things, then, whose matter is of this sort, e.g. stones, cannot be moved in the particular way required, except by something else, but in another way they can move themselves—and so it is with fire. Therefore some things will not exist apart from some one who has the art of making them, while others will; for motion will be started by these things which have not the art but can themselves be moved by other things which have not the art or with a motion starting from a part of the product.

And it is clear also from what has been said that in a sense every product of art is produced from a thing which shares its name (as natural products are produced), or from a part of itself which shares its name (e.g. the house is produced from a house, *qua* produced by reason; for the art of building is the form of the house), or from something which contains a part of it—if we exclude things produced by accident; for the cause of the thing's producing the product directly *per se* is a part of the product. The heat in the movement caused heat in the body, and this is either health, or a part of health, or is followed by a part of health or by health itself. And so it is said to cause health, because it causes that to which health attaches as a consequence.

· · · · ·

Things which are formed by nature are in the same case as these products of art. For the seed is productive in the same way as the things that work by art; for it has the form potentially, and that from which the seed comes has in a sense the same name as the off- 1034ᵇ spring—only in a sense, for we must not expect parent and offspring always to have exactly the same name, as in the production of 'human being' from 'human being'; for a 'woman' also can be produced by a 'man'—unless the offspring be an imperfect form; which is the reason why the parent of a mule is not a mule. The natural things which (like the artificial objects previously consid- 5 ered) can be produced spontaneously are those whose matter can be moved even by itself in the way in which the seed usually moves it; those things which have not such matter cannot be produced except from the parent animals themselves.

· · · · ·

STANDARD OF ARTISTIC GOODNESS

FROM *Nicomachean Ethics*
(1106ᵃ 14-1106ᵇ 17; 1094ᵃ 1-1094ᵇ 10)

BOOK II

6 Every virtue or excellence both brings into good condition the 1106ᵃ thing of which it is the excellence and makes the work of that thing be done well; e.g. the excellence of the eye makes both the eye and its work good; for it is by the excellence of the eye that we see well. Similarly the excellence of the horse makes a horse both 20 good in itself and good at running and at carrying its rider and at awaiting the attack of the enemy. Therefore, if this is true in every case, the virtue of man also will be the state of character which

makes a man good and which makes him do his own work well.

How this is to happen we have stated already, but it will be
25 made plain also by the following consideration of the specific nature of virtue. In everything that is continuous and divisible it is
possible to take more, less, or an equal amount, and that either in
terms of the thing itself or relatively to us; and the equal is an intermediate between excess and defect. By the intermediate in the
30 object I mean that which is equidistant from each of the extremes,
which is one and the same for all men; by the intermediate relatively to us that which is neither too much nor too little—and this
is not one, nor the same for all. For instance, if ten is many and
two is few, six is the intermediate, taken in terms of the object; for
35 it exceeds and is exceeded by an equal amount; this is intermediate according to arithmetical proportion. But the intermediate rela-
1106ᵇ tively to us is not to be taken so; if ten pounds are too much for a
particular person to eat and two too little, it does not follow that
the trainer will order six pounds; for this also is perhaps too much
for the person who is to take it, or too little—too little for Milo,
5 too much for the beginner in athletic exercises. The same is true of
running and wrestling. Thus a master of any art avoids excess and
defect, but seeks the intermediate and chooses this—the intermediate not in the object but relatively to us.

If it is thus, then, that every art does its work well—by looking to
the intermediate and judging its works by this standard (so that we
10 often say of good works of art that it is not possible either to take
away or to add anything, implying that excess and defect destroy
the goodness of works of art, while the mean preserves it; and good
artists, as we say, look to this in their work), and if, further, virtue
is more exact and better than any art, as nature also is, then virtue
15 must have the quality of aiming at the intermediate. I mean moral
virtue; for it is this that is concerned with passions and actions, and
in these there is excess, defect, and the intermediate.

. . . . .

BOOK I

1094ᵃ 1 Every art and every inquiry, and similarly every action and pursuit, is thought to aim at some good; and for this reason the good
has rightly been declared to be that at which all things aim. But a
certain difference is found among ends; some are activities, others
5 are products apart from the activities that produce them. Where

there are ends apart from the actions, it is the nature of the products to be better than the activities. Now, as there are many actions, arts, and sciences, their ends also are many; the end of the medical art is health, that of shipbuilding a vessel, that of strategy victory, that of economics wealth. But where such arts fall under a single capacity—as bridle-making and the other arts concerned with the equipment of horses fall under the art of riding, and this and every military action under strategy, in the same way other arts fall under yet others—in all of these the ends of the master arts are to be preferred to all the subordinate ends; for it is for the sake of the former that the latter are pursued. It makes no difference whether the activities themselves are the ends of the actions, or something else apart from the activities, as in the case of the sciences just mentioned.

2   If, then, there is some end of the things we do, which we desire for its own sake (everything else being desired for the sake of this), and if we do not choose everything for the sake of something else (for at that rate the process would go on to infinity, so that our desire would be empty and vain), clearly this must be the good and the chief good. Will not the knowledge of it, then, have a great influence on life? Shall we not, like archers who have a mark to aim at, be more likely to hit upon what is right? If so, we must try, in outline at least to determine what it is, and of which of the sciences or capacities it is the object. It would seem to belong to the most authoritative art and that which is most truly the master art. And politics appears to be of this nature; for it is this that ordains which of the sciences should be studied in a state, and which each class of citizens should learn and up to what point they should learn them; and we see even the most highly esteemed of capacities to fall under this, e.g. strategy, economics, rhetoric; now, since politics uses the rest of the sciences, and since, again, it legislates as to what we are to do and what we are to abstain from, the end of this science must include those of the others, so that this end must be the good for man. For even if the end is the same for a single man and for a state, that of the state seems at all events something greater and more complete whether to attain or to preserve; though it is worth while to attain the end merely for one man, it is finer and godlike to attain it for a nation or for city-states.

· · · · ·

BEAUTY

FROM *Metaphysics*
(1078ª 31-1078ᵇ 6)

BOOK XIII

Now since the good and the beautiful are different (for the former always implies conduct as its subject, while the beautiful is found also in motionless things), those who assert that the mathematical sciences say nothing of the beautiful or the good are in error. For
35 these sciences say and prove a great deal about them; if they do not expressly mention them, but prove attributes which are their results or their definitions, it is not true to say that they tell us
1078ᵇ nothing about them. The chief forms of beauty are order and symmetry and definiteness, which the mathematical sciences demonstrate in a special degree. And since these (e.g. order and definiteness) are obviously causes of many things, evidently these sciences must treat this sort of causative principle also (i.e. the
5 beautiful) as in some sense a cause. But we shall speak more plainly elsewhere about these matters.*

FROM *Rhetoric*
(1361ᵇ 2-1361ᵇ 15)

BOOK I

1361ᵇ   . . . Beauty varies with the time of life. In a young man beauty is the possession of a body fit to endure the exertion of running and of contests of strength; which means that he is pleasant to
10 look at; and therefore all-round athletes are the most beautiful, being naturally adapted both for contests of strength and for speed also. For a man in his prime, beauty is fitness for the exertion of warfare, together with a pleasant but at the same time formidable appearance. For an old man, it is to be strong enough for such exertion as is necessary, and to be free from all those deformities of
15 old age which cause pain to others.

· · · · ·

_____

* [See *Poetics*, Chap. 7, for further remarks on beauty.]

THE IMITATIVE ART
OF POETRY

FROM *Poetics*
(1447^a 7-1462^b 20, with omissions)

1 Our subject being Poetry, I propose to speak not only of the 1447^a
art in general but also of its species and their respective capacities;
of the structure of plot required for a good poem; of the number
and nature of the constituent parts of a poem; and likewise of 10
any other matters in the same line of inquiry. Let us follow the
natural order and begin with the primary facts.

Epic poetry and Tragedy, as also Comedy, Dithyrambic poetry,
and most flute-playing and lyre-playing, are all, viewed as a whole, 15
modes of imitation. But at the same time they differ from one another in three ways, either by a difference of kind in their means,
or by differences in the objects, or in the manner of their imitations.

I. Just as colour and form are used as means by some, who
(whether by art or constant practice) imitate and portray many
things by their aid, and the voice is used by others; so also in the 20
above-mentioned group of arts, the means with them as a whole
are rhythm, language, and harmony—used, however, either singly
or in certain combinations. A combination of harmony and rhythm
alone is the means in flute-playing and lyre-playing, and any
other arts there may be of the same description, e.g. imitative 25
piping. Rhythm alone, without harmony, is the means in the
dancer's imitations; for even he, by the rhythms of his attitudes,
may represent men's characters, as well as what they do and suffer.
There is further an art which imitates by language alone, without
harmony, in prose or in verse, and if in verse, either in some one or 1447^b
in a plurality of metres. This form of imitation is to this day without a name. We have no common name for a mime of Sophron or 10
Xenarchus and a Socratic Conversation; and we should still be
without one even if the imitation in the two instances were in
trimeters or elegiacs or some other kind of verse—though it is the
way with people to tack on 'poet' to the name of a metre, and
talk of elegiac-poets and epic-poets, thinking that they call them

15 poets not by reason of the imitative nature of their work, but indiscriminately by reason of the metre they write in. Even if a theory of medicine or physical philosophy be put forth in a metrical form, it is usual to describe the writer in this way; Homer and Empedocles, however, have really nothing in common apart from their metre; so that, if the one is to be called a poet, the other

20 should be termed a physicist rather than a poet. We should be in the same position also, if the imitation in these instances were in all the metres, like the *Centaur* (a rhapsody in a medley of all metres) of Chaeremon; and Chaeremon one has to recognize as a poet. So much, then, as to these arts. There are, lastly, certain

25 other arts, which combine all the means enumerated, rhythm, melody, and verse, e.g. Dithyrambic and Nomic poetry, Tragedy and Comedy; with this difference, however, that the three kinds of means are in some of them all employed together, and in others brought in separately, one after the other. These elements of difference in the above arts I term the means of their imitation.

1448ᵃ 2 II. The objects the imitator represents are actions, with agents who are necessarily either good men or bad—the diversities of human character being nearly always derivative from this primary distinction, since the line between virtue and vice is one dividing the whole of mankind. It follows, therefore, that the agents represented must be either above our own level of goodness, or be-

5 neath it, or just such as we are; in the same way as, with the painters, the personages of Polygnotus are better than we are, those of Pauson worse, and those of Dionysius just like ourselves. It is clear that each of the above-mentioned arts will admit of these differences, and that it will become a separate art by representing objects with this point of difference. Even in dancing, flute-playing,

10 and lyre-playing such diversities are possible; and they are also possible in the nameless art that uses language, prose or verse without harmony, as its means; Homer's personages, for instance, are better than we are; Cleophon's are on our own level; and those of Hegemon of Thasos, the first writer of parodies, and Nicochares

15 the author of the *Diliad*, are beneath it. The same is true of the Dithyramb and the Nome: the personages may be presented in them with the difference exemplified in the . . . of . . . and Argas, and in the Cyclopses of Timotheus and Philoxenus. This difference it is that distinguishes Tragedy and Comedy also; the one

would make its personages worse, and the other better, than the men of the present day.

3 III. A third difference in these arts is in the manner in which 20 each kind of object is represented. Given both the same means and the same kind of object for imitation, one may either (1) speak at one moment in narrative and at another in an assumed character, as Homer does; or (2) one may remain the same throughout, without any such change; or (3) the imitators may represent the whole story dramatically, as though they were actually doing the things described.

As we said at the beginning, therefore, the differences in the imitation of these arts come under three heads, their means, their objects, and their manner.

So that as an imitator Sophocles will be on one side akin to 25 Homer, both portraying good men; and on another to Aristophanes, since both present their personages as acting and doing. This in fact, according to some, is the reason for plays being termed dramas, because in a play the personages act the story. Hence too both Tragedy and Comedy are claimed by the Dorians 30 as their discoveries; Comedy by the Megarians—by those in Greece as having arisen when Megara became a democracy, and by the Sicilian Megarians on the ground that the poet Epicharmus was of their country, and a good deal earlier than Chionides and Magnes; even Tragedy also is claimed by certain of the Peloponnesian Dorians. In support of this claim they point to the words 35 'comedy' and 'drama'. Their word for the outlying hamlets, they say, is *comae*, whereas Athenians call them *demes*—thus assuming that comedians got the name not from their *comoe* or revels, but from their strolling from hamlet to hamlet, lack of appreciation keeping them out of the city. Their word also for 'to act', they 1448ᵇ say, is *dran*, whereas Athenians use *prattein*.

So much, then, as to the number and nature of the points of difference in the imitation of these arts.

4 It is clear that the general origin of poetry was due to two causes, each of them part of human nature. Imitation is natural to 5 man from childhood, one of his advantages over the lower animals being this, that he is the most imitative creature in the world, and learns at first by imitation. And it is also natural for all to de-

10 light in works of imitation. The truth of this second point is shown by experience: though the objects themselves may be painful to see, we delight to view the most realistic representations of them in art, the forms for example of the lowest animals and of dead bodies. The explanation is to be found in a further fact: to be learning something is the greatest of pleasures not only to the

15 philosopher but also to the rest of mankind, however small their capacity for it; the reason of the delight in seeing the picture is that one is at the same time learning—gathering the meaning of things, e.g. that the man there is so-and-so; for if one has not seen the thing before, one's pleasure will not be in the picture as an

20 imitation of it, but will be due to the execution or colouring or some similar cause. Imitation, then, being natural to us—as also the sense of harmony and rhythm, the metres being obviously species of rhythms—it was through their original aptitude, and by a series of improvements for the most part gradual on their first efforts, that they created poetry out of their improvisations.

Poetry, however, soon broke up into two kinds according to the

25 differences of character in the individual poets; for the graver among them would represent noble actions, and those of noble personages; and the meaner sort the actions of the ignoble. The latter class produced invectives at first, just as others did hymns and panegyrics. We know of no such poem by any of the pre-Homeric poets, though there were probably many such writers among them; instances, however, may be found from Homer

30 downwards, e.g. his *Margites*, and the similar poems of others. In this poetry of invective its natural fitness brought an iambic metre into use; hence our present term 'iambic', because it was the metre of their 'iambs' or invectives against one another. The result was that the old poets became some of them writers of heroic and others of iambic verse. Homer's position, however, is peculiar:

35 just as he was in the serious style the poet of poets, standing alone not only through the literary excellence, but also through the dramatic character of his imitations, so too he was the first to outline for us the general forms of Comedy by producing not a dramatic invective, but a dramatic picture of the Ridiculous; his *Margites*

1449[a] in fact stands in the same relation to our comedies as the *Iliad* and *Odyssey* to our tragedies. As soon, however, as Tragedy and Comedy appeared in the field, those naturally drawn to the one

5 line of poetry became writers of comedies instead of iambs, and those naturally drawn to the other, writers of tragedies instead of

epics, because these new modes of art were grander and of more esteem than the old.

If it be asked whether Tragedy is now all that it need be in its formative elements, to consider that, and decide it theoretically and in relation to the theatres, is a matter for another inquiry.

It certainly began in improvisations—as did also Comedy; the one originating with the authors of the Dithyramb, the other with those of the phallic songs, which still survive as institutions in many of our cities. And its advance after that was little by little, through their improving on whatever they had before them at each stage. It was in fact only after a long series of changes that the movement of Tragedy stopped on its attaining to its natural form. (1) The number of actors was first increased to two by Aeschylus, who curtailed the business of the Chorus, and made the dialogue, or spoken portion, take the leading part in the play. (2) A third actor and scenery were due to Sophocles. (3) Tragedy acquired also its magnitude. Discarding short stories and a ludicrous diction, through its passing out of its satyric stage, it assumed, though only at a late point in its progress, a tone of dignity; and its metre changed then from trochaic to iambic. The reason for their original use of the trochaic tetrameter was that their poetry was satyric and more connected with dancing than it now is. As soon, however, as a spoken part came in, nature herself found the appropriate metre. The iambic, we know, is the most speakable of metres, as is shown by the fact that we very often fall into it in conversation, whereas we rarely talk hexameters, and only when we depart from the speaking tone of voice. (4) Another change was a plurality of episodes or acts. As for the remaining matters, the superadded embellishments and the account of their introduction, these must be taken as said, as it would probably be a long piece of work to go through the details.

5 As for Comedy, it is (as has been observed) an imitation of men worse than the average; worse, however, not as regards any and every sort of fault, but only as regards one particular kind, the Ridiculous, which is a species of the Ugly. The Ridiculous may be defined as a mistake or deformity not productive of pain or harm to others; the mask, for instance, that excites laughter, is something ugly and distorted without causing pain.

Though the successive changes in Tragedy and their authors are not unknown, we cannot say the same of Comedy; its early stages

1449ᵇ passed unnoticed, because it was not as yet taken up in a serious way. It was only at a late point in its progress that a chorus of comedians was officially granted by the archon; they used to be mere volunteers. It had also already certain definite forms at the time when the record of those termed comic poets begins. Who it was who supplied it with masks, or prologues, or a plurality of ac-
5 tors and the like, has remained unknown. The invented Fable, or Plot, however, originated in Sicily with Epicharmus and Phormis; of Athenian poets Crates was the first to drop the Comedy of invective and frame stories of a general and non-personal nature, in other words, Fables or Plots.

Epic poetry, then, has been seen to agree with Tragedy to this ex-
10 tent, that of being an imitation of serious subjects in a grand kind of verse. It differs from it, however, (1) in that it is in one kind of verse and in narrative form; and (2) in its length—which is due to its action having no fixed limit of time, whereas Tragedy endeavours to keep as far as possible within a single circuit of the sun, or something near that. This, I say, is another point of differ-
15 ence between them, though at first the practice in this respect was just the same in tragedies as in epic poems. They differ also (3) in their constituents, some being common to both and others peculiar to Tragedy—hence a judge of good and bad in Tragedy is a judge of that in epic poetry also. All the parts of an epic are included in Tragedy; but those of Tragedy are not all of them to be found in the Epic.

20 6   Reserving hexameter poetry and Comedy for consideration hereafter, let us proceed now to the discussion of Tragedy; before doing so, however, we must gather up the definition resulting from what has been said. A tragedy, then, is the imitation of an action
25 that is serious and also, as having magnitude, complete in itself; in language with pleasurable accessories, each kind brought in separately in the parts of the work; in a dramatic, not in a narrative form; with incidents arousing pity and fear, wherewith to accomplish its catharsis of such emotions. Here by 'language with pleasureable accessories' I mean that with rhythm and harmony or song
30 superadded; and by 'the kinds separately' I mean that some portions are worked out with verse only, and others in turn with song.

I.   As they act the stories, it follows that in the first place the Spectacle (or stage-appearance of the actors) must be some part of the whole; and in the second Melody and Diction, these two being the means of their imitation. Here by 'Diction' I mean merely this, the composition of the verses; and by 'Melody', what is too 35 completely understood to require explanation. But further: the subject represented also is an action; and the action involves agents, who must necessarily have their distinctive qualities both of character and thought, since it is from these that we ascribe certain qualities to their actions. There are in the natural order of things, therefore, two causes, Thought and Character, of their actions, and consequently of their success or failure in their lives. Now the action (that which was done) is represented in the play by the Fable or Plot. The Fable, in our present sense of the term, is simply this, the combination of the incidents, or things done in the story; whereas Character is what makes us ascribe certain moral 5 qualities to the agents; and Thought is shown in all they say when proving a particular point or, it may be, enunciating a general truth. There are six parts consequently of every tragedy, as a whole (that is) of such or such quality, viz. a Fable or Plot, Characters, Diction, Thought, Spectacle, and Melody; two of them arising 10 from the means, one from the manner, and three from the objects of the dramatic imitation; and there is nothing else besides these six. Of these, its formative elements, then, not a few of the dramatists have made due use, as every play, one may say, admits of Spectacle, Character, Fable, Diction, Melody, and Thought.

II. The most important of the six is the combination of the in- 15 cidents of the story. Tragedy is essentially an imitation not of persons but of action and life, of happiness and misery. All human happiness or misery takes the form of action; the end for which we live is a certain kind of activity, not a quality. Character gives us qualities, but it is in our actions—what we do—that we are happy or the reverse. In a play accordingly they do not act in order to 20 portray the Characters; they include the Characters for the sake of the action. So that it is the action in it, i.e. its Fable or Plot, that is the end and purpose of the tragedy; and the end is everywhere the chief thing. Besides this, a tragedy is impossible without action, but there may be one without Character. The tragedies of most of 25 the moderns are characterless—a defect common among poets of all kinds, and with its counterpart in painting in Zeuxis as compared with Polygnotus; for whereas the latter is strong in character, the work of Zeuxis is devoid of it. And again: one may string together a series of characteristic speeches of the utmost finish as regards Diction and Thought, and yet fail to produce the true tragic 30 effect; but one will have much better success with a tragedy which, however inferior in these respects, has a Plot, a combination of incidents, in it. And again: the most powerful elements of attraction in Tragedy, the Peripeties and Discoveries, are parts of the Plot. A further proof is in the fact that beginners succeed earlier with the Diction and Characters than with the construction of a story; and the same may be said of nearly all the early dramatists. We maintain, therefore, that the first essential, the life and soul, so to speak, of Tragedy is the Plot; and that the Characters come second—compare the parallel in painting, where the most beautiful colours laid on without order will not give one the same pleasure as a simple black-and-white sketch of a portrait. We maintain that Tragedy is primarily an imitation of action, and that it is mainly for the sake of the action that it imitates the personal agents. Third comes the element of Thought, i.e. the power of saying whatever can be said, or what is appropriate to the occasion. This is what, in the speeches in Tragedy, falls under the arts of Politics and Rhetoric; for the older poets make their personages discourse like statesmen, and the modern like rhetoricians. One must not confuse it with Character. Character in a play is that which reveals the moral purpose of the agents, i.e. the sort of thing they seek or avoid, where that is not obvious—hence there is no room for Character in a speech on a purely indifferent subject. Thought, on the other hand, is shown in all they say when proving or disproving some particular point, or enunciating some universal proposition. Fourth among the literary elements is the Diction of the personages, i.e., as before explained, the expression of their thoughts in words, which is practically the same thing with verse as with prose. As for the two remaining parts, the Melody is the greatest of the pleasurable accessories of Tragedy. The Spectacle, though an attraction, is the least artistic of all the parts, and has least to do with the art of poetry. The tragic effect is quite possible without a public performance and actors; and besides, the getting-up of the Spectacle is more a matter for the costumier than the poet.

7 Having thus distinguished the parts, let us now consider the proper construction of the Fable or Plot, as that is at once the first and the most important thing in Tragedy. We have laid it down that a tragedy is an imitation of an action that is complete in itself, as a whole of some magnitude; for a whole may be of no mag-

nitude to speak of. Now a whole is that which has beginning, middle, and end. A beginning is that which is not itself necessarily after anything else, and which has naturally something else after it; an end is that which is naturally after something itself, either as its 30 necessary or usual consequent, and with nothing else after it; and a middle, that which is by nature after one thing and has also another after it. A well-constructed Plot, therefore, cannot either begin or end at any point one likes; beginning and end in it must be of the forms just described. Again: to be beautiful, a living creature, and every whole made up of parts, must not only present a 35 certain order in its arrangement of parts, but also be of a certain definite magnitude. Beauty is a matter of size and order, and therefore impossible either (1) in a very minute creature, since our perception becomes indistinct as it approaches instantaneity; or (2) in a creature of vast size—one, say, 1,000 miles long—as in that case, instead of the object being seen all at once, the unity and 1451ᵃ wholeness of it is lost to the beholder. Just in the same way, then, as a beautiful whole made up of parts, or a beautiful living creature, must be of some size, but a size to be taken in by the eye, 5 so a story or Plot must be of some length, but of a length to be taken in by the memory. As for the limit of its length, so far as that is relative to public performances and spectators, it does not fall within the theory of poetry. If they had to perform a hundred tragedies, they would be timed by water-clocks, as they are said to have been at one period. The limit, however, set by the actual nature of the thing is this: the longer the story, consistently with 10 its being comprehensible as a whole, the finer it is by reason of its magnitude. As a rough general formula, 'a length which allows of the hero passing by a series of probable or necessary stages from misfortune to happiness, or from happiness to misfortune', may suffice as a limit for the magnitude of the story. 15

8 The Unity of a Plot does not consist, as some suppose, in its having one man as its subject. An infinity of things befall that one man, some of which it is impossible to reduce to unity; and in like manner there are many actions of one man which cannot be made to form one action. One sees, therefore, the mistake of all 20 the poets who have written a *Heracleid*, a *Theseid*, or similar poems; they suppose that, because Heracles was one man, the story also of Heracles must be one story. Homer, however, evidently understood this point quite well, whether by art or instinct, just in the same

way as he excels the rest in every other respect. In writing an
25 *Odyssey*, he did not make the poem cover all that ever befell his
hero—it befell him, for instance, to get wounded on Parnassus and
also to feign madness at the time of the call to arms, but the two
incidents had no necessary or probable connexion with one another—instead of doing that, he took as the subject of the *Odyssey*,
30 as also of the *Iliad*, an action with a Unity of the kind we are describing. The truth is that, just as in the other imitative arts one
imitation is always of one thing, so in poetry the story, as an imitation of action, must represent one action, a complete whole, with
its several incidents so closely connected that the transposal or
withdrawal of any one of them will disjoin and dislocate the whole.
For that which makes no perceptible difference by its presence or
35 absence is no real part of the whole.

9   From what we have said it will be seen that the poet's function is to describe, not the thing that has happened, but a kind of
thing that might happen, i.e. what is possible as being probable or
1451ᵇ necessary. The distinction between historian and poet is not in
the one writing prose and the other verse—you might put the work
of Herodotus into verse, and it would still be a species of history; it
consists really in this, that the one describes the thing that has
5 been, and the other a kind of thing that might be. Hence poetry is
something more philosophic and of graver import than history,
since its statements are of the nature rather of universals, whereas
those of history are singulars. By a universal statement I mean
one as to what such or such a kind of man will probably or necessarily say or do—which is the aim of poetry, though it affixes
10 proper names to the characters; by a singular statement, one as to
what, say, Alcibiades did or had done to him. In Comedy this has
become clear by this time; it is only when their plot is already
made up of probable incidents that they give it a basis of proper
names, choosing for the purpose any names that may occur to
15 them, instead of writing like the old iambic poets about particular persons. In Tragedy, however, they still adhere to the historic
names; and for this reason: what convinces is the possible; now
whereas we are not yet sure as to the possibility of that which has
not happened, that which has happened is manifestly possible, else
it would not have come to pass. Nevertheless even in Tragedy there
20 are some plays with but one or two known names in them, the rest
being inventions; and there are some without a single known

name, e.g. Agathon's *Antheus*, in which both incidents and names
are of the poet's invention; and it is no less delightful on that account. So that one must not aim at a rigid adherence to the traditional stories on which tragedies are based. It would be absurd, in   25
fact, to do so, as even the known stories are only known to a few,
though they are a delight none the less to all.

It is evident from the above that the poet must be more the poet
of his stories or Plots than of his verses, inasmuch as he is a poet by
virtue of the imitative element in his work, and it is actions that he
imitates. And if he should come to take a subject from actual history, he is none the less a poet for that; since some historic occur-   30
rences may very well be in the probable and possible order of
things; and it is in that aspect of them that he is their poet.

Of Simple Plots and actions the episodic are the worst. I call a
Plot episodic when there is neither probability nor necessity in the
sequence of its episodes. Actions of this sort bad poets construct   35
through their own fault, and good ones on account of the players.
His work being for public performance, a good poet often stretches
out a Plot beyond its capabilities, and is thus obliged to twist the
sequence of incident.

Tragedy, however, is an imitation not only of a complete action,   1452ᵃ
but also of incidents arousing pity and fear. Such incidents have
the very greatest effect on the mind when they occur unexpect-
edly and at the same time in consequence of one another; there is
more of the marvellous in them then than if they happened of   5
themselves or by mere chance. Even matters of chance seem most
marvellous if there is an appearance of design as it were in them; as
for instance the statue of Mitys at Argos killed the author of Mitys'
death by falling down on him when a looker-on at a public spectacle; for incidents like that we think to be not without a meaning.   10
A Plot, therefore, of this sort is necessarily finer than others.

10   Plots are either simple or complex, since the actions they represent are naturally of this twofold description. The action, proceeding in the way defined, as one continuous whole, I call sim-   15
ple, when the change in the hero's fortunes takes place without
Peripety or Discovery; and complex, when it involves one or the
other, or both. These should each of them arise out of the structure of the Plot itself, so as to be the consequence, necessary or
probable, of the antecedents. There is a great difference between a   20
thing happening *propter hoc* and *post hoc*.

11   A Peripety is the change of the kind described from one state of things within the play to its opposite, and that too in the way we are saying, in the probable or necessary sequence of events; as it is for instance in *Oedipus:* here the opposite state of things is produced by the Messenger, who, coming to gladden Oedipus and to remove his fears as to his mother, reveals the secret of his birth. And in *Lynceus:* just as he is being led off for execution, with Danaus at his side to put him to death, the incidents preceding this bring it about that he is saved and Danaus put to death. A Discovery is, as the very word implies, a change from ignorance to knowledge, and thus to either love or hate, in the personages marked for good or evil fortune. The finest form of Discovery is one attended by Peripeties, like that which goes with the Discovery in *Oedipus.* There are no doubt other forms of it; what we have said may happen in a way in reference to inanimate things, even things of a very casual kind; and it is also possible to discover whether some one has done or not done something. But the form most directly connected with the Plot and the action of the piece is the first-mentioned. This, with a Peripety, will arouse either pity or fear—actions of that nature being what Tragedy is assumed to represent; and it will also serve to bring about the happy or unhappy ending. The Discovery, then, being of persons, it may be that of one party only to the other, the latter being already known; or both parties may have to discover themselves. Iphigenia, for instance, was discovered to Orestes by sending the letter; and another Discovery was required to reveal him to Iphigenia.

10   Two parts of the Plot, then, Peripety and Discovery, are on matters of this sort. A third part is Suffering; which we may define as an action of a destructive or painful nature, such as murders on the stage, tortures, woundings, and the like. The other two have been already explained.

12   The parts of Tragedy to be treated as formative elements in the whole were mentioned in a previous Chapter. From the point of view, however, of its quantity, i.e. the separate sections into which it is divided, a tragedy has the following parts: Prologue, Episode, Exode, and a choral portion, distinguished into Parode and Stasimon; these two are common to all tragedies, whereas songs from the stage and *Commoe* are only found in some. The Prologue is all that precedes the Parode of the chorus; an Episode all that comes in between two whole choral songs; the Exode all that fol-

lows after the last choral song. In the choral portion the Parode is the whole first statement of the chorus; a Stasimon, a song of the chorus without anapaests or trochees; a *Commos*, a lamentation sung by chorus and actor in concert. The parts of Tragedy to be 25 used as formative elements in the whole we have already mentioned; the above are its parts from the point of view of its quantity, or the separate sections into which it is divided.

13 The next points after what we have said above will be these: (1) What is the poet to aim at, and what is he to avoid, in constructing his Plots? and (2) What are the conditions on which the tragic effect depends?

We assume that, for the finest form of Tragedy, the Plot must be 30 not simple but complex; and further, that it must imitate actions arousing fear and pity, since that is the distinctive function of this kind of imitation. It follows, therefore, that there are three forms of Plot to be avoided. (1) A good man must not be seen passing from happiness to misery, or (2) a bad man from misery to happiness. The first situation is not fear-inspiring or piteous, but simply 35 odious to us. The second is the most untragic that can be; it has no one of the requisites of Tragedy; it does not appeal either to the human feeling in us, or to our pity, or to our fears. Nor, on the 1453ᵃ other hand, should (3) an extremely bad man be seen falling from happiness into misery. Such a story may arouse the human feeling in us, but it will not move us to either pity or fear; pity is occasioned 5 by undeserved misfortune, and fear by that of one like ourselves; so that there will be nothing either piteous or fear-inspiring in the situation. There remains, then, the intermediate kind of personage, a man not pre-eminently virtuous and just, whose misfortune, however, is brought upon him not by vice and depravity but by some error of judgement, of the number of those in the enjoyment of 10 great reputation and prosperity; e.g. Oedipus, Thyestes, and the men of note of similar families. The perfect Plot, accordingly, must have a single, and not (as some tell us) a double issue; the change in the hero's fortunes must be not from misery to happiness, but on the contrary from happiness to misery; and the cause of it must lie 15 not in any depravity, but in some great error on his part; the man himself being either such as we have described, or better, not worse, than that. Fact also confirms our theory. Though the poets began by accepting any tragic story that came to hand, in these days the finest tragedies are always on the story of some few 20

houses, on that of Alcmeon, Oedipus, Orestes, Meleager, Thyestes, Telephus, or any others that may have been involved, as either agents or sufferers, in some deed of horror. The theoretically best tragedy, then, has a Plot of this description. The critics, therefore,
25 are wrong who blame Euripides for taking this line in his tragedies, and giving many of them an unhappy ending. It is, as we have said, the right line to take. The best proof is this: on the stage, and in the public performances, such plays, properly worked out, are seen to be the most truly tragic; and Euripides, even if his execution be faulty in every other point, is seen to be nevertheless the
30 most tragic certainly of the dramatists. After this comes the construction of Plot which some rank first, one with a double story (like the *Odyssey*) and an opposite issue for the good and the bad personages. It is ranked as first only through the weakness of the
35 audiences; the poets merely follow their public, writing as its wishes dictate. But the pleasure here is not that of Tragedy. It belongs rather to Comedy, where the bitterest enemies in the piece (e.g. Orestes and Aegisthus) walk off good friends at the end, with no slaying of any one by any one.

1453^b 14 The tragic fear and pity may be aroused by the Spectacle; but they may also be aroused by the very structure and incidents of the play—which is the better way and shows the better poet. The Plot in fact should be so framed that, even without seeing the
5 things take place, he who simply hears the ˄ccount of them shall be filled with horror and pity at the incidents; which is just the effect that the mere recital of the story in *Oedipus* would have on one. To produce this same effect by means of the Spectacle is less artistic, and requires extraneous aid. Those, however, who make use of the Spectacle to put before us that which is merely monstrous and not
10 productive of fear, are wholly out of touch with Tragedy; not every kind of pleasure should be required of a tragedy, but only its own proper pleasure.

The tragic pleasure is that of pity and fear, and the poet has to produce it by a work of imitation; it is clear, therefore, that the causes should be included in the incidents of his story. Let us see,
15 then, what kinds of incident strike one as horrible, or rather as piteous. In a deed of this description the parties must necessarily be either friends, or enemies, or indifferent to one another. Now when enemy does it on enemy, there is nothing to move us to pity

either in his doing or in his meditating the deed, except so far as the actual pain of the sufferer is concerned; and the same is true when the parties are indifferent to one another. Whenever the tragic deed, however, is done within the family—when murder or 20 the like is done or meditated by brother on brother, by son on father, by mother on son, or son on mother—these are the situations the poet should seek after. The traditional stories, accordingly, must be kept as they are, e.g. the murder of Clytaemnestra by Orestes and of Eriphyle by Alcmeon. At the same time even with 25 these there is something left to the poet himself; it is for him to devise the right way of treating them. Let us explain more clearly what we mean by 'the right way'. The deed of horror may be done by the doer knowingly and consciously, as in the old poets, and in Medea's murder of her children in Euripides. Or he may do it, but in ig- 30 norance of his relationship, and discover that afterwards, as does the Oedipus in Sophocles. Here the deed is outside the play; but it may be within it, like the act of the Alcmeon in Astydamas, or that of the Telegonus in *Ulysses Wounded*. A third possibility is for one meditating some deadly injury to another, in ignorance of his 35 relationship, to make the discovery in time to draw back. These exhaust the possibilities, since the deed must necessarily be either done or not done, and either knowingly or unknowingly.

The worst situation is when the personage is with full knowledge on the point of doing the deed, and leaves it undone. It is odious and also (through the absence of suffering) untragic; hence it is that no one is made to act thus except in some few instances, e.g. 1454ᵃ Haemon and Creon in *Antigone*. Next after this comes the actual perpetration of the deed meditated. A better situation than that, however, is for the deed to be done in ignorance, and the relationship discovered afterwards, since there is nothing odious in it, and the Discovery will serve to astound us. But the best of all 5 is the last; what we have in *Cresphontes*, for example, where Merope, on the point of slaying her son, recognizes him in time; in *Iphigenia*, where sister and brother are in a like position; and in *Helle*, where the son recognizes his mother, when on the point of giving her up to her enemy.

This will explain why our tragedies are restricted (as we said just now) to such a small number of families. It was accident rather 10 than art that led the poets in quest of subjects to embody this kind of incident in their Plots. They are still obliged, accordingly, to

have recourse to the families in which such horrors have occurred.
On the construction of the Plot, and the kind of Plot required for
15 Tragedy, enough has now been said.

15 In the Characters there are four points to aim at. First and
foremost, that they shall be good. There will be an element of
character in the play, if (as has been observed) what a personage
says or does reveals a certain moral purpose; and a good element
of character, if the purpose so revealed is good. Such goodness is
20 possible in every type of personage, even in a woman or a slave,
though the one is perhaps an inferior, and the other a wholly worth-
less being. The second point is to make them appropriate. The
Character before us may be, say, manly; but it is not appropriate
in a female Character to be manly, or clever. The third is to make
25 them like the reality, which is not the same as their being good and
appropriate, in our sense of the term. The fourth is to make them
consistent and the same throughout; even if inconsistency be part of
the man before one for imitation as presenting that form of character, he should still be consistently inconsistent. We have an instance of baseness of character, not required for the story, in the
30 Menelaus in *Orestes*; of the incongruous and unbefitting in the
lamentation of Ulysses in *Scylla*, and in the (clever) speech of
Melanippe; and of inconsistency in *Iphigenia at Aulis*, where Iphigenia the suppliant is utterly unlike the later Iphigenia. The right
thing, however, is in the Characters just as in the incidents of the
35 play to endeavour always after the necessary or the probable; so that
whenever such-and-such a personage says or does such-and-such a
thing, it shall be the necessary or probable outcome of his character; and whenever this incident follows on that, it shall be either
the necessary or the probable consequence of it. From this one
1454ᵇ sees (to digress for a moment) that the Dénouement also should
arise out of the plot itself, and not depend on a stage-artifice, as in
Medea, or in the story of the (arrested) departure of the Greeks in
the *Iliad*. The artifice must be reserved for matters outside the play
5 —for past events beyond human knowledge, or events yet to come,
which require to be foretold or announced; since it is the privilege
of the Gods to know everything. There should be nothing improbable among the actual incidents. If it be unavoidable, however,
it should be outside the tragedy, like the improbability in the *Oedipus* of Sophocles. But to return to the Characters. As Tragedy is
an imitation of personages better than the ordinary man, we in our

way should follow the example of good portrait-painters, who re- 10
produce the distinctive features of a man, and at the same time,
without losing the likeness, make him handsomer than he is. The
poet in like manner, in portraying men quick or slow to anger,
or with similar infirmities of character, must know how to represent
them as such, and at the same time as good men, as Agathon and Homer have represented Achilles.

All these rules one must keep in mind throughout, and, further, 15
those also for such points of stage-effect as directly depend on the
art of the poet, since in these too one may often make mistakes.
Enough, however, has been said on the subject in one of our published writings.

16 Discovery in general has been explained already. As for the
species of Discovery, the first to be noted is (1) the least artistic 20
form of it, of which the poets make most use through mere lack
of invention, Discovery by signs or marks. Of these signs some are
congenital, like the 'lance-head which the Earth-born have on them',
or 'stars', such as Carcinus brings in his *Thyestes*; others acquired
after birth—these latter being either marks on the body, e.g. scars,
or external tokens, like necklaces, or (to take another sort of in- 25
stance) the ark in the Discovery in *Tyro*. Even these, however, admit of two uses, a better and a worse; the scar of Ulysses is an instance; the Discovery of him through it is made in one way by the
nurse and in another by the swineherds. A Discovery using signs
as a means of assurance is less artistic, as indeed are all such as
imply reflection; whereas one bringing them in all of a sudden, as 30
in the *Bath-story*, is of a better order. Next after these are (2) Discoveries made directly by the poet; which are inartistic for that
very reason; e.g. Orestes' Discovery of himself in *Iphigenia*: whereas
his sister reveals who she is by the letter, Orestes is made to say 35
himself what the poet rather than the story demands. This, therefore, is not far removed from the first-mentioned fault, since he
might have presented certain tokens as well. Another instance is
the 'shuttle's voice' in the *Tereus* of Sophocles. (3) A third species
is Discovery through memory, from a man's consciousness being 1455ᵃ
awakened by something seen. Thus in *The Cyprioe* of Dicae-
ogenes, the sight of the picture makes the man burst into tears; and
in the *Tale of Alcinous*, hearing the harper Ulysses is reminded of
the past and weeps; the Discovery of them being the result. (4)
A fourth kind is Discovery through reasoning; e.g. in *The Cho-* 5

ephoroe; 'One like me is here; there is no one like me but Orestes; he, therefore, must be here.' Or that which Polyidus the Sophist suggested for *Iphigenia*; since it was natural for Orestes to reflect: 'My sister was sacrificed, and I am to be sacrificed like her.' Or that in the *Tydeus* of Theodectes: 'I came to find a son, and am to die
10 myself.' Or that in *The Phinidae*: on seeing the place the women inferred their fate, that they were to die there, since they had also been exposed there. (5) There is, too, a composite Discovery arising from bad reasoning on the side of the other party. An instance of it is in *Ulysses the False Messenger*: he said he should know
15 the bow—which he had not seen; but to suppose from that that he would know it again (as though he had once seen it) was bad reasoning. (6) The best of all Discoveries, however, is that arising from the incidents themselves, when the great surprise comes about through a probable incident, like that in the *Oedipus* of Sophocles; and also in *Iphigenia*; for it was not improbable that she should wish to have a letter taken home. These last are the only Discov-
20 eries independent of the artifice of signs and necklaces. Next after them come Discoveries through reasoning.

17   At the time when he is constructing his Plots, and engaged on the Diction in which they are worked out, the poet should remember (1) to put the actual scenes as far as possible before his eyes. In
25 this way, seeing everything with the vividness of an eye-witness as it were, he will devise what is appropriate, and be least likely to overlook incongruities. This is shown by what was censured in Carcinus, the return of Amphiaraus from the sanctuary; it would have passed unnoticed, if it had not been actually seen by the audience; but on the stage his play failed, the incongruity of the incident offending the spectators. (2) As far as may be, too, the poet
30 should even act his story with the very gestures of his personages. Given the same natural qualifications, he who feels the emotions to be described will be the most convincing; distress and anger, for instance, are portrayed most truthfully by one who is feeling them at the moment. Hence it is that poetry demands a man with a special gift for it, or else one with a touch of madness in him; the former can easily assume the required mood, and the latter may be actually beside himself with emotion. (3) His story, again, whether already made or of his own making, he should first simplify
1455ᵇ and reduce to a universal form, before proceeding to lengthen it out by the insertion of episodes. The following will show how the

universal element in *Iphigenia*, for instance, may be viewed: A certain maiden having been offered in sacrifice, and spirited away from her sacrificers into another land, where the custom was to sacrifice all strangers to the Goddess, she was made there the priestess of this rite. Long after that the brother of the priestess happened to come; the fact, however, of the oracle having for a certain reason bidden him go thither, and his object in going, are outside the Plot of the play. On his coming he was arrested, and about to be sacrificed, when he revealed who he was—either as Euripides puts it, or (as suggested by Polyidus) by the not improbable exclamation, 'So I too am doomed to be sacrificed, as my sister was'; and the disclosure led to his salvation. This done, the next thing, after the proper names have been fixed as a basis for the story, is to work in episodes or accessory incidents. One must mind, however, that the episodes are appropriate, like the fit of madness in Orestes, which led to his arrest, and the purifying, which brought about his salvation. In plays, then, the episodes are short; in epic poetry they serve to lengthen out the poem. The argument of the *Odyssey* is not a long one. A certain man has been abroad many years; Poseidon is ever on the watch for him, and he is all alone. Matters at home too have come to this, that his substance is being wasted and his son's death plotted by suitors to his wife. Then he arrives there himself after his grievous sufferings; reveals himself, and falls on his enemies; and the end is his salvation and their death. This being all that is proper to the *Odyssey*, everything else in it is episode.

18 (4) There is a further point to be borne in mind. Every tragedy is in part Complication and in part Dénouement; the incidents before the opening scene, and often certain also of those within the play, forming the Complication; and the rest the Dénouement. By Complication I mean all from the beginning of the story to the point just before the change in the hero's fortunes; by Dénouement, all from the beginning of the change to the end. In the *Lynceus* of Theodectes, for instance, the Complication includes, together with the presupposed incidents, the seizure of the child and that in turn of the parents; and the Dénouement all from the indictment for the murder to the end. Now it is right, when one speaks of a tragedy as the same or not the same as another, to do so on the ground before all else of their Plot, i.e. as having the same or not the same Complication and Dénouement. Yet there are many

dramatists who, after a good Complication, fail in the Dénoue-
1455^b32 ment. But it is necessary for both points of construction to be always duly mastered. (5) There are four distinct species of Tragedy
—that being the number of the constituents also that have been
mentioned: first, the complex Tragedy, which is all Peripety and
Discovery; second, the Tragedy of suffering, e.g. the *Ajaxes* and *Ixi-*
1456^a *ons*; third, the Tragedy of character, e.g. *The Phthiotides* and *Pe-
leus*. The fourth constituent is that of 'Spectacle', exemplified in
The Phorcides, in *Prometheus*, and in all plays with the scene laid in
the nether world. The poet's aim, then, should be to combine every
element of interest, if possible, or else the more important and the
major part of them. This is now especially necessary owing to the
5 unfair criticism to which the poet is subjected in these days. Just
because there have been poets before him strong in the several
species of tragedy, the critics now expect the one man to surpass
10 that which was the strong point of each one of his predecessors.
(6) One should also remember what has been said more than once,
and not write a tragedy on an epic body of incident (i.e. one with a
plurality of stories in it), by attempting to dramatize, for instance,
the entire story of the *Iliad*. In the epic owing to its scale every
part is treated at proper length; with a drama, however, on the
15 same story the result is very disappointing. This is shown by the
fact that all who have dramatized the fall of Ilium in its entirety,
and not part by part, like Euripides, or the whole of the Niobe story,
instead of a portion, like Aeschylus, either fail utterly or have but
ill success on the stage; for that and that alone was enough to ruin
even a play by Agathon. Yet in their Peripeties, as also in their sim-
20 ple plots, the poets I mean show wonderful skill in aiming at the
kind of effect they desire—a tragic situation that arouses the
human feeling in one, like the clever villain (e.g. Sisyphus) deceived, or the brave wrongdoer worsted. This is probable, however,
only in Agathon's sense, when he speaks of the probability of even
25 improbabilities coming to pass. (7) The Chorus too should be regarded as one of the actors; it should be an integral part of the
whole, and take a share in the action—that which it has in Sophocles, rather than in Euripides. With the later poets, however, the
songs in a play of theirs have no more to do with the Plot of that
than of any other tragedy. Hence it is that they are now singing in-
30 tercalary pieces, a practice first introduced by Agathon. And yet
what real difference is there between singing such intercalary pieces,

and attempting to fit in a speech, or even a whole act, from one play into another?

19 The Plot and Characters having been discussed, it remains to consider the Diction and Thought. As for the Thought, we may assume what is said of it in our Art of Rhetoric, as it belongs more 35 properly to that department of inquiry. The Thought of the personages is shown in everything to be effected by their language—in every effort to prove or disprove, to arouse emotion (pity, fear, anger, and the like), or to maximize or minimize things. It is clear, 1456ᵇ also, that their mental procedure must be on the same lines in their actions likewise, whenever they wish them to arouse pity or horror, or to have a look of importance or probability. The only difference 5 is that with the act the impression has to be made without explanation; whereas with the spoken word it has to be produced by the speaker, and result from his language. What, indeed, would be the good of the speaker, if things appeared in the required light even apart from anything he says?

. . . . .

22 The perfection of Diction is for it to be at once clear and not mean. The clearest indeed is that made up of the ordinary words for 20 things, but it is mean, as is shown by the poetry of Cleophon and Sthenelus. On the other hand the Diction becomes distinguished and non-prosaic by the use of unfamiliar terms, i.e. strange words, metaphors, lengthened forms, and everything that deviates from the ordinary modes of speech.—But a whole statement in such terms will be either a riddle or a barbarism, a riddle, if made up 25 of metaphors, a barbarism, if made up of strange words. The very nature indeed of a riddle is this, to describe a fact in an impossible combination of words (which cannot be done with the real names for things, but can be with their metaphorical substitutes); e.g. 'I saw a man glue brass on another with fire', and the 30 like. The corresponding use of strange words results in a barbarism. —A certain admixture, accordingly, of unfamiliar terms is necessary. These, the strange word, the metaphor, the ornamental equivalent, &c., will save the language from seeming mean and prosaic, while the ordinary words in it will secure the requisite clearness. What helps most, however, to render the Diction at 1458ᵇ once clear and non-prosaic is the use of the lengthened, curtailed,

and altered forms of words. Their deviation from the ordinary
words will, by making the language unlike that in general use, give
it a non-prosaic appearance; and their having much in common
5 with the words in general use will give it the quality of clearness. It
is not right, then, to condemn these modes of speech, and ridicule the poet for using them, as some have done; e.g. the elder
Euclid, who said it was easy to make poetry if one were to be allowed to lengthen the words in the statement itself as much
10 as one likes—a procedure he caricatured by reading Ἐπιχάρην εἶδον
Μαραθῶνάδε βαδίζοντα, and οὐκ ἂν γ' ἐράμενος τὸν ἐκείνου ἐλλέβορον as
verses. A too apparent use of these licenses has certainly a ludicrous
effect, but they are not alone in that; the rule of moderation applies
to all the constituents of the poetic vocabulary; even with metaphors, strange words, and the rest, the effect will be the same, if one
15 uses them improperly and with a view to provoking laughter. The
proper use of them is a very different thing. To realize the difference one should take an epic verse and see how it reads when the
normal words are introduced. The same should be done too with
the strange word, the metaphor, and the rest; for one has only
to put the ordinary words in their place to see the truth of what
we are saying. The same iambic, for instance, is found in Aeschylus
and Euripides, and as it stands in the former it is a poor line;
20 whereas Euripides, by the change of a single word, the substitution
of a strange for what is by usage the ordinary word, has made it
seem a fine one. Aeschylus having said in his *Philoctetes:*

φαγέδαινα ἥ μου σάρκας ἐσθίει ποδός

Euripides has merely altered the ἐσθίει here into θοινᾶται.
Or suppose

25 νῦν δέ μ' ἐὼν ὀλίγος τε καὶ οὐτιδανὸς καὶ ἀεικής

to be altered, by the substitution of the ordinary words, into

νῦν δέ μ' ἐὼν μικρός τε καὶ ἀσθενικὸς καὶ ἀειδής.

Or the line

δίφρον ἀεικέλιον καταθεὶς ὀλίγην τε τράπεζαν

into

30 δίφρον μοχθηρὸν καταθεὶς μικράν τε τράπεζαν.

Or ἠιόνες βοόωσιν into ἠιόνες κράζουσιν. Add to this that Ariphrades
used to ridicule the tragedians for introducing expressions unknown

in the language of common life, δωμάτων ἄπο (for ἀπὸ δωμάτων), σέθεν, ἐγὼ δέ νιν, ᾿Αχιλλέως πέρι (for πέρι ᾿Αχιλλέως), and the like. The mere fact of their not being in ordinary speech gives the Diction a non-prosaic character; but Ariphrades was unaware of that. It is a great thing, indeed, to make a proper use of these poetical forms, as also of compounds and strange words. But the greatest thing by far is to be a master of metaphor. It is the one thing that cannot be learnt from others; and it is also a sign of genius, since a good metaphor implies an intuitive perception of the similarity in dissimilars.

Of the kinds of words we have enumerated it may be observed that compounds are most in place in the dithyramb, strange words in heroic, and metaphors in iambic poetry. Heroic poetry, indeed, may avail itself of them all. But in iambic verse, which models itself as far as possible on the spoken language, only those kinds of words are in place which are allowable also in an oration, i.e. the ordinary word, the metaphor, and the ornamental equivalent.

Let this, then, suffice as an account of Tragedy, the art imitating by means of action on the stage.

23 As for the poetry which merely narrates, or imitates by means of versified language (without action), it is evident that it has several points in common with Tragedy.

I. The construction of its stories should clearly be like that in a drama; they should be based on a single action, one that is a complete whole in itself, with a beginning, middle, and end, so as to enable the work to produce its own proper pleasure with all the organic unity of a living creature. Nor should one suppose that there is anything like them in our usual histories. A history has to deal not with one action, but with one period and all that happened in that to one or more persons, however disconnected the several events may have been. Just as two events may take place at the same time, e.g. the sea-fight off Salamis and the battle with the Carthaginians in Sicily, without converging to the same end, so too of two consecutive events one may sometimes come after the other with no one end as their common issue. Nevertheless most of our epic poets, one may say, ignore the distinction.

Herein, then, to repeat what we have said before, we have a further proof of Homer's marvellous superiority to the rest. He did not attempt to deal even with the Trojan war in its entirety, though it was a whole with a definite beginning and end—through a feeling apparently that it was too long a story to be

35 taken in in one view, or if not that, too complicated from the variety of incident in it. As it is, he has singled out one section of the whole; many of the other incidents, however, he brings in as episodes, using the Catalogue of the Ships, for instance, and other episodes to relieve the uniformity of his narrative.

. . . . .

1459b 24 II. Besides this, Epic poetry must divide into the same species as Tragedy; it must be either simple or complex, a story of character or one of suffering. Its parts, too, with the exception of Song
10 and Spectacle, must be the same, as it requires Peripeties, Discoveries, and scenes of suffering just like Tragedy. Lastly, the Thought and Diction in it must be good in their way. All these elements appear in Homer first; and he has made due use of them. His two poems are each examples of construction, the *Iliad* simple and
15 a story of suffering, the *Odyssey* complex (there is Discovery throughout it) and a story of character. And they are more than this since in Diction and Thought too they surpass all other poems.

There is, however, a difference in the Epic as compared with Tragedy, (1) in its length, and (2) in its metre. (1) As to its length,
20 the limit already suggested will suffice: it must be possible for the beginning and end of the work to be taken in in one view—a condition which will be fulfilled if the poem be shorter than the old epics, and about as long as the series of tragedies offered for one hearing. For the extension of its length epic poetry has a special advantage, of which it makes large use. In a play one cannot represent an action with a number of parts going on simultaneously;
25 one is limited to the part on the stage and connected with the actors. Whereas in epic poetry the narrative form makes it possible for one to describe a number of simultaneous incidents; and these, if germane to the subject, increase the body of the poem. This then is a gain to the Epic, tending to give it grandeur, and also variety of
30 interest and room for episodes of diverse kinds. Uniformity of incident by the satiety it soon creates is apt to ruin tragedies on the stage. (2) As for its metre, the heroic has been assigned it from experience; were any one to attempt a narrative poem in some one, or in several, of the other metres, the incongruity of the thing would be apparent. The heroic in fact is the gravest and weightiest
35 of metres—which is what makes it more tolerant than the rest of strange words and metaphors, that also being a point in which the narrative form of poetry goes beyond all others. The iambic and

trochaic, on the other hand, are metres of movement, the one representing that of life and action, the other that of the dance. Still **1460ª**
more unnatural would it appear, if one were to write an epic in a medley of metres, as Chaeremon did. Hence it is that no one has ever written a long story in any but heroic verse; nature herself, as we have said, teaches us to select the metre appropriate to such a story.

Homer, admirable as he is in every other respect, is especially so **5**
in this, that he alone among epic poets is not unaware of the part to be played by the poet himself in the poem. The poet should say very little *in propria persona*, as he is no imitator when doing that. Whereas the other poets are perpetually coming forward in person, and say but little, and that only here and there, as imitators, Homer after a brief preface brings in forthwith a man, a woman, **10**
or some other Character—no one of them characterless, but each with distinctive characteristics.

The marvellous is certainly required in Tragedy. The Epic, however, affords more opening for the improbable, the chief factor in the marvellous, because in it the agents are not visibly before one. The scene of the pursuit of Hector would be ridiculous on **15**
the stage—the Greeks halting instead of pursuing him, and Achilles shaking his head to stop them; but in the poem the absurdity is overlooked. The marvellous, however, is a cause of pleasure, as is shown by the fact that we all tell a story with additions, in the belief that we are doing our hearers a pleasure.

Homer more than any other has taught the rest of us the art of framing lies in the right way. I mean the use of paralogism. When- **20**
ever, if A is or happens, a consequent, B, is or happens, men's notion is that, if the B is, the A also is—but that is a false conclusion. Accordingly, if A is untrue, but there is something else, B, that on the assumption of its truth follows as its consequent, the right thing then is to add on the B. Just because we know the truth of the consequent, we are in our own minds led on to the erroneous inference of the truth of the antecedent. Here is an instance, from the **25**
Bath-story in the *Odyssey*.

A likely impossibility is always preferable to an unconvincing possibility. The story should never be made up of improbable incidents; there should be nothing of the sort in it. If, however, such incidents are unavoidable, they should be outside the piece, like the hero's ignorance in *Oedipus* of the circumstances of Laius' **30**
death; not within it, like the report of the Pythian games in *Electra*,

or the man's having come to Mysia from Tegea without uttering a word on the way, in *The Mysians*. So that it is ridiculous to say that one's Plot would have been spoilt without them, since it is fundamentally wrong to make up such Plots. If the poet has taken such a Plot, however, and one sees that he might have put it in a more
35 probable form, he is guilty of absurdity as well as a fault of art. Even in the *Odyssey* the improbabilities in the setting-ashore of Ulysses
1460b would be clearly intolerable in the hands of an inferior poet. As it is, the poet conceals them, his other excellences veiling their absurdity. Elaborate Diction, however, is required only in places where there is no action, and no Character or Thought to be revealed. Where there is Character or Thought, on the other hand, an over-
5 ornate Diction tends to obscure them.

25 As regards Problems and their Solutions, one may see the number and nature of the assumptions on which they proceed by viewing the matter in the following way. (1) The poet being an imitator just like the painter or other maker of likenesses, he must
10 necessarily in all instances represent things in one or other of three aspects, either as they were or are, or as they are said or thought to be or to have been, or as they ought to be. (2) All this he does in language, with an admixture, it may be, of strange words and metaphors, as also of the various modified forms of words, since the use of these is conceded in poetry. (3) It is to be remembered, too, that there is not the same kind of correctness in poetry as in poli-
15 tics, or indeed any other art. There is, however, within the limits of poetry itself a possibility of two kinds of error, the one directly, the other only accidentally connected with the art. If the poet meant to describe the thing correctly, and failed through lack of power of expression, his art itself is at fault. But if it was through his having meant to describe it in some incorrect way (e.g. to make the horse in movement have both right legs thrown forward) that the tech-
20 nical error (one in a matter of, say, medicine or some other special science), or impossibilities of whatever kind they may be, have got into his description, his error in that case is not in the essentials of the poetic art. These, therefore, must be the premisses of the Solutions in answer to the criticisms involved in the Problems.

I. As to the criticisms relating to the poet's art itself. Any impossibilities there may be in his descriptions of things are faults. But from another point of view they are justifiable, if they serve the end
25 of poetry itself—if (to assume what we have said of that end) they

make the effect of either that very portion of the work or some other portion more astounding. The Pursuit of Hector is an instance in point. If, however, the poetic end might have been as well or better attained without sacrifice of technical correctness in such matters, the impossibility is not to be justified, since the description should be, if it can, entirely free from error. One may ask, too, whether the 30 error is in a matter directly or only accidentally connected with the poetic art; since it is a lesser error in an artist not to know, for instance, that the hind has no horns, than to produce an unrecognizable picture of one.

II. If the poet's description be criticized as not true to fact, one may urge perhaps that the object ought to be as described—an answer like that of Sophocles, who said that he drew men as they ought to be, and Euripides as they were. If the description, how- 35 ever, be neither true nor of the thing as it ought to be, the answer must be then, that is in accordance with opinion. The tales about Gods, for instance, may be as wrong as Xenophanes thinks, neither true nor the better thing to say; but they are certainly in ac- 1461ᵃ cordance with opinion. Of other statements in poetry one may per- 1461ᵃ haps say, not that they are better than the truth, but that the fact was so at the time; e.g. the description of the arms: 'their spears stood upright, butt-end upon the ground'; for that was the usual way of fixing them then, as it is still with the Illyrians. As for the question whether something said or done in a poem is morally right or not, in dealing with that one should consider not only the intrinsic quality 5 of the actual word or deed, but also the person who says or does it, the person to whom he says or does it, the time, the means, and the motive of the agent—whether he does it to attain a greater good, or to avoid a greater evil.

III. Other criticisms one must meet by considering the language of the poet.   10

. . . . .

Speaking generally, one has to justify (1) the Impossible by ref- 1461ᵇ erence to the requirements of poetry, or to the better, or to opin- 10 ion. For the purposes of poetry a convincing impossibility is preferable to an unconvincing possibility; and if men such as Zeuxis depicted be impossible, the answer is that it is better they should be like that, as the artist ought to improve on his model. (2) The Improbable one has to justify either by showing it to be in accordance with opinion, or by urging that at times it is not improb-

15 able; for there is a probability of things happening also against probability. (3) The contradictions found in the poet's language one should first test as one does an opponent's confutation in a dialectical argument, so as to see whether he means the same thing, in the same relation, and in the same sense, before admitting that he has contradicted either something he has said himself or what a man of sound sense assumes as true. But there is no possible apology for improbability of Plot or depravity of character,
20 when they are not necessary and no use is made of them, like the improbability in the appearance of Aegeus in *Medea* and the baseness of Menelaus in *Orestes*.

The objections, then, of critics start with faults of five kinds: the allegation is always that something is either (1) impossible, (2) improbable, (3) corrupting, (4) contradictory, or (5) against technical correctness. The answers to these objections must be sought
25 under one or other of the above-mentioned heads, which are twelve in number.

26 The question may be raised whether the epic or the tragic is the higher form of imitation. It may be argued that, if the less vulgar is the higher, and the less vulgar is always that which addresses the better public, an art addressing any and every one is of a very vulgar order. It is a belief that their public cannot see the meaning,
30 unless they add something themselves, that causes the perpetual movements of the performers—bad flute-players, for instance, rolling about, if quoit-throwing is to be represented, and pulling at the conductor, if Scylla is the subject of the piece. Tragedy, then, is said to be an art of this order—to be in fact just what the later actors were in the eyes of their predecessors; for Mynniscus used to
35 call Callippides 'the ape', because he thought he so overacted his
1462ª parts; and a similar view was taken of Pindarus also. All Tragedy, however, is said to stand to the Epic as the newer to the older school of actors. The one, accordingly, is said to address a cultivated audience, which does not need the accompaniment of ges-
5 ture; the other, an uncultivated one. If, therefore, Tragedy is a vulgar art, it must clearly be lower than the Epic.

The answer to this is twofold. In the first place, one may urge (1) that the censure does not touch the art of the dramatic poet, but only that of his interpreter; for it is quite possible to overdo the gesturing even in an epic recital, as did Sosistratus, and in a singing contest, as did Mnasitheus of Opus. (2) That one should not condemn all movement, unless one means to condemn even the dance, but only that of ignoble people—which is the point of the criticism passed on Callippides and in the present day on oth- 10 ers, that their women are not like gentlewomen. (3) That Tragedy may produce its effect even without movement or action in just the same way as Epic poetry; for from the mere reading of a play its quality may be seen. So that, if it be superior in all other respects, this element of inferiority is no necessary part of it.

In the second place, one must remember (1) that Tragedy has everything that the Epic has (even the epic metre being admissible), together with a not inconsiderable addition in the shape of 15 the Music (a very real factor in the pleasure of the drama) and the Spectacle. (2) That its reality of presentation is felt in the play as read, as well as in the play as acted. (3) That the tragic imitation requires less space for the attainment of its end; which is a 1462ᵇ great advantage, since the more concentrated effect is more pleasurable than one with a large admixture of time to dilute it—consider the *Oedipus* of Sophocles, for instance, and the effect of expanding it into the number of lines of the *Iliad*. (4) That there is less unity in the imitation of the epic poets, as is proved by the fact that any one work of theirs supplies matter for several trage- 5 dies; the result being that, if they take what is really a single story, it seems curt when briefly told, and thin and waterish when on the scale of length usual with their verse. In saying that there is less unity in an epic, I mean an epic made up of a plurality of actions, in the same way as the *Iliad* and *Odyssey* have many such parts, each one of them in itself of some magnitude; yet the struc- 10 ture of the two Homeric poems is as perfect as can be, and the action in them is as nearly as possible one action. If, then, Tragedy is superior in these respects, and also, besides these, in its poetic effect (since the two forms of poetry should give us, not any or every pleasure, but the very special kind we have mentioned), it is clear that, as attaining the poetic effect better than the Epic, it 15 will be the higher form of art.

So much for Tragedy and Epic poetry—for these two arts in general and their species; the number and nature of their constituent parts; the causes of success and failure in them; the Objections of the critics, and the Solutions in answer to them.

Fear and Pity

FEAR

FROM *Rhetoric*
(1382ᵃ 19-1383ᵇ 11)

BOOK II

1382ᵃ 5 To turn next to Fear, what follows will show the things and
20 persons of which, and the states of mind in which, we feel afraid.
Fear may be defined as a pain or disturbance due to a mental picture of some destructive or painful evil in the future. Of destructive
or painful evils only; for there are some evils, e.g. wickedness or
stupidity, the prospect of which does not frighten us: I mean only
such as amount to great pains or losses. And even these only if
25 they appear not remote but so near as to be imminent: we do not
fear things that are a very long way off: for instance, we all know we
shall die, but we are not troubled thereby, because death is not
close at hand. From this definition it will follow that fear is caused
by whatever we feel has great power of destroying us, or of harming
30 us in ways that tend to cause us great pain. Hence the very indications of such things are terrible, making us feel that the terrible
thing itself is close at hand; the approach of what is terrible is just
what we mean by 'danger'. Such indications are the enmity and anger of people who have power to do something to us; for it is plain
that they have the will to do it, and so they are on the point of do-
35 ing it. Also injustice in possession of power; for it is the unjust
man's will to do evil that makes him unjust. Also outraged virtue
1382ᵇ in possession of power; for it is plain that, when outraged, it always
has the will to retaliate, and now it has the power to do so. Also
fear felt by those who have the power to do something to us, since
such persons are sure to be ready to do it. And since most men tend
5 to be bad—slaves to greed, and cowards in danger—it is, as a rule,
a terrible thing to be at another man's mercy; and therefore, if
we have done anything horrible, those in the secret terrify us with
the thought that they may betray or desert us. And those who can
do us wrong are terrible to us when we are liable to be wronged;
for as a rule men do wrong to others whenever they have the
10 power to do it. And those who have been wronged, or believe

themselves to be wronged, are terrible; for they are always looking out for their opportunity. Also those who have done people wrong, if they possess power, since they stand in fear of retaliation: we have already said that wickedness possessing power is terrible. Again, our rivals for a thing cause us fear when we cannot both have it at once; for we are always at war with such men. We also fear those who are to be feared by stronger people than ourselves: 15 if they can hurt those stronger people, still more can they hurt us; and, for the same reason, we fear those whom those stronger people are actually afraid of. Also those who have destroyed people stronger than we are. Also those who are attacking people weaker than we are: either they are already formidable, or they will be so when they have thus grown stronger. Of those we have wronged, and of our enemies or rivals, it is not the passionate and outspoken 20 whom we have to fear, but the quiet, dissembling, unscrupulous; since we never know when they are upon us, we can never be sure they are at a safe distance. All terrible things are more terrible if they give us no chance of retrieving a blunder—either no chance at all, or only one that depends on our enemies and not ourselves. Those things are also worse which we cannot, or cannot easily, help. 25 Speaking generally, anything causes us to feel fear that when it happens, or threatens, others causes us to feel pity.

The above are, roughly, the chief things that are terrible and are feared. Let us now describe the conditions under which we ourselves feel fear. If fear is associated with the expectation that something destructive will happen to us, plainly nobody will be 30 afraid who believes nothing can happen to him; we shall not fear things that we believe cannot happen to us, nor people who we believe cannot inflict them upon us; nor shall we be afraid at times when we think ourselves safe from them. It follows therefore that fear is felt by those who believe something to be likely to happen to them, at the hands of particular persons, in a particular form, 35 and at a particular time. People do not believe this when they are, 1383a or think they are, in the midst of great prosperity, and are in consequence insolent, contemptuous, and reckless—the kind of character produced by wealth, physical strength, abundance of friends, power: nor yet when they feel they have experienced every kind of horror already and have grown callous about the future, like men 5 who are being flogged and are already nearly dead—if they are to feel the anguish of uncertainty, there must be some faint expectation of escape. This appears from the fact that fear sets us thinking what can be done, which of course nobody does when things are hopeless. Consequently, when it is advisable that the audience should be frightened, the orator must make them feel that they really are in danger of something, pointing out that it has happened to others who were stronger than they are, and is happening, or has happened, to people like themselves, at the hands of unexpected people, in an unexpected form, and at an unexpected time.

Having now seen the nature of fear, and of the things that cause it, and the various states of mind in which it is felt, we can also see what Confidence is, about what things we feel it, and under what conditions. It is the opposite of fear, and what causes it is the opposite of what causes fear; it is, therefore, the expectation associated with a mental picture of the nearness of what keeps us safe and the absence or remoteness of what is terrible: it may be due either to the near presence of what inspires confidence or to the absence of what causes alarm. We feel it if we can take steps—many, or important, or both—to cure or prevent trouble; if we have neither wronged others nor been wronged by them; if we have either no rivals at all or no strong ones; if our rivals who are strong are our friends or have treated us well or been treated well by us; or if those whose interest is the same as ours are the more numerous party, or the stronger, or both.

As for our own state of mind, we feel confidence if we believe we have often succeeded and never suffered reverses, or have often met danger and escaped it safely. For there are two reasons why human beings face danger calmly: they may have no experience of it, or they may have means to deal with it: thus when in danger at sea people may feel confident about what will happen either because they have no experience of bad weather, or because their experience gives them the means of dealing with it. We also feel confident whenever there is nothing to terrify other people like ourselves, or people weaker than ourselves, or people than whom we believe ourselves to be stronger—and we believe this if we have conquered them, or conquered others who are as strong as they are, or stronger. Also if we believe ourselves superior to our rivals in the number and importance of the advantages that make men formidable—wealth, physical strength, strong bodies of supporters, extensive territory, and the possession of all, or the most important, appliances of war. Also if we have wronged no one, or not many, or not those of whom we are afraid; and generally, if our relations with the gods are satisfactory, as will be shown especially by signs and oracles. The fact is that anger makes us confident—that anger is excited by our knowledge that we are not the wrongers but the wronged, and that the divine power is always supposed to be on the side of the wronged. Also when, at the outset of an enterprise, we believe that we cannot and shall not fail, or that we shall suc- 10 ceed completely.—So much for the causes of fear and confidence.

P I T Y

FROM *Rhetoric*
(1385^b 11-1386^b 9)

B O O K   I I

8   Let us now consider Pity, asking ourselves what things excite 1385^b pity, and for what persons, and in what states of our mind pity is felt. Pity may be defined as a feeling of pain caused by the sight of some evil, destructive or painful, which befalls one who does not deserve it, and which we might expect to befall ourselves or some 15 friend of ours, and moreover to befall us soon. In order to feel pity, we must obviously be capable of supposing that some evil may happen to us or some friend of ours, and moreover some such evil as is stated in our definition or is more or less of that kind. It is therefore not felt by those completely ruined, who suppose that 20 no further evil can befall them, since the worst has befallen them already; nor by those who imagine themselves immensely fortunate—their feeling is rather presumptuous insolence, for when they think they possess all the good things of life, it is clear that the impossibility of evil befalling them will be included, this being one of the good things in question. Those who think evil *may* befall them are such as have already had it befall them and have safely es- 25 caped from it; elderly men, owing to their good sense and their experience; weak men, especially men inclined to cowardice; and also educated people, since these can take long views. Also those who have parents living, or children, or wives; for these are our own, and the evils mentioned above may easily befall them. And those who are neither moved by any courageous emotion such as anger 30 or confidence (these emotions take no account of the future), nor by a disposition to presumptuous insolence (insolent men, too, take no account of the possibility that something evil will hap-

pen to them), nor yet by great fear (panic-stricken people do not feel pity, because they are taken up with what is happening to themselves); only those feel pity who are between these two ex-
35 tremes. In order to feel pity we must also believe in the goodness
1386ᵃ of at least some people; if you think nobody good, you will believe that everybody deserves evil fortune. And, generally, we feel pity whenever we are in the condition of remembering that similar misfortunes have happened to us or ours, or expecting them to happen in future.

So much for the mental conditions under which we feel pity. What we pity is stated clearly in the definition. All unpleasant and
5 painful things excite pity if they tend to destroy and annihilate; and all such evils as are due to chance, if they are serious. The painful and destructive evils are: death in its various forms, bodily injuries and afflictions, old age, diseases, lack of food. The evils
10 due to chance are: friendlessness, scarcity of friends (it is a pitiful thing to be torn away from friends and companions), deformity, weakness, mutilation; evil coming from a source from which good ought to have come; and the frequent repetition of such misfortunes. Also the coming of good when the worst has happened: e.g. the arrival of the Great King's gifts for Diopeithes after his death.
15 Also that either no good should have befallen a man at all, or that he should not be able to enjoy it when it has.

The grounds, then, on which we feel pity are these or like these. The people we pity are: those whom we know, if only they are not very closely related to us—in that case we feel about them as if we were in danger ourselves. For this reason Amasis did not
20 weep, they say, at the sight of his son being led to death, but did weep when he saw his friend begging: the latter sight was pitiful, the former terrible, and the terrible is different from the pitiful; it tends to cast out pity, and often helps to produce the opposite of pity. Again, we feel pity when the danger is near ourselves. Also
25 we pity those who are like us in age, character, disposition, social standing, or birth; for in all these cases it appears more likely that the same misfortune may befall us also. Here too we have to remember the general principle that what we fear for ourselves excites our pity when it happens to others. Further, since it is when the sufferings of others are close to us that they excite our pity (we cannot remember what disasters happened a hundred centuries ago,
30 nor look forward to what will happen a hundred centuries hereafter, and therefore feel little pity, if any, for such things): it follows that

those who heighten the effect of their words with suitable gestures, tones, dress, and dramatic action generally, are especially successful in exciting pity: they thus put the disasters before our eyes, and make them seem close to us, just coming or just past. Anything 1386ᵇ that has just happened, or is going to happen soon, is particularly piteous: so too therefore are the tokens and the actions of sufferers—the garments and the like of those who have already suffered; the words and the like of those actually suffering—of those, for instance, who are on the point of death. Most piteous of all is it when, in such times of trial, the victims are persons of noble character: 5 whenever they are so, our pity is especially excited, because their innocence, as well as the setting of their misfortunes before our eyes, makes their misfortunes seem close to ourselves.

THEORY OF MUSIC

FROM *Politics*
(1339ᵃ 11-1342ᵇ 34)

BOOK VIII

5 Concerning music there are some questions which we have al- 1339ᵃ ready raised; these we may now resume and carry further; and our remarks will serve as a prelude to this or any other discussion of the subject. It is not easy to determine the nature of music, or 15 why any one should have a knowledge of it. Shall we say, for the sake of amusement and relaxation, like sleep or drinking, which are not good in themselves, but are pleasant, and at the same time 'make care to cease', as Euripides says? And for this end men also appoint music, and make use of all three alike—sleep, drinking, 20 music—to which some add dancing. Or shall we argue that music conduces to virtue, on the ground that it can form our minds and habituate us to true pleasures as our bodies are made by gymnastic to be of a certain character? Or shall we say that it con- 25 tributes to the enjoyment of leisure and mental cultivation, which is a third alternative? Now obviously youths are not to be instructed with a view to their amusement, for learning is no amusement, but is accompanied with pain. Neither is intellectual en- 30

joyment suitable to boys of that age, for it is the end, and that which is imperfect cannot attain the perfect or end. But perhaps it may be said that boys learn music for the sake of the amusement which they will have when they are grown up. If so, why should they
35 learn themselves, and not, like the Persian and Median kings, enjoy the pleasure and instruction which is derived from hearing others? (for surely persons who have made music the business and profession of their lives will be better performers than those who practise
40 only long enough to learn). If they must learn music, on the same principle they should learn cookery, which is absurd. And even granting that music may form the character, the objection
1339b still holds: why should we learn ourselves? Why cannot we attain true pleasure and form a correct judgment from hearing others, like the Lacedaemonians?—for they, without learning music, nevertheless can correctly judge, as they say, of good and bad melodies.
5 Or again, if music should be used to promote cheerfulness and refined intellectual enjoyment, the objection still remains—why should we learn ourselves instead of enjoying the performances of others? We may illustrate what we are saying by our conception of the Gods; for in the poets Zeus does not himself sing or play on the lyre. Nay, we call professional performers vulgar; no freeman would play or sing unless he were intoxicated or in jest. But these matters
10 may be left for the present.

The first question is whether music is or is not to be a part of education. Of the three things mentioned in our discussion, which does it produce?—education or amusement or intellectual enjoyment, for it may be reckoned under all three, and seems to share
15 in the nature of all of them. Amusement is for the sake of relaxation, and relaxation is of necessity sweet, for it is the remedy of pain caused by toil: and intellectual enjoyment is universally acknowledged to contain an element not only of the noble but of the
20 pleasant, for happiness is made up of both. All men agree that music is one of the pleasantest things, whether with or without song; as Musaeus says,

'Song is to mortals of all things the sweetest.'

Hence and with good reason it is introduced into social gatherings and entertainments, because it makes the hearts of men glad: so
25 that on this ground alone we may assume that the young ought to be trained in it. For innocent pleasures are not only in harmony with the perfect end of life, but they also provide relaxation. And

whereas men rarely attain the end, but often rest by the way and amuse themselves, not only with a view to a further end, but also for the pleasure's sake, it may be well at times to let them find a refreshment in music. It sometimes happens that men make amusement the end, for the end probably contains some element of pleasure, though not any ordinary or lower pleasure; but they mistake the lower for the higher, and in seeking for the one find the other, since every pleasure has a likeness to the end of action. For the end is not eligible for the sake of any future good, nor do the pleasures which we have described exist for the sake of any future good but of the past, that is to say, they are the alleviation of past toils and pains. And we may infer this to be the reason why men seek happiness from these pleasures.

But music is pursued, not only as an alleviation of past toil, but also as providing recreation. And who can say whether, having this use, it may not also have a nobler one? In addition to this common pleasure, felt and shared in by all (for the pleasure given by music is natural, and therefore adapted to all ages and characters), may it not have also some influence over the character and the soul? It must have such an influence if characters are affected by it. And that they are so affected is proved in many ways, and not least by the power which the songs of Olympus exercise; for beyond question they inspire enthusiasm, and enthusiasm is an emotion of the ethical part of the soul. Besides, when men hear imitations, even apart from the rhythms and tunes themselves, their feelings move in sympathy. Since then music is a pleasure, and virtue consists in rejoicing and loving and hating aright, there is clearly nothing which we are so much concerned to acquire and to cultivate as the power of forming right judgments, and of taking delight in good dispositions and noble actions. Rhythm and melody supply imitations of anger and gentleness, and also of courage and temperance, and of all the qualities contrary to these and of the other qualities of character, which hardly fall short of the actual affections, as we know from our own experience, for in listening to such strains our souls undergo a change. The habit of feeling pleasure or pain at mere representations is not far removed from the same feeling about realities; for example, if any one delights in the sight of a statue for its beauty only, it necessarily follows that the sight of the original will be pleasant to him. The objects of no other sense, such as taste or touch, have any resemblance to moral qualities; in visible objects there is only a little, for

there are figures which are of a moral character, but only to a slight extent, and all do not participate in the feeling about them. Again, figures and colours are not imitations, but signs, of moral habits,
35 indications which the body gives of states of feeling. The connexion of them with morals is slight, but in so far as there is any, young men should be taught to look, not at the works of Pauson, but at those of Polygnotus, or any other painter or sculptor who expresses moral ideas. On the other hand, even in mere melodies
40 there is an imitation of character, for the musical modes differ essentially from one another, and those who hear them are differently
1340^b affected by each. Some of them make men sad and grave, like the so-called Mixolydian, others enfeeble the mind, like the relaxed modes, another, again, produces a moderate and settled temper, which appears to be the peculiar effect of the Dorian; the Phrygian
5 inspires enthusiasm. The whole subject has been well treated by philosophical writers on this branch of education, and they confirm their arguments by facts. The same principles apply to rhythms; some have a character of rest, others of motion, and of
10 these latter again, some have a more vulgar, others a nobler movement. Enough has been said to show that music has a power of forming the character, and should therefore be introduced into the
15 education of the young. The study is suited to the stage of youth, for young persons will not, if they can help, endure anything which is not sweetened by pleasure, and music has a natural sweetness. There seems to be in us a sort of affinity to musical modes and rhythms, which makes some philosophers say that the soul is a tuning, others, that it possesses tuning.

20 6   And now we have to determine the question which has been already raised, whether children should be themselves taught to sing and play or not. Clearly there is a considerable difference made in the character by the actual practice of the art. It is difficult, if not impossible, for those who do not perform to be good judges
25 of the performance of others. Besides, children should have something to do, and the rattle of Archytas, which people give to their children in order to amuse them and prevent them from breaking anything in the house, was a capital invention, for a young thing
30 cannot be quiet. The rattle is a toy suited to the infant mind, and education is a rattle or toy for children of a larger growth. We conclude then that they should be taught music in such a way as to become not only critics but performers.

The question what is or is not suitable for different ages may be easily answered; nor is there any difficulty in meeting the objection of those who say that the study of music is vulgar. We reply (1) in 35 the first place, that they who are to be judges must also be performers, and that they should begin to practise early, although when they are older they may be spared the execution; they must have learned to appreciate what is good and to delight in it, thanks to the knowledge which they acquired in their youth. As to (2) 40 the vulgarizing effect which music is supposed to exercise, this is a question which we shall have no difficulty in determining, when we have considered to what extent freemen who are being trained to political virtue should pursue the art, what melodies and what 1341ᵃ rhythms they should be allowed to use, and what instruments should be employed in teaching them to play; for even the instrument makes a difference. The answer to the objection turns upon these distinctions; for it is quite possible that certain methods of teaching and learning music do really have a degrading effect. It 5 is evident then that the learning of music ought not to impede the business of riper years, or to degrade the body or render it unfit for civil or military training, whether for bodily exercises at the time or for later studies.

The right measure will be attained if students of music stop 10 short of the arts which are practised in professional contests, and do not seek to acquire those fantastic marvels of execution which are now the fashion in such contests, and from these have passed into education. Let the young practise even such music as we have prescribed, only until they are able to feel delight in noble melodies and rhythms, and not merely in that common part of music 15 in which every slave or child and even some animals find pleasure.

From these principles we may also infer what instruments should be used. The flute, or any other instrument which requires great skill, as for example the harp, ought not to be admitted into education, but only such as will make intelligent students of music or of 20 the other parts of education. Besides, the flute is not an instrument which is expressive of moral character; it is too exciting. The proper time for using it is when the performance aims not at instruction, but at the relief of the passions. And there is a further objection; the impediment which the flute presents to the use of the voice detracts from its educational value. The ancients therefore were right 25 in forbidding the flute to youths and freemen, although they had once allowed it. For when their wealth gave them a greater in-

clination to leisure, and they had loftier notions of excellence, be-
30 ing also elated with their success, both before and after the Persian
War, with more zeal than discernment they pursued every kind of
knowledge, and so they introduced the flute into education. At
Lacedaemon there was a choragus who led the chorus with a flute,
and at Athens the instrument became so popular that most freemen could play upon it. The popularity is shown by the tablet
35 which Thrasippus dedicated when he furnished the chorus to
Ecphantides. Later experience enabled men to judge what was or
was not really conducive to virtue, and they rejected both the flute
40 and several other old-fashioned instruments, such as the Lydian
harp, the many-stringed lyre, the 'heptagon', 'triangle', 'sambuca',
1341ᵇ and the like—which are intended only to give pleasure to the
hearer, and require extraordinary skill of hand. There is a meaning
also in the myth of the ancients, which tells how Athene invented
5 the flute and then threw it away. It was not a bad idea of theirs,
that the Goddess disliked the instrument because it made the face
ugly; but with still more reason may we say that she rejected it because the acquirement of flute-playing contributes nothing to the
mind, since to Athene we ascribe both knowledge and art.

Thus then we reject the professional instruments and also the
professional mode of education in music (and by professional
10 we mean that which is adopted in contests), for in this the performer practises the art, not for the sake of his own improvement,
but in order to give pleasure, and that of a vulgar sort, to his
hearers. For this reason the execution of such music is not the part
of a freeman but of a paid performer, and the result is that the per-
15 formers are vulgarized, for the end at which they aim is bad. The
vulgarity of the spectator tends to lower the character of the music
and therefore of the performers; they look to him—he makes them
what they are, and fashions even their bodies by the movements
which he expects them to exhibit.

20 7   We have also to consider rhythms and modes, and their use in
education. Shall we use them all or make a distinction? and shall
the same distinction be made for those who practise music with
a view to education, or shall it be some other? Now we see that
music is produced by melody and rhythm, and we ought to know
25 what influence these have respectively on education, and whether
we should prefer excellence in melody or excellence in rhythm. But
as the subject has been very well treated by many musicians of the

present day, and also by philosophers who have had considerable experience of musical education, to these we would refer the more 30 exact student of the subject; we shall only speak of it now after the manner of the legislator, stating the general principles.

We accept the division of melodies proposed by certain philosophers into ethical melodies, melodies of action, and passionate or inspiring melodies, each having, as they say, a mode corresponding to it. But we maintain further that music should be 35 studied, not for the sake of one, but of many benefits, that is to say, with a view to (1) education, (2) purgation (the word 'purgation' we use at present without explanation, but when hereafter we speak of poetry, we will treat the subject with more precision); music may also serve (3) for intellectual enjoyment, for relaxation 40 and for recreation after exertion. It is clear, therefore, that all the 1342ᵃ modes must be employed by us, but not all of them in the same manner. In education the most ethical modes are to be preferred, but in listening to the performances of others we may admit the 5 modes of action and passion also. For feelings such as pity and fear, or, again, enthusiasm, exist very strongly in some souls, and have more or less influence over all. Some persons fall into a religious frenzy, whom we see as a result of the sacred melodies— 10 when they have used the melodies that excite the soul to mystic frenzy—restored as though they had found healing and purgation. Those who are influenced by pity or fear, and every emotional nature, must have a like experience, and others in so far as each is 15 susceptible to such emotions, and all are in a manner purged and their souls lightened and delighted. The purgative melodies likewise give an innocent pleasure to mankind. Such are the modes and the melodies in which those who perform music at the theatre should be invited to compete. But since the spectators are of two kinds—the one free and educated, and the other a vulgar crowd composed of mechanics, labourers, and the like—there ought to 20 be contests and exhibitions instituted for the relaxation of the second class also. And the music will correspond to their minds; for as their minds are perverted from the natural state, so there are perverted modes and highly strung and unnaturally coloured melodies. A man receives pleasure from what is natural to him, and 25 therefore professional musicians may be allowed to practise this lower sort of music before an audience of a lower type. But, for the purposes of education, as I have already said, those modes and melodies should be employed which are ethical, such as the

30 Dorian, as we said before; though we may include any others
which are approved by philosophers who have had a musical education. The Socrates of the *Republic* is wrong in retaining only the
1342ᵇ Phrygian mode along with the Dorian, and the more so because he
rejects the flute; for the Phrygian is to the modes what the flute is
to musical instruments—both of them are exciting and emotional.
5 Poetry proves this, for Bacchic frenzy and all similar emotions are
more suitably expressed by the flute, and are better set to the
Phrygian than to any other mode. The dithyramb, for example,
acknowledged to be Phrygian, a fact of which the connoisseurs of
music offer many proofs, saying, among other things, that Philoxenus, having attempted to compose his *Mysians* as a dithyramb in
10 the Dorian mode, found it impossible, and fell back by the very nature of things into the more appropriate Phrygian. All men agree
15 that the Dorian music is the gravest and manliest. And whereas we
say that the extremes should be avoided and the mean followed,
and whereas the Dorian is a mean between the other modes, it is
evident that our youth should be taught the Dorian music.

· · · · ·

PLOTINUS

Despite his affinities with Plato, Plotinus extracts only a metaphysics of beauty from his classical predecessor and never develops a philosophy of art. Yet the metaphysics of beauty which he elaborated has had the most profound influence on generations of artists, philosophers, and critics. Plotinus succeeds in giving poetic completeness and lyric grandeur to the doctrines of beauty which so fascinated the ancient and the Hellenistic world. From these speculations both early Christian philosophy and Italian Renaissance Humanism draw their conceptions of beauty. In Augustine, the philosophy of Plotinus finds its Christian elaboration, and in Ficino his doctrines of art's relation to transcendent beauty are read back into a Renaissance Symposium, but one in which the artist of genius usurps the leadership of the philosopher.

Strangely enough, Plotinus' views are reasserted strongly at the moment when modern aesthetic theory makes its appearance, for the seventeenth-century Platonism of the Cambridge school and nineteenth-century German romantic idealism drew heavily upon Plotinus. It is through Ralph Cudworth and the Earl of Shaftesbury that Plotinus comes once more to exercise his poetic power over the philosophies of beauty. These writers revivify two strands in Plotinus' thought: the mysticism of divine harmony which en-

tails the participation of all finite things in infinite beauty, and the ultimate intelligibility of the universe (in Cudworth); *and secondly, the symbolic nature of all human products* (in nineteenth-century German philosophy). *It is in terms of the concepts of Beauty and Symbol that Plotinus is best understood.*

The beauty of art and nature is a manifestation of the unity of being. In his metaphysics, Plotinus ascends from the unity of individual souls to the unity of the general or world soul, and from that to the intellect thinking itself. Ultimately all dualities of knowing and known, subject and object, are overcome by the self-identity of the self-reflective thought. It is to this wholeness that all orders of creation aspire, and from it that all have been created. From the simple Good of the intellect all order is generated by a process of emanation: *from the One comes Mind, from Mind comes Soul, and Soul forms and enters into body. The world of body or nature exhibits an order and harmony which itself is an emanation from the One. When Soul encounters sensible beauty it experiences pleasure because it perceives there a communal nature which carries it back to the possibility of the ultimate harmony of the One. But this beauty of objects is also an emanation of Beauty itself, and that in turn is an emanation from the Good of the intellect. Hence individual beauty is, as it were, a symbol of cosmic harmony and a symbol of the higher reality to which all beautiful things are related and upon which all individual experiences of beauty depend.*

Artists' products are therefore valuable chiefly as symbols. It is with Plotinus that the symbolic nature of art receives its first comprehensive formulation. Not only is the beautiful object a symbol of cosmic harmony, but the cosmic order is best alluded to by metaphors themselves of a poetic nature. The emanations from the one are likened to an overflowing spring (Ennead V, 2.1), *and to a light which permeates the Whole from its source in the One* (Ennead V, 1.6). *An interesting use of art as an image of a metaphysical principle is Plotinus' reference to the dance in explaining the harmony of nature as a living whole* (Ennead IV, 4.33). *The Good radiates beauty from itself and is the source of beauty, while Beauty itself is second in the order of emanations. Thus the beauty of a man-made object* (statue) *is an imitation of Beauty and ultimately of the Good. And below the beauty of the created are the incomplete beauties of natural things which the arts are able to perfect. Hence, works of art stand midway between the somewhat obscured beauties of nature, which they ennoble and bring to fulfillment, and Beauty itself, which the mind can know through its ascent beyond the*

beautiful object. Art is a symbol in a double sense: of that lower
reality which it perfects, and that ultimate reality which it mir-
rors.

ENNEAD I

Sixth Tractate

BEAUTY

1. Beauty addresses itself chiefly to sight; but there is a beauty for the
hearing too, as in certain combinations of words and in all kinds of
music, for melodies and cadences are beautiful; and minds that lift
themselves above the realm of sense to a higher order are aware of
beauty in the conduct of life, in actions, in character, in the pursuits
of the intellect; and there is the beauty of the virtues. What loftier
beauty there may be, yet, our argument will bring to light.

What, then, is it that gives comeliness to material forms and draws
the ear to the sweetness perceived in sounds, and what is the secret of
the beauty there is in all that derives from Soul?

Is there some One Principle from which all take their grace, or is
there a beauty peculiar to the embodied and another for the bodiless?
Finally, one or many, what would such a Principle be?

Consider that some things, material shapes for instance, are gracious not by anything inherent but by something communicated,
while others are lovely of themselves, as, for example, Virtue.

The same bodies appear sometimes beautiful, sometimes not; so
that there is a good deal between being body and being beautiful.

What, then, is this something that shows itself in certain material
forms? This is the natural beginning of our inquiry.

What is it that attracts the eyes of those to whom a beautiful object
is presented, and calls them, lures them, towards it, and fills them with
joy at the sight? If we possess ourselves of this, we have at once a
standpoint for the wider survey.

Almost everyone declares that the symmetry of parts towards each
other and towards a whole, with, besides, a certain charm of colour,
constitutes the beauty recognized by the eye, that in visible things, as
indeed in all else, universally, the beautiful thing is essentially symmetrical, patterned.

But think what this means.

Only a compound can be beautiful, never anything devoid of parts; and only a whole; the several parts will have beauty, not in themselves, but only as working together to give a comely total. Yet beauty in an aggregate demands beauty in details: it cannot be constructed out of ugliness; its law must run throughout.

All the loveliness of colour and even the light of the sun, being devoid of parts and so not beautiful by symmetry, must be ruled out of the realm of beauty. And how comes gold to be a beautiful thing? And lightning by night, and the stars, why are these so fair?

In sounds also the simple must be proscribed, though often in a whole noble composition each several tone is delicious in itself.

Again since the one face, constant in symmetry, appears sometimes fair and sometimes not, can we doubt that beauty is something more than symmetry, that symmetry itself owes its beauty to a remoter principle?

Turn to what is attractive in methods of life or in the expression of thought; are we to call in symmetry here? What symmetry is to be found in noble conduct, or excellent laws, in any form of mental pursuit?

What symmetry can there be in points of abstract thought?

The symmetry of being accordant with each other? But there may be accordance or entire identity where there is nothing but ugliness: the proposition that honesty is merely a generous artlessness chimes in the most perfect harmony with the proposition that morality means weakness of will; the accordance is complete.

Then again, all the virtues are a beauty of the Soul, a beauty authentic beyond any of these others; but how does symmetry enter here? The Soul, it is true, is not a simple unity, but still its virtue cannot have the symmetry of size or of number: what standard of measurement could preside over the compromise or the coalescence of the Soul's faculties or purposes?

Finally, how by this theory would there be beauty in the Intellectual-Principle, essentially the solitary?

2.   Let us, then, go back to the source, and indicate at once the Principle that bestows beauty on material things.

Undoubtedly this Principle exists; it is something that is perceived at the first glance, something which the Soul names as from an ancient knowledge and, recognizing, welcomes it, enters into unison with it.

But let the Soul fall in with the Ugly and at once it shrinks within itself, denies the thing, turns away from it, not accordant, resenting it.

Our interpretation is that the Soul—by the very truth of its nature, by its affiliation to the noblest Existents in the hierarchy of Being—when it sees anything of that kin, or any trace of that kinship, thrills with an immediate delight, takes its own to itself, and thus stirs anew to the sense of its nature and of all its affinity.

But, is there any such likeness between the loveliness of this world and the splendours in the Supreme? Such a likeness in the particulars would make the two orders alike: but what is there in common between beauty here and beauty There?

We hold that all the loveliness of this world comes by communion in Ideal-Form.

All shapelessness whose kind admits of pattern and form, as long as it remains outside of Reason and Idea, is ugly by that very isolation from the Divine-Thought. And this is the Absolute Ugly: an ugly thing is something that has not been entirely mastered by pattern, that is by Reason, the Matter not yielding at all points and in all respects to Ideal-Form.

But where the Ideal-Form has entered, it has grouped and co-ordinated what from a diversity of parts was to become a unity: it has rallied confusion into co-operation: it has made the sum one harmonious coherence: for the Idea is a unity and what it moulds must come to unity as far as multiplicity may.

And on what has thus been compacted to unity, Beauty enthrones itself, giving itself to the parts as to the sum: when it lights on some natural unity, a thing of like parts, then it gives itself to that whole. Thus, for an illustration, there is the beauty, conferred by craftsmanship, of all a house with all its parts, and the beauty which some natural quality may give to a single stone.

This, then, is how the material thing becomes beautiful—by communicating in the thought that flows from the Divine.

3. And the Soul includes a faculty peculiarly addressed to Beauty—one incomparably sure in the appreciation of its own, when Soul entire is enlisted to support its judgement.

Or perhaps the Soul itself acts immediately, affirming the Beautiful where it finds something accordant with the Ideal-Form within itself, using this Idea as a canon of accuracy in its decision.

But what accordance is there between the material and that which antedates all Matter?

On what principle does the architect, when he finds the house standing before him correspondent with his inner ideal of a house, pronounce it beautiful? Is it not that the house before him, the stones apart, is the inner idea stamped upon the mass of exterior matter, the indivisible exhibited in diversity?

So with the perceptive faculty: discerning in certain objects the Ideal-Form which has bound and controlled shapeless matter, opposed in nature to Idea, seeing further stamped upon the common shapes some shape excellent above the common, it gathers into unity what still remains fragmentary, catches it up and carries it within, no longer a thing of parts, and presents it to the Ideal-Principle as something concordant and congenial, a natural friend: the joy here is like that of a good man who discerns in a youth the early signs of a virtue consonant with the achieved perfection within his own soul.

The beauty of colour is also the outcome of a unification: it derives from shape, from the conquest of the darkness inherent in Matter by the pouring-in of light, the unembodied, which is a Rational-Principle and an Ideal-Form.

Hence it is that Fire itself is splendid beyond all material bodies, holding the rank of Ideal-Principle to the other elements, making ever upwards, the subtlest and sprightliest of all bodies, as very near to the unembodied; itself alone admitting no other, all the others penetrated by it: for they take warmth but this is never cold; it has colour primally; they receive the Form of colour from it: hence the splendour of its light, the splendour that belongs to the Idea. And all that has resisted and is but uncertainly held by its light remains outside of beauty, as not having absorbed the plenitude of the Form of colour.

And harmonies unheard in sound create the harmonies we hear and wake the Soul to the consciousness of beauty, showing it the one essence in another kind: for the measures of our sensible music are not arbitrary but are determined by the Principle whose labour is to dominate Matter and bring pattern into being.

Thus far of the beauties of the realm of sense, images and shadow-pictures, fugitives that have entered into Matter—to adorn, and to ravish, where they are seen.

4. But there are earlier and loftier beauties than these. In the sense-bound life we are no longer granted to know them, but the Soul, taking no help from the organs, sees and proclaims them. To the vision of these we must mount, leaving sense to its own low place.

As it is not for those to speak of the graceful forms of the material world who have never seen them or known their grace—men born blind let us suppose—in the same way those must be silent upon the beauty of noble conduct and of learning and all that order who have never cared for such things, nor may those tell of the splendour of virtue who have never known the face of Justice and of Moral-Wisdom beautiful beyond the beauty of Evening and of Dawn.

Such vision is for those only who see with the Soul's sight—and at the vision, they will rejoice, and awe will fall upon them and a trouble deeper than all the rest could ever stir, for now they are moving in the realm of Truth.

This is the spirit that Beauty must ever induce, wonderment and a delicious trouble, longing and love and a trembling that is all delight. For the unseen all this may be felt as for the seen; and this the Souls feel for it, every Soul in some degree, but those the more deeply that are the more truly apt to this higher love—just as all take delight in the beauty of the body but all are not stung as sharply, and those only that feel the keener wound are known as Lovers.

5. These Lovers, then, lovers of the beauty outside of sense, must be made to declare themselves.

What do you feel in presence of the grace you discern in actions, in manners, in sound morality, in all the works and fruits of virtue, in the beauty of Souls? When you see that you yourselves are beautiful within, what do you feel? What is this Dionysiac exultation that thrills through your being, this straining upwards of all your soul, this longing to break away from the body and live sunken within the veritable self?

These are no other than the emotions of Souls under the spell of love.

But what is it that awakens all this passion? No shape, no colour, no grandeur of mass: all is for a Soul, something whose beauty rests upon no colour, for the moral wisdom the Soul enshrines and all the other hueless splendour of the virtues. It is that you find in yourself, or admire in another, loftiness of spirit; righteousness of life; disciplined purity; courage of the majestic face; gravity, modesty that goes fearless and tranquil and passionless; and, shining down upon all, the light of god-like Intellection.

All these noble qualities are to be reverenced and loved, no doubt, but what entitles them to be called beautiful?

They exist: they manifest themselves to us: anyone that sees them must admit that they have reality of Being; and is not Real-Being really beautiful?

But we have not yet shown by what property in them they have wrought the Soul to loveliness: what is this grace, this splendour as of Light, resting upon all the virtues?

Let us take the contrary, the ugliness of the Soul, and set that against its beauty: to understand, at once, what this ugliness is and how it comes to appear in the Soul will certainly open our way before us.

Let us then suppose an ugly Soul, dissolute, unrighteous: teeming with all the lusts; torn by internal discord; beset by the fears of its cowardice and the envies of its pettiness; thinking, in the little thought it has, only of the perishable and the base; perverse in all its impulses; the friend of unclean pleasures; living the life of abandonment to bodily sensation and delighting in its deformity.

What must we think but that all this shame is something that has gathered about the Soul, some foreign bane outraging it, soiling it, so that encumbered with all manner of turpitude, it has no longer a clean activity or a clean sensation, but commands only a life smouldering dully under the crust of evil; that, sunk in manifold death, it no longer sees what a Soul should see, may no longer rest in its own being, dragged ever as it is towards the outer, the lower, the dark?

An unclean thing, I dare to say; flickering hither and thither at the call of objects of sense, deeply infected with the taint of body, occupied always in Matter, and absorbing Matter into itself; in its commerce with the Ignoble it has trafficked away for an alien nature its own essential Idea.

If a man has been immersed in filth or daubed with mud, his native comeliness disappears and all that is seen is the foul stuff besmearing him: his ugly condition is due to alien matter that has encrusted him, and if he is to win back his grace it must be his business to scour and purify himself and make himself what he was.

So, we may justly say, a Soul becomes ugly—by something foisted upon it, by sinking itself into the alien, by a fall, a descent into body, into Matter. The dishonour of the Soul is in its ceasing to be clean and apart. Gold is degraded when it is mixed with earthy particles; if these be worked out, the gold is left and is beautiful, isolated from all that is foreign, gold with gold alone. And so the Soul; let it be but cleared of the desires that come by its too intimate converse with the body, emancipated from all the passions, purged of all that embodiment has thrust upon it, withdrawn, a solitary, to itself again—in that moment the ugliness that came only from the alien is stripped away.

6.   For, as the ancient teaching was, moral-discipline and courage and every virtue, not even excepting Wisdom itself, all is purification.

Hence the Mysteries with good reason adumbrate the immersion of the unpurified in filth, even in the Nether-World, since the unclean loves filth for its very filthiness, and swine foul of body find their joy in foulness.

What else is Sophrosyny, rightly so-called, but to take no part in the pleasures of the body, to break away from them as unclean and unworthy of the clean? So too, Courage is but being fearless of the death which is but the parting of the Soul from the body, an event which no one can dread whose delight is to be his unmingled self. And Magnanimity is but disregard for the lure of things here. And Wisdom is but the Act of the Intellectual-Principle withdrawn from the lower places and leading the Soul to the Above.

The Soul thus cleansed is all Idea and Reason, wholly free of body, intellective, entirely of that divine order from which the wellspring of Beauty rises and all the race of Beauty.

Hence the Soul heightened to the Intellectual-Principle is beautiful to all its power. For Intellection and all that proceeds from Intellection are the Soul's beauty, a graciousness native to it and not foreign, for only with these is it truly Soul. And it is just to say that in the Soul's becoming a good and beautiful thing is its becoming like to God, for from the Divine comes all the Beauty and all the Good in beings.

We may even say that Beauty *is* the Authentic-Existents and Ugliness is the Principle contrary to Existence: and the Ugly is also the primal evil; therefore its contrary is at once good and beautiful, or is Good and Beauty: and hence the one method will discover to us the Beauty-Good and the Ugliness-Evil.

And Beauty, this Beauty which is also The Good, must be posed as The First: directly deriving from this First is the Intellectual-Principle which is pre-eminently the manifestation of Beauty; through the Intellectual-Principle Soul is beautiful. The beauty in things of a lower order—actions and pursuits for instance—comes by operation of the shaping Soul which is also the author of the beauty found in the world of sense. For the Soul, a divine thing, a fragment as it were of the Primal Beauty, makes beautiful to the fullness of their capacity all things whatsoever that it grasps and moulds.

7.   Therefore we must ascend again towards the Good, the desired of

every Soul. Anyone that has seen This, knows what I intend when I say that it is beautiful. Even the desire of it is to be desired as a Good. To attain it is for those that will take the upward path, who will set all their forces towards it, who will divest themselves of all that we have put on in our descent: so, to those that approach the Holy Celebrations of the Mysteries, there are appointed purifications and the laying aside of the garments worn before, and the entry in nakedness—until passing, on the upward way, all that is other than the God, each in the solitude of himself shall behold that solitary-dwelling Existence, the Apart, the Unmingled, the Pure, that from Which all things depend, for Which all look and live and act and know, the Source of Life and of Intellection and of Being.

And one that shall know this vision—with what passion of love shall he not be seized, with what pang of desire, what longing to be molten into one with This, what wondering delight! If he that has never seen this Being must hunger for It as for all his welfare, he that has known must love and reverence It as the very Beauty; he will be flooded with awe and gladness, stricken by a salutary terror; he loves with a veritable love, with sharp desire; all other loves than this he must despise, and disdain all that once seemed fair.

This, indeed, is the mood even of those who, having witnessed the manifestation of Gods or Supernals, can never again feel the old delight in the comeliness of material forms: what then are we to think of one that contemplates Absolute Beauty in Its essential integrity, no accumulation of flesh and matter, no dweller on earth or in the heavens—so perfect Its purity—far above all such things in that they are nonessential, composite, not primal but descending from This?

Beholding this Being—the Choragus of all Existence, the Self-Intent that ever gives forth and never takes—resting, rapt, in the vision and possession of so lofty a loveliness, growing to Its likeness, what Beauty can the Soul yet lack? For This, the Beauty supreme, the absolute, and the primal, fashions Its lovers to Beauty and makes them also worthy of love.

And for This, the sternest and the uttermost combat is set before the Souls; all our labour is for This, lest we be left without part in this noblest vision, which to attain is to be blessed in the blissful sight, which to fail of is to fail utterly.

For not he that has failed of the joy that is in colour or in visible forms, not he that has failed of power or of honours or of kingdom has failed, but only he that has failed of only This, for Whose winning he should renounce kingdoms and command over earth and ocean and sky, if only, spurning the world of sense from beneath his feet, and straining to This, he may see.

8. But what must we do? How lies the path? How come to vision of the inaccessible Beauty, dwelling as if in consecrated precincts, apart from the common ways where all may see, even the profane?

He that has the strength, let him arise and withdraw into himself, foregoing all that is known by the eyes, turning away for ever from the material beauty that once made his joy. When he perceives those shapes of grace that shown in body, let him not pursue: he must know them for copies, vestiges, shadows, and hasten away towards That they tell of. For if anyone follow what is like a beautiful shape playing over water—is there not a myth telling in symbol of such a dupe, how he sank into the depths of the current and was swept away to nothingness? So too, one that is held by material beauty and will not break free shall be precipitated, not in body but in Soul, down to the dark depths loathed of the Intellective-Being, where, blind even in the Lower-World, he shall have commerce only with shadows, there as here.

'Let us flee then to the beloved Fatherland': this is the soundest counsel. But what is this flight? How are we to gain the open sea? For Odysseus is surely a parable to us when he commands the flight from the sorceries of Circe or Calypso—not content to linger for all the pleasure offered to his eyes and all the delight of sense filling his days.

The Fatherland to us is There whence we have come, and There is The Father.

What then is our course, what the manner of our flight? This is not a journey for the feet; the feet bring us only from land to land; nor need you think of coach or ship to carry you away; all this order of things you must set aside and refuse to see: you must close the eyes and call instead upon another vision which is to be waked within you, a vision, the birth-right of all, which few turn to use.

9. And this inner vision, what is its operation?

Newly awakened it is all too feeble to bear the ultimate splendour. Therefore the Soul must be trained—to the habit of remarking, first, all noble pursuits, then the works of beauty produced not by the labour of the arts but by the virtue of men known for their goodness: lastly, you must search the souls of those that have shaped these beautiful forms.

But how are you to see into a virtuous Soul and know its loveliness?

Withdraw into yourself and look. And if you do not find yourself beautiful yet, act as does the creator of a statue that is to be made beautiful: he cuts away here, he smoothes there, he makes this line lighter, this other purer, until a lovely face has grown upon his work. So do you also: cut away all that is excessive, straighten all that is crooked, bring light to all that is overcast, labour to make all one glow of beauty and never cease chiselling your statue, until there shall shine out on you from it the godlike splendour of virtue, until you shall see the perfect goodness surely established in the stainless shrine.

When you know that you have become this perfect work, when you are self-gathered in the purity of your being, nothing now remaining that can shatter that inner unity, nothing from without clinging to the authentic man, when you find yourself wholly true to your essential nature, wholly that only veritable Light which is not measured by space, not narrowed to any circumscribed form nor again diffused as a thing void of term, but ever unmeasurable as something greater than all measure and more than all quantity—when you perceive that you have grown to this, you are now become very vision: now call up all your confidence, strike forward yet a step—you need a guide no longer —strain, and see.

This is the only eye that sees the mighty Beauty. If the eye that adventures the vision be dimmed by vice, impure, or weak, and unable in its cowardly blenching to see the uttermost brightness, then it sees nothing even though another point to what lies plain to sight before it. To any vision must be brought an eye adapted to what is to be seen, and having some likeness to it. Never did eye see the sun unless it had first become sunlike, and never can the Soul have vision of the First Beauty unless itself be beautiful.

Therefore, first let each become godlike and each beautiful who cares to see God and Beauty. So, mounting, the Soul will come first to the Intellectual-Principle and survey all the beautiful Ideas in the Supreme and will avow that this is Beauty, that the Ideas are Beauty. For by their efficacy comes all Beauty else, by the offspring and essence of the Intellectual-Being. What is beyond the Intellectual-Principle we affirm to be the nature of Good radiating Beauty before it. So that, treating the Intellectual-Cosmos as one, the first is the Beautiful: if we make distinction there, the Realm of Ideas constitutes the Beauty of the Intellectual Sphere; and The Good, which lies beyond, is the Fountain at once and Principle of Beauty: the Primal Good and the Primal Beauty have the one dwelling-place and, thus, always, Beauty's seat is There.

ENNEAD V

Eighth Tractate

ON THE INTELLECTUAL BEAUTY

1. It is a principle with us that one who has attained to the vision of the Intellectual Beauty and grasped the beauty of the Authentic Intellect will be able also to come to understand the Father and Transcendent of that Divine Being. It concerns us, then, to try to see and say, for ourselves and as far as such matters may be told, how the Beauty of the divine Intellect and of the Intellectual Cosmos may be revealed to contemplation.

Let us go to the realm of magnitudes:—suppose two blocks of stone lying side by side: one is unpatterned, quite untouched by art; the other has been minutely wrought by the craftsman's hands into some statue of god or man, a Grace or a Muse, or if a human being, not a portrait but a creation in which the sculptor's art has concentrated all loveliness.

Now it must be seen that the stone thus brought under the artist's hand to the beauty of form is beautiful not as stone—for so the crude block would be as pleasant—but in virtue of the Form or Idea introduced by the art. This form is not in the material; it is in the designer before ever it enters the stone; and the artificer holds it not by his equipment of eyes and hands but by his participation in his art. The beauty, therefore, exists in a far higher state in the art; for it does not come over integrally into the work; that original beauty is not transferred; what comes over is a derivative and a minor: and even that shows itself upon the statue not integrally and with entire realization of intention but only in so far as it has subdued the resistance of the material.

Art, then, creating in the image of its own nature and content, and working by the Idea or Reason-Principle of the beautiful object it is to produce, must itself be beautiful in a far higher and purer degree since it is the seat and source of that beauty, indwelling in the art, which must naturally be more complete than any comeliness of the external. In the degree in which the beauty is diffused by entering into matter, it is so much the weaker than that concentrated in unity; everything that reaches outwards is the less for it, strength less strong, heat less hot, every power less potent, and so beauty less beautiful.

Then again every prime cause must be, within itself, more powerful than its effect can be: the musical does not derive from an unmusical source but from music; and so the art exhibited in the material work derives from an art yet higher.

Still the arts are not to be slighted on the ground that they create by imitation of natural objects; for, to begin with, these natural objects are themselves imitations; then, we must recognize that they give no bare reproduction of the thing seen but go back to the Reason-Principles from which Nature itself derives, and, furthermore, that much of their work is all their own; they are holders of beauty and add where nature is lacking. Thus Pheidias wrought the Zeus upon no model among things of sense but by apprehending what form Zeus must take if he chose to become manifest to sight.

2.   But let us leave the arts and consider those works produced by Nature and admitted to be naturally beautiful which the creations of art are charged with imitating, all reasoning life and unreasoning things alike, but especially the consummate among them, where the moulder and maker has subdued the material and given the form he desired. Now what is the beauty here? It has nothing to do with the blood or the menstrual process: either there is also a colour and form apart from all this or there is nothing unless sheer ugliness or (at best) a bare recipient, as it were the mere Matter of beauty.

Whence shone forth the beauty of Helen, battle-sought; or of all those women like in loveliness to Aphrodite; or of Aphrodite herself; or of any human being that has been perfect in beauty; or of any of these gods manifest to sight, or unseen but carrying what would be beauty if we saw?

In all these is it not the Idea, something of that realm but communicated to the produced from within the producer, just as in works of art, we held, it is communicated from the arts to their creations? Now we can surely not believe that, while the made thing and the Idea thus impressed upon Matter are beautiful, yet the Idea not so alloyed but resting still with the creator—the Idea primal, immaterial, firmly a unity—is not Beauty.

If material extension were in itself the ground of beauty, then the creating principle, being without extension, could not be beautiful: but beauty cannot be made to depend upon magnitude since, whether in a large object or a small, the one Idea equally moves and forms the mind by its inherent power. A further indication is that as long as the object remains outside us we know nothing of it; it affects us by entry; but only as an Idea can it enter through the eyes which are not of scope to take an extended mass: we are, no doubt, simultaneously possessed of the magnitude which, however, we take in not as mass but by an elaboration upon the presented form.

Then again the principle producing the beauty must be, itself, ugly, neutral, or beautiful: ugly, it could not produce the opposite; neutral, why should its product be the one rather than the other? The Nature, then, which creates things so lovely must be itself of a far earlier beauty; we, undisciplined in discernment of the inward, knowing nothing of it, run after the outer, never understanding that it is the inner which stirs us; we are in the case of one who sees his own reflection but not realizing whence it comes goes in pursuit of it.

But that the thing we are pursuing is something different and that the beauty is not in the concrete object is manifest from the beauty there is in matters of study, in conduct and custom; briefly, in soul or mind. And it is precisely here that the greater beauty lies, perceived whenever you look to the wisdom in a man and delight in it, not wasting attention on the face, which may be hideous, but passing all appearance by and catching only at the inner comeliness, the truly personal; if you are still unmoved and cannot acknowledge beauty under such conditions, then looking to your own inner being you will find no beauty to delight you and it will be futile in that state to seek the greater vision, for you will be questing it through the ugly and impure.

This is why such matters are not spoken of to everyone; you, if you are conscious of beauty within, remember.

3. Thus there is in the Nature-Principle itself an Ideal archetype of the beauty that is found in material forms, and, of that archetype again, the still more beautiful archetype in Soul, source of that in Nature. In the proficient soul this is brighter and of more advanced loveliness: adorning the soul and bringing to it a light from that greater light which is Beauty primally, its immediate presence sets the soul reflecting upon the quality of this prior, the archetype which has no such entries, and is present nowhere but remains in itself alone, and thus is not even to be called a Reason-Principle but is the creative source of the very first Reason-Principle which is the Beauty to which Soul serves as Matter.

This prior, then, is the Intellectual-Principle, the veritable, abiding and not fluctuant since not taking intellectual quality from outside itself. By what image, thus, can we represent it? We have nowhere to go but to what is less. Only from itself can we take an image of it; that is, there can be no representation of it, except in the sense that we represent gold by some portion of gold—purified, either actually or mentally, if it be impure—insisting at the same time that this is not the total thing gold, but merely the particular gold of a particular parcel. In the same way we learn in this matter from the purified Intellect in ourselves or, if you like, from the gods and the glory of the Intellect in them.

For assuredly all the gods are august and beautiful in a beauty beyond our speech. And what makes them so? Intellect, and especially Intellect operating within them (the divine sun and stars) to visibility. It is not through the loveliness of their corporeal forms: even those that have body are not gods by that beauty; it is in virtue of Intellect that they, too, are gods, and as gods beautiful. They do not veer between wisdom and folly: in the immunity of Intellect unmoving and pure, they are wise always, all-knowing, taking cognizance not of the human but of their own being and of all that lies within the contemplation of Intellect. Those of them whose dwelling is in the heavens are ever in this meditation—what task prevents them?—and from afar they look, too, into that further heaven by a lifting of the head. The gods belonging to that higher Heaven itself, they whose station is upon it and in it, see and know in virtue of their omnipresence to it. For all There is heaven; earth is heaven, and sea heaven; and animal and plant and man; all is the heavenly content of that heaven: and the gods in it, despising neither men nor anything else that is there where all is of the heavenly order, traverse all that country and all space in peace.

4. To 'live at ease' is There; and to these divine beings verity is mother and nurse, existence and sustenance; all that is not of process but of authentic being they see, and themselves in all: for all is transparent, nothing dark, nothing resistant; every being is lucid to every other, in breadth and depth; light runs through light. And each of them contains all within itself, and at the same time sees all in every other, so that everywhere there is all, and all is all and each all, and infinite the glory. Each of them is great; the small is great; the sun, There, is all the stars; and every star, again, is all the stars and sun. While some one manner of being is dominant in each, all are mirrored in every other.

Movement There is pure (as self-caused), for the moving principle is not a separate thing to complicate it as it speeds.

So, too, Repose is not troubled, for there is no admixture of the unstable; and the Beauty is all beauty since it is not resident in what is not beautiful. Each There walks upon no alien soil; its place is its essential self; and, as each moves, so to speak, towards what is Above, it is attended by the very ground from which it starts: there is no distinguishing between the Being and the Place; all is Intellect, the Principle and the ground on which it stands, alike. Thus we might think that our visible sky (the ground or place of the stars), lit as it is, produces the light which reaches us from it, though of course this is really produced by the stars (as it were, by the Principles of light alone, not also by the ground as the analogy would require).

In our realm all is part rising from part and nothing can be more than partial; but There each being is an eternal product of a whole and is at once a whole and an individual manifesting as part but, to the keen vision There, known for the whole it is.

The myth of Lynceus seeing into the very deeps of the earth tells us of those eyes in the divine. No weariness overtakes this vision which yet brings no such satiety as would call for its ending; for there never was a void to be filled so that, with the fullness and the attainment of purpose, the sense of sufficiency be induced: nor is there any such incongruity within the divine that one Being There could be repulsive to another: and of course all There are unchangeable. This absence of satisfaction means only a satisfaction leading to no distaste for that which produces it; to see is to look the more, since for them to continue in the contemplation of an infinite self and of infinite objects is but to acquiesce in the bidding of their nature.

Life, pure, is never a burden; how then could there be weariness There where the living is most noble? That very life is wisdom, not a wisdom built up by reasonings but complete from the beginning, suffering no lack which could set it inquiring, a wisdom primal, unborrowed, not something added to the Being, but its very essence. No wisdom, thus, is greater; this is the authentic knowing, assessor to the divine Intellect as projected into manifestation simultaneously with it; thus, in the symbolic saying, Justice is assessor to Zeus.

(Perfect wisdom:) for all the Principles of this order, dwelling There, are as it were visible images projected from themselves, so that all becomes an object of contemplation to contemplators immeasurably blessed. The greatness and power of the wisdom There we may know from this, that it embraces all the real Beings, and has made all and all follow it, and yet that it is itself those beings, which sprang into being with it, so that all is one and the essence There is wisdom. If we have failed to understand, it is that we have thought of knowledge as a mass of theorems and an accumulation of propositions, though that is false even for our sciences of the sense-realm. But in case this should be questioned, we may leave our own sciences for the present, and deal with the knowing in the Supreme at which Plato glances where he speaks of 'that knowledge which is not a stranger in something strange to it'—though in what sense, he leaves us to examine and declare, if we boast ourselves worthy of the discussion. This is probably our best starting-point.

5. All that comes to be, work of nature or of craft, some wisdom has made: everywhere a wisdom presides at a making.

No doubt the wisdom of the artist may be the guide of the work; it is sufficient explanation of the wisdom exhibited in the arts; but the artist himself goes back, after all, to that wisdom in Nature which is embodied in himself; and this is not a wisdom built up of theorems but one totality, not a wisdom consisting of manifold detail coordinated into a unity but rather a unity working out into detail.

Now, if we could think of this as the primal wisdom, we need look no further, since, at that, we have discovered a principle which is neither a derivative nor a 'stranger in something strange to it.' But if we are told that, while this Reason-Principle is in Nature, yet Nature itself is its source, we ask how Nature came to possess it; and, if Nature derived it from some other source, we ask what that other source may be; if, on the contrary, the principle is self-sprung, we need look no further: but if (as we assume) we are referred to the Intellectual-Principle we must make clear whether the Intellectual-Principle engendered the wisdom: if we learn that it did, we ask whence: if from itself, then inevitably it is itself Wisdom.

The true Wisdom, then (found to be identical with the Intellectual-Principle), is Real Being; and Real Being is Wisdom; it is wisdom that gives value to Real Being; and Being is Real in virtue of its origin in wisdom. It follows that all forms of existence not possessing wisdom are, indeed, Beings in right of the wisdom which went to their forming, but as not in themselves possessing it, are not Real Beings.

We cannot, therefore, think that the divine Beings of that sphere, or the other supremely blessed There, need look to our apparatus of science: all of that realm (the very Beings themselves), all is noble image, such images as we may conceive to lie within the soul of the wise—but There not as inscription but as authentic existence. The ancients had this in mind when they declared the Ideas (Forms) to be Beings, Essentials.

6. Similarly, as it seems to me, the wise of Egypt—whether in precise knowledge or by a prompting of nature—indicated the truth where, in their effort towards philosophical statement, they left aside the writing-forms that take in the detail of words and sentences—those characters that represent sounds and convey the propositions of reasoning—and drew pictures instead, engraving in the temple-inscriptions a separate image for every separate item: thus they exhibited the absence of discursiveness in the Intellectual Realm.

For each manifestation of knowledge and wisdom is a distinct image, an object in itself, an immediate unity, not an aggregate of discursive reasoning and detailed willing. Later from this wisdom in unity there appears, in another form of being, an image, already less compact, which announces the original in terms of discourse and seeks the causes by which things are such that the wonder rises how a generated world can be so excellent.

For, one who knows must declare his wonder that this Wisdom, while not itself containing the causes by which Being exists and takes such excellence, yet imparts them to the entities produced in Being's realm. This excellence, whose necessity is scarcely or not at all manifest to search, exists, if we could but find it out, before all searching and reasoning.

What I say may be considered in one chief thing, and thence applied to all the particular entities:

7. Consider the universe: we are agreed that its existence and its nature come to it from beyond itself; are we, now, to imagine that its maker first thought it out in detail—the earth, and its necessary situation in the middle; water and, again, its position as lying upon the earth; all the other elements and objects up to the sky in due place and order; living beings with their appropriate forms as we know them, their inner organs and their outer limbs—and that having thus appointed every item beforehand, he then set about the execution?

Such designing was not even possible; how could the plan for a universe come to one that had never looked outward? Nor could he work on material gathered from elsewhere as our craftsmen do, using hands and tools; feet and hands are of the later order.

One way, only, remains: all things must exist in something else; of that prior—since there is no obstacle, all being continuous within the realm of reality—there has suddenly appeared a sign, an image, whether given forth directly or through the ministry of soul or of some phase of soul, matters nothing for the moment: thus the entire aggregate of existence springs from the divine world, in greater beauty There because There unmingled but mingled here.

From the beginning to end all is gripped by the Forms of the Intellectual Realm: Matter itself is held by the Ideas of the elements and to these Ideas are added other Ideas and others again, so that it is hard to work down to crude Matter beneath all that sheathing of Idea. Indeed since Matter itself is, in its degree, an Idea—the lowest—all this universe is Idea and there is nothing that is not Idea as the archetype was. And all is made silently, since nothing had part in the making but Being and Idea—a further reason why creation went without toil. The Exemplar was the Idea of an All and so an All must come into being.

Thus nothing stood in the way of the Idea, and even now it dominates, despite all the clash of things: the creation is not hindered on its way even now; it stands firm in virtue of being All. To me, moreover, it seems that if we ourselves were archetypes, Ideas, veritable Being, and the Idea with which we construct here were our veritable Essence, then our creative power, too, would toillessly effect its purpose: as man now stands, he does not produce in his work a true image of himself: become man, he has ceased to be the All; ceasing to be man—we read—'he soars aloft and administers the Cosmos entire'; restored to the All he is maker of the All.

But—to our immediate purpose—it is possible to give a reason why the earth is set in the midst and why it is round and why the ecliptic runs precisely as it does, but, looking to the creating principle, we cannot say that because this was the way therefore things were so planned: we can say only that because the Exemplar is what it is, therefore the things of this world are good; the causing principle, we might put it, reached the conclusion before all formal reasoning and not from any premises, not by sequence or plan but before either, since all of that order, is later, all reason, demonstration, persuasion.

Since there is a Source, all the created must spring from it and in accordance with it; and we are rightly told not to go seeking the causes impelling a Source to produce, especially when this is the perfectly sufficient Source and identical with the Term: a Source which is Source and Term must be the All-Unity, complete in itself.

8. This then is Beauty primally; it is entire and omnipresent as an entirety; and therefore in none of its parts or members lacking in beauty; beautiful thus beyond denial. Certainly it cannot be anything (be, for example, Beauty) without being wholly that thing; it can be nothing which it is to possess partially or in which it utterly fails (and therefore it must entirely be Beauty entire).

If this principle were not beautiful, what other could be? Its prior does not deign to be beautiful; that which is the first to manifest itself —Form and object of vision to the intellect—cannot but be lovely to see. It is to indicate this that Plato, drawing on something well within our observation, represents the Creator as approving the work he has achieved: the intention is to make us feel the lovable beauty of the archetype and of the Divine Idea; for to admire a representation is to admire the original upon which it was made.

It is not surprising if we fail to recognize what is passing within us: lovers, and those in general that admire beauty here, do not stay to reflect that it is to be traced, as of course it must be, to the Beauty There. That the admiration of the Demiurge is to be referred to the Ideal Exemplar is deliberately made evident by the rest of the passage: 'He admired; and determined to bring the work into still closer likeness with the Exemplar': he makes us feel the magnificent beauty of the Exemplar by telling us that the Beauty sprung from this world is, itself, a copy from That.

And indeed if the divine did not exist, the transcendently beautiful, in a beauty beyond all thought, what could be lovelier than the things we see? Certainly no reproach can rightly be brought against this world save only that it is not That.

9. Let us, then, make a mental picture of our universe: each member shall remain what it is, distinctly apart; yet all is to form, as far as possible, a complete unity so that whatever comes into view, say the outer orb of the heavens, shall bring immediately with it the vision, on the one plane, of the sun and of all the stars with earth and sea and all living things as if exhibited upon a transparent globe.

Bring this vision actually before your sight, so that there shall be in your mind the gleaming representation of a sphere, a picture holding all the things of the universe moving or in repose or (as in reality) some at rest, some in motion. Keep this sphere before you, and from it imagine another, a sphere stripped of magnitude and of spatial differences; cast out your inborn sense of Matter, taking care not merely to attenuate it: call on God, maker of the sphere whose image you now hold, and pray Him to enter. And may He come bringing His own Universe with all the gods that dwell in it—He who is the one God and all the gods, where each is all, blending into a unity, distinct in powers but all one god in virtue of that one divine power of many facets.

More truly, this is the one God who is all the gods; for, in the coming to be of all those, this, the one, has suffered no diminishing. He and all have one existence, while each again is distinct. It is distinction by state without interval: there is no outward form to set one here and another there and to prevent any from being an entire identity; yet there is no sharing of parts from one to another. Nor is each of those divine wholes a power in fragment, a power totalling to the sum of the measurable segments: the divine is one all-power, reaching out to infinity, powerful to infinity: and so great is God that his very members are infinites. What place can be named to which He does not reach?

Great, too, is this firmament of ours and all the powers constellated within it, but it would be greater still, unspeakably, but that there is inbound in it something of the petty power of body; no doubt the powers of fire and other bodily substances might themselves be thought very great, but in fact, it is through their failure in the true power that we see them burning, destroying, wearing things away, and slaving towards the production of life; they destroy because they are themselves in process of destruction, and they produce because they belong to the realm of the produced.

The power in that other world has merely Being and Beauty of Being. Beauty without Being could not be, nor Being voided of beauty: abandoned of Beauty, Being loses something of its essence. Being is desirable because it is identical with Beauty; and Beauty is loved because it is Being. How then can we debate which is the cause of the other, where the nature is one? The very figment of Being needs some imposed image of Beauty to make it passable, and even to ensure its existence; it exists to the degree in which it has taken some share in the beauty of Idea; and the more deeply it has drawn on this, the less imperfect it is, precisely because the nature which is essentially the beautiful has entered into it the more intimately.

10. This is why Zeus, although the oldest of the gods and their sovereign, advances first (in the Phaedrus myth) towards that vision, fol-

lowed by gods and demigods and such souls as are of strength to see.
That Being appears before them from some unseen place and rising
loftily over them pours its light upon all things, so that all gleams in
its radiance; it upholds some beings, and they see; the lower are daz-
zled and turn away, unfit to gaze upon that sun, the trouble falling
the more heavily on those most remote.

Of those looking upon that Being and its content, and able to see,
all take something but not all the same vision always: intently gazing,
one sees the fount and principle of Justice, another is filled with the
sight of Moral Wisdom, the original of that quality as found, sometimes at least, among men, copied by them in their degree from the
divine virtue which, covering all the expanse, so to speak, of the Intel-
lectual-Realm is seen, last attainment of all, by those who have known
already many splendid visions.

The gods see, each singly and all as one. So, too, the souls; they see
all There in right of being sprung, themselves, of that universe and
therefore including all from beginning to end and having their existence There if only by that phase which belongs inherently to the Divine, though often too they are There entire, those of them that have
not incurred separation.

This vision Zeus takes and it is for such of us, also, as share his love
and appropriate our part in the Beauty There, the final object of all
seeing, the entire beauty upon all things; for all There sheds radiance,
and floods those that have found their way thither so that they too
become beautiful; thus it will often happen that men climbing heights
where the soil has taken a yellow glow will themselves appear so, bor-
rowing colour from the place on which they move. The colour flowering on that other height we speak of is Beauty; or rather all There is
light and beauty, through and through, for the beauty is no mere
bloom upon the surface.

To those that do not see entire, the immediate impression is alone
taken into account; but those drunken with this wine, filled with the
nectar, all their soul penetrated by this beauty, cannot remain mere
gazers: no longer is there a spectator outside gazing on an outside spectacle; the clear-eyed hold the vision within themselves,
though, for the most part, they have no idea that it is within but look
towards it as to something beyond them and see it as an object of vision caught by a direction of the will.

All that one sees as a spectacle is still external; one must bring the
vision within and see no longer in that mode of separation but as we
know ourselves; thus a man filled with a god—possessed by Apollo or

by one of the Muses—need no longer look outside for his vision of the divine being; it is but finding the strength to see divinity within.

11. Similarly any one, unable to see himself, but possessed by that God, has but to bring that divine-within before his consciousness and at once he sees an image of himself, himself lifted to a better beauty: now let him ignore that image, lovely though it is, and sink into a perfect self identity, no such separation remaining; at once he forms a multiple unity with the God silently present; in the degree of his power and will, the two become one; should he turn back to the former duality, still he is pure and remains very near to the God; he has but to look again and the same presence is there.

This conversion brings gain: at the first stage, that of separation, a man is aware of self; but retreating inwards, he becomes possessor of all; he puts sense away behind him in dread of the separated life and becomes one in the Divine; if he plans to see in separation, he sets himself outside.

The novice must hold himself constantly under some image of the Divine Being and seek in the light of a clear conception; knowing thus, in a deep conviction, whither he is going into what a sublimity he penetrates—he must give himself forthwith to the inner and, radiant with the Divine Intellections (with which he is now one), be no longer the seer, but, as that place has made him, the seen.

Still, we will be told, one cannot be in beauty and yet fail to see it. The very contrary: to see the divine as something external is to be outside of it; to become it is to be most truly in beauty: since sight deals with the external, there can here be no vision unless in the sense of identification with the object.

And this identification amounts to a self-knowing, a self-consciousness guarded by the fear of losing the self in the desire of a too wide awareness.

It must be remembered that sensations of the ugly and evil impress us more violently than those of what is agreeable and yet leave less knowledge as the residue of the shock: sickness makes the rougher mark, but health, tranquilly present, explains itself better; it takes the first place, it is the natural thing, it belongs to our being; illness is alien, unnatural, and thus makes itself felt by its very incongruity, while the other conditions are native and we take no notice. Such being our nature, we are most completely aware of ourselves when we are most completely identified with the object of our knowledge.

This is why in that other sphere, when we are deepest in that knowledge by intellection, we are aware of none; we are expecting some impression on sense, which has nothing to report since it has seen nothing and never could in that order see anything. The unbelieving element is sense; it is the other, the Intellectual-Principle, that sees; and if this too doubted, it could not even credit its own existence, for it can never stand away and with bodily eyes apprehend itself as a visible object.

12. We have told how this vision is to be procured, whether by the mode of separation or in identity: now, seen in either way, what does it give to report?

The vision has been of God in travail of a beautiful offspring, God engendering a universe within himself in a painless labour and—rejoiced in what he has brought into being, proud of his children—keeping all closely by Him, for the pleasure He has in his radiance and in theirs.

Of this offspring—all beautiful, but most beautiful those that have remained within—only one has become manifest without; from him (Zeus, sovran over the visible universe), the youngest born, we may gather, as from some image, the greatness of the Father and of the Brothers that remain within the Father's house.

Still the manifested God cannot think that he has come forth in vain from the father; for through him another universe has arisen, beautiful as the image of beauty, and it could not be lawful that Beauty and Being should fail of a beautiful image.

This second Cosmos at every point copies the archetype: it has life and being in copy, and has beauty as springing from that diviner world. In its character of image it holds, too, that divine perpetuity without which it would only at times be truly representative and sometimes fail like a construction of art; for every image whose existence lies in the nature of things must stand during the entire existence of the archetype.

Hence it is false to put an end to the visible sphere as long as the Intellectual endures, or to found it upon a decision taken by its maker at some given moment.

That teaching shirks the penetration of such a making as is here involved: it fails to see that as long as the Supreme is radiant there can be no failing of its sequel but, that existing, all exists. And—since the necessity of conveying our meaning compels such terms—the Supreme has existed for ever and for ever will exist.

13. The God fettered (as in the Kronos Myth) to an unchanging identity leaves the ordering of this universe to his son (to Zeus), for it could not be in his character to neglect his rule within the divine sphere, and, as though sated with the Authentic-Beauty, seek a lordship too recent and too poor for his might. Ignoring this lower world, Kronos (Intellectual-Principle) claims for himself his own father (Ouranos, the Absolute, or One) with all the upward-tending between them: and he counts all that tends to the inferior, beginning from his son (Zeus, the All-Soul), as ranking beneath him. Thus he holds a mid-position determined on the one side by the differentiation implied in the severance from the very highest and, on the other, by that which keeps him apart from the link between himself and the lower: he stands between a greater father and an inferior son. But since that father is too lofty to be thought of under the name of Beauty, the second God remains the primally beautiful.

Soul also has beauty, but is less beautiful than Intellect as being its image and therefore, though beautiful in nature, taking increase of beauty by looking to that original. Since then the All-Soul—to use the more familiar term—since Aphrodite herself is so beautiful, what name can we give to that other? If Soul is so lovely in its own right, of what quality must that prior be? And since its being is derived, what must that power be from which the Soul takes the double beauty, the borrowed and the inherent?

We ourselves possess beauty when we are true to our own being; our ugliness is in going over to another order; our self-knowledge, that is to say, is our beauty; in self-ignorance we are ugly.

Thus beauty is of the Divine and comes Thence only.

Do these considerations suffice to a clear understanding of the Intellectual Sphere or must we make yet another attempt by another road?

ENNEAD VI

Seventh Tractate

MULTIPLICITY OF THE IDEAL-FORMS

31. But since the beauty and light in all come from That which is before all, it is Thence that Intellectual-Principle took the brilliance of

the Intellectual Energy which flashed Nature (Soul?) into being; Thence soul took power towards life, in virtue of that fuller life streaming into it. Intellectual-Principle was raised thus to that Supreme and remains with it, happy in that presence. Soul too, that soul which as possessing knowledge and vision was capable, clung to what it saw; and as its vision so its rapture; it saw and was stricken; but having in itself something of that principle it felt its kinship and was moved to longing like those stirred by the image of the beloved to desire of the veritable presence. Lovers here mould themselves to the beloved; they seek to increase their attraction of person and their likeness of mind; they are unwilling to fall short in moral quality or in other graces lest they be distasteful to those possessing such merit—and only among such can true love be. In the same way the soul loves the Supreme Good, from its very beginnings stirred by it to love. The soul which has never strayed from this love waits for no reminding from the beauty of our world: holding that love—perhaps unawares—it is ever in quest, and, in its longing to be borne Thither, passes over what is lovely here and with one glance at the beauty of the universe dismisses all; for it sees that all is put together of flesh and Matter, befouled by its housing, made fragmentary by corporal extension, not the Authentic Beauty which could never venture into the mud of body to be soiled, annulled.

By only noting the flux of things it knows at once that from elsewhere comes the beauty that floats upon them and so it is urged Thither, passionate in pursuit of what it loves: never—unless someone robs it of that love—never giving up till it attain.

There indeed all it saw was beautiful and veritable; it grew in strength by being thus filled with the life of the True; itself becoming veritable Being and attaining veritable knowledge, it enters by that neighbouring into conscious possession of what it has long been seeking.

32. Where, then? where exists the author of this beauty and life, the begetter of the veritable?

You see the splendour over all the manifold Forms or Ideas; well might we linger here: but amid all these things of beauty we cannot but ask whence they come and whence the beauty. This source can be none of the beautiful objects; were it so, it too would be a mere part. It can be no shape, no power, nor the total of powers and shapes that have had the becoming that has set them here; it must stand above all the powers, all the patterns. The origin of all this must be the formless

—formless not as lacking shape but as the very source of even shape Intellectual.

In the realm of process anything coming to be must come to be something; to every thing its distinctive shape: but what shape can that have which no one has shaped? It can be none of existing things; yet it is all: none, in that beings are later; all, as the wellspring from which they flow. That which can make all can have, itself, no extension; it must be limitless and so without magnitude; magnitude itself is of the Later and cannot be an element in that which is to bring it into being. The greatness of the Authentic cannot be a greatness of quantity; all extension must belong to the subsequent: the Supreme is great in the sense only that there can be nothing mightier, nothing to equal it, nothing with anything in common with it: how then could anything be equal to any part of its content? Its eternity and universal reach entail neither measure nor measurelessness; given either, how could it be the measure of things? So with shape: granted beauty, the absence of shape or form to be grasped is but enhancement of desire and love; the love will be limitless as the object is, an infinite love.

Its beauty, too, will be unique, a beauty above beauty: it cannot be beauty since it is not a thing among things. It is lovable and the author of beauty; as the power to all beautiful shape, it will be the ultimate of beauty, that which brings all loveliness to be; it begets beauty and makes it yet more beautiful by the excess of beauty streaming from itself, the source and height of beauty. As the source of beauty it makes beautiful whatsoever springs from it. And this conferred beauty is not itself in shape; the thing that comes to be is without shape, though in another sense shaped; what is denoted by shape is, in itself, an attribute of something else, shapeless at first. Not the beauty but its participant takes the shape.

33. When therefore we name beauty, all such shape must be dismissed; nothing visible is to be conceived, or at once we descend from beauty to what but bears the name in virtue of some faint participation. This formless Form is beautiful as Form, beautiful in proportion as we strip away all shape, even that given in thought to mark difference, as for instance the difference between Justice and Sophrosyny, beautiful in their difference.

The Intellectual-Principle is the less for seeing things as distinct, even in its act of grasping in unity the multiple content of its Intellectual realm; in its knowing of the particular it possesses itself of one Intellectual shape; but, even thus, in this dealing with variety as unity, it leaves us still with the question how we are to envisage that which stands beyond this all-lovely, beyond this principle at once multiple and above multiplicity, the Supreme for which the soul hungers though unable to tell why such a being should stir its longing—reason, however, urging that This at last is the Authentic Term because the Nature best and most to be loved may be found there only where there is no least touch of Form. Bring something under Form and present it so before the mind; immediately we ask what Beyond imposed that shape; reason answers that while there exists the giver having shape to give—a giver that is shape, idea, an entirely measured thing—yet this is not alone, is not adequate in itself, is not beautiful in its own right but is a mingled thing. Shape and idea and measure will always be beautiful, but the Authentic Beauty, or rather the Beyond-Beauty, cannot be under measure and therefore cannot have admitted shape or be Idea: the primal Beauty, The First, must be without Form; the beauty of that higher realm must be, simply, the Nature of the Intellectual Good.

Take an example from love: so long as the attention is upon the visible form, love has not entered: when from that outward form the lover elaborates within himself, in his own partless soul, an immaterial image, then it is that love is born, then the lover longs for the sight of the beloved to make that fading image live again. If he could but learn to look elsewhere, to the more nearly formless, his longing would be for that: his first experience was loving a great luminary by way of some thin gleam from it.

Shape is an impress from the unshaped; it is the unshaped that produces shape, not shape the unshaped; and Matter is needed for the producing; Matter, in the nature of things, is the furthest away, since of itself it has not even the lowest degree of shape. Thus lovableness does not belong to Matter but to that which draws upon Form: the Form upon Matter comes by way of soul; soul is more nearly Form and therefore more lovable; Intellectual-Principle, nearer still, is even more to be loved: by these steps we are led to know that the primary nature of Beauty must be formless.

. . . . .

ENNEAD III

Eighth Tractate

NATURE, CONTEMPLATION, AND THE ONE

3. But if this Reason-Principle (Nature) is in act—and produces by the process indicated—how can it have any part in Contemplation?

To begin with, since in all its production it is stationary and intact, a Reason-Principle self-indwelling, it is in its own nature a Contemplative act. All doing must be guided by an Idea, and will therefore be distinct from that Idea: the Reason-Principle then, as accompanying and guiding the work, will be distinct from the work; not being action but Reason-Principle it is, necessarily, Contemplation. Taking the Reason-Principle, the Logos, in all its phases, the lowest and last springs from a mental act (in the higher Logos) and is itself a contemplation, though only in the sense of being contemplated (i.e. of being object and not subject), but above it stands the total Logos with its two distinguishable phases, first, that identified not as Nature but as All-Soul and, next, that operating in Nature and being itself the Nature-Principle.

And does this Reason-Principle, Nature, spring from a contemplation?

Wholly and solely.

From self-contemplation, then? Or what are we to think? It derives from a Contemplation and some contemplating Being; how are we to suppose it to have Contemplation itself?

The Contemplation springing from the reasoning faculty—that, I mean, of planning its own content—it does not possess.

But why not, since it is a phase of Life, a Reason-Principle, and a creative Power?

Because to plan for a thing is to lack it: Nature does not lack; it creates because it possesses. Its creative act is simply its possession of its own characteristic Essence; now its Essence, since it is a Reason-Principle, is to be at once an act of contemplation and an object of contemplation. In other words, the Nature-Principle produces by virtue of being an act of contemplation, an object of contemplation, and a Reason-Principle; on this triple character depends its creative efficacy.

Thus the act of production is seen to be in Nature an act of contemplation, for creation is the outcome of a contemplation which never becomes anything else, which never does anything else, but creates by simply being a contemplation.

4. And Nature, asked why it brings forth its works, might answer if it cared to listen and to speak:

'It would have been more becoming to put no question but to learn in silence just as I myself am silent and make no habit of talking. And what is your lesson? This; that whatsoever comes into being is my vision, seen in my silence, the vision that belongs to my character who, sprung from vision, am vision-loving and create vision by the vision-seeing faculty within me. The mathematicians from their vision draw their figures: but I draw nothing: I gaze and the figures of the material world take being as if they fell from my contemplation. As with my Mother (the All-Soul) and the Beings that begot me so it is with me: they are born of a Contemplation and my birth is from them, not by their Act but by their Being; they are the loftier Reason-Principles, they contemplate themselves and I am born.'

Now what does this tell us?

It tells: that what we know as Nature is a Soul, offspring of a yet earlier Soul of more powerful life; that it possesses, therefore, in its repose, a vision within itself; that it has no tendency upward nor even downward but is at peace, steadfast, in its own Essence; that, in this immutability accompanied by what may be called Self-Consciousness, it possesses—within the measure of its possibility—a knowledge of the realm of subsequent things perceived in virtue of that understanding and consciousness; and, achieving thus a resplendent and delicious spectacle, has no further aim.

Of course, while it may be convenient to speak of 'understanding' or 'perception' in the Nature-Principle, this is not in the full sense applicable to other beings; we are applying to sleep a word borrowed from the wake.

For the Vision on which Nature broods, inactive, is a self-intuition, a spectacle laid before it by virtue of its unaccompanied self-concentration and by the fact that in itself it belongs to the order of intuition. It is a Vision silent but somewhat blurred, for there exists another, a clearer, of which Nature is the image: hence all that Nature produces is weak; the weaker act of intuition produces the weaker object.

In the same way, human beings, when weak on the side of contemplation, find in action their trace of vision and of reason: their spiritual feebleness unfits them for contemplation; they are left with a void, because they cannot adequately seize the vision; yet they long for it; they are hurried into action as their way to the vision which they cannot attain by intellection. They act from the desire of seeing their action, and of making it visible and sensible to others when the result shall prove fairly well equal to the plan. Everywhere, doing and making will be found to be either an attenuation or a complement of vision—attenuation if the doer was aiming only at the thing done; complement if he is to possess something nobler to gaze upon than the mere work produced.

Given the power to contemplate the Authentic, who would run, of choice, after its image?

The relation of action to contemplation is indicated in the way duller children, inapt to study and speculation, take to crafts and manual labour.

• • • • •

AUGUSTINE

When one turns to St. Augustine after reading in the classical tradition of philosophy of art one is struck by the radical shift which has taken place in the foundation of art evaluation. Where Plato and Aristotle approach art from a political and metaphysical point of view, where the question of truth is determined by reference to the polis and a doctrine of Being, Augustine begins his analysis from the foundation of faith, the faith of Christianity. Scripture, not philosophy, is the arbiter. The production and consumption of art are matters of interest to the church. For Plato they were of interest to the city administration. The degree to which the artist may be said to be a knower is established by reference to the doctrines of the Christian religion. The Christian thinker faces the same problems as the pagan: What is the function and purpose of art? How are we to understand artistic creativity? How can the subject matter of art be evaluated? But he seeks answers in a different direction: What do Scripture and tradition teach us? What is the relation of God to the world? What are the ways of knowing God's design? What is the mission of the church? In order to answer these questions, Augustine had to resolve difficult conflicts. His treatises are remarkable for their unremitting efforts to satisfy the demands of faith and to do justice to the natural gratifications of art. Four basic conflicts, the resolutions of which give him the answers he seeks, are: 1) pagan vs. Christian; 2) Nature vs. art; 3) imitation vs. symbol; 4) creation vs. begetting.

The immediate sensuous gratification of art remains a problem even when conflicts are resolved, for though the Divine order and harmony are reflected in nature and to some extent in art, perceptual objects tie the senses down to earthly things and prevent the mind from contemplating what is eternal and unchanging. Art and the beauties of nature have their place in the ascent to God, but better guides for the soul's return are to be found in objects which do not require the use of sight. Those human arts which participate least in the sensible are the best mirrors of Divine order. Thus music, Augustine believes, is a higher art than painting. But better than music as a teacher are the words of Scripture. In the Bible we find statements about God and His works, and these words are especially adapted to the powers of human comprehension. Yet to understand requires a method, for Christian interpretation must not read the figure in the literal sense alone; the mind must transcend the mere image. Augustine not only discussed the methods for interpreting Scripture, but provided extended interpretations of a great many books of the Bible. (See De Doctrina Christiana, De Utilitate Credendi.)

Therefore, according to Augustine, Scripture properly interpreted provides the most direct knowledge of Divine purpose and order, but the arts of music and painting can make their contribution toward our understanding, too. It is the direct deliverances of art that interest Augustine far more than any adornment or glorification of places of worship that it can provide. This latter use of art in relation to the church develops in Eastern Christianity several centuries after Augustine and brings with it the iconoclastic controversy. For Augustine this issue is only a possibility realized in his exhortations against pagan idolatry. As long as art agrees with the truths of faith and reflects the harmony of God's creative power it has a justification.

The fullest exploitation to which art is properly subject is in the manifestation of Beauty. In fact, Augustine's philosophy of art is more properly a philosophy of Beauty, developing out of the Neoplatonic tradition, for human making when subject to the Divine Will can participate in what Augustine calls "number." The term "number" (numerus) has several meanings for Augustine: 1) mathematical proportion; 2) rhythmic organization; 3) fittingness of parts (in both the elements of an object and the faculties of the human soul); 4) the Divine, i.e., the *plenitude, unity, law, and beauty of God. Further, the nature of number is apprehended by man through an experience at first physical (felt number or rhythm), then intellectual (the number of thought and memory), and finally innate number (the judgment of the soul by means of a harmony bestowed upon it by God). Augustine's clearest statement of this metaphysics of Beauty is to be found in De Musica.*

DE ORDINE

Chapter Eleven

30. Reason is a mental operation capable of distinguishing and connecting the things that are learned. But only a rare class of men is capable of using it as a guide to the knowledge of God or of the soul; either of the soul within us or of the world-soul. And this is due to nothing else than the fact that for anyone who has advanced towards objects of sense, it is difficult to return to himself. Wherefore, although men strive to act entirely with reason in those things which are liable to deceive, yet only a very few know what reason *is*, or what its qualities are. This seems strange, but that is how the matter stands. For the present, however, it is enough to have said that much; for even if I should wish to expound the matter to you as it should be understood, my incompetence would be equaled by my arrogance if I should profess that I myself have grasped it already. Nevertheless, insofar as it has deigned to reveal itself in the things that appear familiar to you, let us now examine it to the best of our ability, in accordance with the demands of the discussion we have undertaken.

31. And first of all, let us see in what connection this word which is called *reason*, is wont to be used. Of particular interest to us ought to be the fact that man has been defined thus by the ancient philosophers: *Man is an animal, rational and mortal.* In this definition, when the genus which is called *animal,* has been given, then we notice that two distinguishing notes are added. And by those distinguishing notes, man, I believe, was to be admonished both whither he is to return and what he ought to flee; for just as the soul's forward movement has fallen down to the things that are mortal, so ought its return be to reason. By the term, *rational,* it is distinguished from God.

Therefore, unless it holds fast to the rational element, it will be a beast; and unless it turns aside from the mortal element, it will not be divine.

But because very learned men are wont to distinguish keenly and ingeniously between the rational [*rationale*] and the reasonable [*rationabile*], such distinction is by no means to be ignored in view of what we have undertaken. They designate as *rational*, whatever uses reason or possesses the faculty of reasoning; but whatever has been done or spoken according to reason, *that* they call *reasonable*. Accordingly, we could call these baths or our discourse *reasonable*; but him who constructed the baths, or ourselves who are now discoursing, we could term *rational*. Reason, then proceeds from a rational soul into reasonable things which are done or spoken.

32. I see therefore two things wherein the faculty and power of reason can even be brought before the senses. Namely, the works of man which are seen and his words which are heard. In each case the mind uses a twin messenger, the ocular and the auricular, according to the needs of the body. Thus when we behold something formed with well-fitting parts, not absurdly do we say that it appears reasonably [fashioned]. In like manner, when we hear a melody harmonize well, we do not hesitate to say that it sounds reasonably [harmonized]. But anyone would be laughed at if he should say that something smells reasonably or tastes reasonably or is reasonably tender, unless perchance in those things which for some purpose have been contrived by men so to smell or taste or glow, or anything else. For instance, if someone, considering the reason why it was done, should say that a place whence serpents are put to flight by pungent odors, emits smells reasonably; or that a potion which a physician hàs prepared, is reasonably bitter or sweet; or that the bath which he ordered regulated for a sickly person, is reasonably warm or tepid. But no one, entering a garden and lifting a rose to his nose, would venture to say: "How reasonably sweet it smells!" No, not even if a physician should order him to smell it—indeed in that case, it is said to have been prescribed or offered reasonably, but not to smell reasonably—and still not, because that odor is a natural one. And even though food be seasoned by a cook, we still may say that it is reasonably seasoned. But in accordance with accepted usage, it is not said to taste reasonably whenever without any extrinsic cause it satisfies a momentary craving. But if he to whom a physician has given a potion should be asked why he ought to think it sweet, then something else is implied as the rea-

son for his thinking so, namely, the nature of his illness, which is not in the sense but is otherwise present in the body. On the other hand, if one is licking something because he is incited by the stimulus of the palate—if he should be asked why it is sweet, and if he should reply: "Because it is pleasant" or "Because I like it," no one will call it reasonably sweet unless perhaps its delight is necessary for something, and what he is chewing has been sweetened for that very purpose.

33. In so far as we have been able to investigate, we now detect certain traces of reason in the senses; and with regard to sight and hearing, we find it in pleasure itself. Other senses, however, usually demand this attribute, not because of the pleasure they afford, but on account of something else; for a purposeful act is the characteristic of a rational animal. With regard to the eyes, that is usually called *beautiful*, in which the harmony of parts is wont to be called reasonable; and with regard to the ears, when we say that a harmony is reasonable and that a rhythmic poem is reasonably composed, we properly call it *sweet*. But we are not wont to pronounce it reasonable, when the color in beautiful objects allures us or when a vibrant chord sounds pure and liquid, so to speak. We must therefore acknowledge that in the pleasure of those senses, what pertains to reason is that in which there is a certain rhythmic measure.

34. Wherefore, considering carefully the parts of this very building, we cannot but be displeased because we see one doorway towards the side and another situated almost, but not exactly, in the middle. In things constructed, a proportion of parts that is faulty, without any compelling necessity, unquestionably seems to inflict, as it were, a kind of injury upon one's gaze. But the fact that three windows inside, one in the middle and two at the sides, pour light at equal intervals on the bathing place—how much that delights and enraptures us as we gaze attentively, is a thing already manifest, and need not be shown to you in many words. In their own terminology, architects themselves call this *design*; and they say that parts unsymmetrically placed, are without *design*.

This is very general; it pervades all the arts and creations of man. Who indeed does not see that in songs—and we likewise say that in them there is a sweetness that pertains to the ears—rhythm is the producer of all this sweetness? But when an actor is dancing, although a certain rhythmic movement of his limbs may indeed afford delight by that same rhythm, yet, since to the attentive spectators all his gestures are signs of things, the dance itself is called *reasonable*, because it aptly signifies and exhibits something over and above the delight of the senses. And even if he should represent a winged Venus and a cloaked Cupid, how skillfully so ever he may depict it by a wonderful movement and posture of the body, he does not seem to offend the eyes; but through the eyes he would offend the mind, to which those signs of things are exhibited. The eyes would be offended if the movements were not graceful; for that pertains to the sense, in which the soul perceives delight precisely because it is united with the body.

Therefore delight *of* the sense is one thing; delight *through* the sense is something else. Graceful movement delights the sense; but the timely import of the movement delights the mind alone through the sense. This is more easily noticed in the case of hearing: whatever has a pleasing sound, that it is which pleases and entices the hearing itself; but what is really signified by that sound, that is what is borne to the mind, though by the messenger of our hearing. And so when we hear these lines:

> *Why do the suns in the winter rapidly sink in the ocean? What is the hindrance that holds back late-coming nights in the summer?* [1]

our praise of the meter is one thing, but our praise of the meaning is something else. Neither is it in the same sense of the term that we say: "It sounds reasonably" and "It is spoken reasonably."

Chapter Twelve

35. There are then three classes of things in which that "something reasonable" is to be seen. One is in actions directed towards an end; the second, in discourse; the third, in pleasure. The first admonishes us to do nothing without purpose; the second, to teach correctly; the last, to find delight in contemplation. The first deals with right living; the other two, with those branches of learning which we are now considering. Now that which is rational in us, that which uses reason and either produces or seeks after the things that are reasonable—since by a certain natural bond it was held fast in the fellowship of those with whom it possessed reason as a common heritage, and since men could not be most firmly associated unless they conversed and thus poured, so to speak, their minds and thoughts back and forth to one another—saw that names, or meaningful sounds, had to be assigned to things, so that men might use the sense almost as an interpreter to link them

---

[1] [Vergil, *Georgics*, II, 480-481.]

together, inasmuch as they could not perceive one another's minds. But they could not hear the words of those not present. Therefore reason, having carefully noted and discriminated all the sounds of the mouth and tongue, invented letters. But it could have done neither of these, if the vast number of things seemed to extend endlessly without any fixed limit. Therefore the great utility of enumerating was brought to mind by its very necessity. And when these two discoveries had been made, then arose the profession of copyists and calculators —the infancy of grammar, so to speak, which Varro calls *literatio*. What it is called in Greek, I do not recall just now.

36. When reason had gone further, it noticed that of those oral sounds which we used in speaking and which it had already designated by letters, there were some which by a varied modulation of the parted lips flowed clear and pure from the throat without any friction; that others acquired a certain kind of sound from the diversified pressure of the lips; and that there were still other sounds, which could not issue forth unless they were conjoined with these. Accordingly, it denominated the letters in the order of their exposition: vowels, semivowels, and mutes. In the next place, it took account of syllables. Then words were grouped into eight classes and forms; and their entire evolvement, purity, and articulation were skillfully and minutely differentiated. And then furthermore, not unmindful of numbers and measure, it directed the mind to the different *morae* of vocal sounds and syllables; and thereby it discovered that of the time-intervals through which the long and the short syllables were extended, some were double and other were simple. It noted these points as well, and reduced them to fixed rules.

37. The science of grammar could now have been complete. But since by its very name it proclaims that it knows letters—indeed on this account it is called "Literature" in Latin—it came to pass that whatever was committed to letters as worth remembering, necessarily pertained to it. And in this way history—whose name is one, but whose subject matter is undefined and many-sided, and which is filled more with cares than with enjoyment or truth, and more burdensome to grammarians than to the historians themselves—was added to this science. Who indeed would tolerate the imputing of ignorance to a man who has not heard that Daedalus flew, and not the imputing of mendacity to the man who invented the fable, folly to anyone who believed it, and impudence to him who questions anyone about it? Or

the case in which I always feel great pity for those of our household who are accused of ignorance if they cannot answer what the name of the mother of Euryalus was, since they, in turn, would not dare to call their questioners vain, absurd, or unduly inquisitive?

Chapter Thirteen

38. And when the science of grammar had been perfected and systematized, reason was then reminded to search out and consider the very power by which it produced art; for by definition, division, and synthesis, it not only had made it orderly and syntactical, but had also guarded it against every subtle encroachment of error. How therefore would it pass on to other discoveries, unless it first classified, noted, and arranged its own resources—its tools and machines, so to speak—and bring into being that discipline of disciplines which they call *dialectics?* This science teaches both how to teach and how to learn. In it, reason itself exhibits itself, and reveals its own nature, its desires, its powers. It knows what knowledge is; and by itself, it not only wishes to make men learned, but also can make them so. Yet, because in the pursuit of the things which are rightly commended as useful and upright, unwise men generally follow their own feelings and habits rather than the very marrow of truth—which indeed only a very exceptional mind beholds—it behooved that they be not only taught to the extent of their ability, but also frequently and strongly aroused as to their emotions. To the portion of itself which would accomplish this —a portion more replete with lack than with enlightenment, its lap heaped high with charms which it would scatter to the crowd so that the crowd might deign to be influenced for its own good—to this portion, it gave the name of *rhetoric.* And so the part which is called reasonable in discourse, has been advanced to this point by the liberal arts and disciplines.

Chapter Fourteen

39. From this point, reason wished to be straightway transported to the most blessed contemplation of things divine. But, lest it fall from on high, it sought steps of ascent, and it devised an orderly path for itself through the slopes it had already won. It longed for a beauty which it alone could by itself behold without these eyes of ours; but it was impeded by the senses. Therefore it turned its gaze slightly towards those senses; for they, shouting with noisy importunity that they possessed truth, kept calling it back when it fain would hasten to other things. And it began with the ears, because they claimed as their

own the very words from which it had fashioned grammar, dialectic, and rhetoric. But reason, being endowed with the keenest powers of discernment, quickly saw what difference there was between sound itself and that of which it was a symbol. It saw that to the jurisdiction of the ears pertained nothing more than sound, and that this was threefold: sound in the utterance of an animate being, or sound in what breath produces in musical instruments, or sound in what is given forth by percussion. It saw that to the first class pertained actors of tragedy and comedy or stageplayers of this kind, and in fact all who give vocal renditions; that the second class was restricted to flutes and similar instruments; and that to the third class were attributed the cithara, the lyre, cymbals, and everything that would be tonal on being struck.

40. Reason saw, however, that this material was of very little value, unless the sounds were arranged in a fixed measure of time and in modulated variation of high and low pitch. It realized that it was from this source that those elements came which it had called *feet* and *accents* when, in grammar, it was treating of syllables with diligent consideration. And because in words themselves it was easy to notice the syllabic *longs* and *shorts*, interspersed with almost equal frequency in a discourse, reason endeavored to arrange and conjoin them into definite series. And at first it followed the sense of hearing itself in this, and superimposed measured link-units, which it called *segments* and *members*. And lest the series of feet be carried further than its discernment could continue, it set a limit at which *reversion* to the beginning should be made: and precisely on this account, called it *verse*. But whatever was not restricted by a definite limit, and yet ran according to methodically arranged feet—that, it designated by the term *rhythm*; and in Latin this can be called nothing other than *number*. And thus poets were begotten of reason. And when it saw in them great achievements, not in sound alone, but in words also and realities, it honored them to the utmost, and gave them license for whatever reasonable fictions they might desire. And yet, because they took their origin from the first of the liberal disciplines, it permitted grammarians to be their critics.

41. Reason understood, therefore, that in this fourth step of ascent— whether in particular rhythm or in modulation in general—numeric proportions held sway and produced the finished product. With the utmost diligence it investigated as to what their nature might be; and,

chiefly because by their aid it had elaborated all the aforesaid developments, it concluded that they were divine and eternal. And from then onwards, it most reluctantly endured their splendor and serenity to be clouded by the material stuff of vocal utterances. And because whatever the mind is able to see is always present and is acknowledged to be immortal, numeric proportions seemed to be of this nature. But because sound is something sensible, it flows away into the past and is imprinted on the memory. By a reasonable fiction it was fabled that the Muses were the daughters of Jupiter and Memory. Now with reason bestowing its favor on the poets, need it be asked what the offspring likewise contained? And since this branch of learning partakes as well of sense as of the intellect, it received the name of *music*.

Chapter Fifteen

42. From this stage, reason advanced to the province of the eyes. And scanning the earth and the heavens, it realized that nothing pleased it but beauty; and in beauty, design; and in design, dimensions; and in dimensions, number. And it asked itself whether any line or curve or any other form or shape in that realm was of such kind as intelligence comprehended. It found that they were far inferior; and that nothing which the eyes beheld, could in any way be compared with what the mind discerned. These distinct and separate realities, it also reduced to a branch of learning, and called it geometry.

The movement of the heavens also aroused and invited reason to consider it diligently. And there, too, on account of the most constant alternations of the seasons, as well as the fixed and unerring courses of the stars and the regulated spacing of distance, it understood that nothing other than dimension and number held sway. Linking these also into an orderly whole by definition and division, it gave rise to astrology—a great subject for the God-fearing, but a torment for the curious.

43. In all these branches of study, therefore, all things were being presented to reason as numerically proportioned. And they were all the more clearly visible in those dimensions which reason, by reflection and contemplation, beheld as most true; but it used to recall rather the shadows and vestiges of those dimensions in the things that are perceived by the senses. Then reason gained much courage and preconceived a great achievement: it ventured to prove the soul immortal. It treated diligently of all things. It came to feel that it possessed great power, and that it owed all its power to numerical pro-

portions. Something wondrous urged it on. And it began to suspect that it itself was perhaps the very number by which all things are numbered; or if not, that this number was there whither it was striving to arrive. And he of whom Alypius made mention when we were treating of the Skeptics, grasped with all his might—as if Proteus were in his hands—this number which would be the discloser of universal truth. But false images of the things which we number, drift away from that most hidden something by which we enumerate, snatch our attention to themselves, and frequently make that hidden something slip away even when it has been already in our grasp.

Chapter Sixteen

44. If a man does not yield to these images, and if he reduces to a simple, true and certain unity all the things that are scattered far and wide throughout so many branches of study, then he is most deserving of the attribute *learned*. Then, without being rash, he can search after things divine—not merely as truths to be believed, but also as matters to be contemplated, understood, and retained. But whoever is still a slave to his passions or is keenly desirous of perishable goods, or, even though he flee from these and live a virtuous life, yet if he does not know what pure nothing is, what formless matter is, what a lifeless informed being is, what a body is, what species in a body is, what place and time are, what *in a place* and *at a time* signify, what local motion is, what non-local motion is, what stable motion is, what eternity is, what it is to be neither in a place nor nowhere, what is beyond time and forever, what it is to be nowhere and nowhere not to be, what it is to be never and never not to be—anyone who does not know these matters, and yet wishes to question and dispute about even his own soul—let alone investigating about the Most High God, Who is better known by knowing what He is not—such a one will fall into every possible error.

But then, whoever has grasped the meaning of simple and intelligible numbers, will readily understand these matters. Furthermore, anyone of good talents and leisure—through the privilege of age or any kind of good fortune—if he be eagerly devoted to study and if he follow the above-mentioned order of studies in so far as is required, will certainly comprehend such numbers. But since all the liberal arts are learned partly for practical use and partly for the knowledge and contemplation of things, to attain the use of them is very difficult except for some very gifted person who from very boyhood has earnestly and constantly applied himself.

Chapter Eighteen

47. And lest anyone think that we have embraced something very extensive, I say this plainly and in a few words: that no one ought to aspire to a knowledge of those matters without that twofold science, so to speak,—the science of right reasoning and that of the power of numbers. And if anyone thinks that this is indeed a great deal, let him master either numbers alone or only dialectics. But if even this seems limitless, let him merely get a thorough understanding of what unity in numbers is, and what its import is—not yet in that supreme law and order of all things—but in the things that we think and do here and there every day. The science of philosophy has already adopted this learning, and has discovered in it nothing more than what unity is, but in a manner far more profound and sublime.

To philosophy pertains a twofold question: the first treats of the soul; the second, of God. The first makes us know ourselves; the second, to know our origin. The former is the more delightful to us; the latter, more precious. The former makes us fit for a happy life; the latter renders us happy. The first is for beginners; the latter, for the well instructed. This is the order of wisdom's branches of study by which one becomes competent to grasp the order of things and to discern two worlds and the very Author of the universe, of Whom the soul has no knowledge save to know how it knows Him not.

48. The soul therefore, holding fast to this order, and now devoted to philosophy, at first introspects itself; and—as soon as that mode of learning has persuaded it that reason either is the soul itself or belongs to it, and that there is in reason nothing more excellent or dominant than numbers, or that reason is nothing else than number—soliloquizes thus: "By some kind of inner and hidden activity of mine, I am able to analyze and synthesize the things that ought to be learned; and this faculty of mine is called reason." As a matter of fact, what ought to be analyzed except what is reputed to have unity, but either has no unity whatever or has less of it than it is believed to have? And likewise, why must something be synthesized, unless in order that it become *one*, in so far as it is capable? Therefore, both in analyzing and in synthesizing, it is oneness that I seek, it is oneness that I love. But when I analyze, I seek a homogeneous unit; and when I synthesize, I look for an integral unit. In the former case, foreign elements are avoided; in the latter, proper elements are conjoined to form some-

thing united and perfect. In order that a stone be a stone, all its parts and its entire nature have been consolidated into one. What about a tree? Is it not true that it would not be a tree if it were not *one?* What about the members and entrails of any animate being, or any of its component parts? Of a certainty, if they undergo a severance of unity, it will no longer be an animal. And what else do friends strive for, but to be *one?* And the more they are one, so much the more are they friends. A population forms a city, and dissension is full of danger for it: to dissent [dis-sentire]—what is that, but to think diversely? An army is made up of many soldiers. And is not any multitude so much the less easily defeated in proportion as it is the more closely united? In fact, the joining is itself called a coin, a co-union, as it were. What about every kind of love? Does it not wish to become one with what it is loving? And if it reaches its object, does it not become one with it? Carnal pleasure affords such ardent delight for no other reason than because the bodies of lovers are brought into union. Why is sorrow distressful? Because it tries to rend what used to be one. Therefore it is troublesome and dangerous to become one with what can be separated.

Chapter Nineteen

49. Out of several pieces of material hitherto lying around in scattered fashion and then assembled into one design, I can make a house. If indeed I am the maker and it is made, then I am the more excellent; and the more excellent precisely because I am the maker. There is no doubt but that I am on that account more excellent than a house. But not on that account am I more excellent than a swallow or a small bee; for skilfully does the one build nests, and the other construct honeycombs. I am, however, more excellent than they, because I am a rational creature.

Now if reason is found in calculated measurements, does it follow that the work of birds is not accurately and aptly measured? Nay, it is most accurately and aptly proportioned. Therefore, it is not by making well measured things, but by grasping the nature of numbers, that I am the more excellent. What then? Have the birds been able to build carefully constructed nests without knowing it? Assuredly, they have. How is this shown? By the fact that we, too, accommodate the tongue to the teeth and palate by fixed measurements, so that letters and words rush forth from the mouth; and when we are speaking, we are not thinking of the oral movement by which we ought to do that. Moreover, what good singer, even though he be unskilled in the art of music, would not, by that same natural sense, keep in his singing both the rhythm and the melody known by memory? And what can become more subject to measure than this? The uninstructed man has no knowledge of it. Nevertheless, he does it by nature's doing. But why is man superior to brute animals, and why is he to be ranked above them? Because he understands what he does. Nothing else ranks me above the brute animal except the fact that I am a rational animal.

50. Then how is it that reason is immortal, and I am defined as something both rational and mortal at the same time? Perhaps reason is not immortal? But one to two, or two to four, is a ratio in the truest sense. That ratio was no truer yesterday than today, nor will it be truer tomorrow or a year hence. Even if the whole world should fall in ruins, that ratio will always necessarily be: it will always be such as it is now. Contrariwise, what the world has today, it did not have yesterday and it will not have it tomorrow. In fact, not even for the course of an hour during this very day has it had the sun in the same position. And so, since nothing in it is permanent, it does not have anything in the same way for even the shortest interval of time.

Therefore, if reason is immortal, and if I who analyze and synthesize all those things, am reason, then that by which I am called mortal is not mine. Or if the soul is not the same as reason, and I nevertheless use reason, and if through reason I am superior, then we ought to take flight from the lesser good to the greater, from the mortal to the immortal. The well instructed soul tells itself all this and more besides, and ponders over them. But I prefer to attend to them no further now, lest, while I am longing to teach you order, I myself should exceed moderation, the parent of order. Indeed, it is not by faith alone, but by trustworthy reason, that the soul leads itself little by little to most virtuous habits and the perfect life. For to the soul that diligently considers the nature and the power of numbers, it will appear manifestly unfitting and most deplorable that it should write a rhythmic line and play the harp by virtue of this knowledge, and that its life and very self —which is the soul—should nevertheless follow a crooked path and, under the domination of lust, be out of tune by the clangor of shameful vices.

51. But when the soul has properly adjusted and disposed itself, and has rendered itself harmonious and beautiful, then will it venture to see God, the very source of all truth and the very Father of Truth. O

great God, What kind of eyes shall those be! How pure! How beautiful! How powerful! How constant! How serene! How blessed! And what is that which they can see! What is it? I ask. What should we surmise? What should we believe? What should we say? Everyday expressions present themselves, but they have been rendered sordid by things of least worth. I shall say no more, except that to us is promised a vision of beauty—the beauty of whose imitation all other things are beautiful, and by comparison with which all other things are unsightly. Whosoever will have glimpsed this beauty —and he will see it, who lives well, prays well, studies well—how will it ever trouble him why one man, desiring to have children, has them not, while another man casts out his own offspring as being unduly numerous; why one man hates children before they are born, and another man loves them after birth; or how it is not absurd that nothing will come to pass which is not with God—and therefore it is inevitable that all things come into being in accordance with order—and nevertheless God is not petitioned in vain?

Finally, how will any burdens, dangers, scorns, or smiles of fortune disturb a just man? In this world of sense, it is indeed necessary to examine carefully what time and place are, so that what delights in a portion of place or time, may be understood to be far less beautiful than the whole of which it is a portion. And furthermore, it is clear to a learned man that what displeases in a portion, displeases for no other reason than because the whole with which that portion harmonizes wonderfully, is not seen; but that in the intelligible world, every part is as beautiful and perfect as the whole.

These matters will be discussed at greater length if, as I earnestly advise and hope, your zeal will have decided to follow either that order mentioned by us or perhaps another order more concise and appropriate—but at any rate, a right order—and will have seriously and consistently held it.

DE MUSICA

BOOK VI

We must not hate what is below us, but rather with God's help   x. 29
put it in its right place, setting in right order what is below us, our-

selves, and what is above us, and not being offended by the lower, but delighting only in the higher. "The soul is weighed in the balance by what delights her", *delectatio quippe pondus est animae*. Delight or enjoyment sets the soul in her ordered place. "Where your treasure is, there will your heart be also" (Matth. 6 21). Where the delight is, there is the treasure; where the heart is, there is the blessedness or misery. The higher things are those in which equality resides, supreme, unshaken, unchangeable, eternal; where there is no time, because no mutability; whence, in imitation of eternity, times in our world are made, ordered, and modified, as long as the circling sky continually returns to its place of starting, recalling thither the heavenly bodies too, with the days, months, years, periods of five years, *lustra*, and other cycles of time which are marked by the stars, according to the laws of equality, unity, and order. So earthly things are subject to heavenly things, seeming to associate the cycles of their own durations in rhythmic succession with the song of the great whole, *universitatis*.

xi. 30   In this array there are many things which to us appear out of order and confused, because we have been attached, *assuti* [nearly all MSS *assueti*], to their order, their station in existence, according to our own limited merits, not knowing the glorious plan which Divine Providence has in operation, *gerat*, concerning us. It is as if some one were put to stand like a statue in a corner of a fine, large house, and found that, being a part of it himself, he could not perceive the beauty of the structure, *fabrica*. A soldier on the battlefield cannot see the dispositions of the whole army. If syllables in a poem had life and perception for just as long as their sounds lasted, the rhythmicality and beauty of the whole intricately inwoven work could not give them pleasure. They could not review and approve the whole poem, which is built of their own transient selves. God made sinful man ugly; but it was not an ugly act to make him so. Man became ugly by his own wish. He lost the whole, which, in obedience to God's laws, he once possessed, and was given his place in part of it, since he is unwilling to practise, *agere*, the law, and therefore is governed by the law instead. Lawful acts are just, and just acts are not essentially ugly. Even in our bad deeds there are good works of God. Man, as man, is good. Adultery is bad. But from adultery, a bad act of man, is born a man, a good act of God.

xi. 31   To return, those rhythms excel by virtue of the beauty of reason, which, if we were cut off from them altogether when we incline towards the body, would cease to govern the Progressive Rhythm perceptible to sense, and to create perceptible beauties of temporal durations by bodily movement. Occursive Rhythm is also thus created, when it goes to meet Sonant Rhythm [*sic*—but the term Corporeal Rhythm has been substituted for Sonant Rhythm]. It is the same psyche which receives all these impulses, which are in fact its own, multiplying them in some sense within itself, and making them capable of being remembered. This particular power of the psyche is called memory, and it is an instrument of great assistance in the busy activities of human life, *magnum, quoddam adiutorium in huius vitae negotiosissimis actibus.*

Whatever things are retained by memory from movements of the   xi. 32 psyche performed in response to the body's affects, *passiones*, are called in Greek phantasies, φαντασίαι, for which there is no satisfactory equivalent in Latin. To treat these phantasies as things ascertained and understood, *pro cognitis atque pro perceptis*, is to live the life of mere opinion, *opinabilis vita est*, the life that is set at the very point where error has entry, *introitu*. For such phantasies, moving within the psyche, a seething welter at the mercy of diverse and contradictory blasts from the wind of attention, *intentionis*, come into mutual contact and from one another procreate new movements within the psyche, which are no longer things delivered by impressions from, *de*, the senses, resulting from impacts delivered by bodily affects, *ex occursionibus passionum corporis impressi de sensibus*, and retained afterwards by the psyche, but are now rather the images of images, *imaginum imagines*, to which the conventional name of phantasms has been given, *quae phantasmata dici placuit*. I think differently about my father whom I have seen and about my grandfather whom I have never seen. My thought of my father comes from memory, but my thought of my grandfather comes from mental movements arising out of other mental movements which are contained in memory. Their origin is hard to discover and to explain. I think that, if I had never seen any human bodies, I could not imagine, *figurare*, them. Whatever I make out of anything which I have seen, I make by means of memory. There is a difference between finding a phantasy in memory and making a phantasm from, *de*, memory. The power, *uis*, of the psyche can do all of this. But it is the greatest error to mistake even true phantasms for ascertained facts; though there is, *quamquam sit*, in both these classes of being something which we can without absurdity say that we know, that is, either something which we have perceived, or else something of which we can form a mental image, *imaginari*. I am not rash to assert that I had a father and a grandfather, but it would be utter insanity if I ventured to say, *dementissime dixerim*, that they were the very men whom my mind, *animus*, holds, either in phantasy or in a phantasm. There are people who follow their phantasms in headlong haste; and indeed we can say that the universal cause of false opinion is the mistake of regarding phantasies or phantasms as true facts ascertained by sense-perception, *per sensum*. We should, of course, resist them; we must not accommodate to them our mental activity, *mens*, wrongly thinking that, just because there is, *dum est*, an element of thought in them, therefore it is by our understanding, *intelligentia*, that we apprehend them.

xi. 33   But, if rhythm of this sort, occurring in a˙ soul, *anima*, abandoned to temporal things, has a beauty within the limitations of its own kind, even though it is only transiently that it stimulates that soul, *quamquam eam transeundo actitent*, why would Divine Providence regard this kind of beauty with jealous disapproval, *inuideat*? This kind of beauty is formed out of, *de*, our penal mortality, which, by a law of God, a law most just, we have fully deserved. But he has not so forsaken us that we cannot be recalled from carnal delight, and quickly retrace our way, *recurrere*, for His pity stretches out its hand. Carnal delight powerfully fixes in the memory all that it derives from our treacherous senses. This intimacy, *consuetudo*, between our souls and the flesh, the result of carnal affection, is called the flesh in the Divine Scriptures. The flesh wrestles with the mental part of us, *mens*, and so the Apostle could say, *cum iam dici potest apostolicum illud*, "With the mind I myself serve the law of God; but with the flesh the law of sin" (Rom. 7 [25]). But when the mental part of us is uplifted to attachment to spiritual things, the impulse of this intimacy is broken; it is gradually suppressed, and then extinguished. It was stronger when we followed it; when we bridle it, it still has some strength, but it is now weaker. If we with firm steps draw back from every lascivious thought, in which there must always be a reduction of the soul's full existence, our delight in the Rhythm of Reason is restored, and our whole life is turned to God, not now receiving pleasure from the body, but giving to it a rhythm of health. This result happens because the outer man is consumed away, and the man himself is transformed into something finer.

xii. 34   But memory gathers, *excipit*, not only the carnal movements of the mind, *animi,* that constitute the rhythm of which we have just spoken, but also spiritual movements, which we have now shortly to treat. Being simple, they have need of fewer words; but they have the utmost need of undisturbed mental activity, *plurimum seuerae mentis.* That equality which we failed to find, fixed and enduring, in perceptible rhythm, but which we recognized as shadowed in it while it passed us by, would nowhere have been an object of our mind's aspiration, *appeteret,* if somewhere it had not become known to our mind. But it cannot have been somewhere in the world of space and time, *locorum et temporum.* Spatial things expand, *tument;* temporal things pass, *praetereunt.* Where then can it have been? Not in bodily forms, which can never be called truly equal to one another if they are fairly weighed by free judgment, *liquido examine,* nor in intervals of time, in which we never know whether something is longer or shorter in duration than something else, the inequality being unobserved by our perception. Where then is that equality at which we must be looking, if we are so led to desire equality in bodily things and their movements, and yet dare not trust them, when we consider them with care? Presumably it is in the place which is higher and finer than any bodily things, *ibi puto quod est corporibus excellentius;* but whether that is in the soul, or above it, is obscure.

Our rhythmic or metric art, which is used by makers of verses, comprises certain rhythmical measurements, *numeri,* according to which they make the verses. The measurements, that is, the rhythm, remain when the verses stop or pass. The verse or rhythm which passes is really manufactured, *fabricari,* by the rhythm which remains. The art is an active conformation, *affectio,* of the mind, *animus,* of the artist. This conformation is not in the mind of any man who is unskilled, or who has forgotten the art. Now one who has forgotten a rhythm can be reminded of it by questions asked of him. The rhythm returns to his memory, but obviously not from the questioner. The man who had forgotten makes movements within the sphere of his own mental activity, *apud mentem suam,* in response to something, and hence the forgotten thing may be restored, *redhibeatur.* Can he even be reminded of the quantities of syllables, which vary in their temporal duration according to the decree of the ancients? For if these quantities had been stable, securely fixed by nature or doctrine, modern scholars would not have been committing the errors in quantity which they do commit. We cannot say that everything forgotten can be recalled to

xii. 35

memory by questions; we could not be made by questions to remember a dinner eaten a year ago, *ante annum;* nor could questions recall to memory detailed quantities of syllables. The *I* of
Italia, Italy, was made short ⌣ in the past by the wish of some individual men. Now it is long —, *Ī, Ītalia,* made long by the wish of
others. This is convention. But no one, past, present, or future, can
by his wish make 1 + 2 anything but 3, or prevent 2 from being
twice 1, *ut duo uni non duplo respondeant.* If one who has never
learnt rhythm, that is, not one who has learnt and then forgotten
it, is thoroughly questioned about it, and answers are elicited from
him, then, just as arithmetical answers about 1 and 2 and the rest
can be elicited by questions, so too the learner may learn the art of
rhythm, except the quantities of syllables, which depend on authority. The questioner does not impart anything, but the learner
acts within himself in such a way as to understand what is asked,
and answers. Through this mental movement rhythm is imprinted
on his faculty of mental activity, *mens,* and he achieves the active
conformation, *affectio,* which is called art.

xii. 36   This rhythm is immutable and eternal, with no inequality possible in it. Therefore it must come from God. The learner who is
questioned moves inwardly to God to understand immutable
truth; and unless he retains in memory the same movement which
once he made, the learner cannot be recalled to an apprehension
of that same immutable truth without external help.

xiii. 37   Presumably the learner had abandoned thoughts of that truth,
and needed to be recalled by memory, because he was intent,
attentus, on something else. What distracted him from thoughts of
the supreme, immutable equality, must have been either equal in
value, *par,* or higher, or lower. Obviously it must have been lower.
[Not necessarily.] The soul admits that immutable equality exists,
but also that it is itself lower than it, because it looks sometimes
at this equality and sometimes at something else. Set on various
objects, the soul performs a variety of temporal rhythms, with no
existence, *nulla est,* in the realm of eternal and immutable things.
This active conformation, *affectio,* by which the soul first understands what are eternal things, then realizes that temporal things
are inferior to them even when they are in itself, and finally knows
that the higher is more to be sought than the lower, is wisdom,
prudentia.

xiii. 38   The soul has, then, the power to know eternal things as things
to which it should cling fast, *inhaerendum,* but it has not at the

same time the power to do so. To find the reason, we must observe what we notice most attentively, and for what we show great care, for that is what we love much. We love the beautiful. True, some love ugly things, the "lovers of putrefaction", in Greek σαπρόφιλοι. But what matters is how much more beautiful are the things which most people like. Clearly no one loves what disgusts the perception, that is, sheer repulsiveness, *foeditas*. Beautiful things please by proportion, *numero*, and here as we have shewn equality is not found only in sounds for the ear and in bodily movements, but also in visible forms, in which hitherto equality has been identified with beauty even more customarily than in sounds. Nothing can be proportionate or rhythmic, *numerosus*, without equality, with pairs of equivalent members responding to each other, *paria paribus*. All that is single, *singula*, must have some central place, so that equality may be preserved in the intervals extending to the central individual part, *ad ea*, from either side, *de utraque parte*. Visible light has the presidency, *principatum*, over all colours, colour of course being a source of delight in bodily forms. And in all light and all colours we aspire to something which is in harmony, *congruit*, with our eyes. We turn away from too bright a light, and dislike looking at what is too dark, just as we shrink from too loud a sound and do not like a whisper. Nothing here depends on intervals of time, but everything on the actual sound which is here the very light of the rhythm, *numerorum*, the sound to which silence is the contrary, just as darkness is the contrary to light. In all this we act according to our nature's capacity, *modo*, seeking according to agreeability or rejecting according to disagreeability, though we perceive that what is disagreeable to us is often agreeable to the other animals; and we are in fact here too rejoicing in what is really a code, *quodam iure*, of equality, discovering that, in ways remote from our usual thinking, equivalences have yet been furnished to match one another, *paria paribus tributa*. In smell, taste, and touch this may equally be observed, and could easily be explored, but it would take too long to unravel the secret in detail, *enucleatius persequi*. Every perceptible thing which pleases us, pleases us by equality or similitude. Where there is equality or similitude, there is rhythmicality, *numerositas*, for nothing is so equal or so similar to anything as one is to one.

All this, as we have discovered, is not passively sustained by the soul from physical bodies, but actively performed by the soul in physical bodies. Love of active performance, in reaction to the xiii. 39

affects of its own body, diverts the soul from contemplation of eternal things, and care for the pleasure of perception calls its attention away, *auocans intentionem*. This it [the love of active performance] effects by Occursive Rhythm. The love of operating in concern with, *de*, physical bodies diverts the soul and renders it restless, *inquietam*, by means of Progressive Rhythm. Further, both phantasies and phantasms divert the soul by means of Recordable Rhythm. Lastly, it is diverted also by a love of the knowledge about such things, a knowledge that is entirely vain, *uanissimae cognitionis*; and this results from Perceptive Rhythm, in which there are some rough and imperfect rules of art, rules which rejoice in mere imitation. From these pursuits is born an anxious curiosity, *curiositas*, called by the very name of anxious care, *cura*, the enemy to quiet assurance, *securitas*, and, through its vanity, incapable of truth, *impos veritatis*.

xiii. 40   The general love of activity, *generalis amor actionis*, which diverts us from truth, starts from pride, *superbia*, the vice which made the soul prefer to imitate God rather than to serve God. Rightly it is written in the Holy Books, "The beginning of a man's pride is to revolt, *apostatare*, from God", and "The beginning of all sin is pride". No statements show better what pride is than this—"Why is earth and ashes proud, because in his life he hath cast away his bowels?" (Ecclesiasticus 10 [9]). The soul by itself is nothing, or it would not have been mutable, and suffered default from its own essence, *defectum ab essentia*. The whole quality of the soul's existence, *quicquid autem illi esse est* [Aristotle's τὸ τί ἦν εἶναι αὐτῷ·[is from God, and therefore, while it remains within its own order of being, it is enlivened, *uegetatur*, in mental activity and in self-consciousness, *mente atque conscientia*, by God's presence. Such goodness the soul has deeply within it. To become distended with pride is to move towards the external and to become empty within, that is, to exist less and less fully, *quod est minus minusque esse*. To move away to what is outside is to sacrifice what is deeply inside, and to put God far away, by a distance not of space but of mental condition, *mentis affectu*.

xiii. 41   Such a soul's appetite is to have other souls subjected to it, not the souls of animals, *pecorum*, which is allowed by Divine law, but rational souls, the souls that are its relatives and friends and partners under the same law, *id est proximas suas et sub eadem lege socias atque consortes*. The soul has conceived the desire to behave concerning, *de*, them with pride, regarding this behaviour concerning them as so much more excellent than behaviour concerning physical bodies as every soul is better than every body. But only God can act upon rational souls directly and not through the body. Yet it so transpires through our condition of sinfulness that souls are permitted to act concerning other souls, *ut permittantur animae de animis aliquid agere*, moving them by signals conveyed by the physical body of either of the souls involved, *significando eas mouentes per alterutra corpora*, either with natural gestures, as facial expression or a nod, or by conventional indications, *placitis*, such as words. We give orders and apply persuasion, and carry out all other actions by which souls act concerning, *de*, or with, *cum*, other souls, by means of signs. Now it follows from the code by which we live that whatever, in pride, desires to excel all else rules not even its own parts and its own body without difficulty, *difficultate*, and pain, partly because of stupidity within itself and partly because it is depressed by the weight of mortal members. By these rhythmical movements, by means of which souls behave in response to, *agunt ad*, one another, they are diverted, through aspiration to honours and tributes of praise, from any deep understanding, *perceptione*, of that other truth, the truth that is pure and unsullied, *sincera*. It is only from God that a soul can win true honour. He can render it blessed, living in His presence in unseen life of righteousness and piety.

Accordingly, the movements extruded by a soul in concern with,   xiii. 42
de, what clings to itself, and in concern with other souls subject to it, are like Progressive Rhythm, for the soul is acting as if upon its own body. The movements which it extrudes, in its desire to gather souls into its flock, *aggregare*, or to subject them, *subdere*, to itself, are counted among Occursive Rhythm. For the soul is acting virtually in the realm of the senses, straining, *id moliens*, to compel something, which is fetched to it from outside, to become one with itself, or alternatively, if it cannot become one with itself, to repel it. Memory now gathers, *excipit*, both kinds of movement, and renders them recordable, that is, capable of being recollected, as the phantasies and phantasms of past actions, in a seething welter. Involved with this is something which can be called a "Weighing Rhythm", *tamquam examinatores numeri*, whose task is to discern which activities prove convenient to the active soul and which inconvenient. This rhythm we should not be sorry to call "Perceptive Rhythm", *sensuales numeri*, for it consists of the perceptible indications, *sensibilia signa*, by means of which

souls behave in response to, *agunt ad,* other souls. When a soul is involved, *implicata,* with all these serious distractions, *intentiones,* it is scarcely surprising if it is diverted from the contemplation of truth, only possible for it in so far as it has respite, *respirat,* from them. It is not allowed to remain in the truth, because it has not won final victory over them, *euicit.* That is why the soul has not inherently and simultaneously both the power to know on what it should take its stand, *consistendum,* and also the power to do so.

xiv. 43   After thus considering, as well as we could, how the soul is tainted with defilement and weighted by its load, it remains for us to see that action, *actio,* is commanded of the soul by Divine authority, *divinitus,* so that through such action it may be purged and unburdened, and may then fly back to peace, and may enter into the joy of its Lord. But of course the Holy Scriptures, with the authority that is theirs, are all the time telling us to love God, our Lord, from our whole heart, our whole soul, and our whole mind, *ex toto corde, ex tota anima, et ex tota mente,* and our neighbour, *proximum,* as ourself. So there is scarcely much for us to say. If we were to refer all the movements of human action and all the rhythms, which we have examined, to this great end, without doubt we shall be cleansed, *mundabimur.* Yet on the other hand the difficulty of practical obedience is as great as the time taken to hear the command is short.

xiv. 44   It is easy to love colours, musical sounds, *uoces,* cakes, roses and the body's soft, smooth surface, *corpora leniter mollia.* In all of them the soul is in quest of nothing except equality and similitude, and even when it reflects with some thoughtfulness it scarcely detects, amid such dark shadows, the trace of it *eius* [the text may be corrupt]. If so, it must indeed be easy to love God. For when the soul thinks of Him, as well as it can with the wounds and the stains impeding its thoughts, even so it cannot believe, *suspicatur,* that in Him there is anything unequal, or unlike Himself, or divided by space, *seclusum locis,* or varied in time. Our soul delights in the construction of tall houses, and indulgence in the efforts involved, *extendi,* in such operations. Here, if it is the proportion, *numeri,* which is the source of pleasure, and I find nothing else that can be, all the equality and similitude discernible would be derided by the arguments of true and methodical reason, *ratio disciplinae.* Why, then, does our soul slip from the truest citadel of equality, and then, with the mere débris which it drags from it, *ruinis suis,* erect terrestial structures, *machinas,* instead? The reason is not the promise of Him who knows not, *ignorat,* to deceive, "For my yoke is easy" (Matth. 11 [30]). Indeed, the love of this world is far more laborious. In this world the soul looks for permanence, *constantia,* and eternity, but never finds them, because only the lowest kind of beauty can be achieved by such transience, and whatever there is in this world which in any decree copies, *imitatur,* permanence, is transmitted, *traicitur,* through, *per,* our soul by God; for an appearance, *species,* which is changeable only in time, is precedent, *prior,* to an appearance which is changeable both in time and in space. The Lord has taught the soul of men what they should not love. "Love not the world. . . . For all that is in the world, the lust of the flesh, and lust of the eyes, and the pride of life <is not of the Father, but is of the world>" (I John 2 [15-16]).

Now consider what kind of man he is, who finds a better xiv. 45 method with which to meet these occurrences. A man who relates, not to mere pleasure, but to the preservation of his bodily self all such rhythms whose source is in the body and in the responses to the affects of the body, and who brings into use, *redigit,* the residue from such rhythms retained in the memory, and others operating from, *de,* other souls in the vicinity, or extruded in order to attach, *adiungere,* to the soul those other souls, or their residue retained in memory, not for its own proud ambition to excel, but for the advantage of those other souls themselves; and who employs that other rhythm, which presides, with an examiner's control, over such rhythms of either kind which subsist in the transience of perception, not for the purpose of satisfying an unjustifiable and harmful curiosity, *curiositas,* but only for essential proof or disproof —such a man, surely, performs every rhythm without being entrapped in their entanglements. His choice is that bodily health should not be obstructed, *ut non impediatur,* and he refers every action to the advantage of his neighbour, whom by the bond of nature he must love as himself. He would obviously be a great man and a great gentleman, *humanissimus.*

Rhythm which does not attain the level of reason is devoid of xiv. 46 beauty; and any love of the lower beauty defiles the soul. The soul loves not only equality but order also. It has lost its true order. But it still resides in the order of things where, and how, truest order requires it to reside. There is a difference between possessing, *tenere,* order, and being possessed, *teneri,* by order. The soul possesses order by itself, *seipsa*, loving all that is higher than itself, that is, in fact, God, and also the souls that are its companions, loving them as itself. By virtue of this love it orders, that is, sets in right order, all that is lower than itself, without becoming defiled. What defiles the soul is not evil, for even the body, though it is very low in the scale, is a creature of God, and is only scorned when it is compared with the dignity of the soul. Gold is defiled even by the purest silver, if it is alloyed with it. We must not deny to rhythm which is concerned with our penal mortality its inclusion within the works of the Divine fabrication, for such rhythm is within its own kind beautiful. But we must not love such rhythm as if it could make us blessed. We must treat it as we would a plank amid the waves of the sea, not casting it away as a burden, but not embracing it and clinging to it as if we imagined it firmly fixed. We must use such rhythm well, so that eventually we may dispense with it. For love of our neighbour, a love as strong as, according to the command, it must be, is the surest step towards an ability to cling to God; indeed, we should not, *et non*, only be possessed by the order which He imposes, but also possess our own order sure.

xiv. 47   Even on the evidence of Perceptive Rhythm, the soul is proved to like order. Why else is the first foot a pyrrhic ⌣ ⌣, the second an iamb ⌣ —, the third a trochee — ⌣, and so on? It may be said that this is not a matter of intuitive perception, but of reason. Yet Perceptive Rhythm has at least the credit for the equivalence by which eight long syllables occupy the same duration as sixteen short syllables; though it prefers a mixture, *misceri exspectat*, of long and short syllables together. Reason, in fact, judges perception. Proceleumatics ⌣ ⌣ ⌣ ⌣ are reported by perception as equal to spondees — —. Here reason finds only a potentiality, *potentia* [δύναμις], of order. Long syllables are only long by comparison with short syllables, and short syllables short by comparison with long syllables. Iambic ⌣ — verse, however, slowly pronounced, is always in ratio 1 : 2, and remains iambic ⌣ —. But purely pyrrhic ⌣ ⌣ verse, pronounced slowly enough, becomes spondaic — —, not, of course, according to any rule of grammar, but according to the requirement of music [or metre]. Dactyls — ⌣ ⌣ and anapaests ⌣ ⌣ — remain dactyls and anapaests, on account of the comparison between long and short syllables which is always present, however long the duration, *mora*, in pronunciation may be. Again, at the ends and beginnings of sequences of feet, half-feet are added according to different laws, all needing to have the same *ictus*, *plausus*, as the contiguous feet, and the final half-foot requiring to have sometimes two short syllables in place of one long syllable. Throughout sense-perception applies its modifications. Now here quantitative equality will not account for everything, for either choice might have been made without loss of equality. Decisions are enforced by the bond of right order. It would take too long to display here the rest of the evidence for this, which is provided by durations of time. So too perception, in dealing with visible forms, rejects some of them, for example a figure bending over too far or standing on its head, and so on, when there is no loss of equality, but there is some fault of order. In all that we perceive and in all that we make, we gradually get used to what at first we rejected. It is by order that we weave our pleasure into one. We only like what has a beginning harmoniously woven on to the middle part, and a middle part harmoniously woven on to the end.

Therefore we must not place our joys in carnal pleasure, nor in honour and tributes of praise, nor in our thought for anything extrinsic to our body, *forinsecus*; for we have God within us, and there all that we love is fixed and changeless. Temporal things are with us, but we are not ourselves involved in them, and we feel no pain in being parted from all that is outside our bodies. Even our bodies themselves can be taken from us without pain, or at least without much pain, and restored where, by the death of their old nature, they may be formed anew. The concentration, *attentio*, of the soul, fixed on some part of the body, becomes readily involved in transactions in which is no peace, and in a devotion to some private operation in neglect of universal law, though even such an operation can never be quite estranged from the totality ruled by God. Thus even he who does not love the laws is still subjected to them. xiv. 48

Now if we normally think with closest attention about immaterial, changeless things, and if it happens that, at the time, we are performing temporal rhythm in one of the kinds of bodily movement which are ordinary and quite easy, such as walking or singing, we may never notice the rhythm, though it depends on our own activity, and so, too, if we are occupied in our own vain phantasms, again we perform the rhythm, but do not notice it. Now how much more, and how much more constantly, when this "corruptible must put on incorruption, and this mortal must put xv. 49

on immortality" (I Cor. 15 ⁵³), that is, when God has revived our mortal bodies, as the Apostle says, "by his Spirit that dwelleth in" us (Rom. 8 ¹¹), how much more, concentrated on the One God, and on truth seen perspicuous, or, as we are told, "face to face", shall we perceive, with joy, the rhythm by which we actuate, *agimus*, our bodies with no unpeacefulness? For we can hardly be expected to believe that the soul, which can derive joy from the things which are good through its own self only, cannot derive joy from the things from which its own goodness comes.

xv. 50   By this action, *actio*, by which the soul with the help of God escapes from the love of the lower beauty, fighting down and killing its own habit which is warring against it, and is destined to celebrate the victory in itself by conquest of the powers of the air, *huius aeris*, it flies at last to God, its stability, its firmament, when those opposing powers in their envy desire to hinder it. Such is the virtue of temperance. The soul, advancing, and feeling in anticipation the eternal joys, and indeed almost grasping them, cannot be deterred by the loss of temporal things or death in any form, when it has strength to say, "For I am in a strait betwixt two, having a desire to depart, and to be with Christ; which is far better: nevertheless to abide in the flesh is more needful for you" (Philipp. 1 ²³⁻²⁴). This conformation, *affectio*, by which the soul has no dread of any adversities, *adversitates*, or any death, is fortitude, *fortitudo*. Its practice of order, by which it serves none but the One God, and desires equality only with the purest of souls, and has no wish to dominate anyone, but only the bestial and bodily nature, is the virtue of justice.

xvi. 51   We have agreed already that it is by prudence that the soul knows where to take its stand, *consistendum*. To this station it raises itself by temperance; that is, by turning its love to God, and turning away from this world, *ab hoc saeculo*. This love, now a righteous love, is called charity, *caritas*, and fortitude and justice go with it. The soul now attains the goal of its loving aspiration; with a perfect sanctification and enlivenment of its body, the multitude of phantasms deleted from its memory, it begins to live with God by God alone, when the promise divinely given has been fulfilled, *completum*. "Beloved, now are we the sons of God, and it does not yet appear what we shall be. But we know that, when he shall appear, we shall be like Him; since we shall see Him as He is" (I John 3 ²). Now will these same virtues continue to exist in Heaven? It might seem not, since prudence, temperance, fortitude, and justice all operate in adversity, *in aduersis*, and should thus hardly be needed there.

Such a view is rational, and has been held by learned men. But xvi. 52 consulting the Books, which no authority excels, I find "O taste and see that the Lord is good, *suauis*" (Ps. 34 [8]). The apostle Peter has added, *interposuit*. ". . . If so be ye have tasted that the Lord is gracious" (I Peter 2 [3]). Here is the truth of what happens, *quod agitur*, in the operation of these virtues which purge the soul in conversion. The love of temporal things could only have been taken by storm, *expugnaretur*, by some sweetness, *suauitas*, in eternal things. When we find in the psalm, *quod canitur*, ". . . Therefore the children of men put their trust under the shadow of Thy wings. They shall be abundantly satisfied with the fatness of Thy house; and Thou shalt make them drink of the river of Thy pleasures. For with Thee is the fountain of life" (Ps. 36 [7-9]), the writer is not now saying that the Lord will be sweet, *suauis*, to the taste, but it is clear enough how abundant is the overflow of the eternal fountain which he indicates, followed even by something like intoxication, a wonderful figure for signifying forgetfulness of secular vanities and phantasms. He adds, "In Thy light we shall see light. O continue Thy loving kindness to those who know Thee" (Ps. 36 [9-10]). "In light", means no doubt, *scilicet*, "in Christ", Who is the Wisdom of God, and so is often called Light; so therefore when it is said, "We shall see", and "Who know Thee . . .", here obviously prudence is implied. Can the true good of the soul be seen and heard where there is no prudence? Prudence, therefore, must exist in the heavenly world.

Next, people cannot be upright in heart without justice. The xvi. 53 same Prophet [that is, "David"] writes, "And Thy righteousness to the upright in heart" (Ps. 36 [10]). We have seen that it is by pride that the soul falls away to some of the actions which are within its power, sinking to certain acts of private individual concern in neglect of universal law. This is to become an apostate from God. To avoid a recurrence of such failure, the soul must fix its love on God, and live a life quite free from all defilement, in perfect chastity and exempt from every care. The Prophet [that is, "David"] further adds, "Let not the foot of pride come against me". By "foot" he means our fall when we depart from God. Refraining, the soul clings to God and lives for eternity.

Now temperance guards against sins arising from the free will, xvi. 54 and fortitude guards against temptation from without. In Scripture, this coercion is called "hand". Coercion is inflicted by no one but sinners. Fortitude, *id*, in itself fortifies the soul, that this infliction may in no way, *ut nullo modo*, occur, and that it may be guarded by the strengthening power, *firmamentum*, of God. Fortitude has stability, and offers resistance which may not be passed. It is indicated in "And let not the hand of the wicked remove me" (Ps. 36 [11]).

xvi. 55   Whether that is or is not the meaning of these words, this is the perfection and this the blessedness in which the soul can be firmly secure, can see truth, suffer no unpleasant thing, *et nihil molestiae pati*, remain subject to God, and excel others. We may conclude that in Eternal Life there will be a place for these four virtues, contemplation, sanctification, serenity, *impassibilitas*, and good order, *ordinatio*; or, since we must not worry over names when there is agreement on, *conueniunt*, the things which they are meant to signify, we may say that some such virtues as these are to be expected.

xvii. 56   God has arranged that even a sinful and sorrowful soul can be moved by rhythm and can rightly perform it, even down to the lowest corruption of the flesh. So degraded, rhythm becomes less and less beautiful, but it must always have some beauty. God is jealous of no beauty due to the soul's damnation, regression, or persistence, *permansione*. Number, the base of rhythm, begins from unity. It has beauty by equality and by similitude, and it has interconnection by order. All nature requires order. It seeks to be like itself, and it possesses its own safety and its own order, in spaces or in times or in bodily form, by methods of balance. We have to admit that in number and rhythm all, without exception and without limit, starting from the single origin of unity, is complete and secure, in a structure of equality and similitude and wealth of goodness, cohering from unity onwards in most intimate affection.

xvii. 57   *Deus creator omnium* has a pleasant rhythm for the ear, but the soul loves the sequence far more for the health and truth in it. We must not believe the dull wits, to use no harsher term, *ut mitius loquar*, of those who say that nothing can come from nothing, for God Almighty is said to have by His act disproved it. A craftsman, *faber*, operates rationally with rhythm in his art, using Perceptive Rhythm in the artistic tradition, *consuetudine*, and, besides that, Progressive Rhythm, with which he makes bodily movements, according to intervals of time, or visible forms in wood, rhythmic with intervals of space. If so, surely nature, in obedience to God, can in the ultimate beginning make the wood used by the crafts-man, and make it from nothing. Of course it can. The numerical or rhythmic structure of a tree is spatial, and it must be preceded by a numerical or rhythmic structure which is temporal. All growing things in the vegetable world, *stirpes*, grow by temporal dimensions, and it is from some deeply abstruse numerical system in them that they put forth their reproductive power. Such, perhaps even more truly such, is the growth of physical bodies in the animal world, where the disposition of limbs and all else is based on rhythmic in-tervals and equality. Every tiny particle must be distended beyond the size of an indivisible point, *impertili nota*. They are all made from elements, and the elements themselves must be made from nothing. It cannot be supposed that they contain anything of less worth or lowlier than earth. But even earth has its equality of parts, and its length, breadth, and height. In it there is a regular progres-sion, *analogia*, which may be Latinized as "corrationality", from point, *impertilis nota*, through length to breadth and height. All is due to the supreme eternal presidency of numerical rhythm, simili-tude, equality, and order. If this presidency of mathematical struc-ture is taken from earth, nothing remains. Clearly God in the be-ginning made earth out of nothing at all.

The specific appearance of earth, which distinguishes it from the xvii. 58 other elements, shews a kind of unity in so far as so base an ele-ment is capable of it. No part of it, *et nulla pars*, is unlike the whole of it. This element occupies the lowest place, which is en-tirely suited to its well-being, so harmoniously are its parts inter-connected. The nature of water is spread all over earth. Water is a unity, all the more beautiful and transparent on account of a yet greater similitude of its parts, *speciosior et perlucidior propter maiorem similitudinem partium*, on guard over its order and its security. Air has still greater unity and internal regularity than water. Finally the sky, where the totality of visible things ends, is the highest of all the elements, and has the greatest well-being. Anything which the ministry of carnal perception can count, and anything contained in it, cannot be furnished with, or possess, any numerical rhythm in space which can be estimated, unless pre-viously a numerical rhythm in time has preceded in silent move-ment. Before even that, there comes vital movement, agile with temporal intervals, and it modifies what it finds, serving the Lord of All Things. Its numerical structure is undistributed into intervals of time; the durations are supplied by potentiality; here, beyond, *supra quam*, even the rational and intellectual rhythm of blessed and saintly souls, here is the very Law of God, by which a leaf falls not, and for which, *cui*, the very hairs of our head are numbered; and, no nature intervening, *excipientes*, they transmit them to the law of earth, and the law below.

Conclusion

This work has far less vigour in its style, *infirmioribus litteris*, than other books, the books on God and the Trinity, the product not of my poor reason, but of the purifying fire of Charity. I have proceeded more slowly than have some holy men. Indeed I only dared to write the work at all, because I had observed pious men of the Church, men concerned with education, writing on such subjects in order to confute heretics.

Marsilio
FICINO

One of the most influential works of the Renaissance Neoplatonic Humanist Marsilio Ficino is his commentary on Plato's Symposium (1475), parts of which are presented here. The original title of Ficino's work was de Amore (of love) but like Plato, he treats love as the power which impels one to seek the beautiful. This is in large part, therefore, a treatise on beauty. But it is also an interpretation of Plato through which we can understand the distinctive originality of Italian Humanism which gave a new direction to the understanding and interpretation of art. One of the dominant interests of the Neoplatonists was the interpretation of the ancient texts, myths, and stories according to an elaborate allegorizing. To Ficino, Plato becomes richly suggestive when his dialogues are interpreted to bring out the concealed meanings. Through a re-examination of the arguments in the Symposium *the true nature of beauty can be discovered, i.e., Plato can be read in the light of Plotinus and the whole, by now extensive, Neoplatonic tradition.*

Consistent with this tradition, Ficino envisions a universe in which the dominant process is creation ordered by the necessity of love, that moving current of divine spirituality which travels from God to the world and from the world to God. Because God creates in beauty he must love what he creates, and each subordinate part of the created must love its superior. In this circle of superabundant spiritual potency the individual comes to know what love is and why the attainment of beauty is his highest realization. "Love is the desire for the fruition of beauty" is the way Ficino states his vision.

The movement to intelligible beauty is by way of visible beauty. The latter is realized by what Ficino calls human love, as distinguished from the former which is realized in divine love. The two kinds of love are symbolized by the Celestial Venus and the Natural Venus who, allegorically presented, appear in Renaissance Italian painting. The beauty of art, in making evident the formal properties of objects, leads from the lower to the higher beauty. Ficino wrote to Giovanni Cavalcanti: "The beauty of bodies does not consist in the shadow of materiality, but in the clarity and gracefulness of form, not in the hidden bulk, but in a kind of luminous harmony, not in an inert and stupid weight, but in a fitting number and measure. Light, gracefulness, proportion, number, and measure which we apprehend by thought, vision, and hearing [are the beautiful]. It is toward these that the true ardor of the genuine lover strives."

Ficino, in his re-establishment of Plato's dialogue of inquiry into love and beauty, sets the tone for the Renaissance evaluation of classical Greek art and thought. Like Renaissance painting and sculpture, Renaissance philosophy of art and beauty proves itself to be an original rediscovery of the ancient world.

COMMENTARY ON PLATO'S *SYMPOSIUM*

First Speech

THE ORIGIN OF LOVE OUT OF CHAOS

Chapter III

. . . By "Chaos" the Platonists mean the world in its formless state; but by "world" they mean Chaos endowed with form. For the Platonists, there are three worlds; therefore, there will be three Chaoses. First of all is God, the author of everything, who we say is the Good Itself. He created first the Angelic Mind, then the Soul of this World as Plato would have it, and last, the Body of the World. That highest realm we call God, not a "world," because *world* means *fabrication*, composed of many, whereas that ought to be perfectly simple, and we affirm it to be the beginning and end of all the worlds. The first world made by God was the Angelic Mind. The second was the Soul of the Universe; the third was this whole structure which we perceive sensibly. In these three worlds there are considered to be three chaoses.

In the beginning, God created the substance of the Angelic Mind, which we also call Essence. This, in the first moment of its creation, was formless and dark, but since it was born from God, it turned toward God, its own source, with a certain innate desire. When turned toward God, it was illumined by the glory of God Himself. In the glow of His radiance its own passion was set ablaze. When its whole passion was kindled, it drew close to God, and in cleaving to Him, assumed form. For God, who is omnipotent, created in the Angelic Mind, as it cleaved to Him, the forms of all things to be created. In this Mind, therefore, in some spiritual way was painted, so to speak, everything which we sense in these bodies [of the material world]. In those forms were conceived the globes of heaven and the elements, the stars, the kinds of vapors, the forms of stones, metals, plants, and animals. These Prototypes or Forms of everything conceived by the dispensation of God in the Angelic Mind are, we cannot doubt, the Ideas. That Form or Idea of the heavens we call the god Uranus, the form of the first planet we call the god Saturn, of the second Jove, and so on with all the rest of the planets. Likewise, the Idea of fire we call the god Vulcan, of the air Jupiter and Juno, of the sea Neptune, and of the earth Pluto. In this way all the gods are assigned to certain parts of the lower world; the Ideas of those parts are collected together in the Angelic Mind, but the drawing near of the Mind to God preceded the completed reception of the Ideas from God who created them. Before the approach came the kindling of passion, before that the illumination by the divine light, before that the first inclination of desire, and before that the substance of the disorderly Mind. It is that still formless substance which we mean by Chaos; that first turning toward God we call the birth of Love; the infusion of the divine light, the nourishing of love; the ensuing conflagration, the increment of love; the approach to God, the impact of love; and the giving of the forms, the completion of love. This composite of all the Forms and

Ideas we call in Latin a *mundus*, and in Greek, a *cosmos*, that is, Orderliness. The attractiveness of this *Orderliness* is Beauty. To beauty,
Love, as soon as it was born, drew the Mind, and led the Mind formerly un-beautiful to the same Mind made beautiful. And so we may
say that the nature of Love is this, that it attracts to beauty and links
the un-beautiful with the beautiful. Who, therefore, will doubt that
Love immediately followed Chaos, and preceded the world and all the
gods who were assigned to the various parts of the world? The more
so, since the passion of the Angelic Mind preceded its own acquisition
of form, and in that Mind, once it had taken form, were born the
gods and the world. And so Orpheus was right in naming Love the
oldest of the gods, and also calling him "perfect in himself," as much
as to say "self-completing," since that first instinct of the Angelic
Mind by its own nature seems to have drawn its own completion from
God, and to have shown that completion to the Mind, which took
form from it, and likewise to the gods, who rose from it.

Phaedrus also called Love "most wise," and rightly so, for omnis-
cience, whence all wisdom properly derives, is attributed to the Angelic Mind, because the Mind (when it was turned toward God by
Love,) glowed with the light of God Himself. The Angelic Mind was
turned toward God in the same way in which the eye is directed toward the light of the sun. For first it looks away, then it sees only the
light of the sun, then third, in the light of the sun it perceives the colors and shapes of things. The eye is at first blind, and, like Chaos,
formless. When it sees the light, it loves the light and is, in turn,
lighted up in looking at it; in receiving the glow, it receives form in
the colors and shapes of things.

Now in the same way that the Angelic Mind, just born and formless,
was turned by love toward God and received from Him its form, so
also the World-Soul turned toward the Mind and toward God, from
whom it was born. And, although it was at first formless and a chaos,
it was directed by love toward the Angelic Mind, and of forms received from the Mind became a world; and so with the matter of this
world, although in the beginning it lay a formless chaos without the
ornament of forms, attracted by innate love, it turned toward the Soul
and offered itself submissively to it, and by the mediation of this love,
it found ornament, from the Soul, of all the forms which are seen in
this world; and thus out of a chaos was made a world.

Therefore, there are three worlds, and also three chaoses. Finally,
in each case, Love accompanies the chaos, precedes the world,

wakens the drowsy, lights the obscure, revives the dead, gives form to the formless, and finishes the incomplete. Certainly no greater praises than these can be spoken of, or even conceived.

ON THE BENEFITS OF LOVE

Chapter IV

But thus far we have discussed only the origin and nobility of Love. I think we ought now to discuss his benefits. To refer individually to the separate benefits of Love to mankind is superfluous, especially since they can all be dealt with as a whole. The principle of them all is, that by avoiding evil, we pursue the good. The evil deeds of man are the same as his ugly deeds. Likewise, the good are the same as the beautiful. Certainly all the laws and codes provide nothing but instruction to man himself to avoid the ugly and cleave to the beautiful. But this state of moral rectitude, which almost innumerable laws and codes after a long time and with great difficulty succeed only partly in bringing about, Love accomplishes in a moment. For shame frightens men away from evil deeds, and the desire of being superior summons them to good deeds. Nothing lays these two before men more sharply and clearly than Love. When we say Love, we mean by that term the desire for beauty, for this is the definition of Love among all philosophers. Beauty is, in fact, a certain charm which is found chiefly and predominantly in the harmony of several elements. This charm is threefold: there is a certain charm in the soul, in the harmony of several virtues; charm is found in material objects, in the harmony of several colors and lines; and likewise charm in sound is the best harmony of several tones. There is, therefore, this triple beauty: of the soul, of the body, and of sound. That of the soul is perceived by the mind; that of the body, by the eyes; and that of sound, by the ear alone. Since, therefore, the mind, the sight, and the hearing are the only means by which we are able to enjoy beauty, and since Love is the desire for enjoying beauty, Love is always limited to [the pleasures of] the mind, the eyes, and the ears. What need is there of the senses of smell, taste, and touch? Odors, flavors, heat, cold, softness hardness, and like qualities are the objects of these senses. None of these is human beauty, since these qualities are simple, and human beauty of the body requires a harmony of various parts. Love regards as its end the enjoyment of beauty; beauty pertains only to the mind, sight, and hearing. Love, therefore, is limited to these three, but desire which rises from the other senses is called, not love, but lust or madness.

Further, if love in relation to man desires human beauty itself, and the beauty of the human body consists in a certain harmony; and if that harmony is a kind of temperance, it follows that love seeks only what is temperate, moderate, and decorous. Pleasures and sensations which are so impetuous and irrational that they jar the mind from its stability and unbalance a man, love does not only not desire, but hates and shuns, because these sensations, being so intemperate, are the opposites of beauty. A mad lasciviousness drags a man down to intemperance and disharmony, and hence seems to attract him to ugliness, whereas love attracts to beauty. Ugliness and beauty are opposites. The impulses, therefore, which attract to these two, seem to be mutually opposites. It follows that love and the desire for physical union are not only not identical impulses, but are proved to be opposite ones.

. . . . .

Second Speech

GOD IS GOODNESS, BEAUTY, AND JUSTICE, THE BEGINNING, MIDDLE, AND END

Chapter I

The Pythagorean philosophers believed that a trinity was the measure of everything, for the reason, I think, that God governs things in threes, and also that things themselves are defined according to a triple classification; hence that statement of Virgil that "God rejoices in odd numbers." Certainly the great Creator first creates everything, then He attracts, and third He finishes. Everything also, when it is born, flows from that eternal source; then it flows back to the same source when it seeks its own origin; and finally it is finished when it has returned to its own source. Orpheus explained this and called Jupiter the beginning, the middle, and the end of the universe: the beginning inasmuch as he produces it, the middle inasmuch as he attracts his products back to himself, and the end inasmuch as he finishes the things that return to him. Hence we can now call the ruler of the universe, Good, Beautiful, and Just, as He is spoken of in Plato: Good, I say, when He creates; Beautiful, when He attracts to Himself; and Just, when He finishes according to the desert of each thing. Beauty, then, whose property it is to attract, is placed between Goodness and Justice: from Goodness it flows out, and to Justice it proceeds.

HOW DIVINE BEAUTY INSPIRES LOVE

Chapter II

This Divine Beauty creates in everything love, that is, desire for itself, because if God draws the world to Himself, and the world is drawn [from Him] there is one continuous attraction, beginning with God, going to the world and ending at last in God, an attraction which returns to the same place whence it began as though in a kind of circle. This single circle, from God to the world and from the world to God, is identified by three names. Inasmuch as it begins in God and attracts to Him, it is Beauty; inasmuch as, going across into the world, it captivates the world, we call it Love; and inasmuch as it returns to its source and with Him joins its labors, then we call it Pleasure. In this way Love begins in Beauty and ends in Pleasure. It is this that Hierotheus and Dionysius the Areopagite mean in the famous hymn in which they sing, "Love is a circle of good, revolving from good to good perpetually." For Love is necessarily Good, since from good, whence He is born, He returns to good again. For He is the same God, whose beauty everything desires, in whose possession everything is content; by whom our desire is kindled; and in whom the passion of lovers finds rest, not because it is spent, but because it is satisfied.

Further, Dionysius is quite justified in comparing God to the sun, because just as the sun illuminates and warms the body, so God provides to our spirits the light of truth and the ardor of love. At any rate, we find this comparison also in the sixth book of Plato's *Republic*, something like this: "The sun generates both visible bodies and seeing eyes: to the eyes, so that they may see, it supplies a clear humor; and the bodies, so that they may be seen, it paints with colors." But still the light possessed by the eyes and the colors possessed by bodies are not enough to make vision complete unless they are aroused and strengthened by the presence and glow of the one light itself above the many, from which the many lights peculiar to the eyes and the bodies were sent out. In the same way, that prime actuality of all, who is called God, gave to everything, as He produced it, activity and form. Certainly this activity, when it was first received by the new creation, and by the waiting object, was weak and incapable of performing any work, but the perpetual and invisible light of the divine sun is always present to everything; it sustains, stimulates, arouses, completes, and strengthens. About it Orpheus in a moment of inspiration says, "sustaining everything and raising itself high above all." Insofar as it is the activity and strength of everything, it is called the Good; insofar as it stimulates and calms, soothes and arouses [everything according to its deserts and in as spiritual a way as possible] it is called the beautiful; and insofar as in objects of cognition it charms those three cognitive powers of the soul (the Mind, the Sight, and the Hearing), it is called Beauty. Insofar as it is in the power of learning, and applies this to an object of cognition, it is called Truth. Finally, as the Good, it creates, rules, and completes; as the Beautiful, it illuminates and pours forth pleasure.

BEAUTY IS THE RADIANCE OF THE DIVINE GOODNESS, AND GOD IS THE CENTER OF FOUR CIRCLES

Chapter III

The ancient theologians were not far wrong when they placed Goodness in the center and Beauty on the circumference of a circle; goodness, I say, is in a single center, and Beauty is in four circles. The single center of everything is God. Around this continually revolve four circles: Mind, Soul, Nature, and Matter. Mind is a fixed circle; Soul moves of itself; Nature moves in another, but not by another; and Matter moves both by another and in another. I shall explain why we call God the center of them all, and why we call these four "circles."

The center of the circle is a point, single, indivisible, and stationary. From it, many divisible mobile lines strike out to their respective circumferences. This divisible circumference revolves around the center as though on a hinge, and the nature of the center is such that, although it is single, indivisible, and fixed, nevertheless, it is found in many or, rather, all of the separate moving lines, for in every direction that point is in one of the lines. But since nothing can be touched by anything unlike itself, the lines drawn from the circumference to the center cannot touch a midpoint of this kind except as each one touches one certain, simple, motionless midpoint of its own. Who will deny that God is rightly called the center of everything, since He is located, single, simple, and motionless within them all; but that everything that is produced from Him is multiple, complex, and movable, and that as these things flow from Him, they flow back to Him in the image of the lines and circumference? Thus Mind, Soul, Nature, and Matter, proceeding from God, strive to return to Him, and they revolve toward Him from every possible direction. Just as the central point is found everywhere in the lines and in the whole circle, and through this central point, the separate lines touch the middle point of the circle, so God, the center of everything, who is the simplest unity and the purest actuality, is infused into everything—not only because He is present to the whole, but also because He endowed everything He created with some particular function or power, completely simple and distinctive, which is called the identity of that thing, and from which and to which, as from and to its own center [God], the rest of its parts and powers hang. It is certainly fitting that these things, as soon as they have been created, should gather around their own center, this identity of their own, before they turn to their creator, so that through their own center they may cling, as we have now several times repeated, to the center of everything. The Angelic Mind rises to its own apex and head before it ascends to God, and it is the same with the Soul and the other two circles. Of those invisible circles of the Mind, that is, and of the Soul, and of Nature, this visible circle of the material world is an image, for bodies are the shadows and traces of souls and minds, and shadows and traces show the shape of the thing which they represent.

. . . . .

HOW PLATO EXPLAINS DIVINITY

Chapter IV

Plato explained this mystery in a letter to King Dionysius, when he affirmed that God is the source of everything beautiful, the beginning and origin, so to speak, of all beauty:

> About the King of all are all things, and they exist for his sake. He is the cause of everything beautiful. About the Second are the second things, and about the Third, the third. What these things are, the human soul tries to learn by looking at things of the same sort as itself, none of which is adequate. About the King Himself and the things of which I spoke, nothing is of that sort. What follows this the soul says.

"About the King" means not within the King, but outside him, for in God there is no complexity. What that word "about" really means,

Plato explains when he adds that everything exists "because of God." He Himself is "the cause of everything beautiful," as much as to say, "Around the King of all are all things because everything of its very nature turns to God as its own end, just as it was produced from that source."

"Of all beautiful things," that is, of all Beauty, which shines out in the circles mentioned. For the shapes of things are led back to God through seeds, these through concepts, and these through Ideas, and they are produced from God in the same stages. Quite rightly, then, when Plato speaks of "all things" he means the sum of Ideas, because in them the rest are included.

"The second about the Second, and the third about the Third." Zoroaster posited three world-rulers, the masters of three orders: Onomasis, Mithris, and Arimanis. These Plato calls God, Mind, and Soul, and he posits three categories of divine Forms: Ideas, Concepts, and Seeds. The first type, that is, the Ideas, therefore, revolve around the first, that is, God, since they are given to the Mind by God, and they draw back to Him the Mind to which they were given. The second type revolves around the second, that is, the Concepts revolve around the Mind, since they cross the Mind into the Soul, and attract the Soul toward the Mind. The third type revolves around the third, that is, the Seeds of things around the Soul, for they go through the Soul into Nature, that is, into the power of generation, and again join Nature to the Soul. In the same order forms descend from Nature into Matter, but Plato does not include them in the order listed here because Dionysius' inquiry was about the divine, and Plato explains as divine the three orders pertaining to the incorporeal Ideas, but he leaves out corporeal forms. He was unwilling to call God the first King, but rather he called him "the King of all," lest he should seem perchance, if he called Him "the First," to put Him in some kind of numerical order on a level of equality with subordinate leaders. Moreover, he does not say that the first things only revolve around Him, but rather that the whole does, lest we think that He is the governor of some one of the three orders rather than King of the whole universe.

"The human soul tries to understand what these are." In close order after these three splendors of the divine beauty shining in the three circles, he adds love of the soul for them; for thence the passion of the soul is kindled. For it is certainly appropriate that the divine seek divine things, "by looking at what is related to itself." Since human thought rises from the senses, we invariably judge the divine on the basis of what seems to us highest in physical bodies. In the strength of corporeal bodies we look for the power of God; in their orderliness we look for His wisdom; and in their usefulness, for His goodness.

Moreover, Plato speaks of the shapes of bodies as related to the soul, as though next of kin, for the shapes of bodies are ranked in the next level after the soul. "Of these things none is adequate." Forms of this kind neither sufficiently are divine things, nor adequately represent them to us, for the true things are the Ideas, Concepts, and Seeds, whereas the Forms of bodies seem to be the shadows of things rather than the true things themselves. In fact, just as the shadow of a body does not give a clear and exact image of the body, so the bodies themselves do not represent the true nature of the divine.

"About the King Himself, and the objects I mentioned, nothing is of that sort." How indeed can mortal things be like immortal? or the false like the true? "But the soul speaks of what follows this." That is, the soul, as long as it judges divine things by mortal, speaks falsely of divinity, and describes not divine, but mortal things.

THE DIVINE BEAUTY SHINES THROUGH EVERYTHING AND IS LOVED IN EVERYTHING

Chapter V

At any rate, to put a great deal into a few words, Goodness is said to be the outstanding characteristic of God. Beauty is a kind of force or light, shining from Him through everything, first through the Angelic Mind, second through the World-Soul and the rest of the souls, third through Nature, and fourth through corporeal Matter. It fits the Mind with a system of Ideas; it fills the Soul with a series of Concepts; it sows Nature with Seeds; and it provides Matter with Forms. In much the same way, in fact, that the single light of the sun lights up four bodies, fire, air, water, and earth, so the single light of God illumines the Mind, Soul, Nature, and Matter. Anyone seeing the light in these four elements sees a beam of the sun, and through this beam is directed to the perception of the supreme light of the sun itself. In the same way, whoever sees and loves the beauty in these four, Mind, Soul, Nature, and Body, seeing the glow of God in these, through this kind of glow sees and loves God Himself.

Third Speech

THAT LOVE IS THE TEACHER AND RULER
OF THE ARTS

Chapter III

After this discussion it remains for us to show in what way Love is the teacher and master of all the arts. We shall easily understand that He is indeed the teacher of the arts if only we consider that no one can ever discover or invent a new art except as the pleasure of investigation and the desire of finding [the truth] motivate him; and except as he who teaches loves his students, and as those students most eagerly thirst after that learning.

Moreover, Love is justly called Ruler of the Arts, for a man fashions works of art carefully and completes them thoroughly, who esteems highly both the works themselves and the people for whom they are made. There is, then, this fact, that artists in each of the arts seek after and care for nothing but love.

Let us now briefly run through those arts which Eryximachus lists in Plato. With what else does Medicine deal than the way in which the four humors of the body become and remain mutual friends; and what foods and drinks and other necessities of life or what types of remedy nature loves and requires? Here also those two loves, the Heavenly and the Earthly, which Pausanias had distinguished above, Eryximachus comes upon through a kind of coincidence; for a temperate complexion of the body has a moderate love for moderate and agreeable things, but an intemperate complexion has an opposite love for opposite things. The former, of course, ought to be indulged, but the latter ought never to be submitted to, but ought to be investigated in gymnastic exercise, to see which bodily habits it prefers and demands, which methods of exercising and which gestures; in agriculture, to see what kind of soil, seeds, and cultivation it demands, or what method of cultivation is preferred by certain trees.

It may likewise be observed in music, in which artists investigate what ratios love, to a greater or lesser degree, what other ratios; they find the least affection between the first and second steps in the scale and between the first and the seventh. They find a rather strong affinity between the first and third, fourth, fifth, or sixth, but the strongest between the first and eighth. By certain intervals and modes they make high and low voices, naturally different, blend together better. From this, smoothness and sweetness of harmony derive. They so resolve slower and faster tempos that they become the fastest friends and produce agreeable rhythms.

But there are said to be two types of melody in music: one serious and steady, the other soft and sensuous. The former is beneficial to those who hear it; the latter, Plato says, (in the *Republic* and the *Laws*) is harmful. In the *Symposium* he assigns to the former the name Urania, and to the latter, Polymnia. Some prefer the first type and others the second. The love of the former people ought to be indulged, and the sounds which they long for should be invited; but the desire of the latter should be resisted, for the passion of the former is heavenly love, and that of the latter, earthly love.

There is a kind of friendship among the stars and four elements which is the subject matter of astronomy. Here, too, these two loves are found, for there is a moderate love among them in which they blend their forces together most temperately; and there is also an immoderate love in which each of them loves itself too much and leaves the others, so to speak. From the moderate love derive a pleasant temperature in the air, tranquillity of the sea, fertility of the earth, and health of animals; from the immoderate, the opposite conditions.

Finally, the power of seers and prophets seems to consist principally in this, that they tell us what services of man are agreeable to God, how men become friends of God, and what kind of love and reverence is to be shown toward God, one's own country, and one's own parents, and to others both living and dead.

It is possible to infer the same thing in the rest of the arts and to conclude summarily that Love is in everything, and for everything, that He is the creator and preserver of everything and the teacher and master of all the arts.

The divine Orpheus justly called Him, "inventive of mind, double-natured, holding the keys to everything." You have already heard how Love is "double-natured" from both Pausanias and Eryximachus. Now we can well understand from what has been said why He is said by Orpheus "to hold the keys to the world." As we have shown, this desire for the spread of its own perfection which is innate in everything, explains the innate and latent fecundity of everything. This desire compels seeds to sprout out into shoots; it draws out from the heart of each thing the powers of that thing, and conceives offspring; and opening the thing as though with a kind of key, it leads the offspring forth into the light.

Wherefore, all the parts of the world, because they are the works of one artist, the parts of one creation, like each other in life and essence, are bound to each other by a certain mutual affection so that it may justly be said that love is a perpetual knot and binder of the world, the immovable support of its parts and the firm foundation of the whole creation.

Fifth Speech

LOVE IS MOST BLESSED BECAUSE HE IS BOTH BEAUTIFUL AND GOOD

Chapter I

Carlo Marsuppini, our worthy disciple of the Muses, following the poet Landino, took up the speech of Agathon thus:

Our Agathon thinks that Love is a most blessed God because He is both most good and most beautiful. He carefully enumerates what is required for Love to be both most beautiful and most good. In the course of this enumeration, he describes Love Himself. After he has told what sort of God He is, he lists the benefits which He gives to mankind, and this is the sum of his speech.

It is our business to inquire first for what reason Agathon said, in order to prove Love blessed, that Love is beautiful as well as good, and what the difference is between goodness and beauty.

In the *Philebus*, Plato would have it that the blessed is that which lacks nothing, that is to say, that which is perfect in every detail. But there is both an interior and an exterior perfection: the interior we call goodness, and the exterior, beauty; and therefore, whatever is completely good and beautiful, since it is perfect, as it were, in every part, we call most blessed.

We notice this distinction in everything. For example, in precious stones, as the natural philosophers claim, a well-balanced combination of the four elements in the interior produces the sparkle of the exterior. Likewise, an innate fecundity in the heart and roots clothes plants and trees with the most pleasing variety of fruit and foliage; and in animals, a salutary complexion of humors provides an appearance pleasing both in shape and color. Virtue of the soul likewise manifests itself in a most noble kind of beauty in words, actions, and deeds. The heavens, too, are bathed in brilliant light by their own sublime essence.

In all these cases, it is an internal perfection which produces the external. The former we call goodness, the latter beauty. For just this reason, we say that beauty is the blossom, so to speak, of goodness. By the allurements of this blossom, as though by a kind of bait, the latent interior goodness attracts all who see it. But since the cognition of our minds has its origin in the senses, we would never know the goodness hidden away in the inner nature of things, nor desire it, unless we were led to it by its manifestations in exterior appearance. In this fact is apparent the wonderful usefulness of this beauty and of [love, which is] its associate.

In these examples, I think it has been sufficiently shown that there is as much difference between real goodness and its mere appearance as there is between a seed and its flower, and that as the blooms of trees grow from their seeds, and themselves produce seeds, so with this beauty which is the blossom of goodness: as it grows out of goodness, so it leads those who love it to the good. Indeed, our Hero has abundantly proved this in the preceding discussion.

HOW LOVE IS PICTURED, AND WITH WHAT PARTS OF THE SOUL BEAUTY IS RECOGNIZED AND LOVE IS CREATED

Chapter II

After this, Agathon lists in more detail the essential qualities in the beautiful appearance of this God. Love is young, he says, tender, agile, well-proportioned, and handsome. But we must first find out what these qualities contribute to beauty, and second, how they should be interpreted when they are applied to this God.

Men have faculties of both reason and sensation; reason through itself grasps the incorporeal principles of everything; sensation, through the five instruments of its body, grasps the shapes and qualities of the body; colors through the eyes, sounds through the ears, odors through the nostrils, tastes through the tongue, and through the nerves the simple qualities of the elements, such as heat, cold, and the rest.

Therefore, so far as we are concerned here, there are six powers of the soul pertaining to cognition: reason, sight, hearing, smell, taste, and touch. Reason is assigned to supreme divinity, sight to fire, hearing to the air, smell to vapors, taste to water, and touch to the earth.

Reason, indeed, pursues the heavenly and does not have its seat in any part of the body, just as divinity does not have a definite seat in any part of the world. Sight is located in the highest part of the body, just as fire is located in the highest part of the world, and by its very nature perceives light, which is the peculiar property of fire. Hearing likewise, following sight in the same way in which the pure air follows fire, drinks in sounds, which rise when the air is broken and glide through the interval in the air into the ears. The sense of smell is assigned altogether to the humid air, and to vapors composed of air and water. Because it is placed between the ears and the tongue, as though between air and water, it easily catches those vapors, and prizes especially those which result from the mixture of air and water; of this sort are the pleasant smelling odors of herbs, flowers and fruits. Who will hesitate to relate the sense of taste to the liquidity of water? This sense follows upon the sense of smell, as upon a denser air; and, imbued with the ever-flowing liquor of saliva, it takes great delight in drinking and in moist flavors. Likewise, who will hesitate to ascribe the sense of touch to the earth, since touch comes into being in all parts of the body, which is earthly, and is completed in the nerves, which are very earthly, and since it easily feels anything which has solidity and weight, which the earth gives to bodies.

Hence it also happens that touch, taste, and smell sense only what is very near them, and they are very much affected in the process of sensation, although the sense of smell does seem to detect things more remote than touch and taste.

Hearing, however, recognizes still more remote things and so it is not so limited. Sight perceives even farther than hearing and catches in a moment what the ear catches only with time, for lightning is seen long before the thunder is heard.

Reason catches the most remote things of all, for it perceives not only what is in the world and the present, as the senses do, but also what is above the heavens, in the past, and in the future.

From this it is apparent to anyone that of those six powers of the soul, three pertain to body and matter, that is, touch, taste, and smell; but the other three, that is, reason, sight, and hearing, pertain to the soul. Therefore the first three, inclining more to the body, are more closely related to it than to the soul; the things which they perceive, since they move the body (which is related to these senses), scarcely ever reach as far as the soul; and they please it least because they are the least like it. But the three higher senses, most remote from the material, are much more closely related to the soul, and they perceive those things which move the body very little, but the soul very much.

Certainly, odors, flavors, temperatures, and the like either harm or help the body a great deal, but they have little effect on the admiration or censure of the soul, and so are only moderately desired by it. On the other hand, the concept of incorporeal truth, colors, shapes and sounds, move the body either not at all or very little, and with difficulty, but they rouse the soul to avid pursuit, and attract the desire of the soul to themselves.

The food of the soul is Truth. To the discovery of it the eyes contribute greatly, and to the learning of it, the ears; therefore, what pertains to reason, sight, and hearing, the soul strives after for its own sake, like its own food. But things which move the other three senses are necessary rather to the body for nutrition, or comfort, or generation, than to the soul, and so the soul desires these things, not for itself, but for another, that is, its body, and we are said to love only those things which we desire for ourselves, and not to love those which we desire for the sake of something else.

Therefore we say correctly that love pertains only to knowledge, shapes, and sounds, and hence that that is beauty only which is found in these three: virtue of the soul, shape, and sound; because that beauty greatly arouses the soul, is called κάλλος, 'arousing,' from the Greek word καλέω, which means *to call*: κάλλος in Greek is equivalent to *pulchritudo* in Latin.

For we derive pleasure from the noble disposition of the soul, the comely appearance of a beautiful body, and the harmony of sounds, and since the soul considers these three (inasmuch as they are related to it and in a measure incorporeal) of more value than the other three, it is fitting that it should accept them more readily, embrace them more ardently, and admire them more eagerly. This pleasing quality, whether of virtue, shape, or sound, which summons and attracts the soul to itself through reason, sight, or hearing, is most rightly called Beauty. These are the three graces about which Orpheus speaks thus: "Splendor, Youth, and Abundant Happiness."

He calls "splendor" that charm and beauty of the soul which consists of brightness of truth and virtue; "youth" he applies to charm of shape and color, for this shines especially in the greenness of youth; and finally, by "happiness," he means that pure, salutary, and perpetual delight which we feel in music.

BEAUTY IS SOMETHING INCORPOREAL

Chapter III

Since this is the case, then, beauty must necessarily be something which is common to virtue, appearance, and sound, for we would certainly not call any of those three beautiful in the same sense unless one definition of beauty were inherent in all three.

Hence it happens that the principle itself of beauty cannot be body, since, if beauty were corporeal, it would have nothing in common with the virtues of the soul, which are incorporeal; in fact, beauty is so far from being body that not only is such beauty as that in the virtues of the soul unable to be corporeal, but also that which is in bodies and sounds. For although we say that certain bodies are beautiful, nevertheless, they are not beautiful because of their matter itself, since one and the same body of a man may be whole and handsome today and tomorrow be deformed by some disfiguring misfortune, as though it were one thing to be a body, and quite another to be handsome. Nor are things beautiful from mere quantity, since both large and small things may seem beautiful. Often the large are ugly and the small attractive, and vice versa: the small ugly, and the great most handsome. It also happens sometimes that a similar beauty is in both great and small bodies. Now, if, in a quantity remaining uniformly the same, the beauty may be changed by some accident, and if the beauty may remain in some changed quantity, and may seem identical in great and small alike, then certainly these two, beauty and quantity, must be completely separate.

But if the beauty of every body consisted in thickness itself of the body, being in a certain sense corporeal, it would nevertheless still not please the onlooker insofar as it was corporeal. The beauty of some person pleases the soul not insofar as it exists in exterior matter, but insofar as its image is comprehended or grasped by the soul through sight. That image in the sight and in the soul, since these two are incorporeal, cannot itself be material, for how could the small pupil of the eye take in the whole heaven, for example, if the eye received the heaven in a corporeal way? Not at all, certainly. But the soul, in a single point, takes in the whole breadth of the body in a spiritual way and in an incorporeal image, and that beauty only pleases the soul which is taken in by it. Moreover, though the image may be a likeness of an external body, it is itself incorporeal in the soul.

Therefore, it is an incorporeal quality which pleases. What pleases is attractive to anyone, and what is attractive, is, in short, beautiful. And so it is brought about that love has reference to something incorporeal, and beauty itself is rather a spiritual image of a thing than its corporeal form.

But there are some who think that beauty consists in a disposition of parts, or, [to use their own language,] size and proportion together with a certain agreeableness of colors. We do not agree with their opinion because, since this kind of disposition of parts would exist in composite things only, there could be no such thing as a beautiful simplicity. But we call "beautiful" the pure colors, the sun and moon, one sound, the glow of gold, the gleam of silver, wisdom, and the soul, of all which are simple, and they certainly please us like beautiful things. Added to this is the fact that the whole proportion includes the composite parts of the body and does not lie in them individually, but in them as a whole, and so the single parts will not be beautiful in themselves. But from the individual particulars, the proportion of the composite whole arises, whence follows something absurd: that things which are not beautiful in their own natures produce beauty. But it also happens time and again that though the proportion and size of its parts remains the same, the body does not please as it did before. Certainly the shape of your body is the same today as it was last year, but the beauty is not the same; nothing grows old more slowly than shape and more quickly than beauty. From this it is clearly established that beauty and shape are not the same.

Then, too, we often see a more orderly disposition and size of parts in one person than in another, and yet the other person, we know not why, is nevertheless adjudged more beautiful, and loved more ardently. This fact seems to warn us sufficiently to consider beauty as something other than the disposition of parts.

Likewise, the same principle advises us not to think that beauty consists in agreeableness of color, for very often the color is more attractive in an old person, and the beauty greater in the young. It sometimes happens among those of equal age that one who surpasses another in color is yet surpassed by the other in charm and beauty.

Nor would anyone dare affirm that beauty is a kind of mixture of shape and colors, for, according to that standard, neither knowledge and sounds, which lack both shape and color, nor colors and lights, which have no definite shape, could be judged worthy of love.

Now, the desire of anyone is satisfied by the possession of that which he wants. For example, hunger and thirst are satisfied by food and drink. Love is satisfied by no sight or embrace of a body; therefore, it desires nothing bodily, but seeks beauty; whence it happens that beauty cannot be anything corporeal.

From these arguments it is concluded that if those who, aroused by love, thirst after beauty, wish to quench their burning thirst with a draught of this liquor, they must seek elsewhere than in the river of matter, or in the streams of quantity, shape, or colors for the sweet potion of this beauty [to quench their thirst by which their thirst is aroused.] Whither, then, will you poor lovers turn? Who was it who kindled the white-hot flames of your hearts? Who will quench so great a fire? That is the need, this the labor; I shall answer you soon, but listen.

BEAUTY IS THE SPLENDOR OF THE
DIVINE COUNTENANCE

Chapter IV

As soon as the Angelic Mind and the World-Soul were born from Him, the Divine Power over everything beneficently infused into them as His offspring that light in which lay the power of creating everything. In these two, because they were nearest, he depicted the pattern of the whole world much more exactly than it is in the material world. Whence this picture of the world which we see shines whole and more clearly in the Angelic Mind and in the World-Soul. For in these two are the Forms of each planet, the sun, the moon, the rest of the stars, the elements, stones, plants, and each of the animals. Representations of this sort the Platonists call Prototypes, or Ideas in the Angelic Mind, Concepts or mental images in the World-Soul, and Forms or physical images in the material world. They are bright in the material world, brighter in the soul, and brightest in the Angelic Mind. Therefore the single face of God shines successively in these three mirrors, placed according to their rank: the Angelic Mind, the World-Soul, and the Body of the World. In the first, because it is the nearest to God, the light is most bright; in the second, more remote, it is somewhat darker, and in the last, the farthest away, compared with the others, it is very dark.

Hence the holy Angelic Mind, because it is unimpeded by any attendance upon the body, reflects upon itself where it sees the face of God engraved within its own breast, and seeing there, is struck with awe, and clings most avidly to it forever. The charm of that divine countenance we call beauty; the passion of the Angelic Mind seeking inwardly the face of God, we call love. O, that it might touch us also: but our soul, born into a condition in which it is encased by an earthly body, is inclined to the function of generation. Weighed down by this preoccupation, it neglects the treasure-house concealed within itself, and so, involved in an earthly body, it is servant to the needs of the body for a very long time. To this labor it accommodates sense indeed continuously, and reason also more often than it should. Hence it happens that though it does not notice the glow of that divine countenance shining forever within it until the body has at length become mature and the soul purged, it may with reflection contemplate the countenance of God revealed to our eyes in the handiwork of God. Through just this kind of contemplation we advance to beholding Him who shines forth from within His handiwork. In this kind of reflection, then, it is finally raised to the recognition of God who shines within itself. But since the countenance of the parent is pleasing to the children, it necessarily follows that the countenance of God the Father is most pleasing to souls. The glory and glow of His countenance, to indulge in tiresome repetition, whether in the Angelic Mind, in the Soul, or in the material world, is to be called universal Beauty, and the desire for it is to be called universal Love.

We do not doubt that this beauty is everywhere incorporeal, for it is obviously incorporeal in the Angelic Mind and in the Soul. That it is also incorporeal in bodies we have both shown above and now most clearly understand from this: that the eye sees nothing but the light of the sun, for the shapes and colors of bodies are never seen unless illuminated with light, nor do they come to the eyes with their own matter itself. Yet it seems necessary for them to be in the eyes in order to be seen by them. Therefore, one light of the sun, painted with the colors and shapes of everything illuminated by it, presents itself to the eyes. The eyes, with the help of a certain light of their own, perceive the light thus affected; they see both the perceived light itself, and everything which is in it. Wherefore, this whole order of the visible world is presented [to view], not in the way in which it is infused in the matter of bodies, but in the way in which it is infused in the light streaming into the eyes. In this light, since it is separate from matter, that order is completely independent of body.

This is also evident from the fact that the light itself cannot be body, since it completely fills the whole world in a moment, from its rising to its setting. It penetrates the body of water and air everywhere, without opposition, and though spread over filthy things, it is nowhere soiled.

But these qualities do not in any way correspond with the nature of bodies, since body does not move in a moment, but in time, nor do two things penetrate each other without opposition from one, the other, or both, but two bodies mixed together stain each other with mutual contagion. We see this in the mixture of water and wine, and of fire and earth. Since, therefore, the light of the sun is incorporeal, whatever it assumes, it does so in the manner of its own nature; therefore, it assumes the colors and shapes of bodies in an incorporeal way, and in the same way it is itself seen, when taken in by the eyes. Hence it happens that this whole earthly beauty, which is the third face of God, presents itself incorporeally to the eyes, through the incorporeal light of the sun.

HOW HATE AND LOVE ARE BORN, OR THAT BEAUTY IS INCORPOREAL

Chapter V

From all these arguments it follows that the entire charm of the divine countenance, which is called universal beauty, is incorporeal, not only in the Angelic Mind and in the World-Soul, but also in the sight of the eyes. Nor do we love only this whole beauty all at once; but moved by our admiration, we love also its parts. There is born a particular love for a particular beauty, and so we are attracted to some man, a part of the world order, especially when in him a spark of the divine beauty clearly shines. Love of this kind springs from two causes: first, the image of the Father's countenance pleases us, and second, the appearance and shape of a well-proportioned man agrees most clearly with that concept of mankind which our soul catches and retains from the author of everything. Whence, if an image of the outer man, received through the senses and going across into the soul, disagrees with the Idea of man which the soul possesses, he immediately displeases us, and is disliked as being ugly. If the image agrees, he thereby pleases us and is loved, as being beautiful. Whence it happens that some men, meeting us, immediately please or displease us, and we do not know the cause of such feeling; and naturally so, since the soul, impeded by its attendance upon the body, by no means reflects upon those Ideas which are innate in it; but, by some natural, mysterious congruity or incongruity, it happens that the exterior form of a thing, striking with its own image the Idea of the same thing painted within the soul, agrees or disagrees with it, and moved by this mysterious agreement or disagreement, the soul either hates or loves the thing itself.

Clearly that divine ray [which we mentioned above] implants in the Angelic Mind and the World-Soul the true pattern of man to be created, but in the matter of the World, since matter is far removed from that divine artificer, the nature of man degenerates from that true Idea of man. But he becomes more like it according as the matter is better disposed, and more unlike in other matter.

As the closer imitation agrees with the Force in God, and the Idea in the Angelic Mind, so it corresponds and agrees with the Concept in the Soul. The soul approves this agreement; indeed, in this very agreement consists beauty, and in this approval consists the passion of love. But since Idea and Concept are foreign to material body, the nature of a man is judged "like," not on the basis of its matter or quantity, but rather on the basis of something incorporeal. As it is like, it agrees with those; as it agrees, it is beautiful; for that reason, body and beauty are different.

If anyone asks how the form of the body can be like the concept of the soul and the Idea of the mind, let him consider, I pray, the building of an architect. In the beginning, an architect conceives an idea of the building, like an Idea in the soul. Then he builds, as nearly as possible, the kind of house he has thought out. Who will deny that the house is a body, and that it is very much like the incorporeal idea of the builder in likeness to which it was made? Furthermore, it is to be judged like the idea more because of a certain incorporeal plan than because of its matter. Therefore, subtract its matter, if you can. You can indeed subtract it in thought, but leave the plan; nothing material or corporeal will remain to you. On the contrary, these two will be exactly the same internally, both the plan which comes forth from the builder [into the physical house], and the plan which remains [unmaterialized] in [the mind of] the builder. You may do the same with any human body. You will find that its form, agreeing with the concept in the soul, is simple, and is completely independent of matter.

HOW MANY THINGS ARE REQUIRED OF A
THING TO BE BEAUTIFUL AND THAT
BEAUTY IS A SPIRITUAL GIFT

Chapter VI

What, then, is the beauty of the body? Activity, vivacity, and a certain grace shining in the body because of the infusion of its own idea. This kind of glow does not descend into matter until the matter has been carefully prepared. The preparation of the living body consists in these three things: Arrangement, Proportion, and Adornment. Arrangement means the intervals of its parts, Proportion means their quantity, and Adornment means its shape and color.

In the first place, it is fitting that all the parts of the body should have a natural place: that the ears be in their proper place, the eyes in theirs, the nostrils in theirs, etc., and that the eyes should be at equal distances on either side of the nose, and likewise that both ears be equally distant from the eyes.

Nor is this balance pertaining to the plan of the intervals enough unless there is added a Proportion of parts, to give to each part, keeping the proper proportions of the whole body, its mean size, so that three noses placed end to end will equal the length of one face, and the semi-circles of both ears joined together will equal the circle of the open mouth; the joining of the eyebrows will also give the same result; the length of the nose will match the length of the lips, and so also will that of the ears; the two circles of the eyes will equal one opening of the mouth; eight heads will compass the height of the body: the same distance will also be measured by the spread of the arms, to the side, and likewise of the legs and feet.

Besides these, we consider Adornment necessary, so that the skillful drawing of lines, wrinkles, and the sparkle of the eyes may decorate that Arrangement and Proportion of the parts.

Now, though these three may be in matter, they cannot themselves be any part of the body. The arrangement of the parts is certainly not one of the parts, for the arrangement is found in all the parts, but no one part is found in all of them. There is added the fact that arrangement is nothing else than the appropriate spacing of parts. But what shall we say spacing is but the distance between the parts? Distance, finally, is either nothing, perfectly empty space, or the mere drawing lines, but who will say that lines, which lack breadth and depth, the qualities necessary to body, are bodies?

In the same way, Proportion is not quantity, but the limit of quantity; these limits are surfaces, lines, and points, which, since they lack mass and depth, are not considered bodies. Adornment also, we place in a pleasing harmony of lights and shades and lines, not in matter. From all this it is clear that beauty is so foreign to matter that it never imparts itself to matter unless the matter has been treated with the three incorporeal preparations which we have discussed.

But the basis of these is a temperate combination of the four elements, such that the body is most like heaven, whose substance is temperate, and does not interfere by any excess of humors, with the soul's work of incarnation. For thus the heavenly glow will easily light up in a body much like heaven, and that perfect Form of man which the soul possesses will turn out more accurately in the quiet and compliant matter.

Moreover, in exactly the same way, sounds are prepared to receive their beauty. The Arrangement of sounds is from the low to the octave, and thence descending again. Their Proportion is a progression restricted to thirds, fourths, fifths and sixths, tones and half-tones; their Adornment is the rich quality of a good tone.

By these three elements, as it were, then, the bodies constructed out of many parts, such as plants, animals, combinations of several sounds, etc., are prepared to receive beauty. But simpler bodies, like the four elements, stones, metals, and single voices are sufficiently well-adapted for the same purpose by a certain inner balance, a richness and clarity of their own natures. Moreover, the soul is the most effectively accommodated to this purpose by its own nature for this reason: that it is both spirit and a mirror, so to speak, next to God, in which, as we have said above, the image of the divine countenance is reflected. Therefore, just as nothing need be added to gold to make it appear beautiful, but if any earthly stains touch it, they must be removed, so the soul needs nothing added to it in order to be beautiful, but anxious care and solicitude for the body must be removed from it, and the disturbance of desire and fear must be dispelled from it; then immediately the natural beauty of the soul will shine out. But lest our speech digress further, let us conclude briefly from what we have said above, that beauty is a certain vital and spiritual charm first infused in the Angelic Mind by the illuminating light of God, thence in the souls of men, the shapes of bodies, and sounds; through reason, sight, and hearing, it moves our souls and delights them; in delighting them, it carries them away, and in so doing, inflames them with burning love.

WHICH GODS BESTOW WHICH ARTS
UPON MEN

Chapter XIII

Agathon thinks that the arts were given to humanity by the Gods because of love: the art of ruling by Jupiter; of archery, prophecy, and medicine by Apollo; bronze-work by Vulcan; the art of weaving by Minerva; and music by the Muses. Twelve gods are in charge of the twelve signs of the Zodiac: Pallas of Aries, Venus of Taurus, Apollo of Gemini, Mercury of Cancer, Jupiter of Leo, Ceres of Virgo, Vulcan of Libra, Mars of Scorpio, Diana of Sagittarius, Vesta of Capricornus, Juno of Aquarius, and Neptune of Pisces.

By these all the arts are handed down to mankind. The signs confer the powers for each of the arts upon the body, and the Gods who are in charge of them bestow them upon the soul: so Jupiter, through Leo, makes a man most fit for the governing of Men and Gods, that is, fit to manage well both divine affairs and human; Apollo, through Gemini, teaches prophecy, medicine, and archery; Pallas, through Aries, teaches the skill of weaving; Vulcan, through Libra, teaches bronze-working; and the others the rest of the arts. But because the gifts of Providence are showered upon us by His beneficence, we say they are given at the instigation of Love.

Moreover, we think that musical harmony is born in that swift and orderly revolution of the heavens: eight tones from the eight orbits, but out of them all a certain ninth harmony is produced. And so we name the nine sounds of the heavens, from their musical harmony, the Muses. Our soul was from the beginning endowed with the principle of this music, for the heavenly harmony is rightly said to be innate in anything whose origin is heavenly. This harmony is then imitated by various instruments and songs. This gift like the rest was given us through the love of the divine providence. Therefore, my noble friends, let us love this God because He is most beautiful; because He is most good, let us imitate Him; because He is most blessed, let us revere Him, so that by His bounty and mercy to us, He will grant us possession of His own Beauty, Goodness, and Bliss.

Sixth Speech

WHAT THE COMPARISON IS BETWEEN GOD, THE ANGELIC MIND, THE SOUL, AND THE BODY

Chapter XVI

Therefore, we ascend from the Body to the Soul, from this to the Angelic Mind, and from this to God. God is above eternity, the Angelic Mind is wholly in eternity. Clearly its operation, like its essence, remains stable. Stability, moreover, is the peculiar property of eternity.

The Soul is partly in eternity, and partly in time, for its substance always remains the same, untouched by any change of increase or decrease; but its operation, as we showed a little while ago, runs through intervals of time.

The Body is completely subject to time. For its substance is changed, and its every operation requires the passage of time.

Therefore the One Itself exists above rest or motion; the Angelic Mind is at rest; the Soul equally at rest and in motion; and the Body is placed in motion alone.

Again, the One alone remains above number, motion, and space. The Angelic Mind is in number, but above motion and space; the Soul is in number and motion, but above space; the Body is subject to number, motion, and space. The One Itself has neither number nor any composition of parts and is not changed in any way from what it is, nor is it restricted to any space. The Angelic Mind has indeed a number of parts or forms, but it is free from motion and space. The Soul has a multitude of parts and feelings and is altered by the process of reasoning and by a variety of emotional disturbances but is exempt from the limits of space. But the Body is subject to all these.

WHAT THE COMPARISON IS BETWEEN THE BEAUTIES OF GOD, OF THE ANGELIC MIND, OF THE SOUL, AND OF THE BODY

Chapter XVII

The same comparison which exists among these four exists among their respective beauties. Certainly, the beauty of the Body consists in the composition of its many parts; it is bound by space, and moves along in time. The beauty of the Soul suffers the changes of time, of course, and contains a multitude of parts, but is free from the limits of space. The beauty of the Angelic Mind, on the other hand, has number alone; it is immune to the other two [space and time]. But the beauty of God suffers none of these limitations.

You see the beauty of the Body. Do you wish to see also the beauty of the Soul? Subtract the weight of the matter itself from the bodily form and the limits of space; leave the rest; now you have the beauty of the Soul. Do you wish to see the beauty of the Angelic Mind? Take away now, please, not only the spacial limit of place, but also the sequence of time; keep the multiple composition, and you will find there the beauty of the Angelic Mind. Do you wish still to see the beauty of God? Take away, in addition to those above, that multiple composition of forms, leave the simple form, and there you will have found the beauty of God.

But what shall I have left after subtracting those qualities? Do you think beauty is anything else but light? Certainly the beauty of all bodies is that light of the sun which you see, adulterated with these three: multiplicity of form (for you see it imprinted with many shapes and colors), the spaciality of place, and change of time. Take away its place in matter so that it keeps the other two besides space; of this nature is the beauty of the soul. Take from it the change of time, if you please, and give it the rest; the light remains most bright without place or motion, but engraven in all the concepts of everything. That is the Angelic Mind, and its beauty. Finally, take away that number of different ideas; leave one simple and clear light, the image of that light, which remains in the very globe of the sun and is not dispersed through the air; now you comprehend in a measure the beauty of God, which certainly excels the rest of the beauties as much as the true light of the sun in itself, pure, single, and inviolate, surpasses the splendor of the sun, which is split up, divided, adulterated, and obscured through the cloudy air.

And so the source of all beauty and love is God, and the light of the sun in the water is as a shadow compared with its brighter light in the air. The glow in the air, likewise, is as a shadow compared with its glow in fire. The glow in fire is as a shadow compared with the light of the sun, glowing in the very sun itself.

There is the same comparison among those four beauties of Body, Soul, Angelic Mind, and God. God is never so deceived as to love the shadow of his own beauty in the Angelic Mind, and to neglect his own true beauty. Nor is the Angelic Mind so taken by the beauty of the Soul, which is the shadow of itself, that it should desert its own beauty, seduced by its shadow. But our soul (and this is greatly to be lamented, since it is the cause of all our woe), the soul, I say, alone, is so carried away by the charms of bodily beauty that it puts aside its own beauty and worships the beauty of the body, which is its shadow, completely forgetting its own beauty. Hence it is that we read in Orpheus of the cruel fate of Narcissus. Hence the fateful misfortune of man in general. A certain young man, Narcissus, that is, the soul of bold and inexperienced man, does not see his own countenance, he never notices his own substance and virtue, but pursues its reflection in the water, and tries to embrace it; that is, the soul admires the beauty in the weak body, an image in the flowing water, which is but the reflection of itself. It deserts its own beauty and never catches its shadow, since the soul neglects itself in worshipping the body, and is never satisfied by enjoyment of the body. For it does not really seek the body itself, but only its own beauty, [and is] seduced by bodily beauty, which is the image of its own beauty. In this way Narcissus desires, and since he pays no heed to that [true beauty] while he desires and pursues something else, he cannot satisfy his desire. Therefore he is destroyed, melted into tears; that is, the soul, so placed outside itself, and having fallen into the body, is racked by terrible disturbances, or infected by the diseases of the body, and dies, so to speak, since it already seems to be more body than soul. So that Socrates might avoid this death, Diotima led him from Body to Soul, from that to the Angelic Mind, and from that back to God.

HOW THE SOUL IS RAISED FROM BODILY
BEAUTY TO THE BEAUTY OF GOD
Chapter XVIII

Now, dear fellow-guests, imagine Diotima addressing Socrates thus. "No body is beautiful in all parts, O Socrates." For it is either beautiful in one part and ugly in another, or beautiful today and ugly tomorrow, or is judged beautiful by one person and ugly by another. Therefore the beauty of the body, polluted by the contagion of ugliness, cannot be pure, true, and prime beauty; of course, no one suspects beauty of being ugly anywhere, any more than he suspects wisdom of being foolish. But we one time think the appearance of a body is handsome and another time think it ugly, and various people may think differently about it at the same moment. Therefore the prime and true beauty is not in bodies. Consider also the fact that many bodies are called by the same name, Beauty. Therefore, there must be in many bodies one common nature of beauty through which they are alike called beautiful. But consider that this one nature, as it is in another, that is, matter, must also be dependent from another, for certainly what is not able to support itself is much less able to depend from itself. It will not depend from matter, will it? Never. For nothing ugly and imperfect is able to beautify and perfect itself. But that which is one ought to spring from one; therefore, the one beauty of many bodies depends from some one incorporeal maker. The one artificer of everything is God, who continually renders all worldly matter beautiful through the Angelic Mind and the Souls. Therefore, we ought to expect to find that true concept of beauty in God and in his assistants, rather than in an earthly body. To this, I think, you will easily ascend again, dear Socrates, by these steps. If nature had given you the eyes of a lynx, dear Socrates, so that you might penetrate with your sight to the inside of anything which came in your way, that outwardly most handsome body of your Alcibiades would seem most ugly. How much of him do you love, my friend? His surface appearance only; nay, rather his color wins you; nay, a certain reflection of lights, and a most insignificant shadow. Or else vain imagination deceives you; you love what you dream rather than what you see.

Now, lest I seem to oppose you in earnest, let us say that Alcibiades certainly is handsome. But in what part handsome? In all his parts except his pug-nose, and his eyebrows, which are higher than they ought to be. Nevertheless, these are beautiful in Phaedrus; but in him the thickness of his legs is not pleasing. These are charming in Charmides, unless perhaps his thin neck might displease you. So, if you observe men individually, you will praise none of them in every detail. Whatever is right anywhere you will gather together and you will make up a whole figure in your mind from the observation of all [the details], so that the absolute beauty of the human species, which is found here and there in many bodies, will be gathered together in your soul in the conception of one image. You value little the beauty of each man, dear Socrates, if you compare it with your Idea. You possess that (Idea), not thanks to the bodies, but thanks to your own soul. So love that image which your soul created and that soul itself, its creator, rather than that crippled and scattered exterior.

But what do I bid you love in the soul?—the beauty of the soul. The beauty of bodies is a visible light, the beauty of the soul is an invisible light; the light of the soul is truth. This alone is what your friend Plato seems to ask of God in his prayers. "Grant," he says, "O

God, that my soul may be beautiful and that those things which pertain to my body may not impair the beauty of my soul, and that I may think only the wise man rich." In this Plato declares that the beauty of the soul consists in truth and wisdom; and that this is given men by God. One and the same Truth given to us all by God, acquires the names of various virtues according to its various powers. According as it shows divine things, it is called Wisdom, which Plato asked of God above all else. According as it shows natural things, it is called Knowledge; as human things, Prudence; as it makes men equal, Justice; as it makes them unconquered, Courage; and as tranquil, Temperance.

Hence, two kinds of virtues are delineated: moral virtues, so to speak, and intellectual virtues, prior to them. The intellectual virtues are: Wisdom, Knowledge, and Prudence; the moral virtues: Justice, Courage, and Temperance. The moral virtues, because of their functions and public applications, are better known. The intellectual virtues, because of their recondite truth, are more esoteric. But he who is brought up with noble breeding, because he is purer than others, is easily raised to the intellectual virtues. Therefore I bid you consider the beauty of the soul, which consists in moral virtues, to be the first beauty, so that you may understand that there is one principle of all moral virtues, through which men are called alike, noble. That is, there is one truth of the pure life, which, through exercise of Justice, Courage, and Temperance, leads us to true happiness. Therefore, esteem as highest this one truth of moral virtue and the beautiful light of the soul. Know also that you will rise immediately above moral virtue to the clear truth of wisdom, knowledge, and prudence, if you will consider these to be conceded to the soul brought up in the best virtues, and that in them is the best rule of a moral life; but however varied are the doctrines of wisdom, knowledge, and prudence you see, nevertheless, remember that there is one single light of truth in them all, through which all alike are called beautiful. I charge you to love this supremely as the supreme beauty of the soul. But this one truth in the numerous doctrines, first of all, cannot be the supreme truth, since it is in another (being distributed in many doctrines). Whatever lies in another certainly depends upon another. But one truth is never born from a multitude of doctrines, for what is one ought to rise from one. Therefore there must be one wisdom above the soul of man, which is not divided among many diverse doctrines, but is one Wisdom from whose single truth the multiform truth of man springs.

O Socrates, remember that that single light of the single truth is the beauty of the Angelic Mind, which you must worship above the beauty of the soul. This, as we have shown in the foregoing discussion, excels the beauty of bodies, because it is neither limited to space nor divided according to the parts of matter, nor is it corrupted. It excels the beauty of the soul because it is fundamentally eternal and is not disturbed by the passage of time, but since the light of the Angelic Mind shines in the series of innumerable ideas, and it is fitting that there be a unity above all the multitude of everything, a unity which is the origin of all number, this light necessarily flows from one single principle of everything, which we call the One Itself.

So the simple light of the One Itself in everything is infinite beauty, because it is neither soiled by the stains of matter, like the beauty of the body, nor, like the form of the soul, is it changed by the passage of time, nor, like the beauty of the Angelic Mind, is it spent in vast number; and every quality separate from extraneous additions is called infinite by the natural philosophers. If there is heat in itself, not limited by cold and moisture and not weighted down with the weight of matter, the heat is called infinite, because its force is free and is not limited by any additional restrictions. Similarly, the light from every body is free and infinite, for it shines without measure or limit, because it shines of its own nature and is limited very little by the body. So the light and beauty of God, which is pure, freed from all other things, is called, without the slightest question, infinite beauty. But infinite beauty demands a vast love also. Wherefore, I ask you, Socrates, to esteem other things with a definite limit and restriction; but you must worship God truly with infinite love, and let there be no limit to divine love.

HOW GOD IS TO BE LOVED

Chapter XIX

This, [we have supposed,] is what Diotima said to Socrates. But, my virtuous friend, we shall not only love God without limit as Diotima is depicted as commanding, but God alone. For as the eyes are to the sun, so the mind is to God. But the eye seeks not only light before other things, but the light alone. If we love bodies, the Soul, or the Angelic Mind, we do not really love these, but God in them: the shadow of God in bodies, the likeness of God in the Soul, and the Image of God in the Angelic Mind. So in the present we shall love God in everything, so that in the future we may love everything in God, for so we set out from there as living beings to see God and everything in Him, and whoever in the present will devote himself with love completely to God, will finally recover himself in God. Certainly he will return to his own Idea through which he was created. There, if anything is lacking, it will be supplied again; he will cling forever to the Idea of himself. [I see that you realize that.] True man and the Idea of man are one and the same; therefore each of us separated from God on earth is not a true man since he is separated from the Form and Idea of himself. To this Idea divine love and piety will lead us, although we are here divided and mutilated. Joined then, by love, to our own Idea, we shall become whole men, so that we shall seem first to have worshipped God in things, in order later to worship things in God; and shall seem to worship things in God in order to recover ourselves above all, and seem, in loving God, to have loved ourselves.

Seventh Speech

HOW USEFUL IS DIVINE LOVE AND THE
FOUR KINDS OF DIVINE MADNESS

Chapter XIII

[Finally, then, this is the source of the kind of madness which springs from physical disease.] But by divine madness, man is raised above the nature of man and passes over into God. The divine madness is a kind of illumination of the rational soul, through which God draws the soul slipping down to the lower world back to the higher. The fall of the soul from the one very beginning itself of everything into bodies, is brought about through four stages, through Mind, Reason, Opinion, and Nature.

For in the whole order of things, there are six grades, of which the highest is the One Itself, and the lowest is body; in the middle are the four which we have mentioned. It is necessary for anything that falls from the first to the last to descend through the middle four. The One Itself is the limit and measure of everything, having no part in mixture and multiplicity. The Angelic Mind is a multitude, to be sure, of ideas, but [it is] stable and eternal. The Reason of the Soul is an unstable but orderly multitude of notions and arguments. Opinion, however, which is beneath reason, is an unstable and unordered multitude of images, but is a unity in one substance and in one point, since the Soul itself, in which opinion exists, is one substance occupying no space. It is the same with Nature, that is, the nutritive force from the soul, and the vital complexion except that it is diffused throughout the points of the body. Body, however, is an undetermined multitude of parts and circumstances subject to motion and divided into substance, points, and moments. All these our Soul looks back upon; through these it descended and through these it ascends. For, since it is produced from the One Itself, which is the source of everything, it has obtained a certain unity which unites its whole being and its powers and functions, from which and to which other parts of the soul are related, like the lines from the center and to the center of a circle. However, it unites not only the parts of the soul together and with the whole soul, but also the whole soul to the One Itself, the cause of everything.

Moreover, inasmuch as it is illumined by the light of the divine Mind, the same soul contemplates through the Mind the ideas of everything in stable actuality. As it looks back upon itself, it contemplates the universal concepts of things and by reasoning proceeds from beginnings to conclusions. As it looks back upon bodies, it considers by opinion the particular forms and images of movable things received through the senses. As it is related to matter, it uses nature as an instrument by which it unites, moves, and forms matter. Whence generations, increases, and their opposites arise. You see therefore that from the One which is above eternity, the soul falls into eternal multiplicity, from eternity into time, from time into space and matter. It falls, I say, since in embracing the body too much it goes a long way from that purity in which it was born.

BY WHAT STEPS THE DIVINE MADNESSES
RAISE THE SOUL

Chapter XIV

Wherefore, just as it descends through four steps, it must necessarily ascend through four, but that madness is divine which raises the soul to the heights as stated in its definition; therefore there are four kinds of divine madness. The first is the poetic madness, the second is that of the mysteries, the third is that of prophecy, and the fourth is that of love. Moreover, the poetry is from the Muses, the mystery from Dionysus, the prophecy from Apollo, and the love from Venus.

Certainly the Soul cannot return to the One unless it itself becomes one. But it was created multiple; because it has fallen into the body, it is distributed among many functions, and it looks back upon an infinite multiplicity of corporeal things. Hence its higher parts are almost asleep and its lower parts dominate the others. The former are affected by stupefaction, the latter by excitation. But the whole soul is filled with discord and dissonance; therefore the first need is for the poetic madness, which through musical tones arouses what is sleeping, through harmonic sweetness calms what is in turmoil, and finally, through the blending of different things, quells dissonant discord and tempers the various parts of the soul.

Nor is that enough, for multiplicity and diversity still remain in the soul. There is added therefore the mystery of Dionysus which, by expiation, sacrifices, and by every form of divine worship, directs the attention of all the parts to the Mind, by which God is worshipped. Whence, since the single parts of the soul have been reorganized into one Mind, the soul is now made a single whole out of many. But there is needed still a third madness to lead the mind back to the Unity Itself, the head of the soul. This Apollo brings about through prophecy, for when the soul rises above Mind into Unity, it sees into the future.

Finally, when the soul has been made one, one, I say, which is in itself the very nature and essence of soul, it remains that immediately it recovers itself into the One which is above essence, that is, God. This the heavenly Venus completes through Love, that is, through the desire for the divine beauty, and the passion for Good.

So the first kind of madness tempers dissonant and unharmonious parts. The second makes the tempered parts one out of many. The third makes it one above all parts; and the fourth into One which is above essence and above the whole.

In the *Phaedrus*, Plato calls the Mind directed to the divine, the charioteer in the soul of man. Oneness of soul is the head of the driver. Reason and Opinion, running through natural things, are his good steed. Confused Fancy and Sense Appetite are his bad horse. The nature of the whole soul is called the wheel itself, because its own motion like that of a wheel, beginning in itself, finally returns to itself when it perceives its own nature, that is, when its contemplation, having begun from the soul, returns to the same thing. Plato attributes wings to the soul, by which it may be borne to the sublime; of these we think one is the inquiry by which the mind strives assiduously for the Truth, and the other the desire for the Good by which our will is always influenced. These parts of the soul lose their order when they are confused by the disturbing body.

So the first kind of madness separates the good horse, that is, reason and opinion, from the bad horse, from confused fancy and sense desire. The second madness subjects the bad horse to the good, and the good horse to the driver, that is, to the Mind. The third madness directs the driver to his own head, that is, to the unity which is the head of his Mind. The last madness turns the head of the driver toward the head of all things; that is, when the driver is blest and is driving his horses, that is, accommodating all parts of the soul subject to him, toward the stable, that is, toward divine beauty, and presents them with ambrosia and, even more, nectar to drink, that is, shows them the vision of beauty, and from that vision, happiness. These are the functions of the four kinds of madness. About them there is a general discussion in the *Phaedrus*, but specifically about the poetic madness in the *Ion*, and on the amatory madness in the *Symposium*. The books of Orpheus are all testimony that he was seized by all four madnesses. We have already learned that Anacreon and Socrates and Sappho were all seized with the amatory madness particularly.

LOVE IS THE NOBLEST OF ALL THESE

Chapter XV

Of all these, the most powerful and most noble is the amatory madness. "Most powerful," I say, because all the others necessarily depend upon it. For we achieve neither the poetic, the religious, nor the prophetic madness without a great zeal, flaming piety, and sedulous worship of the divine. But zeal, piety, and worship, what else do we call them but love? Therefore all the madnesses depend upon the power of Love. It is also most noble, since to it as to an end, the others are referred; moreover, it is this which joins us most closely with God.

· · · · ·

Anthony Ashley Cooper, Third Earl of SHAFTESBURY

With the writings of Shaftesbury a new problem emerges as a crucial one for the philosophy of art, a problem generated by the impressive advances of the physical sciences and by the new philosophy of Descartes and Hobbes. In its simplest terms, the problem is how to reconcile science and religion; and in its relevance to the philosophy of art the problem is how aesthetic values can be defended against the attacks of relativism and mechanistic conceptions of the universe. Shaftesbury is not the first to consider the problem—he inherits and carries further defenses put up by the group known as the Cambridge Platonists—but his solutions, though unsystematic, are of the greatest influence on both the Continent and England. Both directly and indirectly he provides many of the ideas which bear fruit in the German philosophies of art of the eighteenth and early nineteenth centuries.

Shaftesbury's writings were gathered together during his life-

time and published in three volumes with the general title: Characteristics of Men, Manners, Opinions, Times. *The purpose of the essays was, in the words of a recent critic, the "reassertion of man's feeling for natural beauty and an attempt to free the human spirit from both the asceticism of the Puritans and the crippling influence of the mechanical philosophy"* (Brett, *page* 61). *Shaftesbury does this by presenting an organic, spiritualistic interpretation of nature. He rhapsodizes about nature, its artistic organization which implies a divine artist, and its spiritual qualities which make it beautiful to the human consciousness. In doing this he rejects mechanistic materialism and opens the way for beauty to be asserted as an independent value. Nature is beautiful in itself, and man—all men—can appreciate nature through a special sensitivity of aesthetic judgment.*

The creative power of nature is mirrored in the creative power of the poetic mind; the beauty of nature is recaptured in the beauty of artistic creation. Man then, in his artistic efforts, enlarges upon and realizes the values of nature. Nature and art are corresponding manifestations of divine harmony. But that harmony is seen also in the exercise of taste; judgments of beauty are creative too, and in asserting that nature or art is beautiful, the critic affirms that he shares a universal appreciation for and celebration of value in the cosmos.

God's creation of the cosmos is an exercise of a constant plastic power in which the divine mind molds natural materials. In like manner, the artist impresses ideas upon stuff, and hence Shaftesbury refers to the artist as "a just Prometheus under Jove." The process of divine and artistic production culminates in an organic form which requires interpretation. Art, like nature, is a composite of symbols wrought by the imagination to which Shaftesbury gives the name "emblematic" symbol, and which he distinguishes from conventional signs on the one hand and iconic signs (i.e., imitative signs) on the other.

Nature manifests not only beauty but also sublimity, and it is from Shaftesbury's interest in the sublime (deriving from Boileau) that the problem is articulated for Burke and Kant. The experience of the sublime provides the religious experience upon which man's positive conception of the infinite rests. For nature in its sublime aspects attests to the power and mystery of God as well as to His goodness. Since for Shaftesbury the sublime is essentially an aesthetic and not, as with Kant, a moral experience, God in His awful as well as harmonious aspects is known through nature as it is evaluated according to an aesthetic faculty.

If follows, therefore, that man's sense of his place in the universe is due to a judgment about the beautiful. And this judg-

ment follows upon an immediate apprehension that must be distinguished from the moral, the pleasurable, and the useful. In this insistence on the purity and disinterestedness of aesthetic judgments Shaftesbury showed Kant the way to a fundamental principle in all philosophies of art. Indeed, one reason to include Shaftesbury here is because of his extensive influence. But more important than that is the vision of a truly philosophic mind. Shaftesbury was too much a British writer devoted to the essay as an approach to the philosophical to produce a system. Yet the very charm of his writing is increased by his inquiring on the basis of facts without insisting upon consistent comprehensiveness. His strong conviction that only in observation of reality could the ultimate philosophy be found led him, as illustrated in the passage below from his unfinished Second Characters, to be at once remarkably "modern" and profoundly "classical" in his philosophic temperament. Indeed, he succeeded in finding that mean which the battle of ancients and moderns demanded.

(All footnotes have been retained so that readers may return to passages in the original text referred to but not included here.)

CHARACTERISTICS

Freedom of Wit and Humour

Part IV, Section III

And thus, after all, the most natural beauty in the world is honesty and moral truth. For all beauty is truth. True features make the beauty of a face; and true proportions the beauty of architecture; as true measures that of harmony and music. In poetry, which is all fable, truth still is the perfection. And whoever is scholar enough to read the ancient philosopher, or his modern copyists,[1] upon the nature of a dramatic and epic poem, will easily understand this account of truth.[2]

A painter, if he has any genius, understands the truth and unity of design; and knows he is even then unnatural when he follows Nature

---

[1] The French translator, no doubt, has justly hit our author's thought, by naming in his margin the excellent Bossu *Du poème épique*; who in that admirable comment and explanation of Aristotle, has perhaps not only shown himself the greatest of the French critics, but presented the world with a view of ancient literature and just writing beyond any other modern of whatever nation.

[2] *Misc.* iii. ch. ii. and v. ch. i.

too close, and strictly copies Life. For his art allows him not to bring all nature into his piece, but a part only. However, his piece, if it be beautiful, and carries truth, must be a whole, by itself, complete, independent, and withal as great and comprehensive as he can make it. So that particulars, on this occasion, must yield to the general design, and all things be subservient to that which is principal; in order to form a certain easiness of sight, a simple, clear, and united view,[3] which would be broken and disturbed by the expression of any thing peculiar or distinct.

---

[3] The τὸ εὐσύνοπτον, as the great Master of arts calls it in his *Poetics*, ch. xxiii. but particularly ch. vii., where he shows "that the τὸ καλόν, the beautiful, or the sublime, in these above-mentioned arts, is from the expression of greatness with order: that is to say, exhibiting the principal or main of what is designed, in the very largest proportions in which it is capable of being viewed. For when it is gigantic, 'tis in a manner out of sight, and can be no way comprehended in that simple and united view. As, on the contrary, when a piece is of the miniature kind; when it runs into the detail and nice delineation of every little particular; 'tis as it were invisible, for the same reason; because the summary beauty, the whole itself, cannot be comprehended in that one united view; which is broken and lost by the necessary attraction of the eye to every small and subordinate part. In a poetic system, the same regard must be had to the memory as in painting to the eye. The dramatic kind is confined within the convenient and proper time of a spectacle. The epic is left more at large. Each work, however, must aim at vastness, and be as great, and of as long duration as possible; but so as to be comprehended (as to the main of it) by one easy glance or retrospect of memory. And this the philosopher calls, accordingly, the τὸ εὐμνημόνευτον." I cannot better translate the passage than as I have done in these explanatory lines. For besides what relates to mere art, the philosophical sense of the original is so majestic, and the whole treatise so masterly, that when I find even the Latin interpreters come so short, I should be vain to attempt anything in our language. I would only add a small remark of my own, which may perhaps be noticed by the studiers of statuary and painting: that the greatest of the ancient as well as modern artists, were ever inclined to follow this rule of the philosopher; and when they erred in their designs, or draughts, it was on the side of greatness, by running into the unsizable and gigantic, rather than into the minute and delicate. Of this, Mich. Angelo, the great beginner and founder among the moderns, and Zeuxis the same among the ancients, may serve as instances. See Pliny, xxxv. 9, concerning Zeuxis, and the notes of Father Hardouin in his edition *in usum Delphini*, p. 200, on the words, *deprehenditur tamen Zeuxis*, etc. And again Pliny himself upon Euphranor, in the same book, ch. 11, p. 226, *docilis ac laboriosus ante omnes, et in quocumque genere excellens, ac sibi aequalis. Hic primus videtur expressisse dignitates heroum, et usurpasse symmetriam. Sed fuit universitate corporum exilior, capitibus articulisque grandior. Volumina quoque composuit de symmetria et coloribus,* etc. ["A good learner and painstaking, uniformly excellent in every branch. He is thought to have first done justice to the majesty of heroes and first mastered proportion, but his bodies were over-slender, his heads and limbs over-large. He wrote too on proportion and colouring." Pliny, *H. N.* xxxv. 128.] Vide infra, *Advice to an Author*, part iii. § 3, in the notes.

Now the variety of Nature is such, as to distinguish everything she forms, by a peculiar original character, which, if strictly observed, will make the subject appear unlike to anything extant in the world besides. But this effect the good poet and painter seek industriously to prevent. They hate minuteness, and are afraid of singularity; which would make their images, or characters, appear capricious and fantastical. The mere face-painter, indeed, has little in common with the poet; but, like the mere historian, copies what he sees, and minutely traces every feature and odd mark. 'Tis otherwise with the men of invention and design. 'Tis from the many objects of nature, and not from a particular one, that those geniuses form the idea of their work. Thus the best artists are said to have been indefatigable in studying the best statues: as esteeming them a better rule than the perfectest human bodies could afford. And thus some considerable wits[4] have recommended the best poems as preferable to the best of histories: and better teaching the truth of characters and nature of mankind.

Nor can this criticism be thought high-strained. Though few confine themselves to these rules, few are insensible of them. Whatever quarter we may give to our vicious poets, or other composers of irregular and short-lived works, we know very well that the standing pieces of good artists must be formed after a more uniform way. Every just work of theirs comes under those natural rules of proportion and truth. The creature of their brain must be like one of Nature's formation. It must have a body and parts proportionable; or the very vulgar will not fail to criticise the work when it has neither head nor tail. For so common sense (according to just philosophy) judges of those works which want the justness of a whole, and show their author, however curious and exact in particulars, to be in the main a very bungler—

> Infelix operis summa, quia ponere totum
> Nesciet.[5]

Such is poetical and such (if I may so call it) graphical or plastic truth. Narrative or historical truth must needs be highly estimable; especially when we consider how mankind, who are become so deeply interested in the subject, have suffered by the want of clearness in it.

---

4 Thus the great Master himself in his *Poetics* above cited, viii., διὸ καὶ φιλοσοφώτερον καὶ σπουδαιότερον ποίησις ἱστορίας ἐστιν· ἡ μὲν γὰρ ποίησις μᾶλλον τὰ καθόλου, ἡ δ᾽ ἱστορία τὰ καθ᾽ ἕκαστον λέγει. ["Poetry is both a more philosophic and a more real thing than history; for poetry tells rather the universal, history the particular."—Arist. *Poet.* xcvi.]

5 Hor. *De Arte Poet.* 34.

'Tis itself a part of moral truth. To be a judge in one, requires a judgment in the other. The morals, the character, and genius of an author must be thoroughly considered; and the historian or relator of things important to mankind must, whoever he be, approve himself many ways to us, both in respect of his judgment, candour, and disinterestedness, ere we are bound to take anything on his authority. And as for critical truth,[6] or the judgment and determination of what commentators, translators, paraphrasts, grammarians and others have, on this occasion, delivered to us; in the midst of such variety of style, such different readings, such interpolations and corruptions in the originals; such mistakes of copyists, transcribers, editors, and a hundred such accidents to which ancient books are subject; it becomes, upon the whole, a matter of nice speculation, considering withal that the reader, though an able linguist, must be supported by so many other helps from chronology, natural philosophy, geography, and other sciences.

And thus many previous truths are to be examined and understood in order to judge rightly of historical truth, and of the past actions and circumstances of mankind, as delivered to us by ancient authors of different nations, ages, times, and different in their characters and interests. Some moral and philosophical truths there are withal so evident in themselves, that 'twould be easier to imagine half mankind to have run mad, and joined precisely in one and the same species of folly, than to admit anything as truth which should be advanced against such natural knowledge, fundamental reason, and common sense.

The Moralists

Part III, Section II

Methinks, said he, Philocles (changing to a familiar voice), we had better leave these unsociable places whither our fancy has transported us, and return to ourselves here again in our more conversable woods and temperate climates. Here no fierce heats nor colds annoy us, no precipices nor cataracts amaze us. Nor need we here be afraid of our own voices whilst we hear the notes of such a cheerful choir, and find the echoes rather agreeable and inviting us to talk.

I confess, said I, those foreign nymphs (if there were any belonging to those miraculous woods) were much too awful beauties to please

---

[6] *Misc.* v. ch. iii.

me. I found our familiar home-nymphs a great deal more to my humour. Yet for all this, I cannot help being concerned for your breaking off just when we were got half the world over, and wanted only to take America in our way home. Indeed, as for Europe, I could excuse your making any great tour there, because of the little variety it would afford us. Besides that, it would be hard to see it in any view without meeting still that politic face of affairs which would too much disturb us in our philosophical flights. But for the western tract, I cannot imagine why you should neglect such noble subjects as are there, unless perhaps the gold and silver, to which I find you such a bitter enemy, frighted you from a mother-soil so full of it. If these countries had been as bare of those metals as old Sparta, we might have heard more perhaps of the Perus and Mexicos than of all Asia and Africa. We might have had creatures, plants, woods, mountains, rivers, beyond any of those we have passed. How sorry am I to lose the noble Amazon! How sorry——

Here, as I would have proceeded, I saw so significant a smile on Theocles's face that it stopped me, out of curiosity, to ask him his thought.

Nothing, said he; nothing but this very subject itself. Go on—I see you'll finish it for me. The spirit of this sort of prophecy has seized you. And Philocles, the cold indifferent Philocles, is become a pursuer of the same mysterious beauty.

'Tis true, said I, Theocles, I own it. Your genius, the genius of the place, and the Great Genius have at last prevailed. I shall no longer resist the passion growing in me for things of a natural kind, where neither art nor the conceit or caprice of man has spoiled their genuine order by breaking in upon that primitive state. Even the rude rocks, the mossy caverns, the irregular unwrought grottos and broken falls of waters, with all the horrid graces of the wilderness itself, as representing Nature more, will be the more engaging, and appear with a magnificence beyond the formal mockery of princely gardens. . . . But tell me, I entreat you, how comes it that, excepting a few philosophers of your sort, the only people who are enamoured in this way, and seek the woods, the rivers, or seashores, are your poor vulgar lovers?

Say not this, replied he, of lovers only. For is it not the same with poets, and all those other students in nature and the arts which copy after her? In short, is not this the real case of all who are lovers either of the Muses or the Graces?

However, said I, all those who are deep in this romantic way are looked upon, you know, as a people either plainly out of their wits, or overrun with melancholy and enthusiasm.[1] We always endeavour to recall them from these solitary places. And I must own that often when I have found my fancy run this way, I have checked myself, not knowing what it was possessed me, when I was passionately struck with objects of this kind.

No wonder, replied he, if we are at a loss when we pursue the shadow for the substance. For if we may trust to what our reasoning has taught us, whatever in Nature is beautiful or charming is only the faint shadow of that first beauty. So that every real love depending on the mind, and being only the contemplation of beauty either as it really is in itself or as it appears imperfectly in the objects which strike the sense, how can the rational mind rest here, or be satisfied with the absurd enjoyment which reaches the sense alone?

From this time forward then, said I, I shall no more have reason to fear those beauties which strike a sort of melancholy, like the places we have named, or like these solemn groves. No more shall I avoid the moving accents of soft music, or fly from the enchanting features of the fairest human face.

If you are already, replied he, such a proficient in this new love that you are sure never to admire the representative beauty except for the sake of the original, nor aim at other enjoyment than of the rational kind, you may then be confident. I am so, and presume accordingly to answer for myself. However, I should not be ill satisfied if you explained yourself a little better as to this mistake of mine you seem to fear. Would it be any help to tell you, "That the absurdity lay in seeking the enjoyment elsewhere than in the subject loved"? The matter, I must confess, is still mysterious. Imagine then, good Philocles, if being taken with the beauty of the ocean, which you see yonder at a distance, it should come into your head to seek how to command it, and, like some mighty admiral, ride master of the sea, would not the fancy be a little absurd?

Absurd enough, in conscience. The next thing I should do, 'tis likely, upon this frenzy, would be to hire some bark and go in nuptial ceremony, Venetian-like, to wed the gulf, which I might call perhaps as properly my own.

Let who will call it theirs, replied Theocles, you will own the enjoyment of this kind to be very different from that which should naturally follow from the contemplation of the ocean's beauty. The bridegroom-Doge, who in his stately Bucentaur floats on the bosom of his Thetis,

---

[1] See *Letter of Enthusiasm*, towards the end. See also above, *Inquiry*, bk. i. part iii. § 3; and *Misc.* ii. ch. 1.

has less possession than the poor shepherd, who from a hanging rock or point of some high promontory, stretched at his ease, forgets his feeding flocks, while he admires her beauty. But to come nearer home, and make the question still more familiar. Suppose (my Philocles) that, viewing such a tract of country as this delicious vale we see beneath us, you should, for the enjoyment of the prospect, require the property or possession of the land.

The covetous fancy, replied I, would be as absurd altogether as that other ambitious one.

O Philocles! said he, may I bring this yet a little nearer, and will you follow me once more? Suppose that, being charmed as you seem to be with the beauty of those trees under whose shade we rest, you should long for nothing so much as to taste some delicious fruit of theirs; and having obtained of Nature some certain relish by which these acorns or berries of the wood became as palatable as the figs or peaches of the garden, you should afterwards, as oft as you revisited these groves, seek hence the enjoyment of them by satiating yourself in these new delights.

The fancy of this kind, replied I, would be sordidly luxurious, and as absurd, in my opinion, as either of the former.

Can you not then, on this occasion, said he, call to mind some other forms of a fair kind among us, where the admiration of beauty is apt to lead to as irregular a consequence?

I feared, said I, indeed, where this would end, and was apprehensive you would force me at last to think of certain powerful forms in human kind which draw after them a set of eager desires, wishes, and hopes; no way suitable, I must confess, to your rational and refined contemplation of beauty. The proportions of this living architecture, as wonderful as they are, inspire nothing of a studious or contemplative kind. The more they are viewed, the further they are from satisfying by mere view. Let that which satisfies be ever so disproportionable an effect, or ever so foreign to its cause, censure it as you please; you must allow, however, that it is natural. So that you, Theocles, for aught I see, are become the accuser of Nature by condemning a natural enjoyment.

Far be it from us both, said he, to condemn a joy which is from Nature. But when we spoke of the enjoyment of these woods and prospects, we understood by it a far different kind from that of the inferior creatures, who, rifling in these places, find here their choicest food. Yet we too live by tasteful food, and feel those other joys of sense in common with them. But 'twas not here (my Philocles) that we had agreed to place our good, nor consequently our enjoyment. We who were rational, and had minds, methought, should place it rather in those minds which were indeed abused, and cheated of their real good, when drawn to seek absurdly the enjoyment of it in the objects of sense, and not in those objects they might properly call their own, in which kind, as I remember, we comprehended all which was truly fair, generous, or good.

So that beauty, said I, and good with you, Theocles, I perceive, are still [2] one and the same.

'Tis so, said he. And thus are we returned again to the subject of our yesterday's morning conversation. Whether I have made good my promise to you in showing[3] the true good, I know not. But so, doubtless, I should have done with good success had I been able in my poetic ecstasies, or by any other efforts, to have led you into some deep view of Nature and the sovereign genius. We then had proved the force of divine beauty, and formed in ourselves an object capable and worthy of real enjoyment.

O Theocles! said I, well do I remember now the terms in which you engaged me that morning when you bespoke my love of this mysterious beauty. You have indeed made good your part of the condition, and may now claim me for a proselyte. If there be any seeming extravagance in the case I must comfort myself the best I can, and consider that all sound love and admiration is enthusiasm:[4] "The transports of poets, the sublime of orators, the rapture of musicians, the high strains of the virtuosi—all mere enthusiasm! Even learning itself, the love of arts and curiosities, the spirit of travellers and adventurers, gallantry, war, heroism—all, all enthusiasm!" 'Tis enough; I am content to be this new enthusiast in a way unknown to me before.

And I, replied Theocles, am content you should call this love of ours enthusiasm, allowing it the privilege of its fellow-passions. For is there a fair and plausible enthusiasm, a reasonable ecstasy and transport allowed to other subjects, such as architecture, painting, music; and shall it be exploded here? Are there senses by which all those other graces and perfections are perceived, and none by which this higher perfection and grace is comprehended? Is it so preposterous to bring that enthusiasm hither, and transfer it from those secondary and scanty objects to this original and comprehensive one? Observe how the case stands in all those other subjects of art or science. What diffi-

---

[2] *Moralists*, part ii. § 1.
[3] 1*b*.
[4] *Letter of Enthusiasm*, towards the end.

culty to be in any degree knowing! How long ere a true taste is gained! How many things shocking, how many offensive at first, which afterwards are known and acknowledged the highest beauties! For 'tis not instantly we acquire the sense by which these beauties are discoverable. Labour and pains are required, and time to cultivate a natural genius ever so apt or forward. But who is there once thinks of cultivating this soil, or of improving any sense or faculty which Nature may have given of this kind? And is it a wonder we should be dull then, as we are, confounded and at a loss in these affairs, blind as to this higher scene, these nobler representations? Which way should we come to understand better? which way be knowing in these beauties? Is study, science, or learning necessary to understand all beauties else? And for the sovereign beauty, is there no skill or science required? In painting there are shades and masterly strokes which the vulgar understand not, but find fault with; in architecture there is the rustic; in music the chromatic kind, and skilful mixture of dissonancies: and is there nothing which answers to this in the whole?

I must confess, said I, I have hitherto been one of those vulgar who could never relish the shades, the rustic, or the dissonancies you talk of. I have never dreamt of such masterpieces in Nature. 'Twas my way to censure freely on the first view. But I perceive I am now obliged to go far in the pursuit of beauty, which lies very absconded and deep; and if so, I am well assured that my enjoyments hitherto have been very shallow. I have dwelt, it seems, all this while upon the surface, and enjoyed only a kind of slight superficial beauties, having never gone in search of beauty itself, but of what I fancied such. Like the rest of the unthinking world, I took for granted that what I liked was beautiful, and what I rejoiced in was my good. I never scrupled loving what I fancied, and aiming only at the enjoyment of what I loved; I never troubled myself with examining what the subjects were, nor ever hesitated about their choice.

Begin then, said he, and choose. See what the subjects are, and which you would prefer, which honour with your admiration, love, and esteem. For by these again you will be honoured in your turn. Such, Philocles, as is the worth of these companions, such will your worth be found. As there is emptiness or fulness here, so will there be in your enjoyment. See therefore where fulness is, and where emptiness. See in what subject resides the chief excellence, where beauty reigns, where 'tis entire, perfect, absolute; where broken, imperfect, short. View these terrestrial beauties and whatever has the appearance of excellence and is able to attract. See that which either really is, or stands as in the room of fair, beautiful, and good. "A mass of metal, a tract of land, a number of slaves, a pile of stones, a human body of certain lineaments and proportions." Is this the highest of the kind? Is beauty founded then in body only, and not in action, life, or operation? . . .

Hold! hold! said I, good Theocles, you take this in too high a key above my reach. If you would have me accompany you, pray lower this strain a little, and talk in a more familiar way.

Thus then, said he (smiling), whatever passion you may have for other beauties, I know, good Philocles, you are no such admirer of wealth in any kind as to allow much beauty to it, especially in a rude heap or mass. But in medals, coins, embossed work, statues, and well-fabricated pieces, of whatever sort, you can discover beauty and admire the kind. True, said I, but not for the metal's sake. 'Tis not then the metal or matter which is beautiful with you? No. But the art? Certainly. The art then is the beauty? Right. And the art is that which beautifies? The same. So that the beautifying, not the beautified, is the really beautiful? It seems so. For that which is beautified, is beautiful only by the accession of something beautifying, and by the recess or withdrawing of the same, it ceases to be beautiful? Be it. In respect of bodies therefore, beauty comes and goes? So we see. Nor is the body itself any cause either of its coming or staying? None. So that there is no principle of beauty in body? None at all. For body can no way be the cause of beauty to itself? No way. Nor govern nor regulate itself? Nor yet this. Nor mean nor intend itself? Nor this neither. Must not that, therefore, which means and intends for it, regulates and orders it, be the principle of beauty to it? Of necessity. And what must that be? Mind, I suppose, for what can it be else?

Here then, said he, is all I would have explained to you before. "That the beautiful, the fair, the comely, were never in the matter, but in the art and design; never in body itself, but in the form or forming power." Does not the beautiful form confess this, and speak the beauty of the design whenever it strikes you? What is it but the design which strikes? What is it you admire but mind, or the effect of mind? 'Tis mind alone which forms. All which is void of mind is horrid, and matter formless is deformity itself.

Of all forms then, said I, those (according to your scheme) are the most amiable, and in the first order of beauty, which have a power of making other forms themselves. From whence methinks they may be styled the forming forms. So far I can easily concur with you, and gladly give the advantage to the human form, above those other beauties of man's formation. The palaces, equipages and estates shall never in my account be brought in competition with the original living forms of flesh and blood. And for the other, the dead forms of Nature, the metals and stones, however precious and dazzling, I am resolved to resist their splendour, and make abject things of them, even in their highest pride, when they pretend to set off human beauty, and are officiously brought in aid of the fair.

Do you not see then, replied Theocles, that you have established three degrees or orders of beauty? As how? Why first, the dead forms, as you properly have called them, which bear a fashion, and are formed, whether by man or Nature, but have no forming power, no action, or intelligence. Right. Next, and as the second kind, the forms which form, that is, which have intelligence, action, and operation. Right still. Here therefore is double beauty. For here is both the form (the effect of mind) and mind itself. The first kind low and despicable in respect of this other, from whence the dead form receives its lustre and force of beauty. For what is a mere body, though a human one, and ever so exactly fashioned, if inward form be wanting, and the mind be monstrous or imperfect, as in an idiot or savage? This too I can apprehend, said I, but where is the third order?

Have patience, replied he, and see first whether you have discovered the whole force of this second beauty. How else should you understand the force of love, or have the power of enjoyment? Tell me, I beseech you, when first you named these the forming forms, did you think of no other productions of theirs besides the dead kinds, such as the palaces, the coins, the brazen or the marble figures of men? Or did you think of something nearer life?

I could easily, said I, have added, that these forms of ours had a virtue of producing other living forms like themselves. But this virtue of theirs, I thought, was from another form above them, and could not properly be called their virtue or art, if in reality there was a superior art or something artist-like, which guided their hand, and made tools of them in this specious work.

Happily thought, said he; you have prevented a censure which I hardly imagined you could escape. And here you have unawares discovered that third order of beauty, which forms not only such as we call mere forms but even the forms which form. For we ourselves are notable architects in matter, and can show lifeless bodies brought into form, and fashioned by our own hands, but that which fashions even minds themselves, contains in itself all the beauties fashioned by those minds, and is consequently the principle, source, and fountain of all beauty.

It seems so.

Therefore whatever beauty appears in our second order of forms, or whatever is derived or produced from thence, all this is eminently, principally, and originally in this last order of supreme and sovereign beauty.

True.

Thus architecture, music, and all which is of human invention, resolves itself into this last order.

Right, said I; and thus all the enthusiasms of other kinds resolve themselves into ours. The fashionable kinds borrow from us, and are nothing without us. We have undoubtedly the honour of being originals.

Now therefore say again, replied Theocles: whether are those fabrics of architecture, sculpture, and the rest of that sort the greatest beauties which man forms, or are there greater and better? None which I know, replied I. Think, think again, said he; and setting aside those productions which just now you excepted against, as masterpieces of another hand; think what there are which more immediately proceed from us, and may more truly be termed our issue. I am barren, said I, for this time; you must be plainer yet, in helping me to conceive. How can I help you? replied he. Would you have me be conscious for you, of that which is immediately your own, and is solely in and from yourself? You mean my sentiments, said I. Certainly, replied he, and together with your sentiments, your resolutions, principles, determinations, actions; whatsoever is handsome and noble in the kind; whatever flows from your good understanding, sense, knowledge, and will; whatever is engendered in your heart (good Philocles!) or derives itself from your parent-mind, which, unlike to other parents, is never spent or exhausted, but gains strength and vigour by producing. So you, my friend, have proved it, by many a work, not suffering that fertile part to remain idle and unactive. Hence those good parts, which from a natural genius you have raised by due improvement. And here, as I cannot but admire the pregnant genius and parent-beauty, so am I satisfied of the offspring, that it is and will be ever beautiful.

I took the compliment, and wished (I told him) the case were really as he imagined, that I might justly merit his esteem and love. My study therefore should be to grow beautiful, in his way of beauty, and from this time forward I would do all I could to propagate that lovely race of mental children, happily sprung from such a high enjoyment and from a union with what was fairest and best. But 'tis you, Theocles, continued I, must help my labouring mind, and be as it were the midwife to those conceptions; which else, I fear, will prove abortive.

You do well, replied he, to give me the midwife's part only; for the mind conceiving of itself, can only be, as you say, assisted in the birth. Its pregnancy is from its nature. Nor could it ever have been thus impregnated by any other mind than that which formed it at the beginning; and which, as we have already proved, is original to all mental as well as other beauty.

Do you maintain then, said I, that these mental children, the notions and principles of fair, just, and honest, with the rest of these ideas, are innate?

Anatomists, said he, tell us that the eggs, which are principles in body, are innate, being formed already in the foetus before the birth. But when it is, whether before, or at, or after the birth, or at what time after, that either these or other principles, organs of sensation, or sensations themselves, are first formed in us, is a matter, doubtless, of curious speculation, but of no great importance. The question is, whether the principles spoken of are from art or Nature? If from Nature purely, 'tis no matter for the time; nor would I contend with you though you should deny life itself to be innate, as imagining it followed rather than preceded the moment of birth. But this I am certain of, that life and the sensations which accompany life, come when they will, are from mere Nature, and nothing else. Therefore if you dislike the word innate, let us change it, if you will, for instinct, and call instinct that which Nature teaches, exclusive of art, culture, or discipline.

Content, said I.

Leaving then, replied he, those admirable speculations to the virtuosi, the anatomists, and school divines, we may safely aver, with all their consents, that the several organs, particularly those of generation, are formed by Nature. Whether is there also from Nature, think you, any instinct for the after use of them? or whether must learning and experience imprint this use? 'Tis imprinted, said I, enough in conscience. The impression or instinct is so strong in the case, that 'twould be absurdity not to think it natural, as well in our own species as in other creatures, amongst whom (as you have already taught me) not only the mere engendering of the young, but the various and almost infinite means and methods of providing for them, are all foreknown.

For thus much we may indeed discern in the preparatory labours and arts of these wild creatures, which demonstrate their anticipating fancies, pre-conceptions, or pre-sensations, if I may use a word you taught me yesterday.

I allow your expression, said Theocles, and will endeavour to show you that the same pre-conceptions, of a higher degree, have place in human kind. Do so, said I, I entreat you; for so far am I from finding in myself these pre-conceptions of fair and beautiful, in your sense, that methinks, till now of late, I have hardly known of anything like them in Nature. How then, said he, would you have known that outward fair and beautiful of human kind, if such an object (a fair fleshly one) in all its beauty had for the first time appeared to you, by yourself, this morning, in these groves? Or do you think perhaps you should have been unmoved, and have found no difference between this form and any other, if first you had not been instructed?

I have hardly any right, replied I, to plead this last opinion, after what I have owned just before.

Well then, said he, that I may appear to take no advantage against you, I quit the dazzling form which carries such a force of complicated beauties, and am contented to consider separately each of those simple beauties, which taken all together create this wonderful effect. For you will allow, without doubt, that in respect of bodies, whatever is commonly said of the unexpressible, the unintelligible, the I-know-not-what of beauty, there can lie no mystery here, but what plainly belongs either to figure, colour, motion or sound. Omitting therefore the three latter, and their dependent charms, let us view the charm in what is simplest of all, mere figure. Nor need we go so high as sculpture, architecture, or the designs of those who from this study of beauty have raised such delightful arts. 'Tis enough if we consider the simplest of figures, as either a round ball, a cube, or dye. Why is even an infant pleased with the first view of these proportions? Why is the sphere or globe, the cylinder and obelisk preferred; and the irregular figures, in respect of these, rejected and despised?

I am ready, replied I, to own there is in certain figures a natural beauty,[5] which the eye finds as soon as the object is presented to it.

Is there then, said he, a natural beauty of figures? and is there not as natural a one of actions? No sooner the eye opens upon figures, the ear to sounds, than straight the beautiful results and grace and har-

---

[5] *Inquiry*, bk. i. part ii. § 3.

mony are known and acknowledged. No sooner are actions viewed, no sooner the human affections and passions discerned (and they are most of them as soon discerned as felt) than straight an inward eye distinguishes, and sees the fair and shapely, the amiable and admirable, apart from the deformed, the foul, the odious, or the despicable. How is it possible therefore not to own "that as these distinctions have their foundation in Nature, the discernment itself is natural, and from Nature alone"?

If this, I told him, were as he represented it, there could never, I thought, be any disagreement among men concerning actions and behaviour, as which was base, which worthy; which handsome, and which deformed. But now we found perpetual variance among mankind, whose differences were chiefly founded on this disagreement in opinion; "The one affirming, the other denying that this, or that, was fit or decent."

Even by this, then, replied he, it appears there is fitness and decency in actions; since the fit and decent is in this controversy ever pre-supposed. And whilst men are at odds about the subjects, the thing itself is universally agreed. For neither is there agreement in judgments about other beauties. 'Tis controverted "which is the finest pile, the loveliest shape or face": but without controversy 'tis allowed "there is a beauty of each kind." This no one goes about to teach: nor is it learnt by any, but confessed by all. All own the standard, rule, and measure: but in applying it to things disorder arises, ignorance prevails, interest and passion breed disturbance. Nor can it otherwise happen in the affairs of life, whilst that which interests and engages men as good, is thought different from that which they admire and praise as honest. But with us, Philocles, 'tis better settled, since for our parts we have already decreed "that beauty and good are still the same."

I remember, said I, what you forced me to acknowledge more than once before. And now, good Theocles, that I am become so willing a disciple, I want not so much to be convinced, methinks, as to be confirmed and strengthened. And I hope this last work may prove your easiest task.

Not unless you help in it yourself, replied Theocles, for this is necessary as well as becoming. It had been indeed shameful for you to have yielded without making good resistance. To help oneself to be convinced is to prevent reason, and bespeak error and delusion. But upon fair conviction to give our heart up to the evident side, and reinforce the impression, this is to help reason heartily. And thus we may be said honestly to persuade ourselves. Show me then how I may best persuade myself.

Have courage, said he, Philocles (raising his voice), be not offended that I say, have courage! 'Tis cowardice alone betrays us. For whence can false shame be, except from cowardice? To be ashamed of what one is sure can never be shameful, must needs be from the want of resolution. We seek the right and wrong in things; we examine what is honourable, what shameful; and having at last determined, we dare not stand to our own judgment, and are ashamed to own there is really a shameful and an honourable. "Hear me" (says one who pretends to value Philocles, and be valued by him), "there can be no such thing as real valuableness or worth; nothing in itself estimable or amiable, odious or shameful. All is opinion. 'Tis opinion which makes beauty, and unmakes it. The graceful or ungraceful in things, the decorum and its contrary, the amiable and unamiable, vice, virtue, honour, shame, all this is founded in opinion only. Opinion is the law and measure. Nor has opinion any rule besides mere chance, which varies it, as custom varies; and makes now this, now that, to be thought worthy, according to the reign of fashion and the ascendant power of education." What shall we say to such a one? How represent to him his absurdity and extravagance? Will he desist the sooner? Or shall we ask, what shame, of one who acknowledges no shameful? Yet he derides, and cries, ridiculous! By what right? what title? For thus, if I were Philocles, would I defend myself: "Am I ridiculous? As how? What is ridiculous? Everything? or nothing?" Ridiculous indeed! But something, then, something there is ridiculous; and the notion, it seems, is right, "of a shameful and ridiculous in things."

How then shall we apply the notion? For this being wrong applied, cannot itself but be ridiculous. Or will he who cries shame refuse to acknowledge any in his turn? Does he not blush, nor seem discountenanced on any occasion? If he does, the case is very distinct from that of mere grief or fear. The disorder he feels is from a sense of what is shameful and odious in itself, not of what is hurtful or dangerous in its consequences. For the greatest danger in the world can never breed shame; nor can the opinion of all the world compel us to it, where our own opinion is not a party. We may be afraid of appearing impudent, and may therefore feign a modesty. But we can never really blush for anything beside what we think truly shameful, and what we should still blush for were we ever so secure as to our interest, and out of the reach of all inconvenience which could happen to us from the thing we were ashamed of.

Thus, continued he, should I be able by anticipation to defend myself, and looking narrowly into men's lives, and that which influenced them on all occasions, I should have testimony enough to make me say within myself, "Let who will be my adversary in this opinion, I shall find him some way or other prepossessed with that of which he would endeavour to dispossess me." Has he gratitude or resentment, pride or shame? Whichever way it be, he acknowledges a sense of just and unjust, worthy and mean. If he be grateful or expects gratitude, I ask "why? and on what account?" If he be angry, if he indulges revenge, I ask "how? and in what case? Revenged of what? of a stone, or madman?" Who is so mad? "But for what? For a chance hurt? an accident against thought or intention?" Who is so unjust? Therefore there is just and unjust; and belonging to it a natural presumption or anticipation on which the resentment or anger is founded. For what else should make the wickedest of mankind often prefer the interest of their revenge to all other interests, and even to life itself, except only a sense of wrong natural to all men, and a desire to prosecute that wrong at any rate? Not for their own sakes, since they sacrifice their very being to it, but out of hatred to the imagined wrong and from a certain love of justice, which even in unjust men is by this example shown to be beyond the love of life itself.

Thus as to pride, I ask, "why proud? why conceited? and of what? Does any one who has pride think meanly or indifferently of himself?" No; but honourably. And how this, if there be no real honour or dignity pre-supposed? For self-valuation supposes self-worth; and in a person conscious of real worth, is either no pride, or a just and noble one. In the same manner self-contempt supposes a self-meanness or defectiveness; and may be either a just modesty or unjust humility. But this is certain, that whoever is proud must be proud of something. And we know that men of thorough pride will be proud even in the meanest circumstances, and when there is no visible subject for them to be proud of. But they descry a merit in themselves which others cannot: and 'tis this merit they admire. No matter whether it be really in them, as they imagine, it is a worth still, an honour or merit which they admire, and would do, wherever they saw it, in any subject besides. For then it is, then only, that they are humbled, "when they see in a more eminent degree in others what they respect and admire so much in themselves." And thus as long as I find men either angry or revengeful, proud or ashamed, I am safe. For they conceive an honourable and dishonourable, a foul and fair, as well as I. No matter where they place it, or how they are mistaken in it, this hinders not my being satisfied "that the thing is, and is universally acknowledged; that it is of nature's impression, naturally conceived, and by no art or counter-nature to be eradicated or destroyed."

And now, what say you, Philocles (continued he), to this defence I have been making for you? 'Tis grounded, as you see, on the supposition of your being deeply engaged in this philosophical cause. But perhaps you have yet many difficulties to get over, ere you can so far take part with beauty as to make this to be your good.

I have no difficulty so great, said I, as not to be easily removed. My inclinations lead me strongly this way, for I am ready enough to yield there is no real good beside the enjoyment of beauty. And I am as ready, replied Theocles, to yield there is no real enjoyment of beauty beside what is good. Excellent! but upon reflection I fear I am little beholden to you for your concession. As how? Because should I offer to contend for any enjoyment of beauty out of your mental way, you would, I doubt, call such enjoyment of mine absurd, as you did once before. Undoubtedly I should. For what is it should enjoy or be capable of enjoyment, except mind? or shall we say, body enjoys? By the help of sense, perhaps, not otherwise. Is beauty, then, the object of sense? Say how? Which way? For otherwise the help of sense is nothing in the case; and if body be of itself incapable, and sense no help to it to apprehend or enjoy beauty, there remains only the mind which is capable either to apprehend or to enjoy.

True, said I, but show me, then, "Why beauty may not be the object of the sense?" Show me first, I entreat you, "Why, where, or in what you fancy it may be so?" Is it not beauty which first excites the sense, and feeds it afterwards in the passion we call love? Say in the same manner, "That it is beauty first excites the sense, and feeds it afterwards in the passion we call hunger." . . . You will not say it. The thought, I perceive, displeases you. As great as the pleasure is of good eating, you disdain to apply the notion of beauty to the good dishes which create it. You would hardly have applauded the preposterous fancy of some luxurious Romans of old, who could relish a fricassee the better for hearing it was composed of birds which wore a beautiful feather or had sung deliciously. Instead of being incited by such a historical account of meats, you would be apt, I believe, to have less appetite the more you searched their origin, and descended into the kitchen science, to learn the several forms and changes they had undergone ere they were served at this elegant voluptuous table. But though the kitchen forms be ever so disgraceful, you will allow that the materials of the kitchen, such, for instance, as the garden furnishes, are really fair and beautiful in their kind. Nor will you deny beauty to the wild field, or to these flowers which grow around us on this verdant couch. And yet, as lovely as are these forms of Nature, the shining grass or silvered moss, the flowery thyme, wild rose or honeysuckle; 'tis not their beauty allures the neighbouring herds, delights the browsing fawn or kid, and spreads the joy we see amidst the feeding flocks; 'tis not the form rejoices, but that which is beneath the form; 'tis savouriness attracts, hunger impels, and thirst better allayed by the clear brook than the thick puddle, makes the fair nymph to be preferred, whose form is otherwise slighted. For never can the form be of real force where it is uncontemplated, unjudged of, unexamined, and stands only as the accidental note or token of what appeases provoked sense, and satisfies the brutish part. Are you persuaded of this, good Philocles? or, rather than not give brutes the advantage of enjoyment, will you allow them also a mind and rational part?

Not so, I told him.

If brutes, therefore, said he, be incapable of knowing and enjoying beauty, as being brutes, and having sense only (the brutish part) for their own share, it follows "that neither can man by the same sense or brutish part conceive or enjoy beauty; but all the beauty and good he enjoys is in a nobler way, and by the help of what is noblest, his mind and reason." Here lies his dignity and highest interest, here his capacity toward good and happiness. His ability or incompetency, his power of enjoyment or his impotence, is founded in this alone. As this is sound, fair, noble, worthy, so are its subjects, acts and employments. For as the riotous mind, captive to sense, can never enter in competition, or contend for beauty with the virtuous mind of reason's culture; so neither can the objects which allure the former compare with those which attract and charm the latter. And when each gratifies itself in the enjoyment and possession of its object, how evidently fairer are the acts which join the latter pair, and give a soul the enjoyment of what is generous and good? This at least, Philocles, you will surely allow, that when you place a joy elsewhere than in the mind, the enjoyment itself will be no beautiful subject, nor of any graceful or agreeable appearance. But when you think how friendship is enjoyed, how honour, gratitude, candour, benignity, and all internal beauty; how all the social pleasures, society itself, and all which constitutes the worth and happiness of mankind; you will here surely allow beauty in the act, and think it worthy to be viewed and passed in review often by the glad mind, happily conscious of the generous part, and of its own advancement and growth in beauty.

Thus, Philocles (continued he, after a short pause), thus have I presumed to treat of beauty before so great a judge, and such a skilful admirer as yourself. For, taking rise from Nature's beauty, which transported me, I gladly ventured further in the chase, and have accompanied you in search of beauty, as it relates to us, and makes our highest good in its sincere and natural enjoyment. And if we have not idly spent our hours, nor ranged in vain through these deserted regions, it should appear from our strict search that there is nothing so divine as beauty, which belonging not to body, nor having any principle or existence except in mind and reason, is alone discovered and acquired by this diviner part, when it inspects itself, the only object worthy of itself. For whatever is void of mind, is void and darkness to the mind's eye. This languishes and grows dim whenever detained on foreign subjects, but thrives and attains its natural vigour when employed in contemplation of what is like itself. 'Tis thus the improving mind, slightly surveying other objects, and passing over bodies and the common forms (where only a shadow of beauty rests), ambitiously presses onward to its source, and views the original of form and order in that which is intelligent. And thus, O Philocles, may we improve and become artists in the kind; learning "to know ourselves, and what that is, which by improving, we may be sure to advance our worth and real self-interest." For neither is this knowledge acquired by contemplation of bodies, or the outward forms, the view of pageantries, the study of estates and honours; nor is he to be esteemed that self-improving artist who makes a fortune out of these, but he (he only) is the wise and able man, who with a slight regard to these things, applies himself to cultivate another soil, builds in a different matter from that of stone or marble; and having righter models in his eye, becomes in truth the architect of his own life and fortune, by laying within himself the lasting and sure foundations of order, peace, and concord. . . . But now 'tis time to think of returning home. The morning is far spent. Come! let us away and leave these uncommon subjects, till we retire again to these remote and unfrequented places.

At these words Theocles, mending his pace, and going down the hill, left me at a good distance, till he heard me calling earnestly after him. Having joined him once again, I begged he would stay a little longer, or if he were resolved so soon to leave both the woods and that philosophy which he confined to them, that he would let me, however, part with them more gradually, and leave the best impression on me he could against my next return. For as much convinced as I was, and as great a convert to his doctrine, my danger still, I owned to him, was very great, and I foresaw that when the charm of these places and his company was ceased, I should be apt to relapse and weakly yield to that too powerful charm, the world. Tell me, continued I, how is it possible to hold out against it and withstand the general opinion of mankind, who have so different a notion of that which we call good? Say truth now, Theocles, can anything be more odd or dissonant from the common voice of the world than what we have determined in this matter?

Whom shall we follow, then? replied he. Whose judgment or opinion shall we take concerning what is good, what contrary? If all or any part of mankind are consonant with themselves, and can agree in this, I am content to leave philosophy and follow them. If otherwise, why should we not adhere to what we have chosen? . . . Let us, then, in another view consider how this matter stands.

Miscellaneous Reflections

MISCELLANY III

Chapter 2

. . . Let us therefore proceed in this view, addressing ourselves to the grown youth of our polite world. Let the appeal be to these whose relish is retrievable, and whose taste may yet be formed in morals, as it seems to be already in exterior manners and behaviour.

That there is really a standard of this latter kind will immediately, and on the first view, be acknowledged. The contest is only, "which is right; which the unaffected carriage and just demeanour; and which the affected and false." Scarce is there any one who pretends not to know and to decide what is well-bred and handsome. There are few so affectedly clownish as absolutely to disown good breeding, and renounce the notion of a beauty in outward manners and deportment. With such as these, wherever they should be found, I must confess I could scarce be tempted to bestow the least pains or labour towards convincing them of a beauty in inward sentiments and principles.

Whoever has any impression of what we call gentility or politeness is already so acquainted with the decorum and grace of things that he will readily confess a pleasure and enjoyment in the very survey and contemplation of this kind. Now if in the way of polite pleasure the study and love of beauty be essential, the study and love of symmetry and order, on which beauty depends, must also be essential in the same respect.

'Tis impossible we can advance the least in any relish or taste of outward symmetry and order, without acknowledging that the proportionate and regular state is the truly prosperous and natural in every subject. The same features which make deformity create incommodiousness and disease. And the same shapes and proportions which make beauty afford advantage by adapting to activity and use. Even in the imitative or designing arts (to which our author so often refers) the truth or beauty of every figure or statue is measured from the perfection of Nature in her just adapting of every limb and proportion to the activity, strength, dexterity, life and vigour of the particular species or animal designed.

Thus beauty and truth are plainly joined with the notion of utility and convenience,[1] even in the apprehension of every ingenious artist, the architect,[2] the statuary, or the painter. 'Tis the same in the physician's way. Natural health is the just proportion, truth, and regular course of things in a constitution. 'Tis the inward beauty of the body. And when the harmony and just measures of the rising pulses, the circulating humours, and the moving airs or spirits, are disturbed or lost, deformity enters, and with it, calamity and ruin.

Should not this (one would imagine) be still the same case and hold equally as to the mind? Is there nothing there which tends to

---

[1] Treatise II. part iv. § 3.

[2] In Graecis operibus nemo sub mutulo denticulos constituit, etc. Quod ergo supra cantherios et templa in veritate debet esse collocatum, id in imaginibus, si infra constitutum fuerit, mendosam habebit operis rationem. Etiamque antiqui non probaverunt, neque instituerunt, etc. Ita quod non potest in veritate fieri, id non putaverunt in imaginibus factum, posse certam rationem habere. Omnia enim certa proprietate et a veris naturae deductis moribus traduxerunt in operum perfectiones: et ea probaverunt quorum explicationes in disputationibus rationem possunt habere veritatis. Itaque ex eis originibus symmetrias et proportiones uniuscujusque generis constitutas reliquerunt. ["In Greek buildings no one placed denticules under mutules. . . . What therefore ought in reality to be put above beams and small timbers will, if in imitations it be put below, be faulty in theory: and so the ancients did not approve of this or practise it. . . . Thus they thought that what cannot be done in reality cannot be correct if done in a copy thereof. For they transferred everything to their perfect works with exact accuracy and attention to the true laws of Nature, and approved only those points the explanation of which can, when discussed, show truthfulness. And so from this beginning they left us proportions and canons ready established in every kind."] Vitruvius, iv. 2, whose commentator Philander may be also read on this place. See above, Treatise III. part i., end; part iii. § 3; and below, *Misc.* v. ch. i.

disturbance and dissolution? Is there no natural tenour, tone, or order of the passions or affections? No beauty or deformity in this moral kind? Or allowing that there really is, must it not, of consequence, in the same manner imply health or sickliness, prosperity or disaster? Will it not be found in this respect, above all, "that what is beautiful is harmonious and proportionable;[3] what is harmonious and propor-

---

[3] This is the honestum, the pulchrum, τὸ καλόν, on which our author lays the stress of virtue, and the merits of this cause; as well in his other Treatises as in this of *Soliloquy* here commented. This beauty the Roman orator, in his rhetorical way, and in the majesty of style, could express no otherwise than as a mystery. "Honestum igitur id intelligimus, quod tale est, ut, detracta omni utilitate, sine ullis praemiis fructibusve, per seipsum possit jure laudari. Quod quale sit, non tam definitione qua sum usus intelligi potest (quanquam aliquantum potest) quam communi omnium judicio, et optimi cujusque studiis, atque factis; qui permulta ob eam unam causam faciunt, quia decet, quia rectum, quia honestum est; etsi nullum consecuturum emolumentum vident." ["By *right* therefore I understand what is such that, apart from expediency, without any reward or profit, it can properly be praised on its own account. What sort of thing, that is, may be understood, not so much from the definition I have given (though to some extent it may be so understood) as from the general agreement of all, and from the enthusiasm and acts of the best men; they do many a thing for this one reason, that it is becoming. is proper, is right, even though they see no gain likely to follow." —Cicero, *De Finibus*, ii. 45.] Our author. on the other side, having little of the orator, and less of the constraint of formality belonging to some graver characters, can be more familiar on this occasion; and accordingly descending without the least scruple into whatever style or humour, he refuses to make the least difficulty or mystery of this matter. He pretends, on this head, to claim the assent not only of orators, poets, and the higher virtuosi, but even of the beaux themselves, and such as go no farther than the dancing-master to seek for grace and beauty. He pretends, we see, to fetch this natural idea from as familiar amusements as dress, equipage, the tiring-room, or toy-shop. And thus in his proper manner of soliloquy or self-discourse, we may imagine him running on, beginning perhaps with some particular scheme or fancied scale of beauty, which, according to his philosophy, he strives to erect by distinguishing, sorting, and dividing into things animate, inanimate, and mixed, as thus:—

In the inanimate: beginning from those regular figures and symmetries with which children are delighted, and proceeding gradually to the proportions of architecture and the other arts. The same in respect of sounds and music. From beautiful stones, rocks, minerals, to vegetables, woods, aggregate parts of the world, seas, rivers, mountains, vales. The globe. Celestial bodies and their order. The higher architecture of Nature. Nature herself considered as inanimate and passive.

In the animate: from animals and their several kinds, tempers, sagacities, to men. And from single persons of men, their private characters, understandings, geniuses, dispositions, manners, to public societies, communities or commonwealths. From flocks, herds, and other natural assemblages or groups of living creatures, to human intelligencies and correspondencies, or whatever is higher in the kind. The correspondence, union and harmony of Nature herself, considered as animate and intelligent.

In the mixed: as in a single person (a body and a mind) the union and harmony of this kind, which constitutes the real person; and the friendship, love, or

tionable is true; and what is at once both beautiful and true is, of consequence, agreeable and good?"

Where then is this beauty or harmony to be found? How is this
symmetry to be discovered and applied? Is it any other art than that of
philosophy or the study of inward numbers and proportions which can
exhibit this in life? If no other, who then can possibly have a taste of
this kind, without being beholden to philosophy? Who can admire the
outward beauties and not recur instantly to the inward, which are the
most real and essential, the most naturally affecting, and of the highest pleasure, as well as profit and advantage?

---

whatever other affection is formed on such an object. A household, a city or
nation, with certain lands, buildings, and other appendices or local ornaments
which jointly form that agreeable idea of home, family, country.

"And what of this?" says an airy spark, no friend to meditation or deep thought.
"What means this catalogue or scale, as you are pleased to call it? Only, sir, to
satisfy myself that I am not alone or single in a certain fancy I have of a thing
called beauty; that I have almost the whole world for my companions; and that
each of us admirers and earnest pursuers of beauty (such as in a manner we all
are) if peradventure we take not a certain sagacity along with us, we must err
widely, range extravagantly, and run ever upon a false scent. We may (in the
sportsman's phrase) have many hares afoot, but shall stick to no real game, nor
be fortunate in any capture which may content us.

"See with what ardour and vehemence the young man, neglecting his proper
race and fellow-creatures, and forgetting what is decent, handsome, or becoming
in human affairs, pursues these species in those common objects of his affection,
a horse, a hound, a hawk! What doting on these beauties! What admiration of
the kind itself! And of the particular animal, what care, and in a manner idolatry
and consecration, when the beast beloved is (as often happens) even set apart
from use, and only kept to gaze on and feed the enamoured fancy with highest
delight! See in another youth, not so forgetful of human kind, but remembering it
still in a wrong way! a φιλόκαλος of another sort, a Chaerea. Quam elegans for-
marum spectator! See as to other beauties, where there is no possession, no enjoyment or reward, but barely seeing and admiring; as in the virtuoso-passion, the love
of painting and the designing arts of every kind so often observed. How fares it
with our princely genius, our grandee who assembles all these beauties, and within
the bounds of his sumptuous palace incloses all these graces of a thousand kinds?
What pains! study! science! Behold the disposition and order of these finer sorts
of apartments, gardens, villas! The kind of harmony to the eye from the various
shapes and colours agreeably mixed and ranged in lines, intercrossing without confusion, and fortunately coincident. A parterre, cypresses, groves, wildernesses. Statues here and there of virtue, fortitude, temperance. Heroes' busts, philosophers'
heads, with suitable mottoes and inscriptions. Solemn representations of things
deeply natural—caves, grottoes, rocks, urns and obelisks in retired places and disposed at proper distances and points of sight, with all those symmetries which
silently express a reigning order, peace, harmony, and beauty! . . . But what is
there answerable to this in the minds of the possessors? What possession or propriety is theirs? What constancy or security of enjoyment? What peace, what
harmony within?"

In so short a compass does that learning and knowledge lie on which manners and life depend. 'Tis we ourselves create and form our taste. If we resolve to have it just, 'tis in our power. We may esteem and resolve, approve and disapprove, as we would wish. For who would not rejoice to be always equal and consonant to himself, and have constantly that opinion of things which is natural and proportionable? But who dares search opinion to the bottom, or call in question his early and prepossessing taste? Who is so just to himself as to recall his fancy from the power of fashion and education to that of reason? Could we, however, be thus courageous, we should soon settle in ourselves such an opinion of good as would secure to us an invariable, agreeable, and just taste in life and manners.

Thus have I endeavoured to tread in my author's steps, and prepare the reader for the serious and downright philosophy which even in this[4] last commented treatise, our author keeps still as a mystery and dares not formally profess. His pretence has been to advise authors and polish styles, but his aim has been to correct manners and regulate lives. He has affected soliloquy, as pretending only to censure

---

Thus our monologist, or self-discoursing author, in his usual strain, when incited to the search of Beauty and the Decorum by vulgar admiration and the universal acknowledgment of the species in outward things, and in the meaner and subordinate subjects. By this inferior species, it seems, our strict inspector disdains to be allured; and refusing to be captivated by anything less than the superior, original, and genuine kind, he walks at leisure, without emotion, in deep philosophical reserve, through all these pompous scenes; passes unconcernedly by those court pageants, the illustrious and much envied potentates of the place; overlooks the rich, the great, and even the fair, feeling no other astonishment than what is accidentally raised in him by the view of these impostures and of this specious snare. For here he observes those gentlemen chiefly to be caught and fastest held who are the highest ridiculers of such reflections as his own, and who in the very height of this ridicule prove themselves the impotent contemners of a species which, whether they will or no, they ardently pursue, some in a face and certain regular lines or features, others in a palace and apartments, others in an equipage and dress. "O effeminacy, effeminacy! Who would imagine this could be the vice of such as appear no inconsiderable men? But person is a subject of flattery which reaches beyond the bloom of youth. The experienced senator and aged general can in our days dispense with a toilet and take his outward form into a very extraordinary adjustment and regulation. All embellishments are affected, besides the true. And thus, led by example, whilst we run in search of elegancy and neatness, pursuing beauty, and adding, as we imagine, more lustre and value to our own person, we grow, in our real character and true self, deformed and monstrous, servile and abject, stooping to the lowest terms of courtship, and sacrificing all internal proportion, all intrinsic and real beauty and worth for the sake of things which carry scarce a shadow of the kind." *Supra, Moralists,* part iii. § 2; *Wit and Humour,* part iv. § 2; *Advice,* part iii. § 3.

[4] Treatise iii. (*Advice to an Author*).

himself, but he has taken occasion to bring others into his company and make bold with personages and characters of no inferior rank. He has given scope enough to raillery and humour, and has intrenched very largely on the province of us miscellanarian writers. But the reader is[5] now about to see him in a new aspect, 'a formal and professed philosopher, a system-writer, a dogmatist and expounder." Habes confitentem reum.

So to his philosophy I commit him. Though, according as my genius at present disposition will permit, I intend still to accompany him at a distance, keep him in sight, and convoy him, the best I am able, through the dangerous seas he is about to pass.

SECOND CHARACTERS

TREATISE IV. PLASTICS OR THE ORIGINAL PROGRESS AND POWER OF DESIGNATORY ART

3. *Rise, Progress, Declension and Revival of Second Characters*[1]

Politeness in figures helped still to polish grace. So music. But Plato and other philosophers and sages look wistfully towards the Egyptian laws (as lovers of rarities for such the Athenians, such the Greeks in general, and so humoured even by a Xenophon) admiring mystery, hiding secrets from the vulgar. This, as being frighted by the popular spirit, felt so severely in the person of their master Socrates. Besides Plato's and Pythagoras' affectation of legislatourship and pulse beating towards that noble ambition, to which the first a sacrifice and the second often tempted, and in state affairs under Dion brought in considerable danger. Hence his emulation with Homer, envious and somewhat detracting way, too truly objected by Dionysius Halicarnassus.

---

[5] Treatise IV. (*The Inquiry*).
[1] Quere from Herodotus, Diodorus Siculus . . . : Marsham, etc., about the records of the Egyptians: how far back. Hierarcho-political reason, as below, p. 125 for retaining the first ancient and hieroglyphic forms and statues of the gods, etc.

True indeed that by this ungenerous and hierarchical polity the state of longer duration.[2] For of what duration Egypt? But then what a state! What barbarity! Superstition! And when enervated once: how perpetual a slavery, from Mede and Persian, to Marmaluke and Turk.

Insinuation from hence, as to the last and present grand hierarchy of Romish Church. Whether not better to have followed the Egyptian in this (as in many other things) and keep the orthodox forms horrid, savage, and consequently inspiring superstition, as in reality their first were from the Gothic times or last feces of the Empire and of Arts, when images, etc., were introduced.

And though Protestants take the contrary weapon (and very justly from the present period), yet for the larger and more extensive period of time. Quere. Whether this may not weaken and supplant, as it polishes and refines, *emollit mores*. Nothing more true in nature can be said. So chiefly a fine picture or statue frontispiece, a fine piece of music, effeminacy indeed, an evil consequent: but not necessarily so, if the magistrate provides, without totally banishing (as Lycurgus some sorts of music and most arts, because of his local and specific commonwealth), or prohibiting as Plato in the case of Homer.

Therefore as beauteous forms polish (taking politeness with its consequences), so ugly barbarise.[3] None impossible; or if practicable, still equally barbarous.

Moses (*non obstante* 2d commandment) raised a serpent, and after him the arch and *sanctus sanctorum*, their cherubs, etc., the brazen tree, its buds, etc.

Prohibition therefore such as Egyptian, Jewish, (or suppose Scythian or Persian), and absolute abhorrence of figure or temple, a savage and barbarising enthusiasm.

Apology and protestation against entering into the decision of the Egyptian and Chinese pretensions to antiquity (so far beyond Mo-

---

[2] Proof of this from the hierarchical policy and hope always to engage sovereign and bring over and reconcile even the conqueror partly by superstition (sin and pleasure), partly by policy as assistant to him. Hence easy betrayer of their national form, prince and people. Trust to spiritual weapons for their own preservation at least (come what will of nobles, prince or people), as when Attila was met and Alexander by the Jewish priests (see Arrianus). Hence the oracles (though a Grecian and much limited priesthood) after they had stood steady all along, yet when things desperate and almost all Greece conquered, (Athens not resisting but driven to sea), began to faint and preach submission. This Herodotus saw and honestly noted. Though for this and other freedoms, i.e. poetic liberty as complaining of the gods, lashed by honest Plutarch, himself a priest.

[3] *Infra*, p. 123.

ses') in their records,[4] though recite the authorities. But this assert: that neither Jew, Egyptian, nor Chinese polite.

This a judgment of politeness. If polite: show me a picture, a statue, coin, proportion, nature. But arabesque! Japan! Indian! Savage. Monstrous. Even in their portraiture, pleasure-pieces, wanton pieces. Also gods monstrous, frightful according to Egyptian[5] and Syrian models; or Turkish mosques, no architecture, or statuary, or figures: or as bad as none.

Frightful, horrid, cruel ideas entertained, advanced by such divine forms; soft, gentle, humane ideas, by truly human forms, and divinity represented after the best, sweetest, and perfectest idea of humanity to the vulgar. But without application to divinities, and simply viewed and contemplated in cities, groves, high-ways, places, gardens, forums, etc., *emollit mores.*

"Bad figures: bad minds." "Crooked designs: crooked fancies." "No designs: no thought." So Turks, etc. "No imitation: no poetry." No arts of this kind: no letters, or at least in a poor degree. So politeness always holds proportion with laws and liberty. So that where the one is with a tolerable progress in the first species (viz. 1st Characters), the other (viz. 2d Characters) will soon prevail. And where it ceases and tyranny (such as the Eastern monarchies, ancient and modern) prevails, art and 2d Characters accordingly sink. See Japan! Mogul! China! Turk and Tartar! Show me amongst their infinite delicacy of other work a single 2d Character, a *form*, even but a single figure, a perspective, a statue, coin, palace, architecture—that is not worse than Gothic. Show but so much as a vase! till in China taught by us and the Dutch.

4.   *Instinct, Natural Ideas, etc.*

Those philosophers (modern) the poorest and most shifting, for the sake of a system, hypothesis, who, surpassing all ancient conceits and extravagances of the kind, deny ideas, sense, perception, (i.e. life) to animals. But those yet poorer and more shifting, who impugn natural ideas and ridicule instinct and innate ideas, because perhaps abused, misapplied, carried too far by some modern preceding writers, or by Plato.

The same philosophers would confound the very notion of species,

---

[4] *Supra,* p. 103.
[5] *Infra,* p. 125.

specific ideas (sad virtuosos!)[6] But had not the creatrix or sovereign plastic nature set the boundaries, the caprice (i.e. wantonness and bestiality) of corrupt man would long since have gone beyond any of the worst painters, grotesque ῥυπαρογράφοι, etc. as well beyond any of the poets in composing new complicated forms of satires, etc., with which the breed would have run out and been lost. But now even in the inward, several species (within the genus) as in dogs and fowls, which breed with one another, a natural propensity for like joining with like; so that the breed when mixed and blended, in time and after several consequent generations displays and opens itself, and the orders return to their first natural secretions, purity and simplicity of form.[7]

An ingenious author and notable metaphysician[8] about twenty years ago took such an advantage from the affected fulsome and common use of instinct and innate ideas, that being extremely well received and heard on account of his excellent genius and capacity in other writings, these words grew so out of fashion that a man of sense durst hardly use them on the most proper and most obvious occasion. And it was safer for a gentleman who was a lover of sports to say seriously upon the subject of his chase, that his dog, jowler, or tomboy reasoned or meditated, than that he had *natural sagacity* or *instinct*. We were allowed, indeed, to say that the poor turner's pot had sense and feeling above the iron-jack which supplied his room, (for Cartesianism was not admitted in its strict sense). But it was dangerous to talk of breeds, either of dogs, or hogs, or horses, lest we should betray our ignorance in imagining according to the vulgar error, that passions, affections, intincts, inclinations, impressions, impulses, ideas, imaginations (ready for the object when prescribed, and even raising or calling up a feigned and false object when the season or ripeness came) should possibly be delivered down in descent and extract to particular species. Nay even the species themselves were called in question, and more than called in question, flatly denied.

As thus poor Horace and other poets, even in their epicurean and

---

[6] See McC.

[7] Memorandum. Room here for demonstration of the young swallow. First flight precipitated, viz. from a rock over the sea, or an eminence over a paved court, or place fatal to fall. Yet the equilibrium instantly found and the art known, not learnt. Strength only failing when supported by the old ones, not art wanting. To the birds' nest, as well or better, more exact the first than afterwards as in Charac-ks, vol. II, pp. 307, 411, 412, etc.

[8] The same as above.

least theological fits, were very credulous and superstitious and foolish, when they said for instance:

Est in juvencis . . . patrum virtus.[9]

[The merit of the sire survives in the offspring.]

The *rictus* and gapings of noxious creatures, bears, lions, wolves, crocodiles, dragons, even small serpents and insects (as vipers) imprinted, previous mould or sockets to speak by analogy (as no other way in cases of sensation, intelligence, perception, egoity, not confined to place or determined by it).

So on the other hand who can doubt the contraries, viz. beauteous faces (especially in the same kind) to be equally imprinted by innate characters, moulds, preparatory sockets for reception and recognition of such joyous forms, as in the passion between the sexes.

Who would charge human nature with this dullness and so readily clear and acquit the bestial? unless perhaps the senseless modern philosophy and fool hypothesis of insensibility be brought in play for cavil's sake.

What more certain than that the poorest ignoramus of our species, being kept from seeing anything but old males, and clothed bodies (as in monkish cloister, or barbarous hermitage) would in a clear light, when brought to see nudities, distinguish between the true and natural, and the unnatural deformed kind.

Thus the species of horses and other animals, the kind being once seen and nature helped (changes not seen in perfection, but far off), the idea of beauty and perfection is raised, and when reduced to this idea of instinct by the able artist, recognised presently by the good eye of every spectator.

If a female of our own species (to pass by the love of babies and that shrewd propensity) should after a great belly got she scarce knew how, not find herself inclined to pick straws, or make a nest: no wonder, because of the second string to the bow, reason, discourse, community, the reserve.[10] Nor is it a wonder any more, that coming to lose the same great belly, and the season at hand for suckling, etc., that she has not the *conatus* or effort, that she calls not for the babies newly left off, nor does what is answerable to the hen, bustling about, swelling her wings, stretching her legs, picking and scraping like a thing mad and in fury.

---

[9] Horace's *Carmina*, Lib. iv, Ode iv, l. 30.
[10] As in 'Moralists,' p. 307.

5. Taste, Relish, Eye, Judgment, Criticism

. . . Reasons why a gentleman's taste if practical and empirical [11] necessarily false:

First Reason. Becomes interested, makes himself a party, espouses a manner, style, mannerist in lowest degree and below the painter by trade and profession. Also judge and party in the cause unfair. So Nero's [12] voice and acting (remember Agrippinus, etc.) in the divine man, and so again the governour of the Grecian province and the people differing about the actor or advice.

Dilemma. Either has an idea or not. If an idea: a hand to come up to it or not. If a hand obedient and answering, then a painter *omnibus numeris*; if a hand inferiour unanswering, then being not obliged to pursue as a professor, or for maintenance, but wholly voluntary and for pleasure only, must lose his end, and hate his products. For if loves and pleasure come by degrees, through self love, conceit, or flattery; then here comes the corruption, here the taste inevitably miscarries, grows awry, warps, turns crooked, perverse. Carry this reasoning into music.

Second Reason. Extravagant fondness for *one* master, *one* particular hand, *one* piece (a hundred to one, if a good one). Besides that, no one master yet of the moderns after Raphael has deserved anything like this; and even as to Raphael see reasons . . .

So Nero's Greek statue. See Pliny.

Third Reason. That if our gentleman besides his superiour knowledge, learning, education and converse, has not withal a particular genius, idea, and hand superiour to the trading artists and of a degree distinguishable from the common road and style of painting: he must naturally by his study and practice be brought upon a level and familiarized with the set of painters of his time; and as he is subject to their flattery and emulous of their praise be brought into society and sympathy with this race, so as to be in a manner *one of them*, and of their club and fraternity; a circumstance which will prove as little advantageous to his fame and reputation as to his manners, his interest, family and estate. [13]

---

[11] Exception for gentlemen quite painters as Fabius Pictor.

[12] So also the good emperor Adrian, his great weakness and blemish; only cause and subject of tyranny in him.

[13] Mem^d. Exception for Fabius Pictor, etc., as above, p. 112, and the whole man as below, p. 176. Definition of a pedant and how formed in painting, etc., as in other science. Adrian Emperour, as above, p. 112.

The case being the same with this company as with that of players, musicians, songsters, minstrels, dancers, and the rest of those trades and their conspiring crew: all holding together.

Nothing even of natural beings worthy of wonder or admiration, but as they show nature's real and highest art, best hand, supreme touches, nature's magnificence, symmetry, proportions, highest orders, supreme order (beyond doric or ionic, beyond corinthian). For what are all these but imitations? Or as in united and conspiring forms, of actual unity and concurrence in one, means to an end, harmony agreement.

Ergo a tree or even a leaf, beautiful not as a green, not as regularly shaped; for then a mere turf or cut bush would equal and surpass an old oak, or cedar, or pine. But a rough bit of rock more beautiful in reality than a pearl or diamond. No bribe to make those relished by almost all, and lastingly relished. The other but for a moment, as a rarity, or as set off itself or helping to set off other forms in dress, equipage, etc., of the lowest human caprice and misconception of beauty. Thus grottos, caves, etc., the finest imitations of finest gardening. For this is *truth*; the rest *false*.

Thus even in nature, the rainbow a mere jewel, an accidental species, refraction, etc. No real *unit*: no being, form, design, end, concurrence. Ergo, a nothing, a non-entity in virtuosoship. A mere miracle or prodigy (without *moral* or *doctrine*); a nothing, a juggle. The passion of those who run after monsters in fairies and the θαυμᾶτοποιοί. Prestidigitators.

Therefore the same here as in life and true wisdom in order to avoid deceit and imposture.

The great business in this (as in our lives, or in the whole of life) is "to correct our taste." [14] For whither will not *taste*[15] lead us? ἀπέχειν, arrest, suspend, defer, delay, proceed gradually, wait, expect, improve . . . Else we are run away with. The man upon the runaway horse in Lucian's cynic (if so good a piece as that be Lucian's), "Whither away! Whither *this* pleases," viz. his horse, pointing to it. Therefore stop it in its full career, cross it, turn it; and sometimes when lazy even give it the spur; just as in horsemanship, as in breaking the colt.

Animum rege: qui nisi paret,
Imperat: hunc frenis, hunc tu compesce catena.[16]

---

[14] *Infra*, p. 144.
[15] τὸ δοκεῖν.
[16] Horat. *Epistola*, Lib. i, Ep. 2, ll. 62, 63.

["Check your temper, which if not ruled, will sternly rule. Hold it hard in with bit and rein."]

From hence it follows: "That pleasure (in order to reap true pleasure) not to be indulged." Ask, inquire of self. "What sort of pleasure have I? What would I have? Quaere, if the true? if *truth*? to what end? What do I contemplate? What inspect? What to understand, reap, learn?" [17]

Is it to see flesh painted as flesh?—No. This artificial, empirical, the artisan, and even least part of the artisan!—Is it drapery?—No. This of the same kind.—Is it fore-shortnings, academy postures, etc.? —No. This still empirical.—Is it fine forms in a vicious sense? This false and more so than ever the ryparographics. Since this deforms the beautiful nature; whereas the *cacatorio*, a boor, or soldier, under a hedge or on a dunghill, more nauseating.—Exciting appetite, a horrid reason. Who dares give this for a reason? If so: paint sauces and dishes for the table, smoking pastys, etc. A thought never as yet pursued (I think) any more than curtsying ladies, or bowing beaus, except in the French court. Pictures of the pretty princes and princesses, and court-airs as hung in toy shops.

Observe the difference of a right and liberal eye from a mechanic, false: the same in painting and figures, etc., as in real life and *persons*. "What *person*, what form, character, species of a man, do we see? Who was he whom we saw in such a company, in such an action, circumstance, reading, writing, talking, hearkening, musing, exercising?"

A tailor who is asked: he answers (according to his eye). "A gentleman in such a coloured stuff, of such a cut."

If it be a dancing master: he answers (according to his eye). "A gentleman with such a gait or tread, his leg turned so or so."

If it be a fop: he answers (according to his eye) still, and as uniting the two latter tastes. "A gentleman so or so dressed, coming into a room with such or such an air, etc., such coloured lips, such teeth."

But if a man of sense, with an eagle's eye: he answers from his memory and recollection (for so he gathers, collects, imprints, and such is his imagery, history, invention). "A gentleman of such a behaviour, speech, action, such an address, such manners, aspect, and seeming note or character of sense and understanding, temper, mind, soul, and inward complexion."

The artificial, witty, far-fetched, refined, hypercritical taste (what is apt to be commended as ingenuous and merely speculative) is the

----

[17] *Supra*, p. 92.

worst in the world, being half-way, and like half-thinkers (in Char-cks, III, 302). The same in fencing, riding, dancing. The *natural* best, till well and truly formed (see again Char-cks, I, 190, at the end), and the original first rude taste corrected by rule, and reduced to a yet more simple and natural measure. Otherwise an innocent child's eye (of good parts and not spoilt already by pictures of the common sort) always found the best, as I have found experimentally, in such a one not of the higher gentry but liberal, and out of the way of prints, and such costly playthings of imagery, etc. The same experienced as to likeness in portraiture.

Ergo. Better mere nature than half-way, illaborate, artful, merely critical judgment; as it were in wantonness, *gayeté de coeur*, with indifference, superciliousness, neglect, scoff, as may be seen even in the manners, and in the way itself of censuring by these false-censurers, pseudo critiques, answerable to the French *pretieuses*, etc.

Better be the mere *je ne sais quoi* of the French. Though this not in our language: nor I hope ever will. But for us (I hope) something better reserved.

Docti rationem artis intelligunt, indocti voluptatem.[18]
["The learned understand the art of composition, the unlearned enjoy pleasure from it."]

6. Discouragements in Art

Compare moderns with ancients. Consider the latter, their care and culture of bodies themselves by exercises, the Greek discipline. Wrestling, even of the wrestlers in state (remember Pericles in Plutarch). So a Scipio, when first Rome took the polite way. See the passage of Livy when the commissioners from the Senate were sent as inquisitors into his athletic and other Greek manners.

Consider after the bodies and forms themselves, the opportunity of viewing these forms of the finer sort (not porters or beggars) in nudity, and in easy, familiar, as well as strenuous exercising action. For as in a hot country, so in quotidian baths. In private families, wives, children. Whereas now none but painters (as Albani) used to such views, and these constrained and awkward as being lucrative only, necessitous, mercenary, and a reproach and shame in the passive parties.

Also distortions by dress, unnatural bandages, ligatures: as cravats, garterings, women's bodice and contraction of waist, pressure of hips, swellings and unnatural disfigurations of necks, breasts, paps. Borings

---

[18] Quintilian's *Institutiones Oratoriae*, Lib. IX, cap. 4, l. 116, cited by Junius in *de pictura veterum*, p. 38.

and lugging down of ears by jewels, (well that it is not nostrils as with the other barbarians), perukes, cravats.

Also props or stilts under the heel or hind part of the foot, relaxing the hinder tendon and muscles; and extending, stretching unnaturally those of the fore part and instep, setting us young a tiptoe. So women's figures of feet and legs wholly destroyed in China by small shoes, till they are unable to stand. Our case even among the lower sort very near the same; a degree or two only removed from the same barbarism.

Hence no modern figure (of the noble kind) now extant in the world, which can be seen standing naturally on the ground.

Idea therefore must be taken from nature and drawn; instinct and what is innate; or from the ancient trunks and broken remains.

What little help from Academy in this respect, viz. of nudity's, i.e. naked porters, or privately from diseased courtesans. Whereas those who know nature understand well what difference debauch soon makes in the youngest female, and how deflowering is soon deflowering in this sense also: the *flos* instantly vanishing.

Statuary[19] the mother art to painting. In the first place on account of religion and civil government (as these stood among the ancients), the families, heroes, patricians, patriots, etc. as well as *penates*. ("He deserves his statue in gold!" Modern expressions which show the nature of the thing.) And in the next place on account of the profound learning, muscles, anatomy, physique, symmetry, (a statue viewed all round), simplicity, purity.

Remember also what pity: Raphael forced to paint walls;[20] cartoons for tapestry; an underwork man for false work; altar pieces as the priests commanded; popes enjoined (witness the transfiguration-piece,[21] called the first picture of the world) saints with lights

---

[19] *Infra*, p. 127.
[20] *Infra*, p. 148.
[21] This transfiguration-piece of Raphael would have made an excellent marble or piece of relief-work (and such Raphael always carried in head: those of the ancients in default of pictures having been his great school and lesson). But as it is, in the illusive art 'tis so far from that sweet persuasiveness and illusion (sweet as it is in other respects) that it not only breaks all rule of perspective, but everything of general order, position or collocation. The mountain a mole-hill, at most a mountebank's stage. Those figures below which should be seen by the upper parts (supposing the point of sight to be above the flat of the mountain as it must be for the sake of the lying figures there) are not at all in the air. Every figure a point of light by itself may be cut out of the cloth, or stuck on any other cloth, anywhere as well as where they are. No *one* principal, no subjection, subordination,

about their heads: sometimes gold and silver! rare works in art! [22]

False[23] criticism another discouragement in art. Upstart affected critics: Why this? Why that? General topics which they think mighty ingenious as: lights whence? How here and yet there?—Answer: Flying clouds, a thunder storm covering one spot; sun shining the stronger and brighter on another. A reflection from the rocks unseen. Other objects out of the picture in the very place of the spectator, whence new various mixed tints[24] of which nothing appears,—but the effect in the picture itself.

Also that other pert question of these sprightly critics, viz. "How does that garment hang on?" Answer: "It does not hang at all. 'Tis dropping. You catch sight only in an instant." So in running figures, in a horse full speed, in the gladiator Farnese. Whoever saw either of these subjects precisely and distinctly in any such attitude? So a man falling from a precipice. An angel, mercury flying. Michael Angelo's natural attraction of his resurrection figures upwards (ill represented in the print, a poor one). All these instantaneous. All is invention (the first part of painting), creation, divining, a sort of prophesying and inspiration, the poetical ecstatic and rapture. Things that were never seen; no nor that ever were: yet feigned. Painter as poet, a second maker.[25]

But without all this apology and defense. The poem and fiction is answer sufficient: the hyperbole, the invention, essential; the probable, plausible; the poetic, truth. What else would be every line in epic exaggerated continually beyond all possibility if narrowly searched. And see most particularly (what is of infinite curiosity and of usefulest speculation to us in the research of painting) the Homerical and Virgilian description of the shields, where the figures at last insensibly begin to stir and move and do what is absurd and impossible to imagine. Yet this is right.

. . . . .

---

unity or integrity: no piece: no whole. All disposition and order sacrificed in this transfiguration-work, as all colouring in the cartoons.

[22] Quere. Whether no instance of this in Raphael's? Where or what other master's besides. Answer. . . .

[23] Of true criticism (of which an art must be found) see 'Soliloquy,' vol. 1, p. 240. "For to all music there must be an ear proportionable. There must be an art of hearing found." So of seeing, etc.

[24] *Infra*, p. 147.

[25] See Char-cks, vol. I, p. 207.

Immanuel
KANT

Kant, like all the very greatest figures in human culture, sums up
a past age and inaugurates a new one. His earliest reading and
correspondence gives evidence of wide familiarity with the aesthetic and critical theories of German, French, and English
thinkers. From Leibniz, Baumgarten, Winckelmann, Sulzer,
Lessing, and Mendelssohn; from Fontenelle, Dubos, Rousseau,
Batteux, and Diderot; from Shaftesbury, Young, Hutcheson,
Kames, Hogarth, Burke, and Hume he learned much and often
borrowed ideas. So impressed was he by the problems of art and
aesthetics that as early as 1772, in a letter to Marcus Herz, he
anticipated writing a treatise on criticism and taste. He devoted
one essay prior to the writing of the Critique of Pure Reason
(1781) to Observations on the Feeling of the Beautiful and the
Sublime (1764). Although this early work, as well as the reading
which lay behind it, prepared Kant for his later philosophical inquiry into beauty and art, it was only after the mature philosophical reflections of the first two critiques that he was ready to
elaborate a philosophy of art. When he did come to write that

in his final critique, he had so transcended the limited theories of taste characteristic of his day that he set the course for the richest development in philosophical aesthetics.

Kant is important for us because it is in his thought that the philosophy of art in the modern sense is adumbrated, and it is in his Critique of Judgment that many of the key ideas of modern aesthetics are first set forth. To be sure, in the French and British writers of the eighteenth century there is a great deal of incisive and critical thinking about art, but it is of the sort characterized by Dilthey's expression "psychological analytical aesthetics." The dimension of a philosophy of art is lacking in that work which was addressed to analyzing the aesthetic impression and establishing its conditions both objective and subjective. Kant's great step is in going beyond empirical analysis to the identification of the aesthetic as a domain of human experience equal in dignity to the theoretical and the practical (i.e., the cognitive and the moral). For Kant the existence of a genuine domain of human experience was signalized by the presence of a unique form of the a priori. To illustrate this we need only turn to the end of the introduction to the Critique of Judgment, where there is a brief table giving a complete view of the sphere of philosophy. There the three great domains, nature, freedom, art, are distinguished; each has its own a priori principles. To nature belongs the principle of conformity to law; to freedom belongs the principle of final purpose; to art belongs the principle of purposiveness. These correspond to the employment of the three fundamental cognitive faculties of understanding, reason, judgment; and these in turn correspond to the three faculties of the human mind itself: the faculty of cognition, the faculty of desire, and the faculty of pleasure and pain. For each of the three Kant discovers a fundamental mode of universal necessity and validity in human experience. Each of his three great critiques is devoted to a detailed examination of these a priori principles.

What Kant attempts to do in the "Critique of Aesthetic Judgment" (the first part of the third critique and that which alone interests us here) is to give an explication of the unique validity of judgments of beauty and sublimity. This accounts for the extreme formalism of sections 1-22. Kant argues that since the judgment of beauty or of taste must be universally and necessarily valid for all men, its ground must be something identical in all men. But as Kant points out, only knowledge is communicable (section 14) and therefore the only thing in experience which can be supposed to be the same for all men is the

*form and not the sensations of representations. With this posi-
tion we first encounter modern formalism.*

Each of the moments of the judgment of taste contributes
to the total picture of the aesthetic judgment of the beautiful.
The first moment, according to quality, explains how the judgment of taste is disinterested, i.e., how it is to be distinguished
from judgments of the pleasant and the good. The second moment, according to quantity, stresses universality which is one of
the two essential characteristics of the a priori. As is to be expected this universality is subjective, not objective. The third
moment, according to relation, develops the idea of purposiveness without a purpose, arguing the independence of judgments
of beauty from the sensuous, emotional, and conceptual. The
fourth moment, according to modality, explains how the necessity of the judgment of taste must be a peculiar necessity distinct
from that of the theoretical and the moral. Since necessity is the
second essential characteristic of the a priori, the second and
fourth moments exhibit fully the a priori nature of judgments of
taste. The first and third moments distinguish the aesthetic from
the nonaesthetic, thus emphasizing that autonomy of the aesthetic which was to remain a lasting theme in modern thought.
In addition, the fourth moment introduces the concept of a
common sense which later forms the key idea of the deduction
of aesthetic judgment.

The analysis of judgments of taste is followed by a discussion
of the nature of art. The artist produces an art object for the
purpose of submitting it to aesthetic judgment and thereby satisfying taste. His task is to produce an object under the specific
conditions of the particular art (e.g., painting, architecture, etc.)
which will at the same time be beautiful. The artist as a genius,
then, has to produce an object that fulfills the purpose of the
particular art but also simultaneously fulfills the generic aesthetic
purpose of satisfying taste. For instance, an architect must produce a building which will accommodate itself to its use and at
the same time be beautiful. Likewise, a musical composition
must both express and excite emotions, and at the same time be
beautiful. The two purposes, it must be stressed, are not the
same for Kant. Insofar as a work is beautiful it is like nature;
hence Kant says that art can only be called beautiful if we are
conscious of it as art while yet it looks like nature (section 45).
Beautiful art is possible only through genius, which Kant defines
as the "innate mental disposition through which nature gives
the rule to art" (section 46).

Through genius the real foundation of human nature speaks

to human feeling. *The genius operates by providing in his imagination what Kant calls an aesthetic idea, i.e., a representation of the imagination that arouses much thought but cannot be encompassed by any body of concepts. This is the first modern definition of the art symbol. Genius thus becomes the faculty of aesthetic ideas. These aesthetic ideas must be expressed in the work so that a work of art is the outward expression of the aesthetic idea in the artist's mind. This outward expression of aesthetic ideas Kant identifies in the latter part of the passages here presented with the beauty he had earlier defined in terms of purposiveness without a purpose. The outward expression of aesthetic ideas is therefore a form—whether musical, architectural, poetic, etc.—which is the proper object of a judgment of taste.*

This form is at the same time a symbol of the morally good, for as Kant shows, there is a thoroughgoing analogy between our judgment of such a form as beautiful and our judgment of the morally good. As a result, the education of moral feeling is a propaedeutic for the cultivation of taste.

CRITIQUE OF JUDGMENT

Critique of the Aesthetical Judgment

FIRST DIVISION

ANALYTIC OF THE AESTHETICAL JUDGMENT

First Book

ANALYTIC OF THE BEAUTIFUL

FIRST MOMENT

Of the Judgment of Taste,[1] According to Quality

§ 1.   The Judgment of Taste Is Aesthetical

In order to distinguish whether anything is beautiful or not, we refer the representation, not by the understanding to the object for cogni-

---

[1] The definition of "taste" which is laid down here is that it is the faculty of judging of the beautiful. But the analysis of judgments of taste must show what

tion, but by the imagination (perhaps in conjunction with the understanding) to the subject and its feeling of pleasure or pain. The judgment of taste is therefore not a judgment of cognition, and is consequently not logical but aesthetical, by which we understand that whose determining ground can be *no other than subjective*. Every reference of representations, even that of sensations, may be objective (and then it signifies the real [element] of an empirical representation), save only the reference to the feeling of pleasure and pain, by which nothing in the object is signified, but through which there is a feeling in the subject as it is affected by the representation.

To apprehend a regular, purposive building by means of one's cognitive faculty (whether in a clear or a confused way of representation) is something quite different from being conscious of this representation as connected with the sensation of satisfaction. Here the representation is altogether referred to the subject and to its feeling of life, under the name of the feeling of pleasure or pain. This establishes a quite separate faculty of distinction and of judgment, adding nothing to cognition, but only comparing the given representation in the subject with the whole faculty of representations, of which the mind is conscious in the feeling of its state. Given representations in a judgment can be empirical (consequently, aesthetical); but the judgment which is formed by means of them is logical, provided they are referred in the judgment to the object. Conversely, if the given representations are rational, but are referred in a judgment simply to the subject (to its feeling), the judgment is so far always aesthetical.

§ 2. The Satisfaction Which Determines the Judgment of Taste Is Disinterested

The satisfaction which we combine with the representation of the existence of an object is called "interest." Such satisfaction always has reference to the faculty of desire, either as its determining ground or as necessarily connected with its determining ground. Now when the question is if a thing is beautiful, we do not want to know whether anything depends or can depend on the existence of the thing, either for myself or for anyone else, but how we judge it by mere observation (intuition or reflection). If anyone asks me if I find that palace

---

is required in order to call an object beautiful. The moments to which this judgment has regard in its reflection I have sought in accordance with the guidance of the logical functions of judgment (for in a judgment of taste a reference to the understanding is always involved). I have considered the moment of quality first because the aesthetical judgment upon the beautiful first pays attention to it.

beautiful which I see before me, I may answer: I do not like things of that kind which are made merely to be stared at. Or I can answer like that Iroquois Sachem, who was pleased in Paris by nothing more than by the cook shops. Or again, after the manner of Rousseau, I may rebuke the vanity of the great who waste the sweat of the people on such superfluous things. In fine, I could easily convince myself that if I found myself on an uninhabited island without the hope of ever again coming among men, and could conjure up just such a splendid building by my mere wish, I should not even give myself the trouble if I had a sufficiently comfortable hut. This may all be admitted and approved, but we are not now talking of this. We wish only to know if this mere representation of the object is accompanied in me with satisfaction, however indifferent I may be as regards the existence of the object of this representation. We easily see that, in saying it is *beautiful* and in showing that I have taste, I am concerned, not with that in which I depend on the existence of the object, but with that which I make out of this representation in myself. Everyone must admit that a judgment about beauty, in which the least interest mingles, is very partial and is not a pure judgment of taste. We must not be in the least prejudiced in favor of the existence of the things, but be quite indifferent in this respect, in order to play the judge in things of taste.

. . . . .

§ 3. The Satisfaction in the Pleasant Is Bound Up with Interest

That which pleases the senses in sensation is "pleasant." Here the opportunity presents itself of censuring a very common confusion of the double sense which the word "sensation" can have, and of calling attention to it. All satisfaction (it is said or thought) is itself sensation (of a pleasure). Consequently everything that pleases is pleasant because it pleases (and according to its different degrees or its relations to other pleasant sensations it is *agreeable, lovely, delightful, enjoyable,* etc.) But if this be admitted, then impressions of sense which determine the inclination, fundamental propositions of reason which determine the will, mere reflective forms of intuition which determine the judgment, are quite the same as regards the effect upon the feeling of pleasure. For this would be pleasantness in the sensation of one's state; and since in the end all the operations of our faculties must issue in the practical and unite in it as their goal, we could suppose no other way of estimating things and their worth than that which consists in the gratification that they promise. It is of no consequence at all how this is attained, and since then the choice of means alone could make a difference, men could indeed blame one another for stupidity and indiscretion, but never for baseness and wickedness. For thus they all, each according to his own way of seeing things, seek one goal, that is, gratification.

If a determination of the feeling of pleasure or pain is called sensation, this expression signifies something quite different from what I mean when I call the representation of a thing (by sense, as a receptivity belonging to the cognitive faculty) sensation. For in the latter case the representation is referred to the object, in the former simply to the subject, and is available for no cognition whatever, not even for that by which the subject *cognizes* itself.

In the above elucidation we understand by the word "sensation" an objective representation of sense; and, in order to avoid misinterpretation, we shall call that which must always remain merely subjective and can constitute absolutely no representation of an object by the ordinary term "feeling." The green color of the meadows belongs to *objective* sensation, as a perception of an object of sense; the pleasantness of this belongs to *subjective* sensation by which no object is represented, i.e. to feeling, by which the object is considered as an object of satisfaction (which does not furnish a cognition of it).

Now that a judgment about an object by which I describe it as pleasant expresses an interest in it, is plain from the fact that by sensation it excites a desire for objects of that kind; consequently the satisfaction presupposes, not the mere judgment about it, but the relation of its existence to my state, so far as this is affected by such an object. Hence we do not merely say of the pleasant, *it pleases*, but, *it gratifies*. I give to it no mere assent, but inclination is aroused by it; and in the case of what is pleasant in the most lively fashion there is no judgment at all upon the character of the object, for those [persons] who always lay themselves out for enjoyment (for that is the word describing intense gratification) would fain dispense with all judgment.

§ 4. *The Satisfaction in the Good Is Bound Up with Interest*
Whatever by means of reason pleases through the mere concept is *good*. That which pleases only as a means we call *good for something* (the useful), but that which pleases for itself is *good in itself*. In

both there is always involved the concept of a purpose, and consequently the relation of reason to the (at least possible) volition, and thus a satisfaction in the *presence* of an object or an action, i.e. some kind of interest.

In order to find anything good, I must always know what sort of a thing the object ought to be, i.e. I must have a concept of it. But there is no need of this to find a thing beautiful. Flowers, free delineations, outlines intertwined with one another without design and called [conventional] foliage, have no meaning, depend on no definite concept, and yet they please. Satisfaction in the good must depend on reflection upon an object that leads to some concept (however indefinite), and it is thus distinguished from the pleasant, which rests entirely upon sensation.

It is true, the pleasant seems in many cases to be the same as the good. Thus people are accustomed to say that all gratification (especially if it lasts) is good in itself, which is very much the same as to say that lasting pleasure and the good are the same. But we can soon see that this is merely a confusion of words, for the concepts which properly belong to these expressions can in no way be interchanged. The pleasant, which, as such, represents the object simply in relation to sense, must first be brought by the concept of a purpose under principles of reason, in order to call it good, as an object of the will. But that there is [involved] a quite different relation to satisfaction in calling that which gratifies at the same time *good* may be seen from the fact that, in the case of the good, the question always is whether it is mediately or immediately good (useful or good in itself); but on the contrary in the case of the pleasant, there can be no question about this at all, for the word always signifies something which pleases immediately. (The same is applicable to what I call beautiful.)

·　·　·　·　·

However, notwithstanding all this difference between the pleasant and the good, they both agree in this that they are always bound up with an interest in their object; so are not only the pleasant (§ 3), and the mediate good (the useful) which is pleasing as a means toward pleasantness somewhere, but also that which is good absolutely and in every aspect, viz. moral good, which brings with it the highest interest. For the good is the object of will (i.e. of a faculty of desire determined by reason). But to wish for something and to have a satisfaction in its existence, i.e. to take an interest in it, are identical.

§ 5. Comparison of the Three Specifically Different Kinds of Satisfaction

The pleasant and the good have both a reference to the faculty of desire, and they bring with them, the former a satisfaction pathologically conditioned (by impulses, *stimuli*), the latter a pure practical satisfaction which is determined not merely by the representation of the object but also by the represented connection of the subject with the existence of the object. [It is not merely the object that pleases, but also its existence.] [2] On the other hand, the judgment of taste is merely *contemplative*; i.e., it is a judgment which, indifferent as regards the existence of an object, compares its character with the feeling of pleasure and pain. But this contemplation itself is not directed to concepts; for the judgment of taste is not a cognitive judgment (either theoretical or practical), and thus is not *based* on concepts, nor has it concepts as its *purpose*.

The pleasant, the beautiful, and the good designate then three different relations of representations to the feeling of pleasure and pain, in reference to which we distinguish from one another objects or methods of representing them. And the expressions corresponding to each, by which we mark our complacency in them, are not the same. That which *gratifies* a man is called *pleasant*; that which merely *pleases* him is *beautiful*; that which is *esteemed* [or *approved*] [3] by him, i.e. that to which he accords an objective worth, is *good*. Pleasantness concerns irrational animals also, but beauty only concerns men, i.e. animal, but still rational, beings—not merely *quâ* rational (e.g. spirits), but *quâ* animal also—and the good concerns every rational being in general. This is a proposition which can only be completely established and explained in the sequel. We may say that, of all these three kinds of satisfaction, that of taste in the beautiful is alone a disinterested and *free* satisfaction; for no interest, either of sense or of reason, here forces our assent. Hence we may say of satisfaction that it is related in the three aforesaid cases to *inclination*, to *favor*, or to *respect*. Now *favor* is the only free satisfaction. An object of inclination and one that is proposed to our desire by a law of reason leave us no freedom in forming for ourselves anywhere an object of pleasure. All interest presupposes or generates a want, and, as the

---

[2] [Second edition.]
[3] [Second edition.]

determining ground of assent, it leaves the judgment about the object no longer free.

. . . . .

Explanation of the Beautiful Resulting from the First Moment

Taste is the faculty of judging of an object or a method of representing it by an *entirely disinterested* satisfaction or dissatisfaction. The object of such satisfaction is called *beautiful.*

SECOND MOMENT

Of the Judgment of Taste, According to Quantity

§ 6. *The Beautiful Is That Which Apart from Concepts Is Represented as the Object of a Universal Satisfaction*

This explanation of the beautiful can be derived from the preceding explanation of it as the object of an entirely disinterested satisfaction. For the fact of which everyone is conscious, that the satisfaction is for him quite disinterested, implies in his judgment a ground of satisfaction for all men. For since it does not rest on any inclination of the subject (nor upon any other premeditated interest), but since the person who judges feels himself quite *free* as regards the satisfaction which he attaches to the object, he cannot find the ground of this satisfaction in any private conditions connected with his own subject, and hence it must be regarded as grounded on what he can presuppose in every other person. Consequently he must believe that he has reason for attributing a similar satisfaction to everyone. He will therefore speak of the beautiful as if beauty were a characteristic of the object and the judgment logical (constituting a cognition of the object by means of concepts of it), although it is only aesthetical and involves merely a reference of the representation of the object to the subject. For it has this similarity to a logical judgment that we can presuppose its validity for all men. But this universality cannot arise from concepts; for from concepts there is no transition to the feeling of pleasure or pain (except in pure practical laws, which bring an interest with them such as is not bound up with the pure judgment of taste). Consequently the judgment of taste, accompanied with the consciousness of separation from all interest, must claim validity for every man, without this universality depending on objects. That is, there must be bound up with it a title to subjective universality.

§ 7. Comparison of the Beautiful with the Pleasant and the Good by Means of the Above Characteristic

As regards the pleasant, everyone is content that his judgment, which he bases upon private feeling and by which he says of an object that it pleases him, should be limited merely to his own person. Thus he is quite contented that if he says, "Canary wine is pleasant," another man may correct his expression and remind him that he ought to say, "It is pleasant *to me*." And this is the case not only as regards the taste of the tongue, the palate, and the throat, but for whatever is pleasant to anyone's eyes and ears. To one, violet color is soft and lovely; to another, it is washed out and dead. One man likes the tone of wind instruments, another that of strings. To strive here with the design of reproving as incorrect another man's judgment which is different from our own, as if the judgments were logically opposed, would be folly. As regards the pleasant, therefore, the fundamental proposition is valid: *everyone has his own taste* (the taste of sense).

The case is quite different with the beautiful. It would (on the contrary) be laughable if a man who imagined anything to his own taste thought to justify himself by saying: "This object (the house we see, the coat that person wears, the concert we hear, the poem submitted to our judgment) is beautiful *for me*." For he must not call it *beautiful* if it merely pleases him. Many things may have for him charm and pleasantness—no one troubles himself at that—but if he gives out anything as beautiful, he supposes in others the same satisfaction; he judges not merely for himself, but for everyone, and speaks of beauty as if it were a property of things. Hence he says "the *thing* is beautiful"; and he does not count on the agreement of others with this his judgment of satisfaction, because he has found this agreement several times before, but he *demands* it of them. He blames them if they judge otherwise and he denies them taste, which he nevertheless requires from them. Here, then, we cannot say that each man has his own particular taste. For this would be as much as to say that there is no taste whatever, i.e. no aesthetical judgment which can make a rightful claim upon everyone's assent.

At the same time we find as regards the pleasant that there is an agreement among men in their judgments upon it in regard to which we deny taste to some and attribute it to others, by this not meaning one of our organic senses, but a faculty of judging in respect of the pleasant generally. Thus we say of a man who knows how to entertain his guests with pleasures (of enjoyment for all the senses), so that they are all pleased, "he has taste." But here the universality is only taken comparatively; and there emerge rules which are only *general* (like all empirical ones), and not *universal*, which latter the judgment of taste upon the beautiful undertakes or lays claim to. It is a judgment in reference to sociability, so far as this rests on empirical rules. In respect of the good it is true that judgments make rightful claim to validity for everyone; but the good is represented only *by means of a concept* as the object of a universal satisfaction, which is the case neither with the pleasant nor with the beautiful.

§ 8. *The Universality of the Satisfaction Is Represented in a Judgment of Taste Only as Subjective*

This particular determination of the universality of an aesthetical judgment, which is to be met with in a judgment of taste, is noteworthy, not indeed for the logician, but for the transcendental philosopher. It requires no small trouble to discover its origin, but we thus detect a property of our cognitive faculty which without this analysis would remain unknown.

First, we must be fully convinced of the fact that in a judgment of taste (about the beautiful) the satisfaction in the object is imputed to *everyone*, without being based on a concept (for then it would be the good). Further, this claim to universal validity so essentially belongs to a judgment by which we describe anything as *beautiful* that, if this were not thought in it, it would never come into our thoughts to use the expression at all, but everything which pleases without a concept would be counted as pleasant. In respect of the latter, everyone has his own opinion; and no one assumes in another agreement with his judgment of taste, which is always the case in a judgment of taste about beauty. I may call the first the taste of sense, the second the taste of reflection, so far as the first lays down mere private judgments and the second judgments supposed to be generally valid (public), but in both cases aesthetical (not practical) judgments about an object merely in respect of the relation of its representation to the feeling of pleasure and pain. Now here is something strange. As regards the taste of sense, not only does experience show that its judgment (of pleasure or pain connected with anything) is not valid universally, but everyone is content not to impute agreement with it to others (although actually there is often found a very extended concurrence in these judgments). On the other hand, the taste of reflection has its claim to the universal validity of its judgments (about the beautiful) rejected often enough, as experience teaches, although it may find it possible (as it actually does) to represent judgments which can demand this universal agreement. In fact it imputes this to everyone for each of its judgments of taste, without the persons that judge disputing as to the possibility of such a claim, although in particular cases they cannot agree as to the correct application of this faculty.

Here we must, in the first place, remark that a universality which does not rest on concepts of objects (not even on empirical ones) is not logical but aesthetical; i.e. it involves no objective quantity of the judgment, but only that which is subjective. For this I use the expression *general validity*, which signifies the validity of the reference of a representation, not to the cognitive faculty, but to the feeling of pleasure and pain for every subject. (We can avail ourselves also of the same expression for the logical quantity of the judgment, if only we prefix "objective" to "universal validity," to distinguish it from that which is merely subjective and aesthetical.)

A judgment with *objective universal validity* is also always valid subjectively; i.e. if the judgment holds for everything contained under a given concept, it holds also for everyone who represents an object by means of this concept. But from a *subjective universal validity*, i.e. aesthetical and resting on no concept, we cannot infer that which is logical because that kind of judgment does not extend to the object. But, therefore, the aesthetical universality which is ascribed to a judgment must be of a particular kind, because it does not unite the predicate of beauty with the concept of the object, considered in its whole logical sphere, and yet extends it to the whole sphere of judging persons.

In respect of logical quantity, all judgments of taste are *singular* judgments. For because I must refer the object immediately to my feeling of pleasure and pain, and that not by means of concepts, they cannot have the quantity of objective generally valid judgments. Nevertheless, if the singular representation of the object of the judgment of taste, in accordance with the conditions determining the latter, were transformed by comparison into a concept, a logically universal judgment could result therefrom. E.g., I describe by a judgment of taste the rose that I see as beautiful. But the judgment which results from the comparison of several singular judgments, "Roses in general are beautiful," is no longer described simply as aesthetical, but as a logical judgment based on an aesthetical one. Again the judgment, "The rose is pleasant" (to use) is, although aesthetical and singular, not a judgment of taste but of sense. It is distinguished from the former by the fact that the judgment of taste carries with it an *aesthetic quantity* of universality, i.e. of validity for everyone, which cannot be found in a judgment about the pleasant. It is only judgments about the good which, although they also determine satisfaction in an object, have logical and not merely aesthetical universality, for they are valid of the object as cognitive of it, and thus are valid for everyone.

If we judge objects merely according to concepts, then all representation of beauty is lost. Thus there can be no rule according to which anyone is to be forced to recognize anything as beautiful. We cannot press [upon others] by the aid of any reasons or fundamental propositions our judgment that a coat, a house, or a flower is beautiful. People wish to submit the object to their own eyes, as if the satisfaction in it depended on sensation; and yet, if we then call the object beautiful, we believe that we speak with a universal voice, and we claim the assent of everyone, although on the contrary all private sensation can only decide for the observer himself and his satisfaction.

We may see now that in the judgment of taste nothing is postulated but such a *universal voice*, in respect of the satisfaction without the intervention of concepts, and thus the *possibility* of an aesthetical judgment that can, at the same time, be regarded as valid for everyone. The judgment of taste itself does not *postulate* the agreement of everyone (for that can only be done by a logically universal judgment because it can adduce reasons); it only *imputes* this agreement to everyone, as a case of the rule in respect of which it expects, not confirmation by concepts, but assent from others. The universal voice is, therefore, only an idea (we do not yet inquire upon what it rests). It may be uncertain whether or not the man who believes that he is laying down a judgment of taste is, as a matter of fact, judging in conformity with that idea; but that he refers his judgment thereto, and consequently that it is intended to be a judgment of taste, he announces by the expression "beauty." He can be quite certain of this for himself by the mere consciousness of the separating off everything belonging to the pleasant and the good from the satisfaction which is left; and this is all for which he promises himself the agreement of everyone—a claim which would be justifiable under these conditions, provided only he did not often make mistakes, and thus lay down an erroneous judgment of taste.

§ 9. Investigation of the Question Whether in the Judgment of Taste the Feeling of Pleasure Precedes or Follows the Judging of the Object

The solution of this question is the key to the critique of taste, and so is worthy of all attention.

If the pleasure in the given object precedes, and it is only its universal communicability that is to be acknowledged in the judgment of taste about the representation of the object, there would be a contradiction. For such pleasure would be nothing different from the mere pleasantness in the sensation, and so in accordance with its nature could have only private validity, because it is immediately dependent on the representation through which the object *is given*.

Hence it is the universal capability of communication of the mental state in the given representation which, as the subjective condition of the judgment of taste, must be fundamental and must have the pleasure in the object as its consequent. But nothing can be universally communicated except cognition and representation, so far as it belongs to cognition. For it is only thus that this latter can be objective, and only through this has it a universal point of reference, with which the representative power of everyone is compelled to harmonize. If the determining ground of our judgment as to this universal communicability of the representation is to be merely subjective, i.e. is conceived independently of any concept of the object, it can be nothing else than the state of mind, which is to be met with in the relation of our representative powers to each other, so far as they refer a given representation to *cognition in general*.

The cognitive powers, which are involved by this representation, are here in free play, because no definite concept limits them to a definite[4] rule of cognition. Hence the state of mind in this representation must be a feeling of the free play of the representative powers in a given representation with reference to a cognition in general. Now a representation by which an object is given that is to become a cognition in general requires *imagination* for the gathering together the manifold of intuition, and *understanding* for the unity of the concept uniting the representations. This state of *free play* of the cognitive faculties in a representation by which an object is given must be universally communicable, because cognition, as the determination of the

---

[4] [First edition has "particular."]

object with which given representations (in whatever subject) are to agree, is the only kind of representation which is valid for everyone.

The subjective universal communicability of the mode of representation in a judgment of taste, since it is to be possible without presupposing a definite concept, can refer to nothing else than the state of mind in the free play of the imagination and the understanding (so far as they agree with each other, as is requisite for *cognition in general*). We are conscious that this subjective relation, suitable for cognition in general, must be valid for everyone, and thus must be universally communicable, just as if it were a definite cognition, resting always on that relation as its subjective condition.

This merely subjective (aesthetical) judging of the object, or of the representation by which it is given, precedes the pleasure in the same and is the ground of this pleasure in the harmony of the cognitive faculties; but on that universality of the subjective conditions for judging of objects is alone based the universal subjective validity of the satisfaction bound up by us with the representation of the object that we call beautiful.

That the power of communicating one's state of mind, even though only in respect of the cognitive faculties, carries a pleasure with it, this we can easily show from the natural propension of man toward sociability (empirical and psychological). But this is not enough for our design. The pleasure that we feel is, in a judgment of taste, necessarily imputed by us to everyone else, as if, when we call a thing beautiful, it is to be regarded as a characteristic of the object which is determined in it according to concepts, though beauty, without a reference to the feeling of the subject, is nothing by itself. But we must reserve the examination of this question until we have answered that other—if and how aesthetical judgments are possible *a priori*.

We now occupy ourselves with the easier question, in what way we are conscious of a mutual subjective harmony of the cognitive powers with one another in the judgment of taste—is it aesthetically by mere internal sense and sensation, or is it intellectually by the consciousness of our designed activity, by which we bring them into play?

If the given representation which occasions the judgment of taste were a concept uniting understanding and imagination in the judging of the object, into a cognition of the object, the consciousness of this relation would be intellectual (as in the objective schematism of the judgment of which the *Critique* treats). But then the judgment would not be laid down in reference to pleasure and pain, and consequently would not be a judgment of taste. But the judgment of taste, independently of concepts, determines the object in respect of satisfaction and of the predicate of beauty. Therefore that subjective unity of relation can only make itself known by means of sensation. The excitement of both faculties (imagination and understanding) to indeterminate but yet, through the stimulus of the given sensation, harmonious activity, viz. that which belongs to cognition in general, is the sensation whose universal communicability is postulated by the judgment of taste. An objective relation can only be thought, but yet, so far as it is subjective according to its conditions, can be felt in its effect on the mind; and, of a relation based on no concept (like the relation of the representative powers to a cognitive faculty in general), no other consciousness is possible than that through the sensation of the effect, which consists in the more lively play of both mental powers (the imagination and the understanding) when animated by mutual agreement. A representation which, as individual and apart from comparison with others, yet has an agreement with the conditions of universality which it is the business of the understanding to supply, brings the cognitive faculties into that proportionate accord which we require for all cognition, and so regard as holding for everyone who is determined to judge by means of understanding and sense in combination (i.e. for every man).

Explanation of the Beautiful Resulting from the Second Moment
The *beautiful* is that which pleases universally without [requiring] a concept.

THIRD MOMENT

Of Judgments of Taste, According to the Relation of the Purposes Which Are Brought into Consideration in Them

§ 10. *Of Purposiveness in General*

If we wish to explain what a purpose is according to its transcendental determinations (without presupposing anything empirical like the feeling of pleasure), [we say that] the purpose is the object of a concept, in so far as the concept is regarded as the cause of the object (the real ground of its possibility); and the causality of a *concept* in respect of its *object* is its purposiveness (*forma finalis*). Where then not merely the cognition of an object but the object itself (its form and existence) is thought as an effect only possible by means of the concept of this latter, there we think a purpose. The representation of the effect is here the determining ground of its cause and precedes it. The consciousness of the causality of a representation, for *maintaining* the subject in the same state, may here generally denote what we call pleasure; while on the other hand pain is that representation which contains the ground of the determination of the state of representations into their opposite [of restraining or removing them].[5]

The faculty of desire, so far as it is determinable to act only through concepts, i.e. in conformity with the representation of a purpose, would be the will. But an object, or a state of mind, or even an action is called purposive, although its possibility does not necessarily presuppose the representation of a purpose, merely because its possibility can be explained and conceived by us only so far as we assume for its ground a causality according to purposes, i.e. in accordance with a will which has regulated it according to the representation of a certain rule. There can be, then, purposiveness without purpose, so far as we do not place the causes of this form in a will, but yet can only make the explanation of its possibility intelligible to ourselves by deriving it from a will. Again, we are not always forced to regard what we observe (in respect of its possibility) from the point of view of reason. Thus we can at least observe a purposiveness according to form, without basing it on a purpose (as the material of the *nexus finalis*), and remark it in objects, although only by reflection.

§ 11. *The Judgment of Taste Has Nothing at Its Basis but the Form of the Purposiveness of an Object (or of Its Mode of Representation)*

Every purpose, if it be regarded as a ground of satisfaction, always carries with it an interest—as the determining ground of the judgment— about the object of pleasure. Therefore no subjective purpose can lie at the basis of the judgment of taste. But also the judgment of taste can be determined by no representation of an objective purpose, i.e. of the possibility of the object itself in accordance with principles of purposive combination, and consequently by no concept of the good, because it is an aesthetical and not a cognitive judgment. It therefore has to do with no *concept* of the character and internal or external possibility of the object by means of this or that cause, but merely with the relation of the representative powers to one another, so far as they are determined by a representation.

Now this relation in the determination of an object as beautiful is

---

[5] [Second edition.]

bound up with the feeling of pleasure, which is declared by the judgment of taste to be valid for everyone; hence a pleasantness [merely] accompanying the representation can as little contain the determining ground [of the judgment] as the representation of the perfection of the object and the concept of the good can. Therefore it can be nothing else than the subjective purposiveness in the representation of an object without any purpose (either objective or subjective), and thus it is the mere form of purposiveness in the representation by which an object is *given* to us, so far as we are conscious of it, which constitutes the satisfaction that we without a concept judge to be universally communicable; and, consequently, this is the determining ground of the judgment of taste.

§ 12. *The Judgment of Taste Rests on a* Priori *Grounds*

To establish *a priori* the connection of the feeling of a pleasure or pain as an effect, with any representation whatever (sensation or concept) as its cause, is absolutely impossible, for that would be a [particular] [6] causal relation which (with objects of experience) can always only be cognized *a posteriori* and through the medium of experience itself. We actually have, indeed, in the *Critique of Practical Reason,* derived from universal moral concepts *a priori* the feeling of respect (as a special and peculiar modification of feeling which will not strictly correspond either to the pleasure or the pain that we get from empirical objects). But there we could go beyond the bounds of experience and call in a causality which rested on a supersensible attribute of the subject, viz. freedom. And even there, properly speaking, it was not this *feeling* which we derived from the idea of the moral as cause, but merely the determination of the will. But the state of mind which accompanies any determination of the will is in itself a feeling of pleasure and identical with it, and therefore does not follow from it as its effect. This last must only be assumed if the concept of the moral as a good precede the determination of the will by the law, for in that case the pleasure that is bound up with the concept could not be derived from it as from a mere cognition.

Now the case is similar with the pleasure in aesthetical judgments, only that here it is merely contemplative and does not bring about an interest in the object, while on the other hand in the moral judgment it is practical. The consciousness of the mere formal purposiveness in the play of the subject's cognitive powers, in a representation through

---

[6] [First edition.]

which an object is given, is the pleasure itself, because it contains a determining ground of the activity of the subject in respect of the excitement of its cognitive powers, and therefore an inner causality (which is purposive) in respect of cognition in general, without however being limited to any definite cognition, and consequently contains a mere form of the subjective purposiveness of a representation in an aesthetical judgment. This pleasure is in no way practical, neither like that arising from the pathological ground of pleasantness, nor that from the intellectual ground of the presented good. But yet it involves causality, viz. of *maintaining* without further design the state of the representation itself and the occupation of the cognitive powers. We *linger* over the contemplation of the beautiful because this contemplation strengthens and reproduces itself, which is analogous to (though not of the same kind as) that lingering which takes place when a [physical] charm in the representation of the object repeatedly arouses the attention, the mind being passive.

§ 13. *The Pure Judgment of Taste Is Indifferent of Charm and Emotion*

Every interest spoils the judgment of taste and takes from its impartiality, especially if the purposiveness is not, as with the interest of reason, placed before the feeling of pleasure but grounded on it. This last always happens in an aesthetical judgment upon anything, so far as it gratifies or grieves us. Hence judgments so affected can lay no claim at all to a universally valid satisfaction, or at least so much the less claim, in proportion as there are sensations of this sort among the determining grounds of taste. That taste is always barbaric which needs a mixture of *charms* and *emotions* in order that there may be satisfaction, and still more so if it make these the measure of its assent.

Nevertheless charms are often not only taken account of in the case of beauty (which properly speaking ought merely to be concerned with form) as contributory to the aesthetical universal satisfaction, but they are passed off as in themselves beauties; and thus the matter of satisfaction is substituted for the form. This misconception, however, which like so many others, has something true at its basis, may be removed by a careful determination of these concepts.

A judgment of taste on which charm and emotion have no influence (although they may be bound up with the satisfaction in the beautiful)—which therefore has as its determining ground merely the purposiveness of the form—is a *pure judgment of taste.*

§ 14. *Elucidation by Means of Examples*

Aesthetical judgments can be divided just like theoretical (logical) judgments into empirical and pure. The first assert pleasantness or unpleasantness; the second assert the beauty of an object or of the manner of representing it. The former are judgments of sense (material aesthetical judgments); the latter [as formal] [7] are alone strictly judgments of taste.

A judgment of taste is therefore pure only so far as no merely empirical satisfaction is mingled with its determining ground. But this always happens if charm or emotion have any share in the judgment by which anything is to be described as beautiful.

Now here many objections present themselves which fallaciously put forward charm not merely as a necessary ingredient of beauty, but as alone sufficient [to justify] a thing's being called beautiful. A mere color, e.g. the green of a grass plot, a mere tone (as distinguished from sound and noise), like that of a violin, are by most people described as beautiful in themselves, although both seem to have at their basis merely the matter of representations, viz. simply sensation, and therefore only deserve to be called pleasant. But we must at the same time remark that the sensations of colors and of tone have a right to be regarded as beautiful only in so far as they are *pure*. This is a determination which concerns their form and is the only [element] of these representations which admits with certainty of universal communicability; for we cannot assume that the quality of sensations is the same in all subjects, and we can hardly say that the pleasantness of one color or the tone of one musical instrument is judged preferable to that of another in the same[8] way by everyone.

· · · · ·

In painting, sculpture, and in all the formative arts—in architecture and horticulture, so far as they are beautiful arts—the *delineation* is the essential thing; and here it is not what gratifies in sensation but what pleases by means of its form that is fundamental for taste. The colors which light up the sketch belong to the charm; they may indeed enliven[9] the object for sensation, but they cannot make it worthy of contemplation and beautiful. In most cases they are rather limited by

---

[7] [Second edition.]

[8] [First edition has *"gleiche"*; second edition has *"solche."*]

[9] [*"Belebt machen"*; first edition had *"beliebt."*]

the requirements of the beautiful form, and even where charm is permissible it is ennobled solely by this.

Every form of the objects of sense (both of external sense and also mediately of internal) is either *figure* or *play*. In the latter case it is either play of figures (in space, viz. pantomime and dancing) or the mere play of sensations (in time). The *charm* of colors or of the pleasant tones of an instrument may be added, but the *delineation* in the first case and the composition in the second constitute the proper object of the pure judgment of taste. To say that the purity of colors and of tones, or their variety and contrast, seem to add to beauty does not mean that they supply a homogeneous addition to our satisfaction in the form because they are pleasant in themselves; but they do so because they make the form more exactly, definitely, and completely, intuitible, and besides, by their charm [excite the representation, while they] [10] awaken and fix our attention on the object itself.

Even what we call "ornaments" [*parerga*],[11] i.e. those things which do not belong to the complete representation of the object internally as elements, but only externally as complements, and which augment the satisfaction of taste, do so only by their form; as, for example, [the frames of pictures[12] or] the draperies of statues or the colonnades of palaces. But if the ornament does not itself consist in beautiful form, and if it is used as a golden frame is used, merely to recommend the painting by its *charm*, it is then called *finery* and injures genuine beauty.

Emotion, that is a sensation in which pleasantness is produced by means of a momentary checking and a consequent more powerful outflow of the vital force, does not belong at all to beauty. But sublimity [with which the feeling of emotion is bound up] [13] requires a different standard of judgment from that which is at the foundation of taste; and thus a pure judgment of taste has for its determining ground neither charm nor emotion—in a word, no sensation as the material of the aesthetical judgment.

§ 15. *The Judgment of Taste Is Quite Independent of the Concept of Perfection*

Objective purposiveness can only be cognized by means of the reference of the manifold to a definite purpose, and therefore only

---

[10] [Second edition.]
[11] [Second edition.]
[12] [Second edition.]
[13] [Second edition.]

through a concept. From this alone it is plain that the beautiful, the judging of which has at its basis a merely formal purposiveness, i.e. a purposiveness without purpose, is quite independent of the concept of the good, because the latter presupposes an objective purposiveness, i.e. the reference of the object to a definite purpose.

Objective purposiveness is either external, i.e. the *utility*, or internal, i.e. the *perfection* of the object. That the satisfaction in an object, on account of which we call it beautiful, cannot rest on the representation of its utility is sufficiently obvious from the two preceding sections; because in that case it would not be an immediate satisfaction in the object, which is the essential condition of a judgment about beauty. But objective internal purposiveness, i.e. perfection, comes nearer to the predicate of beauty; and it has been regarded by celebrated philosophers as the same as beauty, with the proviso, *if it is thought in a confused way*. It is of the greatest importance in a critique of taste to decide whether beauty can thus actually be resolved into the concept of perfection.

To judge of objective purposiveness we always need, not only the concept of a purpose, but (if that purposiveness is not to be external utility but internal) the concept of an internal purpose which shall contain the ground of the internal possibility of the object. Now as a purpose in general is that whose *concept* can be regarded as the ground of the possibility of the object itself; so, in order to represent objective purposiveness in a thing, the concept of *what sort of thing it is to be* must come first. The agreement of the manifold in it with this concept (which furnishes the rule for combining the manifold) is the *qualitative perfection* of the thing. Quite different from this is *quantitative* perfection, the completeness of a thing after its kind, which is a mere concept of magnitude (of totality). In this *what the thing ought to be* is conceived as already determined, and it is only asked if it has *all* its requisites. The formal [element] in the representation of a thing, i.e. the agreement of the manifold with a unity (it being undetermined what this ought to be), gives to cognition no objective purposiveness whatever. For since abstraction is made of this unity as *purpose* (what the thing ought to be), nothing remains but the subjective purposiveness of the representations in the mind of the intuiting subject. And this, although it furnishes a certain purposiveness of the representative state of the subject, and so a facility of apprehending a given form by the imagination, yet furnishes no perfection of an object, since the object is not here conceived by means of the concept of a purpose. For example, if in a forest I come across a plot of sward around which trees stand in a circle and do not then represent to myself a purpose, viz. that it is intended to serve for country dances, not the least concept of perfection is furnished by the mere form. But to represent to oneself a formal *objective* purposiveness without purpose, i.e. the mere form of a *perfection* (without any matter and without the *concept* of that with which it is accordant, even if it were merely the idea of conformity to law in general),[14] is a veritable contradiction.

Now the judgment of taste is an aesthetical judgment, i.e. such as rests on subjective grounds, the determining ground of which cannot be a concept, and consequently cannot be the concept of a definite purpose. Therefore by means of beauty, regarded as a formal subjective purposiveness, there is in no way thought a perfection of the object, as a purposiveness alleged to be formal but which is yet objective. And thus to distinguish between the concepts of the beautiful and the good as if they were only different in logical form, the first being a confused, the second a clear concept of perfection, but identical in content and origin, is quite fallacious. For then there would be no *specific* difference between them, but a judgment of taste would be as much a cognitive judgment as the judgment by which a thing is described as good; just as when the ordinary man says that fraud is unjust he bases his judgment on confused grounds, while the philosopher bases it on clear grounds, but both on identical principles of reason. I have already, however, said that an aesthetical judgment is unique of its kind and gives absolutely no cognition (not even a confused cognition) of the object; this is only supplied by a logical judgment. On the contrary, it simply refers the representation, by which an object is given, to the subject, and brings to our notice no characteristic of the object, but only the purposive form in the determination of the representative powers which are occupying themselves therewith. The judgment is called aesthetical just because its determining ground is not a concept, but the feeling (of internal sense) of that harmony in the play of the mental powers, so far as it can be felt in sensation. On the other hand, if we wish to call confused concepts and the objective judgment based on them aesthetical, we will have an understanding judging sensibly or a sense representing its objects by means of concepts [both of which are contradictory].[15] The faculty of concepts, be they confused or clear, is the understanding; and although understanding has to do with the judgment of taste as an aesthetical judgment (as it has with all judgments), yet it has to do with it, not as a faculty by which an object is cognized, but as the faculty which de-

---

[14] [The words "even if . . . general" were added in the second edition.]
[15] [Second edition.]

termines the judgment and its representation (without any concept) in accordance with its relation to the subject and the subject's internal feeling, in so far as this judgment may be possible in accordance with a universal rule.

. . . . .

Explanation of the Beautiful Derived from this Third Moment

Beauty is the form of the *purposiveness* of an object, so far as this is perceived in it *without any representation of a purpose*.[16]

FOURTH MOMENT

Of the Judgment of Taste, According to the Modality of the Satisfaction in the Object

§ 18. What the Modality in a Judgment of Taste Is

I can say of every representation that it is at least *possible* that (as a cognition) it should be bound up with a pleasure. Of a representation that I call *pleasant* I say that it *actually* excites pleasure in me. But the *beautiful* we think as having a *necessary* reference to satisfaction. Now this necessity is of a peculiar kind. It is not a theoretical objective necessity, in which case it would be cognized *a priori* that everyone *will feel* this satisfaction in the object called beautiful by me. It is not a practical necessity, in which case, by concepts of a pure rational will serving as a rule for freely acting beings, the satisfaction is the necessary result of an objective law and only indicates that we absolutely (without any further design) ought to act in a certain way. But the necessity which is thought in an aesthetical judgment can only be called exemplary, i.e. a necessity of the assent of *all* to a judgment which is regarded as the example of a universal rule that we cannot state. Since an aesthetical judgment is not an objective cognitive judgment, this necessity cannot be derived from definite concepts and is therefore not apodictic. Still less can it be inferred from the

---

[16] It might be objected to this explanation that there are things in which we see a purposive form without cognizing any purpose in them, like the stone implements often gotten from old sepulchral tumuli with a hole in them, as if for a handle. These, although they plainly indicate by their shape a purposiveness of which we do not know the purpose, are nevertheless not described as beautiful. But if we regard a thing as a work of art, that is enough to make us admit that its shape has reference to some design and definite purpose. And hence there is no immediate satisfaction in the contemplation of it. On the other hand a flower, e.g. a tulip, is regarded as beautiful, because in perceiving it we find a certain purposiveness which, in our judgment, is referred to no purpose at all.

universality of experience (of a complete agreement of judgments as to the beauty of a certain object). For not only would experience hardly furnish sufficiently numerous vouchers for this, but also, on empirical judgments, we can base no concept of the necessity of these judgments.

§ 19. *The Subjective Necessity, Which We Ascribe to the Judgment of Taste, Is Conditioned*

The judgment of taste requires the agreement of everyone, and he who describes anything as beautiful claims that everyone *ought* to give his approval to the object in question and also describe it as beautiful. The *ought* in the aesthetical judgment is therefore pronounced in accordance with all the data which are required for judging, and yet is only conditioned. We ask for the agreement of everyone else, because we have for it a ground that is common to all; and we could count on this agreement, provided we were always sure that the case was correctly subsumed under that ground as rule of assent.

§ 20. *The Condition of Necessity Which a Judgment of Taste Asserts Is the Idea of a Common Sense*

If judgments of taste (like cognitive judgments) had a definite objective principle, then the person who lays them down in accordance with this latter would claim an unconditioned necessity for his judgment. If they were devoid of all principle, like those of the mere taste of sense, we would not allow them in thought any necessity whatever. Hence they must have a subjective principle which determines what pleases or displeases only by feeling and not by concepts, but yet with universal validity. But such a principle could only be regarded as a *common sense*, which is essentially different from common understanding which people sometimes call common sense (*sensus communis*); for the latter does not judge by feeling but always by concepts, although ordinarily only as by obscurely represented principles.

Hence it is only under the presupposition that there is a common sense (by which we do not understand an external sense, but the effect resulting from the free play of our cognitive powers)—it is only under this presupposition, I say, that the judgment of taste can be laid down.

§ 21. *Have We Ground for Presupposing a Common Sense?*

Cognitions and judgments must, along with the conviction that accompanies them, admit of universal communicability; for otherwise there would be no harmony between them and the object, and they would be collectively a mere subjective play of the representative powers, exactly as scepticism desires. But if cognitions are to admit of communicability, so must also the state of mind—i.e. the accordance of the cognitive powers with a cognition generally and that proportion of them which is suitable for a representation (by which an object is given to us) in order that a cognition may be made out of it—admit of universal communicability. For without this as the subjective condition of cognition, cognition as an effect could not arise. This actually always takes place when a given object by means of sense excites the imagination to collect the manifold, and the imagination in its turn excites the understanding to bring about a unity of this collective process in concepts. But this accordance of the cognitive powers has a different proportion according to the variety of the objects which are given. However, it must be such that this internal relation, by which one mental faculty is excited by another, shall be generally the most beneficial for both faculties in respect of cognition (of given objects); and this accordance can only be determined by feeling (not according to concepts). Since now this accordance itself must admit of universal communicability, and consequently also our feeling of it (in a given representation), and since the universal communicability of a feeling presupposes a common sense, we have grounds for assuming this latter. And this common sense is assumed without relying on psychological observations, but simply as the necessary condition of the universal communicability of our knowledge, which is presupposed in every logic and in every principle of knowledge that is not sceptical.

§ 22. *The Necessity of the Universal Agreement That Is Thought in a Judgement of Taste Is a Subjective Necessity, Which Is Represented as Objective Under the Presupposition of a Common Sense*

In all judgments by which we describe anything as beautiful, we allow no one to be of another opinion, without, however, grounding our judgment on concepts, but only on our feeling, which we therefore place at its basis, not as a private, but as a communal feeling. Now this common sense cannot be grounded on experience, for it aims at justifying judgments which contain an *ought*. It does not say that everyone *will* agree with my judgment, but that he *ought*. And so common sense, as an example of whose judgment I here put forward my judgment of taste and on account of which I attribute to the latter an *exemplary* validity, is a mere ideal norm, under the supposition of which I have a right to make into a rule for everyone a judgment that accords therewith, as well as the satisfaction in an object expressed in such judgment. For the principle which concerns the agreement of different judging persons, although only subjective, is yet assumed as subjectively universal (an idea necessary for everyone), and thus can claim universal assent (as if it were objective) provided we are sure that we have correctly subsumed [the particulars] under it.

This indeterminate norm of a common sense is actually presupposed by us, as is shown by our claim to lay down judgments of taste. Whether there is in fact such a common sense, as a constitutive principle of the possibility of experience, or whether a yet higher principle of reason makes it only into a regulative principle for producing in us a common sense for higher purposes; whether, therefore, taste is an original and natural faculty or only the idea of an artificial one yet to be acquired, so that a judgment of taste with its assumption of a universal assent in fact is only a requirement of reason for producing such harmony of sentiment; whether the ought, i.e. the objective necessity of the confluence of the feeling of any one man with that of every other, only signifies the possibility of arriving at this accord, and the judgment of taste only affords an example of the application of this principle—these questions we have neither the wish nor the power to investigate as yet; we have now only to resolve the faculty of taste into its elements in order to unite them at last in the idea of a common sense.

Explanation of the Beautiful Resulting from the Fourth Moment

The *beautiful* is that which without any concept is cognized as the object of a *necessary* satisfaction.

GENERAL REMARK ON THE FIRST SECTION OF THE ANALYTIC

If we seek the result of the preceding analysis, we find that everything runs up into this concept of taste—that it is a faculty for judging an object in reference to the imagination's *free conformity to law*. Now, if in the judgment of taste the imagination must be considered in its freedom, it is in the first place not regarded as reproductive, as it is subject to the laws of association, but as productive and spontaneous (as the author of arbitrary forms of possible intuition). And although in the apprehension of a given object of sense it is tied to a definite form of this object and so far has no free play (such as that of poetry), yet it may readily be conceived that the object can furnish it with such a form containing a collection of the manifold as the imagination itself, if it were left free, would project in accordance with the *conformity to law of the understanding* in general. But that the *imaginative power* should be *free* and yet *of itself conformed to law*, i.e. bringing autonomy with it, is a contradiction. The understanding alone gives the law. If, however, the imagination is compelled to proceed according to a definite law, its product in respect of form is determined by concepts as to what it ought to be. But then, as is above shown, the satisfaction is not that in the beautiful, but in the good (in perfection, at any rate in mere formal perfection), and the judgment is not a judgment of taste. Thus only a conformity to law without law and a subjective agreement of imagination with understanding—without an objective agreement, where the representation is referred to a definite concept of an object—will be able to subsist together with the free conformity to law of the understanding (which has also been called purposiveness without purpose) and with the peculiar character of a judgment of taste.

Now geometrically regular figures, such as a circle, a square, a cube, etc., are commonly adduced by critics of taste as the simplest and most indisputable examples of beauty, and yet they are called regular because we can only represent them by regarding them as mere presentations of a definite concept which prescribes the rule for the figure (according to which alone it is possible). One of these two must be wrong, either that judgment of the critic which ascribes beauty to the said figures, or ours which regards purposiveness apart from a concept as requisite for beauty.

Hardly anyone will say that a man must have taste in order that he should find more satisfaction in a circle than in a scrawled outline, in an equilateral and equiangular quadrilateral than in one which is oblique, irregular, and as it were deformed, for this belongs to the ordinary understanding and is not taste at all. Where, e.g., our design is to judge of the size of an area or to make intelligible the relation of the parts of it, when divided, to one another and to the whole, then regular figures and those of the simplest kind are needed, and the satisfaction does not rest immediately on the aspect of the figure, but on its availability for all kinds of possible designs. A room whose walls form oblique angles, or a parterre of this kind, even every violation of symmetry in the figure of animals (e.g. being one-eyed), of buildings, or of flower beds, displeases because it contradicts the purpose of the thing, not only practically in respect of a definite use of it, but also when we pass judgment on it as regards any possible design. This is not the case in the judgment of taste, which when pure combines satisfaction or dissatisfaction—without any reference to its use or to a purpose—with the mere *consideration* of the object.

The regularity which leads to the concept of an object is indeed the indispensable condition (*conditio sine qua non*) for grasping the object in a single representation and determining the manifold in its form. This determination is a purpose in respect of cognition, and in reference to this it is always bound up with satisfaction (which accompanies the execution of every, even problematical, design). There is here, however, merely the approval of the solution satisfying a problem, and not a free and indefinite purposive entertainment of the mental powers with what we call beautiful, where the understanding is at the service of imagination, and not *vice versa*.

In a thing that is only possible by means of design—a building, or even an animal—the regularity consisting in symmetry must express the unity of the intuition that accompanies the concept of purpose, and this regularity belongs to cognition. But where only a free play of the representative powers (under the condition, however, that the understanding is to suffer no shock thereby) is to be kept up, in pleasure gardens, room decorations, all kinds of tasteful furniture, etc., regularity that shows constraint is avoided as much as possible. Thus in the English taste in gardens or in bizarre taste in furniture, the freedom of the imagination is pushed almost near to the grotesque, and in this separation from every constraint of rule we have the case where taste can display its greatest perfection in the enterprises of the imagination.

All stiff regularity (such as approximates to mathematical regularity) has something in it repugnant to taste; for our entertainment in the contemplation of it lasts for no length of time, but it rather, in so far as it has not expressly in view cognition or a definite practical purpose, produces weariness. On the other hand, that with which imagination can play in an unstudied and purposive manner is always new to us, and one does not get tired of looking at it. Marsden, in his description of Sumatra, makes the remark that the free beauties of nature surround the spectator everywhere and thus lose their attraction for him. On the other hand, a pepper garden, where the stakes on which this plant twines itself form parallel rows, had much attractiveness for him if he met with it in the middle of a forest. And he hence infers that wild beauty, apparently irregular, only pleases as a variation from the regular beauty of which one has seen enough. But he need only have made the experiment of spending one day in a pepper garden to have been convinced that, if the understanding has put itself in accordance with the order that it always needs by means of regularity, the object will not entertain for long—nay, rather it will impose a burdensome constraint upon the imagination. On the other hand, nature, which there is prodigal in its variety even to luxuriance, that is subjected to no constraint of artificial rules, can supply constant food for taste. Even the song of birds, which we can bring under no musical rule, seems to have more freedom, and therefore more for taste, than a song of a human being which is produced in accordance with all the rules of music; for we very much sooner weary of the latter if it is repeated often and at length. Here, however, we probably confuse our participation in the mirth of a little creature that we love with the beauty of its song, for if this were exactly imitated by man (as sometimes the notes of the nightingale are), it would seem to our ear quite devoid of taste.

Again, beautiful objects are to be distinguished from beautiful views of objects (which often on account of their distance cannot be more clearly cognized). In the latter case taste appears, not so much in what the imagination *apprehends* in this field, as in the impulse it thus gets to *fiction*, i.e. in the peculiar fancies with which the mind entertains itself, while it is continually being aroused by the variety which strikes the eye. An illustration is afforded, e.g. by the sight of the changing shapes of a fire on the hearth or of a rippling brook; neither of these has beauty, but they bring with them a charm for the imagination because they entertain it in free play.

Second Book

ANALYTIC OF THE SUBLIME

Deduction of [Pure]¹ Aesthetical Judgments

§ 31. *Of the Method of Deduction of Judgments of Taste*

A deduction, i.e. the guarantee of the legitimacy of a class of judgments, is only obligatory if the judgment lays claim to necessity. This it does if it demands even subjective universality or the agreement of everyone, although it is not a judgment of cognition, but only one

---

¹ [Second edition.]

of pleasure or pain in a given object, i.e. it assumes a subjective purposiveness thoroughly valid for everyone, which must not be based on
any concept of the thing, because the judgment is one of taste.

We have before us in the latter case no cognitive judgment—neither a theoretical one based on the concept of a *nature* in general
formed by the understanding, nor a (pure) practical one based on the
idea of *freedom*, as given *a priori* by reason. Therefore we have to
justify *a priori* the validity, neither of a judgment which represents
what a thing is, nor of one which prescribes that I ought to do something in order to produce it. We have merely to prove for the judgment generally the *universal validity* of a singular judgment that expresses the subjective purposiveness of an empirical representation of
the form of an object, in order to explain how it is possible that a
thing can please in the mere act of judging it (without sensation or
concept) and how the satisfaction of one man can be proclaimed as a
rule for every other, just as the act of judging of an object for the sake
of a *cognition* in general has universal rules.

· · · · ·

§ 34. There Is No Objective Principle of Taste Possible

By a principle of taste I mean a principle under the condition of which
we could subsume the concept of an object and thus infer, by means
of a syllogism, that the object is beautiful. But that is absolutely impossible. For I must immediately feel pleasure in the representation
of the object, and of that I can be persuaded by no grounds of proof
whatever. Although, as Hume says, all critics can reason more plausibly
than cooks, yet the same fate awaits them. They cannot expect the
determining ground of their judgment [to be derived] from the force
of the proofs, but only from the reflection of the subject upon its own
proper state (of pleasure or pain), all precepts and rules being rejected.

But although critics can and ought to pursue their reasonings so
that our judgments of taste may be corrected and extended, it is not
with a view to set forth the determining ground of this kind of aesthetical judgments in a universally applicable formula, which is impossible; but rather to investigate the cognitive faculties and their exercise
in these judgments, and to explain by examples the reciprocal subjective purposiveness, the form of which, as has been shown above, in
a given representation, constitutes the beauty of the object.

· · · · ·

§ 36. *Of the Problem of a Deduction of Judgments of Taste*

The concept of an object in general can immediately be combined with the perception of an object, containing its empirical predicates, so as to form a cognitive judgment; and it is thus that a judgment of experience is produced. At the basis of this lie *a priori* concepts of the synthetical unity of the manifold of intuition, by which the manifold is thought as the determination of an object. These concepts (the categories) require a deduction, which is given in the *Critique of Pure Reason*; and by it we can get the solution of the problem: how are synthetical *a priori* cognitive judgments possible? This problem concerns then the *a priori* principles of the pure understanding and its theoretical judgments.

But with a perception there can also be combined a feeling of pleasure (or pain) and a satisfaction, that accompanies the representation of the object and serves instead of its predicate; thus there can result an aesthetical noncognitive judgment. At the basis of such a judgment —if it is not a mere judgment of sensation but a formal judgment of reflection, which imputes the same satisfaction necessarily to everyone —must lie some *a priori* principle, which may be merely subjective (if an objective one should prove impossible for judgments of this kind), but also as such may need a deduction, that we may thereby comprehend how an aesthetical judgment can lay claim to necessity. On this is founded the problem with which we are now occupied: how are judgments of taste possible? This problem, then, has to do with the *a priori* principles of the pure faculty of judgment in *aesthetical* judgments, i.e. judgments in which it has not (as in theoretical ones) merely to subsume under objective concepts of understanding and in which it is subject to a law, but in which it is itself, subjectively, both object and law.

This problem then may be thus represented: how is a judgment possible in which merely from *our own* feeling of pleasure in an object, independently of its concept, we judge that this pleasure attaches to the representation of the same object *in every other subject,* and that *a priori* without waiting for the accordance of others?

It is easy to see that judgments of taste are synthetical, because they go beyond the concept and even beyond the intuition of the object, and add to that intuition as predicate something that is not a cognition, viz. a feeling of pleasure (or pain). Although the predicate (of the *personal* pleasure bound up with the representation) is empirical, nevertheless, as concerns the required assent of *everyone* the judgments are *a priori*, or desire to be regarded as such; and this is already involved in the expressions of this claim. Thus this problem of the *Critique of Judgment* belongs to the general problem of transcendental philosophy: how are synthetical *a priori* judgments possible?

§ 37. *What Is Properly Asserted* a Priori *of an Object in a Judgment of Taste*

That the representation of an object is immediately bound up with pleasure can only be internally perceived; and if we did not wish to indicate anything more than this, it would give a merely empirical judgment. For I cannot combine a definite feeling (of pleasure or pain) with any representation, except where there is at bottom an *a priori* principle in the reason determining the will. In that case the pleasure (in the moral feeling) is the consequence of the principle, but cannot be compared with the pleasure in taste, because it requires a definite concept of a law; and the latter pleasure, on the contrary, must be bound up with the mere act of judging, prior to all concepts. Hence also all judgments of taste are singular judgments, because they do not combine their predicate of satisfaction with a concept, but with a given individual empirical representation.

And so it is not the pleasure, but the *universal validity of this pleasure*, perceived as mentally bound up with the mere judgment upon an object, which is represented *a priori* in a judgment of taste as a universal rule for the judgment and valid for everyone. It is an empirical judgment [to say] that I perceive and judge an object with pleasure. But it is an *a priori* judgment [to say] that I find it beautiful, i.e. I attribute this satisfaction necessarily to everyone.

§ 38. *Deduction of Judgments of Taste*

If it be admitted that, in a pure judgment of taste, the satisfaction in the object is combined with the mere act of judging its form, it is nothing else than its subjective purposiveness for the judgment which we feel to be mentally combined with the representation of the object. The judgment, as regards the formal rules of its action, apart from all matter (whether sensation or concept), can only be directed to the subjective conditions of its employment in general (it is applied [2] neither to a particular mode of sense nor to a particular concept of the understanding), and consequently to that subjective [element]

---

[2] [First edition has "limited."]

which we can presuppose in all men (as requisite for possible cognition in general). Thus the agreement of a representation with these conditions of the judgment must be capable of being assumed as valid *a priori* for everyone. That is, we may rightly impute to everyone the pleasure or the subjective purposiveness of the representation for the relation between the cognitive faculties in the act of judging a sensible object in general.[3]

Remark

This deduction is thus easy, because it has no need to justify the objective reality of any concept, for beauty is not a concept of the object and the judgment of taste is not cognitive. It only maintains that we are justified in presupposing universally in every man those subjective conditions of the judgment which we find in ourselves; and further, that we have rightly subsumed the given object under these conditions. The latter has indeed unavoidable difficulties which do not beset the logical judgment. There we subsume under concepts, but in the aesthetical judgment under a merely sensible relation between the imagination and understanding mutually harmonizing in the representation of the form of the object—in which case the subsumption may easily be deceptive. Yet the legitimacy of the claim of the judgment in counting upon universal assent is not thus annulled; it reduces itself merely to judging as valid for everyone the correctness of the principle from subjective grounds. For as to the difficulty or doubt concerning the correctness of the subsumption under that principle, it makes the legitimacy of the claim of an aesthetical judgment in general to such validity and the principle of the same as little doubtful as the alike (though neither so commonly nor readily) faulty subsumption of the logical judgment under its principle can make the latter, an objective principle, doubtful.

. . . . .

---

[3] In order to be justified in claiming universal assent for an aesthetical judgment that rests merely on subjective grounds, it is sufficient to assume: (1) That the subjective conditions of the judgment, as regards the relation of the cognitive powers thus put into activity to a cognition in general, are the same in all men. This must be true, because otherwise men would not be able to communicate their representations or even their knowledge. (2) The judgment must merely have reference to this relation (consequently to the *formal condition* of the judgment) and be pure, i.e. not mingled either with concepts of the object or with sensations, as determining grounds. If there has been any mistake as regards this latter condition, then there is only an inaccurate application of the privilege, which a law gives us, to a particular case; but that does not destroy the privilege itself in general.

§ 40. *Of Taste as a Kind of* Sensus Communis

We often give to the judgment, if we are considering the result rather than the act of its reflection, the name of a sense, and we speak of a sense of truth, or of a sense of decorum, of justice, etc. And yet we know, or at least we ought to know, that these concepts cannot have their place in sense, and further, that sense has not the least capacity for expressing universal rules; but that no representation of truth, fitness, beauty, or justice, and so forth could come into our thoughts if we could not rise beyond sense to higher faculties of cognition. *The common understanding of men*, which, as the mere healthy (not yet cultivated) understanding, we regard as the least to be expected from anyone claiming the name of man, has therefore the doubtful honor of being given the name of "common sense" (*sensus communis*); and in such a way that, by the name "common" (not merely in our language, where the word actually has a double signification, but in many others), we understand "vulgar," that which is everywhere met with, the possession of which indicates absolutely no merit or superiority.

But under the *sensus communis* we must include the idea of a sense *common to all*, i.e. of a faculty of judgment which, in its reflection, takes account (*a priori*) of the mode of representation of all other men in thought, in order, as it were, to compare its judgment with the collective reason of humanity, and thus to escape the illusion arising from the private conditions that could be so easily taken for objective, which would injuriously affect the judgment. This is done by comparing our judgment with the possible rather than the actual judgments of others, and by putting ourselves in the place of any other man, by abstracting from the limitations which contingently attach to our own judgment. This again is brought about by leaving aside as much as possible the matter of our representative state, i.e. sensation, and simply having respect to the formal peculiarities of our representation or representative state. Now this operation of reflection seems perhaps too artificial to be attributed to the faculty called *common sense*, but it only appears so when expressed in abstract formulae. In itself there is nothing more natural than to abstract from charm or emotion if we are seeking a judgment that is to serve as a universal rule.

· · · · ·

I take up again the threads interrupted by this digression, and I say that taste can be called *sensus communis* with more justice than sound understanding can, and that the aesthetical judgment rather than the intellectual may bear the name of a sense common to all,[4] if we are willing to use the word "sense" of an effect of mere reflection upon the mind, for then we understand by sense the feeling of pleasure. We could even define taste as the faculty of judging of that which makes *universally communicable*, without the mediation of a concept, our feeling in a given representation.

The skill that men have in communicating their thoughts requires also a relation between the imagination and the understanding in order to associate intuitions with concepts, and concepts again with those concepts, which then combine in a cognition. But in that case the agreement of the two mental powers is *according to law*, under the constraint of definite concepts. Only where the imagination in its freedom awakens the understanding and is put by it into regular play, without the aid of concepts, does the representation communicate itself, not as a thought, but as an internal feeling of a purposive state of the mind.

Taste is then the faculty of judging *a priori* of the communicability of feelings that are bound up with a given representation (without the mediation of a concept).

If we could assume that the mere universal communicability of a feeling must carry in itself an interest for us with it (which, however, we are not justified in concluding from the character of a merely reflective judgment), we should be able to explain why the feeling in the judgment of taste comes to be imputed to everyone, so to speak, as a duty.

§ 45. *Beautiful Art Is an Art in So Far as It Seems Like Nature*

In a product of beautiful art, we must become conscious that it is art and not nature; but yet the purposiveness in its form must seem to be as free from all constraint of arbitrary rules as if it were a product of mere nature. On this feeling of freedom in the play of our cognitive faculties, which must at the same time be purposive, rests that pleasure which alone is universally communicable, without being based on concepts. Nature is beautiful because it looks like art, and art can only

---

[4] We may designate taste as *sensus communis aestheticus*, common understanding as *sensus communis logicus*.

be called beautiful if we are conscious of it as art while yet it looks like nature.

For whether we are dealing with natural or with artificial beauty, we can say generally: *That is beautiful which pleases in the mere act of judging it* (not in the sensation of it or by means of a concept). Now art has always a definite design of producing something. But if this something were bare sensation (something merely subjective), which is to be accompanied with pleasure, the product would please in the act of judgment only by mediation of sensible feeling. And again, if the design were directed toward the production of a definite object, then, if this were attained by art, the object would only please by means of concepts. But in both cases the art would not please *in the mere act of judging*, i.e. it would not please as beautiful but as mechanical.

Hence the purposiveness in the product of beautiful art, although it is designed, must not seem to be designed, i.e. beautiful art must *look* like nature, although we are conscious of it as art. But a product of art appears like nature when, although its agreement with the rules, according to which alone the product can become what it ought to be, is *punctiliously* observed, yet this is not *painfully* apparent; [the form of the schools does not obtrude itself] [5]—it shows no trace of the rule having been before the eyes of the artist and having fettered his mental powers.

§ 46. *Beautiful Art Is the Art of Genius*

Genius is the talent (or natural gift) which gives the rule to art. Since talent, as the innate productive faculty of the artist, belongs itself to nature, we may express the matter thus: Genius is the innate mental disposition (*ingenium*) *through which* nature gives the rule to art.

Whatever may be thought of this definition, whether it is merely arbitrary or whether it is adequate to the concept that we are accustomed to combine with the word *genius* (which is to be examined in the following paragraphs), we can prove already beforehand that, according to the signification of the word here adopted, beautiful arts must necessarily be considered as arts of *genius*.

For every art presupposes rules by means of which in the first instance a product, if it is to be called artistic, is represented as possible. But the concept of beautiful art does not permit the judgment upon the beauty of a product to be derived from any rule which has a *con-*

---

[5] [Second edition.]

cept as its determining ground, and therefore has at its basis a concept of the way in which the product is possible. Therefore beautiful art cannot itself devise the rule according to which it can bring about its product. But since at the same time a product can never be called art without some precedent rule, nature in the subject must (by the harmony of its faculties) give the rule to art; i.e. beautiful art is only possible as a product of genius.

We thus see (1) that genius is a *talent* for producing that for which no definite rule can be given; it is not a mere aptitude for what can be learned by a rule. Hence *originality* must be its first property. (2) But since it also can produce original nonsense, its products must be models, i.e. *exemplary*, and they consequently ought not to spring from imitation, but must serve as a standard or rule of judgment for others. (3) It cannot describe or indicate scientifically how it brings about its products, but it gives the rule just as nature does. Hence the author of a product for which he is indebted to his genius does not know himself how he has come by his ideas; and he has not the power to devise the like at pleasure or in accordance with a plan, and to communicate it to others in precepts that will enable them to produce similar products. (Hence it is probable that the word "genius" is derived from *genius*, that peculiar guiding and guardian spirit given to a man at his birth, from whose suggestion these original ideas proceed.) (4) Nature, by the medium of genius, does not prescribe rules to science but to art, and to it only in so far as it is to be beautiful art.

§ 48. *Of the Relation of Genius to Taste*

For *judging* of beautiful objects as such, *taste* is requisite; but for beautiful art, i.e. for the *production* of such objects, *genius* is requisite.

If we consider genius as the talent for beautiful art (which the special meaning of the word implies) and in this point of view analyze it into the faculties which must concur to constitute such a talent, it is necessary in the first instance to determine exactly the difference between natural beauty, the judging of which requires only taste, and artificial beauty, the possibility of which (to which reference must be made in judging such an object) requires genius.

A natural beauty is a *beautiful thing*; artificial beauty is a *beautiful representation* of a thing.

In order to judge of a natural beauty as such, I need not have beforehand a concept of what sort of thing the object is to be; i.e. I need not know its material purposiveness (the purpose), but its mere form pleases by itself in the act of judging it without any knowledge of the purpose. But if the object is given as a product of art and as such is to be declared beautiful, then, because art always supposes a purpose in the cause (and its causality), there must be at bottom in the first instance a concept of what the thing is to be. And as the agreement of the manifold in a thing with its inner destination, its purpose, constitutes the perfection of the thing, it follows that in judging of artificial beauty the perfection of the thing must be taken into account; but in judging of natural beauty (as *such*) there is no question at all about this. It is true that in judging of objects of nature, especially objects endowed with life, e.g. a man or a horse, their objective purposiveness also is commonly taken into consideration in judging of their beauty; but then the judgment is no longer purely aesthetical, i.e. a mere judgment of taste. Nature is no longer judged inasmuch as it appears like art, but in so far as it *is* actual (although superhuman) art; and the teleological judgment serves as the basis and condition of the aesthetical, as a condition to which the latter must have respect. In such a case, e.g. if it is said "That is a beautiful woman," we think nothing else than this: nature represents in her figure the purposes in view in the shape of a woman's figure. For we must look beyond the mere form to a concept, if the object is to be thought in such a way by means of a logically conditioned aesthetical judgment.

Beautiful art shows its superiority in this, that it describes as beautiful things which may be in nature ugly or displeasing. The Furies, diseases, the devastations of war, etc., may [even regarded as calamitous] [6] be described as very beautiful, as they are represented in a picture. There is only one kind of ugliness which cannot be represented in accordance with nature without destroying all aesthetical satisfaction, and consequently artificial beauty, viz. that which excites *disgust*. For in this singular sensation, which rests on mere imagination, the object is represented as it were obtruding itself for our enjoyment, while we strive against it with all our might. And the artistic representation of the object is no longer distinguished from the nature of the object itself in our sensation, and thus it is impossible that it can be regarded as beautiful. The art of sculpture again, because in its products art is almost interchangeable with nature, excludes from its creations the immediate representation of ugly objects; e.g. it represents death by a beautiful genius, the warlike spirit by Mars, and permits [all such things] to be represented only by an allegory or attribute that has a pleasing effect, and thus only indirectly by the aid of

---

[6] [Second edition.]

the interpretation of reason, and not for the mere aesthetical judgment.

So much for the beautiful representation of an object, which is properly only the form of the presentation of a concept, by means of which this latter is communicated universally. But to give this form to the product of beautiful art, mere taste is requisite. By taste the artist estimates his work after he has exercised and corrected it by manifold examples from art or nature, and after many, often toilsome, attempts to content himself he finds that form which satisfies him. Hence this form is not, as it were, a thing of inspiration or the result of a free swing of the mental powers, but of a slow and even painful process of improvement, by which he seeks to render it adequate to his thought, without detriment to the freedom of the play of his powers.

But taste is merely a judging and not a productive faculty, and what is appropriate to it is therefore not a work of beautiful art. It can only be a product belonging to useful and mechanical art or even to science, produced according to definite rules that can be learned and must be exactly followed. But the pleasing form that is given to it is only the vehicle of communication and a mode, as it were, of presenting it, in respect of which we remain free to a certain extent, although it is combined with a definite purpose. Thus we desire that table appointments, a moral treatise, even a sermon, should have in themselves this form of beautiful art, without it seeming to be *sought*; but we do not therefore call these things works of beautiful art. Under the latter class are reckoned a poem, a piece of music, a picture gallery, etc.; and in some works of this kind asserted to be works of beautiful art we find genius without taste, while in others we find taste without genius.

§ 49. *Of the Faculties of the Mind That Constitute Genius*

We say of certain products of which we expect that they should at least in part appear as beautiful art, they are without *spirit*, although we find nothing to blame in them on the score of taste. A poem may be very neat and elegant, but without spirit. A history may be exact and well arranged, but without spirit. A festal discourse may be solid and at the same time elaborate, but without spirit. Conversation is often not devoid of entertainment, but yet without spirit; even of a woman we say that she is pretty, an agreeable talker, and courteous, but without spirit. What then do we mean by spirit?

Spirit, in an aesthetical sense, is the name given to the animating principle of the mind. But that by means of which this principle animates the soul, the material which it applies to that [purpose], is what puts the mental powers purposively into swing, i.e. into such a play as maintains itself and strengthens the mental powers in their exercise.

Now I maintain that this principle is no other than the faculty of presenting *aesthetical ideas*. And by an aesthetical idea I understand that representation of the imagination which occasions much thought, without however any definite thought, i.e. any *concept*, being capable of being adequate to it; it consequently cannot be completely compassed and made intelligible by language. We easily see that it is the counterpart (pendant) of a *rational idea*, which conversely is a concept to which no *intuition* (or representation of the imagination) can be adequate.

The imagination (as a productive faculty of cognition) is very powerful in creating another nature, as it were, out of the material that actual nature gives it. We entertain ourselves with it when experience becomes too commonplace, and by it we remold experience, always indeed in accordance with analogical laws, but yet also in accordance with principles which occupy a higher place in reason (laws, too, which are just as natural to us as those by which understanding comprehends empirical nature). Thus we feel our freedom from the law of association (which attaches to the empirical employment of imagination), so that the material supplied to us by nature in accordance with this law can be worked up into something different which surpasses nature.

Such representations of the imagination we may call *ideas*, partly because they at least strive after something which lies beyond the bounds of experience and so seek to approximate to a presentation of concepts of reason (intellectual ideas), thus giving to the latter the appearance of objective reality, but especially because no concept can be fully adequate to them as internal intuitions. The poet ventures to realize to sense, rational ideas of invisible beings, the kingdom of the blessed, hell, eternity, creation, etc.; or even if he deals with things of which there are examples in experience—e.g. death, envy and all vices, also love, fame, and the like—he tries, by means of imagination, which emulates the play of reason in its quest after a maximum, to go beyond the limits of experience and to present them to sense with a completeness of which there is no example in nature. This is properly speaking the art of the poet, in which the faculty of aesthetical ideas can manifest itself in its entire strength. But this faculty, considered in itself, is properly only a talent (of the imagination).

If now we place under a concept a representation of the imagination belonging to its presentation, but which occasions in itself more thought than can ever be comprehended in a definite concept and which consequently aesthetically enlarges the concept itself in an unbounded fashion, the imagination is here creative, and it brings the faculty of intellectual ideas (the reason) into movement; i.e. by a representation more thought (which indeed belongs to the concept of the object) is occasioned than can in it be grasped or made clear.

Those forms which do not constitute the presentation of a given concept itself but only, as approximate representations of the imagination, express the consequences bound up with it and its relationship to other concepts, are called (aesthetical) *attributes* of an object whose concept as a rational idea cannot be adequately presented. Thus Jupiter's eagle with the lightning in its claws is an attribute of the mighty king of heaven, as the peacock is of his magnificent queen. They do not, like *logical attributes*, represent what lies in our concepts of the sublimity and majesty of creation, but something different, which gives occasion to the imagination to spread itself over a number of kindred representations that arouse more thought than can be expressed in a concept determined by words. They furnish an *aesthetical idea*, which for that rational idea takes the place of logical presentation; and thus, as their proper office, they enliven the mind by opening out to it the prospect into an illimitable field of kindred representations. But beautiful art does this not only in the case of painting or sculpture (in which the term "attribute" is commonly employed); poetry and rhetoric also get the spirit that animates their works simply from the aesthetical attributes of the object, which accompany the logical and stimulate the imagination, so that it thinks more by their aid, although in an undeveloped way, than could be comprehended in a concept and therefore in a definite form of words. For the sake of brevity, I must limit myself to a few examples only.

When the great King in one of his poems expresses himself as follows:

> Oui, finissons sans trouble et mourons sans regrets,
> En laissant l'univers comblé de nos bienfaits.
> Ainsi l'astre du jour au bout de sa carrière,
> Répand sur l'horizon une douce lumière;
> Et les derniers rayons qu'il darde dans les airs,
> Sont les derniers soupirs qu'il donne à l'univers;

he quickens his rational idea of a cosmopolitan disposition at the end of life by an attribute which the imagination (in remembering all the pleasures of a beautiful summer day that are recalled at its close by a serene evening) associates with that representation, and which excites a number of sensations and secondary representations for which no expression is found. On the other hand, an intellectual concept may serve conversely as an attribute for a representation of sense, and so can quicken this latter by means of the idea of the supersensible, but only by the aesthetical [element], that subjectively attaches to the concept of the latter, being here employed. Thus, for example, a certain poet says, in his description of a beautiful morning:

> The sun arose
> As calm from virtue springs.

The consciousness of virtue, if we substitute it in our thoughts for a virtuous man, diffuses in the mind a multitude of sublime and restful feelings, and a boundless prospect of a joyful future, to which no expression that is measured by a definite concept completely attains.[7]

In a word, the aesthetical idea is a representation of the imagination associated with a given concept, which is bound up with such a multiplicity of partial representations in its free employment that for it no expression marking a definite concept can be found; and such a representation, therefore, adds to a concept much ineffable thought, the feeling of which quickens the cognitive faculties, and with language, which is the mere letter, binds up spirit also.

The mental powers, therefore, whose union (in a certain relation) constitutes genius are imagination and understanding. In the employment of the imagination for cognition, it submits to the constraint of the understanding and is subject to the limitation of being conformable to the concept of the latter. On the contrary, in an aesthetical point of view it is free to furnish unsought, over and above that agreement with a concept, abundance of undeveloped material for the understanding, to which the understanding paid no regard in its concept but which it applies, though not objectively for cognition, yet subjectively to quicken the cognitive powers and therefore also indirectly to cognitions. Thus genius properly consists in the happy relation [between these faculties], which no science can teach and no industry

---

[7] Perhaps nothing more sublime was ever said and no sublimer thought ever expressed than the famous inscription on the Temple of Isis (Mother Nature): "I am all that is and that was and that shall be, and no mortal hath lifted my veil." Segner availed himself of this idea in a *suggestive* vignette prefixed to his *Natural Philosophy*, in order to inspire beforehand the pupil whom he was about to lead into that temple with a holy awe, which should dispose his mind to serious attention.

can learn, by which ideas are found for a given concept; and, on the other hand, we thus find for these ideas the expression by means of which the subjective state of mind brought about by them, as an accompaniment of the concept, can be communicated to others. The latter talent is, properly speaking, what is called spirit; for to express the ineffable element in the state of mind implied by a certain representation and to make it universally communicable—whether the expression be in speech or painting or statuary—this requires a faculty of seizing the quickly passing play of imagination and of unifying it in a concept (which is even on that account original and discloses a new rule that could not have been inferred from any preceding principles or examples) that can be communicated without any constraint [of rules].[8]

If, after this analysis, we look back to the explanation given above of what is called *genius*, we find: first, that it is a talent for art, not for science, in which clearly known rules must go beforehand and determine the procedure. Secondly, as an artistic talent it presupposes a definite concept of the product as the purpose, and therefore understanding; but it also presupposes a representation (although an indeterminate one) of the material, i.e. of the intuition, for the presentment of this concept, and, therefore, a relation between the imagination and the understanding. Thirdly, it shows itself, not so much in the accomplishment of the proposed purpose in a presentment of a definite concept, as in the enunciation or expression of aesthetical ideas which contain abundant material for that very design; and consequently it represents the imagination as free from all guidance of rules and yet as purposive in reference to the presentment of the given concept. Finally, in the fourth place, the unsought undesigned subjective purposiveness in the free accordance of the imagination with the legality of the understanding presupposes such a proportion and disposition of these faculties as no following of rules, whether of science or of mechanical imitation, can bring about, but which only the nature of the subject can produce.

In accordance with these suppositions, genius is the exemplary originality of the natural gifts of a subject in the *free* employment of his cognitive faculties. In this way the product of a genius (as regards what is to be ascribed to genius and not to possible learning or schooling) is an example, not to be imitated (for then that which in it is genius and constitutes the spirit of the work would be lost), but to

---

[8] [Second edition.]

be followed by another genius, whom it awakens to a feeling of his own originality and whom it stirs so to exercise his art in freedom from the constraint of rules, that thereby a new rule is gained for art; and thus his talent shows itself to be exemplary. But because a genius is a favorite of nature and must be regarded by us as a rare phenomenon, his example produces for other good heads a school, i.e. a methodical system of teaching according to rules, so far as these can be derived from the peculiarities of the products of his spirit. For such persons beautiful art is so far imitation, to which nature through the medium of a genius supplied the rule.

· · · · ·

§ 50. *Of the Combination of Taste with Genius in the Products of Beautiful Art*

To ask whether it is more important for the things of beautiful art that genius or taste should be displayed is the same as to ask whether in it more depends on imagination or on judgment. Now since in respect of the first an art is rather said to be *full of spirit,* but only deserves to be called a *beautiful* art on account of the second, this latter is at least, as its indispensable condition (*conditio sine qua non*), the most important thing to which one has to look in the judging of art as beautiful art. Abundance and originality of ideas are less necessary to beauty than the accordance of the imagination in its freedom with the conformity to law of the understanding. For all the abundance of the former produces in lawless freedom nothing but nonsense; on the other hand, the judgment is the faculty by which it is adjusted to the understanding.

Taste, like the judgment in general, is the discipline (or training) of genius; it clips its wings, it makes it cultured and polished; but, at the same time, it gives guidance as to where and how far it may extend itself if it is to remain purposive. And while it brings clearness and order into the multitude of the thoughts [of genius], it makes the ideas susceptible of being permanently and, at the same time, universally assented to, and capable of being followed by others, and of an ever progressive culture. If, then, in the conflict of these two properties in a product something must be sacrificed, it should be rather on the side of genius; and the judgment, which in the things of beautiful art gives its decision from its own proper principles, will rather sacrifice the freedom and wealth of the imagination than permit anything prejudicial to the understanding.

For beautiful art, therefore, *imagination, understanding, spirit,* and *taste* are requisite.[9]

§ 51. *Of the Division of the Beautiful Arts*

We may describe beauty in general (whether natural or artificial) as the expression of aesthetical ideas; only that in beautiful art this idea must be occasioned by a concept of the object, while in beautiful nature the mere reflection upon a given intuition, without any concept of what the object is to be, is sufficient for the awakening and communicating of the idea of which that object is regarded as the expression.

If, then, we wish to make a division of the beautiful arts, we cannot choose a more convenient principle, at least tentatively, than the analogy of art with the mode of expression of which men avail themselves in speech, in order to communicate to one another as perfectly as possible not merely their concepts but also their sensations.[10] This is done by *word, deportment,* and *tone* (articulation, gesticulation, and modulation). It is only by the combination of these three kinds of expression that communication between the speaker [and his hearers] can be complete. For thus thought, intuition, and sensation are transmitted to others simultaneously and conjointly.

There are, therefore, only three kinds of beautiful arts: the arts of *speech,* the *formative* arts, and the art of the *play of sensations* (as external sensible impressions). We may also arrange a division by dichotomy: thus beautiful art may be divided into the art of expression of thoughts and of intuitions, and these further subdivided in accordance with their form or their matter (sensation). But this would appear to be too abstract, and not so accordant with ordinary concepts.

(1) The arts of speech are *rhetoric* and *poetry. Rhetoric* is the art of carrying on a serious business of the understanding as if it were a free play of the imagination; *poetry,* the art of conducting a free play of the imagination as if it were a serious business of the understanding.

---

[9] The three former faculties are *united* in the first instance by means of the fourth. Hume gives us to understand in his *History of England* that although the English are inferior in their productions to no people in the world as regards the evidences they display of the three former properties, *separately* considered, yet they must be put after their neighbors the French as regards that which unites these properties.

[10] The reader is not to judge this scheme for a possible division of the beautiful arts as a deliberate theory. It is only one of various attempts which we may and ought to devise.

The *orator*, then, promises a serious business, and in order to entertain his audience conducts it as if it were a mere *play* with ideas. The *poet* merely promises an entertaining play with ideas, and yet it has the same effect upon the understanding as if he had only intended to carry on its business. The combination and harmony of both cognitive faculties, sensibility and understanding, which cannot dispense with each other but which yet cannot well be united without constraint and mutual prejudice, must appear to be undesigned and so to be brought about by themselves; otherwise it is not *beautiful* art. Hence, all that is studied and anxious must be avoided in it, for beautiful art must be free art in a double sense. It is not a work like a mercenary employment, the greatness of which can be judged according to a definite standard, which can be attained or paid for; and again, though the mind is here occupied, it feels itself thus contented and aroused without looking to any other purpose (independently of reward).

The orator therefore gives something which he does not promise, viz. an entertaining play of the imagination; but he also fails to supply what he did promise, which is indeed his announced business, viz. the purposive occupation of the understanding. On the other hand, the poet promises little and announces a mere play with ideas; but he supplies something which is worth occupying ourselves with, because he provides in this play food for the understanding and, by the aid of imagination, gives life to his concepts. [Thus the orator on the whole gives less, the poet more, than he promises.] [11]

(2) The formative arts, or those by which expression is found for ideas in *sensible intuition* (not by representations of mere imagination that are aroused by words), are either arts of *sensible truth* or of *sensible illusion*. The former is called *plastic*, the latter *painting*. Both express ideas by figures in space: the former makes figures cognizable by two senses, sight and touch (although not by the latter as far as beauty is concerned); the latter only by one, the first of these. The aesthetical idea (the archetype or original image) is fundamental for both in the imagination, but the figure which expresses this (the ectype or copy) is either given in its bodily extension (as the object itself exists) or as it paints itself on the eye (according to its appearance when projected on a flat surface). In the first case the condition given to reflection may be either the reference to an actual purpose or only the semblance of it.

---

[11] [Second edition.]

To *plastic*, the first kind of beautiful formative art, belong *sculpture* and *architecture*. The first presents corporeally concepts of things, *as they might have existed in nature* (though as beautiful art it has regard to aesthetical purposiveness). The second is the art of presenting concepts of things that are possible *only through art* and whose form has for its determining ground, not nature, but an arbitrary purpose, with the view of presenting them with aesthetical purposiveness. In the latter the chief point is a certain *use* of the artistic object, by which condition the aesthetical ideas are limited. In the former the main design is the mere *expression* of aesthetical ideas. Thus statues of men, gods, animals, etc., are of the first kind; but temples, splendid buildings for public assemblies, even dwelling houses, triumphal arches, columns, mausoleums, and the like, erected in honorable remembrance, belong to architecture. Indeed all house furniture (upholsterer's work and such like things which are for use) may be reckoned under this art, because the suitability of a product for a certain use is the essential thing in an *architectural work*. On the other hand, a mere *piece of sculpture*, which is simply made for show and which is to please in itself, is as a corporeal presentation a mere imitation of nature, though with a reference to aesthetical ideas; in it *sensible truth* is not to be carried so far that the product ceases to look like art and looks like a product of the elective will.

Painting, as the second kind of formative art, which presents a *sensible illusion* artificially combined with ideas, I would divide into the art of the beautiful *depicting of nature* and that of the beautiful *arrangement of its products*. The first is *painting proper*, the second is the art of *landscape gardening*. The first gives only the illusory appearance of corporeal extension; the second gives this in accordance with truth, but only the appearance of utility and availableness for other purposes than the mere play of the imagination in the contemplation of its forms.[12] This latter is nothing else than the ornamenta-

---

[12] That landscape gardening may be regarded as a species of the art of painting, although it presents its forms corporeally, seems strange. But since it actually takes its forms from nature (trees, shrubs, grasses, and flowers from forest and field—at least in the first instance) and so far is not an art like plastic, and since it also has no concept of the object and its purpose (as in architecture) conditioning its arrangements, but involves merely the free play of the imagination in contemplation, it so far agrees with mere aesthetical painting which has no definite theme (which arranges sky, land, and water so as to entertain us by means of light and shade only). In general the reader is only to judge of this as an attempt to combine the beautiful arts under one principle, viz. that of the expression of aesthetical ideas (according to the analogy of speech), and not to regard it as a definitive analysis of them.

tion of the soil with a variety of those things (grasses, flowers, shrubs, trees, even ponds, hillocks, and dells) which nature presents to an observer, only arranged differently and in conformity with certain ideas. But, again, the beautiful arrangement of corporeal things is only apparent to the eye, like painting; the sense of touch cannot supply any intuitive presentation of such a form. Under painting in the wide sense I would reckon the decoration of rooms by the aid of tapestry, bric-a-brac, and all beautiful furniture which is merely available to be *looked* at; and the same may be said of the art of tasteful dressing (with rings, snuffboxes, etc.). For a bed of various flowers, a room filled with various ornaments (including under this head even ladies' finery), make at a fête a kind of picture which, like pictures properly so called (that are not intended to *teach* either history or natural science), has in view merely the entertainment of the imagination in free play with ideas and the occupation of the aesthetical judgment without any definite purpose. The detailed work in all this decoration may be quite distinct in the different cases and may require very different artists, but the judgment of taste upon whatever is beautiful in these various arts is always determined in the same way, viz. it only judges the forms (without any reference to a purpose) as they present themselves to the eye, either singly or in combination, according to the effect they produce upon the imagination. But that formative art may be compared (by analogy) with deportment in speech is justified by the fact that the spirit of the artist supplies by these figures a bodily expression to his thought and its mode, and makes the thing itself, as it were, speak in mimic language. This is a very common play of our fancy, which attributes to lifeless things a spirit suitable to their form by which they speak to us.

(3) The art of the beautiful play of sensations (externally stimulated), which admits at the same time of universal communication, can be concerned with nothing else than the proportion of the different degrees of the disposition (tension) of the sense to which the sensation belongs, i.e. with its tone. In this far-reaching signification of the word it may be divided into the artistic play of the sensations of hearing and sight, i.e. into *music* and the *art of color*. It is noteworthy that these two senses, beside their susceptibility for impressions so far as these are needed to gain concepts of external objects, are also capable of a peculiar sensation bound up therewith of which we cannot strictly decide whether it is based on sense or reflection. This susceptibility may sometimes be wanting, although in other re-

spects the sense, as regards its use for the cognition of objects, is not at all deficient but is peculiarly fine. That is, we cannot say with certainty whether colors or tones (sounds) are merely pleasant sensations or whether they form in themselves a beautiful play of sensations, and as such bring with them in aesthetical judgment a satisfaction in the form [of the object]. If we think of the velocity of the vibrations of light or in the second case of the air, which probably far surpasses all our faculty of judging immediately in perception the time interval between them, we must believe that it is only the *effect* of these vibrations upon the elastic parts of our body that is felt, but that the *time interval* between them is not remarked or brought into judgment; and thus that only pleasantness, and not beauty of composition, is bound up with colors and tones. But on the other hand, first, we think of the mathematical [element] which enables us to pronounce on the proportion between these oscillations in music and thus to judge of them; and by analogy with which we easily may judge of the distinctions between colors. Secondly, we recall instances (although they are rare) of men who, with the best sight in the world, cannot distinguish colors and, with the sharpest hearing, cannot distinguish tones; while for those who can do this the perception of an altered quality (not merely of the degree of sensation) in the different intensities in the scale of colors and tones is definite; and further, the very number of these is fixed by *intelligible* differences. Thus we may be compelled to see that both kinds of sensations are to be regarded, not as mere sensible impressions, but as the effects of a judgment passed upon the form in the play of divers sensations. The difference in our definition, according as we adopt the one or the other opinion in judging of the grounds of music, would be just this: either, as we have done, we must explain it as the beautiful play of sensations (of hearing), or else as a play of *pleasant* sensations. According to the former mode of explanation, music is represented altogether as a *beautiful* art; according to the latter, as a *pleasant* art (at least in part).

§ 53. Comparison of the Respective Aesthetical Worth of the Beautiful Arts

Of all the arts *poetry* (which owes its origin almost entirely to genius and will least be guided by precept or example) maintains the first rank. It expands the mind by setting the imagination at liberty and by offering, within the limits of a given concept, amid the unbounded variety of possible forms according therewith, that which unites the presentment of this concept with a wealth of thought to which no verbal expression is completely adequate, and so rising aesthetically to ideas. It strengthens the mind by making it feel its faculty—free, spontaneous, and independent of natural determination—of considering and judging nature as a phenomenon in accordance with aspects which it does not present in experience either for sense or understanding, and therefore of using it on behalf of, and as a sort of schema for, the supersensible. It plays with illusion, which it produces at pleasure, but without deceiving by it; for it declares its exercise to be mere play, which however can be purposively used by the understanding. Rhetoric, in so far as this means the art of persuasion, i.e. of deceiving by a beautiful show (*ars oratoria*), and not mere elegance of speech (eloquence and style), is a dialectic which borrows from poetry only so much as is needful to win minds to the side of the orator before they have formed a judgment and to deprive them of their freedom; it cannot therefore be recommended either for the law courts or for the pulpit. For if we are dealing with civil law, with the rights of individual persons, or with lasting instruction and determination of people's minds to an accurate knowledge and a conscientious observance of their duty, it is unworthy of so important a business to allow a trace of any luxuriance of wit and imagination to appear, and still less any trace of the art of talking people over and of captivating them for the advantage of any chance person. For although this art may sometimes be directed to legitimate and praiseworthy designs, it becomes objectionable when in this way maxims and dispositions are spoiled in a subjective point of view, though the action may objectively be lawful. It is not enough to do what is right; we should practice it solely on the ground that it is right. Again, the mere concept of this species of matters of human concern, when clear and combined with a lively presentation of it in examples, without any offense against the rules of euphony of speech or propriety of expression, has by itself for ideas of reason (which collectively constitute eloquence) sufficient influence upon human minds; so that it is not needful to add the machinery of persuasion, which, since it can be used equally well to beautify or to hide vice and error, cannot quite lull the secret suspicion that one is being artfully overreached. In poetry everything procceds with honesty and candor. It declares itself to be a mere entertaining play of the imagination, which wishes to proceed as regards form in harmony with the laws of the understanding;

and it does not desire to steal upon and ensnare the understanding by the aid of sensible presentation.[13]

After poetry, *if we are to deal with charm and mental movement,* I would place that art which comes nearest to the art of speech and can very naturally be united with it, viz, *the art of tone.* For although it speaks by means of mere sensations without concepts, and so does not, like poetry, leave anything over for reflection, it yet moves the mind in a greater variety of ways and more intensely, although only transitorily. It is, however, rather enjoyment than cultivation (the further play of thought that is excited by its means is merely the effect of a kind of mechanical association), and in the judgment of reason it has less worth than any other of the beautiful arts. Hence, like all enjoyment, it desires constant change and does not bear frequent repetition without producing weariness. Its charm, which admits of universal communication, appears to rest on this that every expression of speech has in its context a tone appropriate to the sense. This tone indicates more or less an affection of the speaker and produces it also in the hearer, which affection excites in its turn in the hearer the idea that is expressed in speech by the tone in question. Thus as modulation is, as it were, a universal language of sensations intelligible to every man, the art of tone employs it by itself alone in its full force, viz. as language of the affections, and thus communicates universally according to the laws of association the aesthetical ideas naturally combined therewith. Now these aesthetical ideas are not concepts or determinate thoughts. Hence the form of the composition of these sensations (har-

---

[13] I must admit that a beautiful poem has always given me a pure gratification, while the reading of the best discourse, whether of a Roman orator or of a modern parliamentary speaker or of a preacher, has always been mingled with an unpleasant feeling of disapprobation of a treacherous art which means to move men in important matters like machines to a judgment that must lose all weight for them on quiet reflection. Readiness and accuracy in speaking (which taken together constitute rhetoric) belong to beautiful art, but the art of the orator (*ars oratoria*), the art of availing oneself of the weaknesses of men for one's own designs (whether these be well meant or even actually good does not matter), is worthy of no *respect*. Again, this art only reached its highest point, both at Athens and at Rome at a time when the state was hastening to its ruin and true patriotic sentiment had disappeared. The man who, along with a clear insight into things, has in his power a wealth of pure speech, and who with a fruitful imagination capable of presenting his ideas unites a lively sympathy with what is truly good, is the *vir bonus dicendi peritus,* the orator without art but of great impressiveness, as Cicero has it, though he may not always remain true to this ideal.

mony and melody) only serves instead of the form of language, by means of their proportionate accordance, to express the aesthetical idea of a connected whole of an unspeakable wealth of thought, corresponding to a certain theme which produces the dominating affection in the piece. This can be brought mathematically under certain rules, because it rests in the case of tones on the relation between the number of vibrations of the air in the same time, so far as these tones are combined simultaneously or successively. To this mathematical form, although not represented by determinate concepts, alone attaches the satisfaction that unites the mere reflection upon such a number of concomitant or consecutive sensations with this their play, as a condition of its beauty valid for every man. It is this alone which permits taste to claim in advance a rightful authority over everyone's judgment.

But in the charm and mental movement produced by music, mathematics has certainly not the slightest share. It is only the indispensable condition (*conditio sine qua non*) of that proportion of the impressions in their combination and in their alternation by which it becomes possible to gather them together and prevent them from destroying each other, and to harmonize them so as to produce a continual movement and animation of the mind, by means of affections consonant therewith, and thus a delightful personal enjoyment.

If, on the other hand, we estimate the worth of the beautiful arts by the culture they supply to the mind and take as a standard the expansion of the faculties which must concur in the judgment for cognition, music will have the lowest place among them (as it has perhaps the highest among those arts which are valued for their pleasantness), because it merely plays with sensations. The formative arts are far before it in this point of view, for in putting the imagination in a free play, which is also accordant with the understanding, they at the same time carry on a serious business. This they do by producing a product that serves for concepts as a permanent self-commendatory vehicle for promoting their union with sensibility and thus, as it were, the urbanity of the higher cognitive powers. These two species of art take quite different courses; the first proceeds from sensations to indeterminate ideas, the second from determinate ideas to sensations. The latter produce *permanent*, the former only *transitory* impressions. The imagination can recall the one and entertain itself pleasantly therewith; but the other either vanish entirely, or, if they are recalled involuntarily by the imagination, they are rather wearisome than pleasant.[14] Besides, there attaches to music a certain want of urbanity from the fact that, chiefly from the character of its instruments, it extends its influence further than is desired (in the neighborhood), and so as it were obtrudes itself and does violence to the freedom of others who are not of the musical company. The arts which appeal to the eyes do not do this, for we need only turn our eyes away if we wish to avoid being impressed. The case of music is almost like that of the delight derived from a smell that diffuses itself widely. The man who pulls his perfumed handkerchief out of his pocket attracts the attention of all around him, even against their will, and he forces them, if they are to breathe at all, to enjoy the scent; hence this habit has gone out of fashion.[15]

Among the formative arts I would give the palm to painting, partly because as the art of delineation it lies at the root of all the other formative arts, and partly because it can penetrate much further into the region of ideas and can extend the field of intuition in conformity with them further than the others can.

SECOND DIVISION

DIALECTIC OF THE AESTHETICAL JUDGMENT

§ 55

A faculty of judgment that is to be dialectical must in the first place be rationalizing, i.e. its judgments must claim universality[1] and that *a priori*, for it is in the opposition of such judgments that dialectic consists. Hence the incompatibility of aesthetical judgments of sense (about the pleasant and the unpleasant) is not dialectical. And again, the conflict between judgments of taste, so far as each man depends merely on his own taste, forms no dialectic of taste, because no one

---

[14] [From this to the end of the paragraph, and the next note, were added in the second edition.]

[15] Those who recommend the singing of spiritual songs at family prayers do not consider that they inflict a great hardship upon the public by such *noisy* (and therefore in general pharisaical) devotions, for they force the neighbors either to sing with them or to abandon meditations.

[1] We may describe as a rationalizing judgment (*judicium ratiocinans*) one which proclaims itself as universal, for as such it can serve as the major premise of a syllogism. On the other hand, we can only speak of a judgment as rational (*judicium ratiocinatum*) which is thought as the conclusion of a syllogism, and consequently as grounded *a priori*.

proposes to make his own judgment a universal rule. There remains, therefore, no other concept of a dialectic which has to do with taste than that of a dialectic of the critique of taste (not of taste itself) in respect of its *principles*, for here concepts that contradict one another (as to the ground of the possibility of judgments of taste in general) naturally and unavoidably present themselves. The Transcendental Critique of Taste will therefore contain a part which can bear the name of a Dialectic of the Aesthetical Judgment, only if and so far as there is found an antinomy of the principles of this faculty which renders its conformity to law, and consequently also its internal possibility, doubtful.

§ 56. *Representation of the Antinomy of Taste*

The first commonplace of taste is contained in the proposition, with which every tasteless person proposes to avoid blame: *everyone has his own taste.* That is as much as to say that the determining ground of this judgment is merely subjective (gratification or grief), and that the judgment has no right to the necessary assent of others.

The second commonplace invoked even by those who admit for judgments of taste the right to speak with validity for everyone is: *there is no disputing about taste.* That is as much as to say that the determining ground of a judgment of taste may indeed be objective, but that it cannot be reduced to definite concepts; and that consequently about the judgment itself nothing can be *decided* by proofs, although much may rightly be *contested.* For *contesting* [quarreling] and *disputing* [controversy] are doubtless the same in this, that, by means of the mutual opposition of judgments they seek to produce their accordance, but different in that the latter hopes to bring this about according to definite concepts as determining grounds, and consequently assumes *objective concepts* as grounds of the judgment. But where this is regarded as impracticable, controversy is regarded as alike impracticable.

We easily see that, between these two commonplaces, there is a proposition wanting which, though it has not passed into a proverb, is yet familiar to everyone, viz. *there may be a quarrel about taste* (although there can be no controversy). But this proposition involves the contradictory of the former one. For wherever quarreling is permissible, there must be a hope of mutual reconciliation; and consequently we can count on grounds of our judgment that have not merely private validity, and therefore are not merely subjective. And to this the proposition, *everyone has his own taste,* is directly opposed.

There emerges therefore in respect of the principle of taste the following antinomy:

(1) *Thesis.* The judgment of taste is not based upon concepts, for otherwise it would admit of controversy (would be determinable by proofs).

(2) *Antithesis.* The judgment of taste is based on concepts, for otherwise, despite its diversity, we could not quarrel about it (we could not claim for our judgment the necessary assent of others).

§ 57. Solution of the Antinomy of Taste

There is no possibility of removing the conflict between these principles that underlie every judgment of taste . . . except by showing that the concept to which we refer the object in this kind of judgment is not taken in the same sense in both maxims of the aesthetical judgment. This twofold sense or twofold point of view is necessary to our transcendental judgment, but also the illusion which arises from the confusion of one with the other is natural and unavoidable.

The judgment of taste must refer to some concept; otherwise it could make absolutely no claim to be necessarily valid for everyone. But it is not therefore capable of being proved *from* a concept, because a concept may be either determinable or in itself undetermined and undeterminable. The concepts of the understanding are of the former kind; they are determinable through predicates of sensible intuition which can correspond to them. But the transcendental rational concept of the supersensible, which lies at the basis of all sensible intuition, is of the latter kind, and therefore cannot be theoretically determined further.

Now the judgment of taste is applied to objects of sense, but not with a view of determining a *concept* of them for the understanding; for it is not a cognitive judgment. It is thus only a private judgment, in which a singular representation intuitively perceived is referred to the feeling of pleasure, and so far would be limited as regards its validity to the individual judging. The object is *for me* an object of satisfaction; by others it may be regarded quite differently—everyone has his own taste.

Nevertheless there is undoubtedly contained in the judgment of taste a wider reference of the representation of the object (as well as of the subject), whereon we base an extension of judgments of this kind as necessary for everyone. At the basis of this there must necessarily be a concept somewhere, though a concept which cannot be determined through intuition. But through a concept of this sort we know nothing, and consequently it can *supply no proof* for the judgment of taste. Such a concept is the mere pure rational concept of the supersensible which underlies the object (and also the subject judging it), regarded as an object of sense and thus as phenomenal. For if we do not admit such a reference, the claim of the judgment of taste to universal validity would not hold good. If the concept on which it is based were only a mere confused concept of the understanding, like that of perfection, with which we could bring the sensible intuition of the beautiful into correspondence, it would be at least possible in itself to base the judgment of taste on proofs, which contradicts the thesis.

But all contradiction disappears if I say: the judgment of taste is based on a concept (viz. the concept of the general ground of the subjective purposiveness of nature for the judgment); from which, however, nothing can be known and proved in respect of the object, because it is in itself undeterminable and useless for knowledge. Yet at the same time and on that very account the judgment has validity for everyone (though, of course, for each only as a singular judgment immediately accompanying his intuition), because its determining ground lies perhaps in the concept of that which may be regarded as the supersensible substrate of humanity.

The solution of an antinomy only depends on the possibility of showing that two apparently contradictory propositions do not contradict each other in fact, but that they may be consistent, although the explanation of the possibility of their concept may transcend our cognitive faculties. That this illusion is natural and unavoidable by human reason, and also why it is so and remains so, although it ceases to deceive after the analysis of the apparent contradiction, may be thus explained.

In the two contradictory judgments we take the concept on which the universal validity of a judgment must be based in the same sense, and yet we apply to it two opposite predicates. In the thesis we mean that the judgment of taste is not based upon *determinate* concepts, and in the antithesis that the judgment of taste is based upon a concept, but an *indeterminate* one (viz. of the supersensible substrate of phenomena). Between these two there is no contradiction.

We can do nothing more than remove this conflict between the claims and counterclaims of taste. It is absolutely impossible to give a definite objective principle of taste in accordance with which its judgments could be derived, examined, and established, for then the judgment would not be one of taste at all. The subjective principle, viz. the indefinite idea of the supersensible in us, can only be put forward as the sole key to the puzzle of this faculty whose sources are hidden from us; it can be made no further intelligible.

The proper concept of taste, that is of a merely reflective aesthetical judgment, lies at the basis of the antinomy here exhibited and adjusted. Thus the two apparently contradictory principles are reconciled—*both can be true*, which is sufficient. If, on the other hand, we assume, as some do, *pleasantness* as the determining ground of taste (on account of the singularity of the representation which lies at the basis of the judgment of taste) or, as others will have it, the principle of perfection (on account of the universality of the same), and settle the definition of taste accordingly, then there arises an antinomy which it is absolutely impossible to adjust except by showing that *both* the contrary (not merely contradictory) *propositions are false*. And this would prove that the concept on which they are based is self-contradictory. Hence we see that the removal of the antinomy of the aesthetical judgment takes a course similar to that pursued by the critique in the solution of the antinomies of pure theoretical reason. And thus here, as also in the *Critique of Practical Reason*, the antinomies force us against our will to look beyond the sensible and to seek in the supersensible the point of union for all our *a priori* faculties, because no other expedient is left to make our reason harmonious with itself.

Remark I

As we so often find occasion in transcendental philosophy for distinguishing ideas from concepts of the understanding, it may be of use to introduce technical terms to correspond to this distinction. I believe that no one will object if I propose some. In the most universal signification of the word, ideas are representations referred to an object, according to a certain (subjective or objective) principle, but so that they can never become a cognition of it. They are either referred to an intuition, according to a merely subjective principle of the mutual harmony of the cognitive powers (the imagination and the understanding), and they are then called *aesthetical*; or they are referred to a concept according to an objective principle, although they can never furnish a cognition of the object, and are called *rational ideas*. In the latter case the concept is a *transcendent* one, which is different from a concept of the understanding, to which an adequately corresponding experience can always be supplied and which therefore is called *immanent*.

An *aesthetical idea* cannot become a cognition because it is an *intuition* (of the imagination) for which an adequate concept can never be found. A *rational idea* can never become a cognition because it involves a concept (of the supersensible) corresponding to which an intuition can never be given.

Now I believe we might call the aesthetical idea an *inexponible* representation of the imagination, and a rational idea an *indemonstrable* concept of reason. It is assumed of both that they are not generated without grounds, but (according to the above explanation of an idea in general) in conformity with certain principles of the cognitive faculties to which they belong (subjective principles in the one case, objective in the other).

Concepts of the understanding must, as such, always be demonstrable [if by demonstration we understand, as in anatomy, merely *presentation*]; [2] i.e. the object corresponding to them must always be capable of being given in intuition (pure or empirical), for thus alone could they become cognitions. The concept of *magnitude* can be given *a priori* in the intuition of space, e.g. of a right line, etc.; the concept of *cause* in impenetrability, in the collision of bodies, etc. Consequently both can be authenticated by means of an empirical intuition, i.e. the thought of them can be proved (demonstrated, verified) by an example; and this must be possible, for otherwise we should not be certain that the concept was not empty, i.e. devoid of any object.

In logic we ordinarily use the expressions "demonstrable" or "indemonstrable" only in respect of *propositions*, but these might be better designated by the titles respectively of *mediately and immediately certain* propositions; for pure philosophy has also propositions of both kinds, i.e. true propositions, some of which are susceptible of proof and others not. It can, as philosophy, prove them on *a priori* grounds, but it cannot demonstrate them, unless we wish to depart entirely from the proper meaning of this word, according to which *to demonstrate* (*ostendere, exhibere*) is equivalent to presenting a concept in intuition (whether in proof or merely in definition). If the intuition is *a priori* this is called construction; but if it is empirical,

---

[2] [Second edition.]

then the object is displayed by means of which objective reality is assured to the concept. Thus we say of an anatomist that he demonstrates the human eye if, by a dissection of this organ, he makes intuitively evident the concept which he has previously treated discursively.

It hence follows that the rational concept of the supersensible substrate of all phenomena in general, or even of that which must be placed at the basis of our arbitrary will in respect of the moral law, viz. of transcendental freedom, is already, in kind, an indemonstrable concept and a rational idea, while virtue is so in degree. For there can be given in experience, as regards its quality, absolutely nothing corresponding to the former, whereas in the latter case no empirical product attains to the degree of that causality which the rational idea prescribes as the rule.

As in a rational idea the *imagination* with its intuitions does not attain to the given concept, so in an aesthetical idea the *understanding* by its concepts never attains completely to that internal intuition which the imagination binds up with a given representation. Since, now, to reduce a representation of the imagination to concepts is the same thing as to *expound* it, the aesthetical idea may be called an *inexponible* representation of the imagination (in its free play). I shall have occasion in the sequel to say something more of ideas of this kind; now I only note that both kinds of ideas, rational and aesthetical, must have their principles and must have them in reason —the one in the objective, the other in the subjective principles of its employment.

We can consequently explain *genius* as the faculty of *aesthetical ideas*, by which at the same time is shown the reason why in the products of genius it is the nature (of the subject), and not a premeditated purpose, that gives the rule to the art (of the production of the beautiful). For since the beautiful must not be judged by concepts, but by the purposive attuning of the imagination to agreement with the faculty of concepts in general, it cannot be rule and precept which can serve as the subjective standard of that aesthetical but unconditioned purposiveness in beautiful art that can rightly claim to please everyone. It can only be that in the subject which is nature and cannot be brought under rules of concepts, i.e. the supersensible substrate of all his faculties (to which no concept of the understanding extends), and consequently that with respect to which it is the final purpose given by the intelligible [part] of our nature to harmonize all our cognitive faculties. Thus alone is it possible that there should be *a priori* at the basis of this purposiveness, for which we can prescribe no objective principle, a principle subjective and yet of universal validity.

Remark II

The following important remark occurs here: There are *three kinds of antinomies* of pure reason, which, however, all agree in this that they compel us to give up the otherwise very natural hypothesis that objects of sense are things in themselves, and force us to regard them merely as phenomena and to supply to them an intelligible substrate (something supersensible of which the concept is only an idea and supplies no proper knowledge). Without such antinomies, reason could never decide upon accepting a principle narrowing so much the field of its speculation and could never bring itself to sacrifices by which so many otherwise brilliant hopes must disappear. For even now, when by way of compensation for these losses a greater field in a practical aspect opens out before it, it appears not to be able without grief to part from those hopes and disengage itself from its old attachment.

That there are three kinds of antinomies has its ground in this that there are three cognitive faculties—understanding, judgment, and reason—of which each (as a superior cognitive faculty) must have its *a priori* principles. For reason, in so far as it judges of these principles and their use, inexorably requires, in respect of them all, the unconditioned for the given conditioned; and this can never be found if we consider the sensible as belonging to things in themselves and do not rather supply to it, as mere phenomenon, something supersensible (the intelligible substrate of nature both external and internal) as the reality in itself [*Sache an sich selbst*]. There are then: (1) *for the cognitive faculty* an antinomy of reason in respect of the theoretical employment of the understanding extended to the unconditioned, (2) *for the feeling of pleasure and pain* an antinomy of reason in respect of the aesthetical employment of the judgment, and (3) *for the faculty of desire* an antinomy in respect of the practical employment of the self-legislative reason; so far as all these faculties have their superior principles *a priori*, and, in conformity with an inevitable requirement of reason, must judge and be able to determine their object, *unconditionally* according to those principles.

As for the two antinomies of the theoretical and practical employment of the superior cognitive faculties, we have already shown their *unavoidableness* if judgments of this kind are not referred to a supersensible substrate of the given objects as phenomena, and also the *possibility of their solution* as soon as this is done. And as for the antinomies in the employment of the judgment, in conformity with the requirements of reason and their solution, which is here given, there are only two ways of avoiding them. Either: we must deny that any *a priori* principle lies at the basis of the aesthetical judgment of taste; we must maintain that all claim to necessary universal agreement is groundless and vain fancy, and that a judgment of taste only deserves to be regarded as correct because *it happens* that many people agree about it; and this, not because we *assume* an *a priori* principle behind this agreement, but because (as in the taste of the palate) of the contingent similar organization of the different subjects. Or: we must assume that the judgment of taste is really a disguised judgment of reason upon the perfection discovered in a thing and the reference of the manifold in it to a purpose, and is consequently only called aesthetical on account of the confusion here attaching to our reflection, although it is at bottom teleological. In the latter case we could declare the solution of the antinomies by means of transcendental ideas to be needless and without point, and thus could harmonize these laws of taste with objects of sense, not as mere phenomena but as things in themselves. But we have shown in several places in the exposition of judgments of taste how little either of these expedients will satisfy.

However, if it be granted that our deduction at least proceeds by the right method, although it be not yet plain enough in all its parts, three ideas manifest themselves. First, there is the idea of the supersensible in general, without any further determination of it, as the substrate of nature. Secondly, there is the idea of the same as the principle of the subjective purposiveness of nature for our cognitive faculty. And thirdly, there is the idea of the same as the principle of the purposes of freedom and of the agreement of freedom with its purposes in the moral sphere.

§ 59. *Of Beauty as the Symbol of Morality*

Intuitions are always required to establish the reality of our concepts. If the concepts are empirical, the intuitions are called *examples*. If they are pure concepts of understanding, the intuitions are called *schemata*. If we desire to establish the objective reality of rational concepts, i.e. of ideas, on behalf of theoretical cognition, then we are asking for something impossible, because absolutely no intuition can be given which shall be adequate to them.

All *hypotyposis* (presentation, *subjectio sub adspectum*), or sensible illustration, is twofold. It is either *schematical,* when to a concept comprehended by the understanding the corresponding intuition is given, or it is *symbolical.* In the latter case, to a concept only thinkable by the reason, to which no sensible intuition can be adequate, an intuition is supplied with which accords a procedure of the judgment analogous to what it observes in schematism, i.e. merely analogous to the rule of this procedure, not to the intuition itself, consequently to the form of reflection merely and not to its content.

There is a use of the word *symbolical* that has been adopted by modern logicians which is misleading and incorrect, i.e. to speak of the *symbolical* mode of representation as if it were opposed to the *intuitive,* for the symbolical is only a mode of the intuitive. The latter (the intuitive, that is), may be divided into the *schematical* and the *symbolical* modes of representation. Both are hypotyposes, i.e. presentations (*exhibitiones*), not mere *characterizations* or designations of concepts by accompanying sensible signs which contain nothing belonging to the intuition of the object and only serve as a means for reproducing the concepts, according to the law of association of the imagination, and consequently in a subjective point of view. These are either words or visible (algebraical, even mimetical) signs, as mere expressions for concepts.[3]

All intuitions which we supply to concepts *a priori* are therefore either *schemata* or *symbols,* of which the former contain direct, the latter indirect, presentations of the concept. The former do this demonstratively; the latter by means of an analogy (for which we avail ourselves even of empirical intuitions) in which the judgment exercises a double function, first applying the concept to the object of a sensible intuition, and then applying the mere rule of the reflection made upon that intuition to a quite different object of which the first is only the symbol. Thus a monarchical state is represented by a living body if it is governed by national laws, and by a mere machine (like a hand mill) if governed by an individual absolute will; but in both cases only *symbolically.* For between a despotic state and a hand mill there is, to be sure, no similarity; but there is a similarity in the rules according to which we reflect upon these two things and their causality. This matter has not been sufficiently analyzed hitherto, for it deserves a deeper investigation; but this is not the place to linger over it. Our language [i.e. German] is full of indirect presentations of

---

[3] The intuitive in cognition must be opposed to the discursive (not to the symbolical). The former is either *schematical,* by *demonstration,* or *symbolical,* as a representation in accordance with a mere *analogy.*

this sort, in which the expression does not contain the proper schema for the concept, but merely a symbol for reflection. Thus the words *ground* (support, basis), *to depend* (to be held up from above), to *flow* from something (instead of, to follow), *substance* (as Locke expresses it, the support of accidents), and countless others are not schematical but symbolical hypotyposes and expressions for concepts, not by means of a direct intuition, but only by analogy with it, i.e. by the transference of reflection upon an object of intuition to a quite different concept to which perhaps an intuition can never directly correspond. If we are to give the name of "cognition" to a mere mode of representation (which is quite permissible if the latter is not a principle of the theoretical determination of what an object is in itself, but of the practical determination of what the idea of it should be for us and for its purposive use), then all our knowledge of God is merely symbolical; and he who regards it as schematical, along with the properties of understanding, will, etc., which only establish their objective reality in beings of this world, falls into anthropomorphism, just as he who gives up every intuitive element falls into deism, by which nothing at all is cognized, not even in a practical point of view.

Now I say the beautiful is the symbol of the morally good, and that it is only in this respect (a reference which is natural to every man and which every man postulates in others as a duty) that it gives pleasure with a claim for the agreement of everyone else. By this the mind is made conscious of a certain ennoblement and elevation above the mere sensibility to pleasure received through sense, and the worth of others is estimated in accordance with a like maxim of their judgment. That is the *intelligible* to which, as pointed out in the preceding paragraph, taste looks, with which our higher cognitive faculties are in accord, and without which a downright contradiction would arise between their nature and the claims made by taste. In this faculty the judgment does not see itself, as in empirical judging, subjected to a heteronomy of empirical laws; it gives the law to itself in respect of the objects of so pure a satisfaction, just as the reason does in respect of the faculty of desire. Hence, both on account of this inner possibility in the subject and of the external possibility of a nature that agrees with it, it finds itself to be referred to something within the subject as well as without him, something which is neither nature nor freedom, but which yet is connected with the supersensible ground of the latter. In this supersensible ground, therefore, the theoretical faculty is bound together in unity with the practical in a way which, though common, is yet unknown. We shall indicate some points of this analogy, while at the same time we shall note the differences.

(1) The beautiful pleases *immediately* (but only in reflective intuition, not, like morality, in its concept). (2) It pleases *apart from any interest* (the morally good is indeed necessarily bound up with an interest, though not with one which precedes the judgment upon the satisfaction, but with one which is first of all produced by it). (3) The *freedom* of the imagination (and therefore of the sensibility of our faculty) is represented in judging the beautiful as harmonious with the conformity to law of the understanding (in the moral judgment the freedom of the will is thought as the harmony of the latter with itself, according to universal laws of reason). (4) The subjective principle in judging the beautiful is represented as *universal*, i.e. as valid for every man, though not cognizable through any universal concept. (The objective principle of morality is also expounded as universal, i.e. for every subject and for every action of the same subject, and thus as cognizable by means of a universal concept). Hence the moral judgment is not only susceptible of definite constitutive principles, but is possible *only* by grounding its maxims on these in their universality.

A reference to this analogy is usual even with the common understanding [of men], and we often describe beautiful objects of nature or art by names that seem to put a moral appreciation at their basis. We call buildings or trees majestic and magnificent, landscapes laughing and gay; even colors are called innocent, modest, tender, because they excite sensations which have something analogous to the consciousness of the state of mind brought about by moral judgments. Taste makes possible the transition, without any violent leap, from the charm of sense to habitual moral interest, as it represents the imagination in its freedom as capable of purposive determination for the understanding, and so teaches us to find even in objects of sense a free satisfaction apart from any charm of sense.

APPENDIX

§ 60. *Of the Method of Taste*

. . . Now taste is at bottom a faculty for judging of the sensible illustration of moral ideas (by means of a certain analogy involved in our reflection upon both these), and it is from this faculty also and from the greater susceptibility grounded thereon for the feeling arising from the latter (called moral feeling) that that pleasure is derived which taste regards as valid for mankind in general and not merely for the private feeling of each. Hence it appears plain that the true propaedeutic for the foundation of taste is the development of moral ideas and the culture of the moral feeling, because it is only when sensibility is brought into agreement with this that genuine taste can assume a definite invariable form.

Friedrich Wilhelm Joseph von
SCHELLING

Schelling's earliest philosophical writing reflects the powerful influence of both Kant and Fichte, though the direction of his later work, with its originality and speculative urgency, is evident even in this derivative period. It did not take long for his own ideas to assert themselves, and they are usually organized under five headings. The first creative period after Schelling broke away from the Fichtean philosophy is devoted to the philosophy of nature (1799), a subject that continued to interest him and to which he returned throughout his life. The continuity of this interest attests to the fact that Schelling never went from one system to another, nor did he move logically from one part of a system to its subsequent stage, but rather carried on a growing, changing philosophy which tried to synthesize his many insights. The second period marks the beginning of his most original thought, that of transcendental idealism (1800), and our selection is from a work of this period known as the System of Transcendental Idealism. The thought of the third period is referred to as the philosophy of identity, in which the philosophy of nature and transcendental idealism are brought into a unitary system. It is at this time that he delivered his lectures on the philosophy of art, the most extensive, systematic writings on art that he produced (Jena 1802-03; repeated at Würzburg 1804-05). In these lectures art is placed in the metaphysical context of the philosophy of identity, which determines for him the subject matter of art, the form of art, as well as a system of the arts. The fourth period is devoted to the philosophy of freedom, and the fifth to the philosophy of religion, including his "positive philosophy" of existence in contrast with his (and Hegel's) earlier "negative," purely rational philosophy.

Schelling's philosophy of transcendental idealism begins with a transformation of the Fichtean ego-philosophy, the central principle of which is that one begins not from the object (Nature) but from the subject (ego). The problem of transcendental idealism is therefore how, starting from the ego, one is to reach a completely realized world. How can the subject arrive at an object that it can know? This is the converse question to that asked by the philosophy of nature, namely, beginning with nature how can one arrive at intelligence? The philosophy of nature starts from an object and endeavors to see how a subject can arise (i.e., how consciousness can arise in the world). In the philosophy of nature Schelling had viewed nature as an evolutionary system, not in the Darwinian sense, but as a system in which nature is a spirit or mind or intelligence that develops according to its own laws. He traces this self-development from matter to the highest stage of consciousness. Thus his explanation of nature was not mechanistic, but rather, as with Goethe, organic. This did not prevent Schelling, any more than it did Goethe, from being keenly interested in science and experimentation.

In the philosophy of transcendental idealism the movement is just the reverse: from ego to world. The ego is at once a productive agent which creates by itself, stage by stage, the total result, and an intuitive agent so that it can grasp what it produces by an intellectual intuition. This grasp by way of intellectual intuition is a process of deepening awareness so that the ego can follow the evolution of its own activity.

Philosophy is therefore able to comprehend this process of the intelligence by a reflection on its own activity, and in this reflection philosophy penetrates to the original production in actually reproducing it. Philosophy is a self-conscious re-creation of the process of the ego. However, the ability to do this is a gift, the counterpart in philosophical insight to the genius of the artist. Only those with the free gift can perform the re-creation.

In doing this the gifted philosopher uses intellectual intuition to follow the mind's progressive reconstruction of the object and understands the mind's coming to agreement with the object. This construction takes place in three stages.

1) *Theoretical.* Intelligence builds up a world of knowledge through three epochs: *a*) From sensation to intelligence; *b*) from productive intuition to reflection; *c*) from reflection to the act of the will. With the act of will practical philosophy begins.

2) *Practical.* Here, in the stage of practical consciousness, Schelling is concerned with the construction of the world of ethical law which leads ultimately into a philosophy of history. History is interpreted as the progressive revelation of the Absolute, a term that functions for Schelling as the term God does for religions. History is like a drama in which God is the chief author, man is the actor and co-author. Although man acts freely in accordance with his own will, nevertheless God's purposes are realized through human action in accord with an unconscious system of providence. It is at this point in the evolution of the history of consciousness that the second half of our selection (Section IV, F) begins. The problem for us here is this: How can a conscious harmony between consciousness and unconsciousness be arrived at? How can harmony between Nature and Freedom be arrived at? How is harmony possible between theoretical and practical mind? This question can be answered only through art. Only art can offer a solution to the problem. (The problem of how to harmonize the two realms Schelling inherits from Kant's *Critique of Judgment*, and it is this problem which underlies the philosophy of what we have come to call the Romantic movement in art.)

3) *Aesthetic.* This is the highest stage of Transcendental Idealism. As Schelling argues, in the work of art the original harmony or identity of object and subject, nature and freedom, unconscious and conscious, is presented objectively (in an object for intuition). This intuition is the aesthetic intuition which Schelling says is intellectual intuition become "objective and universally valid." In short, art is philosophy become objective.

By means of the creative process, the genius is able to solve the problem for aesthetic intuition which the philosopher tries to realize through intellectual intuition. But because philosophy is reflection, it must wait upon art to produce the consciousness of the unity of nature and freedom before it itself (philosophy) is able to grasp this unity by means of reflection in intellectual intuition. Art is therefore the general organon of philosophy, and the keystone of its arch.

SYSTEM OF
TRANSCENDENTAL IDEALISM

Introduction

1. Concept of Transcendental Philosophy

1. All knowledge rests on the agreement of something objective with something subjective. For we *know* only what is true, and truth is universally held to be the agreement of representations with their objects.

2. The sum of all that is purely *objective* in our knowledge we may call *nature*; the sum of everything *subjective* may be called, on the other hand, the *ego* or *intelligence*. The two concepts are mutually opposed. Intelligence is originally conceived of as that which merely represents, nature as that which is merely capable of being represented, the former as that which is conscious, the latter as the unconscious. Now in all knowledge a mutual agreement of the two—the conscious and the intrinsically unconscious—is necessary. The problem is to explain this agreement.

3. In knowledge itself—while I am knowing—the objective and subjective elements are so united that one cannot say which of the two has priority. There is here no first and no second; the two are simultaneous and one. But in my very *attempt to explain* this identity I must already have *dissolved* it. In order to explain it, since nothing else is given to me besides these two factors of knowledge (as principle of explanation), I must necessarily set one of them *before* the other, *proceed* from one of them, in order to go from it to the other. From which of the two I am to start is not itself determined by the problem.

4. There are accordingly only two possible cases.

A. *The objective factor may be taken as prior, and we then ask how a subjective factor that agrees with it can be joined to it.*

The concept of the subjective is not *contained* in the concept of the objective; rather, they mutually exclude each other. The subjective factor must therefore *be joined to* the objective factor. The concept of nature does not entail that there should also be something intelligent representing it. Nature, so it appears, would exist even if there were nothing representing it. The problem can therefore also be expressed thus: How is that which is intelligent joined to nature, or, How does nature come to be represented?

The problem assumes that nature or the objective factor is prior. It is therefore doubtless a problem of natural science, which makes this very assumption. That natural science really at least *approximates* the solution of this problem—and without knowing it—can be shown here only briefly.

If all knowledge has, as it were, two poles that mutually presuppose and require each other, then they must seek each other in all sciences. There must of necessity therefore be *two* basic sciences and it must be impossible to start out from one pole without being driven to the other. The necessary tendency of all *natural science* is consequently to get from nature to the intelligent. This and nothing else lies at the ground of the effort to bring *theory* into the phenomena of nature. The highest perfection of natural science would be the complete intellectualizing of all natural laws into laws of intuition and thought. The phenomena (the material element) would have to disappear fully and only the laws (the formal element) remain. Hence it is that the more the lawful element emerges in nature itself, the more the material husk disappears; the phenomena themselves become more mental and in the end entirely cease to be. Optical phenomena are nothing but a geometry whose lines are drawn by light, and this light itself is already of ambiguous materiality. In the phenomena of magnetism all material traces already disappear; and of the phenomena of gravitation, which natural scientists themselves believed could be understood only as direct mental influence, nothing remains but the law, whose realization in the large is the mechanism of the heavenly motions. A completed theory of nature would be one in virtue of which the whole of nature resolved itself into a single intelligence. The dead and unconscious products of nature are only unsuccessful efforts of nature to reflect itself, and so-called dead nature is really an unripe intelligence; hence in its phenomena, though unconsciously, intelligent character already peers through. Its highest goal, namely, that of becoming wholly objective for itself, nature reaches only by the highest and final reflection. This is nothing other than man or, more generally, what we call reason, by which nature returns completely into herself and by which it becomes evident that nature is originally identical with that which is recognized as the intelligent and conscious principle in us.

This may perhaps suffice to show that natural science has a necessary tendency to make nature intelligent. By this very tendency it becomes *philosophy of nature*, which is one of the two necessary basic sciences of philosophy.

B. *The subjective factor may be taken as prior, and the problem is then how an objective factor that agrees with it can be joined to it.*

If all knowledge rests on the agreement of these two factors, the explanation of this agreement is without doubt the supreme task of all knowledge; and if, as is generally admitted, philosophy is the highest and chief of all the sciences, it is without doubt the main task of philosophy.

But the problem requires only an explanation of that agreement in general, and leaves it completely undetermined where the explanation shall begin—which of the two it is to take as the first factor and which as the second. Moreover, since the two opposites are mutually necessary to each other, the result of the operation must be the same from whichever point we start.

The task of *philosophy of nature,* as has just been shown, is to make the *objective* factor primary and to derive the subjective factor from it.

Hence, if there exists a *transcendental philosophy,* only the opposite course remains for it, to start from the *subjective factor, as from a first and absolute principle, and to let the objective factor arise out of it.* Philosophy of nature and transcendental philosophy have thus separated themselves into two possible directions of philosophy; and if *all* philosophy must aim at making *either* an intelligence out of nature *or* a nature out of intelligence, then transcendental philosophy, which has this latter task, is *the second necessary basic science of philosophy.*

2. Corollaries

In the foregoing remarks we have not only deduced the concept of transcendental philosophy, but have at the same time afforded the reader a view of the entire system of philosophy which, as we see, is composed of two basic sciences that, opposed to each other in principle and direction, reciprocally require and complement each other. The present work sets forth not the whole system of philosophy but only one of its basic sciences, which may first be more precisely characterized in accordance with the concept of it already derived.

1. If for transcendental philosophy the subjective factor is primary, the sole ground of all reality, the sole principle of explanation of all else, it must necessarily begin with universal doubt concerning the reality of the objective factor.

As the natural philosopher, oriented exclusively toward the objective, seeks above all to prevent the entry of the subjective into his cognition, so conversely the transcendental philosopher seeks to prevent the entry of the objective into the purely subjective principle of cognition. The means of segregation is absolute skepticism, not a skepticism that is half-hearted or merely directed against the vulgar prejudices of mankind and which never really gets down to fundamentals, but one that is thoroughgoing, that directs itself not against single prejudices but against the basic prejudice with which all others must stand or fall. For in addition to artificial prejudices into which people are conventionally indoctrinated, there are much more primitive ones, planted in man not by education or art but by nature herself, which are taken by all except the philosopher to be the principles of all cognition and which the merely self-appointed thinker treats as the touchstone of all truth.

The one basic prejudice, to which all others reduce themselves, is none other than that *there exist things outside us*. This supposition, because it rests neither on grounds nor on reasoning (for there is no valid proof for it) and yet cannot be eradicated by any contrary proof (*naturam furca expellas, tamen usque redibit*), makes a claim to immediate certainty. Yet it refers to something altogether different from us, indeed even opposed to us, something of which one cannot at all see how it might enter into immediate consciousness. Hence it cannot be regarded as anything more than a prejudice—one that is indeed innate and original—but nonetheless on that account a prejudice.

The contradiction that a proposition which by its very nature cannot be immediately certain is yet blindly and groundlessly assumed to be so, cannot be resolved by the transcendental philosopher except by assuming that this proposition implicitly, and without our realizing it until now, is not so much connected with as identical with an immediate certainty. *To exhibit this identity* will be the express business of transcendental philosophy.

2. Now even in the ordinary usage of reason itself there is nothing immediately certain except the proposition *I am*. Because *outside* of immediate consciousness this proposition loses even its meaning, it is the most individual of all truths and the absolute prejudgment that must *first* be assumed if anything else is to be certain. The proposition *There exist things outside us* will therefore be certain for the transcendental philosopher only through its identity with the proposition

I am; and its certainty will also only *be equal* to the certainty of the proposition from which it derives its own certainty.

Accordingly, transcendental knowledge would distinguish itself from ordinary knowledge on two points.

First, for transcendental cognition, certainty about the existence of external things is a mere prejudice, beyond which it passes in seeking out the grounds of this certainty. (The transcendental philosopher cannot make it his business to demonstrate the existence of things in themselves, but only that it is a natural and necessary prejudice to asssume external objects as real.)

Second, the two propositions *I am* and *There are things outside me,* which fuse in ordinary consciousness, are separated by transcendental cognition (setting one before the other), precisely in order to be able to prove their identity and to really exhibit the immediate connection that is merely felt in ordinary cognition. By the act of this separation itself, if and when it is complete, the philosopher transposes himself into the transcendental mode of contemplation, which is by no means a natural, but an artificial, one.

3. If for the transcendental philosopher only the subjective factor has primary reality, he will make only the subjective into his immediate object in cognition. The objective will become his object only indirectly, and in contrast with ordinary knowledge where *cognition* itself (the act of knowing) disappears in favor of the object, in transcendental knowledge the object as such vanishes in favor of the act of knowledge. Transcendental cognition is thus a knowing of knowing, insofar as it is purely subjective.

Thus, for example, only the objective factor in intuition reaches ordinary consciousness; the intuition itself loses itself in the object. The transcendental mode of contemplation, on the other hand, catches sight of the intuited object only through the act of intuiting. Thus ordinary knowing is a mechanism in which concepts dominate, without however being distinguished *as* concepts, whereas transcendental thinking interrupts that mechanism and, in becoming conscious to itself of the concept as an act, raises itself to the *concept of the concept.* In ordinary action we forget about the *acting itself* in favor of the object of action; philosophizing is also an *action,* but not merely an action. It is at the same time a continual *self-intuiting* in this action.

The nature of the transcendental mode of contemplation must therefore in general consist in this: *in it, that which escapes con-*

sciousness in all other thinking, knowing, or doing, and is absolutely non-objective, is now also brought to consciousness and becomes objective. In short, it is a continual becoming-object for itself of the subjective.

The transcendental art will consist precisely in the skill of maintaining oneself steadily in this doubleness of action and thought.

3. *Preliminary Division of Transcendental Philosophy*

This division is *preliminary* because the principles of division can be deduced only in the science itself.

We return to the concept of the science.

Transcendental philosophy has to explain how knowledge in general is possible, presupposing that the subjective is taken to be the dominant or primary factor in it.

It is not, therefore, a single part or a particular object of knowledge, but *knowledge itself* and *knowledge in general* that transcendental philosophy makes its object.

Now all knowledge reduces itself to certain original convictions or primitive prejudgments. Transcendental philosophy must reduce these individual convictions to a single primary conviction; this single one, from which all the others are derived, is expressed in the *first principle of this philosophy,* and the task of finding such a principle is nothing other than that of finding the absolute certainty by means of which all further certainty is arrived at.

The division of transcendental philosophy itself is determined by these original convictions, whose credentials it examines. These convictions must first be sought in the ordinary understanding. If, then, we return to the standpoint of ordinary thought, we find the following convictions engraved deeply in the human understanding.

A. That not only does there exist independently of us a world of things outside us, but also that our representations so agree with them that there is *nothing* in things *other than* what we perceive in them. The element of compulsion in our objective representations is explained by the fact that things are unalterably determined and that by this determinacy of things our representations are also mediately determined. The first problem of philosophy is defined by this first and most primitive conviction: to explain how representations can agree absolutely with objects existing in complete independence of them. Now the possibility of all experience rests on the assumption that things are exactly as we perceive them, that in fact we know things as they are *in themselves* (for what would experience be, and in what direction would e.g. physics not go astray without this presupposition of the absolute identity of being and appearing?). Consequently the solution of this problem is identical with *theoretical philosophy*, which is supposed to inquire into the possibility of experience.

B. The second equally primitive conviction is that representations that arise in us *through* freedom *without necessity*, can pass from the world of thought into the actual world and attain to objective reality.

This conviction is contrary to the first. According to the first we assume that objects are *unalterably determined* and that our representations are determined by them; according to the second, objects are alterable, and indeed are so by the causality of representations in us. According to the first conviction a transition occurs from the real world to the world of representation; representations are determined by something objective. According to the second a transition takes place from the world of representation to the real world; something objective is determined by a (freely projected) representation in us.

A second problem is posed by the second conviction: how something objective should be so transformable by something merely thought, that it is brought into complete agreement with what is thought.

Since the possibility of all free action rests on this assumption, the solution of this problem is *practical philosophy*.

C. But with these two problems we see ourselves involved in a contradiction. B calls for the domination of thought (the ideal) over the world of sense; but how is this thinkable if (according to A) our representation is already in its origin merely the slave of the objective factor? Conversely, if the actual world is something completely independent of us, to which (as its archetype) our representation must conform (according to A), it is inconceivable how once again the real world should be able to conform to representations in us (as B requires). In a word, practical certainty disappears in the presence of theoretical certainty, and theoretical certainty disappears in the presence of practical. It is impossible that truth should occur in our cognition and reality in our volition simultaneously.

This contradiction must be resolved if philosophy is to exist at all —and the solution of this problem or the answer to the question *How can we conceive at one and the same time of representations conforming to objects and of objects conforming to representations?* is not the *first* but the *highest* task of transcendental philosophy.

It is easy to see that this problem can be solved neither in theoretical nor in practical philosophy, but in a higher philosophy which is the connecting link between the two, neither theoretical nor practical but *both* at once.

We cannot comprehend how at one and the same time the objective world should adapt itself to representations in us and representations in us to the objective world, unless there exists a *pre-established harmony* between the two worlds, the ideal world and the real. But this pre-established harmony is itself unthinkable unless the activity by which the objective world is produced is originally identical with that which manifests itself in volition, and conversely.

Now, in fact, it is a *productive* activity that manifests itself in volition; all free action is productive, but productive *with consciousness*. If we now suppose, since both activities are to be only one in principle, that the same activity that is productive *with consciousness* in free action is productive *without consciousness* in the production of the world, then this pre-established harmony is real and the contradiction is resolved.

If we suppose that all this is really the case, then the original identity of the activity concerned in the producing of the world with that which manifests itself in volition, will exhibit itself in the products of the former, and these products will have to appear as products of an activity at once *conscious* and *unconscious*.

Nature, as a whole as well as in its individual products, will have to appear to be a work produced with consciousness and yet at the same time a product of the blindest mechanism; *it is purposive without being explicable in purposive terms*. The philosophy of *natural purposes*, or teleology, is thus the required point of union of theoretical and practical philosophy.

D.   Up to this point we have postulated only in general terms the identity of the unconscious activity that has produced nature with the conscious activity that manifests itself in volition, without deciding where the principle of this activity lies, whether in nature or in us.

Now the system of knowledge can be considered complete only when it returns to its principle. Transcendental philosophy would thus be complete only when it could demonstrate that the above *identity* —the final resolution of its whole problem—lies in *its principle* (in the ego).

It is postulated, therefore, that this simultaneously conscious and unconscious activity is to be exhibited in the subjective factor, *in consciousness itself*.

Only *aesthetic* activity is of this kind, and every work of art is intelligible only as the product of such an activity. The ideal world of art and the real world of objects are therefore products of one and the same activity. The confluence of the two (conscious and unconscious activities) *without* consciousness gives rise to the real world, and *with* consciousness to the aesthetic world.

The objective world is only the primitive, as yet unconscious, poetry of the spirit; the general organon of philosophy—and the keystone of its whole arch—is the *philosophy of art*.

4. *Organ of Transcendental Philosophy*

1. The sole immediate object of transcendental contemplation is the subjective. The sole organ for philosophizing in this manner is therefore the *inner sense*, and its object is of such a nature that, unlike the object of mathematics, it can never be the object of outer intuition. To be sure the object of mathematics no more exists *outside* cognition than does that of philosophy. The whole existence of mathematics rests on intuition; it exists therefore only in intuition, but this intuition itself is an external one. In addition, the mathematician never deals immediately with intuition (construction) itself, but only with that which has been constructed, which may indeed be represented externally, whereas the philosopher looks only at the *act of construction itself*, which is absolutely internal.

2. Moreover, the objects of the transcendental philosopher do not exist at all except insofar as they are freely produced. We cannot be constrained to perform such a production as one may, say, be constrained by the external drawing of a mathematical figure to intuit the same inwardly. Nevertheless, just as the existence of a mathematical figure rests on outer sense, so the whole reality of a philosophical concept rests solely on *inner sense*. The whole object of this philosophy is nothing other than the action of intelligence according to definite laws. This action can be apprehended only by a peculiar immediate inner intuition, which again is possible only by way of production. But this is not enough. In philosophizing, we are not merely the object, but also at the same time the subject of contemplation. In order to understand philosophy, therefore, two conditions must be fulfilled, *first*, that we be engaged in a continuous inner activity, in a continuous producing of the primary acts of intelligence, and *second* that we be engaged in continuous reflection upon this productive process, in a word, that we be at once that which is intuited (that which does the producing) and that which intuits.

3. By means of this continuous doubleness of production and in-

tuition, *that which otherwise is reflected by nothing* is to become an object. We cannot prove *here* (though we can in what follows) that this reflection of what is absolutely unconscious and nonobjective is possible only through an *aesthetic act* of the imagination. In the meantime it is at least evident from what has already been shown here that all philosophy is *productive*. Philosophy, as well as art, therefore rests upon the productive faculty, and the difference between the two depends solely on a difference in direction of the productive power. For whereas production in art is directed outward in order to reflect the unconscious in products, philosophical production turns immediately inward so as to reflect the unconscious in intellectual intuition. The appropriate sense by which this kind of philosophy must be comprehended is thus the *aesthetic* sense, and for this very reason the philosophy of art is the true organon of philosophy.

There exist only two ways of passing beyond common reality: poetry, which transports us to an ideal world; and philosophy, which makes the real world disappear wholly before us. It is hard to see why the sense for philosophy should be more universally distributed than that for poetry, especially among the class of people who have completely lost the aesthetic organ, whether because of concentration on memory (nothing more directly kills the productive capacity) or as a result of lifeless speculation destructive of all imagination.

4. It is unnecessary to detain ourselves with commonplaces about the *sense of truth*, or about utter unconcern in regard to consequences, although we might want to ask what other conviction could still be sacred to him who challenges the most certain of all (that there exist things outside us). We may rather cast one more glance at the so-called claims of ordinary understanding.

In matters of philosophy the ordinary or common understanding has no other claims than that which every object under inquiry has, *to be completely explained*.

The task is not to prove that what the common understanding holds to be true is in fact true; it is only to disclose the inevitability of its illusions. It remains the case that the objective world belongs merely to the necessary limitations that make self-consciousness (that which I am) possible. For the ordinary understanding it is sufficient if the necessity of its viewpoint is itself again derived from this philosophical viewpoint.

To this end it is not only necessary that the inner machinery of our mental activity should be laid open, and the mechanism of necessary representation be disclosed; but also the peculiarity of our nature should be exhibited by which it is necessary that what has reality merely in our intuition becomes reflected to us as something present outside us.

Just as natural science engenders idealism out of realism by spiritualizing the laws of nature into laws of intelligence, or adding the formal to the material, so transcendental philosophy engenders realism out of idealism by *materializing the laws of intelligence into laws of nature,* or joining the material to the formal.

Section IV
F.

PROBLEM

to explain how the ego itself can become conscious of the original harmony between the subjective and the objective.

SOLUTION

1.

1. All action can be understood only in terms of a primordial union of freedom and necessity. The proof is that every action, whether of the *individual* or of the whole *species,* must be thought of as free *qua* action, while *qua* objective result it must be thought of as standing under natural laws. Subjectively, then, or for inner appearance, it is we who act; objectively it is never we but something else acting, as it were, through us.

2. This objective entity that acts through *me* should however again be I. Now I am only the conscious factor, whereas that which acts through me is the unconscious factor. Thus the unconscious element in my action should be identical with the conscious element. This identity, however, cannot be demonstrated in free action itself, for it annuls itself precisely for the sake of free action, i.e., in order that the objective factor should become objective. Thus the identity would have to be demonstrated at a point beyond this objectivation. But that which in free action becomes the objective element, independent of us, is *intuition* on our side of appearance. Consequently the identity would have to be demonstrable in intuition.

It cannot however be demonstrated in intuition itself. For either the intuition is simply *subjective*, hence not objective at all, or it becomes objective in action, and then the identity has been canceled in the action precisely for the sake of the objectivation. Hence it would seem that the identity could be demonstrated only in the products of intuition.

This identity cannot be shown in the objective of the second order,[1] since it comes about only by the dissolution of that identity and by a division that is infinite. This objective factor, to be sure, cannot be explained except by the assumption that what divides itself in free action for the sake of appearance is something originally posited in harmony. This identity, however, should first be shown for the ego itself, and since it is the ground of explanation of history, it cannot also be demonstrated from history.

The identity therefore can only be shown in the objective of the first order.[2]

We supposed the objective world to arise through a completely blind mechanism of intelligence. But how such a mechanism is possible in a nature whose basic character is consciousness would be difficult to conceive if the mechanism were not already determined beforehand by free and conscious activity. It would be just as hard to conceive how any realization at all of our aims in the external world is possible by means of conscious and free activity unless a susceptibility to such an action were already laid down in the world, even before it becomes the object of a conscious action, by virtue of the original identity of unconscious and conscious activity.

If, however, all conscious activity is purposive, then this coincidence of conscious and unconscious activity can be demonstrated only in a product that is *purposive without having been purposively produced*. Nature must be such a product, and this is precisely the principle of all teleology, in which alone the solution of the given problem can be sought.

---

1 [The lawfulness of history which is the providential revelation of the divine.]
2 [Nature as objective.]

Section V

THE MAIN PROPOSITIONS OF TELEOLOGY
ACCORDING TO THE PRINCIPLES OF
TRANSCENDENTAL IDEALISM

1.

The appearance of freedom can be conceived only in terms of a single identical activity that has divided itself into conscious and unconscious factors solely for the sake of appearing. Nature, as that which lies beyond this division and which is brought forth without freedom, must just as certainly appear as a product that is purposive without having been produced according to a purpose. It must appear, therefore, as a product that looks as though it were produced with conscious intention, although it is the work of blind mechanism.

(a) *Nature must appear as a purposive product.* Transcendental proof of this proposition is derived from the necessary harmony of unconscious and conscious activity. Proof from experience does not belong in transcendental philosophy. We therefore proceed to the second proposition. Namely,

(b) *Nature is not purposive in its production,* i.e., although it bears in itself all the characteristics of a purposive product it is nevertheless not purposive in its origin, and the character of nature, and precisely what makes it nature, is denied by the attempt to explain it in terms of purposive production. For the uniqueness of nature rests precisely on the fact that it is purposive in its mechanism even though this is nothing but blind mechanism. If I cancel its mechanism, I cancel nature itself. The whole magical charm, for instance, that surrounds organic nature and that can be fully penetrated only with the aid of transcendental idealism, rests on the contradiction that nature, although a product of blind natural forces, is nevertheless through and through purposive. But this contradiction, which may be deduced *a priori* by means of transcendental principles, is contravened by teleological modes of explanation.

Nature, says Kant, speaks figuratively to us in its purposive forms. The appearance of freedom in ourselves gives us the interpretation of nature's symbolic language. What has divided itself in free action for the sake of appearing is still unseparated in the natural product. Every plant is wholly what it ought to be; what is free in it is necessary, and what is necessary, free. Man is an eternal fragment, for his action is either necessary and then not free, or free and then not necessary and lawful. Thus only organic nature gives me the complete appearance of a united freedom and necessity in the external world, and this could be inferred in advance from the place organic nature assumes in the series of productions in theoretical philosophy. For, according to our deductions, organic nature is itself already a producing that has become objective; hence, to that extent, it borders on free action; yet it is an unconscious intuiting of this productive process, and to that extent again itself a blind producing.

Now this contradiction, that one and the same product is simultaneously a blind product and yet purposive, simply cannot be explained in any system other than transcendental idealism, since every other system must deny either the purposiveness of the products or the mechanism in their production, thus doing away with the coexistence of the two.

Either we assume that matter spontaneously shapes itself into purposive products. Then at least it becomes conceivable how matter and purposive concept interpenetrate in the products. We then either ascribe absolute reality to matter—as happens in hylozoism, an absurd system, insofar as it assumes that *matter itself* is intelligent—or we do not. In the latter case matter must be thought of as a mere mode of intuition of an intelligent being, so that the purposive concept and the object do not really interpenetrate in matter but in that being's intuition; and then hylozoism itself leads back to transcendental idealism.

Or we assume that matter is absolutely inactive and suppose the purposiveness in its products to be produced by an intelligence outside it, in such a way that the concept of this purposiveness has preceded the production itself. But then it is inconceivable how concept and object interpenetrate to infinity, how in a word the product should be a natural product rather than a product of art. For the difference between the product of art and that of nature lies precisely in the fact that in the former the concept is imprinted only on the surface of the object, whereas in the latter it has entered into the object itself and is completely inseparable from it. This absolute identity of the purposive concept with the object itself is, however, explicable solely in terms of a production in which conscious and unconscious activity unite; but such a production, again, is possible only in an intelligence. Now we can very well conceive how a creative intelligence can represent a world for itself, but not how it can do so for others outside itself. Thus we see ourselves here again driven back to transcendental idealism.

The purposiveness of nature as a whole as well as in its individual products can only be conceived in terms of an intuition in which the concept of the concept and the object itself are originally and indistinguishably united. For then the product will indeed have to appear purposive, since the production itself was already determined by the principle which separates itself into the free and the unfree for the sake of consciousness, and yet, again, the purposive concept cannot be conceived as preceding the production, because in the above-mentioned intuition both were still indistinguishable. Now, teleological modes of explanation suppose that the purposive concept, which corresponds to conscious activity, precedes the object, which corresponds to unconscious activity. That this kind of explanation actually puts an end to all genuine explanation of nature, and thereby becomes injurious to knowledge in its perfection, is so self-evident from what has been said that it needs no further explanation, even by way of illustration.

2.

In its blind and mechanical purposiveness nature represents to me, to be sure, an original identity of conscious and unconscious activity. However, it does not represent this identity to me as one whose ultimate ground lies in the *ego itself*. The transcendental philosopher sees perfectly well that the principle of this identity or harmony is that which is ultimate in us, which divides itself already in the first act of self-consciousness and is charged with the whole of consciousness in all its determinations; but the *ego itself* does not see this. Now the problem of the *whole science* was just this, how the ultimate ground of harmony between the subjective and the objective should become objective *to the ego itself*.

In intelligence itself, therefore, an intuition must be discoverable by which the ego, in *one and the same* appearance, is at once conscious and unconscious *for itself*. Only by way of such an intuition do we bring intelligence, as it were, wholly out of itself; only by means of such an intuition is the whole problem of transcendental philosophy (to explain the agreement of the subjective and the objective) solved.

By the first requirement, namely, that conscious and unconscious activity should become objective in *one and the same intuition*, this intuition distinguishes itself from that which we were able to deduce in practical philosophy, where intelligence was conscious only for inner intuition but was unconscious for outer intuition.

By the second requirement, namely, that the ego should become simultaneously conscious and unconscious in one and the same intuition *for itself*, the intuition here postulated distinguishes itself from that which we have in products of nature, where in fact we apprehend that identity, but not as an identity whose principle lies in the ego itself. Every organization is a monogram of that original identity; but to recognize itself in this reflection the ego must already have known itself immediately in that identity.

We have nothing to do but analyze the characteristic traits of the intuition just deduced in order to discover the intuition itself which, to anticipate, can be no other than *artistic intuition*.

Section VI

DEDUCTION OF A UNIVERSAL ORGAN OF PHILOSOPHY, OR MAIN PROPOSITIONS OF THE PHILOSOPHY OF ART ACCORDING TO PRINCIPLES OF TRANSCENDENTAL IDEALISM

1. *Deduction of the Art Product in General*

The postulated intuition should comprehend what exists separated in the appearance of freedom and in the intuition of the product of nature, namely, *identity of conscious and unconscious in the ego and consciousness of this identity*. The product of this intuition will thus be contiguous on the one side with the product of nature and on the other side with the product of freedom, and it will have to unite within itself the characteristics of both. If we know the product of intuition, then we also know the intuition itself. We therefore need only deduce the product in order to deduce the intuition.

The product will have in common with the product of freedom the fact that it is produced with conscious intent, and with the product of nature that it is produced unconsciously. In the first respect it will consequently be the inverse of the organic product of nature. If unconscious (blind) activity is reflected as conscious by the organic product, then inversely by the product here discussed conscious activity will be reflected as unconscious (objective); or, if the organic product reflects for me unconscious activity as determined by conscious activity, then inversely, the product which is here deduced will reflect conscious activity as determined by unconscious activity. More briefly: nature begins unconscious and ends conscious; its production is not purposive but its product indeed is. The ego, in the activity here discussed, must begin with consciousness (subjectively) and end in the unconscious, or *objectively*; the ego is conscious as regards production, unconscious as regards the product.

How shall *we*, however, explain transcendentally for ourselves an intuition of this nature, in which unconscious activity, as it were, works its way through conscious activity to perfect identity with it? We reflect first on the fact that the activity is supposed to be a conscious one. Now it is plainly impossible that something objective should be produced with consciousness, which nevertheless is here required. Only what arises unconsciously is objective; the genuinely objective element in that intuition therefore cannot be introduced by means of *consciousness*. On this point we may appeal immediately to the proofs that have already been adduced in regard to free action, namely, that the objective element in free action arises in it by force of something independent of freedom. The difference is merely this: (a) that in free action the identity of both activities must be annulled precisely in order that the action should thereby appear as free; here, on the other hand, in *consciousness* itself, and without the negation of consciousness, both should appear as one. Also (b) the two activities in free action can *never* become absolutely identical. Hence, again, the object of free action is necessarily an *infinite* one, never fully realized; for were it fully realized, then the conscious and the objective activity would collapse into one, i.e., the appearance of freedom would vanish. Now what was simply impossible through freedom is to be possible through the action here postulated, which, however, just on this account, must cease to be a free action and become one in which freedom and necessity are absolutely united. But the production was to have occurred with consciousness, which is impossible unless both the activities are separated. Here, therefore, is a clear contradiction. I shall set it forth once more. Conscious and unconscious activity are to be absolutely one in the product, just as they are also in the organic product; but they are to be one in a different way—both are to be one *for the ego itself*. But this is impossible unless the ego is conscious of the production. But if the ego is conscious of the production, then the two activities must be separate, since this is a necessary condition for consciousness of production. The two activities must therefore be one, for otherwise there is no identity; the two must be separate, for otherwise there is identity, but not for the ego. How is this contradiction to be resolved?

Both activities must be separated for the sake of the appearance, the objectivation of production, just as they must be separated in free action for the sake of the objectivation of intuition. But they cannot be separate *to infinity*, as in free action, because the objective phase would then never be a complete representation of the relevant identity. The identity of the two was to have been broken up only for the sake of consciousness, but the production is to end in unconsciousness. Hence there must be a point where both fall together into one; and conversely, where both fall together into one, the production must cease to appear free.

Once this point in the production is arrived at, the productive process must cease absolutely, and it must be impossible for the producer to continue to produce. For the condition of all producing is just the opposition of conscious and unconscious activity, whereas these are here supposed to meet absolutely; so that in intelligence all strife is ended, all contradiction resolved.

Intelligence will thus terminate in full recognition of the identity expressed in the product, as one whose principle lies in itself, i.e., it will terminate in a complete self-intuition. Now since it was the free tendency to self-intuition in this identity that originally brought about the self-estrangement of intelligence, the feeling that accompanies this intuition will be a feeling of infinite satisfaction. The whole productive drive comes to rest with the completion of the product; all contradictions are resolved, all riddles unraveled. Since the production proceeded from freedom, i.e., from an infinite opposition of the two activities, intelligence will not be able to ascribe to *freedom* the absolute unification of the two in which the production ends. For simultaneously with the completion of the product all appearance of freedom is removed; intelligence will feel itself surprised and *blessed* by that unification, i.e., it will regard it as though it were a freely bestowed favor of a higher nature that has by means of it made the impossible possible.

But this unknown, which here brings objective and conscious activity into unexpected harmony, is none other than that Absolute which contains the universal ground of the pre-established harmony between the conscious and the unconscious. If, then, this absolute is reflected from the product, it will appear to intelligence as something above it and which itself, in opposition to freedom, adds the element of purposelessness to that which was begun with consciousness and purposeful intention.

This unchangeable identity, which cannot arrive at consciousness and is only reflected from the product, is for the producer exactly what destiny is for the actor, i.e., an obscure unknown power that adds the element of perfection, completion, or objectivity to the fragmentary work of freedom. And, as the power that realizes nonintended ends by means of our free action without our knowledge is called destiny, so the incomprehensible principle which adds the objective to the conscious without the co-operation of freedom and in a certain way in opposition to freedom, in which what is united in the above-mentioned production eternally flees from itself, is signified by the obscure concept of *genius*.

The postulated product is none other than the product of genius, or, since genius is possible only in art, the *product of art*.

The deduction is finished and we now have nothing to do but show by a complete analysis that all the characteristic traits of the postulated production converge in the aesthetic process.

That all aesthetic production rests on an opposition of activities may properly be inferred from the declaration by all artists that they are involuntarily impelled to the creation of their works, that they merely satisfy an irresistible impulse of their nature through such production. For if every impulse originates in a contradiction in such a way that, given the contradiction, the free activity occurs involuntarily, then the artistic impulse must also proceed from such a feeling of an inner contradiction. But this contradiction, since it sets into motion the whole man with all his powers, is without doubt a contradiction that seizes upon the *ultimate in him*, the root of his entire existence. It is as though in the rare persons who are, above all others, artists in the highest sense of the word, the immutable identity, on which all existence rests, has put off the raiment with which it clothes itself in others and now, just as it is immediately affected by things, with equal immediacy reaffects everything. Consequently it can only be the contradiction between the conscious and the unconscious in free action that sets the artistic impulse into motion, just as, once more, it can only be given to art to satisfy our infinite striving as well as to resolve the ultimate and most extreme contradiction in us.

Just as aesthetic production starts from the feeling of an apparently irresolvable contradiction, so, according to the testimony of all artists and of all who participate in their inspiration, it comes to a close in the feeling of an *infinite* harmony. That this feeling, which accompanies the closure, is at the same time an *emotion* (a being *moved*), already demonstrates that the artist ascribes the complete resolution of the contradiction which he discovers in his work not [alone] to himself but to a spontaneous gift of his nature, which, however inexorably it sets him into contradiction with himself, with equal grace removes the pain of this contradiction from him. For just as the artist is driven to production involuntarily and even against his inner resistance (hence the maxims among the ancients: pati Deum, etc., and hence in general the image of being inspired by a breath from without), so the objective element comes about in his production as though without his co-operation, i.e., itself in a purely objective way. Just as the fateful man does not accomplish what he intends or has in view but rather what he must, by an incomprehensible destiny under whose influence he stands, so the artist, however purposeful he may be, nevertheless, in regard to what is truly objective in his creation, seems to stand under the influence of a power that sets him apart from all other men and compels him to express or represent things he does not himself fully see through and whose meaning is infinite. Now since that absolute confluence of the two mutually fleeing activities is not at all further explicable, but is merely an *appearance*, which, though incomprehensible, cannot be denied, art is the sole and eternal revelation that exists and the miracle which, even if it had existed only once, must have persuaded us of the absolute reality of that highest principle.

Moreover, if art is brought to completion by two thoroughly different activities, then genius is neither the one nor the other but that which is above both. If we must seek in one of these two activities, namely conscious activity, for what is usually called *art*, but which is merely one part of art, namely, the part that is practiced with consciousness, deliberation, and reflection, which can also be taught and learned, received from others, and attained by one's own practice, then, on the other hand, we must seek in the unconscious, which also enters into art, for that in art which cannot be learned, cannot be attained by practice or in any other way, but can only be inborn by the free gift of nature, and which is what we may call in one word the *poetry* in art.

Obviously, then, it would be utterly futile to ask which of the two constituents is prior to the other; for in fact either without the other has no value and only the two in conjunction can bring forth the highest. For though that which cannot be achieved by practice but is native with us is generally considered the nobler of the two, the gods have so firmly tied the exercise of that original power to painstaking human effort, to industry and deliberation, that without art, poetry, even where it is innate, produces only products that appear lifeless, in which no human understanding can take delight, and which repel all judgment and even intuition by the completely blind force at work in them. On the contrary, it is rather to be expected that art might be able to accomplish something without poetry than poetry without art, partly because a person can hardly be by nature devoid of poetry, while many have no art, and partly because persistent study of the ideas of the great masters can to some degree compensate for an original lack of objective power. Still, only a semblance of poetry can arise in this way, which is easily distinguishable by its superficiality, in contrast with the inexhaustible depth which the true artist, though he works with the greatest presence of mind, puts into his work involuntarily and which neither he nor anyone else is able to penetrate completely. There are also many other characteristics by which such mere semblance of poetry is distinguishable, e.g., the great value it places on the merely mechanical features of art, the poverty of the form in which it moves itself, etc.

It is evident also that as neither poetry nor art can produce a perfected work singly each by itself, so the two existing in separation cannot produce such a work. Consequently, because the identity of the two can only be original, and is absolutely impossible and unattainable through freedom, the complete work of art is possible only through genius, which for this reason is for aesthetics what the ego is for philosophy, namely, that which is highest, absolutely real, which itself never becomes objective but is the cause of everything objective.

2. Character of the Art Product

A) The work of art reflects for us the identity of conscious and unconscious activity. But the opposition of the two is infinite, and it is removed without any contribution of freedom. The basic character of the work of art is thus an *unconscious infinity* [synthesis of nature and freedom]. The artist seems to have presented in his work, as if instinctively, apart from what he has put into it with obvious intent, an infinity which no finite understanding can fully unfold. To make this clear to ourselves merely by one example, Greek mythology—of which it is undeniable that it includes within itself an infinite meaning and symbols for all Ideas—arose among a people and in a manner both of which make it impossible to assume any thoroughgoing intentionality in its discovery and in the harmony with which everything is unified into a single great whole. So it is with every true work of art: each is susceptible of infinite interpretation, as though there were an infinity of intentions within it, yet we cannot at all tell whether this infinity lay in the artist himself or whether it resides solely in the art-work. On the other hand, in a product that merely simulates the character of a work of art, intention and rule lie on the surface and appear so limited and bounded that the product is nothing other than a faithful impression of the conscious activity of the artist and is altogether merely an object for reflection, but not for intuition, which loves to immerse itself in what it intuits and can come to rest only in the infinite.

B) Every aesthetic production starts from the feeling of an infinite contradiction. Hence also the feeling that accompanies the completion of the art product must be the feeling of such a satisfaction, and this feeling must in turn go over into the work of art itself. The outward expression of the work of art is therefore the expression of repose and of quiet grandeur, even where the greatest tension of pain or of joy is to be expressed.

C) Every aesthetic production starts from an intrinsically infinite separation of both activities, which are separated in every free production. Since, however, both these activities are to be presented in the product as united, an infinite will be finitely presented by this product. But the infinite finitely presented is beauty. The basic character of every work of art, which comprehends within itself both of the foregoing characters, is therefore *beauty*, and without beauty there is no work of art. For although there are sublime works of art as well, and beauty and sublimity are in a certain respect opposite (in that a natural scene, for instance, can be beautiful without thereby being sublime, and conversely), still the opposition between beauty and sublimity is one that occurs only in regard to the object and not in regard to the subject of intuition. For the difference between a beautiful and a sublime work of art rests only on the fact that where beauty exists the infinite contradiction is resolved in the object itself, whereas where sublimity exists the contradiction is not unified in the object itself but is merely raised to a level at which it involuntarily removes itself in the intuition, which then is as good as if it were removed from the object. It can also be shown easily that sublimity rests on the same contradiction as beauty. For whenever an object is called sublime, a magnitude is apprehended by unconscious activity which cannot be apprehended in conscious activity; the ego is thereby set into a conflict with itself which can end only in an aesthetic intuition that places both activities in an unanticipated harmony. However, the intuition, which lies here not in the artist but in the intuiting subject itself, is completely involuntary, because the sublime (quite unlike the merely marvelous, which likewise poses the imagination with a contradiction which, however, it is not worth the effort to resolve) sets all the powers of the mind in motion in order to resolve the contradiction that threatens one's entire intellectual existence.

Now that the characteristics of the work of art have been derived, its *difference* from all other products has also been brought to light.

For the work of art distinguishes itself from the organic product of nature chiefly by the fact that a) the organic being presents still unseparated what aesthetic production presents after separation but united; b) organic production does not start out from consciousness, hence also not from an infinite contradiction, which is a condition of aesthetic production. The organic product of nature will therefore also not necessarily be beautiful if beauty is exclusively the resolution of an infinite contradiction; and if it is beautiful, then its beauty will seem simply accidental, because the condition of its existence cannot be thought of as existing in nature. From this the altogether unique interest in natural beauty—not insofar as it is beauty in general, but insofar as it is definitely *natural beauty*—can be explained. Our view regarding the imitation of nature as the principle of art becomes clear from the foregoing. For far from its being the case that a merely accidentally beautiful nature should give the rule to art, what art produces in its perfection is the principle and the norm for judging the beauty of nature.

It is easy to determine what the distinction is between the aesthetic product and the *ordinary art product*. In its principle, all aesthetic production is absolutely free, since the artist can indeed be impelled to produce by a contradiction, but only by one that lies in the highest region of his own nature, whereas all other production is occasioned by a contradiction that lies outside the real producer and hence all such production has its end outside itself. From its independence of external ends there springs the sanctity and purity of art. This goes so far that it excludes not only affinity with everything that is merely sensuous enjoyment (to demand which of art is the peculiar characteristic of barbarism), or with the useful (to demand which is possible only to an age that places the highest efforts of the human spirit in economic discoveries), but even affinity with everything that belongs to morality. Indeed, it leaves far below it science itself, which in view of its disinterestedness borders most closely upon art, merely because it is always directed to a goal beyond itself and in the end must itself serve as a mere means for the highest (art).

As for the relation of art to science in particular, they are both so opposed in tendency that, were science ever to have accomplished its whole task as art always has accomplished its, both would have to converge and become one—which is the proof of completely opposite tendencies. For although science, in its highest function, has one and the same problem as art, yet this problem, because of the manner of its solution, is an infinite one for science. We can thus say that art is the model for science, and wherever art may be, there science must first join it. From this we can see why and to what extent there is no genius in the sciences, not because it would be impossible for a scientific problem to be solved in a "genial" way, but because the very problem whose solution can be discovered by genius is also soluble mechanically. Of such a sort, e.g., is the Newtonian system of gravitation, which could have been a "genial" discovery—and in its first discoverer, Kepler, really was—but could equally well have been a wholly scientific discovery, as it became through Newton. Only what art produces is possible solely and alone through genius, because in every task that art has fulfilled an infinite contradiction has been resolved. What science produces *can* be produced by genius, but it is not necessarily so produced. Genius, therefore, is and remains problematic in science, i.e., one can always definitely say where it is not, but never where it is. There are only a few characteristic traits from which we can infer to genius in science. (That we have to infer to it already demonstrates a wholly unique state of affairs here.) E.g., genius is certainly not present where a whole, such as a system, arises part by part and as if by composition. Conversely, genius would have to be presupposed wherever it is clear that the idea of the whole has preceded the individual parts. For, since the idea of the whole cannot grow distinct except by unfolding itself in the individual parts, while, again, the individual parts are possible only through the idea of the whole, there appears to be a contradiction here which is possible only through an act of genius, i.e., through an unexpected confluence of unconscious and conscious activity. Another reason for imputing genius in science would be if someone were to say and assert things whose meaning he could not have wholly penetrated (whether in view of the time in which he lived or in comparison with his other utterances), where he thus expressed something apparently with consciousness which, nevertheless, he could only have expressed unconsciously. Yet that these grounds of imputation can be highly deceptive can easily be demonstrated in a number of ways.

Genius is differentiated from everything that is mere talent or skill by the fact that it resolves a contradiction which is absolute and resolvable by nothing else. In all production, even in the most ordinary everyday variety, an unconscious activity works together with conscious activity; but only a production whose condition was an infinite opposition of both activities is aesthetic and is possible *only* through genius.

3. *Corollaries*

Having derived the nature and character of the art product as fully as was required for the present investigation, nothing remains but to give an account of the relation in which the philosophy of art stands to the whole system of philosophy in general.

1. Philosophy as a whole starts from, and must start from a principle that, as the absolute identity, is completely nonobjective. How then is this absolutely nonobjective principle to be evoked in consciousness and understood, which is necessary if it is the condition of understanding the whole of philosophy? No proof is needed of the impossibility of apprehending or presenting it by means of concepts. Nothing remains, therefore, but that it be presented in an immediate intuition; yet this itself seems incomprehensible and, since its object is supposed to be something absolutely nonobjective, even self-contradictory. If, however, there were nevertheless such an intuition, which had as object that which was absolutely identical, in itself neither subjective nor objective, and if on behalf of this intuition, which can only be an intellectual intuition, one were to appeal to immediate experience, by what means could this intuition be established as objective, i.e., how could we establish beyond doubt that it does not rest on a merely subjective illusion, unless there were an objectivity belonging to the intuition which was universal and acknowledged by all men? This universally acknowledged and thoroughly undeniable objectivity of intellectual intuition is art itself. For aesthetic intuition is precisely intellectual intuition become objective.[1] The work of art

---

[1] Philosophy as a whole proceeds, and must proceed, from a principle that, as the absolute principle, is also at the same time the simply identical. An absolutely simple, identical entity cannot be apprehended or communicated by description or, in general, by concepts. It can only be intuited. Such an intuition is the organ of all philosophy. But this intuition, which is not sensuous but intellectual and which has for its object not the objective or the subjective but the absolutely identical, the in-itself neither subjective nor objective, is itself merely something

merely reflects to me what is otherwise reflected by nothing, that absolutely identical principle which has already divided itself in the ego. Thus what for the philosopher divides itself already in the first act of consciousness, and which is otherwise inaccessible to any intuition, shines back to us from its products by the miracle of art.

But not only the first principle of philosophy and the first intuition from which it proceeds, but also the whole mechanism that philosophy deduces and on which it itself rests, becomes objective for the first time through aesthetic production.

Philosophy starts out from an infinite dichotomy of opposed activities; but all aesthetic production rests on the same dichotomy, which latter is completely resolved by each artistic representation. What then is the marvelous faculty by which, according to the assertions of philosophers, an infinite opposition annuls itself in productive intuition? We have until now been unable to make this mechanism fully comprehensible because it is only the faculty of art that can fully disclose it. This productive faculty under consideration is the same as that by which art also attains to the impossible, namely, to resolve an infinite contradiction in a finite product. It is the poetic faculty which, in the first potency, is original intuition, and conversely it is only productive intuition repeating itself in the highest potency that we call the poetic faculty. It is one and the same thing that is active in both, the sole capacity by which we are able to think and comprehend even what is contradictory—the imagination. Hence also it is products of one and the same activity that appear to us beyond consciousness as real and on the hither side of consciousness as ideal or as a world of art. But precisely this fact, that under otherwise entirely identical conditions of origin, the genesis of one lies beyond consciousness and that of the other on this side of consciousness, constitutes the eternal and ineradicable difference between the two.

For while the real world proceeds wholly from the same original opposition as that from which the world of art must proceed (bearing in mind that the art world must also be thought of as a single great whole, and presents in all of its individual productions only the one infinite), nevertheless the opposition beyond consciousness is infinite only to the extent that an infinite is presented by the objective world as a *whole* and never by the individual object, whereas for art the opposition is infinite in regard to *each individual object*, and every single

---

inward which cannot again become objective for itself: it can become objective only through a second intuition. This second intuition is aesthetic intuition. [Alternate version by Schelling.]

product of art presents infinity. For if aesthetic production proceeds from freedom, and if the opposition of conscious and unconscious activity is absolute precisely for freedom, then there exists really only a single absolute work of art, which can to be sure exist in entirely different exemplars but which yet is only one, even though it should not yet exist in its most original form. To this view it cannot be objected that it would be inconsistent with the great freedom with which the predicate "work of art" is used. That which does not present an infinite immediately or at least in reflection is not a work of art. Shall we, e.g., also call poems works of art that by their nature present merely what is individual and subjective? Then we shall also have to apply the name to every epigram that records a merely momentary feeling or current impression. Yet the great masters who worked in these literary types sought to achieve objectivity only through the *whole* of their writings, and used them only as means whereby to represent a whole infinite life and to reflect it by a many-faceted mirror.

2. If aesthetic intuition is only intellectual intuition become objective, then it is evident that art is the sole true and eternal organon as well as document of philosophy, which sets forth in ever fresh forms what philosophy cannot represent outwardly, namely, the unconscious in action and production and its original identity with the conscious. For this very reason art occupies the highest place for the philosopher, since it opens to him, as it were, the holy of holies where in eternal and primal union, as in a single flame, there burns what is sundered in nature and history and what must eternally flee from itself in life and action as in thought. The view of nature which the philosopher composes artificially is, for art, original and natural. What we call nature is a poem that lies hidden in a mysterious and marvelous book. Yet if the riddle could reveal itself, we would recognize in it the Odyssey of the spirit which, in a strange delusion, seeking itself flees itself; for the land of fantasy toward which we aspire gleams through the world of sense only as through a half-transparent mist, only as a meaning does through words. When a great painting comes into being it is as though the invisible curtain that separates the real from the ideal world is raised; it is merely the opening through which the characters and places of the world of fantasy, which shimmers only imperfectly through the real world, fully come upon the stage. Nature is nothing more to the artist than it is to the philosopher; it is merely the ideal world appearing under unchanging limitations, or it is merely the imperfect reflection of a world that exists not outside but within him.

What is the derivation of this affinity of philosophy and art, despite their opposition? This question is already sufficiently answered by the foregoing.

We conclude therefore with the following observation. A system is completed when it has returned to its starting point. But this is precisely the case with our system. For it is just that original ground of all harmony of the subjective and the objective which could be presented in its original identity only by intellectual intuition, that was fully brought forth from the subjective and became altogether objective by means of the work of art, in such a way that we have conducted our object, the ego itself, gradually to the point at which we ourselves stood when we began to philosophize.

But now, if it is art alone that can succeed in making objective with universal validity what the philosopher can only represent subjectively, then it is to be expected (to draw this further inference) that as philosophy, and with it all the sciences that were brought to perfection by it, was born from and nurtured by poetry in the childhood of science, so now after their completion they will return as just so many individual streams to the universal ocean of poetry from which they started out. On the whole it is not difficult to say what will be the intermediate stage in the return of science to poetry, since one such intermediate stage existed in mythology before this seemingly irresolvable breach occurred. But how a new mythology (which cannot be the invention of an individual poet but only of a new generation that represents things as if it were a single poet) can itself arise, is a problem for whose solution we must look to the future destiny of the world and the further course of history alone.

General Observation on the Whole System

If the reader who has followed our progress attentively up to this point once more contemplates the organization of the whole, he will doubtless make the following observations.

The entire system falls between two extremes, of which one is characterized by intellectual and the other by aesthetic intuition. What intellectual intuition is for the philosopher, aesthetic intuition is for his object. The former, since it is necessary merely for the particular orientation of mind adopted in philosophizing, does not at all occur in ordinary consciousness. The latter, since it is nothing but intellectual intuition become objective or universally valid, *can* at least occur in every consciousness. But this also makes it possible to see that and why philosophy *as* philosophy can never be universally valid.

Absolute objectivity is given to art alone. If art is deprived of objectivity, one may say, it ceases to be what it is and becomes philosophy; give objectivity to philosophy, it ceases to be philosophy and becomes art. Philosophy, to be sure, reaches the highest level, but it brings only, as it were, a fragment of man to this point. Art brings *the whole man*, as he is, to that point, namely to a knowledge of the highest of all, and on this rests the eternal difference and the miracle of art.

Furthermore, the whole continuity of transcendental philosophy rests merely on a continuous potentiation of self-intuition, from the first, simplest stage in self-consciousness to the highest stage, the aesthetic.

The following are the potencies that the object of philosophy traverses so as to produce the total structure of self-consciousness.

The act of self-consciousness in which at the beginning the absolutely identical principle divides itself is nothing but an act of *self-intuition in general*. Consequently, nothing definite can yet be posited by this act in the ego, since it is only through it that all definiteness in general is posited. In this first act the identity first becomes subject and object simultaneously, i.e., it becomes in general ego—not for itself but for philosophizing reflection.

(What the identity is abstracted from and, as it were, *before* this act, cannot at all be asked. For it is that which can reveal itself *only* through self-consciousness and can in no way separate itself from this act.)

The second self-intuition is that by which the ego intuits the definiteness posited in the objective aspect of its activity, which occurs in sensation. In this intuition the ego is *an object for itself*, whereas in the preceding one it was object and subject only for the philosopher.

In the third self-intuition the ego becomes an object for itself also as sensing, i.e., the previously subjective phase in the ego is transposed into an objective phase. Everything in the ego, consequently, is now objective, or the ego is *wholly* objective and *as* objective it is simultaneously subject and object.

From this moment of consciousness nothing will therefore be able to remain behind except what exists, in accordance with the consciousness that has already arisen, as the absolutely-objective (the external world). In this intuition, which is already potentiated and for that very reason productive, there is contained in addition to the objective and subjective activities which are *both* objective here, still a third, a genuinely intuiting or *ideal* activity, the very same as later comes to view as *conscious* activity. But since it is merely the third of the other two, it cannot separate itself from them nor be set in opposition to them. Thus there is a conscious activity already comprised in this intuition, or the unconscious objective element is determined by a conscious activity, except that the latter is not differentiated as such.

The following intuition will be that by which the ego intuits itself as productive. However, since the ego is now *merely* objective, this intuition will also be *merely* objective, i.e., once again unconscious. There is indeed in this intuition an ideal activity which has as its object the intuiting, virtually ideal activity comprised within the preceding intuition; the intuiting activity here is thus an ideal one to the second power, i.e., a purposive activity which is, however, unconsciously purposive. What remains behind of this intuition in consciousness will thus indeed appear as purposive, but not as a purposively produced product. Such a result is *organization* throughout its entire range.

By the way of these four stages the ego is completed as intelligence. It is apparent that up to this point nature keeps pace with the ego, and hence that nature doubtless lacks only the final feature, whereby all the intuitions attain for it the same significance they have for the ego. But what this final feature may be will become evident from what follows.

If the ego were to continue to be *merely* objective, self-intuition could potentiate itself on and on to infinity; in this way the series of products in nature would merely be increased, but consciousness would never arise. Consciousness is possible only in so far as the merely objective element in the ego becomes objective *for the ego itself*. But the ground of this *cannot lie in the ego itself*. For the ego is absolutely identical with that *merely* objective phase. The ground, therefore, can only lie outside the ego, which is gradually narrowed, by progressive delimitation, to intelligence and even to individuality. *Outside* the individual, however, i.e., independent of it, there is only *intelligence itself*. But intelligence itself must (according to the deduced mechanism) limit itself, where it is, to individuality. The ground sought outside the individual can therefore lie only in *another individual*.

That which is absolutely objective can become an object *for the ego itself* only by means of the influence of another rational being. But the design of such an influence must already have lain in this latter being. Thus freedom is always already presupposed in nature (nature does not generate it), and where it is not already present as a first principle it can never arise. Here, therefore, it becomes evident that although nature is completely equal to intelligence up to this point and runs through the same potencies as intelligence, nevertheless freedom, *if* it exists (*that* it exists, however, cannot be proved theoretically), must be superior to nature (*natura prior*).

Hence a new sequence of actions, which are not possible by means of nature but leave it behind, begins at this point.

The absolutely-objective element or the lawfulness of intuition becomes an object for the ego itself. But intuition becomes an object for the intuiting agent only by means of will. The objective element in will is intuition itself, or the pure lawfulness of nature; the subjective element is an ideal activity directed upon that lawfulness in itself; the act in which this happens is the *absolute act of will*.

For the ego the absolute act of will itself becomes once more an object in that, for the ego, the objective element in will, directed toward something external, becomes object in the form of natural impulse, while the subjective element, directed toward lawfulness in itself, becomes object in the form of absolute will, i.e., categorical imperative. But this, again, is not possible without an activity superior to both. This activity is free choice or free will, or consciously free activity.

Now if this consciously free activity (which is opposed to the objective activity present in action, although it has to become one with it immediately) is intuited in its original identity with the objective activity (which is absolutely impossible by means of freedom) then there arises thereby the highest potency of self-intuition. Since this itself already lies above and beyond the *conditions* of consciousness and rather is itself consciousness self-creative from the beginning, it must appear to be simply accidental wherever it is; and this simply accidental feature in the highest potency of self-intuition is what is signified by the idea of *genius*.

These are the moments in the history of self-consciousness, invariable and fixed for all knowledge, which are expressed in experience by a continuous sequence of levels that can be exhibited and pursued from simple matter to organization (by which unconsciously productive nature returns into itself) and from that point through reason and free choice up to the highest union of freedom and necessity in art (by which nature, become consciously productive, closes and consummates itself in itself.)

Georg Wilhelm Friedrich
HEGEL

Hegel thought of himself as completing the movement, initiated by modern philosophy, which viewed reality as spirit or mind. Schelling, the last representative of this movement, had interpreted reason (in his transcendental idealism) as a form of intellectual intuition whose ultimate object is art. Hegel, on the contrary, considered art one of the ultimate forms, but not the last form of mind. Rather, for Hegel, philosophy is the final, and art but one previous step toward truth.

In the Phenomenology of Mind Hegel points out that the true is not merely substance but also subject, a living and self-developing identity, that this truth is the whole whose essence completes itself through its own development. The true can therefore be considered actual only as it is a self-determining spiritual whole whose fundamental character is self-knowledge, or self-consciousness. The highest level of the evolution of the spirit or mind, Hegel called "the Absolute." At the lower stage, which Hegel called "objective mind"—the stage of law, morality, the state, and world history—Spirit has realized itself in actuality, and now in the stage of Absolute Mind, its task becomes

*that of knowing itself in its own essence. In this self-knowledge
it becomes for itself its own Being. Yet this summit of self-
reinstating identity is joined with the historical actuality in a
curious way, for Absolute Spirit is essentially religion. But it is
religion in an inclusive sense that comprehends three forms: art,
religion proper, and philosophy. While Spirit rises above historical actuality in realizing itself in these ultimate stages of its self-
knowledge, the process of self-realization is historical, i.e., occurs
in time. Thus the highest stages of Spirit unify the eternal and
the historical.*

*Absolute mind, Hegel maintained, is the stage of self-conscious
freedom in which Mind is reconciled with its opposite. This is
truth; and how Hegel compared it with truth in the more usual
sense is evident in this passage:*

Truth is at first taken to mean that I *know* how something *is*.
This is truth, however, only in reference to consciousness; it is
formal truth, bare correctness. Truth in the deeper sense consists
in the identity between objectivity and the notion. It is in this
deeper sense of truth that we speak of a true state, or of a true
work of art. These objects are true, if they are as they ought to
be, i.e., if their reality corresponds to their notion. When thus
viewed, to be untrue means much the same as to be bad. A bad
man is an untrue man, a man who does not behave as his notion
or his vocation requires. Nothing however can subsist, if it be
wholly devoid of identity between the notion and reality. Even
bad and untrue things have being, insofar as their reality still,
somehow, conforms to their notion. Whatever is thoroughly bad
or contrary to the notion, is for that very reason on the way to
ruin. It is by the notion alone that the things in the world have
their subsistence; or, as it is expressed in the language of religious
conception, things are what they are, only in virtue of the divine
and thereby creative thought which dwells within them.

("Logic" from the *Encyclopedia*, 1817)

*Hegel's own name for truth is the Idea, which he defines as
follows: "The Idea is truth in itself and for itself—the absolute
unity of the notion and objectivity. . . . The Idea is the truth;
for truth is the correspondence of objectivity with the notion:
—not of course the correspondence of external things with my
conceptions,—for these are only correct conceptions, held by
me, the individual person." (Ibid.) The Absolute Idea, or the
Idea in its absolute form, is what we have spoken of above as
Mind or Spirit, and Mind or Spirit in its absolute form begins
at the stage of art.*

Art aims essentially at beauty, which is one way in which truth is expressed. Hence Hegel defines beauty as "the sensuous appearance or show" of the Idea. The Idea, Hegel points out, is true in itself as Idea and not true merely in its sensuous, outer existence. But at the same time the Idea is beautiful insofar as truth becomes immediately accessible to consciousness in outward form, so that the concept or idea is unified with its outer appearance. It is in this sense that beauty is the sensuous appearance of the Idea, or the show of the Absolute Concept. The concept which shows itself for itself is art.

Hegel's Lectures on Aesthetics, *gathered and organized after his death, constitutes one of the richest books in the Western literary tradition. It is also, unfortunately, one of the most neglected, for its very bulk and systematic exposition have prevented many people from knowing its comprehensiveness and sampling the wealth of concrete historical material contained in it. Indeed, much of what is still vital in the historical and stylistic inquiry into art can be traced to this book. While Hegel may do violence to the history of art through his formal, schematic a priori structuring of his subject, the great sensitivity of his interpretations, the profound attempt to realize a "science of art" led him to write a history and metaphysics of beauty. The story is one of a vital process, for the Idea evolves into the particular forms of artistic beauty, classified as "symbolic," "classic," and "romantic," by Hegel; and within each one and through all taken together he is able to discern a system of the individual arts, i.e., architecture, sculpture, painting, music, and poetry.*

Each of the particular forms of art derives its significance from the fact that in beauty, because it is the sensuous appearance of the Idea of the Absolute, there must occur a conformity between the ideal content and the sensuous, imaginative configuration. Hence the value and meaning of the arts depends on understanding the position of each in the unfolding of the Idea toward complete self-consciousness. Each of the individual arts is specifically suited to the expression of one of the art stages (symbolic, classic, romantic) though it is theoretically capable of expressing all three. In symbolic art the ideal content is less than sensuous imaginative material can express. It is too abstract and immediate to determine for itself a thoroughly individual sensuous form. The characteristic symbolic art is architecture, especially that architecture in which the object symbolically manifests the ideal content in its outward form. Hegel cites as an example Egyptian architecture—the pyramids, which he speaks of as "enormous crystals which secrete an In-

ward within them; and they so enclose an external form which is the product of art that we are made aware they stand there for this very Inward in its separation from the mere actuality of nature, and that their entire significance depends on that relation."

In Classical art the ideal content reaches the highest level that sensuous imaginative material can concretely express. Hence the Idea is completely at home in the sensuous realm only in the form of classical art. In this sense classic art represents the perfection of artistic beauty. Here the Idea is developed exactly to the degree which is most suitable for sensuous presentation. The essential classic art is that of sculpture, and Hegel thinks of sculpture, as the Greeks did, as concerned with the human form. Only the human form can reveal Spirit in sensuous fashion, an assertion that goes back to Kant, who maintained that only man is capable of an ideal of beauty, and to Winckelmann, who saw in Greek sculpture the perfection of beauty. But Hegel maintained further that Greek religion realized a concept of the divine which harmonized the ethical and the natural. Hence the Greek gods, the subject of Greek sculpture, are the perfect expression of a religion of art itself.

In Romantic art, finally, the ideal content is so evolved that it contains more than any sensuous imaginative material can expressly embody. Here too then, but in a manner converse to that of symbolic art, the Idea becomes somewhat alien to the sensuous, but now on a higher level. Romantic art is the art of subjectivity; its content is the Absolute that knows itself in its own infinite spirituality. This Hegel identifies with the God of Christianity. Romantic art takes three forms, each progressively more spiritualized: painting, whose medium is already idealized by the fact that it represents three-dimensional space in two dimensions; music, whose medium is constantly fleeting, and highly expressive of inward light; and finally poetry, whose medium of language is the most spiritual of all, the universal art which includes within itself the totality of art.

THE PHILOSOPHY OF FINE ART

Introduction

I

The present inquiry has for its subject-matter *Aesthetic*. It is a subject co-extensive with the entire *realm of the beautiful;* more specifically described, its province is that of *Art*, or rather, we should say, of *Fine Art*.

For a subject-matter such as this the term "Aesthetic" is no doubt not entirely appropriate, for "Aesthetic" denotes more accurately the science of the senses or emotion. It came by its origins as a science, or rather as something that to start with purported to be a branch of philosophy, during the period of the school of Wolff, in other words when works of art were generally regarded in Germany with reference to the feelings they were calculated to evoke, as, for example, the feelings of pleasure, admiration, fear, pity, and so forth. It is owing to the unsuitability or, more strictly speaking, the superficiality of this term that the attempt has been made by some to apply the name "Callistic" to this science. Yet this also is clearly insufficient inasmuch as the science here referred to does not investigate beauty in its general signification, but the beauty of art pure and simple. For this reason we shall accommodate ourselves to the term Aesthetic, all the more so as the mere question of nomenclature is for ourselves a matter of indifference. It has as such been provisionally accepted in ordinary speech, and we cannot do better than retain it. The *term*, however, which fully expresses our science is "Philosophy of Art," and, with still more precision, "Philosophy of Fine Art."

(*a*) In virtue of this expression we at once exclude the beauty of Nature from the scientific exposition of Fine Art. Such a limitation of our subject may very well appear from a certain point of view as an arbitrary boundary line, similar to that which every science is entitled to fix in the demarcation of its subject-matter. We must not, however, understand the limitation of "Aesthetic" to the beauty of art in this sense. We are accustomed, no doubt, in ordinary life to speak of a beautiful colour, a beautiful heaven, a beautiful stream, to say nothing of beautiful flowers, animals, and, above all, of beautiful human beings. Without entering now into the disputed question how far the quality of beauty can justly be predicated of such objects, and consequently the beauty of Nature comes generally into competition with that of art, we are justified in maintaining categorically that the beauty of art stands *higher* than Nature. For the beauty of art is a beauty begotten, a new birth of mind; and to the extent that Spirit and its creations stand higher than Nature and its phenomena, to that extent the beauty of art is more exalted than the beauty of Nature. Indeed, if we regard the matter in its formal aspect, that is to say, according to the way it is there, any chance fancy that passes through any one's head, is of higher rank than any product of Nature. For in every case intellectual conception and freedom are inseparable from such a conceit. In respect to *content* the sun appears to us an absolutely necessary constituent of actual fact, while the perverse fancy passes away as something accidental and evanescent. None the less in its own independent being a natural existence such as the sun possesses no power of self-differentiation; it is neither essentially free nor self-aware; and, if we regard it in its necessary cohesion with other things, we do not regard it independently for its own sake, and consequently not as beautiful.

Merely to maintain, in a general way, that mind and the beauty of art which originates therefrom stand *higher* than the beauty of Nature is no doubt to establish next to nothing. The expression *higher* is obviously entirely indefinite; it still indicates the beauty of Nature and art as standing juxtaposed in the field of conception, and emphasizes the difference as a quantitative and accordingly external difference. But in predicating of mind and its artistic beauty a higher place in contrast to Nature, we do not denote a distinction which is merely relative. Mind, and mind alone, is pervious to truth, comprehending all in itself, so that all which is beautiful can only be veritably beautiful as partaking in this higher sphere and as begotten of the same. Regarded under this point of view it is only a reflection of the beauty appertinent to mind, that is, we have it under an imperfect and incomplete mode, and one whose substantive being is already contained in the mind itself.

And apart from this we shall find the restriction to the beauty of art only natural, for in so far as the beauties of Nature may have come under discussion—a rarer occurrence among ancient writers than among ourselves—yet at least it has occurred to no one to insist emphatically on the beauty of natural objects to the extent of proposing a science, or systematic exposition of such beauties. It is true that the point of view of *utility* has been selected for such exclusive treatment. We have, for example, the conception of a science of natural objects in so far as they are useful in the conflict with diseases, in other words a description of minerals, chemical products, plants, animals, which subserve the art of healing. We do not find any analogous exploitation and consideration of the realm of Nature in its aspect of beauty. In the case of natural beauty we are too keenly conscious that we are dealing with an indefinite subject-matter destitute of any real criterion. It is for this reason that such an effort of comparison would carry with it too little interest to justify the attempt.

These preliminary observations over beauty in Nature and art, over the relation of both, and the exclusion of the first-mentioned from the province of our real subject-matter are intended to disabuse us of the notion that the limitation of our science is simply a question of capricious selection. We have, however, not reached the point where a *demonstration* of this fact is feasible for the reason that such an investigation falls within the limits of our science itself, and it is therefore only at a later stage that we can either discuss or prove the same.

Assuming, however, that we have, by way of prelude, limited our inquiry to the beauty of art, we are merely by this first step involved in fresh difficulties.

(*b*) What must first of all occur to us is the question whether Fine Art in itself is truly susceptible to a scientific treatment. It is a simple fact that beauty and art pervade all the affairs of life like some friendly genius, and embellish with their cheer all our surroundings, mental no less than material. They alleviate the strenuousness of such relations, the varied changes of actual life; they banish the tedium of our existence with their entertainment; and where nothing really worth having is actually achieved it is at least an advantage that they occupy the place of actual vice. Yet while art prevails on all sides with its pleasing shapes, from the crude decorations of savage tribes up to the splendours of the sacred shrine adorned with every conceivable beauty of design, none the less such shapes themselves appear to fall outside the real purposes of life, and even where the imaginative work of art is not impervious to such serious objects, nay, rather at times even appear to assist them, to the extent at least of removing what is evil to a distance, yet for all that art essentially belongs to the *relaxation* and *recreation* of spiritual life, whereas its substantive interests rather make a call upon its strained energy. On such grounds an attempt to treat that which on its own account is not of a serious character with all the gravity of scientific exposition may very possibly appear to be unsuitable and pedantic. In any case from such a point of view art appears a *superfluity* if contrasted with the essential needs and interests of life, even assuming that the *softening* of the soul which a preoccupation with the beauty of objects is capable of producing, does not actually prove injurious in its effeminate influence upon the serious quality of those *practical* interests. Owing to this fundamental assumption that they are a luxury it has often appeared necessary to undertake the defence of the fine arts relatively to the necessities of practical life, and in particular relatively to morality and piety; and inasmuch as this harmlessness is incapable of demonstration, the idea has been at least to make it appear credible, that this luxury of human experience contributes a larger proportion of *advantages* than *disadvantages*. In this respect serious aims have been attributed to art, and in many quarters it has been commended as a mediator between reason and sensuous associations, between private inclinations and duty, personified in short as a reconciler of these forces in the strenuous conflict and opposition which this antagonism generates. But it is just conceivable that, even assuming the presence of such aims with all their indubitably greater seriousness, neither reason nor duty come by much profit from such mediation, for the simple reason that they are incapable by their very nature of any such interfusion or compromise, demanding throughout the same purity which they intrinsically possess. And we might add that art does not become in any respect more worthy thereby of scientific discussion, inasmuch as it remains still on two sides a menial, that is, subservient to idleness and frivolity, if also to objects of more elevated character. In such service, moreover, it can at most merely appear as a means instead of being an object for its own sake. And, in conclusion, assuming that art is a means, it still invariably labours under the formal defect, that so far as it in fact is subservient to more serious objects, and produces results of like nature, the means which actually brings this about is *deception*. For beauty is made vital in the *appearance*. Now it can hardly be denied that aims which are true and serious ought not to be achieved by deception; and though such an effect is here and there secured by this means, such ought only to be the case in a restricted degree; and even in the exceptional case we are not justified in regarding deception as the right means. For the means ought to correspond with the dignity of the aim. Neither semblance nor deception, but only what is itself real and true, possesses a title to create what is real and true. Just in the same way science has to investigate the true interests of the mind in accordance with the actual process of the real world and the manner of conceiving it as we actually find it.

We may possibly conclude from the above grounds that the art of beauty is unworthy of philosophical examination. It is after all, it may be said, only a pleasant pastime, and, though we may admit more serious aims are also in its purview, nevertheless it is essentially opposed to such aims in their seriousness. It is at the most merely the servant of specific amusements no less than the exceptional serious objects, and for the medium of its existence as also for the means of its operations can merely avail itself of deception and show.

But yet further in the *second* place, it is a still more plausible contention that even supposing fine art to be compatible generally with philosophical disquisition, none the less it would form no really adequate subject-matter for scientific enquiry in the strict sense. For the beauty of art is presented to sense, feeling, perception, and imagination: its field is not that of thought, and the comprehension of its activity and its creations demands another faculty than that of the scientific intelligence. Furthermore, what we enjoy in artistic beauty is just the *freedom* of its creative and plastic activity. In the production and contemplation of these we appear to escape the principle of rule and system. In the creations of art we seek for an atmosphere of repose and animation as some counterpoise to the austerity of the realm of law and the sombre self-concentration of thought; we seek for blithe and powerful reality in exchange for the shadow-world of the Idea. And, last of all, the free activity of the imagination is the source of the fair works of art, which in this world of the mind are even more free than Nature is herself. Not only has art at its service the entire wealth of natural form in all their superabundant variety, but the creative imagination is able inexhaustibly to extend the realm of form by its *own* productions and modifications. In the presence of such an immeasurable depth of inspired creation and its free products, it may not unreasonably be supposed that thought will lose the courage to apprehend such in their apparent *range*, to pronounce its verdict thereon, and to appropriate such beneath its universal formulae.

Science, on the other hand, everyone must admit, is formally bound to occupy itself with thinking which abstracts from the mass of particulars: and for this very reason, from one point of view, the imagination and its contingency and caprice, in other words the organ of artistic activity and enjoyment, is excluded from it. On the other hand, when art gives joyous animation to just this gloomy and arid dryness of the notion, bringing its abstractions and divisions into reconciliation with concrete fact, supplementing with its detail what is wanting to the notion in this respect, even in that case a *purely* contemplative reflection simply removes once more all that has been added, does away with it, conducting the notion once again to that simplicity denuded of positive reality which belongs to it and its shadowland of abstraction. It is also a possible contention that science in respect to content is concerned with what is essentially *necessary*. If our science of Aesthetic places on one side natural beauty, not merely have we apparently made no advance, but rather separated ourselves yet further from what is necessary. The expression *Nature* implies from the first the ideas of *necessity* and *uniformity*, that is to say a constitution which gives every expectation of its proximity and adaptability to scientific inquiry. In mental operations generally, and most of all in the imagination, if contrasted in this respect with Nature, caprice and superiority to every kind of formal restriction, caprice, it is here assumed, is uniquely in its right place, and these at once put out of court the basis of a scientific inquiry.

From each and all these points of view consequently, in its origin, that is to say, in its effect and in its range, fine art, so far from proving itself fitted for scientific effort, rather appears fundamentally to resist the regulative principle of thought, and to be ill-adapted for exact scientific discussion.

Difficulties of this kind, and others like them, which have been raised in respect to a thoroughly scientific treatment of fine art have been borrowed from current ideas, points of view, and reflection, the more systematic expansion of which we may read *ad nauseam* in previous literature, in particular French literature, upon the subject of beauty and the fine arts. Such contain to some extent facts which have their justification; in fact, elaborate arguments are deduced therefrom, which also are not without their tincture of apparent plausibility. In this way, for instance, there is the fact that the configuration of beauty is as multifold as the phenomenon of beauty is of universal extension: from which we may conclude, if we care to do so, that a universal impulse towards beauty is enclosed in our common nature, and may yet further conceivably infer, that because the conceptions of beauty are so countless in their variety and withal are obviously something *particular*, it is impossible to secure laws of *universal* validity either relatively to beauty or our taste for it.

Before turning away from such theories to the subject, as we ourselves conceive it, it will be a necessary and preliminary task to discuss the questions and objections raised above.

First, as to the *worthiness* of art to form the object of scientific inquiry, it is no doubt the case that art can be utilized as a mere pas-

time in the service of pleasure and entertainment, either in the em-
bellishment of our surroundings, the imprinting of a delight-giving
surface to the external conditions of life, or the emphasis placed by
decoration on other objects. In these respects it is unquestionably no
independent or free art, but an art subservient to certain objects.
The kind of art, however, which *we* ourselves propose to examine is
one which is *free* in its aim and its means. That art in general can
serve other objects, and even be merely a pastime, is a relation which
it possesses in common with thought itself. From one point of view
thought likewise, as science subservient to other ends, can be used in
just the same way for finite purposes and means as they chance to
crop up, and as such serviceable faculty of science is not self-deter-
mined, but determined by something alien to it. But, further, as
distinct from such subservience to particular objects, science is raised
of its own essential resources in free independence to truth, and exclusively united with its own aims in discovering the true fulfilment in
that truth.

Fine art is not art in the true sense of the term until it is also thus
free, and its *highest* function is only then satisfied when it has established itself in a sphere which it shares with religion and philosophy, becoming thereby merely one mode and form through which the
Divine, the profoundest interests of mankind, and spiritual truths of
widest range, are brought home to consciousness and expressed. It is
in works of art that nations have deposited the richest intuitions and
ideas they possess; and not infrequently fine art supplies a key of
interpretation to the wisdom and religion of peoples; in the case of
many it is the only one. This is an attribute which art shares in common with religion and philosophy, the peculiar distinction in the case
of art being that its presentation of the most exalted subject-matter is
in sensuous form, thereby bringing them nearer to Nature and her
mode of envisagement, that is closer to our sensitive and emotional
life. The world, into the profundity of which thought penetrates, is a
supersensuous one, a world which to start with is posited as a Beyond
in contrast to the immediacy of ordinary conscious life and present
sensation. It is the freedom of reflecting consciousness which disengages itself from this immersion in the "*this side*," or immediacy, in
other words sensuous reality and finitude. But the mind is able, too,
to heal the *fracture* which is thus created in its progression. From the
wealth of its own resources it brings into being the works of fine art as
the primary bond of mediation between that which is exclusively external, sensuous and transitory, and the medium of pure thought, be-

tween Nature and its finite reality, and the infinite freedom of a reason which comprehends. Now it was objected that the *element of art* was, if we view it as a whole, of an *unworthy* character, inasmuch as it consisted of appearance and deceptions inseparable from such. Such a contention would of course be justifiable, if we were entitled to assume that appearance had no *locus standi* at all. An appearance or show is, however, essential to actuality. There could be no such thing as truth if it did not appear, or, rather, let itself appear, were it not further true for some *one* thing or person, *for* itself as also *for* spirit. Consequently it cannot be appearance in general against which such an objection can be raised, but the particular mode of its manifestation under which art makes actual what is essentially real and true. If, then, the appearance, in the medium of which art gives determinate existence to its creations, be defined as *deception*, such an objection is in the first instance intelligible if we compare it with the *external world* of a phenomena, and its *immediate* relation to ourselves as material substance, or view it relatively to our own world of emotions, that is our inward sensuous life. Both these are worlds to which in our everyday life, the life, that is, of visible experience, we are accustomed to attach the worth and name of reality, actuality and truth as contrasted with that of art, which fails to possess such reality as we suppose. Now it is just this entire sphere of the empirical world, whether on its personal side or its objective side, which we ought rather to call in a stricter sense than when we apply the term to the world of art, merely a show or appearance, and an even more unyielding form of deception. It is only beyond the immediacy of emotional life and that world of external objects that we shall discover reality in any true sense of the term. Nothing is actually real but that which is actual in its own independent right and substance, that which is at once of the substance of Nature and of mind, which, while it is actually *here* in present and determinate existence, yet retains under such limitation an essential and self-concentred being, and only in virtue of such is truly real. The predominance of these universal powers is precisely that which art accentuates and manifests. In the external and soul-world of ordinary experience we have also no doubt this essence of actuality, but in the chaotic congeries of particular detail, encumbered by the immediacy of sensuous envisagement, and every kind of caprice of condition, event, character, and so forth. Now it is just the show and deception of this false and evanescent world which art disengages from the veritable significance of phenomena to which we have referred, implanting in the same a reality of more exalted rank born of mind. The phenomena of art therefore are not merely not appearance and nothing more; we are justified in ascribing to them, as contrasted with the realities of our ordinary life, an actually higher reality and more veritable existence. To as little extent are the representations of art a deceptive appearance as compared with the assumed truer delineations of historical writing. For immediate existence also does not belong to historical writing. It only possesses the intellectual appearance of the same as the medium of its delineations, and its content remains charged with the entire contingent *materia* of ordinary reality and its events, developments and personalities, whereas the work of art brings us face to face with the eternal powers paramount in history with this incidental association of the immediate sensuous present and its unstable appearance expunged.

If, however, it is in contrast with philosophic thought and religious and ethical principles, that the mode of appearance of the shapes of art, is described as a deception, there is certainly this in support of the view that the mode of revelation attained by a content in the realm of thought is the truest reality. In comparison, nevertheless, with the appearance of immediate sensuous existence and that of historical narration, the show of art possesses the advantage that, in its own virtue, it points beyond itself, directing us to a somewhat spiritual, which it seeks to envisage to the conceptive mind. Immediate appearance, on the contrary, does not give itself out to be thus illusive, but rather to be the true and real, though as a matter of fact such truth is contaminated and obstructed by the immediately sensuous medium. The hard rind of Nature and the everyday world offer more difficulty to the mind in breaking through to the Idea than do the products of art.

But if from this particular point of view we place art thus highly, we must not, on the other hand, fail to remember that neither in respect to content or form is art either the highest or most absolute mode of bringing the true interests of our spiritual life to consciousness. The very form of art itself is sufficient to limit it to a definite content. It is only a particular sphere and grade of truth which is capable of being reproduced in the form of a work of art. Such truth must have the power in its own determinate character to go out freely into sensuous shape and remain adequate to itself therein, if it is to be the genuine content of art, as is the case, for example, with the gods of Greece. On the other hand there is a profounder grasp of truth, in which the form is no longer on such easy and friendly terms with the sensuous material as to be adequately accepted and expressed by that medium.

Of such a type is the Christian conception of truth; and above all it is the prevailing spirit of our modern world, or, more strictly, of our religion and our intellectual culture, which have passed beyond the point at which art is the highest mode under which the absolute is brought home to human consciousness. The type peculiar to art-production and its products fails any longer to satisfy man's highest need. We are beyond the stage of reverence for works of art as divine and objects deserving our worship. The impression they produce is one of a more reflective kind, and the emotions which they arouse require a higher test and a further verification. Thought and reflection have taken their flight above fine art. To those who are fond of complaint and grumbling such a condition of things may be held as a form of decadence; it may be ascribed to the obsession of passion and selfish interests, which scare away the seriousness of art no less than its blithesomeness. Or we may find the fault to lie in the exigencies of the present day, the complex conditions of social and political life, which prevent the soul, entangled as it is in microscopic interests, from securing its freedom in the nobler objects of art, a condition, too, in which the intelligence itself becomes a menial to such trifling wants and the interests they excite in sciences, which subserve objects of a like nature, and are seduced into the voluntary exile of such a wilderness.

But however we may explain the fact it certainly is the case that Art is no longer able to discover that satisfaction of spiritual wants, which previous epochs and nations have sought for in it and exclusively found in it, a satisfaction which, at least on the religious side, was associated with art in the most intimate way. The fair days of Greek art, as also the golden time of the later middle ages, are over. The reflective culture of our life of to-day makes it inevitable, both relatively to our volitional power and our judgment, that we adhere strictly to general points of view, and regulate particular matters in consonance with them, so that universal forms, laws, duties, rights, and maxims hold valid as the determining basis of our life and the force within of main importance. What is demanded for artistic interest as also for artistic creation is, speaking in general terms, a vital energy, in which the universal is not present as law and maxim, but is operative in union with the soul and emotions, just as also, in the imagination, what is universal and rational is enclosed only as brought into unity with a concrete sensuous phenomenon. For this reason the present time is not, if we review its conditions in their widest range, favourable to art. And with regard to the executive artist himself it is not merely that reflection on every side, which *will* insist on utterance, owing to the universal habit of critical opinion and judgment, leads him astray from his art and infects his mind with a like desire to accumulate abstract thought in his creations; rather the entire spiritual culture of the times is of such a nature that he himself stands within a world thus disposed to reflection and the conditions it presupposes, and, do what he may, he cannot release himself either by his wish or his power of decision from their influence, neither can he by means of exceptional education, or a removal from the ordinary conditions of life, conjure up for himself and secure a solitude capable of replacing all that is lost.

In all these respects art is and remains for us, on the side of its highest possibilities, a thing of the past. Herein it has further lost its genuine truth and life, and is rather transported to our world of *ideas* than is able to maintain its former necessity and its superior place in reality. What is now stimulated in us by works of art is, in addition to the fact of immediate enjoyment, our judgment. In other words we subject the content, and the means of presentation of the work of art, and the suitability and unsuitability of both, to the contemplation of our thought. A *science* of art is therefore a far more urgent necessity in our own days than in times in which art as art sufficed by itself alone to give complete satisfaction. We are invited by art to contemplate it reflectively, not, that is to say, with the object of recreating such art, but in order to ascertain scientifically its nature.

In doing our best to accept such an invitation we are confronted with the objection already adverted to, that even assuming that art is a subject adapted for philosophical investigation in a general way, yet it unquestionably is not so adapted to the systematic procedure of science. Such an objection, however, implies to start with the false notion that we can have a philosophical inquiry which is at the same time unscientific. In reply to such a point I can only here state summarily my opinion, that whatever ideas other people may have of philosophy and philosophizing, I myself conceive philosophical inquiry of any sort or kind to be inseparable from the methods of science. The function of philosophy is to examine subject-matter in the light of the principle of necessity, not, it is true, merely in accordance with its subjective necessity or external co-ordination, classification, and so forth; it has rather to unfold and demonstrate the object under review out of the necessity of its own intimate nature. Until this essential process is made explicit the scientific quality of such an inquiry is absent. In so far, however, as the objective necessity of an object subsists essentially in its logical and metaphysical nature the isolated examination of art may in such a case, at any rate, or rather inevitably, must be carried forward with a certain relaxation of scientific stringency. For art is based upon many assumptions, part of which relate to its content, part to its material or conceptive medium, in virtue of which art is never far from the borders of contingency and caprice. Consequently it is only relatively to the essential and ideal progression of its content and its means of expression that we are able to recall with advantage the formative principle of its necessity.

The objection that works of fine art defy the examination of scientific thought, because they originate in the unregulated world of imagination and temperament, and assert their effect exclusively on the emotions and the fancy with a complexity and variety which defies exact analysis, raises a difficulty which still carries genuine weight behind it. As a matter of fact the beauty of art does appear in a form which is expressly to be contrasted with abstract thought, a form which it is compelled to disturb in order to exercise its own activity in its own way. Such a result is simply a corollary of the thesis that reality anywhere and everywhere, whether the life of Nature or mind, is defaced and slain by its comprehension; that so far from being brought more close to us by the comprehension of thinking, it is only by this means that it is in the complete sense removed apart from us, so that in his attempt to grasp through thought as a *means* the nature of life, man rather renders nugatory this very aim. An exhaustive discussion of the subject is here impossible; we propose merely to indicate the point of view from which the removal of this difficulty or impossibility and incompatibility might be effected. It will at least be readily admitted that mind is capable of self-contemplation, and of possessing a consciousness, and indeed one that implies a power of thought co-extensive with itself and everything which originates from itself. It is, in fact, precisely *thought,* the process of thinking, which constitutes the most intimate and essential nature of mind. It is in this thinking consciousness over itself and its products, despite all the freedom and caprice such may otherwise and indeed must invariably possess—assuming only mind or spirit to be veritably pregnant therein —that mind exhibits the activity congenial to its essential nature. Art and the creations of art, being works which originate in and are begotten of the spirit, are themselves stamped with the hall-mark of spirit, even though the mode of its presentation accept for its own the phenomenal guise of sensuous reality, permeating as it does the sensuous substance with intelligence. Viewed in this light art is placed from the first nearer to spirit and its thought than the purely external and unintelligent Nature. In the products of art mind is exclusively dealing with that which is its own. And although works of art are not thought and notion simply as such, but an evolution of the notion out of itself, an alienation of the same in the direction of sensuous being, yet for all that the might of the thinking spirit is discovered *not merely* in its ability to grasp *itself* in its most native form as pure thinking, but also, and as completely, to recognize itself in its self-divestment in the medium of emotion and the sensuous, to retain the grasp of itself in that "other" which it transforms but is not, trans-muting the alien factor into thought-expression, and by so doing re-covering it to itself. And moreover in this active and frequent relation to that "other" than itself the reflective mind is not in any way un-true to itself. We have here no oblivion or surrender of itself; neither is it so impotent as to be unable to comprehend what is differentiated from that other; what it actually does is to grasp in the notion *both* itself and its opposite. For the notion is the universal, which maintains itself in its particularizations, which covers in its grasp both itself and its "other," and consequently contains the power and energy to can-cel the very alienation into which it passes. For this reason the work of art, in which thought divests itself of itself, belongs to the realm of comprehending thought; and mind, by subjecting it to scientific contemplation, thereby simply satisfies its most essential nature. For inasmuch as thought is its essence and notion, it can only ultimately find such a satisfaction after passing all the products of its activity through the alembic of rational thought, and in this way making them for the first time in very truth part of its own substance. But though art, as we shall eventually see with yet more distinctness, is far indeed from being the highest form of mind, it is only in the philosophy of art that it comes into all that it may justly claim.

In the same way art is not debarred from a philosophical inquiry by reason of its unregulated caprice. As already intimated, it is its true function to bring to consciousness the highest interests of mind. An immediate consequence of this is that, so far as the *content* of fine art is concerned, it cannot range about in all the wildness of an un-bridled fancy; these interests of spirit posit categorically for the con-tent that embodies them definite points of attachment, however mul-tifold and inexhaustible may be the forms and shapes they assume. The same may be said of the forms themselves. They too do not re-main unaffected by constraining principles. It is not every chance form which is capable of expressing and presenting these interests, capable of assimilating them and reproducing them. It is only through one determinate content that the form adequate to its embodiment is defined.

It is upon grounds such as these that we are also able to discover a track adapted to critical reflection through the apparently endless vistas of artistic creations and shapes.

We have now, I trust, by way of prelude, succeeded in restricting the content of our science on the lines of definition proposed. We have made it clear that neither is fine art unworthy of philosophical study, nor is such a philosophical study incapable of accepting as an object of its cognition the essence of fine art.

II

3. The philosophical idea of the beautiful . . . must combine, that is to say, metaphysical universality with the determinate content of real particularity. It is only by this means that it is grasped in its essential no less than explicit truth. For on the one hand it is then, as contrasted with the sterility of one-sided reflection, fruit-bearing out of its own wealth. It is its function, in consonance with its own notion, to develop into a totality of definite qualities, and this essential conception itself, no less than its detailed explication, comprises the necessary coherence of its particular features as also of the progress and transition of one phase thereof into another. On the other hand, these particulars into which the passage is made essentially carry the universality and essentiality of the fundamental notion as the particulars of which they appear.

. . . . .

III

. . . What in the first instance is known to us under current conceptions of a work of art may be subsumed under the three following determinations:

(1)   A work of art is no product of Nature. It is brought into being through the agency of man.

(2)   It is created essentially *for* man; and, what is more, it is to a greater or less degree delivered from a sensuous medium, and addressed to his *senses*.

(3)   It contains an *end* bound up with it.

1.   With regard to the first point, that a work of art is a product of

human activity, an inference has been drawn from this (*a*) that such an activity, being the conscious production of an external object can also be *known* and *divulged,* and learned and reproduced by others. For that which one is able to effect, another—such is the notion—is able to effect or to imitate, when he has once simply mastered the way of doing it. In short we have merely to assume an acquaintance with the rules of art-production universally shared, and anybody may then, if he cares to do so, give effect to executive ability of the same type, and produce works of art. It is out of reasoning of this kind that the above-mentioned theories, with their provision of rules, and their prescriptions formulated for practical acceptance, have arisen. Unfortunately that which is capable of being brought into effect in accordance with suggestions of this description can only be something formally regular and mechanical. For only that which is mechanical is of so exterior a type that only an entirely empty effort of will and dexterity is required to accept it among our working conceptions, and forthwith to carry it out; an effort, in fact, which is not under the necessity to contribute out of its own resources anything concrete such as is quite outside the prescriptive power of such general rules.

This is apparent with most vividness when precepts of this kind are not limited to what is purely external and mechanical, but extend their pretensions to the activity of the artist in the sense that implies wealth of significance and intelligence. In this field our rules pass off to purely indefinite generalities, such as "the theme ought to be interesting, and each individual person must speak as is appropriate to his status, age, sex and situation." But if rules are really to suffice for such a purpose their directions ought to be formulated with such directness of detail that, without any further co-operation of mind, they could be executed precisely in the manner they are prescribed. Such rules being, in respect to this content, abstract, clearly and entirely fall short of their pretension of being able to complete the artistic consciousness. Artistic production is not a formal activity in accordance with a series of definitions; it is, as an activity of soul, constrained to work out of its own wealth, and to bring before the mind's eye a wholly other and far richer content, and a more embracing and unique creation than ever can be thus prescribed. In particular cases such rules may prove of assistance, in so far, that is, as they contain something really definite and consequently useful for practice. But even here their guidance will only apply to conditions wholly external.

(*b*) This above indicated tendency has consequently been wholly given up; but writers in doing so have only fallen as unreservedly into the opposite extreme. A work of art came to be looked upon, and so far rightly, as no longer the product of an activity *shared by all men*, but rather as a creation of a mind gifted in an extraordinary degree. A mind of this type has in this view *merely* to give free vent to its peculiar endowment, regarded as a specific natural power. It has to free itself absolutely from a pursuit of rules of universal application, as also from any admixture of conscious reflection with its creative and, as thus viewed, wholly instinctive powers, or rather it should be on its guard therefrom, the assumption being that such an exercise of conscious thought can only act on its creations as an infection and a taint. Agreeably to such a view the work of art has been heralded as the product of *talent* and *genius*; and it is mainly the aspect of natural gift inseparable from the ordinary conception of talent and genius, which has been emphasized. There is to some extent real truth in this. Talent is specific, genius universal capacity. With neither of these can a man endow himself *simply* by the exercise of his self-conscious activity.

· · · · ·

. . . The real and indeed sole point to maintain as essential is the thesis that although artistic talent and genius essentially implies an element of natural power, yet it is equally indispensable that it should be thoughtfully cultivated, that reflection should be brought to bear on the particular way it is exercised, and that it should be also kept alive with use and practice in actual work. The fact is that an important aspect of the creating process is merely facility in the use of a medium; that is to say, a work of art possesses a purely technical side, which extends to the borders of mere handicraft. This is most obviously the case in architecture and sculpture, less so in painting and music, least of all in poetry. A facility here is not assisted at all by inspiration; what is solely indispensable is reflection, industry, and practice. Such technical skill an artist simply *must* possess in order that he may be master over the external material, and not be thwarted by its obstinacy.

Add to this that the more exalted the rank of an artist the more profoundly ought he to portray depth of soul and mind; and these are not to be known by flashlight, but are exclusively to be sounded, if at all, by the direction of the man's own intelligence on the world of souls and the objective world. In this respect, therefore, once more *study* is the means whereby the artist brings to consciousness such a

content, and appropriates the material and structure of his conceptions. At the same time no doubt one art will require such a conscious reception and cognitive mastery of the content in question
more than another. Music, for example, which has exclusively to deal
with the entirely undefined motion of the soul within, with the musical tones of that which is, relatively, feeling denuded of positive
thought, has little or no need to bring home to consciousness the
substance of intellectual conception. For this very reason musical
talent declares itself as a rule in very early youth, when the head is
still empty and the emotions have barely had a flutter; it has, in fact,
attained real distinction at a time in the artist's life when both intelligence and life are practically without experience. And for the matter
of that we often enough see very great accomplishment in musical
composition and execution hung together with considerable indigence
of mind and character. It is quite another matter in the case of poetry.
What is of main importance here is a presentation of our humanity
rich in subject-matter and reflective power, of its profounder interests,
and of the forces which move it. Here at least mind and heart must
themselves be richly and profoundly disciplined by life, experience,
and thought before genius itself can bring into being the fruit that is
ripe, the content that has substance, and is essentially consummate.

. . . . .

(c)   A third view, held relatively to the idea of a work of art as a
product of human activity, concerns the position of such towards the
phenomena of Nature. The natural tendency of ordinary thinking in
this respect is to assume that the product of human art is of *subordinate* rank to the works of Nature. The work of art possesses no feeling
of its own; it is not through and through a living thing, but, regarded
as an external object, is a dead thing. It is usual to regard that
which is alive of higher worth than what is dead. We may admit, of
course, that the work of art is not in itself capable of movement and
alive. The living, natural thing is, whether looked at within or without, an organization with the life-purpose of such worked out into
the minutest detail. The work of art merely attains to the show of
animation on its surface. Below this it is ordinary stone, wood, or canvas, or in the case of poetry idea, the medium of such being speech
and letters. But this element of external existence is not that which
makes a work a creation of fine art. A work of art is only truly such
in so far as originating in the human spirit, it continues to belong to
the soil from which it sprang, has received, in short, the baptism of

the mind and soul of man, and only presents that which is fashioned in consonance with such a sacrament. An interest vital to man, the spiritual values which the single event, one individual character, one action possesses in its devolution and final issue, is seized in the work of art and emphasized with greater purity and clarity than is possible on the ground of ordinary reality where human art is not. And for this reason the work of art is of higher rank than any product of Nature whatever, which has not submitted to this passage through the mind. In virtue of the emotion and insight, for example, in the atmosphere of which a landscape is portrayed by the art of painting, this creation of the human spirit assumes a higher rank than the purely natural landscape. Everything which partakes of spirit is better than anything begotten of mere Nature. However this may be, the fact remains that no purely natural existence is able, as art is, to represent divine ideals.

And further, all that the mind borrows from its own ideal content it is able, even in the direction of external existence, to endow with *permanence*. The individual living thing on the contrary is transitory; it vanishes and is unstable in its external aspect. The work of art persists. At the same time it is not mere continuation, but rather the form and pressure thereon of the mintage of soul-life which constitutes its true pre-eminence as contrasted with Nature's reality.

But this higher position we have thus assigned to the work of art is yet further contested by another prevalent conception of ordinary ideas. It is contended that Nature and all that proceeds from her are a work of God, created by His goodness and wisdom. The work of art is on the contrary *merely* a human product fashioned by human hands according to human design. The fallacy implied in this contrast between the products of Nature viewed as a divine creation and human activity as of wholly finite energy consists in the apparent assumption that God is not operative in and through man, but limits the sphere of His activity to Nature alone. We must place this false conception entirely on one side if we are desirous of penetrating to the true idea of art; or rather, as opposed to such a conception we ought to accept the extreme opposite thereto, namely, that God is more honoured by that which mind makes and creates than by everything brought into being and fashioned in the natural process. For not only is there a divinity in man, but it is actually effective in him in a form which is adequate to the essential nature of God in a far higher degree than in the work of Nature. God is a Spirit, and it is only in man that the medium, through which the Divine passes, possesses the form of spirit fully conscious of the activity in which it manifests its ideal presence.

In Nature the medium correspondent to this is the unconscious sensuous and external *materia*, which is by many degrees inferior to consciousness in its worth. In the products of art God works precisely as He works through the phenomena of Nature. The divine substance, however, as it is asserted in the work of art has secured, being begotten of spirit life itself, a highway commensurable to its existence; determinate existence in the unconscious sensuousness of Nature is not a mode of appearance adequate to the Divine Being.

(*d*) Assuming, then, that the work of art is a creation of man in the sense that it is the offspring of mind or spirit we have still a further question in conclusion, which will help us to draw a more profound inference still from our previous discussion. That question is, "What is the human *need* which stimulates art-production?" On the one hand the artistic activity may be regarded as the mere play of accident, or human conceits, which might just as well be left alone as attempted. For, it may be urged, there are other and better means for carrying into effect the aims of art, and man bears within himself higher and more weighty interests, than art is capable of satisfying. In contrast to such a view art appears to originate in a higher impulse, and to satisfy more elevated needs, nay, at certain times the highest and most absolute of all, being, as it has been, united to the most embracing views of entire epochs and nations upon the constitution of the world and the nature of their religion.

· · · · ·

The universal and absolute want from which art on its side of essential form arises originates in the fact that man is a *thinking* consciousness, in other words that he renders explicit *to himself*, and from his own substance, what he is and all in fact that exists. The objects of Nature exist exclusively in immediacy and *once for all*. Man, on the contrary, as mind *reduplicates* himself. He is, to start with, an object of Nature as other objects; but in addition to this, and no less truly, he exists *for himself*; he observes himself, makes himself present to his imagination and thought, and only in virtue of this active power of self-realization is he actually mind or spirit. This consciousness of himself man acquires in a twofold way; in the *first* instance *theoretically*. This is so in so far as he is under a constraint to bring himself in his own inner life to consciousness—all which moves in the human heart, all that surges up and strives therein—and generally, so far as he is impelled to make himself an object of perception and conception, to fix for himself definitively that which thought discovers as essential being, and in all that he summons out of himself, no less than in that which is received from without, to recognize only himself. And *secondly*, this realization is effected through a *practical* activity. In other words man possesses an impulse to assert himself in that which is presented him in immediacy, in that which is at hand as an external something to himself, and by doing so at the same time once more to recognize himself therein. This purpose he achieved by the alteration he effects in such external objects, upon which he imprints the seal of his inner life, rediscovering in them thereby the features of his own determinate nature. And man does all this, in order that he may as a free agent divest the external world of its stubborn alienation from himself—and in order that he may enjoy in the configuration of objective fact an external reality simply of himself. The very first impulse of the child implies in essentials this practical process of deliberate change in external fact. A boy throws stones into the stream, and then looks with wonder at the circles which follow in the water, regarding them as a result in which he sees something of his own doing. This human need runs through the most varied phenomena up to that particular form of self-reproduction in the external fact which is presented us in human art. And it is not merely in relation to external objects that man acts thus. He treats himself, that is, his natural form, in a similar manner: he will not permit it to remain as he finds it; he alters it deliberately. This is the rational ground of all ornament and decoration, though it may be as barbarous, tasteless, entirely disfiguring, nay, as injurious as the crushing of the feet of Chinese ladies, or the slitting of ears and lips. For it is among the really cultured alone that a change of figure, behaviour, and every mode and manner of self-expression will issue in harmony with the dictates of mental elevation.

This universal demand for artistic expression is based on the rational impulse in man's nature to exalt both the world of his soul experience and that of Nature for himself into the conscious embrace of mind as an object in which he rediscovers himself. He satisfies the demand of this spiritual freedom by making explicit to his *inner* life all that exists, no less than from the further point of view giving a realized *external* embodiment to the self made thus explicit. And by this reduplication of what is his own he places before the vision and within the cognition of himself and others what is within him. This is the free rationality of man, in which art as also all action and knowledge originates. We shall investigate at a later stage the specific need for art as compared with that for other political and ethical action, or that for religious ideas and scientific knowledge.

2. We have hitherto considered the work of art under the aspect that it is fashioned by man; we will now pass over to the second part of our definition, that it is produced for his *sense-apprehension*, and consequently is to a more or less degree under obligations to a sensuous medium.

(a) This reflection has been responsible for the inference that the function of fine art is to arouse feeling, more precisely the feeling which suits us—that is, pleasant feeling. From such a point of view writers have converted the investigation of fine art into a treatise on the emotions and asked what kind of feelings art ought to excite—take fear, for example, and compassion—with the further question how such can be regarded as pleasant, how, in short, the contemplation of misfortune can bring satisfaction. This tendency of reflection dates for the most part from the times of Moses Mendelssohn, and many such trains of reasoning may be found in his writings. A discussion of this kind, however, did not carry the problem far. Feeling is the undefined obscure region of spiritual life. What is felt remains cloaked in the form of the separate personal experience under its most abstract persistence; and for this reason the distinctions of feeling are wholly abstract; they are not distinctions which apply to the subject-matter itself. To take examples—fear, anxiety, care, dread, are of course one type of emotion under various modifications; but in part they are purely quantitative degrees of intensity, and in part forms which reflect no light on their content itself, but are indifferent to it. In the case of fear, for instance, an existence is assumed, for which the individual in question possesses an interest, but sees at the same time the negative approach which threatens to destroy this existence, and thereupon discovers in immediate fusion within himself the above interest and the approach of that negative as a contradictory affection of his personal life. A fear of this sort, however, does not on its own account condition any particular content; it may associate with itself subject-matter of the most opposed and varied character. The feeling merely as such is in short a wholly empty form of a subjective state. Such a form may no doubt in certain cases itself be essentially complex, as we find it is with hope, pain, joy, and pleasure; it may also in this very complexity appropriate various modes of content, as, for example, we have a feeling of justice, an ethical feeling, a sublime religious feeling, and so forth; but despite the fact that a content of this kind is present in different modes of feeling, no light whatever is thereby thrown on such content which will disclose its essential and definite character. The feeling throughout remains a purely subjective state which belongs to me, one in which the concrete fact vanishes, as though contracted to a vanishing point in the most abstract of all spheres. For this reason an inquiry over the nature of the emotions which art ought or ought not to arouse, comes simply to a standstill in the undefined; it is an investigation which deliberately abstracts from genuine content and its concrete substance and notion. Reflection upon feeling is satisfied with the observation of the personal emotional state and its singularity, instead of penetrating and sounding the matter for study, in other words the work of art, and in doing so bidding good-bye to the wholly subjective state and its conditions. In feeling, however, it is just this subjective state void of content which is not merely accepted, but becomes the main thing; and that is precisely why people are so proud of having emotions. And for no other reason that is why such an investigation is tedious owing to its indefinite nature and emptiness, and even repellent in its attention to trivial personal idiosyncrasies.

(*b*) Inasmuch, however, as the work of art is not merely concerned with exciting some kind of emotion or other—for this is an object it would share without any valid distinction with eloquence, historical composition, religious edification and much else—but is only a work of art in so far as it is beautiful, it occurred to reflective minds to discover a *specific feeling for beauty*, and a distinct *sense-faculty* correspondent with it. In such an inquiry it soon became clear that a sense of this kind was no definite and mere instinct rigidly fixed by Nature, which was able by itself and independently to distinguish the beautiful. As a consequence the demand was made for *culture* as a condition precedent to such a sense, and the sense of beauty as thus cultivated was called *taste*, which, albeit an instructed apprehension and discovery of the beautiful, was none the less assumed to persist in the character of immediate feeling. We have already discussed the way in which abstract theory attempted to form such a sense of taste, and how external and one-sided that sense remained. While the critical sense generally of the time when such ideas were in currency was lacking in the *universality* of its principles, as a *specific* critique of particular works of art it was less concerned to substantiate a judgment *more decisive* than hitherto—indeed the

material to effectuate this was not as yet forthcoming—than to promote in a general way the *cultivation* of such a taste. Consequently
this educative process also came to a halt in the region of the more
indefinite, and merely busied itself by its reflections in the fitting out
of feeling as a sense of beauty in such a way that beauty could immediately be discovered whenever and wherever it might chance to
appear. The real depth of the subject-matter remained notwithstanding a closed book to such a taste. Profundity of this kind demands not
merely sensitive reception and abstract thought, but the reason in its
concrete grasp and the most sterling qualities of soul-life. Taste on
the contrary is merely directed to the outside surfaces, which are the
playground of the feelings, and upon which one-sided principles may
very well pass as currency. But for this very reason our so-called good
taste is scared by every kind of profounder artistic effect, and is
dumb where the ideal significance is in question, and all mere ex-
ternalities and accessories vanish. For when great passions and the
movements of a profound soul assert themselves, we do not bother
ourselves any more with the finer distinctions of taste and its retail
traffic in trifles. It is conscious that genius leaves such ground far behind it in its stride; and shrinking before that power feels on its part
far from comfortable, not knowing very well which way to turn.

(c)   Thus it is the further change has come about that critics of
art-production no longer have an eye simply to the education of
taste, or are intent upon the illustration of such a sense. The *con-
noisseur*, or art-scholar, has taken the place of the man, or judge of
artistic taste. The positive side of art-scholarship, in so far as it implies
a sound and exhaustive acquaintance with the entire embrace of
what is distinctive and peculiar in a given work of art, we have already maintained to be a necessary condition of artistic research. A
work of art, owing to its nature, which, if it is material from one
point of view, is also related to a particular person, originates from
specific conditions of the most varied kind, among which as excep-
tionally important we may mention the date and place of its origins,
the characteristic personality of the artist, and, above all, the degree
of executive accomplishment secured by the art. All these points of
view have to be taken into consideration if we wish to obtain a
view and knowledge of such a work which is clear in its outlines, and
founded on a true basis, nay, even wish to enjoy it rightly. It is with
these that our art-scholarship is mainly occupied; and all that it can
do for us in this way should be gratefully accepted. Though it is quite

true such art-scholarship must be reckoned as of essential importance, it ought not be regarded as the sole, or indeed the highest, constituent in the relation of the contemplative spirit to a work of art and art generally. Such art-scholarship (this is the defective tendency) may restrict itself wholly to a knowledge of purely external characteristics, either on the side of technique or historical condition, or in other directions; it may continue to possess the barest inkling of the true nature of a given work, or simply no knowledge at all. It may even form a depreciatory verdict on the value of profounder inquiries as compared with purely matter of fact, technical, and historical knowledge. Yet even so an art-scholarship, assuming it to be really genuine and thorough, at least proceeds upon grounds and knowledge which are definite, and an intelligent judgment; and it is association with such that our more accurate review of the distinct, if also to some extent exterior, aspects of a work of art, and our estimate of their relative significance, is secured.

(d) Following the above observations upon the modes of inquiry which were suggested by that aspect of a work of art in which, as itself an object with a material medium, it possessed an essential relation to man as himself receptive through sense, we will now examine this point of view in its more essential connection with art itself. We propose to do ths partly (α) in respect to the art-product viewed as an object, partly (β) as regards the personal characteristics of the artist, his genius, talent, and so forth. We do not, however, propose to enter into matter which can in this connection exclusively proceed from the knowledge of art according to its universal concept. The truth is we are not as yet in the full sense on scientific ground; we have merely reached the province of external reflection.

(α) There is no question, then, that a work of art is presented to sensuous apprehension. It is submitted to the emotional sense, whether outer or inner, to sensuous perception and the imaged sense, precisely as the objective world is so presented around us, or as is our own inward sensitive nature. Even a speech, for example, may be addressed to the sensuous imagination and feeling. Notwithstanding this fact, however, the work of art is not exclusively directed to the *sensuous* apprehension, viewed, that is, as an object materially conditioned. Its position is of the nature, that along with its sensuous presentation it is fundamentally addressed to the *mind*. The mind is intended to be affected by it and to receive some kind of satisfaction in it.

This function of the work of art at once makes it clear how it is that it is in no way intended to be a natural product or, on the side where it impinges on Nature, to possess the living principle of Nature. This, at least, is a fact whether the natural product is ranked lower or higher than a *mere* work of art, as people are accustomed to express themselves in the tone of depreciation.

In other words the sensuous aspect of a work of art has a right to determinate existence only in so far as it exists for the human mind, not, however, in so far as itself, as a material object, exists for itself independently.

If we examine more closely in what way the sensuous *materia* is presented to man we find that what is so can be placed under various relations to the mind.

(aa) The lowest in grade and that least compatible with relation to intelligence is purely sensuous sensation. It consists primarily in mere looking, listening, just as in times of mental overstrain it may often be a relaxation to go about without thought, and merely listen and have a look round. The mind, however, does not rest in the mere apprehension of external objects through sight and hearing; it makes them objective to its own inward nature, which thereupon is impelled itself to give effect to itself in these things as a further step under a sensuous mode, in other words, it relates itself to them as *desire*. In this appetitive relation to the external world man, as a sensuous particular thing, stands in a relation of opposition to things in general as in the same way particulars. He does not address himself to them with open mind and the universal ideas of thought; he retains an isolated position, with its personal impulses and interests, relatively to objects as fixed in their obduracy as himself, and makes himself at home in them by using them, or eating them up altogether, and, in short, gives effect to his self-satisfaction by the sacrifice he makes of them. In this negative relation desire requires for itself not merely the superficial show of external objects, but the actual things themselves in their material concrete existence. Mere pictures of the wood, which it seeks to make use of, or of the animals, which it hopes to eat up, would be of no service to desire. Just as little is it possible for desire to suffer the object to remain in its freedom; its craving is just this to force it to annihilate this self-subsistency and freedom of external facts, and to demonstrate that these things are only there to be destroyed and devoured. But at the same time the particular person is neither himself free, begirt as he is by the particular limited and transitory interests of his desires, for his definite acts do not proceed from the essential universality and rationality of his will, neither is he free relatively to the external world, for desire remains essentially determined by things and related to them.

This relation, then, of desire is not that in which man is related to the work of art. He suffers it to exist in its free independence as an object; he associates himself with it without any craving of this kind, rather as with an object reflective of himself, which exists solely for the contemplative faculty of mind. For this reason, as we have said, the work of art, although it possesses sensuous existence, does not require sensuous concrete existence, nor yet the animated life of such objects. Or, rather, we should add, it *ought* not to remain on such a level, in so far as its true function is exclusively to satisfy spiritual interests, and to shut the door on all approach to mere desire. Hence we can understand how it is that practical desire rates the particular works of Nature in the organic or inorganic world, which are at its service, more highly than works of art, which are obviously useless in this sense, and only contribute enjoyment to other capacities of man's spirit.

($\beta\beta$) A second mode under which the externally present comes before the conscious subject is, as contrasted with the single sensuous perception and active desire, the purely theoretical relation to the *intelligence*. The theoretic contemplation of objects has no interest in consuming the same in their particularity and satisfying or maintaining itself through the sense by their means; its object is to attain a knowledge of them in their *universality*, to seek out their ideal nature and principle, to comprehend them according to their notional idea. Consequently this contemplative interest is content to leave the particular things as they are, and stands aloof from them in their objective singularity, which is not the object of such a faculty's investigation. For the rational intelligence is not a property of the particular person in the sense that desire is so; it appertains to his singularity as being itself likewise essentially universal. So long as it persists in this relation of universality to the objects in question, it is his reason in its universal potency which is attempting to discover *itself* in Nature, and thereby the inward or essential being of the natural objects, which his sensuous existence does not present under its mode of immediacy, although such existence is founded therein. This interest of contemplation, the satisfaction of which is the task of *science*, is, however, shared in this scientic form just as little by art as it shared in the common table of those impulses of the purely practical desire.

Science can, it is true, take as its point of departure the sensuous thing in its singularity, and possess itself of some conception, how this individual thing is present in its specific colour or form. But for all that this isolated thing of sense as such possesses no further relation to mind, inasmuch as the interest of intelligence makes for the universal, the law, the thought and notion of the object, and consequently not only does it forsake it in its immediate singularity, but it actually transforms it within the region of idea, converting a concrete object of sense into an abstract subject-matter of thought, that is converting it into something other than the same object of its sensuous perception actually was. The artistic interest does not follow such a process, and is distinct from that of science for this reason. The contemplation of art restricts its interest simply in the way in which the work of art, as external object, in the directness of its definition, and in the singularity wherein it appears to sense, is manifested in all its features of colour, form, and sound, or as a single isolated vision of the whole; it does not go so far beyond the immediately received objective character as to propose, as is the case with science, the ideal or conceptive thinking of this particular objectivity under the terms of the rational and universal notion which underlies it.

The interest of art, therefore, is distinguishable from the practical interest of desire in virtue of the fact that it suffers its object to remain in its free independence, whereas desire applies it, even to the point of destruction, to its own uses. The contemplation of art, on the other hand, differs from that of a scientific intelligence in an analogous way in virtue of the fact that it cherishes an interest for the object in its isolated existence, and is not concerned to transform the same into terms of universal thought and notion.

(γγ) It follows, then, that, though the sensuous *materia* is unquestionably present in a work of art, it is only as surface or *show* of the sensuous that it is under any necessity to appear. In the sensuous appearance of the work of art it is neither the concrete material stuff, the empirically perceived completeness and extension of the internal organism which is the object of desire, nor is it the universal thought of pure ideality, which in either case the mind seeks for. Its aim is the sensuous presence, which, albeit suffered to persist in its sensuousness, is equally entitled to be delivered from the framework of its purely material substance. Consequently, as compared with the immediately envisaged and incorporated object of Nature, the sensuous presence in the work of art is transmuted to mere semblance or *show*, and the work of art occupies a midway ground, with the directly perceived objective world on one side and the ideality of pure thought on the other. It is not as yet pure thought, but, despite the element of sensuousness which adheres to it, it is no longer purely material existence, in the sense at least that stones, plants, and organic life are such. The sensuous element in a work of art is rather itself somewhat of ideal intension, which, however, as not being actually the ideal medium of thought, is still externally presented at the same time as an object. This semblance of the sensuous presents itself to the mind externally as the form, visible appearance, and harmonious vibration of things. This is always assuming that it suffers the objects to remain in their freedom as objective facts, and does not seek to penetrate into their inward essence by abstract thought, for by doing so they would (as above explained) entirely cease to exist for it in their external singularity.

For this reason the sensuous aspect of art is only related to the two *theoretical* senses of *sight* and *hearing*; smell, on the other hand, taste, and the feeling of touch are excluded from the springs of art's enjoyment. Smell, taste, and touch come into contact with matter simply as such, and with the immediate sensuous qualities of the same; smell with the material volatization through the air; taste with the material dissolution of substance, and touch or mere bodily feeling with qualities such as heat, coldness, smoothness, and so forth. On this account these senses cannot have to do with the objects of art, which ought to subsist in their actual and very independence, admitting of no purely sensuous or rather physical relation. The pleasant for such senses is not the beauty of art. Thus art on its sensuous side brings before us deliberately merely a shadow-world of shapes, tones, and imaged conceptions, and it is quite beside the point to maintain that it is simply a proof of the impotence and limitations of man that he can only present us with the surface of the physical world, mere *schemata*, when he calls into being his creative works. In art these sensuous shapes and tones are not offered as exclusively for themselves and their form to our direct vision. They are presented with the intent to secure in such shape satisfaction for higher and more spiritual interests, inasmuch as they are mighty to summon an echo and response in the human spirit evoked from all depths of its conscious life. In this way the sensuous is *spiritualized* in art, or, in other words, the life of *spirit* comes to dwell in it under sensuous guise.

(β) For this reason, however, a product of art is only possible in so far as it has received its passage through the mind, and has originated from the productive activity of mind. This brings us to another question we have to answer, and it is this: "How is the sensuous or material aspect, which is imperative as a condition of art, operative in the artist as conjoined to his personal productive activity?" Now this mode or manner of artistic production contains, as an activity personal to the artist, in essentials just the same determinants which we found posited in the work of art. It must be a spiritual activity, which, however, at the same time possesses in itself the element of sensuousness and immediacy. It is neither, on the one hand, purely mechanical work, such as is purely unconscious facility in sleight of hand upon physical objects, or a stereotyped activity according to teachable rule of thumb; nor, on the other hand, is it a productive process of science, which tends to pass from sensuous things to abstract ideas and thoughts, or is active exclusively in the medium of pure thought. In contrast to these the two aspects of mental idea and sensuous material must in the artistic product be united. For example, it would be possible in the case of poetical compositions to attempt to embody what was the subject-matter in the form of prosaic thought in the first instance, and only after doing so to attach to the same imaginative ideas rhymes and so on, so that as a net result such imagery would be appendent to the abstract reflections as so much ornament and decoration. An attempt of this kind, however, could only lead us to a poor sort of poetry for in it we should have operative a twofold kind of activity in its *separation*, which in the activity of genuine artistic work only holds good in inseparable unity. It is this true kind of creative activity which forms what is generally described as the artistic *imagination*. It is the rational element, which in its import as spirit only exists, in so far as it actively forces its way into the presence of consciousness, yet likewise, and only subject to this condition, displays all its content to itself under a sensuous form. This activity possesses therefore a spiritual content, but it clothes the same in sensuous image, and for this reason that it is only able to come to a knowledge of the same under this sensuous garb. We may compare such a process with that of a man of experience in life, a man, shall we add, of real geniality and wit, who—while at the same time being fully conscious in what the main importance of life consists, what are the things which essentially bind men together, what moves them and is the mainspring of their lives—nevertheless has neither brought home this content in universal maxims, nor indeed is able to unfold it to others in the generalities of the reflective process, but makes these mature results of his intelligence without exception clear to himself and others in particular cases, whether real or invented, or by examples and such like which hit the mark. For in the ideas of such a man everything shapes itself into the concrete image determinate in its time and place, to which therefore the addition of names and any other detail of external condition causes no difficulty. Yet such a kind of imagination rather rests on the recollection of conditions he has lived through, actual experience, than it is a creative power of itself. Memory preserves and renews the particularity and external fashion of such previous events with all their more distinct circumstances, but on the other hand does not suffer the universal to appear independently. The creative imagination of an artist is the imagination of a great mind and a big heart; it is the grasp and excogitation of ideas and shapes, and, in fact, nothing less than this grasp of the profoundest and most embracing human interests in the wholly definite presentation of imagery borrowed from objective experience. A consequence of this is, that imagination of this type is based in a certain sense on a natural gift, a general talent for it, as we say, because its creative power essentially implies an aspect of sense presentation. It is no doubt not unusual to speak in the same way of scientific "talent." The sciences, however, merely presuppose the general capacity for thought, which does not possess, as imagination does, together with its intellectual activity, a reference to the concrete testimony of Nature, but rather precisely abstracts from the activity that form in which we find it in Nature. It would be, therefore, truer to the mark if we said there is no specific scientific talent in the sense of a purely natural endowment. Imagination, on the other hand, combines within it a mode of instinct-like creativeness. In other words the essential plasticity and material element in a work of art is subjectively present in the artist as part of his native disposition and impulse, and as his unconscious activity belongs in part to that which man receives straight from Nature. No doubt the entire talent and genius of an individual is not wholly exhausted by that we describe as natural capability. The creation of art is quite as much a spiritual and self-cognized process; but for all that we affirm that its spirituality contains an element of plastic or configurative facility which Nature confers on it. For this reason, though almost anybody can reach a certain point in art, yet, in order to pass beyond this—and it is here that the art in question really begins—a talent for art which is inborn and of a higher order altogether is indispensable.

Considered simply as a natural basis a talent of this kind asserts itself for the most part in early youth, and is manifested in the restless persistency, ever intent with vivacity and alertness, to create artistic shapes in some particular sensuous medium, and to make this mode of expression and utterance the unique one or the one of main importance and most suitable. And thus also a virtuosity up to a certain point in the technique of art which is arrived at with ease is a sign of inborn talent. A sculptor finds everything convertible into plastic shape, and from early days takes to modelling clay; and so on generally whatever men of such innate powers have in their minds, whatever excites and moves their souls, becomes forthwith a plastic figure, a drawing, a melody, or a poem.

(γ) Thirdly, and in conclusion: the *content* of art is also in some respects borrowed from the objective world perceived in sense, that is Nature; or, in any case, if the content is also of a spiritual character, it can only be grasped in such a way, that the spiritual element therein, as human relations, for example, are displayed in the form of phenomena which possess objective reality.

3. There is yet another question to solve, namely, what the interest or the *End* is, which man proposes to himself in the creation of the content embodied by a work of art. This was, in fact, the third point of view, which we propounded relatively to the art-product. Its more detailed discussion will finally introduce us to the true notional concept of art itself.

If we take a glance at our ordinary ideas on this subject, one of the most prevalent is obviously

(*a*) The principle of the imitation of Nature. According to this view the essential aim or object of art consists in imitation, by which is understood a facility in copying natural forms as present to us in a manner which shall most fully correspond to such facts. The success of such an exact representation of Nature is assumed to afford us complete satisfaction.

(α) Now in this definition there is to start with absolutely nothing but the formal aim to bring about the bare repetition a second time by man, so far as his means will permit of this, of all that was already in the external world, precisely too in the way it is there. A repetition of this sort may at once be set down as

(αα) A *superfluous* task for the reason that everything which pictures, theatrical performances represent by way of imitation—animals, natural scenery, incidents of human life—we have already elsewhere before us in our gardens or at home, or in other examples of the more restricted or extended reaches of our personal acquaintance. Looked at, moreover, more closely, such a superfluity of energy can hardly appear otherwise than a presumptuous trifling; it is so because

(ββ) It lags so far behind Nature. In other words art is limited in its means of representation. It can only produce one-sided illusions, a semblance, to take one example, of real fact addressed exclusively to *one* sense. And, moreover, if it does wholly rely on the bare aim of *mere* imitation, instead of Nature's life all it gives us ever is the mere pretence of its substance. For some such reason the Turks, who are Mohammedans, will not put up with any pictures or copies of men and other objects. When James Bruce, in his travels through Abyssinia, showed a painted fish to a Turk, that worthy was at first astonished; but, quickly recovering himself, he made answer as follows: "If this fish shall rise up against you at the last day, and say, 'You have certainly given me a body, but no living soul,' how are you going to justify yourself against such a complaint?" The prophet himself, moreover, if we may believe the Sunna, said to the two women Ommi Hubiba and Ommi Selma, who told him of certain pictures in the Æthiopian churches: "These pictures will rise up in judgment against their creators on the Last Day." There are, no doubt, no less examples of completely deceptive imitation. The painted grapes of Zeuxis have been accepted from antiquity and long after as an instance of art's triumph, and also of that of the principle of imitation, because, we are told, actual doves pecked at them. We might add to this ancient example that more modern one of Bültner's monkey, which bit to pieces a painted cockchafer in Rösel's "Diversions of Insects," and was consequently forgiven by his master, although he destroyed by this means a fine copy of the precious work, because he proved thus the excellence of its illustrations. But if we will only reflect a moment on such and other instances we can only come to the conclusion that instead of praising works of art, because they have deceived *even* doves and monkeys, the foolish people ought to be condemned who imagine that the quality of a work of art is enhanced if they are able to proclaim an effect of the same so miserable as the supreme and last word they can say for it. In short, to sum up, we may state emphatically that in the mere business of imitation art cannot maintain its rivalry with Nature, and if it makes the attempt it must look like a worm which undertakes to crawl after an elephant.

(γγ) Having regard, then, to this invariable failure, that is, relative failure of human imitation as contrasted with the natural prototype, we have no end left us but the pleasure offered by sleight of hand in its effort to produce something which resembles Nature. And it is unquestionably a fact that mankind are able to derive enjoyment from the attempt to reproduce with their individual labour, skill, and industry what they find around them. But a delight and admiration of this kind also becomes, if taken alone, indeed just in proportion as the copy follows slavishly the thing copied, so much the more icily null and cold, or brings its reaction of surfeit and repugnance. There are portraits which, as has been drily remarked, are positively shame-less in their likeness; and Kant brings forward a further example of this pleasure in imitation pure and simple to the effect that we are very soon tired of a man—and there really are such—who is able to imitate the nightingale's song quite perfectly; for we no sooner find that it is a man who is producing the strain than we have had enough of it. We then take it to be nothing but a clever trick, neither the free outpouring of Nature, nor yet a work of art. We expect, in short, from the free creative power of men something quite other than a music of this kind, which only retains our interest when, as in the case of the nightingale's note, it breaks forth in unpremeditated fashion, resembling in this respect the rhythmic flood of human feeling, from the native springs of its life. And as a general rule this delight we ex-perience in the skill of imitation can only be of a restricted character; it becomes a man better to derive enjoyment from that which he brings to birth from himself. In this respect the invention of every in-significant technical product is of higher rank; and mankind may feel more proud at having invented the hammer, nail and so forth, than in making themselves adepts as imitators. For this abstract zest in the pursuit of imitation is on the same lines as the feat of the man who had taught himself to throw lentils through a small aperture without missing. He made an exhibition of this feat to Alexander, and Alexander merely made him a present as a reward for this art, empty and useless as it was, of a bushel of lentils.

(β) Inasmuch as, moreover, the principle of imitation is purely formal, *objective beauty* itself disappears, if that principle is accepted as the end. For the question is then no longer what is the *constitu-tion* of that which is to be imitated, but simply whether the copy is *correct* or no. The object and the content of the beautiful come to be regarded as a matter of indifference. When, in other words, putting the principle of mere imitation on one side, we speak, in connection with animals, human beings, places, actions, and characters, of a dis-tinction between beauty and ugliness, it remains none the less the fact that relatively to such a principle we are referring to a distinction which does not properly belong to an art for which we have appropriated this principle of imitation to the exclusion of all others. In such a case, therefore, whenever we select objects and attempt to distinguish between their beauty and ugliness, owing to this absence of a standard we can apply to the infinite forms of Nature, we have in the final resort only left us the *personal taste*, which is fixed by no rule, and admits of no discussion. And, in truth, if we start, in the selection of objects for representation, from that which mankind *generally* discover as beautiful and ugly, and accept accordingly for artistic imitation, in other words, form their particular taste, there is no province in the domain of the objective world which is not open to us, and which is hardly likely to fail to secure its admirer. At any rate, among men we may assume that, though the case of every husband and his wife may be disputed, yet at least every bridegroom regards his bride as beautiful, very possibly being the only person who does so; and that an individual taste for a beauty of this kind admits of no fixed rules at all may be regarded as a bit of luck for both parties. If, moreover, we cast a glance wholly beyond mere individuals and their accidental taste to that of nations, this again is full of diversity and opposition. How often we hear it repeated that a European beauty would not please a Chinaman, or even a Hottentot—a Chinaman having a totally distinct notion of beauty from that of a black man, and the black man in his turn from that of a European. Indeed, if we consider the works of art of those extra-European peoples, their images of gods, for instance, which have been imaginatively conceived as worthy of veneration and sublime, they can only appear to us as frightful idols; their music will merely ring in our ears as an abominable noise, while, from the opposite point of view, such aliens will regard our sculptures, paintings, and musical compositions as having no meaning or actually ugly.

(γ) But even assuming that we abstract from an objective principle of art, and retain the beautiful as established on the subjective and individual taste, we shall soon discover from the point of view of art itself, that the imitation of natural objects, which appeared to be a universal principle, and indeed one secured by important authorities, is not to be relied upon, at least under this general and wholly abstract conception of it. If we look at the particular arts we cannot fail to observe that, albeit painting and sculpture portray objects which resemble those of Nature, or the type of which is essentially borrowed from Nature, the works of architecture on the contrary—and this, too, is one of the *fine* arts—quite as little as the compositions of poetry, to the extent at least that these latter are not restricted to mere description, cannot justly be described as imitations of Nature. At any rate, if we are desirous of maintaining such a thesis with respect to the arts thus excluded, we should find ourselves forced to make important deviations from the track, in order to condition our proposition in various ways, and level down our so-called truth at least to the plane of probability. But once accept probability, and we should again be confronted with a great difficulty in determining precisely what is and what is not probable; and in the end no one could really think of or succeed, even if he did so, in excluding from poetry all compositions of an entirely capricious and completely imaginative character.

The end or object of art must therefore consist in something other than the purely formal imitation of what is given to objective sense, which invariably can merely call into being technical *legerdemain* and not *works* of art. It is no doubt an essential constituent of a work of art that it should have natural forms as a foundation, because the mode of its representation is an external form, and thereby along with it is that of natural phenomena. In painting it is obviously an important study to learn to copy with accuracy colours in their mutual relations, such as light effects and reflections, and so forth, and, with no less accuracy, the forms and shapes of objects carried into their most subtle gradations of line. It is in this respect that in modern times more particularly the principle of the imitation of Nature and naturalism generally has come into vogue. The object has been to recall an art, which has deteriorated into weakness and nebulosity, to the strength and determinate outlines of Nature, or, in yet another direction, as against the purely arbitrary caprice and convention of a studio, which is in truth as remote from Nature as it is from art, and merely indicates the path of art's declension, to assert the claim of the legitimate, direct, and independent, no less than coherent stability of natural fact. But while admitting that from a certain point of view such an effort is reasonable enough, yet for all that the naturalism which it demands, taken by itself, is neither the substantive thing, not yet of primary importance, in the true basis of art; and although the external fact in its natural appearance constitutes an element of essential value, yet the objective fact alone does not supply the *standard* of rightness, nor is the mere imitation of external phenomena, in their external shape that is, the *end* of art.

(*b*)   And as a consequence of this we have the further question— "What is the true *content* of art, and with what aim is that content brought before us?" On this head we are confronted by the common opinion that it is the task and object of art to bring before our sense, feeling, and power of emulation *every thing* that the spirit of man can perceive or conceive. Art has in short to realize for us the well-known saying, "*Nihil humani a me alienum puto.*" Its object is therefore declared to be that of arousing and giving life to slumbering emotions, inclinations, passions of *every* description, of filling the heart up to the brim; of compelling mankind, whether cultured or the reverse, to pass through all that the human soul carries in its most intimate and mysterious chambers, all that it is able to experience and reproduce, all that the heart is able to stir and evoke in its depths and its countlessly manifold possibilities; and yet further to deliver to the domain of feeling and the delight of our vision all that the mind may possess of essential and exalted being in its thought and the Idea—that majestic hierarchy of the noble, eternal, and true; and no less to interpret for us misfortune and misery, wickedness and crime; to make the hearts of men realize through and through all that is atrocious and dreadful, no less than every kind of pleasure and blessedness; and last of all to start the imagination like a rover among the day-dream playing-fields of the fancy, there to revel in the seductive mirage of visions and emotions which captivate the senses. All this infinitely manifold content—so it is held—it is the function of art to explore, in order that by this means the experience of our external life may be repaired of its deficiencies, and yet from a further point of view that the passions we share with all men may be excited, not merely that the experiences of life may not have us unmoved, but that we ourselves may thereafter long to make ourselves open channels of a universal experience. Such a stimulus is not presented on the plane of actual experience itself, but can only come through the semblance of it, that is to say through the illusions which art, in its creations, substitutes for the actual world. And the possibility of such a deception, by means of the semblances of art, depends on the fact that all reality must for man pass through the medium of the vision and imaginative idea; and it is only after such a passage that it penetrates the emotional life and the will. In such a process it is of consequence whether it is immediate external reality which claims his attention, or whether the result is effected by some other way, in other words by means of images, symbols, and ideas, which contain and display the content of such actuality. Men are able to imagine things, which do not actually exist, as if they did exist. Consequently it is precisely the same thing for our emotional life, whether it is the objective world or merely the show of the same, in virtue of which a situation, a relation, or any content of life, in short, is brought home to us. Either mode is equally able to stir in us an echo to the essential secret which it carries, whether it be in grief or joy, in agitation or convulsion, and can cause to flow through us the feelings and passions of anger, hate, pity, anxiety, fear, love, reverence and admiration, honour and fame.

The awakening of every kind of emotion in us, the drawing our soul through every content of life, the realization of all these movements of soul-life by means of a presence which is only external as an illusion—this it is which, in the opinion described, is pre-eminently regarded as the peculiar and transcendent power of artistic creation.

We must not, however, overlook the fact that in this view of art as a means to imprint on the soul and the mind what is good and evil alike, to make man more strong in the pursuit of what is noblest, no less than enervate his definite course, by transporting his emotional life through the most sensuous and selfish desires, the task as yet proposed to art remains throughout of an entirely formal character; without possessing independently an assured aim all that art can offer is the empty form for every possible kind of ideal and formative content.

(c) As a matter of fact art also has this formal side, namely, that it is able to bring before our senses and feeling and artistically adorn every possible kind of material, precisely as the thoughts of ordinary reflection elaborate every possible subject-matter and modes of action, supplying the same with its equipment of reasons and vindications. In the presence, however, of such a variety of content we cannot fail to observe that these diversified emotions and ideas, which it is assumed art has to stimulate or enforce, intersect each other, contradict and mutually cancel each other. Indeed, under this aspect, the more art inspires men to emotions thus opposed, to that extent precisely it merely enlarges the cleavage in their feelings and passions, and sets them staggering about in Bacchantic riot, or passes over into sophistry and scepticism precisely as your ordinary free thinkers do. This variety of the material of art itself compels us, therefore, not to remain satisfied with so formal a determination. Our rational nature forces its way into this motley array of discord, and demands to see the resurrection of a higher and more universal purpose from these elements despite their opposition, and to be conscious of its attainment. Just in a similar manner the social life of mankind and the State are no doubt credited with the aim that in them *all* human capacities and *all* individual potencies should meet with expansion and expression in *all* their features and tendencies. But in opposition to so formal a view there very quickly crops up the question in what *unity* these manifold manifestations are to be concentrated, and what *single end* they must have for their fundamental concept and ultimate end. Just as in the case of the notional concept of the human State so too there arises in that of human art the need, as to a part thereof, for an end *common* to the particular aspects, no less than in part for one which is more exalted and *substantive* in its character.

As such a substantive end the conclusion of reflection is readily brought home to us that art possesses at once the power and function to mitigate the savagery of mere desires.

(*a*) With regard to this first conception we have merely to ascertain what characteristic peculiar to art implies this possibility of eliminating this rawness of desire, and of fettering and instructing the impulses and passions. Coarseness in general has its ground-root in an unmitigated self-seeking of sensuous impulses, which take their plunge off and are exclusively intent on the satisfaction of their concupiscence. Sensual desire is, however, all the more brutal and domineering, in proportion as, in its isolation and confinement, it appropriates the *entire man,* so that he does not retain the power to separate himself in his universal capacity from this determinacy and to maintain the conscious presence of such universality. Even if the man in such a case exclaims, "the passion is mightier than myself," though it is true no doubt that for that man's mind the abstract ego is separate from the particular passion, yet it is purely so in a formal way. All that such a separation amounts to is that as against the force of the passion the ego, in its universal form or competency, is of no account at all. The savageness of passion consists therefore in the fusion of the ego as such a universal with the confined content of its desire, so that a man no longer possesses volitional power outside this single passion. Such savageness and untamed force of the possibilities of passion art mitigates in the first instance to the extent that it brings home to the mind and imagination of man what he does actually feel and carry into effect in such a condition. And even if art restricts itself to this that it places before the vision of the mind pictures of passion, nay, even assuming such to be flattering pictures, yet for all that a power of amelioration is contained therein. At least we may say, that by this means is brought before a man's intelligence what apart from such presentment he merely *is.* The man in this way contemplates his impulses and inclinations; and whereas apart from this they whirl him away without giving him time to reflect, he now sees them outside himself and already, for the reason that they come before him rather as objects than a part of himself, he begins to be free from them as aliens. For this reason it may often happen that an artist, under the weight of grief, mitigates and weakens the intensity of his own emotions in their effect upon him by the artistic representation of them. Comfort, too, is to be found even in tears. The man who to start with is wholly given up to and concentrated in sorrow, is able thus, at any rate, to express that which is merely felt within in a direct way. Yet more alleviating is the utterance of such inner life in words, images, musical sound, and shapes.

It was therefore a good old custom in the case of funerals and layings-out to appoint wailing women, in order to give audible expression to grief, or generally to create an external sympathy. For manifestations of sympathy bring the content of human sorrow to the sufferer in an objective form; he is by their repetition driven to reflect upon it, and the burden is thereby made lighter. And so it has from of old been considered that to weep or to speak oneself out are equally means whereby freedom is secured from the oppressing burden, or at least the heart is appreciably lifted. Consequently the mitigation of the violence of passions admits of this general explanation that man is released from his unmediated confinement in an emotion, becomes aware of it as a thing external to himself, to which he is consequently obliged to place himself in an ideal relation. Art, while still remaining within the sphere of the senses, frees man from the might of his sensitive experience by means of its representations. No doubt we frequently hear that pet phrase of many that it is man's duty to remain in immediate union with Nature. Such union is in its unmediated purity nothing more or less than savagery and wildness; and art, precisely in the way that it dissolves this unity for human beings, lifts them with gentle hands over this inclosure in Nature. The way men are occupied with the objects of art's creation remains throughout of a contemplative character; and albeit in the first instance it educates merely an attention to the actual facts portrayed, yet over and beyond this, and with a power no less decisive, it draws man's attention to their significance, it forces him to compare their content with that of others, and to receive without reserve the general conclusions of such a survey and all the ramifications such imply.

(β) To the characteristic above discussed adheres in natural sequence the second which has been predicated of art as its essential aim, namely, the *purification* of the passions, an instruction, that is, and a building to *moral* completeness. For the defining rôle that art has to bridle savage nature and educate the passions remained one wholly formal and general, so that the further question must arise as to a *specific* kind and an essential and *culminating* point of such an educative process.

(αα) The doctrine of the purification of the passions shares in the defect previously noted as adhering to the mitigation of desires. It does, however, emphasize more closely the fact that the representations of art needed a standard, by means of which it would be possible to estimate their comparative worth and unworth. This standard is just their effectiveness to separate what is pure from that which is the reverse in the passions. Art, therefore, requires a content which is capable of expressing this purifying power, and in so far as the power to assert such effectiveness is assumed to constitute the substantive end of art, the purifying content will consist in asserting that effective power before consciousness in its *universality* and *essentiality*.

(ββ) It is a deduction from the point of view just described that it is the end of art to *instruct*. Thus, on the one hand, the peculiar character of art consists in the movement of the emotions and in the satisfaction which is found in this movement, even in fear, compassion, in painful agitation and shock—that is to say, in the satisfying concern of the feelings and passions, and to that extent in a complacent, delighted, or enthusiastic attitude to the objects of art and their presentation and effect: while, on the other hand, this artistic object is held to discover its higher standard exclusively in its power to instruct, in the *fabula docet*, and thereby in the usefulness, which the work of art is able to exercise on the reicpient. In this respect the Horatian adage

Et prodesse volunt et delectare poetae

contains, concentrated into a few words, all that in after times has been drawn out as a doctrine of art through every conceivable grade of dilution to the last extreme of insipidity.

In respect, then, to such instruction we have to ask whether the idea is that the same ought to be direct or indirect in the work of art, explicit or implicit.

Now if the question at issue is one of general importance to art about a universal rather than contingent purpose, such an ultimate end, on account of the essential spirituality of art, can only be itself of spiritual import; in other words, so far from being of accidental importance it must be true in virtue of its own nature and on its own account. An end of this kind can only apply to instruction in so far as a genuine and essentially explicit content is brought before the mind by means of the work of art. From such a point of view we are entitled to affirm that it is the function of art to accept so much the more of a content of this nature within its compass in proportion to the nobility of its rank, and that only in the verity of such a content will it discover the standard according to which the pertinency of or the reverse of what is expressed is adjudged. Art is in truth the primary *instructress* of peoples.

But, on the other hand, if the object of instruction is so entirely treated as an *end* that the universal nature of the content presented cannot fail to be asserted and rendered bluntly and on its own account explicit as abstract thesis, prosaic reflection or general maxim, rather than merely in an indirect way contained by implication in the concrete embodiment of art, then and in that case, by means of such a separation, the sensuous, plastic configuration, which is precisely that which makes the artistic product a *work of art*, is merely an otiose accessory, a husk, a semblance, which are expressly posited as nothing more than *shell* and semblance. Thereby the very nature of a work of art is abused. For the work of art ought not to bring before the imaginative vision a content in its universality as such, but rather under the mode of individual concreteness and distinctive sensuous particularity. If the work in question does not conform to such a principle, but rather sets before us the generalization of its content with the express object of instruction pure and simple, then the imaginative no less than the material aspect of it are merely an external and superfluous ornament, and the work of art is itself a shattered thing within that ornament, a ruin wherein form and content no longer appear as a mutually adherent growth. For, in the case supposed, the particular object of the senses and the ideal content apprehended by the mind have become external to one another.

Furthermore, if the object of art is assumed to consist in utilitarian *instruction* of this kind, that other aspect of delight, entertainment, and diversion is simply abandoned on its own account as *unessential;* it has now to look for its substance to the utility of the matter of instruction, to which it is simply an accompaniment. But this amounts to saying, that art does not carry its vocation and purpose in itself, but that its fundamental conception is in something else, to which it subserves as a *means.* Art becomes, in short, merely one of the many means, which are either of use, or may be employed to secure, the aim of instruction. This brings us to the boundary line where art can only cease to be an end on its own independent account; it is deliberately deposed either to the mere plaything of entertainment, or a mere means of instruction.

(γγ) The line of this limit is most emphasized when the question is raised as to the end or object of highest rank for the sake of which the passions have to be purified or men have to be instructed. This goal has frequently in modern times been identified with *moral improvement,* and the end of art is assumed to consist in this that its function is to prepare our inclinations and impulses, and generally to conduct us to the supreme goal of moral perfection. In this view we find instruction and purification combined. The notion is that art by the insight it gives us of genuine moral goodness, in other words, through its instruction, at the same time summons us to the process of purification, and in this way alone can and ought to bring about the improvement of mankind as the right use they can make of it and its supreme object.

With reference to the relation in which art stands to the end of improvement, we may practically say the same thing as we did about the didactic end. It may readily be admitted that art as its principle ought not to make the immoral and its advance its end. But it is one thing deliberately to make immorality the aim of its presentation and another not expressly to do so in the case of morality. It is possible to deduce an excellent moral from any work of art whatever; but such depends, of course, on a particular interpretation and consequently on the individual who draws the moral. The defence is made of the most immoral representations on the ground that people ought to become acquainted with evil and sin in order to act morally. Conversely, it has been maintained that the portrayal of Mary Magdalene, the fair sinner, who afterwards repented, has seduced many into sin, because art makes repentance look so beautiful, and you must first sin before you can repent. The doctrine of moral improvement, however logically carried out, is not merely satisfied that a moral should be conceivably deducible from a work of art through interpretation; on the contrary, it would have the moral instruction clearly made to emerge as the substantive aim of the work; nay, further, it would deliberately exclude from art's products all subjects, characters, actions, and events which fail to be moral in its own sense. For art, in distinction from history and the sciences, which have their subject-matter determined for them, has a choice in the selection of its subjects.

· · · · ·

(*d*) When discussing moral improvement as the ultimate end accepted for art it was found that its principle pointed to a higher standpoint. It will be necessary also to vindicate this standpoint for art.

Thereby the false position to which we have already directed attention vanishes, namely, that art has to serve as a means for moral ends and the moral end of the world generally by means of its didactive and ameliorating influence, and by doing so has its essential aim not in itself, but in something else. If we therefore continue still to speak of an end or goal of art, we must at once remove the perverse idea, which in the question, "What is the end?" will still make it include the supplemental query, "What is the use?" The perverseness consists in this that the work of art would then have to be regarded as related to something else, which is presented us as what is essential and ought to be. A work of art would in that case be merely a useful instrument in the realization of an end which possessed real and independent importance outside the realm of art. As opposed to this we must maintain that it is art's function to reveal *truth* under the mode of art's sensuous or material configuration, to display the reconciled antithesis previously described, and by this means to prove that it possesses its final aim in itself, in this representation in short and self-relevation. For other ends such as instruction, purification, improvement, procuring of wealth, struggle after fame and honour have nothing whatever to do with this work of art as such, still less do they determine the fundamental idea of it.

It is then from this point of view, into which the reflective consideration of our subject-matter finally issues, that we have to grasp the fundamental idea of art in terms of its ideal or inward necessity, as it is also from this point of view that historically regarded the true appreciation and acquaintance with art took its origin. For that antithesis, to which we have drawn attention, did not merely assert its presence within the general thought of educated men, but equally in philosophy as such. It was only after philosophy was in a position to overcome this opposition absolutely that it grasped the fundamental notion of its own content, and, to the extent it did so, the idea of Nature and of art.

For this reason, as this point of view implies the reawakening of philosophy in the widest connotation of the term, so also it is the reawakening of the science of art. We may go further and affirm that aesthetic as a science is in a real sense primarily indebted to this reawakening for its true origination, and art for its higher estimation.

V

1. After the above introductory observations we may now pass on to the consideration of our subject itself. We are, however, still within the introduction; and being so I do not propose to attempt anything more than indicate by way of sketch the main outlines of the general course of the scientific inquiry which is to follow it. Inasmuch, however, as we have referred to art as issuing from the absolute Idea itself, and, indeed, have assigned as its end the sensuous presentation of the Absolute itself, it will be incumbent on us to conduct this survey of the entire field in such a way, as at least to disclose generally, how the particular parts originate in the notional concept of the beauty of art. We must therefore attempt to awaken some idea of this notion in its broadest significance.

It has already been stated that the content of art is the Idea, and the form of its display the configuration of the sensuous or plastic image. It is further the function of art to mediate these two aspects under the reconciled mode of free totality. The *first* determinant implied by this is the demand that the content, which has to secure artistic representation, shall disclose an essential capacity for such display. If this is not so all that we possess is a defective combination. A content that, independently, is ill adapted to plastic form and external presentment is compelled to accept this form, or a matter that is of itself prosaic in its character is driven to make the best it can of a mode of presentation which is antagonistic to its nature.

The *second* requirement, which is deducible from the first, is the demand that the content of art should be nothing essentially abstract. This does not mean, however, that it should be merely concrete in the sense that the sensuous object is such in its contrast to all that is spiritual and the content of thought, regarding these as the essentially simple and abstract. Everything that possesses truth for Spirit, no less than as part of Nature, is essentially concrete, and, despite its universality, possesses both ideality and particularity essentially within it. When we state, for example, of God that he is simple One, the Supreme Being as such, we have thereby merely given utterance to a lifeless abstraction of the irrational understanding. Such a God, as He is thus not conceived in His concrete truth, can supply no content for art, least of all plastic art. Consequently neither the Jews nor the Turks have been able to represent their God, who is not even an abstraction of the understanding in the above sense, under the positive mode in which Christians have represented Him. For in Christianity God is conceived in His Truth, and as such essentially concrete, as personality, as the subjective focus of conscious life, or, more accurately defined, as Spirit. And what He is as Spirit is made explicit to the religious apprehension as a trinity of persons, which at the same time are, in their independence, regarded as One. Here is essentiality, universality, and particularity, no less than their reconciled unity, and it is only a unity such as this which gives us the concrete. And inasmuch as a content, in order to unveil truth at all, must be of this concrete character, art makes the demand for a like concreteness, and, for this reason, that a purely abstract universal does not in itself possess the property to proceed to particularity and external manifestation, and to unity with itself therein.

If, then, a sensuous form and configuration is to be correspondent with a true and therefore concrete content, such must in the third place likewise be as clearly individual, entirely concrete and a self-enclosed unity. This character of concreteness, predicable of both aspects of art, the content no less than the representation, is just the point in which both coalesce and fall in with one another. The natural form of the human body is, for example, such a sensuous concrete capable of displaying Spirit in its essential concreteness and of adapting itself wholly to such a presentment. For which reason we must quit ourselves of the idea that it is a matter of mere accident that an actual phenomenon of the objective world is accepted as the mode in which to embody such a form coalescent with truth. Art does not lay hold of this form either because it is simply there or because there is no other. The concrete content itself implies the presence of external and actual, we may even add the sensuous appearance. But to make this possible this sensuous concrete, which is essentially impressed with a content that is open to mind, is also essentially addressed to the inward conscious life, and the external mode of its configuration, whereby it is visible to perception and the world of idea, has for its aim the being there exclusively for the soul and mind of man. This is the sole reason that content and artistic conformation are dovetailed one into the other. The *purely* sensuous concrete, that is external Nature as such, does not exclusively originate in such an end. The variously colored plumage of birds is resplendent unseen; the notes of this song are unheard. The Cereus, which only blossoms for a night, withers away without any admiration from another in the wilderness of the southern forests; and these forests, receptacles themselves of the most beautiful and luxuriant vegetation, with the richest and most aromatic perfumes, perish and collapse in like manner unenjoyed. The work of art has no such naive and independent being. It is essentially a question, an address to the responding soul of man, an appeal to affections and intelligence.

Although the endowment by art of sensuous shape is not in this respect accidental, yet on the other hand it is not the highest mode of grasping the spiritually concrete. Thought is a higher mode of presentment than that of the sensuous concrete. Though abstract in a relative sense; yet it must not be one-sided, but concrete thinking, in order to be true and rational. The extent to which a definite content possesses for its appropriate form sensuous artistic representation, or essentially requires, in virtue of its nature, a higher and more spiritual embodiment is a question of difference exemplified at once if we compare the Greek gods with God as conceived under Christian ideas. The Greek god is not abstract, but individual, and is in close association with the natural human form. The Christian God is also, no doubt, a concrete personality, but under the mode of pure spiritual actuality, who is cognized as Spirit and in Spirit. His medium of determinate existence is therefore essentially knowledge of the mind and not external natural shape, by means of which His representation can only be imperfect, and not in the entire depths of His idea or notional concept.

Inasmuch, however, as it is the function of art to represent the Idea to immediate vision in sensuous shape and not in the form of thought and pure spirituality in the strict sense, and inasmuch as the value and intrinsic worth of this presentment consists in the correspondence and unity of the two aspects, that is the Idea and its sensuous shape, the supreme level and excellence of art and the reality, which is truly consonant with its notion, will depend upon the degree of intimacy and union with which idea and configuration appear together in elaborated fusion. The higher truth consequently is spiritual content which has received the shape adequate to the conception of its essence; and this it is which supplies the principle of division for the philosophy of art. For before the mind can attain to the true notion of its absolute essence, it is constrained to traverse a series of stages rooted in this very notional concept; and to this course of stages which it unfolds to itself, corresponds a coalescent series, immediately related therewith, of the plastic types of art, under the configuration whereof mind as art-spirit presents to itself the consciousness of itself.

This evolution within the art-spirit has further itself two sides in virtue of its intrinsic nature. *First*, that is to say, the development is itself a spiritual and universal one; in other words there are the definite and comprehensive views of the world in their series of gradations which give artistic embodiment to the specific but widely embracing consciousness of Nature, man, and God. *Secondly*, this ideal or *universal* art-development has to provide for itself immediate existence and sensuous configuration, and the definite modes of this art-actualization in the sensuous medium are themselves a totality of necessary distinctions in the realm of art—that is to say, they are the *particular types* of art. No doubt the types of artistic configuration on the one hand are, in respect to their spirituality, of a general character, and not restricted to any one material, and the sensuous existence is similarly itself of varied multiplicity of medium. Inasmuch, however, as this material potentially possesses, precisely as the mind or spirit does, the Idea for its inward soul or significance, it follows that a definite sensuous involves with itself a closer relation and secret bond of association with the spiritual distinctions and specific types of artistic embodiment.

Relatively to these points of view our philosophy will be divided into three fundamental parts.

First, we have a *general* part. It has for its content and object the universal Idea of fine art, conceived here as the Ideal, together with the more elaborated relation under which it is placed respectively to Nature and human artistic production.

Secondly, we have evolved from the notional concept of the beauty of art a *particular part*, in so far as the essential distinctions, which this idea contains in itself, are unfolded in a graduated series of *particular* modes of configuration.

Thirdly, there results a *final* part which has to consider the particularized content of fine art itself. It consists in the advance of art to the sensuous realization of its shapes and its consummation in a system of the several arts and their genera and species.

2. In respect to the first and second of these divisions it is important to recollect, in order to make all that follows intelligible, that the Idea, viewed as the beautiful in art, is not the Idea in the strict sense, that is as a metaphysical Logic apprehends it as the Absolute. It is rather the Idea as carried into concrete form in the direction of express realization, and as having entered into immediate and adequate unity with such reality. For the *Idea as such*, although it is both potentially and explicitly true, is only truth in its universality and not as

yet presented in objective embodiment. The Idea as fine art, how-ever, is the Idea with the more specific property of being essentially individual reality, in other words, an individual configuration of real-ity whose express function it is to make manifest the Idea—in its ap-pearance. This amounts to the demand that the Idea and its forma-tive configuration as concrete realization must be brought together under a mode of complete adequacy. The Idea as so conceived, a re-ality, that is to say, moulded in conformity with the notional concept of the Idea, is the Ideal. The problem of such consonancy might, in the first instance, be understood in the wholly formal sense that the Idea might be any idea so long as the actual shape, it matters not what the shape might be, represented this particular Idea and no other. In that case, however, the required truth of the Ideal is a fact simply interchangeable with mere correctness, a correctness which consists in the expression of any significance in a manner adapted to it, provided that its meaning is thereby directly discoverable in the form. The Ideal, however, is not to be thus understood. According to the standard or test of its own nature any content whatever can re-ceive adequate presentation, but it does not necessarily thereby possess a claim to be the fine art of the Ideal. Nay, more, in com-parison with ideal beauty the presentation will even appear defective. And in this connection we may once for all observe—though actual proof is reserved to a later stage—that the defects of a work of art are not invariably to be attributed to defects of executive skill. *Defective-ness of form* arises also from *defectiveness of content*. The Chinese, Hindoos, and Egyptians, for example, in their artistic images, sculp-tured deities and idols, never passed beyond a formless condition, or a definition of shape that was vicious and false, and were unable to master true beauty. And this was so for the reason that their mytho-logical conceptions, the content and thought of their works of art, were still essentially indeterminate, or only determinate in a false sense, did not, in fact, attain to a content which was absolute in itself. Viewed in this sense the excellence of works of art is so much the greater in the degree that their content and thought is ideal and profound. And in affirming this we have not merely in our mind the degree of executive mastery displayed in the grasp and imitation of natural form as we find it in the objective world. For in certain stages of the artistic consciousness and its reproductive effects the desertion and distortion of the conformations of Nature is not so much due to unintentional technical inexperience or lack of ability, as it is to de-liberate alteration, which originates in the mental content itself, and is demanded by the same. From this point of view there is therefore imperfect art, which, both in technical and other respects, may be quite consummate in its *own specific sphere*, yet if tested with the true notion of art and the Ideal can only appear as defective. Only in the highest are the Idea and the artistic presentation truly consonant with one another in the sense that the objective embodiment of the Idea is in itself essentially and as realized the true configuration, because the content of the Idea thus expressed is itself in truth the genuine content. It is appertinent to this, as already noted, that the Idea must be defined in and through itself as concrete totality, thereby essentially possessing in itself the principle and standard of its particularization and definition as thus manifested objectively. For example, the Christian imagination will only be able to represent God in human form and with man's means of spiritual expression, because it is herein that God Himself is fully known in Himself as mind or Spirit. Determinacy is, as it were, the bridge to phenomenal presence. Where this determinacy is not totality derived from the Idea itself, where the Idea is not conceived as that which is self-definitive and self-differentiating, it remains abstract and possesses its definition, and with it the principle for the particular mode of embodiment adapted to itself not within itself but as something outside it. And owing to this the Idea is also still abstract and the configuration it assumes is not yet posited by itself. The Idea, however, which is essentially concrete, carries the principle of its manifestation in itself, and is thereby the means of its own free manifestation. Thus it is only the truly concrete Idea that is able to evoke the true embodiment, and this appropriate coalescence of both is the Ideal.

3. But inasmuch as in this way the Idea is concrete unity, this unity can only enter the artistic consciousness by the expansion and further mediation of the particular aspects of the Idea; and it is through this evolution that the beauty of art receives a *totality of particular stages and forms*. Therefore, after we have considered fine art in its essence and on its own account, we must see how the beautiful in its entirety breaks up into its particular determinations. This gives, as our second part, the *doctrine of the types of art*. The origin of these types is to be found in the varied ways under which the Idea is conceived as the content of art; it is by this means that a distinction in the mode of form under which it manifests itself is conditioned. These types are therefore simply the different modes of relation which obtain between the Idea and its configuration, relations which emanate from the Idea itself, and thereby present us with the general

basis of division for this sphere. For the principle of division must always be found in the notional concept, the particularization and division of which it is.

We have here to consider *three* relations of the Idea to its external process of configuration.

(*a*) *First*, the origin of artistic creation proceeds from the Idea when, being itself still involved in defective definition and obscurity, or in vicious and untrue determinacy, it becomes embodied in the shapes of art. As indeterminate it does not as yet possess in itself that individuality which the Ideal demands. Its abstract character and one-sidedness leaves its objective presentment still defective and contingent. Consequently this first type of art is rather a mere search after plastic configuration than a power of genuine representation. The Idea has not as yet found the formative principle within itself, and therefore still continues to be the mere effort and strain to find it. We may in general terms describe this form as the *symbolic* type of art. The abstract Idea possesses in it its external shape outside itself in the purely material substance of Nature, from which the shaping process proceeds, and to which in its expression it is entirely yoked. Natural objects are thus in the first instance left just as they are, while, at the same time the substantive Idea is imposed upon them as their significance, so that their function is henceforth to express the same, and they claim to be interpreted, as though the Idea itself was present in them. A rationale of this is to be found in the fact that the external objects of reality do essentially possess an aspect in which they are qualified to express a universal import. But as a completely adequate coalescence is not yet possible, all that can be the outcome of such a relation is an *abstract attribute*, as when a lion is understood to symbolize strength.

On the other hand this abstractness of the relation makes present to consciousness no less markedly how the Idea stands relatively to natural phenomena as an alien; and albeit it expatiates in all these shapes, having no other means of expression among all that is real, and seeks after itself in their unrest and defects of genuine proportion, yet for all that it finds them inadequate to meet its needs. It consequently exaggerates natural shapes and the phenomena of Nature in every degree of indefinite and limitless extension; it flounders about in them like a drunkard, and seethes and ferments, doing violence to their truth with the distorted growth of unnatural shapes, and strives vainly by the contrast, hugeness, and splendour of the forms accepted to exalt the phenomena to the plane of the Idea. For the Idea is here still more or less indeterminate, and unadaptable, while the objects of Nature are wholly definite in their shape.

Hence, on account of the incompatibility of the two sides of ideality and objective form to one another, the relation of the Idea to the other becomes a *negative* one. The former, being in its nature ideal, is unsatisfied with such an embodiment, and posits itself as its inward or ideally universal substance under a relation of *sublimity* over and above all this inadequate superfluity of natural form. In virtue of this sublimity the natural phenomena, of course, and the human form and event are accepted and left simply as they are, but at the same time, recognized as unequal to their significance, which is exalted far above all earthly content.

These features constitute in general terms the character of the primitive artistic pantheism of the East, which, on the one hand, charges the meanest objects with the significance of the absolute Idea, or, on the other, compels natural form, by doing violence to its structure, to express its world-ideas. And, in consequence, it becomes bizarre, grotesque, and deficient in taste, or turns the infinite but abstract freedom of the substantive Idea contemptuously against all phenomenal existence as alike nugatory and evanescent. By such means the significance cannot be completely presented in the expression, and despite all straining and endeavour the final inadequacy of plastic configuration to Idea remains insuperable. Such may be accepted as the first type of art—symbolic art with its yearning, its fermentation, its mystery, and sublimity.

(b) In the *second* type of art, which we propose to call "*Classical*," the twofold defect of symbolic art is annulled. Now the symbolic configuration is imperfect, because, first, the Idea here only enters into consciousness in *abstract* determinacy or indeterminateness: and, secondly, by reason of the fact that the coalescence of import with embodiment can only throughout remain defective, and in its turn also wholly abstract. The classical art-type solves both these difficulties. It is, in fact, the free and adequate embodiment of the Idea in the shape which, according to its notional concept, is uniquely appropriate to the Idea itself. The Idea is consequently able to unite in free and completely assonant concord with it. For this reason the classical type of art is the first to present us with the creation and vision of the complete Ideal, and to establish the same as realized fact.

The conformability, however, of notion and reality in the classical type ought not to be taken in the purely *formal* sense of the coalescence of a content with its external form, any more than this was possible in the case of the Ideal. Otherwise every copy from Nature, and every kind of portrait, every landscape, flower, scene, and so forth, which form the aim of the presentment, would at once become classical in virtue of the fact of the agreement it offers between such content and form. In classical art, on the contrary, the characteristic feature of the content consists in this, that it is itself concrete Idea, and as such the concrete spiritual; for it is only that which pertains to Spirit which is veritable ideality. To secure such a content we must find out that in Nature which on its own account is that which is essentially and explicitly appropriate to the spiritual. It must be the *original* notion itself, which has invented the form for concrete spirituality, and now the *subjective* notion—in the present case the spirit of art—has merely *discovered* it, and made it, as an existence possessed of natural shape, concordant with free and individual spirituality. Such a configuration, which the Idea essentially possesses as spiritual, and indeed as individually determinate spirituality, when it must perforce appear as a temporal phenomenon, is the *human form*. Personification and anthropomorphism have frequently been abused as a degradation of the spiritual. But art, in so far as its function is to bring to vision the spiritual in sensuous guise, must advance to such anthropomorphism, inasmuch as Spirit is only adequately presented to perception in its bodily presence. The transmigration of souls is in this respect an abstract conception, and physiology ought to make it one of its fundamental principles, that life has necessarily, in the course of its evolution, to proceed to the human form, for the reason that it is alone the visible phenomenon adequate to the expression of intelligence.

The human bodily form, then, is employed in the classical type of art not as purely sensuous existence, but exclusively as the existence and natural shape appropriate to mind. It has therefore to be relieved of all the defective excrescences which adhere to it in its purely physical aspect, and from the contingent finiteness of its phenomenal appearance. The external shape must in this way be purified in order to express in itself the content adequate for such a purpose; and, furthermore, along with this, that the coalescence of import and embodiment may be complete, the spirituality which constitutes the content must be of such a character that it is completely able to express itself in the natural form of man, without projecting beyond the limits of such expression within the sensuous and purely physical sphere of existence. Under such a condition Spirit is at the same time defined as particular, the spirit or mind of man, not as simply absolute and eternal. In this latter case it is only capable of asserting and expressing itself as intellectual being.

Out of this latter distinction arises, in its turn, the defect which brings about the dissolution of the classical type of art, and makes the demand for a third and higher form, namely the *romantic* type.

(c) The romantic type of art annuls the completed union of the Idea and its reality, and occurs, if on a higher plane, to the difference and opposition of both sides, which remained unovercome in symbolic art. The classical type of art no doubt attained the highest excellence of which the sensuous embodiment of art is capable. The defect, such as it is, is due to the defect which obtains in art itself throughout, the limitations of its entire province, that is to say. The limitation consists in this, that art in general and, agreeably to its fundamental idea, accepts for its object Spirit, the notion of which is infinite concrete universality, under the guise of sensuously concrete form. In the classical type it sets up the perfected coalescence of spiritual and sensuous existence as adequate conformation of both. As a matter of fact, however, in this fusion mind itself is not represented agreeably to its *true notional concept*. Mind is the infinite subjectivity of the Idea, which as absolute inwardness, is not capable of freely expanding in its entire independence, so long as it remains within the mould of the bodily shape, fused therein as in the existence wholly congenial to it.

To escape from such a condition the romantic type of art once more cancels that inseparable unity of the classical type, by securing a content which passes beyond the classical stage and its mode of expression. This content, if we may recall familiar ideas—is coincident with what Christianity affirms to be true of God as Spirit, in contrast to the Greek faith in gods which forms the essential and most fitting content of classical art. In Greek art the concrete ideal substance is potentially, but not as fully realized, the unity of the human and divine nature; a unity which for the very reason that it is purely *immediate* and not wholly explicit, is manifested without defect under an immediate and *sensuous* mode. The Greek god is the object of naive intuition and sensuous imagination. His shape is therefore the bodily form of man. The sphere of his power and his being is individual and individually limited; and in his opposition to the individual person is an essence and a power with whom the inward life of soul is merely potentially in unity, but does not itself possess this unity as inward subjective knowledge. The higher stage is the *knowledge* of this *implied* unity, which in its latency the classical art-type receives as its content and is able to perfectly represent in bodily shape. This elevation of mere potentiality into self-conscious knowledge constitutes an enormous difference. It is nothing less than the infinite difference which, for example, separates man generally from the animal creation. Man is animal; but even in his animal functions he is not restricted within the potential sphere as the animal is, but becomes conscious of them, learns to understand them, and raises them—as, for instance, the process of digestion—into self-conscious science. By this means man dissolves the boundaries of his merely potential immediacy; in virtue of the very fact that he knows himself to be animal he ceases to be merely animal, and as mind is endowed with self-knowledge.

If, then, in this way the unity of the human and divine nature, which in the previous stage was potential, is raised out of this immediate into a self-conscious unity, it follows that the genuine medium for the reality of this content is no longer the sensuous and immediate existence of what is spiritual, that is, the physical body of man, but the *self-aware* inner life of *soul itself*. Now it is Christianity—for the reason that it presents to mind God as *Spirit*, and not as the particular individual spirit, but as absolute in spirit and in truth—which steps back from the sensuousness of imagination into the inward life of reason, and makes *this* rather than *bodily* form the medium and determinate existence of its content. So also, the unity of the human and divine nature is a conscious unity exclusively capable of realization by means of *spiritual* knowledge, and in *Spirit*. The new content secured thereby is consequently not indefeasibly bound up with the sensuous presentation, as the mode completely adequate, but is rather delivered from this immediate existence, which has to be hypostatized as a negative factor, overcome and reflected back into the spiritual unity. In this way romantic art must be regarded as art transcending itself, albeit within the boundary of its own province, and in the form of art itself.

We may therefore briefly summarize our conclusion that in this third stage the object of art consists in the free and concrete presence of spiritual activity, whose vocation it is to appear as such a presence or activity for the inner world of conscious intelligence. In consonance with such an object art cannot merely work for sensuous perception. It must deliver itself to the inward life, which coalesces with its object simply as though this were none other than itself, in other words, to the intimacy of soul, to the heart, the emotional life, which as the medium of Spirit itself essentially strives after freedom, and seeks and possesses its reconciliation only in the inner chamber of spirit. It is this inward or ideal world which constitutes the content of the romantic sphere: it will therefore necessarily discover its representation as such inner idea or feeling, and in the show or appearance of the same. The world of the soul and intelligence celebrates its triumph over the external world, and, actually in the medium of that outer world, makes that victory to appear, by reason of which the sensuous appearance sinks into worthlessness.

On the other hand, this type of art, like every other, needs an external vehicle of expression. As already stated, the spiritual content has here withdrawn from the external world and its immediate unity into its own world. The sensuous externality of form is consequently accepted and represented, as in the symbolic type, as unessential and transient; furthermore the subjective finite spirit and volition is treated in a similar way; a treatment which even includes the idiosyncrasies or caprice of individuals, character, action, or the particular features of incident and plot. The aspect of external existence is committed to contingency and handed over to the adventurous action of imagination, whose caprice is just as able to reflect the facts given *as* they are, as it can change the shapes of the external world into a medley of its own invention and distort them to mere caricature. For this external element has no longer its notion and significance in its own essential province, as in classical art. It is now discovered in the emotional realm, and this is manifested in the medium of that realm itself rather than in the external and *its* form of reality, and is able to secure or to recover again the condition of reconciliation with itself in every accident, in all the chance circumstance that falls into independent shape, in all misfortune and sorrow, nay, in crime itself.

Hence it comes about that the characteristics of symbolic art, its indifference, incompatibility and severance of Idea from configurative expression, are here reproduced once more, if with essential difference. And this difference consists in the fact that in romantic art the Idea, whose defectiveness, in the case of the symbol, brought with it the defect of external form, has to display itself as Spirit and in the medium of soul-life as essentially self-complete. And it is to complete fundamentally this higher perfection that it withdraws itself from the external element. It can, in short, seek and consummate its true reality and manifestation nowhere but in its own domain.

This we may take to be in general terms the character of the symbolic, classical, and romantic types of art, which in fact constitute the three relations of the Idea to its embodiment in the realm of human art. They consist in the aspiration after, the attainment and transcendency of the Ideal, viewed as the true concrete notion of beauty.

4. In contrast to these two previous divisions of our subject the *third* part presupposes the notional concept of the Ideal, and the universal art-types. It in other words consists in their realization through specific sensuous media. We have consequently no longer to deal with the inner or ideal evolution of the beauty of art in conformity with its widest and most fundamental determinations. What we have now before us to consider is how these ideal determinants pass into actual existence, how they are distinguishable in their external aspect, and how they give an independent and a realized shape to every element implied in the evolution of this Idea of beauty as *a work of art*, and not merely as a *universal type*. Now it is the peculiar differences immanent in the Idea of beauty which are carried over by it into external existence. For this reason in this third fundamental division these general art-types must themselves supply the basic principle for the articulation and definition of the *particular arts*. Or, to put the same thing another way, the several species of art possess in themselves the same essential differences, which we have already become acquainted with as the universal art-types. *External* objectivity, however, to which these types are subjected in a sensuous and consequently *specific* material, necessitates the differentiation of these types into diverse and independent modes of realization, in other words, those of particular arts. Each general type discovers its determinate character in one determinate external material or medium, in which its adequate presentation is secured under the manner it prescribes. But, from another point of view, these types of art, inasmuch as their definition is none the less consistent with the fact of the *universality* of their typical import, break through the boundaries of their *specific* realization in some definite art-species, and achieve an existence in other arts no less, although their position in such is of subordinate importance. For this reason, albeit the particular arts belong specifically to one of these general art-types respectively, the *adequate* external embodiment whereof they severally constitute, yet this does not prevent them, each after its own mode of external configuration, from representing the totality of these art-types. To summarize, then, in this third principal division we are dealing with the beauty of art, as it unveils itself in a world of realized beauty by means of the arts and their creations. The content of this world is the beautiful, and the true beautiful, as we have seen, is spiritual being in concrete form, the Ideal; or apprehended with still more intimacy it is the absolute mind and truth itself. This region of divine truth artistically presented to sensuous

vision and emotion forms the centre of the entire world of art. It is the independent, free and divine Image, which has completely appropriated the externality of form and medium, and now wears them simply as the means of its self-manifestation. Inasmuch, however, as the beautiful is unfolded here as *objective* reality, and in this process is differentiated into particular aspects and phases, this centre posits its extremes, as realized in their peculiar actuality, in antithetical reaction to itself. Thus one of these extremes consists of an objectivity as yet devoid of mind, which we may call the natural environment of God. Here the external element, when it receives form, remains as it was, and does not possess its spiritual aim and content in itself, but in another. The other extreme is the divine as inward, something known, as the manifold particularized *subjective* existence of Deity. It is the truth as operative and vital in sense, soul, and intelligence of particular persons, which does not persist as poured forth into its mould of external shape, but returns into the inward life of individuals. The Divine is under such a mode at once distinguishable from its pure manifestation as Godhead, and passes itself thereby into the variety of particularization which belongs to every kind of particular subjective knowledge, feeling, perception, and emotion. In the analogous province of religion with which art, at its highest elevation, is immediately connected, we conceive the same distinction as follows. First, we imagine the natural life on Earth in its finitude as standing on one side; but then, secondly, the human consciousness accepts God for its object, in which the distinction between objectivity and subjectivity falls away; then, finally, we advance from God as such to the devotion of the *community*, that is to God as He is alive and present in the subjective consciousness. These three fundamental modifications present themselves in the world of art in independent evolution.

(*a*) The *first* of the particular arts with which, according to their fundamental principle, we have to start is architecture considered as a fine art. Its function consists in so elaborating the external material of inorganic Nature that the same becomes intimately connected with Spirit as an artistic and external environment. Its medium is matter itself as an external object, a heavy mass that is subject to mechanical laws; and its forms persist as the forms of inorganic Nature coordinated with the relations of the abstract understanding such as symmetry and so forth. In this material and in these forms the Ideal is incapable of realization as concrete spirituality, and the reality thus presented remains confronting the Idea as an external fabric with which it enters into no fusion, or has only entered so far as to establish an abstract relation. And it is in consequence of this that the fundamental type of the art of building is that of *symbolism*. Architecture is in fact the first pioneer on the highway toward the adequate realization of Godhead. In this service it is put to severe labour with objective nature, that it may disengage it by its effort from the confused growth of finitude and the distortions of contingency. By this means it levels a space for the God, informs His external environment, and builds Him His temple, as a fit place for the concentration of Spirit, and its direction to the absolute objects of intelligent life. It raises an enclosure for the congregation of those assembled, as a defence against the threatening of the tempest, against rain, the hurricane, and savage animals. It in short reveals the will thus to assemble, and although under an external relation, yet in agreement with the principles of art. A significance such as this it can to a greater or less extent import into its material and its forms, in proportion as the determinate content of its fabric, which is the object of its operations and effort, is more or less significant, is more concrete or more abstract, more profound in penetrating its own essential depth, or more obscure and superficial. Indeed architecture may in this respect proceed so far in the execution of such a purpose as to create an adequate artistic existence for such an ideal content in its very forms and material. In doing so, however, it has already passed beyond its peculiar province and is diverted into the stage immediately above it of sculpture. For the boundary of sculpture lies precisely in this that it retains the spiritual as an inward being which persists in direct contrast to the external embodiment of architecture. It can consequently merely point to that which is absorbed in soul-life as to something external to itself.

(b) Nevertheless, as above explained, the external and inorganic world is purified by architecture, it is coordinated under symmetrical laws, and made cognate with mind, and as a result the temple of God, the house of his community, stands before us. Into this temple, in the *second* place, the God himself enters in the lightning-flash of individuality which smites its way into the inert mass, permeating the same with its presence. In other words the infinite and no longer purely symmetrical form belonging to intelligence brings as it were to a focus and informs the shape in which it is most at home. This is the task of *sculpture*. In so far as in it the inward life of Spirit, to which the art of architecture can merely point a way to, makes its dwelling within the sensuous shape and its external material, and to the extent that these two sides come into plastic communion with one another in such a manner that neither is predominant, sculpture receives as its fundamental type the *classical* art-form.

For this reason the sensuous element on its own account admits of no expression here which is not affected by spiritual affinities, just as, conversely, sculpture can reproduce with completeness no spiritual content, which does not maintain throughout adequate presentation to perception in bodily form. What sculpture, in short, has to do is to make the presence of Spirit stand before us in its bodily shape and in immediate union therewith at rest and in blessedness; and this form has to be made vital by means of the content of spiritual individuality. The external sensuous material is consequently no longer elaborated either in conformity with its mechanical quality alone, as a mass of weight, nor in shapes of the inorganic world simply, nor in entire indifference to colour, etc. It is carried into the ideal forms of the human figure, and, we may add, in the completeness of all three spatial dimensions. In other words and relatively to such a process we must maintain for sculpture that in it the inward or ideal content of Spirit are first revealed in their eternal repose and essential self-stability. To such repose and unity with itself there can only correspond that external shape which itself persists in such unity and repose. And this condition is satisfied by configuration viewed in its *abstract spatiality*. The spirit which sculpture represents is that which is essentially sound, not broken up in the play of chance conceits and passions; and for this reason its external form also is not dissolved in the manifold variety of appearance, but exhibits itself under this one presentment only as the abstraction of space in the totality of its dimensions.

Assuming, then, that the art of architecture has executed its temple, and the hand of sculpture has placed therein the image of the god, we have in the *third* place to assume the *community* of the faithful as confronting the god thus presented to vision in the wide chambers of his dwelling-place. Now this community is the spiritual reflection into its own world of that sensuous presence, the subjective and inward animating life of soul, in its union with which, both for the artistic content and the external material which manifests it, the determining principle may be identified with particularization in varied shapes and qualities, individualization and the life of soul which they imply. The downright and solid fact of unity the god possesses in sculpture breaks up into the multiplicity of a world of particular souls, whose union is no longer sensuous but wholly ideal.

Here for the first time God Himself is revealed as veritably Spirit—

viz., the Spirit revealed in His community. Here at last He is seen apprehended as this moving to-and-fro, as this alternation between His own essential unity and His realization in the knowledge of individual persons and that separation which it involves, as also in the universal spiritual being and union of the many. In such a community God is disengaged from the abstraction of His unfolded self-seclusion and self-identity, no less than from the immediate absorption in bodily shape, in which He is presented by sculpture. He is, in a word, lifted into the actual sphere of spiritual existence and knowledge, into the reflected appearance, whose manifestation is essentially inward and the life of heart and soul. Thereby the higher content is now the nature of Spirit, and that in its ultimate or absolute shape. But at the same time the separation to which we have alluded displays this as *particular* spiritual being, a specific emotional life. Moreover, for the reason that the main thing here is not the untroubled repose of the God in himself, but his manifestation simply, the Being which is *for another*, self-revealment in fact, it follows that, on the plane we have now reached, all the varied content of human subjectivity in its vital movement and activity, whether viewed as passion, action, or event, or more generally the wide realm of human feeling, volition and its discontinuance, become one and all for their own sake objects of artistic representation.

Agreeably with such a content the sensuous element of art has likewise to show itself potentially adapted to such particularization and the display of such an inward content of heart and mind. Media of this description are supplied by colour, musical tones, and finally in sound as mere sign for ideal perceptions and conceptions; and we further obtain the means of realizing with the use of such media a content of this kind in the arts of painting, music, and poetry. Throughout this sphere the sensuous medium is found to be essentially disparate in itself and throughout posited as ideal. In this way it responds in the highest degree to the fundamentally spiritual content of art, and the coalescence of spiritual significance and sensuous material attains a more intimate union than was possible either in architecture or sculpture. At the same time such a union is necessarily more near to soul-life, leaning exclusively to the subjective side of human experience; one which, in so far as form and content are thus constrained to particularization and to posit their result as ideal, can only be actually effected at the expense of the objective universality of the content as also of the fusion with the immediately sensuous medium.

The arts, then, which are lifted into a higher strain of ideality, abandoning as they do the symbolism of architecture and the classical Ideal of sculpture, accept their predominant type from the *romantic* art-form; and these are the arts most fitted to express its mode of configuration. They are, however, a totality of arts, because the romantic type is itself essentially the most concrete.

(*c*) The articulation of this *third sphere* of the particular arts may be fixed as follows:

(*a*) The *first* art which comes next to sculpture is that of painting. It avails itself for a medium of its content and the plastic configuration of the same of visibility as such, to the extent that it is differentiated in its own nature, in other words is defined in the continuity of colour. No doubt the material of architecture and sculpture is likewise both visible and coloured. It is, however, not, as in painting, visibility in its pure nature, not the essentially simple light, which by its differentiating of itself in its opposition to darkness, and in association with that darkness gives rise to colour. This quality of visibility made essentially ideal and treated as such no longer either requires, as in architecture, the abstractly mechanical qualities of mass as appropriate to materials of weight, nor, as is the case with sculpture, the complete dimensuration of spatial condition, even when concentrated into organic forms. The visibility and the making apparent, which belong to painting, possess differences of quality under a more ideal mode—that is, in the specific varieties of colour—which liberates art from the objective totality of spatial condition, by being limited to a plane surface.

On the other hand the content also attains the widest compass of particularity. Whatever can find a place in the human heart, as emotion, idea, and purpose, whatever it is capable of actually shaping—all such diversity may form part of the varied presentations of painting. The entire world of particular existence, from the most exalted embodiment of mind to the most insignificant natural fact, finds a place here. For it is possible even for finite Nature, in its particular scenes and phenomena, to form part of such artistic display, provided only that we have some reference to conscious life which makes it akin to human thought and emotion.

(*β*) The *second* art which continues the further realization of the romantic type and forms a distinct contrast to painting is that of *music*. Its medium, albeit still sensuous, yet proceeds into still profounder subjectivity and particularization. We have here, too, the deliberate treatment of the sensuous medium as ideal, and it consists in the negation and idealization into the isolated unity of a single point, the indifferent external collocation of space, whose complete appearance is retained by painting and deliberately feigned in its completeness. This isolated point, viewed as this process of negation, is an essentially concrete and active process of cancellation within the determinate substance of the material medium, viewed, that is, as motion and vibration of the material object within itself and in its relation to itself. Such an inchoate ideality of matter, which no longer appears under the form of space, but as temporal ideality, is sound or tone. We have here the sensuous set down as negated, and its abstract visibility converted into audibility. In other words sound liberates the ideal content from its fetters in the material substance. This earliest secured inwardness of matter and impregnation of it with soul-life supplies the medium for the intimacy and soul of Spirit—itself as yet indefinite—permitting, as it does, the echo and reverberation of man's emotional world through its entire range of feelings and passions. In this way music forms the centre of the romantic arts, just as sculpture represents the midway point of arrest between architecture and the arts of the romantic subjectivity. Thus, too, it forms the point of transition between the abstract, spatial sensuousness of painting and the abstract spirituality of poetry. Music carries within itself, like architecture, and in contrast to the emotional world simply and its inward self-seclusion, a relation of quantity conformable to the principles of the understanding and their modes of coordinated configuration.

(γ)   We must look for our *third* and most spiritual type of artistic presentation among the romantic arts in that of *poetry*. The supreme characteristic of poetry consists in the power with which it brings into vassalage of the mind and its conceptions the sensuous element from which music and painting began to liberate art. For sound, the only remaining external material retained by poetry, is in it no longer the feeling of the sonorous itself, but is a mere sign without independent significance. And it is, moreover, a sign of idea which has become essentially concrete, and not merely of indefinite feeling and its subtle modes and gradations. And this is how sound develops into the Word, as essentially articulate voice, whose intention it is to indicate ideas and thoughts. The purely negative moment to which music advanced now asserts itself as the wholly concrete point, the point which is mind itself, the self-conscious individual, which produces from itself the infinite expansion of its ideas and unites the same with the temporal condition of sound. Yet this sensuous element, which was still in music immediately united to emotion, is in poetry separated from the content of consciousness. Mind, in short, here determines this content for its own sake and apart from all else into the content of idea; to express such idea it no doubt avails itself of sound, but employs it merely as a sign without independent worth or substance. Thus viewed, the sound here may be just as well reproduced by the mere letter, for the audible, like the visible, is here reduced to a mere indication of mind. For this reason, the true medium of poetical representation is the poetical imagination and the intellectual presentation itself; and inasmuch as this element is common to all types of art it follows that poetry is a common thread through them all, and is developed independently in each. Poetry is, in short, the universal art of the mind, which has become essentially free, and which is not fettered in its realization to an externally sensuous material, but which is creatively active in the space and time belonging to the inner world of ideas and emotion. Yet it is precisely in this its highest phase, that art terminates, by transcending itself; it is just here that it deserts the medium of a harmonious presentation of mind in sensuous shape and passes from the poetry of imaginative idea into the prose of thought.

Such we may accept as the articulate totality of the particular arts; they are the external art of architecture, the objective art of sculpture and the subjective arts of painting, music, and poetry. Many other classifications than these have been attempted, for a work of art presents such a wealth of aspects, that it is quite possible, as has frequently been the case, to make first one and then another the basis of division. For instance, you may take the sensuous medium simply. Architecture may then be viewed as a kind of crystallization; sculpture, as the organic configuration of material in its sensuous and spatial totality; painting as the coloured surface and line, while in music, space, as such, passes over into the point or moment of time replete with content in itself, until we come finally to poetry, where the external medium is wholly suppressed into insignificance. Or, again, these differences have been viewed with reference to their purely abstract conditions of space and time. Such abstract divisions of works of art may, as their medium also may be consequentially traced in their characteristic features. They cannot, however, be worked out as the final and fundamental principle, because such aspects themselves derive their origins from a higher principle, and must therefore fall into subordination thereto.

This higher principle we have discovered in the types of art—

symbolic, classical, and romantic—which are the universal stages or phases of the Idea of beauty itself.

Their relation to the individual arts in their concrete manifestation as embodiment is of a kind that these arts constitute the real and positive existence of these general art-types. For *symbolic* art attains its most adequate realization and most pertinent application in *architecture*, in which it expatiates in the full import of its notion, and is not as yet depreciated, as it were, into the merely inorganic nature dealt with by some other art. The *classical* type of art finds its unfettered realization, on the other hand, in sculpture, treating architecture merely as the enclosure which surrounds it, and being unable to elaborate painting and music into the wholly adequate forms of its content. Finally, the *romantic* art-type is supreme in the products of painting and music, and likewise in poetical composition, as their pre-eminent and unconditionally adequate modes of expression. Poetry is, however, conformable to all types of the beautiful, and its embrace reaches them all for the reason that the poetic imagination is its own proper medium, and imagination is essential to every creation of beauty, whatever its type may be.

To sum up, then, what the particular arts realize in particular works of art, are according to their fundamental conception, simply the universal types which constitute the self-unfolding Idea of beauty. It is as the external realization of this Idea that the wide Pantheon of art is being raised; and the architect and builder thereof is the spirit of beauty as it gradually comes to self-cognition, and to complete which the history of the world will require its evolution of centuries.

Arthur
SCHOPENHAUER

If we think of Kant's philosophy of art as the culmination of eighteenth-century philosophical inquiry, we may think of Schelling's philosophy of art as the beginning of the nineteenth-century Romantic interpretation of art. It must be remembered that Hegel's lectures on art did not appear until 1835 and that between the publications of Schelling and Hegel there appeared The World as Will and Idea *(first edition 1819, revised edition 1844). It was, of course, the revised edition that won Schopenhauer so many converts and disciples. While Kant's work was immediately acclaimed, it took twenty-five years before Schopenhauer received serious attention, but now as we read him we see the extent to which his voluntarism has characterized art theories of our own day.*

Schopenhauer accepts Kantian phenomenalism without question, for he sees it as another version of the essential discovery of modern thought originating with Descartes: the world is the elaboration of the human mind. But Schopenhauer does not accept Kant's distinction between noumena and phenomena, nor does he find the Kantian psychology true. All that man knows lies within his own consciousness, though he may posit a knowing subject and an eternal matter as constants behind the flux of experience. A little analysis shows us that these are but artificial notions, for the self is nothing without consciousness, matter is nothing without specific events following one another in time. Hence the reality which makes these two dead concepts alive and meaningful is the cosmic force which enlivens them, and this Schopenhauer calls the Will. We cannot find reality in self or matter, but only in the Will: this is the thing in itself, neither the perceiving subject nor perceived matter, but that which manifests both from itself.

The aesthetic is also a "phenomenon of the brain," dependent upon the peculiarities of the individual who perceives, but remarkable in its perfection and harmony. While I may not agree with you on what is beautiful, I will find in beauty, as do you, the perfection which all else in consciousness lacks. Beauty is "a cathartic to the mind," lifting us for a moment above the tug of desire and the boredom of gratification which are the usual conditions of life. Through art the restless will in man is momentarily stilled. To Schopenhauer nature unaffected by human agents exhibits a quality that human art, since it is the work of a person, cannot match. He favors the English over the French garden, for it thrives on neglect, and therefore can show us "the objectification of the still unconscious will to live." Where art triumphs over nature is in the presentation of truth; it shows us the Ideas of the world as they really are, i.e., in perceptible form, and in music it directly represents the will itself. In art we see the world which we often try to frame, unsuccessfully, in concepts. Art is the highest work of the human consciousness, where mind finally realizes itself, for through art the artist, possessor of an Idea, communicates it to others. Although art can exist only as the perceptible, it releases us from the ordinary conceptualization of the world, and allows us to know the universal. Schopenhauer insists that art is the most universal presentation of reality, while at the same time the most specifically sensuous presentation. It is this paradoxical joining of the sensuous and the universal which accounts for art's power and gratification. Only the universal in phenomenal manifestation could achieve this excellence.

For Schopenhauer, as for Kant, the art work is the product of genius, a peculiar power which enables its possessor to leave his own interests, wishes, aims entirely out of sight and thereby free himself to create a world in imagination. But the arts created by genius are not all equally successful in bringing us to *the truth. There is an unfolding of reality through art which is like that described by Hegel. At the most primitive, the Idea is expressed in architecture; at the most developed the Idea is transcended by music which expresses the will itself. Between them occur sculpture, painting, and literature. All of these try to depict the world and in so doing fail of complete universality. Only music, which leaves the world behind, is able to realize the innermost nature of reality. Yet the seeming abandonment of the world is in fact the ability to represent the world in its deepest truth, for music "is thus by no means like the other arts, the copy of the Ideas, but the copy of the will itself, whose objectivity the Ideas are."*

Art, by providing us with the apprehension of the Ideas, enables us to enter a state of pure objectivity of perception. In this state the will is eliminated from subjective consciousness and we become a pure will-less subject of knowledge. With the withdrawal of subjectivity the possibility of suffering is abolished, the will being quieted. We escape from the world and its troubles through this pure will-less contemplation. And in the case of music we escape from the world through our contemplation of it in its deepest reality, the will. Only the asceticism of the saint can conquer reality in like manner. Hence for most mortals music is the knowledge which in its revelatory power releases us most completely from the world which we think under the concept of the will. With this high valuation, Schopenhauer exhibits the well-known romantic propensity to see in music the ideal condition of art.

Schopenhauer's thought has had a profound influence on contemporary philosophy and letters. Nietzsche begins his analysis of art with a refinement of Schopenhauer's position, and Santayana learned as much from Schopenhauer as from Plato. Most notable in the influence on writers is the conception of art presented in Thomas Mann's Doctor Faustus *and* Felix Krull.

THE WORLD AS WILL AND IDEA

SUPPLEMENTS TO THE FIRST BOOK

Chapter I: *The Standpoint of Idealism*

. . . "The world is my idea" is, like the axioms of Euclid, a proposition which every one must recognise as true as soon as he understands it; although it is not a proposition which every one understands as soon as he hears it. To have brought this proposition to clear consciousness, and in it the problem of the relation of the ideal and the real, *i.e.*, of the world in the head to the world outside the head, together with the problem of moral freedom, is the distinctive feature of modern philosophy. For it was only after men had spent their labour for thousands of years upon a mere philosophy of the object that they discovered that among the many things that make the world so obscure and doubtful the first and chiefest is this, that however immeasurable and massive it may be, its existence yet hangs by a single thread; and this is the actual consciousness in which it exists. This condition, to which the existence of the world is irrevocably subject, marks it, in spite of all *empirical* reality, with the stamp of *ideality*, and therefore of mere *phenomenal appearance*. Thus on one side at least the world must be recognised as akin to dreams, and indeed to be classified along with them. For the same function of the brain which, during sleep, conjures up before us a completely objective, perceptible, and even palpable world must have just as large a share in the presentation of the objective world of waking life. Both worlds, although different as regards their matter, are yet clearly moulded in the one form. This form is the intellect, the function of the brain. Descartes was probably the first who attained to the degree of reflection which this fundamental truth demands, and consequently he made it the starting-point of his philosophy, though provisionally only in the form of a sceptical doubt. When he took his *cogito ergo sum* as alone certain, and provisionally regarded the existence of the world as problematical, he really discovered the essential and only right starting-point of all philosophy, and at the same time its *true* foundation. This foundation is essentially and inevitably the *subjective*, the *individual consciousness*. For this alone is and remains immediate; everything else, whatever it may be, is mediated and conditioned through it, and is therefore dependent upon it. Therefore modern philosophy is rightly regarded as starting with Descartes, who was the father of it. Not long afterwards Berkeley followed the same path further, and attained to *idealism* proper, *i.e.*, to the knowledge that the world which is extended in space, thus the objective, material world in general, exists as such simply and solely in our *idea*, and that it is false, and indeed absurd, to attribute to it, *as such*, an existence apart from all idea and independent of the knowing subject, thus to assume matter as something absolute and possessed of real being in itself. But his correct and profound insight into this truth really constitutes Berkeley's whole philosophy; in it he had exhausted himself.

Thus true philosophy must always be idealistic; indeed, it must be so in order to be merely honest. For nothing is more certain than that no man ever came out of himself in order to identify himself directly with things which are different from him; but everything of which he has certain, and therefore immediate, knowledge lies within his own consciousness. Beyond this consciousness, therefore, there can be no *immediate* certainty; but the first principles of a science must have such certainty. For the empirical standpoint of the other sciences it is quite right to assume the objective world as something absolutely given; but not so for the standpoint of philosophy, which has to go back to what is first and original. Only consciousness is immediately given; therefore the basis of philosophy is limited to facts of consciousness, *i.e.*, it is essentially *idealistic*. Realism which commends itself to the crude understanding, by the appearance which it assumes of being matter-of-fact, really starts from an arbitrary assumption, and is therefore an empty castle in the air, for it ignores or denies the first of all facts, that all that we know lies within consciousness. For that the *objective existence* of things is conditioned through a subject whose ideas they are, and consequently that the objective world exists only as *idea*, is no hypothesis, and still less a dogma, or even a paradox set up for the sake of discussion; but it is the most certain and the simplest truth; and the knowledge of it is only made difficult by the fact that it is indeed so simple, and that it is not every one who has sufficient power of reflection to go back to the first elements of his consciousness of things. There can never be an absolute and independent objective existence; indeed such an existence is quite unintelligible. For the objective, as such, always and essentially has its existence in the consciousness of a subject, is thus the idea of this subject, and consequently is conditioned by it, and also by its forms, the forms of the idea, which depend upon the subject and not on the object.

That *the objective world would exist* even if there existed no conscious being certainly seems at the first blush to be unquestionable, because it can be thought in the abstract, without bringing to light the contradiction which it carries within it. But if we desire to *realise* this abstract thought, that is, to reduce it to ideas of perception, from which alone (like everything abstract) it can have content and truth, and if accordingly we try *to imagine an objective world without a knowing subject*, we become aware that what we then imagine is in truth the opposite of what we intended, is in fact nothing else than the process in the intellect of a knowing subject who perceives an objective world, is thus exactly what we desired to exclude. For this perceptible and real world is clearly a phenomenon of the brain; therefore there lies a contradiction in the assumption that as such it ought also to exist independently of all brains.

. . . . .

The world as idea, the objective world, has thus, as it were, two poles; the simple knowing subject without the forms of its knowledge, and crude matter without form and quality. Both are completely unknowable; the subject because it is that which knows, matter because without form and quality it cannot be perceived. Yet both are fundamental conditions of all empirical perception. Thus the knowing subject, merely as such, which is a presupposition of all experience, stands opposed as its pure counterpart to the crude, formless, and utterly dead (i.e., will-less) matter, which is given in no experience, but which all experience presupposes. This subject is not in time, for time is only the more definite form of all its ideas. The matter which stands over against it is, like it, eternal and imperishable, endures through all time, but is, properly speaking, not extended, for extension gives form, thus it has no spatial properties. Everything else is involved in a constant process of coming into being and passing away, while these two represent the unmoved poles of the world as idea. The permanence of matter may therefore be regarded as the reflex of the timelessness of the pure subject, which is simply assumed as the condition of all objects. Both belong to phenomena, not to the thing in itself, but they are the framework of the phenomenon. Both are arrived at only by abstraction, and are not given immediately, pure and for themselves.

The fundamental error of all systems is the failure to understand this truth. *Intelligence and matter are correlates, i.e.*, the one exists only for the other, both stand and fall together, the one is only the reflex of the other. Indeed they are really *one and the same thing* regarded from two opposite points of view; and this one thing, I am here anticipating, is the manifestation of the will, or the thing in itself.

. . . . .

SUPPLEMENTS TO THE THIRD BOOK

Chapter XXXIV: On the Inner Nature of Art

Not merely philosophy but also the fine arts work at bottom towards the solution of the problem of existence. For in every mind that once gives itself up to the purely objective contemplation of nature a desire has been excited, however concealed and unconscious it may be, to comprehend the true nature of things, of life and existence. For this alone has interest for the intellect as such, *i.e.*, for the pure subject of knowledge which has become free from the aims of the will; as for the subject which knows as a mere individual the aims of the will alone have interest. On this account the result of the purely objective apprehension of things is an expression more of the nature of life and existence, more an answer to the question, "What is life?" Every genuine and successful work of art answers this question in its own way with perfect correctness. But all the arts speak only the naive and childish language of perception, not the abstract and serious language of *reflection*; their answer is therefore a fleeting image: not permanent and general knowledge. Thus for *perception* every work of art answers that question, every painting, every statue, every poem, every scene upon the stage: music also answers it; and indeed more profoundly than all the rest, for in its language, which is understood with absolute directness, but which is yet untranslatable into that of the reason, the inner nature of all life and existence expresses itself. Thus all the other arts hold up to the questioner a perceptible image, and say, "Look here, this is life." Their answer, however correct it may be, will yet always afford merely a temporary, not a complete and final, satisfaction. For they always give merely a fragment, an example instead of the rule, not the whole, which can only be given in the universality of the *conception*. For this, therefore, thus for reflection and in the abstract, to give an answer which just on that account shall be permanent and suffice for always, is the task of philosophy. However, we see here upon what the relationship of philosophy to the fine arts rests, and can conclude from that to what extent the capacity of both, although in its direction and in secondary matters very different, is yet in its root the same.

Every work of art accordingly really aims at showing us life and things as they are in truth, but cannot be directly discerned by every one through the mist of objective and subjective contingencies. Art takes away this mist.

The works of the poets, sculptors, and representative artists in general contain an unacknowledged treasure of profound wisdom; just because out of them the wisdom of the nature of things itself speaks, whose utterances they merely interpret by illustrations and purer repetitions. On this account, however, every one who reads the poem or looks at the picture must certainly contribute out of his own means to bring that wisdom to light; accordingly he comprehends only so much of it as his capacity and culture admit of; as in the deep sea each sailor only lets down the lead as far as the length of the line will allow. Before a picture, as before a prince, every one must stand, waiting to see whether and what it will speak to him; and, as in the case of a prince, so here he must not himself address it, for then he would only hear himself. It follows from all this that in the works of the representative arts all truth is certainly contained, yet only *virtualiter* or *implicite*; philosophy, on the other hand, endeavours to supply the same truth *actualiter* and *explicite*, and therefore, in this sense, is related to art as wine to grapes. What it promises to supply would be, as it were, an already realised and clear gain, a firm and abiding possession; while that which proceeds from the achievements and works of art is one which has constantly to be reproduced anew. Therefore, however, it makes demands, not only upon those who produce its works, but also upon those who are to enjoy them which are discouraging and hard to comply with. Therefore its public remains small, while that of art is large.

The co-operation of the beholder, which is referred to above, as demanded for the enjoyment of a work of art, depends partly upon the fact that every work of art can only produce its effect through the medium of the fancy; therefore it must excite this, and can never allow it to be left out of the play and remain inactive. This is a condition of the aesthetic effect, and therefore a fundamental law of all fine arts. But it follows from this that, through the work of art, everything must not be directly given to the senses, but rather only so much as is demanded to lead the fancy on to the right path; something, and indeed the ultimate thing, must always be left over for the fancy to do. Even the author must always leave something over for the reader to think; for Voltaire has very rightly said, *"Le secret d'être ennuyeux, c'est de tout dire."* But besides this, in art the best of all is too spiritual to be given directly to the senses; it must be born in the imagination of the beholder, although begotten by the work of art. It depends upon this that the sketches of great masters often effect more than their finished pictures; although another advantage certainly contributes to this, namely, that they are completed offhand in the moment of conception; while the perfected painting is only produced through continued effort, by means of skilful deliberation and persistent intention, for the inspiration cannot last till it is completed. From the fundamental aesthetical law we are speaking of, it is further to be explained why wax figures never produce an aesthetic effect, and therefore are not properly works of fine art, although it is just in them that the imitation of nature is able to reach its highest grade. For they leave nothing for the imagination to do. Sculpture gives merely the form without the colour; painting gives the colour, but the mere appearance of the form; thus both appeal to the imagination of the beholder. The wax figure, on the other hand, gives all, form and colour at once; whence arises the appearance of reality, and the imagination is left out of account. Poetry, on the contrary, appeals indeed to the imagination alone, which it sets in action by means of mere words.

An arbitrary playing with the means of art without a proper knowledge of the end is, in every art, the fundamental characteristic of the dabbler. Such a man shows himself in the pillars that support nothing, aimless volutes, juttings and projections of bad architecture, in the meaningless runs and figures, together with the aimless noise of bad music, in the jingling of the rhymes of senseless poetry, &c.

It follows from the preceding chapter, and from my whole view of art, that its aim is the facilitating of the knowledge of the Ideas of the world (in the Platonic sense, the only one which I recognise for the word Idea). The Ideas, however, are essentially something perceptible, which, therefore, in its fuller determinations, is inexhaustible. The communication of such an Idea can therefore only take place on the path of perception, which is that of art. Whoever, therefore, is filled with the comprehension of an Idea is justified if he chooses art as the medium of its communication. The mere conception, on the other hand, is something completely determinable, therefore exhaustible, and distinctly thought, the whole content of which can be coldly and dryly expressed in words. Now to desire to communicate such a conception by means of a work of art is a very useless circumlocution, indeed belongs to that playing with the means of art without knowledge of its end which has just been condemned. Therefore a work of art which has proceeded from mere distinct conceptions is always ungenuine. If now, in considering a work of plastic art, or in reading a poem, or in hearing a piece of music (which aims at describing something definite), we see, through all the rich materials of art, the distinct, limited, cold, dry conception shine out, and at last come to the front, the conception which was the kernel of this work, the whole notion of which consequently consisted in the distinct thinking of it, and accordingly is absolutely exhausted by its communication, we feel disgusted and indignant, for we see ourselves deceived and cheated out of our interest and attention. We are only perfectly satisfied by the impression of a work of art when it leaves something which, with all our thinking about it, we cannot bring down to the distinctness of a conception. The mark of that hybrid origin from mere conceptions is that the author of a work of art could, before he set about it, give in distinct words what he intended to present; for then it would have been possible to attain his whole end through these words. Therefore it is an undertaking as unworthy as it is absurd if, as has often been tried at the present day, one seeks to reduce a poem of Shakespeare's or Goethe's to the abstract truth which it was its aim to communicate. Certainly the artist ought to think in the arranging of his work; but only that thought which was *perceived* before it was thought has afterwards, in its communication, the power of animating or rousing, and thereby becomes imperishable. We shall not refrain from observing here that certainly the work which is done at a stroke, like the sketches of painters already referred to, the work which is completed in the inspiration of its first conception, and as it were unconsciously dashed off, like the melody which comes entirely without reflection, and quite as if by inspiration, and finally, also the lyrical poem proper, the mere song, in which the deeply felt mood of the present, and the impression of the surroundings, as if involuntarily, pours itself forth in words, whose metre and rhyme come about of their own accord—that all these, I say, have the great advantage of being purely the work of the ecstasy of the moment, the inspiration, the free movement of genius, without any admixture of intention and reflection; hence they are through and through delightful and enjoyable, without shell and kernel, and their effect is much more inevitable than that of the greatest works of art, of slower and more deliberate execution. In all the latter, thus in great historical paintings, in long epic poems, great operas, &c., reflection, intention, and deliberate selection has had an important part; understanding, technical skill, and routine must here fill up the gaps which the conception and inspiration of genius has left, and must mix with these all kinds of necessary supplementary work as cement of the only really genuinely brilliant parts. This explains why all such works, only excepting the perfect masterpieces of the very greatest masters (as, for example, "Hamlet," "Faust," the opera of "Don Juan"), inevitably contain an admixture of something insipid and wearisome, which in some measure hinders the enjoyment of them. Proofs of this are the "Messiah," "*Gerusalemme liberata*," even "Paradise Lost" and the "Æneid"; and Horace already makes the bold remark, "*Quandoque dormitat bonus Homerus.*" But that this is the case is the consequence of the limitation of human powers in general.

The mother of the useful arts is. necessity; that of the fine arts superfluity. As their father, the former have understanding; the latter genius, which is itself a kind of superfluity, that of the powers of knowledge beyond the measure which is required for the service of the will.

THIRD BOOK: THE WORLD AS IDEA

Second Aspect: The Idea Independent of the
Principle of Sufficient Reason
The Platonic Idea
The Object of Art

§ 38. In the aesthetical mode of contemplation we have found *two inseparable constituent parts*—the knowledge of the object, not as individual thing but as Platonic Idea, that is, as the enduring form of this whole species of things; and the self-consciousness of the knowing person, not as individual, but as *pure will-less subject of knowledge*. The condition under which both these constituent parts appear always united was found to be the abandonment of the method of knowing which is bound to the principle of sufficient reason, and which, on the other hand, is the only kind of knowledge that is of value for the service of the will and also for science. Moreover, we shall see that the pleasure which is produced by the contemplation of the beautiful arises from these two constituent parts, sometimes more from the one, sometimes more from the other, according to what the object of the aesthetical contemplation may be.

All *willing* arises from want, therefore from deficiency, and therefore from suffering. The satisfaction of a wish ends it; yet for one wish that is satisfied there remain at least ten which are denied. Further, the desire lasts long, the demands are infinite; the satisfaction is short and scantily measured out. But even the final satisfaction is itself only apparent; every satisfied wish at once makes room for a new one; both are illusions; the one is known to be so, the other not yet. No attained object of desire can give lasting satisfaction, but merely a fleeting gratification; it is like the alms thrown to the beggar, that keeps him alive to-day that his misery may be prolonged till the morrow. Therefore, so long as our consciousness is filled by our will, so long as we are given up to the throng of desires with their constant hopes and fears, so long as we are the subject of willing, we can never have lasting happiness nor peace. It is essentially all the same whether we pursue or flee, fear injury or seek enjoyment; the care for the constant demands of the will, in whatever form it may be, continually occupies and sways the consciousness; but without peace no true well-being is possible. The subject of willing is thus constantly stretched on the revolving wheel of Ixion, pours water into the sieve of the Danaids, is the ever-longing Tantalus.

But when some external cause or inward disposition lifts us suddenly out of the endless stream of willing, delivers knowledge from the slavery of the will, the attention is no longer directed to the motives of willing, but comprehends things free from their relation to the will, and thus observes them without personal interest, without subjectivity, purely objectively, gives itself entirely up to them so far as they are ideas, but not in so far as they are motives. Then all at once the peace which we were always seeking, but which always fled from us on the former path of the desires, comes to us of its own accord, and it is well with us. It is the painless state which Epicurus prized as the highest good and as the state of the gods; for we are for the moment set free from the miserable striving of the will; we keep the Sabbath of the penal servitude of willing; the wheel of Ixion stands still.

But this is just the state which I described above as necessary for the knowledge of the Idea, as pure contemplation, as sinking oneself in perception, losing oneself in the object, forgetting all individuality, surrendering that kind of knowledge which follows the principle of sufficient reason, and comprehends only relations; the state by means of which at once and inseparably the perceived particular thing is raised to the Idea of its whole species, and the knowing individual to the pure subject of will-less knowledge, and as such they are both taken out of the stream of time and all other relations. It is then all one whether we see the sun set from the prison or from the palace.

Inward disposition, the predominance of knowing over willing, can produce this state under any circumstances. This is shown by those admirable Dutch artists who directed this purely objective perception to the most insignificant objects, and established a lasting monument of their objectivity and spiritual peace in their pictures of *still life*, which the aesthetic beholder does not look on without emotion; for they present to him the peaceful, still, frame of mind of the artist, free from will, which was needed to contemplate such insignificant things so objectively, to observe them so attentively, and to repeat this perception so intelligently; and as the picture enables the onlooker to participate in this state, his emotion is often increased by the contrast between it and the unquiet frame of mind, disturbed by vehement willing, in which he finds himself. In the same spirit, landscape-painters, and particularly Ruisdael, have often painted very insignificant country scenes, which produce the same effect even more agreeably.

All this is accomplished by the inner power of an artistic nature alone; but that purely objective disposition is facilitated and assisted from without by suitable objects, by the abundance of natural beauty which invites contemplation, and even presses itself upon us. Whenever it discloses itself suddenly to our view, it almost always succeeds in delivering us, though it may be only for a moment, from subjectivity, from the slavery of the will, and in raising us to the state of pure knowing. This is why the man who is tormented by passion, or want, or care, is so suddenly revived, cheered, and restored by a single free glance into nature: the storm of passion, the pressure of desire and fear, and all the miseries of willing are then at once, and in a marvellous manner, calmed and appeased. For at the moment at which, freed from the will, we give ourselves up to pure will-less knowing, we pass into a world from which everything is absent that influenced our will and moved us so violently through it. This freeing of knowledge lifts us as wholly and entirely away from all that, as do sleep and dreams; happiness and unhappiness have disappeared; we are no longer individual; the individual is forgotten; we are only pure subject of knowledge; we are only that *one* eye of the world which looks out from all knowing creatures, but which can become perfectly free from the service of will in man alone. Thus all difference of individuality so entirely disappears, that it is all the same whether the perceiving eye belongs to a mighty king or to a wretched beggar; for neither joy nor complaining can pass that boundary with us. So near us always lies a sphere in which we escape from all our misery; but who has the strength to continue long in it? As soon as any single relation to our will, to our person, even of these objects of our pure contemplation, comes again into consciousness, the magic is at an end; we fall back into the knowledge which is governed by the principle of sufficient reason; we know no longer the Idea, but the particular thing, the link of a chain to which we also belong, and we are again abandoned to all our woe. Most men remain almost always at this standpoint because they entirely lack objectivity, *i.e.*, genius. Therefore they have no pleasure in being alone with nature; they need company, or at least a book. For their knowledge remains subject to their will; they seek, therefore, in objects, only some relation to their will, and whenever they see anything that has no such relation, there sounds within them, like a ground bass in music, the constant inconsolable cry, "It is of no use to me"; thus in solitude the most beautiful surroundings have for them a desolate, dark, strange, and hostile appearance.

Lastly, it is this blessedness of will-less perception which casts an enchanting glamour over the past and distant, and presents them to us in so fair a light by means of self-deception. For as we think of days long gone by, days in which we lived in a distant place, it is only the objects which our fancy recalls, not the subject of will, which bore about with it then its incurable sorrows just as it bears them now; but they are forgotten, because since then they have often given place to others. Now, objective perception acts with regard to what is remembered just as it would in what is present, if we let it have influence over us, if we surrendered ourselves to it free from will. Hence it arises that, especially when we are more than ordinarily disturbed by some want, the remembrance of past and distant scenes suddenly flits across our minds like a lost paradise. The fancy recalls only what was objective, not what was individually subjective, and we imagine that that objective stood before us then just as pure and undisturbed by any relation to the will as its image stands in our fancy now; while in reality the relation of the objects to our will gave us pain then just as it does now. We can deliver ourselves from all suffering just as well through present objects as through distant ones whenever we raise ourselves to a purely objective contemplation of them, and so are able to bring about the illusion that only the objects are present and not we ourselves. Then, as the pure subject of knowledge, freed from the miserable self, we become entirely one with these objects, and, for the moment, our wants are as foreign to us as they are to them. The world as idea alone remains, and the world as will has disappeared.

In all these reflections it has been my object to bring out clearly the nature and the scope of the subjective element in aesthetic pleasure; the deliverance of knowledge from the service of the will, the forgetting of self as an individual, and the raising of the consciousness to the pure will-less, timeless, subject of knowledge, independent of all relations. With this subjective side of aesthetic contemplation, there must always appear as its necessary correlative the objective side, the intuitive comprehension of the Platonic Idea. But before we turn to the closer consideration of this, and to the achievements of art in relation to it, it is better that we should pause for a little at the subjective side of aesthetic pleasure, in order to complete our treatment of this by explaining the impression of the *sublime* which depends altogether upon it, and arises from a modification of it. After that we shall complete our investigation of aesthetic pleasure by considering its objective side.

· · · · ·

§ 39. All these reflections are intended to bring out the subjective part of aesthetic pleasure; that is to say, that pleasure so far as it consists simply of delight in perceptive knowledge as such, in opposition to will. And as directly connected with this, there naturally follows the explanation of that disposition or frame of mind which has been called the sense of the *sublime*.

We have already remarked above that the transition to the state of pure perception takes place most easily when the objects bend themselves to it, that is, when by their manifold and yet definite and distinct form they easily become representatives of their Ideas, in which beauty, in the objective sense, consists. This quality belongs pre-eminently to natural beauty, which thus affords even to the most insensible at least a fleeting aesthetic satisfaction: indeed it is so remarkable how especially the vegetable world invites aesthetic observation, and, as it were, presses itself upon it, that one might say, that these advances are connected with the fact that these organisms, unlike the bodies of animals, are not themselves immediate objects of knowledge, and therefore require the assistance of a foreign intelligent individual in order to rise out of the world of blind will and enter the world of idea, and that thus they long, as it were, for this entrance, that they may attain at least indirectly what is denied them directly. But I leave this suggestion which I have hazarded, and which borders perhaps upon extravagance, entirely undecided, for only a very intimate and devoted consideration of nature can raise or justify it.[1] As long as that which raises us from the knowledge of mere relations subject to the will, to aesthetic contemplation, and thereby exalts us to the position of the subject of knowledge free from will, is this fittingness of nature, this significance and distinctness of its forms, on account of which the Ideas individualised in them readily present themselves to us; so long is it merely *beauty* that affects us and the sense of the *beautiful* that is excited. But if these very objects whose significant forms invite us to pure contemplation, have a hostile relation to the human will in general, as it exhibits itself in its objectivity, the human body, if they are opposed to it, so that it is menaced by the irresistible predominance of their power, or sinks into insignificance before their immeasurable greatness; if, nevertheless, the beholder does not direct his attention to this eminently hostile relation to his will, but, although perceiving and recognising it, turns consciously away from it, forcibly detaches himself from his will and its relations, and, giving himself up entirely to knowledge, quietly contemplates those very objects that are so terrible to the will, comprehends only their Idea, which is foreign to all relation, so that he lingers gladly over its contemplation, and is thereby raised above himself, his person, his will, and all will:—in that case he is filled with the sense of the *sublime*, he is in the state of spiritual exaltation, and therefore the object producing such a state is called *sublime*. Thus what distinguishes the sense of the sublime from that of the beautiful is this: in the case of the beautiful, pure knowledge has gained the upper hand without a struggle, for the beauty of the object, *i.e.*, that property which facilitates the knowledge of its Idea, has removed from consciousness without resistance, and therefore imperceptibly, the will and the knowledge of relations which is subject to it, so that what is left is the pure subject of knowledge without even a remembrance of will. On the other hand, in the case of the sublime that state of pure knowledge is only attained by a conscious and forcible breaking away from the relations of the same object to the will, which are recognised as unfavourable, by a free and conscious transcending of the will and the knowledge related to it.

This exaltation must not only be consciously won, but also consciously retained, and it is therefore accompanied by a constant re-

---

[1] I am all the more delighted and astonished, forty years after I so timidly and hesitatingly advanced this thought, to discover that it has already been expressed by St. Augustine: *Arbusta formas suas varias, quibus mundi hujus visibilis structura formosa est, sentiendas sensibus praebent; ut, pro eo quod* NOSSE *non possunt, quasi* INNOTESCERE *velle videantur.—De civ. Dei, xi, 27.*

membrance of will; yet not of a single particular volition, such as fear or desire, but of human volition in general, so far as it is universally expressed in its objectivity, the human body. If a single real act of will were to come into consciousness, through actual personal pressure and danger from the object, then the individual will thus actually influenced would at once gain the upper hand, the peace of contemplation would become impossible, the impression of the sublime would be lost, because it yields to the anxiety, in which the effort of the individual to right itself has sunk every other thought. A few examples will help very much to elucidate this theory of the aesthetic sublime and remove all doubt with regard to it; at the same time they will bring out the different degrees of this sense of the sublime. It is in the main identical with that of the beautiful, with pure willless knowing, and the knowledge, that necessarily accompanies it of Ideas out of all relation determined by the principle of sufficient reason, and it is distinguished from the sense of the beautiful only by the additional quality that it rises above the known hostile relation of the object contemplated to the will in general. Thus there come to be various degrees of the sublime, and transitions from the beautiful to the sublime, according as this additional quality is strong, bold, urgent, near, or weak, distant, and merely indicated. I think it is more in keeping with the plan of my treatise, first to give examples of these transitions, and of the weaker degrees of the impression of the sublime, although persons whose aesthetical susceptibility in general is not very great, and whose imagination is not very lively, will only understand the examples given later of the higher and more distinct grades of that impression; and they should therefore confine themselves to these, and pass over the examples of the very weak degrees of the sublime that are to be given first.

As man is at once impetuous and blind striving of will (whose pole or focus lies in the genital organs), and eternal, free, serene subject of pure knowing (whose pole is the brain); so, corresponding to this antithesis, the sun is both the source of *light*, the condition of the most perfect kind of knowledge, and therefore of the most delightful of things—and the source of *warmth*, the first condition of life, *i.e.*, of all phenomena of will in its higher grades. Therefore, what warmth is for the will, light is for knowledge. Light is the largest gem in the crown of beauty, and has the most marked influence on the knowledge of every beautiful object. Its presence is an indispensable condition of beauty; its favourable disposition increases the beauty of the most beautiful. Architectural beauty more than any other object is enhanced by favourable light, though even the most insignificant things become through its influence most beautiful. If, in the dead of winter, when all nature is frozen and stiff, we see the rays of the setting sun reflected by masses of stone, illuminating without warming, and thus favourable only to the purest kind of knowledge, not to the will; the contemplation of the beautiful effect of the light upon these masses lifts us, as does all beauty, into a state of pure knowing. But, in this case, a certain transcending of the interests of the will is needed to enable us to rise into the state of pure knowing, because there is a faint recollection of the lack of warmth from these rays, that is, an absence of the principle of life; there is a slight challenge to persist in pure knowing, and to refrain from all willing, and therefore it is an example of a transition from the sense of the beautiful to that of the sublime. It is the faintest trace of the sublime in the beautiful; and beauty itself is indeed present only in a slight degree. The following is almost as weak an example.

Let us imagine ourselves transported to a very lonely place, with unbroken horizon, under a cloudless sky, trees and plants in the perfectly motionless air, no animals, no men, no running water, the deepest silence. Such surroundings are, as it were, a call to seriousness and contemplation, apart from all will and its cravings; but this is just what imparts to such a scene of desolate stillness a touch of the sublime. For, because it affords no object, either favourable or unfavourable, for the will which is constantly in need of striving and attaining, there only remains the state of pure contemplation, and whoever is incapable of this, is ignominiously abandoned to the vacancy of unoccupied will, and the misery of ennui. So far it is a test of our intellectual worth, of which, generally speaking, the degree of our power of enduring solitude, or our love of it, is a good criterion. The scene we have sketched affords us, then, an example of the sublime in a low degree, for in it, with the state of pure knowing in its peace and all-sufficiency, there is mingled, by way of contrast, the recollection of the dependence and poverty of the will which stands in need of constant action. This is the species of the sublime for which the sight of the boundless prairies of the interior of North America is celebrated.

But let us suppose such a scene, stripped also of vegetation, and showing only naked rocks; then from the entire absence of that organic life which is necessary for existence, the will at once becomes uneasy, the desert assumes a terrible aspect, our mood becomes more tragic; the elevation to the sphere of pure knowing takes place with a more decided tearing of ourselves away from the interests of the will; and because we persist in continuing in the state of pure knowing, the sense of the sublime distinctly appears.

The following situation may occasion this feeling in a still higher degree. Nature convulsed by a storm; the sky darkened by black threatening thunder-clouds; stupendous, naked, overhanging cliffs, completely shutting out the view; rushing, foaming torrents; absolute desert; the wail of the wind sweeping through the clefts of the rocks. Our dependence, our strife with hostile nature, our will broken in the conflict, now appears visibly before our eyes. Yet, so long as the personal pressure does not gain the upper hand, but we continue in aesthetic contemplation, the pure subject of knowing gazes unshaken and unconcerned through that strife of nature, through that picture of the broken will, and quietly comprehends the Ideas even of those objects which are threatening and terrible to the will. In this contrast lies the sense of the sublime.

But the impression becomes still stronger, if, when we have before our eyes, on a large scale, the battle of the raging elements, in such a scene we are prevented from hearing the sound of our own voice by the noise of a falling stream; or, if we are abroad in the storm of tempestuous seas, where the mountainous waves rise and fall, dash themselves furiously against steep cliffs, and toss their spray high into the air; the storm howls, the sea boils, the lightning flashes from black clouds, and the peals of thunder drown the voice of storm and sea. Then, in the undismayed beholder, the two-fold nature of his consciousness reaches the highest degree of distinctness. He perceives himself, on the one hand, as an individual, as the frail phenomenon of will, which the slightest touch of these forces can utterly destroy, helpless against powerful nature, dependent, the victim of chance, a vanishing nothing in the presence of stupendous might; and, on the other hand, as the eternal, peaceful, knowing subject, the condition of the object, and, therefore, the supporter of this whole world; the terrific strife of nature only his idea; the subject itself free and apart from all desires and necessities, in the quiet comprehension of the Ideas. This is the complete impression of the sublime. Here he obtains a glimpse of a power beyond all comparison superior to the individual, threatening it with annihilation.

The impression of the sublime may be produced in quite another way, by presenting a mere immensity in space and time; its immeasurable greatness dwindles the individual to nothing. Adhering to Kant's nomenclature and his accurate division, we may call the first kind the dynamical, and the second the mathematical sublime, although we entirely dissent from his explanation of the inner nature of the impression, and can allow no share in it either to moral reflections, or to hypostases from scholastic philosophy.

If we lose ourselves in the contemplation of the infinite greatness of the universe in space and time, meditate on the thousands of years that are past or to come, or if the heavens at night actually bring before our eyes innumerable worlds and so force upon our consciousness the immensity of the universe, we feel ourselves dwindle to nothing; as individuals, as living bodies, as transient phenomena of will, we feel ourselves pass away and vanish into nothing like drops in the ocean. But at once there rises against this ghost of our own nothingness, against such lying impossibility, the immediate consciousness that all these worlds exist only as our idea, only as modifications of the eternal subject of pure knowing, which we find ourselves to be as soon as we forget our individuality, and which is the necessary supporter of all worlds and all times the condition of their possibility. The vastness of the world which disquieted us before, rests now in us; our dependence upon it is annulled by its dependence upon us. All this, however, does not come at once into reflection, but shows itself merely as the felt consciousness that in some sense or other (which philosophy alone can explain) we are one with the world, and therefore not oppressed, but exalted by its immensity. It is the felt consciousness of this that the Upanishads of the Vedas repeatedly express in such a multitude of different ways; very admirably in the saying already quoted: *Hae omnes creaturae in totum ego sum, et praeter me aliud ens non est* (Oupnek'hat, vol. i, p. 122.) It is the transcending of our own individuality, the sense of the sublime.

We receive this impression of the mathematical-sublime, quite directly, by means of a space which is small indeed as compared with the world, but which has become directly perceptible to us, and affects us with its whole extent in all its three dimensions, so as to make our own body seem almost infinitely small. An empty space can never be thus perceived, and therefore never an open space, but only space that is directly perceptible in all its dimensions by means of the limits which enclose it; thus for example a very high, vast dome, like that of St. Peter's at Rome, or St. Paul's in London. The sense of the sublime here arises through the consciousness of the vanishing nothingness of our own body in the presence of a vastness which, from another point of view, itself exists only in our idea, and of which we are as knowing subject, the supporter. Thus here as everywhere it arises from the contrast between the insignificance and dependence of ourselves as individuals, as phenomena of will, and the consciousness of ourselves as pure subject of knowing. Even the vault of the starry heaven produces this if it is contemplated without reflection; but just in the same way as the vault of stone, and only by its apparent, not its real extent. Some objects of our perception excite in us the feeling of the sublime because, not only on account of their spatial vastness, but also of their great age, that is, their temporal duration, we feel ourselves dwarfed to insignificance in their presence, and yet revel in the pleasure of contemplating them: of this kind are very high mountains, the Egyptian pyramids, and colossal ruins of great antiquity.

Our explanation of the sublime applies also to the ethical, to what is called the sublime character. Such a character arises from this, that the will is not excited by objects which are well calculated to excite it, but that knowledge retains the upper hand in their presence. A man of sublime character will accordingly consider men in a purely objective way, and not with reference to the relations which they might have to his will; he will, for example, observe their faults, even their hatred and injustice to himself, without being himself excited to hatred; he will behold their happiness without envy; he will recognise their good qualities without desiring any closer relations with them; he will perceive the beauty of women, but he will not desire them. His personal happiness or unhappiness will not greatly affect him, he will rather be as Hamlet describes Horatio:—

> ". . . for thou hast been,
> As one, in suffering all, that suffers nothing;
> A man that fortune's buffets and rewards
> Hast ta'en with equal thanks," &c. (A. 3. Sc. 2.)

For in the course of his own life and its misfortunes, he will consider less his individual lot than that of humanity in general, and will therefore conduct himself in its regard, rather as knowing than as suffering.

§ 41. The course of the discussion has made it necessary to insert at this point the treatment of the sublime, though we have only half done with the beautiful, as we have considered its subjective side only. For it was merely a special modification of this subjective side that distinguished the beautiful from the sublime. This difference was found to depend upon whether the state of pure will-less knowing, which is presupposed and demanded by all aesthetic contemplation, was reached without opposition, by the mere disappearance of the will from consciousness, because the object invited and drew us towards it; or whether it was only attained through the free, conscious transcending of the will, to which the object contemplated had an unfavourable and even hostile relation, which would destroy contemplation altogether, if we were to give ourselves up to it. This is the distinction between the beautiful and the sublime. In the object they are not essentially different, for in every case the object of aesthetical contemplation is not the individual thing, but the Idea in it which is striving to reveal itself; that is to say, adequate objectivity of will at a particular grade. Its necessary correlative, independent, like itself of the principle of sufficient reason, is the pure subject of knowing; just as the correlative of the particular thing is the knowing individual, both of which lie within the province of the principle of sufficient reason.

When we say that a thing is *beautiful*, we thereby assert that it is an object of our aesthetic contemplation, and this has a double meaning; on the one hand it means that the sight of the thing makes us *objective*, that is to say, that in contemplating it we are no longer conscious of ourselves as individuals, but as pure will-less subjects of knowledge; and on the other hand it means that we recognise in the object, not the particular thing, but an Idea; and this can only happen, so far as our contemplation of it is not subordinated to the principle of sufficient reason, does not follow the relation of the object to anything outside it (which is always ultimately connected with relations to our own will), but rests in the object itself. For the Idea and the pure subject of knowledge always appear at once in consciousness as necessary correlatives, and on their appearance all distinction of time vanishes, for they are both entirely foreign to the principle of sufficient reason in all its forms, and lie outside the relations which are imposed by it; they may be compared to the rainbow and the sun, which have no part in the constant movement and succession of the falling drops. Therefore, if, for example, I contemplate a tree aesthetically, *i.e.*, with artistic eyes, and thus recognise, not it, but its Idea, it becomes at once of no consequence whether it is this tree or its predecessor which flourished a thousand years ago, and whether the observer is this individual or any other that lived anywhere and at any time; the particular thing and the knowing individual are abolished with the principle of sufficient reason, and there remains nothing but the Idea and the pure subject of knowing, which together constitute the adequate objectivity of will at this grade. And the Idea dispenses not only with time, but also with space, for the Idea proper is not this special form which appears before me but its expression, its pure significance, its inner being, which discloses itself to me and appeals to me, and which may be quite the same though the spatial relations of its form be very different.

Since, on the one hand, every given thing may be observed in a purely objective manner and apart from all relations; and since, on the other hand, the will manifests itself in everything at some grade of its objectivity, so that everything is the expression of an Idea; it follows that everything is also *beautiful*.

· · · · ·

§ 43. Matter as such cannot be the expression of an Idea. For, as we found in the first book, it is throughout nothing but causality: its being consists in its causal action. But causality is a form of the principle of sufficient reason; knowledge of the Idea, on the other hand, absolutely excludes the content of that principle. We also found, in the second book, that matter is the common substratum of all particular phenomena of the Ideas, and consequently is the connecting link between the Idea and the phenomenon, or the particular thing. Accordingly for both of these reasons it is impossible that matter can for itself express any Idea. This is confirmed *a posteriori* by the fact that it is impossible to have a perceptible idea of matter as such, but only an abstract conception; in the former, *i.e.*, in perceptible ideas are exhibited only the forms and qualities of which matter is the supporter, and in all of which Ideas reveal themselves. This corresponds also with the fact, that causality (the whole essence of matter) cannot for itself be presented perceptibly, but is merely a definite causal connection. On the other hand, *every phenomenon* of an Idea, because as such it has entered the form of the principle of sufficient reason, or the *principium individuationis*, must exhibit itself in matter, as one of its qualities. So far then matter is, as we have said, the connecting link between the Idea and the *principium individuationis*, which is the form of knowledge of the individual, or the principle of sufficient reason. Plato is therefore perfectly right in his enumeration, for after the Idea and the phenomenon, which include all other things in the world, he gives matter only, as a third thing which is different from both (Timaus, p. 345). The individual, as a phenomenon of the Idea, is always matter. Every quality of matter is also the phenomenon of an Idea, and as such it may always be an object of aesthetic contemplation, *i.e.*, the Idea expressed in it may always be recognised. This holds good of even the most universal qualities of matter, without which it never appears, and which are the weakest objectivity of will. Such are gravity, cohesion, rigidity, fluidity, sensitiveness to light, and so forth.

If now we consider *architecture* simply as a fine art and apart from its application to useful ends, in which it serves the will and not pure knowledge, and therefore ceases to be art in our sense; we can assign to it no other aim than that of bringing to greater distinctness some of those ideas, which are the lowest grades of the objectivity of will; such as gravity, cohesion, rigidity, hardness, those universal qualities of stone, those first, simplest, most inarticulate manifestations of will; the bass notes of nature; and after these light, which in many respects is their opposite. Even at these low grades of the objectivity of will we see its nature revealing itself in discord; for properly speaking the conflict between gravity and rigidity is the sole aesthetic material of architecture; its problem is to make this conflict appear with perfect distinctness in a multitude of different ways. It solves it by depriving these indestructible forces of the shortest way to their satisfaction, and conducting them to it by a circuitous route, so that the conflict is lengthened and the inexhaustible efforts of both forces become visible in many different ways. The whole mass of the building, if left to its original tendency, would exhibit a mere heap or clump, bound as closely as possible to the earth, to which gravity, the form in which the will appears here, continually presses, while rigidity, also objectivity of will, resists. But this very tendency, this effort, is hindered by architecture from obtaining direct satisfaction, and only allowed to reach it indirectly and by roundabout ways. The roof, for example, can only press the earth through columns, the arch must support itself, and can only satisfy its tendency towards the earth through the medium of the pillars, and so forth. But just by these enforced digressions, just by these restrictions, the forces which reside in the crude mass of stone unfold themselves in the most distinct and multifarious ways; and the purely aesthetic aim of architecture can go no further than this. Therefore the beauty, at any rate, of a building lies in the obvious adaptation of every part, not to the outward arbitrary end of man (so far the work belongs to practical architecture), but directly to the stability of the whole, to which the position, dimensions, and form of every part must have so necessary a relation that, where it is possible, if any one part were taken away, the whole would fall to pieces. For just because each part bears just as much as it conveniently can, and each is supported just where it requires to be and just to the necessary extent, this opposition unfolds itself, this conflict between rigidity and gravity, which constitutes the life, the manifestation of will, in the stone, becomes completely visible, and these lowest grades of the objectivity of will reveal themselves distinctly. In the same way the form of each part must not be determined arbitrarily, but by its end, and its relation to the whole. The column is the simplest form of support, determined simply by its end: the twisted column is tasteless; the four-cornered pillar is in fact not so simple as the round column, though it happens that it is easier to make it. The forms also of frieze, rafter, roof, and dome are entirely determined by their immediate end, and explain themselves from it. The decoration of capitals, &c., belongs to sculpture, not to architecture, which admits it merely as extraneous ornament, and could dispense with it. According to what has been said, it is absolutely necessary, in order to understand the aesthetic satisfaction afforded by a work of architecture, to have immediate knowledge through perception of its matter as regards its weight, rigidity, and cohesion, and our pleasure in such a work would suddenly be very much diminished by the discovery that the material used was pumice-stone; for then it would appear to us as a kind of sham building. We would be affected in almost the same way if we were told that it was made of wood, when we had supposed it to be of stone, just because this alters and destroys the relation between rigidity and gravity, and consequently the significance and necessity of all the parts, for these natural forces reveal themselves in a far weaker degree in a wooden building. Therefore no real work of architecture as a fine art can be made of wood, although it assumes all forms so easily; this can only be explained by our theory. If we were distinctly told that a building, the sight of which gave us pleasure, was made of different kinds of material of very unequal weight and consistency, but not distinguishable to the eye, the whole building would become as utterly incapable of affording us pleasure as a poem in an unknown language. All this proves that architecture does not affect us mathematically, but also dynamically, and that what speaks to us through it, is not mere form and symmetry, but rather those fundamental forces of nature, those first Ideas, those lowest grades of the objectivity of will. The regularity of the building and its parts is partly produced by the direct adaptation of each member to the stability of the whole, partly it serves to facilitate the survey and comprehension of the whole, and finally, regular figures to some extent enhance the beauty because they reveal the constitution of space as such. But all this is of subordinate value and necessity, and by no means the chief concern; indeed, symmetry is not invariably demanded, as ruins are still beautiful.

Works of architecture have further quite a special relation to light; they gain a double beauty in the full sunshine, with the blue sky as a background, and again they have quite a different effect by moonlight. Therefore, when a beautiful work of architecture is to be erected, special attention is always paid to the effects of the light and to the climate. The reason of all this is, indeed, principally that all the parts and their relations are only made clearly visible by a bright, strong light; but besides this I am of opinion that it is the function of architecture to reveal the nature of light just as it reveals that of things so opposite to it as gravity and rigidity. For the light is intercepted, confined, and reflected by the great opaque, sharply outlined, and variously formed masses of stone, and thus it unfolds its nature and qualities in the purest and clearest way, to the great pleasure of the beholders, for light is the most joy-giving of things, as the condition and the objective correlative of the most perfect kind of knowledge of perception.

Now, because the Ideas which architecture brings to clear perception, are the lowest grades of the objectivity of will, and consequently their objective significance, which architecture reveals to us, is comparatively small; the aesthetic pleasure of looking at a beautiful building in a good light will lie, not so much in the comprehension of the Idea, as in the subjective correlative which accompanies this comprehension; it will consist pre-eminently in the fact that the beholder, set free from the kind of knowledge that belongs to the individual, and which serves the will and follows the principle of sufficient reason, is raised to that of the pure subject of knowing free from will. It will consist then principally in pure contemplation itself, free from all the suffering of will and of individuality. In this respect the opposite of architecture, and the other extreme of the series of the fine arts, is the drama, which brings to knowledge the most significant Ideas. Therefore in the aesthetic pleasure afforded by the drama the objective side is throughout predominant.

Architecture has this distinction from plastic art and poetry: it does not give us a copy but the thing itself. It does not repeat, as they do, the known Idea, so that the artist lends his eyes to the beholder, but in it the artist merely presents the object to the beholder, and facilitates for him the comprehension of the Idea by bringing the actual, individual object to a distinct and complete expression of its nature.

Unlike the works of the other arts, those of architecture are very seldom executed for purely aesthetic ends. These are generally subordinated to other useful ends which are foreign to art itself. Thus the great merit of the architect consists in achieving and attaining the pure aesthetic ends, in spite of their subordination to other ends which are foreign to them. This he does by cleverly adapting them in a variety of ways to the arbitrary ends in view, and by rightly judging which form of aesthetical architectonic beauty is compatible and may be associated with a temple, which with a palace, which with a prison, and so forth. The more a harsh climate increases these demands of necessity and utility, determines them definitely, and prescribes them more inevitably, the less free play has beauty in architecture. In the mild climate of India, Egypt, Greece, and Rome, where the demands of necessity were fewer and less definite, architecture could follow its aesthetic ends with the greatest freedom. But under a northern sky this was sorely hindered. Here, when caissons, pointed roofs and towers were what was demanded, architecture could only unfold its own beauty within very narrow limits, and therefore it was obliged to make amends by resorting all the more to the borrowed ornaments of sculpture, as is seen in Gothic architecture.

We thus see that architecture is greatly restricted by the demands of necessity and utility; but on the other hand it has in them a very powerful support, for, on account of the magnitude and costliness of its works, and the narrow sphere of its aesthetic effect, it could not continue to exist merely as a fine art, if it had not also, as a useful and necessary profession, a firm and honourable place among the occupations of men. It is the want of this that prevents another art from taking its place beside architecture as a sister art, although in an aesthetical point of view it is quite properly to be classed along with it as its counterpart; I mean artistic arrangements of water. For what architecture accomplishes for the Idea of gravity when it appears in connection with that of rigidity, hydraulics accomplishes for the same Idea, when it is connected with fluidity, *i.e.*, formlessness, the greatest mobility and transparency. Leaping waterfalls foaming and tumbling over rocks, cataracts dispersed into floating spray, springs gushing up as high columns of water, and clear reflecting lakes, reveal the Ideas of fluid and heavy matter, in precisely the same way as the works of architecture unfold the Ideas of rigid matter. Artistic hydraulics, however, obtains no support from practical hydraulics, for, as a rule, their ends cannot be combined; yet, in exceptional cases, this happens; for example, in the Cascata di Trevi at Rome.

§ 44. What the two arts we have spoken of accomplish for these lowest grades of the objectivity of will, is performed for the higher grades of vegetable nature by artistic horticulture. The landscape beauty of a scene consists, for the most part, in the multiplicity of natural objects which are present in it, and then in the fact that they are clearly separated, appear distinctly, and yet exhibit a fitting connection and alternation. These two conditions are assisted and promoted by landscape-gardening, but it has by no means such a mastery over its material as architecture, and therefore its effect is limited. The beauty with which it is concerned belongs almost exclusively to nature; it has done little for it; and, on the other hand, it can do little against unfavourable nature, and when nature works, not for it, but against it, its achievements are small.

The vegetable world offers itself everywhere for aesthetic enjoyment without the medium of art; but so far as it is an object of art, it belongs principally to landscape-painting; to the province of which all the rest of unconscious nature also belongs. In paintings of still life, and of mere architecture, ruins, interiors of churches, &c., the subjective side of aesthetic pleasure is predominant, i.e., our satisfaction does not lie principally in the direct comprehension of the represented Ideas, but rather in the subjective correlative of this comprehension, pure, will-less knowing. For, because the painter lets us see these things through his eyes, we at once receive a sympathetic and reflected sense of the deep spiritual peace and absolute silence of the will, which were necessary in order to enter with knowledge so entirely into these lifeless objects, and comprehend them with such love, i.e., in this case with such a degree of objectivity. The effect of landscape-painting proper is indeed, as a whole, of this kind; but because the Ideas expressed are more distinct and significant, as higher grades of the objectivity of will, the objective side of aesthetic pleasure already comes more to the front and assumes as much importance as the subjective side. Pure knowing as such is no longer the paramount consideration, for we are equally affected by the known Platonic Idea, the world as idea at an important grade of the objectification of will.

But a far higher grade is revealed by animal painting and sculpture. Of the latter we have some important antique remains; for example, horses at Venice, on Monte Cavallo, and on the Elgin Marbles, also at Florence in bronze and marble; the ancient boar, howling wolves, the lions in the arsenal at Venice, also in the Vatican a whole room almost filled with ancient animals, &c. In these representations the objective side of aesthetic pleasure obtains a marked predominance over the subjective. The peace of the subject which knows these Ideas, which has silenced its own will, is indeed present, as it is in all aesthetic contemplation; but its effect is not felt, for we are occupied with the restlessness and impetuosity of the will represented. It is that very will, which constitutes our own nature, that here appears to us in forms, in which its manifestation is not, as in us, controlled and tempered by intellect, but exhibits itself in stronger traits, and with a distinctness that borders on the grotesque and monstrous. For this very reason there is no concealment; it is free, naive, open as the day, and this is the cause of our interest in animals. The characteristics of species appeared already in the representation of plants, but showed itself only in the forms; here it becomes much more distinct, and expresses itself not only in the form, but in the action, position, and mien, yet always merely as the character of the species, not of the individual. This knowledge of the Ideas of higher grades, which in painting we receive through extraneous means, we may gain directly by the pure contemplative perception of plants, and observation of beasts, and indeed of the latter in their free, natural, and unrestrained state. The objective contemplation of their manifold and marvellous forms, and of their actions and behaviour, is an instructive lesson from the great book of nature, it is a deciphering of the true *signatura rerum*.[2] We see in them the manifold grades and modes of the manifestation of will, which in all beings of one and the same grade, wills always in the same way, which objectifies itself as life, as existence in such endless variety, and such different forms, which are all adaptations to the different external circumstances, and may be compared to many variations on the same theme. But if we had to communicate to the observer, for reflection, and in a word, the explanation of their inner nature, it would be best to make use of that Sanscrit formula which occurs so often in the sacred books of the Hindoos, and is called Mahavakya, *i.e.*, the great word: "*Tat twam asi*," which means, "this living thing art thou."

§ 45.　The great problem of historical painting and sculpture is to express directly and for perception the Idea in which the will reaches the highest grade of its objectification. The objective side of the pleasure afforded by the beautiful is here always predominant, and the subjective side has retired into the background. It is further to be observed that at the next grade below this, animal painting, the charac-

---

[2] Jakob Böhm in his book, "de Signatura Rerum," ch. i., § 13-15, says, "There is nothing in nature that does not manifest its internal form externally; for the internal continually labours to manifest itself. . . . Everything has its language by which to reveal itself. . . . And this is the language of nature when everything speaks out of its own property, and continually manifests and declares itself, . . . for each thing reveals its mother, which thus gives *the essence and the will* to the form."

teristic is entirely one with the beautiful; the most characteristic lion, wolf, horse, sheep, or ox, was always the most beautiful also. The reason of this is that animals have only the character of their species, no individual character. In the representation of men the character of the species is separated from that of the individual; the former is now called beauty (entirely in the objective sense), but the latter retains the name, character, or expression, and the new difficulty arises of representing both, at once and completely, in the same individual.

Human beauty is an objective expression, which means the fullest objectification of will at the highest grade at which it is knowable, the Idea of man in general, completely expressed in the sensible form. But however much the objective side of the beautiful appears here, the subjective side still always accompanies it. And just because no object transports us so quickly into pure aesthetic contemplation, as the most beautiful human countenance and form, at the sight of which we are instantly filled with unspeakable satisfaction, and raised above ourselves and all that troubles us; this is only possible because this most distinct and purest knowledge of will raises us most easily and quickly to the state of pure knowing, in which our personality, our will with its constant pain, disappears, so long as the pure aesthetic pleasure lasts. Therefore it is that Goethe says: "No evil can touch him who looks on human beauty; he feels himself at one with himself and with the world." That a beautiful human form is produced by nature must be explained in this way. At this its highest grade the will objectifies itself in an individual; and therefore through circumstances and its own power it completely overcomes all the hindrances and opposition which the phenomena of the lower grades present to it. Such are the forces of nature, from which the will must always first extort and win back the matter that belongs to all its manifestations. Further, the phenomenon of will at its higher grades always has multiplicity in its form. Even the tree is only a systematic aggregate of innumerably repeated sprouting fibres. This combination assumes greater complexity in higher forms, and the human body is an exceedingly complex system of different parts, each of which has a peculiar life of its own, *vita propria*, subordinate to the whole. Now that all these parts are in the proper fashion subordinate to the whole, and coordinate to each other, that they all work together harmoniously for the expression of the whole, nothing superfluous, nothing restricted; all these are the rare conditions, whose result is beauty, the completely expressed character of the species. So is it in nature. But how in art? One would suppose that art achieved the beautiful by imitating nature. But how is the artist to recognise the perfect work which is to be imitated, and distinguish it from the failures, if he does not anticipate the beautiful *before experience?* And besides this, has nature ever produced a human being perfectly beautiful in all his parts? It has accordingly been thought that the artist must seek out the beautiful parts, distributed among a number of different human beings, and out of them construct a beautiful whole; a perverse and foolish opinion. For it will be asked, how is he to know that just these forms and not others are beautiful? We also see what kind of success attended the efforts of the old German painters to achieve the beautiful by imitating nature. Observe their naked figures. No knowledge of the beautiful is possible purely *a posteriori*, and from mere experience; it is always, at least in part, *a priori*, although quite different in kind, from the forms of the principle of sufficient reason, of which we are conscious *a priori*. These concern the universal form of phenomena as such, as it constitutes the possibility of knowledge in general, the universal *how* of all phenomena, and from this knowledge proceed mathematics and pure natural science. But this other kind of knowledge *a priori*, which makes it possible to express the beautiful, concerns, not the form but the content of phenomena, not the *how* but the *what* of the phenomenon. That we all recognise human beauty when we see it, but that in the true artist this takes place with such clearness that he shows it as he has never seen it, and surpasses nature in his representation; this is only possible because *we ourselves are* the will whose adequate objectification at its highest grade is here to be judged and discovered. Thus alone have we in fact an anticipation of that which nature (which is just the will that constitutes our own being) strives to express. And in the true genius this anticipation is accompanied by so great a degree of intelligence that he recognises the Idea in the particular thing, and thus, as it were, *understands the half-uttered speech of nature,* and articulates clearly what she only stammered forth. He expresses in the hard marble that beauty of form which in a thousand attempts she failed to produce, he presents it to nature, saying, as it were, to her, "That is what you wanted to say!" And whoever is able to judge replies, "Yes, that is it." Only in this way was it possible for the genius of the Greeks to find the type of human beauty and establish it as a canon for the school of sculpture; and only by virtue of such an anticipation is it possible for all of us to recognise beauty, when it has actually been achieved by nature in the particular case. This anticipation is the *Ideal.* It is the *Idea* so far as it is known *a priori*, at least half, and it becomes practical for art, because it corresponds to and completes what is given *a posteriori* through nature. The possibility of such an anticipation of the beautiful *a priori* in the artist, and of its recognition *a posteriori* by the critic, lies in the fact that the artist and the critic are themselves the "in-itself" of nature, the will which objectifies itself. For, as Empedocles said, like can only be known by like: only nature can understand itself: only nature can fathom itself: but only spirit also can understand spirit.[3]

The opinion, which is absurd, although expressed by the Socrates of Xenophon (Stobæi Floril, vol. ii. p. 384) that the Greeks discovered the established ideal of human beauty empirically, by collecting particular beautiful parts, uncovering and noting here a knee, there an arm, has an exact parallel in the art of poetry. The view is entertained, that Shakespeare, for example, observed, and then gave forth from his own experience of life, the innumerable variety of the characters in his dramas, so true, so sustained, so profoundly worked out. The impossibility and absurdity of such an assumption need not be dwelt upon. It is obvious that the man of genius produces the works of poetic art by means of an anticipation of what is characteristic, just as he produces the works of plastic and pictorial art by means of a prophetic anticipation of the beautiful; yet both require experience as a pattern or model, for thus alone can that which is dimly known *a priori* be called into clear consciousness, and an intelligent representation of it becomes possible.

Human beauty was explained above as the fullest objectification of will at the highest grade at which it is knowable. It expresses itself through the form; and this lies in space alone, and has no necessary connection with time, as, for example, motion has. Thus far then we may say: the adequate objectification of will through a merely spatial phenomenon is beauty, in the objective sense. A plant is nothing but such a merely spatial phenomenon of will; for no motion, and consequently no relation to time (regarded apart from its development), belongs to the expression of its nature; its mere form expresses its whole being and displays it openly. But brutes and men require, further, for the full revelation of the will which is manifested in them, a series of actions, and thus the manifestation in them takes on a direct relation

---

[3] The last sentence is the German of the *il n'y a que l'esprit qui sente l'esprit*, of Helvetius. In the first edition there was no occasion to point this out, but since then the age has become so degraded and ignorant through the stupefying influence of the Hegelian sophistry, that some might quite likely say that an antithesis was intended here between "spirit and nature." I am therefore obliged to guard myself in express terms against the suspicion of such vulgar sophisms.

to time. All this has already been explained in the preceding book; it is related to what we are considering at present in the following way. As the merely spatial manifestation of will can objectify it fully or defectively at each definite grade,—and it is this which constitutes beauty or ugliness,—so the temporal objectification of will, *i.e.*, the action, and indeed the direct action, the movement, may correspond to the will, which objectifies itself in it, purely and fully without foreign admixture, without superfluity, without defect, only expressing exactly the act of will determined in each case;—or the converse of all this may occur. In the first case the movement is made with *grace*, in the second case without it. Thus as beauty is the adequate representation of will generally, through its merely spatial manifestation; *grace* is the adequate representation of will through its temporal manifestation, that is to say, the perfectly accurate and fitting expression of each act of will, through the movement and position which objectify it. Since movement and position presuppose the body, Winckelmann's expression is very true and suitable, when he says, "Grace is the proper relation of the acting person to the action" (Works, vol. i. p. 258). It is thus evident that beauty may be attributed to a plant, but no grace, unless in a figurative sense; but to brutes and men, both beauty and grace. Grace consists, according to what has been said, in every movement being performed, and every position assumed, in the easiest, most appropriate and convenient way, and therefore being the pure, adequate expression of its intention, or of the act of will, without any superfluity, which exhibits itself as aimless, meaningless bustle, or as wooden stiffness. Grace presupposes as its condition a true proportion of all the limbs, and a symmetrical, harmonious figure; for complete ease and evident appropriateness of all positions and movements are only possible by means of these. Grace is therefore never without a certain degree of beauty of person. The two, complete and united, are the most distinct manifestation of will at the highest grade of its objectification.

It was mentioned above that in order rightly to portray man, it is necessary to separate the character of the species from that of the individual, so that to a certain extent every man expresses an Idea peculiar to himself, as was said in the last book. Therefore the arts whose aim is the representation of the Idea of man, have as their problem, not only beauty, the character of the species, but also the character of the individual, which is called, *par excellence, character.* But this is only the case in so far as this character is to be regarded, not as something accidental and quite peculiar to the man as a single individual, but as a side of the Idea of humanity which is specially apparent in this individual, and the representation of which is therefore of assistance in revealing this Idea. Thus the character, although as such it is individual, must yet be Ideal, that is, its significance in relation to the Idea of humanity generally (the objectifying of which it assists in its own way) must be comprehended and expressed with special prominence. Apart from this the representation is a portrait, a copy of the individual as such, with all his accidental qualities. And even the portrait ought to be, as Winckelmann says, the ideal of the individual.

That *character* which is to be ideally comprehended, as the prominence of a special side of the Idea of humanity, expresses itself visibly, partly through permanent physiognomy and bodily form, partly through passing emotion and passion, the reciprocal modification of knowing and willing by each other, which is all exhibited in the mien and movements. Since the individual always belongs to humanity, and, on the other hand, humanity always reveals itself in the individual with what is indeed peculiar ideal significance, beauty must not be destroyed by character nor character by beauty. For if the character of the species is annulled by that of the individual, the result is caricature; and if the character of the individual is annulled by that of the species, the result is an absence of meaning. Therefore the representation which aims at beauty, as sculpture principally does, will yet always modify this (the character of the species), in some respect, by the individual character, and will always express the Idea of man in a definite individual manner, giving prominence to a special side of it. For the human individual as such has to a certain extent the dignity of a special Idea, and it is essential to the Idea of man that it should express itself in individuals of special significance. Therefore we find in the works of the ancients, that the beauty distinctly comprehended by them, is not expressed in one form, but in many forms of different character. It is always apprehended, as it were, from a different side, and expressed in one way in Apollo, in another way in Bacchus, in another in Hercules, in another in Antinous; indeed the characteristic may limit the beautiful, and finally extend even to hideousness, in the drunken Silenus, in the Faun, &c. If the characteristic goes so far as actually to annul the character of the species, if it extends to the unnatural, it becomes caricature. But we can far less afford to allow grace to be interfered with by what is characteristic than even beauty, for graceful position and movement are demanded for the expression of the character also; but yet it must be achieved in the way which is most fitting, appropriate, and easy for the person. This will be observed, not only by the sculptor and the painter, but also by every good actor; otherwise caricature will appear here also as grimace or distortion.

In sculpture, beauty and grace are the principal concern. The special character of the mind, appearing in emotion, passion, alternations of knowing and willing, which can only be represented by the expression of the countenance and the gestures, is the peculiar sphere of *painting*. For although eyes and colour, which lie outside the province of sculpture, contribute much to beauty, they are yet far more essential to character. Further, beauty unfolds itself more completely when it is contemplated from various points of view; but the expression, the character, can only be completely comprehended from *one* point of view.

Because beauty is obviously the chief aim of sculpture, Lessing tried to explain the fact that the *Laocoon does not cry out*, by saying that crying out is incompatible with beauty. The Laocoon formed for Lessing the theme, or at least the text of a work of his own, and both before and after him a great deal has been written on the subject. I may therefore be allowed to express my views about it in passing, although so special a discussion does not properly belong to the scheme of this work, which is throughout concerned with what is general.

§ 49. The truth which lies at the foundation of all that we have hitherto said about art, is that the object of art, the representation of which is the aim of the artist, and the knowledge of which must therefore precede his work as its germ and source, is an Idea in Plato's sense, and never anything else; not the particular thing, the object of common apprehension, and not the concept, the object of rational thought and of science. Although the Idea and the concept have something in common, because both represent as unity a multiplicity of real things; yet the great difference between them has no doubt been made clear and evident enough by what we have said about concepts in the first book, and about Ideas in this book. I by no means wish to assert, however, that Plato really distinctly comprehended this difference; indeed many of his examples of Ideas, and his discussions of them, are applicable only to concepts. Meanwhile we leave this question alone and go on our own way, glad when we come upon traces of any great and noble mind, yet not following his footsteps but our own aim. The *concept* is abstract, discursive, undetermined within its own sphere, only determined by its limits, attainable and comprehensible by him who has only reason, communicable by words without any other assistance, entirely exhausted by its definition. The

Idea on the contrary, although defined as the adequate representative of the concept, is always object of perception, and although representing an infinite number of particular things, is yet thoroughly determined. It is never known by the individual as such, but only by him who has raised himself above all willing and all individuality to the pure subject of knowing. Thus it is only attainable by the man of genius, and by him who, for the most part through the assistance of the works of genius, has reached an exalted frame of mind, by increasing his power of pure knowing. It is therefore not absolutely but only conditionally communicable, because the Idea, comprehended and repeated in the work of art, appeals to every one only according to the measure of his own intellectual worth. So that just the most excellent works of every art, the noblest productions of genius, must always remain sealed books to the dull majority of men, inaccessible to them, separated from them by a wide gulf, just as the society of princes is inaccessible to the common people. It is true that even the dullest of them accept on authority recognisedly great works, lest otherwise they should argue their own incompetence; but they wait in silence, always ready to express their condemnation, as soon as they are allowed to hope that they may do so without being left to stand alone; and then their long-restrained hatred against all that is great and beautiful, and against the authors of it, gladly relieves itself; for such things never appealed to them, and for that very reason were humiliating to them. For as a rule a man must have worth in himself in order to recognise it and believe in it willingly and freely in others. On this rests the necessity of modesty in all merit, and the disproportionately loud praise of this virtue, which alone of all its sisters is always included in the eulogy of every one who ventures to praise any distinguished man, in order to appease and quiet the wrath of the unworthy. What then is modesty but hypocritical humility, by means of which, in a world swelling with base envy, a man seeks to obtain pardon for excellences and merits from those who have none? For whoever attributes to himself no merits, because he actually has none, is not modest but merely honest.

The *Idea* is the unity that falls into multiplicity on account of the temporal and spatial form of our intuitive apprehension; the *concept*, on the contrary, is the unity reconstructed out of multiplicity by the abstraction of our reason; the latter may be defined as *unitas post rem,* the former as *unitas ante rem.* Finally, we may express the distinction between the Idea and the concept, by a comparison, thus: the *concept* is like a dead receptacle, in which, whatever has been put, actually lies side by side, but out of which no more can be taken (by analytical judgment) than was put in (by synthetical reflection); the (Platonic) *Idea*, on the other hand, develops, in him who has comprehended it, ideas which are new as regards the concept of the same name; it resembles a living organism, developing itself and possessed of the power of reproduction, which brings forth what was not put into it.

It follows from all that has been said, that the concept, useful as it is in life, and serviceable, necessary and productive as it is in science, is yet always barren and unfruitful in art. The comprehended Idea, on the contrary, is the true and only source of every work of art. In its powerful originality it is only derived from life itself, from nature, from the world, and that only by the true genius, or by him whose momentary inspiration reaches the point of genius. Genuine and immortal works of art spring only from such direct apprehension. Just because the Idea is and remains object of perception, the artist is not conscious in the abstract of the intention and aim of his work; not a concept, but an Idea floats before his mind; therefore he can give no justification of what he does. He works, as people say, from pure feeling, and unconsciously, indeed instinctively. On the contrary, imitators, mannerists, *imitatores, servum pecus*, start, in art, from the concept; they observe what pleases and affects us in true works of art; understand it clearly, fix it in a concept, and thus abstractly, and then imitate it, openly or disguisedly, with dexterity and intentionally. They suck their nourishment, like parasite plants, from the works of others, and like polypi, they become the colour of their food. We might carry comparison further, and say that they are like machines which mince fine and mingle together whatever is put into them, but can never digest it, so that the different constituent parts may always be found again if they are sought out and separated from the mixture; the man of genius alone resembles the organised, assimilating, transforming and reproducing body. For he is indeed educated and cultured by his predecessors and their works; but he is really fructified only by life and the world directly, through the impression of what he perceives; therefore the highest culture never interferes with his originality. All imitators, all mannerists, apprehend in concepts the nature of representative works of art; but concepts can never impart inner life to a work. The age, *i.e.*, the dull multitude of every time, knows only concepts, and sticks to them, and therefore receives mannered works of art with ready and loud applause: but after a few years these works become insipid, because the spirit of the age, *i.e.*, the prevailing concepts, in which alone they could take root, have changed. Only true works of art, which are drawn directly from nature and life, have eternal youth and enduring power, like nature and life themselves. For they belong to no age, but to humanity, and as on that account they are coldly received by their own age, to which they disdain to link themselves closely, and because indirectly and negatively they expose the existing errors, they are slowly and unwillingly recognised; on the other hand, they cannot grow old, but appear to us ever fresh and new down to the latest ages. Then they are no longer exposed to neglect and ignorance, for they are crowned and sanctioned by the praise of the few men capable of judging, who appear singly and rarely in the course of ages, and give in their votes, whose slowly growing number constitutes the authority, which alone is the judgment-seat we mean when we appeal to posterity. It is these successively appearing individuals, for the mass of posterity will always be and remain just as perverse and dull as the mass of contemporaries always was and always is. We read the complaints of great men in every century about the customs of their age. They always sound as if they referred to our own age, for the race is always the same. At every time and in every art, mannerisms have taken the place of the spirit, which was always the possession of a few individuals, but mannerisms are just the old cast-off garments of the last manifestation of the spirit that existed and was recognised. From all this it appears that, as a rule, the praise of posterity can only be gained at the cost of the praise of one's contemporaries, and *vice versa.*

§ 50. If the aim of all art is the communication of the comprehended Idea, which through the mind of the artist appears in such a form that it is purged and isolated from all that is foreign to it, and may now be grasped by the man of weaker comprehension and no productive faculty; if further, it is forbidden in art to start from the concept, we shall not be able to consent to the intentional and avowed employment of a work of art for the expression of a concept; this is the case in the *Allegory.* An allegory is a work of art which means something different from what it represents. But the object of perception, and consequently also the Idea, expresses itself directly and completely, and does not require the medium of something else which implies or indicates it. Thus, that which in this way is indicated and represented by something entirely different, because it cannot itself be made object of perception, is always a concept. Therefore through the allegory a conception has always to be signified, and consequently the mind of the beholder has to be drawn away from the expressed perceptible idea to one which is entirely different, abstract and not perceptible, and which lies quite outside the work of art. The picture or statue is intended to accomplish here what is accomplished far more fully by a book. Now, what we hold is the end of art, representation of a perceivable, comprehensible Idea, is not here the end. No great completeness in the work of art is demanded for what is aimed at here. It is only necessary that we should see what the thing is meant to be, for, as soon as this has been discovered, the end is reached, and the mind is now led away to quite a different kind of idea to an abstract conception, which is the end that was in view. Allegories in plastic and pictorial art are, therefore, nothing but hieroglyphics; the artistic value which they may have as perceptible representations, belongs to them not as allegories, but otherwise. That the "Night" of Correggio, the "Genius of Fame" of Hannibal Carracci, and the "Hours" of Poussin, are very beautiful pictures, is to be separated altogether from the fact that they are allegories. As allegories they do not accomplish more than a legend, indeed rather less. We are here again reminded of the distinction drawn above between the real and the nominal significance of a picture. The nominal is here the allegorical as such, for example, the "Genius of Fame." The real is what is actually represented, in this case a beautiful winged youth, surrounded by beautiful boys; this expresses an Idea. But this real significance affects us only so long as we forget the nominal, allegorical significance; if we think of the latter, we forsake the perception, and the mind is occupied with an abstract conception; but the transition from the Idea to the conception is always a fall. Indeed, that nominal significance, that allegorical intention, often injures the real significance, the perceptible truth. For example, the unnatural light in the "night" of Correggio, which, though beautifully executed, has yet a merely allegorical motive, and is really impossible. If then an allegorical picture has artistic value, it is quite separate from and independent of what it accomplishes as allegory. Such a work of art serves two ends at once, the expression of a conception and the expression of an Idea. Only the latter can be an end of art; the other is a foreign end, the trifling amusement of making a picture also do service as a legend, as a hieroglyphic, invented for the pleasure of those to whom the true nature of art can never appeal. It is the same thing as when a work of art is also a useful implement of some kind, in which case it also serves two ends; for example, a statue which is at the same time a candelabrum or a caryatid; or a bas-relief, which is also the shield of Achilles. True lovers of art will allow neither the one nor the other. It is true that an allegorical picture may, because of this quality, produce a vivid impression upon the feelings; but when this is the case, a legend would under the same circumstances produce the same effect. For example, if the desire of fame were firmly and lastingly rooted in the heart of a man, because he regarded it as his rightful possession, which is only withheld from him so long as he has not produced the charter of his ownership; and if the Genius of Fame, with his laurel crown, were to appear to such a man, his whole mind would be excited, and his powers called into activity; but the same effect would be produced if he were suddenly to see the word "fame," in large distinct letters on the wall. Or if a man has made known a truth, which is of importance either as a maxim for practical life, or as insight for science, but it has not been believed; an allegorical picture representing time as it lifts the veil, and discloses the naked figure of Truth, will affect him powerfully; but the same effect would be produced by the legend: *"Le temps découvre la verité."* For what really produces the effect here is the abstract thought, not the object of perception.

If then, in accordance with what has been said, allegory in plastic and pictorial art is a mistaken effort, serving an end which is entirely foreign to art, it becomes quite unbearable when it leads so far astray that the representation of forced and violently introduced subtilties degenerates into absurdity. Such, for example, is a tortoise, to represent feminine seclusion; the downward glance of Nemesis into the drapery of her bosom, signifying that she can see into what is hidden; the explanation of Bellori that Hannibal Carracci represents voluptuousness clothed in a yellow robe, because he wishes to indicate that her lovers soon fade and become yellow as straw. If there is absolutely no connection between the representation and the conception signified by it, founded on subsumption under the concept, or association of Ideas; but the signs and the things signified are combined in a purely conventional manner, by positive, accidentally introduced laws; then I call this degenerate kind of allegory *Symbolism.* Thus the rose is the symbol of secrecy, the laurel is the symbol of fame, the palm is the symbol of peace, the scallop-shell is the symbol of pilgrimage, the cross is the symbol of the Christian religion. To this class also belongs all significance of mere colour, as yellow is the colour of falseness, and blue is the colour of fidelity. Such symbols may often be of use in life, but their value is foreign to art. They are simply to be regarded as hieroglyphics, or like Chinese word-writing, and really belong to the same class as armorial bearings, the bush that indicates a public-house, the key of the chamberlain, or the leather of the mountaineer. If, finally, certain historical or mythical persons, or personified conceptions, are represented by certain fixed symbols, these are properly called *emblems*. Such are the beasts of the Evangelist, the owl of Minerva, the apple of Paris, the Anchor of Hope, &c. For the most part, however, we understand by emblems those simple allegorical representations explained by a motto, which are meant to express a moral truth, and of which large collections have been made by J. Camerarius, Alciatus, and others. They form the transition to poetical allegory, of which we shall have more to say later. Greek sculpture devotes itself to the perception, and therefore it is *aesthetical*; Indian sculpture devotes itself to the conception, and therefore it is merely *symbolical*.

. . . . .

§ 52. Now that we have considered all the fine arts in the general way that is suitable to our point of view, beginning with architecture, the peculiar end of which is to elucidate the objectification of will at the lowest grades of its visibility, in which it shows itself as the dumb unconscious tendency of the mass in accordance with laws, and yet already reveals a breach of the unity of will with itself in a conflict between gravity and rigidity—and ending with the consideration of tragedy, which presents to us at the highest grades of the objectification of will this very conflict with itself in terrible magnitude and distinctness; we find that there is still another fine art which has been excluded from our consideration, and had to be excluded, for in the systematic connection of our exposition there was no fitting place for it—I mean *music*. It stands alone, quite cut off from all the other arts. In it we do not recognise the copy or repetition of any Idea of existence in the world. Yet it is such a great and exceedingly noble art, its effect on the inmost nature of man is so powerful, and it is so entirely and deeply understood by him in his inmost consciousness as a perfectly universal language, the distinctness of which surpasses even that of the perceptible world itself, that we certainly have more to look for in it than an *exercitum arithmeticœ occultum nescientis se numerare animi*, which Leibnitz called it. Yet he was perfectly right, as he considered only its immediate external significance, its form. But if it were nothing more, the satisfaction which it affords would be like that which we feel when a sum in arithmetic comes out right, and could not be that intense pleasure with which we see the deepest recesses of our nature find utterance. From our standpoint, therefore, at which the aesthetic effect is the criterion, we must attribute to music a far more serious and deep significance, connected with the inmost nature of the world and our own self, and in reference to which the arithmetical proportions, to which it may be reduced, are related, not as the thing signified, but merely as the sign. That in some sense music must be related to the world as the representation to the thing represented, as the copy to the original, we may conclude from the analogy of the other arts, all of which possess this character, and affect us on the whole in the same way as it does, only that the effect of music is stronger, quicker, more necessary, and infallible. Further, its representative relation to the world must be very deep, absolutely true, and strikingly accurate, because it is instantly understood by every one, and has the appearance of a certain infallibility, because its form may be reduced to perfectly definite rules expressed in numbers, from which it cannot free itself without entirely ceasing to be music. Yet the point of comparison between music and the world, the respect in which it stands to the world in the relation of a copy or repetition, is very obscure. Men have practised music in all ages without being able to account for this; content to understand it directly, they renounce all claim to an abstract conception of this direct understanding itself.

I gave my mind entirely up to the impression of music in all its forms, and then returned to reflection and the system of thought expressed in the present work, and thus I arrived at an explanation of the inner nature of music and of the nature of its imitative relation to the world—which from analogy had necessarily to be presupposed—an explanation which is quite sufficient for myself, and satisfactory to my investigation, and which will doubtless be equally evident to any one who has followed me thus far and has agreed with my view of the world. Yet I recognise the fact that it is essentially impossible to prove this explanation, for it assumes and establishes a relation of music, as idea, to that which from its nature can never be idea, and music will have to be regarded as the copy of an original which can never itself be directly presented as idea. I can therefore do no more than state here, at the conclusion of this third book, which has been principally devoted to the consideration of the arts, the explanation of the marvellous art of music which satisfies myself, and I must leave the acceptance or denial of my view to the effect produced upon each of my readers both by music itself and by the whole system of thought communicated in this work. Moreover, I regard it as necessary, in order to be able to assent with full conviction to the exposition of the significance of music I am about to give, that one should often listen to music with constant reflection upon my theory concerning it, and for this again it is necessary to be very familiar with the whole of my system of thought.

The (Platonic) Ideas are the adequate objectification of will. To excite or suggest the knowledge of these by means of the representation of particular things (for works of art themselves are always representations of particular things) is the end of all the other arts, which can only be attained by a corresponding change in the knowing subject. Thus all these arts objectify the will indirectly only by means of the Ideas; and since our world is nothing but the manifestation of the Ideas in multiplicity, though their entrance into the *principium individuationis* (the form of the knowledge possible for the individual as such), music also, since it passes over the Ideas, is entirely independent of the phenomenal world, ignores it altogether, could to a certain extent exist if there was no world at all, which cannot be said of the other arts. Music is as *direct* an objectification and copy of the whole *will* as the world itself, nay, even as the Ideas, whose multiplied manifestation constitutes the world of individual things. Music is thus by no means like the other arts, the copy of the Ideas, but the *copy of the will itself*, whose objectivity the Ideas are. This is why the effect of music is so much more powerful and penetrating than that of the other arts, for they speak only of shadows, but it speaks of the thing itself. Since, however, it is the same will which objectifies itself both in the Ideas and in music, though in quite different ways, there must be, not indeed a direct likeness, but yet a parallel, an analogy, between music and the Ideas whose manifestation in multiplicity and incompleteness is the visible world. The establishing of this analogy will facilitate, as an illustration, the understanding of this exposition, which is so difficult on account of the obscurity of the subject.

I recognise in the deepest tones of harmony, in the bass, the lowest grades of the objectification of will, unorganised nature, the mass of the planet. It is well known that all the high notes which are easily sounded, and die away more quickly, are produced by the vibration in their vicinity of the deep bass-notes. When, also, the low notes sound, the high notes always sound faintly, and it is a law of harmony that only those high notes may accompany a bass-note which actually already sound along with it of themselves (its *sons harmoniques*) on account of its vibration. This is analogous to the fact that the whole of the bodies and organisations of nature must be regarded as having come into existence through gradual development out of the mass of the planet; this is both their supporter and their source, and the same relation subsists between the high notes and the bass. There is a limit of depth, below which no sound is audible. This corresponds to the fact that no matter can be perceived without form and quality, *i.e.*, without the manifestation of a force which cannot be further explained, in which an Idea expresses itself, and, more generally, that no matter can be entirely without will. Thus, as a certain pitch is inseparable from the note as such, so a certain grade of the manifestation of will is inseparable from matter. Bass is thus, for us, in harmony what unorganised nature, the crudest mass, upon which all rests, and from which everything originates and develops, is in the world. Now, further, in the whole of the complemental parts which make up the harmony between the bass and the leading voice singing the melody, I recognise the whole gradation of the Ideas in which the will objectifies itself. Those nearer to the bass are the lower of these grades, the still unorganised, but yet manifold phenomenal things; the higher represent to me the world of plants and beasts. The definite intervals of the scale are parallel to the definite grades of the objectification of will, the definite species in nature. The departure from the arithmetical correctness of the intervals, through some temperament, or produced by the key selected, is analogous to the departure of the individual from the type of the species. Indeed, even the impure discords, which give no definite interval, may be compared to the monstrous abortions produced by beasts of two species, or by man and beast. But to all these bass and complemental parts which make up the *harmony* there is wanting that connected progress which belongs only to the high voice singing the melody, and it alone moves quickly and lightly in modulations and runs, while all these others have only a slower movement without a connection in each part for itself. The deep bass moves most slowly, the representative of the crudest mass. Its rising and falling occurs only by large intervals, in thirds, fourths, fifths, never by *one* tone, unless it is a base inverted by double counterpoint. This slow movement is also physically essential to it; a quick run or shake in the low notes cannot even be imagined. The higher complemental parts, which are parallel to animal life, move more quickly, but yet without melodious connection and significant progress. The disconnected course of all the complemental parts, and their regulation by definite laws, is analogous to the fact that in the whole irrational world, from the crystal to the most perfect animal, no being has a connected consciousness of its own which would make its life into a significant whole, and none experiences a succession of mental developments, none perfects itself by culture, but everything exists always in the same way according to its kind, determined by fixed law. Lastly, in the *melody*, in the high, singing, principal voice leading the whole and progressing with unrestrained freedom, in the unbroken significant connection of *one* thought from beginning to end representing a whole, I recognise the highest grade of the objectification of will, the intellectual life and effort of man. As he alone, because endowed with reason, constantly looks before and after on the path of his actual life and its innumerable possibilities, and so achieves a course of life which is intellectual, and therefore connected as a whole; corresponding to this, I say, the *melody* has significant intentional connection from beginning to end. It records, therefore, the history of the intellectually enlightened will. This will expresses itself in the actual world as the series of its deeds; but melody says more, it records the most secret history of this intellectually-enlightened will, pictures every excitement, every effort, every movement of it, all that which the reason collects under the wide and negative concept of feeling, and which it cannot apprehend further through its abstract concepts. Therefore it has always been said that music is the language of feeling and of passion, as words are the language of reason.

. . . . .

Now the nature of man consists in this, that his will strives, is satisfied and strives anew, and so on for ever. Indeed, his happiness and well-being consist simply in the quick transition from wish to satisfaction, and from satisfaction to a new wish. For the absence of satisfaction is suffering, the empty longing for a new wish, languor, *ennui*. And corresponding to this the nature of melody is a constant digression and deviation from the key-note in a thousand ways, not only to the harmonious intervals to the third and dominant, but to every tone, to the dissonant sevenths and to the superfluous degrees; yet there always follows a constant return to the key-note. In all these deviations melody expresses the multifarious efforts of will, but always its satisfaction also by the final return to an harmonious interval, and still more, to the key-note. The composition of melody, the disclosure in it of all the deepest secrets of human willing and feeling, is the work of genius, whose action, which is more apparent here than anywhere else, lies far from all reflection and conscious intention, and may be called an inspiration. The conception is here, as everywhere in art, unfruitful. The composer reveals the inner nature of the world, and expresses the deepest wisdom in a language which his reason does not understand; as a person under the influence of mesmerism tells things of which he has no conception when he awakes. Therefore in the composer, more than in any other artist, the man is entirely separated and distinct from the artist. Even in the explanation of this wonderful art, the concept shows its poverty and limitation. I shall try, however, to complete our analogy. As quick transition from wish to satisfaction, and from satisfaction to a new wish, is happiness and well-being, so quick melodies without great deviations are cheerful; slow melodies, striking painful discords, and only winding back through many bars to the key-note are, as analogous to the delayed and hardly won satisfaction, sad. The delay of the new excitement of will, languor, could have no other expression than the sustained keynote, the effect of which would soon be unbearable; very monotonous and unmeaning melodies approach this effect. The short intelligible subjects of quick dance-music seem to speak only of easily attained common pleasure. On the other hand, the *Allegro maestoso*, in elaborate movements, long passages, and wide deviations, signifies a greater, nobler effort towards a more distant end, and its final attainment. The *Adagio* speaks of the pain of a great and noble effort which despises all trifling happiness. But how wonderful is the effect of the *minor* and *major!* How astounding that the change of half a tone, the entrance of a minor third instead of a major, at once and inevitably forces upon us an anxious painful feeling, from which again we are just as instantaneously delivered by the major. The *Adagio* lengthens in the minor the expression of the keenest pain, and becomes even a convulsive wail. Dance-music in the minor seems to indicate the failure of that trifling happiness which we ought rather to despise, seems to speak of the attainment of a lower end with toil and trouble. The inexhaustibleness of possible melodies corresponds to the inexhaustibless of Nature in difference of individuals, physiognomies, and courses of life. The transition from one key to an entirely different one, since it altogether breaks the connection with what went before, is like death, for the individual ends in it; but the will which appeared in this individual lives after him as before him, appearing in other individuals, whose consciousness, however, has no connection with his.

But it must never be forgotten, in the investigation of all these analogies I have pointed out, that music has no direct, but merely an indirect relation to them, for it never expresses the phenomenon, but only the inner nature, the in-itself of all phenomena, the will itself. It does not therefore express this or that particular and definite joy, this or that sorrow, or pain, or horror, or delight, or merriment, or peace of mind; but joy, sorrow, pain, horror, delight, merriment, peace of mind *themselves*, to a certain extent in the abstract, their essential nature, without accessories, and therefore without their motives. Yet we completely understand them in this extracted quintessence. Hence it arises that our imagination is so easily excited by music, and now seeks to give form to that invisible yet actively moved spirit-world which speaks to us directly, and clothe it with flesh and blood, *i.e.*, to embody it in an analogous example. This is the origin of the song with words, and finally of the opera, the text of which should therefore never forsake that subordinate position in order to make itself the chief thing and the music a mere means of expressing it, which is a great misconception and a piece of utter perversity; for music always expresses only the quintessence of life and its events, never these themselves, and therefore their differences do not always affect it. It is precisely this universality, which belongs exclusively to it, together with the greatest determinateness, that gives music the high worth which it has as the panacea for all our woes. Thus, if music is too closely united to the words, and tries to form itself according to the events, it is striving to speak a language which is not its own. No one has kept so free from this mistake as Rossini; therefore his music speaks *its own language* so distinctly and purely that it requires no words, and produces its full effect when rendered by instruments alone.

. . . . .

In the whole of this exposition of music I have been trying to bring out clearly that it expresses in a perfectly universal language, in a homogeneous material, mere tones, and with the greatest determinateness and truth, the inner nature, the in-itself of the world, which we think under the concept of will, because will is its most distinct manifestation. Further, according to my view and contention, philosophy is nothing but a complete and accurate repetition or expression of the nature of the world in very general concepts, for only in such is it possible to get a view of that whole nature which will everywhere be adequate and applicable. Thus, whoever has followed me and entered into my mode of thought, will not think it so very paradoxical if I say, that supposing it were possible to give a perfectly accurate, complete explanation of music, extending even to particulars, that is to say, a detailed repetition in concepts of what it expresses, this would also be a sufficient repetition and explanation of the world in concepts, or at least entirely parallel to such an explanation, and thus it would be the true philosophy. Consequently the saying of Leibnitz quoted above, which is quite accurate from a lower standpoint, may be parodied in the following way to suit our higher view of music: *Musica est exercitium metaphysices occultum nescientis se philosophari animi*; for *scire*, to know, always means to have fixed in abstract concepts. But further, on account of the truth of the saying of Leibnitz, which is confirmed in various ways, music, regarded apart from its aesthetic or inner significance, and looked at merely externally and purely empirically, is simply the means of comprehending directly and in the concrete large numbers and complex relations of numbers, which otherwise we could only know indirectly by fixing them in concepts. Therefore by the union of these two very different but correct views of music we may arrive at a conception of the possibility of a philosophy of number, such as that of Pythagoras and of the Chinese in Y-King, and then interpret in this sense the saying of the Pythagoreans which Sextus Empiricus quotes (adv. Math., L. vii.): τῳ αριθμῳ δε τα παντ' επεοικεν (*numero cuncta assimilantur*). And if, finally, we apply this view to the interpretation of harmony and melody given above, we shall find that a mere moral philosophy without an explanation of Nature, such as Socrates wanted to introduce, is precisely analogous to a mere melody without harmony, which Rousseau exclusively desired; and, in opposition to this mere physics and metaphysics without ethics, will correspond to mere harmony without melody. Allow me to add to these cursory observations a few more remarks concerning the analogy of music with the phenomenal world. We found in the second book that the highest grade of the objectification of will, man, could not appear alone and isolated, but presupposed the grades below him, as these again presupposed the grades lower still. In the same way music, which directly objectifies the will, just as the world does, is complete only in full harmony. In order to achieve its full effect, the high leading voice of the melody requires the accompaniment of all the other voices, even to the lowest bass, which is to be regarded as the origin of all. The melody itself enters as an integral part into the harmony, as the harmony enters into it, and only thus, in the full harmonious whole, music expresses what it aims at expressing. Thus also the one will outside of time finds its full objectification only in the complete union of all the steps which reveal its nature in the innumerable ascending grades of distinctness. The following analogy is also very remarkable. We have seen in the preceding book that notwithstanding the self-adaptation of all the phenomena of will to each other as regards their species, which constitutes their teleological aspect, there yet remains an unceasing conflict between those phenomena as individuals, which is visible at every grade, and makes the world a constant battle-field of all those manifestations of one and the same will, whose inner contradiction with itself becomes visible through it. In music also there is something corresponding to this. A complete, pure, harmonious system of tones is not only physically but arithmetically impossible. The numbers themselves by which the tones are expressed have inextricable irrationality. There is no scale in which, when it is counted, every fifth will be related to the keynote as 2 to 3, every major third as 4 to 5, every minor third as 5 to 6, and so on. For if they are correctly related to the keynote, they can no longer be so to each other; because, for example, the fifth must be the minor third to the third, &c. For the notes of the scale may be compared to actors who must play now one part, now another. Therefore a perfectly accurate system of music cannot even be thought, far less worked out; and on this account all possible music deviates from perfect purity; it can only conceal the discords essential to it by dividing them among all the notes, *i.e.*, by temperament. On this see Chladni's "Akustik," § 30, and his "Kurze Uebersicht der Schall- und Klanglehre."

I might still have something to say about the way in which music is perceived, namely, in and through time alone, with absolute exclusion of space, and also apart from the influence of the knowledge of causality, thus without understanding; for the tones make the aesthetic impression as effect, and without obliging us to go back to their causes, as in the case of perception. I do not wish, however, to lengthen this discussion, as I have perhaps already gone too much into detail with regard to some things in this Third Book, or have dwelt too much on particulars. But my aim made it necessary, and it will be the less disapproved if the importance and high worth of art, which is seldom sufficiently recognised, be kept in mind. For if, according to our view, the whole visible world is just the objectification, the mirror, of the will, conducting it to knowledge of itself, and, indeed, as we shall soon see, to the possibility of its deliverance; and if, at the same time, the world as idea, if we regard it in isolation, and, freeing ourselves from all volition, allow it alone to take possession of our consciousness, is the most joy-giving and the only innocent side of life; we must regard art as the higher ascent, the more complete development of all this, for it achieves essentially just what is achieved by the visible world itself, only with greater concentration, more perfectly, with intention and intelligence, and therefore may be called, in the full significance of the word, the flower of life. If the whole world as idea is only the visibility of will, the work of art is to render this visibility more distinct. It is the *camera obscura* which shows the objects more purely, and enables us to survey them and comprehend them better. It is the play within the play, the stage upon the stage in "Hamlet."

The pleasure we receive from all beauty, the consolation which art affords, the enthusiasm of the artist, which enables him to forget the cares of life,—the latter an advantage of the man of genius over other men, which alone repays him for the suffering that increases in proportion to the clearness of consciousness, and for the desert loneliness among men of a different race,—all this rests on the fact that the in-itself of life, the will, existence itself, is, as we shall see farther on, a constant sorrow, partly miserable, partly terrible; while, on the contrary, as idea alone, purely contemplated, or copied by art, free from pain, it presents to us a drama full of significance. This purely knowable side of the world, and the copy of it in any art, is the element of the artist. He is chained to the contemplation of the play, the objectification of will; he remains beside it, does not get tired of contemplating it and representing it in copies; and meanwhile he bears himself the cost of the production of that play, *i.e.*, he himself is the will which objectifies itself, and remains in constant suffering. That pure, true, and deep knowledge of the inner nature of the world becomes now for him an end in itself: he stops there. Therefore it does not become to him a quieter of the will, as, we shall see in the next book, it does in the case of the saint who has attained to resignation; it does not deliver him for ever from life, but only at moments, and is therefore not for him a path out of life, but only an occasional consolation in it, till his power, increased by this contemplation and at last tired of the play, lays hold on the real. The St. Cecilia of Raphael may be regarded as a representation of this transition. To the real, then, we now turn in the following book.

Friedrich Wilhelm
NIETZSCHE

The Birth of Tragedy, *Nietzsche's first book, is a revolutionary statement that has had profound effects in both classical studies and philosophy. Here, in a short, sometimes vague, and undeveloped form, is a theory of Greek drama and of the foundations of art which has been taken up again and again in our own day. Nietzsche is the first to look penetratingly at Greek irrationalism; he sees that the origins of art and of all human creativity are to be found in the dual aspects of human nature which he calls dream and song. Boldly developing the meaning this has for our interpretation of reality, he suggests that existence can be understood and justified only in aesthetic terms. This then puts scientific inquiry in a new light: it is either a misleading failure or a rival to art; in the latter case it is itself a kind of illusion similar to the illusion of art.*

Art, science, and philosophy are all forms of illusion, Nietzsche maintains in his close dependence on Schopenhauer. Here life is interpreted and re-enacted so that from the meaningless flux of experience a meaningful whole, ordered world emerges. Most interesting and provocative of all these illusory tactics of the

human mind is tragedy, an art form which appeared and disappeared in the Athenian world of ancient Greece. Tragedy is
distinguished by the vision it presents, a vision of the horror of
nature and the unnatural act which lies behind all that man
takes to be noble in conduct. Tragedy shows us that "Wisdom
is a crime committed on nature." How, Nietzsche asks, could
such a vision come into being? To answer that most difficult
question he makes his famous distinction between the Apollonian and the Dionysiac: the first a fantasy of dreams, the second
a wild, barbaric intoxication. Both are natural to man, but civili-
zations differ in their encouragement of one or both of these
sides of human nature. Through a strange historical process, the
inner working of which we do not understand, the Athenian
poets of the fifth and fourth century B.C. were able to develop
an art form which combined the Apollonian dream and the
Dionysiac intoxication. Thus in the tragic drama the chorus of
dancing satyrs discharges itself upon the stage in a series of
dreamlike images of the God Dionysus. The conflict between
the formal individuation of dream life and the blind merging
of self into oneness of intoxication is resolved for a moment in
the achievement of Attic tragedy. But the resolution must be
momentary: it breaks up into the simple blindness of music on
the one hand, and the Doric rigidity of formal plastic art on the
other. Apollo is in danger of becoming empty; Dionysus of becoming blind. But tragedy in its integration remains one of the
greatest achievements of man.

When the disintegration occurred it occurred in part because
the pessimistic vitality of tragedy was not tolerable to many people. The mystery of being which tragedy proposes for our terrified view is a negation of all that we in our optimistic moments
claim for the human intellect. In response to this challenge
there developed the man whom Nietzsche symbolizes by Socrates
and to whom he gives the name "theoretical man." In short,
tragedy was killed by philosophy which wanted to replace the
tragic vision by a vision of nature as ultimately understandable
and intelligible, fit object of rational inquiry, suitably analyzed
by the art of dialectic. Theoretical man is a dialectician and a
morally virtuous actor who no longer fears death and who claims
nature is ultimately reasonable. Hence he replaces art with inquiry. With this conclusion Nietzsche comes back to the starting
point of his essay. Having asked "What is the meaning of inquiry for life?" he now answers that inquiry is but a way of creating a new, more comforting illusion. Inquiry's aim is a vision of
nature in the mode of "aesthetic socratism." Ever since Socrates

Western man has retained this vision and in so doing has lost the most precious and vital Dionysiac elements of his being. Nietzsche would recall man to the vision of tragedy and would return philosophy to its pre-Socratic subordination to tragedy. Of course it is too late; but today the Nietzschean revaluation of all that the West has prided itself upon is extended by Heidegger, who is at the present time the philosopher closest to Nietzsche's remarkable originality and daring.

THE BIRTH OF TRAGEDY

1

We shall do a great deal for the science of esthetics, once we perceive not merely by logical inference, but with the immediate certainty of intuition, that the continuous development of art is bound up with the *Apollonian* and *Dionysian* duality: just as procreation depends on the duality of the sexes, involving perpetual strife with only periodically intervening reconciliations. The terms Dionysian and Apollonian we borrow from the Greeks, who disclose to the discerning mind the profound mysteries of their view of art, not, to be sure, in concepts, but in the impressively clear figures of their gods. Through Apollo and Dionysus, the two art-deities of the Greeks, we come to recognize that in the Greek world there existed a sharp opposition, in origin and aims, between the Apollonian art of sculpture, and the non-plastic, Dionysian, art of music. These two distinct tendencies run parallel to each other, for the most part openly at variance; and they continually incite each other to new and more powerful births, which perpetuate an antagonism, only superficially reconciled by the common term "Art"; till at last, by a metaphysical miracle of the Hellenic will, they appear coupled with each other, and through this coupling eventually generate the art-product, equally Dionysian and Apollonian, of Attic tragedy.

In order to grasp these two tendencies, let us first conceive of them as the separate art-worlds of *dreams* and *drunkenness*. These physiological phenomena present a contrast analogous to that existing between the Apollonian and the Dionysian. It was in dreams, says Lucretius, that the glorious divine figures first appeared to the souls of men; in dreams the great shaper beheld the splendid corporeal structure of superhuman beings; and the Hellenic poet, if questioned about the mysteries of poetic inspiration, would likewise have suggested dreams and he might have given an explanation like that of Hans Sachs in the *Mastersingers*:

> "*Mein Freund, das grad' ist Dichters Werk,*
> *dass er sein Träumen deut' und merk'.*
> *Glaubt mir, des Menschen wahrster Wahn*
> *wird ihm im Traume aufgethan:*
> *all' Dichtkunst und Poëterei*
> *ist nichts als Wahrtraum-Deuterei.*" [1]

The beautiful appearance of the dream-worlds, in creating which every man is a perfect artist, is the prerequisite of all plastic art, and in fact, as we shall see, of an important part of poetry also. In our dreams we delight in the immediate apprehension of form; all forms speak to us; none are unimportant, none are superfluous. But, when this dream-reality is most intense, we also have, glimmering through it, the sensation of its appearance: at least this is my experience, as to whose frequency, aye, normality, I could adduce many proofs, in addition to the sayings of the poets. Indeed, the man of philosophic mind has a presentiment that underneath this reality in which we live and have our being, is concealed another and quite different reality, which, like the first, is an appearance; and Schopenhauer actually indicates as the criterion of philosophical ability the occasional ability to view men and things as mere phantoms or dream-pictures. Thus the esthetically sensitive man stands in the same relation to the reality of dreams as the philosopher does to the reality of existence; he is a close and willing observer, for these pictures afford him an interpretation of life, and it is by these processes that he trains himself for life. And it is not only the agreeable and friendly pictures that he experiences in himself with such perfect understanding: but the serious, the troubled, the sad, the gloomy, the sudden restraints, the tricks of fate, the uneasy presentiments, in short, the whole Divine Comedy of life, and the Inferno, also pass before him, not like mere shadows on the wall—for in these scenes he lives and suffers—and yet not without that fleeting sensation of appearance. And perhaps many will, like myself, recall that amid the dangers and terrors of dream-life they would at times, cry out in self-encouragement, and not without success: "It is only a dream! I will dream on!" I have likewise heard of

---

[1] ["My friend, that is exactly the poet's task, to mark his dreams and to attach meanings to them. Believe me, man's most profound illusions are revealed to him in dreams; and all versifying and poetizing is nothing but an interpretation of them."]

persons capable of continuing one and the same dream for three and even more successive nights: facts which indicate clearly that our innermost beings, our common subconscious experiences, express themselves in dreams because they must do so and because they take profound delight in so doing.

This joyful necessity of the dream-experience has been embodied by the Greeks in their Apollo: for Apollo, the god of all plastic energies, is at the same time the soothsaying god. He, who (as the etymology of the name indicates) is the "shining one," the deity of light, is also ruler over the fair appearance of the inner world of fantasy. The higher truth, the perfection of these states in contrast to the incompletely intelligible everyday world, this deep consciousness of nature, healing and helping in sleep and dreams, is at the same time the symbolical analogue of the soothsaying faculty and of the arts generally, which make life possible and worth living. But we must also include in our picture of Apollo that delicate boundary, which the dream-picture must not overstep—lest it act pathologically (in which case appearance would impose upon us as pure reality). We must keep in mind that measured restraint, that freedom from the wilder emotions, that philosophical calm of the sculptor-god. His eye must be "sunlike," as befits his origin; even when his glance is angry and distempered, the sacredness of his beautiful appearance must still be there. And so, in one sense, we might apply to Apollo the words of Schopenhauer when he speaks of the man wrapped in the veil of Mâyâ: *Welt als Wille und Vorstellung*, I. p. 416: "Just as in a stormy sea, unbounded in every direction, rising and falling with howling mountainous waves, a sailor sits in a boat and trusts in his frail barque: so in the midst of a world of sorrows the individual sits quietly, supported by and trusting in his *principium individuationis*." In fact, we might say of Apollo, that in him the unshaken faith in this *principium* and the calm repose of the man wrapped therein receive their sublimest expression; and we might consider Apollo himself as the glorious divine image of the *principium individuationis*, whose gestures and expression tell us of all the joy and wisdom of "appearance," together with its beauty.

In the same work Schopenhauer has depicted for us the terrible *awe* which seizes upon man, when he is suddenly unable to account for the cognitive forms of a phenomenon, when the principle of reason, in some one of its manifestations, seems to admit of an exception. If we add to this awe the blissful ecstasy which rises from the innermost depths of man, aye, of nature, at this very collapse of the *principium individuationis*, we shall gain an insight into the nature of the *Dionysian*, which is brought home to us most intimately perhaps by the analogy of *drunkenness*. It is either under the influence of the narcotic draught, which we hear of in the songs of all primitive men and peoples, or with the potent coming of spring penetrating all nature with joy, that these Dionysian emotions awake, which, as they intensify, cause the subjective to vanish into complete self-forgetfulness. So also in the German Middle Ages singing and dancing crowds, ever increasing in number, were whirled from place to place under this same Dionysian impulse. In these dancers of St. John and St. Vitus, we rediscover the Bacchic choruses of the Greeks, with their early history in Asia Minor, as far back as Babylon and the orgiastic Sacaea. There are some, who, from obtuseness, or lack of experience, will deprecate such phenomena as "folk-diseases," with contempt or pity born of the consciousness of their own "healthy-mindedness." But, of course, such poor wretches can not imagine how anemic and ghastly their so-called "healthy-mindedness" seems in contrast to the glowing life of the Dionysian revellers rushing past them.

Under the charm of the Dionysian not only is the union between man and man reaffirmed, but Nature which has become estranged, hostile, or subjugated, celebrates once more her reconciliation with her prodigal son, man. Freely earth proffers her gifts, and peacefully the beasts of prey approach from desert and mountain. The chariot of Dionysus is bedecked with flowers and garlands; panthers and tigers pass beneath his yoke. Transform Beethoven's "Hymn to Joy" into a painting; let your imagination conceive the multitudes bowing to the dust, awestruck—then you will be able to appreciate the Dionysian. Now the slave is free; now all the stubborn, hostile barriers, which necessity, caprice or "shameless fashion" have erected between man and man, are broken down. Now, with the gospel of universal harmony, each one feels himself not only united, reconciled, blended with his neighbor, but as one with him; he feels as if the veil of Mâyâ had been torn aside and were now merely fluttering in tatters before the mysterious Primordial Unity. In song and in dance man expresses himself as a member of a higher community; he has forgotten how to walk and speak; he is about to take a dancing flight into the air. His very gestures bespeak enchantment. Just as the animals now talk, just as the earth yields milk and honey, so from him emanate supernatural sounds. He feels himself a god, he himself now walks about enchanted, in ecstasy, like to the gods whom he saw walking about in his dreams. He is no longer an artist, he has become a work of art: in these paroxysms of intoxication the artistic power of all nature reveals itself to the highest gratification of the Primordial Unity. The noblest clay, the most costly marble, man, is here kneaded and cut, and to the sound of the chisel strokes of the Dionysian world-artist rings out the cry of the Eleusinian mysteries: "Do ye bow in the dust, O millions? Do you divine your creator, O world?"

2

Thus far we have considered the Apollonian and its antithesis, the Dionysian, as artistic energies which burst forth from nature herself, *without the mediation of the human artist*; energies in which nature's art-impulses are satisfied in the most immediate and direct way: first, on the one hand, in the pictorial world of dreams, whose completeness is not dependent upon the intellectual attitude or the artistic culture of any single being; and, on the other hand, as drunken reality, which likewise does not heed the single unit, but even seeks to destroy the individual and redeem him by a mystic feeling of Oneness. With reference to these immediate art-states of nature, every artist is an "imitator," that is to say, either an Apollonian artist in dreams, or a Dionysian artist in ecstasies, or finally—as for example in Greek tragedy—at once artist in both dreams and ecstasies: so we may perhaps picture him sinking down in his Dionysian drunkenness and mystical self-abnegation, alone, and apart from the singing revelers, and we may imagine how now, through Apollonian dream-inspiration, his own state, *i.e.*, his oneness with the primal nature of the universe, is revealed to him in a *symbolical dream-picture*.

So much for these general premises and contrasts. Let us now approach the *Greeks* in order to learn how highly these *art-impulses of nature* were developed in them. Thus we shall be in a position to understand and appreciate more deeply that relation of the Greek artist to his archetypes, which, according to the Aristotelian expression, is "the imitation of nature." In spite of all the dream-literature and the numerous dream-anecdotes of the Greeks, we can speak only conjecturally, though with reasonable assurance, of their *dreams*. If we consider the incredibly precise and unerring plastic power of their eyes, together with their vivid, frank delight in colors, we can hardly refrain (to the shame of all those born later) from assuming even for their dreams a certain logic of line and contour, colors and groups, a certain pictorial sequence reminding us of their finest bas-reliefs, whose perfection would certainly justify us, if a comparison were possible, in designating the dreaming Greeks as Homers and Homer as a dreaming Greek: in a deeper sense than that in which modern man, speaking of his dreams, ventures to compare himself with Shakespeare.

On the other hand, there is no conjecture as to the immense gap which separates the *Dionysian Greek* from the Dionysian barbarian. From all quarters of the Ancient World,—to say nothing here of the modern,—from Rome to Babylon, we can point to the existence of Dionysian festivals, types which bear, at best, the same relation to the Greek festivals as the bearded satyr, who borrowed his name and attributes from the goat, does to Dionysus himself. In nearly every case these festivals centered in extravagant sexual licentiousness, whose waves overwhelmed all family life and its venerable traditions; the most savage natural instincts were unleashed, including even that horrible mixture of sensuality and cruelty which has always seemed to me to be the genuine "witches' brew." For some time, however, it would appear that the Greeks were perfectly insulated and guarded against the feverish excitements of these festivals by the figure of Apollo himself rising here in full pride, who could not have held out the Gorgon's head to any power more dangerous than this grotesquely uncouth Dionysian. It is in Doric art that this majestically-rejecting attitude of Apollo is eternized. The opposition between Apollo and Dionysus became more hazardous and even impossible, when, from the deepest roots of the Hellenic nature, similar impulses finally burst forth and made a path for themselves: the Delphic god, by a seasonably effected reconciliation, now contented himself with taking the destructive weapons from the hands of his powerful antagonist. This reconciliation is the most important moment in the history of the Greek cult: wherever we turn we note the revolutions resulting from this event. The two antagonists were reconciled; the boundary lines thenceforth to be observed by each were sharply defined, and there was to be a periodical exchange of gifts of esteem. At bottom, however, the chasm was not bridged over. But if we observe how, under the pressure of this treaty of peace, the Dionysian power revealed itself, we shall now recognize in the Dionysian orgies of the Greeks, as compared with the Babylonian Sacaea with their reversion of man to the tiger and the ape, the significance of festivals of world-redemption and days of transfiguration. It is with them that nature for the first time attains her artistic jubilee; it is with them that the destruction of the *principium individuationis* for the first time becomes an artistic phenomenon. The horrible "witches' brew" of sensuality and cruelty becomes ineffective: only the curious blending and duality in the emotions of the Dionysian revelers remind us—as medicines remind us of deadly poisons—of the phenomenon that pain begets joy, that ecstasy may wring sounds of agony from us. At the very climax of joy there sounds a cry of horror or a yearning lamentation for an irretrievable loss. In these Greek festivals, nature seems to reveal a sentimental trait; it is as if she were heaving a sigh at her dismemberment into individuals. The song and pantomime of such dually-minded revelers was something new and unheard-of for the Homeric-Grecian world: and the Dionysian *music* in particular excited awe and terror. If music, as it would seem, had been known previously as an Apollonian art, it was so, strictly speaking, only as the wave-beat of rhythm, whose formative power was developed for the representation of Apollonian states. The music of Apollo was Doric architectonics in tones, but in tones that were merely suggestive, such as those of the cithara. The very element which forms the essence of Dionysian music (and hence of music in general) is carefully excluded as un-Apollonian: namely, the emotional power of the tone, the uniform flow of the melos, and the utterly incomparable world of harmony. In the Dionysian dithyramb man is incited to the greatest exaltation of all his symbolic faculties; something never before experienced struggles for utterance—the annihilation of the veil of Mâyâ, Oneness as the soul of the race, and of nature itself. The essence of nature is now to be expressed symbolically; we need a new world of symbols; for once the entire symbolism of the body is called into play, not the mere symbolism of the lips, face, and speech, but the whole pantomime of dancing, forcing every member into rhythmic movement. Thereupon the other symbolic powers suddenly press forward, particularly those of music, in rhythmics, dynamics, and harmony. To grasp this collective release of all the symbolic powers, man must have already attained that height of self-abnegation which wills to express itself symbolically through all these powers: and so the dithyrambic votary of Dionysus is understood only by his peers! With what astonishment must the Apollonian Greek have beheld him! With an astonishment that was all the greater the more it was mingled with the shuddering suspicion that all this was actually not so very alien to him after all, in fact, that it was only his Apollonian consciousness which, like a veil, hid this Dionysian world from his vision.

3

To understand this, it becomes necessary to level the artistic structure of the *Apollonian culture,* as it were, stone by stone, till the foundations on which it rests become visible. First of all we see the glorious *Olympian* figures of the gods, standing on the gables of this structure. Their deeds, pictured in brilliant reliefs, adorn its friezes. We must not be misled by the fact that Apollo stands side by side with the others as an individual deity, without any claim to priority of rank. For the same impulse which embodied itself in Apollo gave birth in general to this entire Olympian world, and so in this sense Apollo is its father. What terrific need was it that could produce such an illustrious company of Olympian beings?

He who approaches these Olympians with another religion in his heart, seeking among them for moral elevation, even for sanctity, for disincarnate spirituality, for charity and benevolence, will soon be forced to turn his back on them, discouraged and disappointed. For there is nothing here that suggests asceticism, spirituality, or duty. We hear nothing but the accents of an exuberant, triumphant life, in which all things, whether good or bad, are deified. And so the spectator may stand quite bewildered before this fantastic superfluity of life, asking himself what magic potion these mad glad men could have imbibed to make life so enjoyable that, wherever they turned, their eyes beheld the smile of Helen, the ideal picture of their own existence, "floating in sweet sensuality." But to this spectator, who has his back already turned, we must perforce cry: "Go not away, but stay and hear what Greek folk-wisdom has to say of this very life, which with such inexplicable gayety unfolds itself before your eyes. There is an ancient story that King Midas hunted in the forest a long time for the wise *Silenus*, the companion of Dionysus, without capturing him. When Silenus at last fell into his hands, the king asked what was the best and most desirable of all things for man. Fixed and immovable, the demigod said not a word; till at last, urged by the king, he gave a shrill laugh and broke out into these words: 'Oh, wretched ephemeral race, children of chance and misery, why do ye compel me to tell you what it were most expedient for you not to hear? What is best of all is beyond your reach forever: not to be born, not to *be*, to be *nothing*. But the second best for you—is quickly to die.' "

How is the Olympian world of deities related to this folk-wisdom? Even as the rapturous vision of the tortured martyr to his suffering.

Now it is as if the Olympian magic mountain had opened before us and revealed its roots to us. The Greek knew and felt the terror and horror of existence. That he might endure this terror at all, he had to interpose between himself and life the radiant dream-birth of the Olympians. That overwhelming dismay in the face of the titanic powers of nature, the Moira enthroned inexorably over all knowledge, the vulture of the great lover of mankind, Prometheus, the terrible fate of the wise Œdipus, the family curse of the Atridae which drove Orestes to matricide: in short, that entire philosophy of the sylvan god, with its mythical exemplars, which caused the downfall of the melancholy Etruscans—all this was again and again overcome by the Greeks with the aid of the Olympian *middle world* of art; or at any rate it was veiled and withdrawn from sight. It was out of the direst necessity to live that the Greeks created these gods. Perhaps we may picture the process to ourselves somewhat as follows: out of the original Titan thearchy of terror the Olympian thearchy of joy gradually evolved through the Apollonian impulse towards beauty, just as roses bud from thorny bushes. How else could this people, so sensitive, so vehement in its desires, so singularly constituted for *suffering*, how could they have endured existence, if it had not been revealed to them in their gods, surrounded with a higher glory? The same impulse which calls art into being, as the complement and consummation of existence, seducing one to a continuation of life, was also the cause of the Olympian world which the Hellenic "will" made use of as a transfiguring mirror. Thus do the gods justify the life of man, in that they themselves live it—the only satisfactory Theodicy! Existence under the bright sunshine of such gods is regarded as desirable in itself, and the real *grief* of the Homeric men is caused by parting from it, especially by early parting: so that now, reversing the wisdom of Silenus, we might say of the Greeks that "to die early is worst of all for them, the next worst—some day to die at all." Once heard, it will ring out again; forget not the lament of the short-lived Achilles, mourning the leaflike change and vicissitude of the race of men and the decline of the heroic age. It is not unworthy of the greatest hero to long for a continuation of life, aye, even though he live as a slave. At the Apollonian stage of development, the "will" longs so vehemently for this existence, the Homeric man feels himself so completely at one with it, that lamentation itself becomes a song of praise.

Here we should note that this harmony which is contemplated with such longing by modern man, in fact, this oneness of man with nature (to express which Schiller introduced the technical term "naïve"), is by no means a simple condition, resulting naturally, and as if inevitably. It is not a condition which, like a terrestrial paradise, *must* necessarily be found at the gate of every culture. Only a romantic age could believe this, an age which conceived of the artist in terms of Rousseau's *Emile* and imagined that in Homer it had found such an artist Emile, reared in Nature's bosom. Wherever we meet with the "naïve" in art, we recognize the highest effect of the Apollonian culture, which in the first place has always to overthrow some Titanic empire and slay monsters, and which, through its potent dazzling representations and its pleasurable illusions, must have triumphed over a terrible depth of world-contemplation and a most keen sensitivity to suffering. But how seldom do we attain to the naïve—that complete absorption in the beauty of appearance! And hence how inexpressibly sublime is *Homer*, who, as individual being, bears the same relation to this Apollonian folk-culture as the individual dream-artist does to the dream-faculty of the people and of Nature in general. The Homeric "naïveté" can be understood only as the complete victory of the Apollonian illusion: an illusion similar to those which Nature so frequently employs to achieve her own ends. The true goal is veiled by a phantasm: and while we stretch out our hands for the latter, Nature attains the former by means of your illusion. In the Greeks the "will" wished to contemplate itself in the transfiguration of genius and the world of art; in order to glorify themselves, its creatures had to feel themselves worthy of glory; they had to behold themselves again in a higher sphere, without this perfect world of contemplation acting as a command or a reproach. Such is the sphere of beauty, in which they saw their mirrored images, the Olympians. With this mirroring of beauty the Hellenic will combated its artistically correlative talent for suffering and for the wisdom of suffering: and, as a monument of its victory, we have Homer, the naïve artist.

4

Now the dream-analogy may throw some light on the problem of the naïve artist. Let us imagine the dreamer: in the midst of the illusion of the dream-world and without disturbing it, he calls out to himself: "It is a dream, I will dream on." What must we infer? That he experiences a deep inner joy in dream-contemplation; on the other hand, to be at all able to dream with this inner joy in contemplation, he must have completely lost sight of the waking reality and its ominous obtrusiveness. Guided by the dream-reading Apollo, we may interpret all these phenomena to ourselves somewhat in this way. Though it is certain that of the two halves of our existence, the waking and the dreaming states, the former appeals to us as infinitely more preferable, important, excellent and worthy of being lived, indeed, as that which alone is lived: yet, in relation to that mysterious substratum of our nature of which we are the phenomenon, I should, paradoxical as it may seem, maintain the very opposite estimate of the value of dream life. For the more clearly I perceive in Nature those omnipotent art impulses, and in them an ardent longing for release, for redemption through release, the more I feel myself impelled to the metaphysical assumption that the Truly-Existent and Primal Unity, eternally suffering and divided against itself, has need of the rapturous vision, the joyful appearance, for its continuous salvation: which appearance we, completely wrapped up in it and composed of it, are compelled to apprehend as the True Non-Being,—*i.e.*, as a perpetual becoming in time, space and causality,—in other words, as empiric reality. If, for the moment, we do not consider the question of our own "reality," if we conceive of our empirical existence, and that of the world in general, as a continuously manifested representation of the Primal Unity, we shall then have to look upon the dream as an *appearance of appearance*, hence as a still higher appeasement of the primordial desire for appearance. And that is why the innermost heart of Nature feels that ineffable joy in the naïve artist and the naïve work of art, which is likewise only "an appearance of appearance." In a symbolic painting, *Raphael*, himself one of these immortal "naïve" ones, has represented for us this devolution of appearance to appearance, the primitive process of the naïve artist and of Apollonian culture. In his "Transfiguration," the lower half of the picture, with the possessed boy, the despairing bearers, the bewildered, terrified disciples, shows us the reflection of suffering, primal and eternal, the sole basis of the world: the "appearance" here is the counter-appearance of eternal contradiction, the father of things. From this appearance now arises, like ambrosial vapor, a new visionary world of appearances, invisible to those wrapped in the first appearance—a radiant floating in purest bliss, a serene contemplation beaming from wide-open eyes. Here we have presented, in the most sublime artistic symbolism, that Apollonian world of beauty and its substratum, the terrible wisdom of Silenus; and intuitively we comprehend their necessary interdependence. Apollo, however, again appears to us as the apotheosis of the *principium individuationis*, in which alone is consummated the perpetually attained goal of the Primal Unity, its redemption through appearance. With his sublime gestures, he shows us how necessary is the entire world of suffering, that by means of it the individual may be impelled to realize the redeeming vision, and then, sunk in contemplation of it, sit quietly in his tossing barque, amid the waves.

If we at all conceive of it as imperative and mandatory, this apotheosis of individuation knows but one law—the individual, *i.e.*, the delimiting of the boundaries of the individual, *measure* in the Hellenic sense. Apollo, as ethical deity, exacts measure of his disciples, and, that to this end, he requires self-knowledge. And so, side by side with the esthetic necessity for beauty, there occur the demands "know thyself" and "nothing overmuch"; consequently pride and excess are regarded as the truly inimical demons of the non-Apollonian sphere, hence as characteristics of the pre-Apollonian age—that of the Titans; and of the extra-Apollonian world—that of the barbarians. Because of his Titan-like love for man, Prometheus must be torn to pieces by vultures; because of his excessive wisdom, which could solve the riddle of the Sphinx, Œdipus must be plunged into a bewildering vortex of crime. Thus did the Delphic god interpret the Greek past.

Similarly the effects wrought by the *Dionysian* seemed "titan-like" and "barbaric" to the Apollonian Greek: while at the same time he could not conceal from himself that he too was inwardly related to these overthrown Titans and heroes. Indeed, he had to recognize even more than this: despite all its beauty and moderation, his entire existence rested on a hidden substratum of suffering and of knowledge, which was again revealed to him by the Dionysian. And lo! Apollo could not live without Dionysus! The "titanic" and the "barbaric" were in the last analysis as necessary as the Apollonian.

And now let us take this artistically limited world, based on appearance and moderation; let us imagine how into it there penetrated, in tones ever more bewitching and alluring, the ecstatic sound of the Dionysian festival; let us remember that in these strains all of Nature's excess in joy, sorrow, and knowledge become audible, even in piercing shrieks; and finally, let us ask ourselves what significance remains to the psalmodizing artist of Apollo, with his phantom harp-sound, once it is compared with this demonic folk-song! The muses of the arts of "appearance" paled before an art which, in its intoxication, spoke the truth. The wisdom of Silenus cried "Woe! woe!" to the serene Olympians. The individual, with all his restraint and proportion, succumbed to the self-oblivion of the Dionysian state, forgetting the precepts of Apollo. Excess revealed itself as truth. Contradiction, the bliss born of pain, spoke out from the very heart of Nature. And so, wherever the Dionysian prevailed, the Apollonian was checked and destroyed. But, on the other hand, it is equally certain that, wherever the first Dionysian onslaught was successfully withstood, the authority and majesty of the Delphic god exhibited itself as more rigid and menacing than ever. For to me the *Doric* state and Doric art are explicable only as a permanent citadel of the Apollonian. For an art so defiantly prim, and so encompassed with bulwarks, a training so warlike and rigorous, a political structure so cruel and relentless, could endure for any length of time only by incessant opposition to the titanic-barbaric nature of the Dionysian.

Up to this point we have simply enlarged upon the observation made at the beginning of this essay: that the Dionysian and the Apollonian, in new births ever following and mutually augmenting one another, controlled the Hellenic genius; that from out the age of "bronze," with its wars of the Titans and its rigorous folk-philosophy, the Homeric world developed under the sway of the Apollonian impulse to beauty; that this "naïve" splendor was again overwhelmed by the influx of the Dionysian; and that against this new power the Apollonian rose to the austere majesty of Doric art and the Doric view of the world. If, then, amid the strife of these two hostile principles, the older Hellenic history thus falls into four great periods of art, we are now impelled to inquire after the *final goal* of these developments and processes, lest perchance we should regard the last-attained period, the period of Doric art, as the climax and aim of these artistic impulses. And here the sublime and celebrated art of *Attic tragedy* and the dramatic dithyramb presents itself as the common goal of both these tendencies, whose mysterious union, after many and long precursory struggles, found glorious consummation in this child,—at once Antigone and Cassandra.

5

We now approach the real goal of our investigation, which is directed towards acquiring a knowledge of the Dionysian-Apollonian genius and its art-product, or at least an anticipatory understanding of its mysterious union. Here we shall first of all inquire after the first evidence in Greece of that new germ which subsequently developed into tragedy and the dramatic dithyramb. The ancients themselves give us a symbolic answer, when they place the faces of *Homer* and *Archilochus* as the forefathers and torchbearers of Greek poetry side by side on gems, sculptures, etc., with a sure feeling that consideration should be given only to these two thoroughly original compeers, from whom a stream of fire flows over the whole of later Greek history. Homer, the aged self-absorbed dreamer, the type of the Apollonian naïve artist, now beholds with astonishment the passionate genius of the war-like votary of the muses, Archilochus, passing through life with fury and violence; and modern esthetics, by way of interpretation, can only add that here the first "objective" artist confronts the first "subjective" artist. But this interpretation helps us but little, because we know the subjective artist only as the poor artist, and throughout the entire range of art we demand specially and first of all the conquest of the Subjective, the release from the ego and the silencing of the individual will and desire; indeed, we find it impossible to believe in any truly artistic production, however insignificant, if it is without objectivity, without pure, detached contemplation. Hence our esthetic must first solve the problem of how the "lyrist" is possible as an artist—he who, according to the experience of all ages, is continually saying "I" and running through the entire chromatic scale of his passions and desires. Compared with Homer, this very Archilochus appalls us by his cries of hatred and scorn, by his drunken outbursts of desire. Therefore is not he, who has been called the first subjective artist, essentially the non-artist? But in this case, how explain the reverence which was shown to him —the poet—in very remarkable utterances by the Delphic oracle itself, the center of "objective" art?

Schiller has thrown some light on the poetic process by a psychological observation, inexplicable to himself, yet apparently valid. He admits that before the act of creation he did not perhaps have before him or within him any series of images accompanied by an ordered thought-relationship; but his condition was rather that of a *musical mood*. ("With me the perception has at first no clear and definite object; this is formed later. A certain musical mood of mind precedes, and only after this ensues the poetical idea.") Let us add to this the natural and most important phenomenon of all ancient lyric poetry, *the union*, indeed, the *identity*, of the *lyrist with the musician,*—compared with which our modern lyric poetry appears like the statue of a god without a head,—with this in mind we may now, on the basis of our metaphysics of esthetics set forth above, explain the lyrist to ourselves in this manner: In the first place, as Dionysian artist he has identified himself with the Primal Unity, its pain and contradiction. Assuming that music has been correctly termed a repetition and a recast of the world, we may say that he produces the copy of this Primal Unity as music. Now, however, under the Apollonian dream-inspiration, this music reveals itself to him again as a *symbolic dream-picture*. The inchoate, intangible reflection of the primordial pain in music, with its redemption in appearance, now produces a second mirroring as a specific symbol or example. The artist has already surrendered his subjectivity in the Dionysian process. The picture which now shows him his identity with the heart of the world, is a dream-scene, which embodies the primordial contradiction and primordial pain, together with the primordial joy, of appearance. The "I" of the lyrist therefore sounds from the depth of his being: its "subjectivity," in the sense of the modern esthetes, is pure imagination. When Archilochus, the first Greek lyrist, proclaims to the daughters of Lycambes both his mad love and his contempt, it is not his passion alone which dances before us in orgiastic frenzy; but we see Dionysus and the Mænads, we see the drunken reveler Archilochus sunk down in slumber—as Euripides depicts it in the *Bacchae*, the sleep on the high mountain pasture, in the noonday sun. And now Apollo approaches and touches him with the laurel. Then the Dionyso-musical enchantment of the sleeper seems to emit picture sparks, lyrical poems, which in their highest form are called tragedies and dramatic dithyrambs.

The plastic artist, as also the epic poet, who is related to him, is sunk in the pure contemplation of images. The Dionysian musician is, without any images, himself pure primordial pain and its primordial reëchoing. The lyric genius is conscious of a world of pictures and symbols—growing out of his state of mystical self-abnegation and oneness. This state has a coloring, a causality and a velocity quite different from that of the world of the plastic artist and the epic poet. For the latter lives in these pictures, and only in them, with joyful satisfaction. He never grows tired of contemplating lovingly even their minutest traits. Even the picture of the angry Achilles is only a picture to him, whose angry expression he enjoys with the dream-joy in appearance. Thus, by this mirror of appearance, he is protected against being united and blended with his figures. In direct contrast to this, the pictures of the *lyrist* are nothing but *his very* self and, as it were, only different projections of himself, by force of which he, as the moving center of this world, may say "I": only of course this self is not the same as that of the waking, empirically real man, but the only truly existent and eternal self resting at the basis of things, and with the help of whose images, the lyric genius can penetrate to this very basis.

Now let us suppose that among these images he also beholds *himself* as non-genius, *i.e.*, his subject, the whole throng of subjective passions and agitations directed to a definite object which appears real to him. It may now seem as if the lyric genius and the allied non-genius were one, as if the former had of its own accord spoken that little word "I." But this identity is but superficial and it will no longer be able to lead us astray, as it certainly led astray those who designated the lyrist as the subjective poet. For, as a matter of fact, Archilochus, the passionately inflamed, loving and hating man, is but a vision of the genius, who by this time is no longer merely Archilochus, but a world-genius expressing his primordial pain symbolically in the likeness of the man Archilochus: while the subjectively willing and desiring man, Archilochus, can never at any time be a poet. It is by no means necessary, however, that the lyrist should see nothing but the phenomenon of the man Archilochus before him as a reflection of eternal being; and tragedy shows how far the visionary world of the lyrist may be removed from this phenomenon, which, of course, is intimately related to it.

Schopenhauer, who did not conceal from himself the difficulty the lyrist presents in the philosophical contemplation of art, thought he had found a solution, with which, however, I am not in entire accord. (Actually, it was in his profound metaphysics of music that he alone held in his hands the means whereby this difficulty might be definitely removed: as I believe I have removed it here in his spirit and to his honor). In contrast to our view, he describes the peculiar nature of song as follows (*Welt als Wille und Vorstellung*, I. 295):

"It is the subject of will, *i.e.*, his own volition, which the consciousness of the singer feels; often as a released and satisfied desire (joy), but still oftener as a restricted desire (grief), always as an emotion, a passion, a moved frame of mind. Besides this, however, and along with it, by the sight of surrounding nature, the singer becomes conscious of himself as the subject of pure will-less knowing, whose unbroken, blissful peace now appears, in contrast to the stress of desire, which is always restricted and always needy. The feeling of this contrast, this alternation, is really what the lyric as a whole expresses and what principally constitutes the lyrical state of mind. In it pure knowing comes to us as it were to deliver us from desire and its strain; we follow, but only for an instant; desire, the remembrance of our own personal ends, tears us anew from peaceful contemplation; yet ever again the next beautiful surrounding in which the pure will-less knowledge presents itself to us, allures us away from desire. Therefore, in the lyric and the lyrical mood, desire (the personal interest of the ends) and pure perception of the surrounding presented are wonderfully mingled with each other; connections between them are sought for and imagined; the subjective disposition, the affection of the will, imparts its own hue to the perceived surrounding, and conversely, the surroundings communicate the reflex of their color to the will. The true lyric is the expression of the whole of this mingled and divided state of mind."

Who could fail to recognize in this description that lyric poetry is here characterized as an incompletely attained art, which arrives at its goal infrequently and only as it were by leaps? Indeed, it is described as a semi-art, whose essence is said to consist in this, that desire and pure contemplation, *i.e.*, the unesthetic and the esthetic condition, are wonderfully mingled with each other. It follows that Schopenhauer still classifies the arts as subjective or objective, using the antithesis as if it were a criterion of value. But it is our contention, on the contrary, that this antithesis between the subjective and the objective is especially irrelevant in esthetics, since the subject, the desiring individual furthering his own egoistic ends, can be conceived of only as the antagonist, not as the origin of art. In so far as the subject is the artist, however, he has already been released from his individual will, and has become as it were the medium through which the one truly existent Subject celebrates his release in appearance. For, above all, to our humiliation *and* exaltation, one thing must be clear to us. The entire comedy of art is neither performed for our betterment or education nor are we the true authors of this art-world. On the contrary, we may assume that we are merely pictures and artistic projections for the true author, and that we have our highest dignity in our significance as works of art—for it is only as an *esthetic phenomenon* that existence and the world are eternally *justified*—while of course our consciousness of our own significance hardly differs from that which the soldiers painted on canvas have of the battle represented on it. Thus all our knowledge of art is basically quite illusory, because as knowing beings we are not one and identical with that Being who, as the sole author and spectator of this comedy of art, prepares a perpetual entertainment for himself. Only in so far as the genius in the act of artistic creation coalesces with this primordial artist of the world, does he catch sight of the eternal essence of art; for in this state he is, in a marvelous manner, like the weird picture of the fairy-tale which can turn its eyes at will and behold itself; he is now at once subject and object, at once poet, actor, and spectator.

6

In connection with Archilochus, scholarly research has discovered that he introduced the *folk-song* into literature, and, on account of this, deserved, according to the general estimate of the Greeks, his unique position beside Homer. But what is the folk-song in contrast to the wholly Apollonian epos? What else but the *perpetuum vestigium* of a union of the Apollonian and the Dionysian? Its enormous diffusion among all peoples, further re-enforced by ever-new births, is testimony to the power of this artistic dual impulse of Nature: which leaves its vestiges in the folk-song just as the orgiastic movements of a people perpetuate themselves in its music. Indeed, it might also be historically demonstrable that every period rich in folk-songs has been most violently stirred by Dionysian currents, which we must always consider the substratum and prerequisite of the folk-song.

First of all, however, we must conceive the folk-song as the musical mirror of the world, as the original melody, now seeking for itself a parallel dream-phenomenon and expressing it in poetry. *Melody is therefore primary and universal,* and so may admit of several objectifications in several texts. Likewise, in the naïve estimation of the people, it is regarded as by far the more important and essential element. Melody generates the poem out of itself by a continuous process. *The strophic form of the folk-song* points to the same thing; a phenomenon which I had always beheld with astonishment, until at last I found this explanation. Any one who in accordance with this theory examines a collection of folk-songs, such as *Des Knaben Wunderhorn*, will find innumerable instances of the way the continuously generating melody scatters picture sparks all around, which in their variegation, their abrupt change, their mad precipitation, manifest a power quite unknown to the epic and its steady flow. From the standpoint of the epos, this unequal and irregular pictorial world of lyric poetry is definitely to be condemned: and it certainly has been thus condemned by the solemn epic rhapsodists of the Apollonian festivals in the age of Terpander.

Accordingly, we observe that in the poetry of the folk-song, language is strained to its utmost that it may *imitate music*; and hence with Archilochus begins a new world of poetry, which is basically opposed to the Homeric. And in saying this we have indicated the only possible relation between poetry and music, between word and tone: the word, the picture, the concept here seeks an expression analogous to music and now feels in itself the power of music. In this sense we may discriminate between two main currents in the history of the language of the Greek people, according to whether their language imitated the world of image and phenomenon, or the world of music. One need only reflect more deeply on the linguistic difference with regard to color, syntactical structure, and vocabulary in Homer and

Pindar, in order to understand the significance of this contrast; indeed, it becomes palpably clear that in the period between Homer and Pindar there must have sounded out the *orgiastic flute tones of Olympus,* which, even in Aristotle's time, when music was infinitely more developed, transported people to drunken ecstasy, and which, in their primitive state of development, undoubtedly incited to imitation all the poetic means of expression of contemporaneous man. I here call attention to a familiar phenomenon of our own times, against which our esthetic raises many objections. We again and again have occasion to observe that a Beethoven symphony compels its individual auditors to use figurative speech in describing it, no matter how fantastically variegated and even contradictory may be the composition and make-up of the different pictorial world produced by a piece of music. To exercise its poor wit on such compositions, and to overlook a phenomenon which is certainly worth explaining, is quite in keeping with this esthetic. Indeed, even when the tone-poet expresses his composition in pictures, when for instance he designates a certain symphony as the "pastoral" symphony, or a passage in it as the "scene by the brook," or another as the "merry gathering of rustics," these too are only symbolical representations born of music —and not perhaps the imitated objects of music—representations which can teach us nothing whatsoever concerning the *Dionysian* content of music, and which indeed have no distinctive value of their own beside other pictorial expressions. We have now to transfer this process of a discharge of music in pictures to some fresh, youthful, linguistically creative people, in order to get a notion of how the strophic faculty of speech is stimulated by this new principle of the imitation of music.

If, therefore, we may regard lyric poetry as the fulguration of music in images and concepts, we should now ask: "In what form does music *appear* in the mirror of symbolism and conception?" *It appears as will,* taking the term in Schopenhauer's sense, *i.e.,* as the antithesis of the esthetic, purely contemplative, and passive frame of mind. Here, however, we must make as sharp a distinction as possible between the concept of essence and the concept of phenomenon; for music, according to its essence, cannot possibly be will. To be will it would have to be wholly banished from the realm of art—for the will is the unesthetic-in-itself. Yet though *essentially* it is not will, *phenomenally* it *appears* as will. For in order to express the phenomenon of music in images, the lyrist needs all the agitations of passion, from the whisper of mere inclination to the roar of madness. Impelled to speak of music in Apollonian symbols, he conceives of all nature, and himself therein, only as eternal Will, Desire, Longing. But in so far as he interprets music by means of images, he himself rests in the quiet calm of Apollonian contemplation, though everything around him which he beholds through the medium of music may be confused and violent. Indeed, when he beholds himself through this same medium, his own image appears to him as an unsatisfied feeling: his own willing, longing, moaning, rejoicing, are to him symbols by which he interprets music. This is the phenomenon of the lyrist: as Apollonian genius he interprets music through the image of the will, while he himself, completely released from the desire of the will, is the pure, undimmed eye of day.

Our whole discussion insists that lyric poetry is dependent on the spirit of music just as music itself in its absolute sovereignty does not need the picture and the concept, but merely *endures* them as accompaniments. The poems of the lyrist can express nothing which did not already lie hidden in the vast universality and absoluteness of the music which compelled him to figurative speech. Language can never adequately render the cosmic symbolism of music, because music stands in symbolic relation to the primordial contradiction and primordial pain in the heart of the Primal Unity, and therefore symbolizes a sphere which is beyond and before all phenomena. Rather are all phenomena, compared with it, merely symbols: hence *language*, as the organ and symbol of phenomena, can never, by any means, disclose the innermost heart of music; language, in its attempt to imitate it, can only be in superficial contact with music; while the deepest significance of the latter cannot with all the eloquence of lyric poetry be brought one step nearer to us.

7

We must now avail ourselves of all the principles of art hitherto considered, in order to find our way through the labyrinth, as we must call it, of *the origin of Greek tragedy*. I do not think I am unreasonable in saying that the problem of this origin has as yet not even been seriously stated, not to say solved, however often the ragged tatters of ancient tradition are sewn together in various combinations and torn apart again. This tradition tells us quite unequivocally, *that tragedy arose from the tragic chorus*, and was originally only chorus and nothing but chorus; and hence we feel it our duty to look into the heart of this tragic chorus as being the real proto-drama. We shall not let ourselves be at all satisfied with that current art-lingo which makes the chorus the "ideal spectator," or has it represent the people in contrast to the aristocratic elements of the scene. This latter explanation has a sublime sound to many a politician. It insists that the immutable moral law was embodied by the democratic Athenians in the popular chorus, which always wins out over the passionate excesses and extravagances of kings. This theory may be ever so forcibly suggested by one of Aristotle's observations; still, it has no influence on the original formation of tragedy, inasmuch as the entire antithesis of king and people, and, in general, the whole politico-social sphere, is excluded from the purely religious origins of tragedy. With this in mind, and remembering the well-known classical form of the chorus in Æschylus and Sophocles, we should even deem it blasphemy to speak here of the anticipation of a "constitutional popular representation." From this blasphemy, however, others have not shrunk. The ancient governments knew of no constitutional representation of the people *in praxi*, and it is to be hoped that they did not "anticipate" it in their tragedy either.

Much more famous than this political interpretation of the chorus is the theory of A. W. Schlegel, who advises us to regard the chorus, in a manner, as the essence and extract of the crowd of spectators, —as the "ideal spectator." This view, when compared with the historical tradition that originally tragedy was only chorus, reveals itself for what it is,—a crude, unscientific, yet brilliant generalization, which, however, acquires that brilliancy only through its epigrammatic form of expression, the deep Germanic bias in favor of anything called "ideal," and our momentary astonishment. For we are certainly astonished the moment we compare our familiar theatrical public with this chorus, and ask ourselves whether it could ever be possible to idealize something analogous to the Greek tragic chorus out of such a public. We tacitly deny this, and now wonder as much at the boldness of Schlegel's assertion as at the totally different nature of the Greek public. For hitherto we had always believed that the true spectator, whoever he may be, must always remain conscious that he was viewing a work of art, and not an empirical reality. But the tragic chorus of the Greeks is forced to recognize *real beings* in the figures of the drama. The chorus of the Oceanides really believes that it sees before it the Titan Prometheus, and considers itself as real as the god of the scene. And are we to designate as the highest and purest type of spectator, one who, like the Oceanides, regards Prometheus as real and present in body? Is it characteristic of the ideal spectator to run on to the stage and free the god from his torments? We had always believed in an esthetic public, we had considered the individual spectator the better qualified the more he was capable of viewing a work of art as art, that is, esthetically. But now Schlegel tells us that the perfect ideal spectator does not at all allow the world of the drama to act on him *esthetically*, but corporeally and empirically. Oh, these Greeks! we sighed; they upset all our esthetics! . . . But once accustomed to it, we have repeated Schlegel's saying whenever the chorus came up for discussion.

Now, the tradition which is quite explicit here, speaks against Schlegel. The chorus as such, without the stage,—the primitive form of tragedy,—and the chorus of ideal spectators do not go together. What kind of art would that be in which the spectator does not enter as a separate concept? What kind of art is that whose true form is identical with the "spectator as such"? The spectator without the play is nonsense. We fear that the birth of tragedy is to be explained neither by the high esteem for the moral intelligence of the multitude nor by the concept of the spectator minus the play. We must regard the problem as too deep to be even touched by such superficial generalizing.

An infinitely more valuable insight into the significance of the chorus had already been displayed by Schiller in the celebrated Preface to his *Bride of Messina*, where he regards the chorus as a living barrier which tragedy constructs round herself to cut off her contact with the world of reality, and to preserve her ideal domain and her poetical freedom.

With this, his chief weapon, Schiller combats the ordinary conception of the natural, the illusion usually demanded in dramatic poetry. Although it is true that the stage day is merely artificial, the architecture only symbolical, and the metrical language purely ideal in character, nevertheless an erroneous view still prevails in the main: that we should not excuse these conventions merely on the ground that they constitute a poetical license. Now in reality these "conventions" form the essence of all poetry. The introduction of the chorus, says Schiller, is the decisive step by which open and honorable war is declared against all naturalism in art. It would seem that to denigrate this view of the matter our would-be superior age has coined the disdainful catchword "pseudo-idealism." I fear, however, that we, on the other hand, with our present adoration of the natural and the real, have reached the opposite pole of all idealism, namely, in the region of wax-work cabinets. There is an art in these too, as certain novels much in vogue at present evidence: but let us not disturb ourselves at the claim that by any such art the Schiller-Goethian "pseudo-idealism" has been vanquished.

It is indeed an "ideal" domain, as Schiller correctly perceived, in which the Greek satyr chorus, the chorus of primitive tragedy, was wont to dwell. It is a domain raised high above the actual path of mortals. For this chorus the Greek built up the scaffolding of a fictitious *natural state* and on it placed fictitious *natural beings*. On this foundation tragedy developed and so, of course, it could dispense from the beginning with a painful portrayal of reality. Yet it is no arbitrary world placed by whim between heaven and earth; rather is it a world with the same reality and credibility that Olympus with its dwellers possessed for the believing Hellene. The satyr, as the Dionysian chorist, lives in a religiously acknowledged reality under the sanction of the myth and the cult. That tragedy should begin with him, that he should be the voice of the Dionysian tragic wisdom, is just as strange a phenomenon as the general derivation of tragedy from the chorus.

Perhaps we shall have a point of departure for our inquiry, if I put forward the proposition that the satyr, the fictitious natural being, bears the same relation to the man of culture that Dionysian music does to civilization. Concerning this latter, Richard Wagner says that it is neutralized by music just as lamplight is neutralized by the light of day. Similarly, I believe, the Greek man of culture felt himself neutralized in the presence of the satyric chorus: and this is the most immediate effect of the Dionysian tragedy, that the state and society, and, in general, the gulfs between man and man give way to an overwhelming feeling of unity leading back to the very heart of nature. The metaphysical comfort—with which, as I have here intimated, every true tragedy leaves us—that, in spite of the flux of phenomena, life at bottom is indestructibly powerful and pleasurable, appears with objective clarity as the satyr chorus, the chorus of natural beings, who as it were live ineradicably behind every civilization, and who, despite the ceaseless change of generations and the history of nations, remain the same to all eternity.

With this chorus the deep-minded Hellene consoles himself, he who is so singularly constituted for the most sensitive and grievous suffering, he who with a piercing glance has penetrated into the very heart of the terrible destructive processes of so-called universal history, as also into the cruelty of nature, and who is in danger of longing for a Buddhistic negation of the will. Art saves him, and through art life saves him—for herself.

For we must realize that in the ecstasy of the Dionysian state, with its annihilation of the ordinary bounds and limits of existence, there is contained a *lethargic* element, in which are submerged all past personal experiences. It is this gulf of oblivion that separates the world of everyday from the world of Dionysian reality. But as soon as we become conscious again of this everyday reality, we feel it as nauseating and repulsive; and an ascetic will-negating mood is the fruit of these states. In this sense the Dionysian man resembles Hamlet: both have for once penetrated into the true nature of things,—they have *perceived*, but it is irksome for them to act; for their action cannot change the eternal nature of things; the time is out of joint and they regard it as shameful or ridiculous that they should be required to set it right. Knowledge kills action, action requires the veil of illusion— it is this lesson which Hamlet teaches, and not the idle wisdom of John-o'-Dreams who from too much reflection, from a surplus of possibilities, never arrives at action at all. Not reflection, no!—true knowledge, insight into the terrible truth, preponderate over all motives inciting to action, in Hamlet as well as in the Dionysian man. There is no longer any use in comfort; his longing goes beyond a world after death, beyond the gods themselves; existence with its glittering reflection in the gods or in an immortal beyond is abjured. In the consciousness of the truth once perceived, man now sees everywhere only the terror or the absurdity of existence; now he can understand the symbolism of Ophelia's fate; now he can realize the wisdom of the sylvan god Silenus: and he is filled with loathing.

But at this juncture, when the will is most imperiled, *art* approaches, as a redeeming and healing enchantress; she alone may transform these horrible reflections on the terror and absurdity of existence into representations with which man may live. These are the representation of the *sublime* as the artistic conquest of the awful, and of the *comic* as the artistic release from the nausea of the absurd. The satyric chorus of the dithyramb is the saving device of Greek art; the paroxysms described above exhaust themselves in the intermediary world of these Dionysian votaries.

8

The satyr, like the idyllic shepherd of our more recent time, is the offspring of a longing for the Primitive and the Natural; but how firmly and fearlessly the Greek embraced the man of the woods, and how timorously and mawkishly modern man dallied with the flattering picture of a sentimental, flute-playing, soft-mannered shepherd! Nature, as yet unchanged by knowledge, maintaining impregnable barriers to culture—that is what the Greek saw in his satyr, which nevertheless was not on this account to be confused with the primitive cave-man. On the contrary, the satyr was the archetype of man, the embodiment of his highest and intensest emotions, the ecstatic reveler enraptured by the proximity of his god, the sympathetic companion in whom is repeated the suffering of the god, wisdom's harbinger speaking from the very heart of nature, emblem of the sexual omnipotence of nature, which the Greek was wont to contemplate with reverence and wonder. The satyr was something sublime and godlike: it was inevitable that he should appear so, especially to the sad downcast glance of the Dionysian man. Our counterfeit tricked-up shepherd would have repulsed the Dionysian; but on the naked and magnificent characters of nature his eye dwelt with rapt satisfaction. Here the illusion of culture was cast off from the archetype of man; here the true man, the bearded satyr, revealed himself, shouting joyfully to his god. Face to face with him the man of culture shrank to a specious caricature. Schiller is right also with regard to these beginnings of tragic art: the chorus is a living bulwark against the onslaught of reality, because it —the satyr chorus—portrays existence more truthfully, more essentially, more perfectly than the cultured man who ordinarily considers himself as the sole reality. The sphere of poetry does not lie outside the world, like some chimera of the poetic imagination; it seeks to be the very opposite, the unvarnished expression of truth, and for this very reason it must reject the false finery of that supposed reality of the cultured man. The contrast between this intrinsic truth of nature and the falsehood of culture, which poses as the only reality, is similar to that existing between the eternal heart of things, the thing in itself, and the collective world of phenomena. And just as tragedy, with its metaphysical comfort, points to the eternal life of this kernel of existence, and to the perpetual dissolution of phenomena, so the symbolism of the satyr chorus already expresses figuratively this primal relation between the thing in itself and the phenomenon. The idyllic shepherd of the modern man is but a copy of the sum of the culture—illusions which he calls nature; the Dionysian Greek desires truth and nature in their most potent form—and so he sees himself metamorphosed into the satyr.

The reveling throng of the votaries of Dionysus rejoices under the influence of such moods and perceptions, the power of which transforms them before their own eyes, so that they imagine they behold themselves as recreated genii of nature, as satyrs. The latter constitution of the tragic chorus is the artistic imitation of this natural phenomenon, which of course necessitated a separation of the Dionysian spectators from the enchanted Dionysians. However, we must always remember that the public of the Attic tragedy rediscovered itself in the chorus of the orchestra, that there was at bottom no opposition of public and chorus: for all was but one great sublime chorus of dancing and singing satyrs, or of such as allowed themselves to be represented by these satyrs. Schlegel's observation in this sense reveals a deeper significance. The chorus *is* the "ideal spectator" [2] in so far as it is the only *beholder*,[3] the beholder of the visionary world of the scene. A public of spectators, as we know it, was unknown to the Greeks. In their theaters the terraced structure of the theatron rising in concentric arcs enabled every one to *overlook*, in an actual sense, the entire world of culture around him, and in an over-abundance of contemplation to imagine himself one of the chorus. According to this view, then, we may call the chorus in its primitive stage in early tragedy a self-mirroring of the Dionysian man: a phenomenon which is most clearly exemplified by the process of the actor, who, if he be truly gifted, sees hovering almost tangibly before his eyes the character he is to represent. The satyr chorus is above all a vision of the Dionysian throng, just as the world of the stage is, in turn, a vision of the satyr chorus. The power of this vision is great enough to render the eye dull and insensible to the impression of "reality," to the presence of the cultured men occupying the tiers of seats on every side. The form of the Greek theater reminds one of a lonesome mountain-valley. The architecture of the scene is a luminous cloud-picture and the Bacchants swarming on the mountains behold this picture from the heights,—the splendid encirclement in the midst of which is visible the image of Dionysus.

Brought in contact with our learned notions of the elementary artistic processes, this artistic proto-phenomenon, here introduced as an explanation of the tragic chorus, is almost shocking: yet nothing can be more certain than that the poet is a poet only in so far as he sees himself surrounded by forms which live and act before him, and into whose innermost being he penetrates. By reason of a peculiar defect in our modern critical faculty, we are inclined to consider the esthetic proto-phenomenon too complexly, too abstractly. For the true poet a metaphor is not a figure of speech, but a vicarious image which ac-

---

[2] [Zuschauer.]
[3] [Schauer.]

tually hovers before him in place of a concept. To him a character is not an aggregate composed of a number of particular traits, but an organic person pressing himself upon his attention, and differing from the similar vision of the painter only in the continuousness of its life and action. Why does Homer describe much more vividly[4] than all the other poets? Because he contemplates[5] much more. We talk so abstractly about poetry, because we are all bad poets. At bottom the esthetic phenomenon is simple: if a man merely has the faculty of seeing perpetual vitality around him, of living continually surrounded by hosts of spirits, he will be a poet. If he but feels the impulse to transform himself and to speak from out the bodies and souls of others, he will be a dramatist.

The Dionysian excitement is able to inspire a whole mass of men with this artistic faculty of seeing themselves surrounded by such a host of spirits with whom they know themselves to be essentially one. This process of the tragic chorus is the *dramatic* protophenomenon: to see yourself transformed before your own eyes, and then to act as if you had actually taken possession of another body and another character. This process stands at the beginning of the development of the drama. Here we have something different from the rhapsodist, who does not unite with his images, but, like the painter, merely views them contemplatively, with detachment. Here we actually have the individual surrendering himself by the fact of his entrance into an alien nature. Moreover, this phenomenon is epidemic in its manifestation: a whole throng experiences this metamorphosis. Hence it is that the dithyramb is essentially different from every other variety of choric song. The virgins, who, laurel branches in hand, solemnly make their way to the temple of Apollo singing a processional hymn, remain what they are and retain their civic names: but the dithyrambic chorus is a chorus of transformed beings, whose civic past and social position are totally forgotten. They have become the timeless servants of their god, living apart from all the life of the community. Every other kind of choric lyric of the Hellenes is nothing but an enormous intensification of the Apollonian unit-singer: while in the dithyramb we have a community of unconscious actors, who mutually regard themselves as transformed among one another.

This enchantment is the prerequisite for all dramatic art. Under its spell the Dionysian reveler sees himself as a satyr, *and as satyr he in turn*

---

4 [Anschaulicher.]
5 [Anschaut.]

beholds the god, that is, in his transformation he sees a new vision outside him as the Apollonian consummation of his own state. With this new vision the drama completes itself.

According to this view, we must understand Greek tragedy as the Dionysian chorus, disburdening itself again and again in an Apollonian image-world. The choric parts, therefore, with which tragedy is interlaced, are in a sense the maternal womb of the entire so-called dialogue, that is, of the whole stage-world, of the drama proper. In several successive outbursts this primal basis of tragedy releases this vision of the drama, which is a dream-phenomenon throughout, and, as such, epic in character: on the other hand, however, as the objectification of a Dionysian state, it represents not the Apollonian redemption in appearance, but, conversely, the dissolution of the individual and his unification with primordial existence. And so the drama becomes the Apollonian embodiment of Dionysian perceptions and influences, and therefore separates itself by a tremendous gap from the epic.

The *chorus* of the Greek tragedy, the symbol of the collectively excited Dionysian throng, thus finds its full explanation in our conception. Accustomed as we were to the function performed by our modern stage chorus, especially an operatic one, we could never comprehend why the tragic chorus of the Greeks should be older, more primitive, indeed, more important than the "action" proper—as has been so plainly declared by the voice of tradition; whereas, furthermore, we could not reconcile with this traditional primacy and primitiveness the fact that the chorus was composed only of humble, attendant beings—indeed, in the beginning, only of goatlike satyrs; and, finally, there remained the riddle of the orchestra before the scene. We have at last realized that the scene, together with the action, was fundamentally and originally thought of only as a *vision*, that the only reality is just the chorus, which of itself generates the vision and celebrates it with the entire symbolism of dancing, music, and speech. In the vision, this chorus beholds its lord and master Dionysus, and so it is forever a chorus that *serves*; it sees how he, the god, suffers and glorifies himself, and therefore does not itself *act*. But though its attitude towards the god is throughout the attitude of ministration, this is nevertheless the highest, that is, the Dionysian, expression of *Nature*, and therefore, like Nature herself in a state of transport, the chorus utters oracles and wise sayings: as *fellow-sufferer* it is at the same time the *sage* who proclaims truth from out the heart of Nature. Thus, then, originates the fantastic figure, seemingly so discordant, of the wise and inspired satyr, who is at the same time "the dumb man" in contrast to the god: who is the image of Nature and her strongest impulses, the very symbol of Nature, and at the same time the *proclaimer* of her art and vision: musician, poet, dancer, and visionary united in one person.

In accordance with this view, and with tradition, *Dionysus*, the proper stage-hero and focus of vision, is in the remotest period of tragedy not at first actually present, but is only so imagined, which means that tragedy is originally only "chorus" and not "drama." Later on the attempt is made to present the god as real and to display the visionary figure together with its aura of splendor before the eyes of all; here the "drama," in the narrow sense of the term, begins. The dithyrambic chorus is now assigned the task of exciting the minds of the audience to such a pitch of Dionysian frenzy, that, when the tragic hero appears on the stage, they do not see in him an unshapely man wearing a mask, but they see a visionary figure, born as it were of their own ecstasy. Picture Admetus, sunk in profound meditation about his lately departed wife, Alcestis, and quite consuming himself in fancied contemplation. Suddenly the veiled figure of a woman, resembling her in form and gait, is led towards him. Picture his sudden trembling anxiety, his excited comparisons, his instinctive conviction —and we shall have a sensation comparable to that with which the dionysiacally excited spectator saw approaching on the stage, the god with whose sufferings he has already become identified. Involuntarily, he transferred the whole image of the god, fluttering magically before his soul, to this masked figure and resolved its reality as it were into a phantasmal unreality. This is the Apollonian dream-state, in which the world of day is veiled, and a new world, clearer, more intelligible, more vivid and yet more shadowy than the old, is, by a perpetual transformation, born and reborn before our eyes. Accordingly we recognize in tragedy a complete stylistic opposition: the language, color, flexibility and movement of the dialogue fall apart into two entirely separate realms of expression, into the Dionysian lyrics of the chorus on the one hand, and the Apollonian dream-world of the scene on the other. The Apollonian appearances, in which Dionysus objectifies himself, are no longer "ein ewiges Meer, ein wechselnd Weben, ein glühend Leben," [6] as is the music of the chorus. They are no longer those forces merely felt, but not condensed into a picture, by which the inspired votary of Dionysus divines the proxim-

---

[6] [An eternal sea, A weaving, flowing, Life, all glowing. *Faust*, Bayard Taylor's Trans.]

ity of his god. Now the clearness and firmness of epic form speak to him from the scene; now Dionysus no longer speaks through forces, but as an epic hero, almost with the tongue of Homer.

9

Whatever rises to the surface in the dialogue of the Apollonian part of Greek tragedy, appears simple, transparent, beautiful. In this sense the dialogue is a reflection of the Hellene, whose nature reveals itself in the dance, because in the dance while the greatest energy is merely potential, it nevertheless betrays itself in the flexibility and exuberance of movement. The language of the Sophoclean heroes, for instance, surprises us so much by its Apollonian precision and clarity, that we at once think we see into the innermost recesses of their being, not a little astounded that the way thereto is so short. But let us, for the moment, disregard the character of the hero which rises to the surface and grows visible—and which at bottom is nothing but the light-picture cast on a dark wall, that is, appearance through and through. Instead, let us enter into the myth which is projected in these bright mirrorings. We shall suddenly experience a phenomenon which has an inverse relation to one familiar in optics. When, after trying hard to look straight at the sun, we turn away blinded, we have dark-colored spots before our eyes as restoratives, so to speak; while, reversing the colors, those light-picture phenomena of the Sophoclean hero,—in short, the Apollonian of the mask,—are the inevitable consequences of a glance into the secret and terrible things of nature. They are shining spots intended to heal the eye which dire night has seared. Only in this sense can we hope to grasp the true meaning of the serious and significant idea of "Greek cheerfulness"; while no matter where we turn at the present time we encounter the false notion that this cheerfulness results from a state of unendangered comfort.

The most sorrowful figure of the Greek stage, the unfortunate Œdipus, is conceived by Sophocles as the type of the noble man who despite his wisdom is fated to error and misery, but who nevertheless, through his extraordinary sufferings, ultimately exerts a magical, healing effect on all around him, which continues even after his death. The noble man does not sin; this is what the profound poet would tell us. All laws, all natural order, yea, the moral world itself, may be destroyed through his action, but through this very action there is brought into play a higher magic circle of influences which build up a new world on the ruins of the old. This is what the poet, in so far as he is at the same time a religious thinker, wishes to tell us: as poet, he first of all discloses to us a wonderfully complicated legal mystery, which slowly, link by link, the judge to his own destruction unravels. The truly Hellenic delight in this dialectical resolution is so great that a touch of surpassing cheerfulness is thereby communicated to the whole play. This touch everywhere softens the edge of the horrible presuppositions of the plot. In the *Œdipus at Colonus* we find this same cheerfulness, only infinitely transfigured. In contrast to the aged king, burdened with an excess of misery, whose relation to all that befalls him is solely that of a sufferer, we have here a supramundane cheerfulness, descending from a divine sphere and making us feel that in his purely passive attitude the hero achieves his highest activity, whose influence extends far beyond his life, while his earlier conscious thought and striving led him only to passivity. Thus, the legal knot of the Œdipus fable, which to mortal eyes appears impossibly complicated, is slowly unraveled—and at this divine counterpart of dialectic we are filled with a profound human joy. If this explanation does justice to the poet, it may still be asked whether the content of the myth is thereby exhausted; and here it becomes evident that the entire conception of the poet is nothing but the light-picture which, after our glance into the abyss, healing nature holds up to our eyes. Œdipus, murderer of his father, husband of his mother, solver of the riddle of the Sphinx! What is the significance of the mysterious triad of these deeds of destiny? There is, especially in Persia, a primitive popular belief that a wise Magian can be born only of incest. With the riddle-solving and mother-marrying Œdipus in mind, we must immediately interpret this to the effect that wherever by some prophetic and magical power the boundary of the present and future, the inflexible law of individuation and, in general, the intrinsic spell of nature, are broken, an extraordinary counternaturalness—in this case, incest—must have preceded as a cause; for how else could one force nature to surrender her secrets but by victoriously opposing her by means of the Unnatural? This is the secret which I see involved in the awful triad of the destiny of Œdipus; the very man who solves the riddle of nature—that doubly-constituted Sphinx—must also, as the murderer of his father and husband of his mother, break the holiest laws of nature. Indeed, it seems as if the myth were trying to whisper into our ears the fact that wisdom, especially Dionysian wisdom, is an unnatural abomination; that whoever, through his own knowledge, plunges nature into an abyss of annihilation, must also expect to experience the dissolution of nature in himself. "The sharpness of wisdom turns upon the sage: wisdom is a crime against nature": such are the terrible expressions the myth cries out to us. But the Hellenic poet, like a sunbeam, touches the sublime and terrible Memnonian statue of the myth, and suddenly it begins to sound—in Sophoclean melodies.

Let me now contrast the glory of passivity with the glory of activity which illuminates the *Prometheus* of Æschylus. What Æschylus the thinker had to tell us here, but which as a poet he only allows us to surmise through his symbolic picture, the youthful Goethe has known how to reveal to us in the bold words of his Prometheus:—

> "Hier sitz' ich, forme Menschen
> Nach meinem Bilde,
> Ein Geschlecht, das mir gleich sei,
> Zu leiden, zu weinen,
> Zu geniessen und zu freuen sich,
> Und dein nicht zu achten,
> Wie ich!" [7]

Man, rising to the level of the Titans, acquires his culture by himself, and compels the gods to ally themselves with him, because in his self-sufficient wisdom he holds in his hands their existence and their limitations. The most wonderful thing, however, in this Prometheus fable, which according to its fundamental conception is an essential hymn of impiety, is the profound Æschylean yearning for *justice*. The infinite tragedy of the bold "individual" on the one hand, and the divine necessity and premonition of a twilight of the gods on the other, the force in these two worlds of suffering operating to produce reconciliation, metaphysical oneness—all this strongly suggests the central and main position of the Æschylean view of the world, which sees Moira as eternal justice enthroned over gods and men. Lest we be surprised at the astounding boldness with which Æschylus weighs the Olympian world in his scales of justice, we must always keep in mind that the thinking Greek had an immovably firm substratum of metaphysical thought in his mysteries, and that all his fits of skepticism could be vented upon the Olympians. When he thought of these

---

[7] ["Here I sit, forming mankind
   In my own image,
   A race resembling me—
   To sorrow, to weep,
   To taste, to have pleasure,
   And to have no need of thee,
   Even as I!"]

deities, the Greek artist in particular had an obscure feeling of *mutual* dependency: and it is precisely in the Prometheus of Æschylus that this feeling is symbolized. The Titanic artist discovered in himself a bold confidence in his ability to create men and at least destroy the gods. He might do this by his superior wisdom, for which, to be sure, he had to atone by eternal suffering. The splendid "I can" of the great genius bought cheaply even at the price of eternal suffering, the stern pride of the artist: this is the essence and soul of Æschylean poetry, while Sophocles in his Œdipus strikes up as prelude the triumphal chant of the *saint*. But even this interpretation which Æschylus has given to the myth does not reveal the astounding depth of its terror. As a matter of fact, the artist's delight in unfolding, the gayety of artistic creation bidding defiance to all calamity, is actually a shining stellar and nebular image reflected in a black sea of sadness. The story of Prometheus is an original possession of the entire Aryan race, and is documentary evidence of its capacity for the profoundly tragic. Indeed, it is not entirely improbable that this myth has the same characteristic significance for the Aryan genius that the myth of the fall of man has for the Semitic, and that the two are related like brother and sister. The presupposition of the Promethean myth is the transcendent value which a naïve humanity attaches to *fire* as the true palladium of every rising culture. That man, however, should not receive this fire only as a gift from heaven, in the form of the igniting lightning or the warming sunshine, but should, on the contrary, be able to control it at will—this appeared to the reflective primitive man as sacrilege, as robbery of the divine nature. And thus the first philosophical problem at once causes a painful, irreconcilable antagonism between man and God, and puts as it were a mass of rock at the gate of every culture. The best and highest that men can acquire they must obtain by a crime, and then they must in turn endure its consequences, namely, the whole flood of sufferings and sorrows with which the offended divinities *must* requite the nobly aspiring race of man. It is a bitter thought, which, by the *dignity* it confers on crime, contrasts strangely with the Semitic myth of the fall of man, in which curiosity, deception, weakness in the face of temptation, wantonness,—in short, a whole series of preëminently feminine passions,—were regarded as the origin of evil. What distinguishes the Aryan conception is the sublime view of *active sin* as the essential Promethean virtue, and the discovery of the ethical basis of pessimistic tragedy in the *justification* of human evil—of human guilt as well as of the suffering incurred thereby. The pain implicit in the very structure of things—which the contemplative Aryan is not disposed to explain away—the antagonism in the heart of the world, manifests itself to him as a medley of different worlds, for instance, a Divine and a human world, both of which are in the right individually, but which, because they exist separately side by side, must suffer for that very individuation. In the heroic effort towards universality made by the individual, in his attempt to penetrate beyond the bounds of individuation and become himself the *one* world-being, he experiences in himself the primordial contradiction concealed in the essence of things, that is, he trespasses and he suffers. Accordingly crime[8] is understood by the Aryans to be masculine, sin[9] by the Semites to be feminine; just as the original crime is committed by man, the original sin by woman. Besides, as the witches' chorus says:

"Wir nehmen das nicht so genau:
Mit tausend Schritten macht's die Frau;
Doch wie sie auch sich eilen kann
Mit einem Sprunge macht's der Mann." [10]

He who understands this innermost core of the Prometheus myth—namely, the necessity for crime imposed on the titanically striving individual—will at once feel the un-Apollonian element in this pessimistic representation. For Apollo seeks to calm individual beings precisely by drawing boundary lines between them, and by again and again, with his requirements of self-knowledge and self-control, recalling these bounds to us as the holiest laws of the universe. However, in order that this Apollonian tendency might not congeal the form to Egyptian rigidity and coldness, in order that the effort to prescribe to the individual wave its path and compass might not ruin the motion of the entire lake, the high tide of the Dionysian tendency destroyed from time to time all those little circles in which the one-sided Apollonian "will" sought to confine the Hellenic world. The suddenly swelling Dionysian tide then takes the separate little wave-mountains of individuals on its back, just as the brother of Prometheus, the Titan Atlas, does with the earth. This Titanic impulse, to become as it were the Atlas of all individuals, and on broad shoulders to

---

[8] [*Der* Frevel.]
[9] [*Die* Sünde.]
[10] [We do not measure with such care:
Woman in thousand steps is there,
But howsoe'er she hasten may,
Man in one leap has cleared the way.
Faust, Bayard Taylor's Trans.]

bear them higher and higher, farther and farther, is what the Promethean and the Dionysian have in common. In this respect the Æschylean Prometheus is a Dionysian mark, while in the aforementioned profound yearning for justice, Æschylus betrays to the intelligent eye his paternal descent from Apollo, the god of individuation, the god who sets the boundaries of justice. And so the double personality of the Æschylean Prometheus, his conjoint Dionysian and Apollonian nature, might be thus expressed in an abstract formula: "Whatever exists is alike just and unjust, and in both cases equally justified."

"Das ist deine Welt! Das heisst eine Welt!" [11]

10

The tradition is undisputed that Greek tragedy in its earliest form had for its sole theme the sufferings of Dionysus, and that for a long time the only stage-hero was simply Dionysus himself. With equal confidence, however, we can assert that, until Euripides, Dionysus never once ceased to be the tragic hero; that in fact all the celebrated figures of the Greek Stage—Prometheus, Œdipus, etc.—are but masks of this original hero, Dionysus. There is godhead behind all these masks; and that is the one essential cause of the typical "ideality," so often wondered at, of these celebrated characters. I know not who it was maintained that all individuals as such are comic and consequently untragic: whence we might infer that the Greeks in general *could* not endure individuals on the tragic stage. And they really seem to have felt this: as, in general, we may note in the Platonic distinction, so deeply rooted in the Hellenic nature, of the "idea" in contrast to the "eidolon," or image. Using Plato's terms we should have to speak of the tragic figures of the Hellenic stage somewhat as follows: the one truly real Dionysus appears in a variety of forms, in the mask of a fighting hero and entangled, as it were, in the net of the individual will. In the latter case the visible god talks and acts so as to resemble an erring, striving, suffering individual. That, generally speaking, he *appears* with such epic precision and clarity is the work of the dream-reading Apollo, who through this symbolic appearance indicates to the chorus its Dionysian state. In reality, however, and behind this appearance, the hero is the suffering Dionysus of the mysteries, the god experiencing in himself the agonies of individuation, of whom wonderful myths tell that as a boy he was torn to pieces by the Titans and has been worshiped in this state as Zagreus: whereby

---

[11] [There is thy world, and what a world!—*Faust*.]

is intimated that this dismemberment, the properly Dionysian *suffering*, is like a transformation into air, water, earth, and fire, that we are therefore to regard the state of individuation as the origin and prime cause of all suffering, as something objectionable in itself. From the smile of this Dionysus sprang the Olympian gods, from his tears sprang man. In this existence as a dismembered god, Dionysus possesses the dual nature of a cruel barbarized demon and a mild, gentle-hearted ruler. But the hope of the epopts looked towards a new birth of Dionysus, which we must now in anticipation conceive as the end of individuation. It was for this coming third Dionysus that the epopts' stormy hymns of joy resounded. And it is this hope alone that casts a gleam of joy upon the features of a world torn asunder and shattered into individuals: as is symbolized in the myth of Demeter, sunk in eternal sorrow, who *rejoices* again only when told that she may *once more* give birth to Dionysus. This view of things already provides us with all the elements of a profound and pessimistic contemplation of the world, together with the *mystery doctrine of tragedy:* the fundamental knowledge of the oneness of everything existent, the conception of individuation as the prime cause of evil, and of art as the joyous hope that the bonds of individuation may be broken in augury of a restored oneness.

We have already pointed out that the Homeric epos is the poem of Olympian culture, in which this culture has sung its own song of victory over the terrors of the war of the Titans. Under the predominating influence of tragic poetry, these Homeric myths are now born anew; and this metempsychosis reveals that in the meantime the Olympian culture also has been conquered by a still deeper view of things. The insolent Titan Prometheus has announced to his Olympian tormentor that some day the greatest danger will menace his rule, unless Zeus ally with him in time. In Æschylus we perceive the terrified Zeus, fearful of his end, allying himself with the Titan. Thus, the former age of the Titans is once more recovered from Tartarus and brought to the light of day. The philosophy of wild and naked nature beholds with the frank, undissembling gaze of truth the myths of the Homeric world as they dance past: they turn pale, they tremble under the piercing glance of this goddess—till the powerful fist of the Dionysian artist forces them into the service of the new deity. Dionysian truth takes over the entire domain of myth as the symbolism of *its* knowledge. This it makes known partly in the public cult of tragedy and partly in the secret celebration of the dramatic mysteries, but always in the old mythical garb. What power was it that freed

Prometheus from his vultures and transformed the myth into a vehicle of Dionysian wisdom? It is the Heracleian power of music: which, having reached its highest manifestation in tragedy, can invest myths with a new and most profound significance. This we have already characterized as the most powerful function of music. For it is the fate of every myth to creep by degrees into the narrow limits of some alleged historical reality, and to be treated by some later generation as a unique fact with historical claims: and the Greeks were already fairly on the way to restamp the whole of their mythical juvenile dream sagaciously and arbitrarily into a historico-pragmatical *juvenile history*. For this is the way in which religions are wont to die out: when under the stern, intelligent eyes of an orthodox dogmatism, the mythical premises of a religion are systematized as a sum total of historical events; when one begins apprehensively to defend the credibility of the myths, while at the same time one opposes any continuation of their natural vitality and growth; when, accordingly, the feeling for myth perishes, and its place is taken by the claim of religion to historical foundations. This dying myth was now seized by the new-born genius of Dionysian music; and in these hands it flourished yet again, with colors such as it had never yet displayed, with a fragrance that awakened a longing anticipation of a metaphysical world. After this final effulgence it collapses, its leaves wither, and soon the mocking Lucians of antiquity catch at the discolored and faded flowers carried away by the four winds. Through tragedy the myth attains its most vital content, its most expressive form; it rises once more like a wounded hero, and its whole excess of strength, together with the philosophic calm of the dying, burns in its eyes with a last powerful gleam.

What didst thou mean, O impious Euripides, in seeking once more to subdue this dying one to your service? Under thy ruthless hands it died: and then thou madest use of counterfeit, masked myth, which like the ape of Heracles could but trick itself out in the old finery. And as myth died in thy hands, so too died the genius of music; though thou didst greedily plunder all the gardens of music—thou didst attain but a counterfeit, masked music. And as thou hast forsaken Dionysus, Apollo hath also forsaken thee; rouse up all the passions from their haunts and conjure them into thy circle, sharpen and whet thy sophistical dialectic for the speeches of thy heroes—thy very heroes have but counterfeit, masked passions, and utter but counterfeit, masked words.

11

Greek tragedy met an end different from that of her older sister arts: she died by suicide, in consequence of an irreconcilable conflict. Accordingly she died tragically, while all the others passed away calmly and beautifully at a ripe old age. If it be consonant with a happy natural state to take leave of life easily, leaving behind a fair posterity, the closing period of these older arts exhibits such a happy natural state: slowly they sink from sight, and before their dying eyes already stand their fairer progeny, who impatiently, with a bold gesture, lift up their heads. But when Greek tragedy died, there rose everywhere the deep feeling of an immense void. Just as the Greek sailors in the time of Tiberius once heard upon a lonesome island the thrilling cry, "Great Pan is dead": so now through the Hellenic world there sounded the grievous lament: "Tragedy is dead! Poetry itself has perished with her! Away with you, ye pale, stunted epigones! Away to Hades, that ye may for once eat your fill of the crumbs of your former masters!"

And when after this death a new Art blossomed forth which revered tragedy as her ancestress and mistress, it was observed with horror that she did indeed bear the features of her mother, but that they were the very features the latter had exhibited in her long death-struggle. It was *Euripides* who fought this death-struggle of tragedy; the later art is known as the *New Attic Comedy*. In it the degenerate form of tragedy lived on as a monument of its painful and violent death.

This connection helps to explain the passionate attachment that the poets of the New Comedy felt for Euripides; so that we are no longer surprised at the wish of Philemon, who would have let himself be hanged at once, merely that he might visit Euripides in the lower world: if he could only be certain that the deceased still had possession of his reason. But if we desire, as briefly as possible, and without claiming to say anything exhaustive, to characterize what Euripides has in common with Menander and Philemon, and what appealed to them so strongly as worthy of imitation, it is sufficient to say that Euripides brought the *spectator* upon the stage. He who has perceived the material out of which the Promethean tragic writers prior to Euripides formed their heroes, and how remote from their purpose it was to bring the true mask of reality on the stage, will also be able to explain the utterly opposite tendency of Euripides. Through him the average man forced his way from the spectators' benches on to the stage itself; the mirror in which formerly only grand and bold traits were represented now showed the painful fidelity that conscientiously reproduces even the abortive outlines of nature. Odysseus, the typical Hellene of the older art, now sank, in the hands of the new poets, to the figure of the Graeculus, who, as the good-naturedly cunning house-slave, henceforth occupies the center of dramatic interest. What Euripides claims credit for in Aristophanes' *Frogs*, namely, that his household medicines have freed tragic art from its pompous corpulency, is apparent above all in his tragic heroes. The spectator now actually saw and heard his double on the Euripidean stage, and rejoiced that he could talk so well. But this joy was not all: you could even learn of Euripides how to speak. He prides himself upon this in his contest with Æschylus: from him the people have learned how to observe, debate, and draw conclusions according to the rules of art and with the cleverest sophistries. In general, through this revolution of the popular speech, he had made the New Comedy possible. For henceforth it was no longer a secret, how—and with what wise maxims—the commonplace was to express itself on the stage. Civic mediocrity, on which Euripides built all his political hopes, was now given a voice, while heretofore the demigod in tragedy and the drunken satyr, or demiman, in comedy, had determined the character of the language. And so the Aristophanean Euripides prides himself on having portrayed the common, familiar, everyday life and activities of the people, about which all are qualified to pass judgment. If now the entire populace philosophizes, manages land and goods and conducts law-suits with unheard-of circumspection, the glory is all his, together with the splendid results of the wisdom with which he has inoculated the rabble.

It was to a populace thus prepared and illuminated that that New Comedy could now address itself, of which Euripides had become as it were the chorus-master; only that this time the chorus of spectators had to be trained. As soon as this chorus was trained to sing in the Euripidean key, there arose that drama which resembles a game of chess—the New Comedy, with its perpetual triumphs of cunning and artfulness. But Euripides—the chorus-master—was still praised continually: indeed, people would have killed themselves in order to learn still more from him, if they had not known that tragic poets were quite as dead as tragedy. But with that death the Hellene had given up his belief in immortality; not only his belief in an ideal past, but also his belief in an ideal future. The words of the well-known epitaph, "frivolous and capricious as an old man," also suit senile Hellenism. The passing moment, wit, levity, and caprice are its highest deities; the fifth estate, that of the slaves, now comes into power, at least in sentiment: and if we may still speak at all of "Greek cheerfulness," it is the cheerfulness of the slave who has nothing of consequence to be responsible for, nothing great to strive for, and who cannot value anything in the past or future higher than the present. It was this semblance of "Greek cheerfulness" which so aroused the deep-minded and formidable natures of the first four centuries of the Christian era: this womanish flight from seriousness and terror, this craven satisfaction with easy enjoyment, seemed to them not only contemptible, but a specifically anti-Christian sentiment. And to influence of that sentiment we must ascribe the fact that the conception of Greek antiquity, which endured for centuries, preserved with almost unconquerable persistency that feverish hue of cheerfulness—as if there had never been a Sixth Century with its birth of tragedy, its Mysteries, its Pythagoras and Heraclitus, as if the very artworks of that great period did not at all exist, though these phenomena can hardly be explained as having originated in any such senile and slavish love of existence and cheerfulness, and though they indicate as the source of their being an altogether different conception of the world.

The assertion made above, that Euripides brought the spectator on the stage that he might better qualify him to pass judgment on the drama, makes it appear as if the old or tragic art had always been in a false relation to the spectator; and one might be tempted to extol as an advance over Sophocles the radical tendency of Euripides to produce a proper relation between art-work and public. But "public," after all, is only a word. In no sense is it a homogeneous and constant quantity. Why should the artist be bound to accommodate himself to a power whose strength lies merely in numbers? And if, by virtue of his endowments and aspirations, he should feel himself superior to every one of these spectators, how should he feel greater respect for the collective expression of all these subordinate capacities than for the relatively highest-endowed individual spectator? In truth, if ever a Greek artist throughout a long life treated his public with arrogance and self-sufficiency, it was Euripides. When the rabble threw themselves at his feet, he openly and with sublime defiance attacked his own tendency, the very tendency with which he had won over the masses. If this genius had had the slightest respect for the noise the mob makes, he would have broken down long before the middle of his career beneath the heavy blows of his own failures. These considerations make it clear that our formula—namely, that Euripides brought the spectator on the stage in order to make him truly competent to pass judgment—was but a provisional one, and that therefore we must penetrate more deeply to understand his tendency. Conversely, it is known beyond any question that Æschylus and Sophocles during the whole of their lives, and indeed, long after their deaths, were in complete possession of the people's favor, and that therefore in the case of these fore-runners of Euripides there was never any question of a false relation between art-work and public. What was it then that thus forcibly drove this artist, so richly endowed, so constantly impelled to production, from the path warmed by the sun of the greatest names in poetry and covered by the cloudless heaven of popular favor? What strange consideration for the spectator led him to oppose the spectator? How could he, out of too great a respect for his public—despise his public?

Euripides—and this is the solution of the riddle just propounded—undoubtedly felt himself, as a poet, superior to the masses in general; but to two of his spectators he did not feel superior. He brought the masses upon the stage; and these two spectators he revered as the only competent judges and masters of his art. Complying with their directions and admonitions, he transferred the entire world of sentiments, passions, and experiences, hitherto present at every festival representation as the invisible chorus on the spectators' benches, into the souls of his stage-heroes. He yielded to their demands, too, when for these new characters he sought out a new language and a new accent. Only in their voices could he hear any conclusive verdict on his work, and also the cheering promise of triumph when he found himself as usual condemned by the public judgment.

Of these two spectators, one is—Euripides himself, Euripides *as thinker*, not as poet. It might be said of him, as of Lessing, that his copious fund of *critical* talent, if it did not create, at least constantly stimulated a corresponding and productive *artistic* impulse. With this faculty, with all the clarity and dexterity of his critical temper, Euripides had sat in the theater and striven to recognize in the masterpieces of his great predecessors, as in faded paintings, feature after feature, line after line. And here he had experienced something which any one initiated in the deeper secrets of Æschylean tragedy might have foretold. He observed something incommensurable in every feature and in every line of the tragedy, a certain deceptive distinctness and at the same time a mysterious depth, almost an infinitude, of background. Even the clearest figure always had a comet's tail attached to it, which seemed to suggest the uncertain, the nebulous. A similar twilight shrouded the structure of the drama, especially the element of the function of the chorus. And how dubious remained the solution of the ethical problems! How questionable the treatment of the myths! How unequal the distribution of good and bad fortune! In the very language of the Old Tragedy there was much that was objectionable to him, or at least puzzling; especially he encountered too much pomp for simple affairs, too many tropes and monstrous expressions to suit the plainness of the characters. So he sat in the theater, pondering uneasily, and as a spectator he confessed to himself that he did not understand his great predecessors. If, however, it was his opinion that the understanding was the essential root of all enjoyment and creation, he must inquire, he must look about to see whether any one else had the same opinion, and whether they also felt this incommensurability. But most people, and among them the finest individuals, answered him only with a distrustful smile; while none could explain why the great masters were still in the right despite his scruples and objections. And in this state of torment, he found *that other spectator*, who did not comprehend tragedy, and therefore did not esteem it. Allied with him, in solitary state, he could now venture to begin the terrific struggle against the art of Æschylus and Sophocles—not as a polemist, but as a dramatic poet, who would oppose *his own* conception of tragedy to the traditional one.

12

Before we name this other spectator, let us pause here a moment in order to recall to our minds our own previously described impression of the discordant and incommensurable elements in the genius of Æschylean tragedy. Let us think of our own surprise at the *chorus* and the *tragic hero* of that tragedy, neither of which we could reconcile with our own customs any more than with tradition—till we rediscovered this duality itself as the origin and essence of Greek tragedy, as the expression of two interwoven artistic impulses, *the Apollonian and the Dionysian.*

To separate this primitive and all-powerful Dionysian element from tragedy, and to construct a new and purified form on the basis of an un-Dionysian art, morality, and conception of the world—this is the tendency of Euripides as it is now clearly revealed to us.

In the evening of his life, Euripides himself composed a myth in which he urgently propounded to his contemporaries the question as to the value and significance of this tendency. Is the Dionysian entitled to exist at all? Should it not be forcibly uprooted from Hellenic soil? Certainly, the poet tells us, if it were only possible: but the god Dionysus is too powerful; his most intelligent adversary—like Pentheus in the *Bacchae*—is unwittingly enchanted by him, and in this enchantment runs to meet his fate. The judgment of the two old prophets, Cadmus and Tiresias, seems also to be the judgment of the aged poet: that the reflection of the wisest individuals does not overthrow old popular traditions, nor the perpetually self-propagating worship of Dionysus; that in fact it is to our interest to display at the very least a diplomatically cautious concern in the presence of such strange forces: although there is always the possibility that the god may take offense at such lukewarm participation, and eventually transform the diplomat—in this case Cadmus—into a dragon. This is what we are told by a poet who opposed Dionysus with heroic valor throughout a long life—and who finally ended his career with a glorification of his adversary, and with suicide, like one staggering from giddiness, who, to escape the horrible vertigo he can no longer endure, casts himself from a tower. This tragedy—the *Bacchae*—is a protest against the practicability of his own tendency; but alas, it has already been put into practice! The surprising thing had happened: when the poet recanted, his tendency had already conquered. Dionysus had already been scared from the tragic stage; he had been scared by a demonic power speaking through Euripides. For even Euripides was, in a sense, only a mask: the deity that spoke through him was neither Dionysus nor Apollo. It was an altogether new-born demon. And it was called *Socrates*. Thus we have a new antithesis—the Dionysian and the Socratic; and on that antithesis the art of Greek tragedy was wrecked. In vain does Euripides seek to comfort us by his recantation. It avails not: the most magnificent temple lies in ruins. Of what use is the lamentation of the destroyer, of what use his confession that it was the most beautiful of all temples? And even if Euripides has been punished by being changed into a dragon by the art-critics of all ages —who could be content with so miserable a compensation?

Let us now examine this *Socratic* tendency with which Euripides combated and vanquished Æschylean tragedy.

We must first ask ourselves, what could be the aim of the Euripidean design, which, in its most ideal form, would wish to base drama exclusively on the un-Dionysian? What other form of drama still remained, if it was not to be born of the womb of music, in the mysterious twilight of the Dionysian? Only *the dramatized epos:* in which Apollonian domain of art the *tragic* effect is of course unattainable. For it is not bound up with the subject-matter of the events represented; indeed, I maintain that it would have been impossible for Goethe in his projected *Nausikaa* to have rendered tragically effective the suicide of the idyllic being, the scene which was to have completed the fifth act. So extraordinary is the power of the epic-Apollonian representation, that before our very eyes it transforms the most terrible things by the joy in appearance and in redemption through appearance. The poet of the dramatized epos cannot blend completely with his pictures any more than the epic rhapsodist can. He is still just the calm, unmoved embodiment of Contemplation whose wide eyes see the picture *before* them. The actor in this dramatized epos still remains fundamentally a rhapsodist: the consecration of the inner dream lies on all his actions, so that he is never wholly an actor.

How, then, is the Euripidean play related to this ideal of the Apollonian drama? Just as the younger rhapsodist is related to the solemn rhapsodist of the old time. In the Platonic *Ion,* the former describes his own nature as follows: "When I am saying anything sad, my eyes fill with tears; when, however, I am saying something awful and terrible, then my hair stands on end with fright and my heart beats quickly." Here we no longer remark anything of the epic absorption in appearance, or of the dispassionate coolness of the true actor, who precisely in his highest activity is wholly appearance and joy in appearance. Euripides is that actor whose heart beats, whose hair stands on end; as Socratic thinker he designs the plan, as passionate actor he executes it. Neither in the designing nor in the execution is he a pure artist. And so the Euripidean drama is a thing both cool and fiery, equally capable of freezing and burning. It is impossible for it to attain the Apollonian effect of the epos, while, on the other hand, it has alienated itself as much as possible from Dionysian elements. Now, in order to develop at all, it requires new stimulants, which can no longer lie within the sphere of the two unique art-impulses, the Apollonian and the Dionysian. These stimulants are cool, paradoxical *thoughts,* replacing Apollonian intuitions—and fiery *passions,* replacing Dionysian ecstasies; and, it may be added, thoughts and passions copied very realistically and in no sense suffused with the atmosphere of art.

Accordingly, having perceived this much, that Euripides did not succeed in establishing the drama exclusively on an Apollonian basis, but rather that his un-Dionysian inclinations deviated into a naturalistic and inartistic tendency, we should now be able to get a nearer view of the character of *esthetic Socratism*, whose supreme law reads about as follows: "To be beautiful everything must be intelligible," as the counterpart to the Socratic identity: "Knowledge is virtue." With this canon in his hands, Euripides measures all the separate elements of the drama—language, characters, dramaturgic structure, and choric music—and corrects them according to his principle. The poetic deficiency and degeneration, which we are so often wont to impute to Euripides in comparison with Sophocles, is for the most part the product of this penetrating critical process, this daring intelligibility. The Euripidean *prologue* may serve as an example of the results of this rationalistic method. Nothing could be more antithetical to the technique of our own stage than the prologue in the drama of Euripides. For a single person to appear at the outset of the play telling us who he is, what precedes the action, what has happened so far, even what will happen in the course of the play, would be condemned by a modern playwright as a willful, inexcusable abandonment of the effect of suspense. We know everything that is going to happen; who cares to wait till it actually does happen?—considering, moreover, that here we do not by any means have the exciting relation of a prophetic dream to a reality taking place later on. But Euripides' speculations took a different turn. The effect of tragedy never depended on epic suspense, on a fascinating uncertainty as to what is to happen now and afterwards: but rather on the great rhetorical-lyric scenes in which the passion and dialectic of the chief hero swelled to a broad and mighty stream. Everything was directed toward pathos, not action: and whatever was not directed toward pathos was considered objectionable. But what interferes most with the hearer's pleasurable satisfaction in such scenes is a missing link, a gap in the texture of the previous history. So long as the spectator has to divine the meaning of this or that person, of the presuppositions of this or that conflict of views and inclinations, his complete absorption in the activities and sufferings of the chief characters is impossible, as is likewise breathless fellow-feeling and fellow-fearing. The Æschylean-Sophoclean tragedy employed the most ingenious devices in the initial scenes to place in the spectator's hands, as if by chance, all the threads necessary for a complete understanding: a trait whereby that noble artistry is approved, which as it were masks the *inevitably* formal element, and makes it appear something accidental. Notwithstanding this, Euripides thought he observed that during these first scenes the spectator was so peculiarly anxious to make out the problem of the previous history, that the poetic beauties and pathos of the exposition were lost to him. Accordingly he put the prologue even before the exposition, and placed it in the mouth of a person who could be trusted: some deity had often as it were to guarantee the particulars of the tragedy to the public, to remove every doubt as to the reality of the myth, just as did Descartes who could prove the reality of the empirical world only by appealing to the truthfulness of God and His inability to utter falsehood. Euripides makes use of this same divine truthfulness once more at the close of his drama, in order to reassure the public as to the future of his heroes; this is the task of the notorious *deus ex machina*. Between this epic retrospect and epic prospect, is placed the dramatico-lyric present, the "drama" as such.

Thus Euripides as a poet is essentially an echo of his own conscious knowledge; and it is precisely on this account that he occupies such a notable position in the history of Greek art. With reference to his critical-productive activity, he must often have felt that he ought to make objective in drama the words at the beginning of the essay of Anaxagoras: "In the beginning all things were mixed together; then came the understanding and created order." Anaxagoras with his "nous" is said to have appeared among philosophers as the only sober person amid a crowd of drunken ones. Euripides may also have conceived his relation to the other tragic poets under a similar figure. As long as the sole ruler and disposer of the universe, the *nous*, remained excluded from artistic activity, things were all mixed together in a primeval chaos. This was what Euripides was obliged to think; and so, as the first "sober" one among them, he was bound to condemn the "drunken" poets. Sophocles said of Æschylus that he did what was right, though he did it unconsciously. This would surely never have been the opinion of Euripides. He would have said, on the contrary, that Æschylus, *because* he created unconsciously, did what was *wrong*. Similarly the divine Plato for the most part speaks but ironically of the creative faculty of the poet, in so far as it is not conscious insight, and places it on a par with the gift of the soothsayer and dream-interpreter. The intimation is that the poet is incapable of composing until he has become unconscious and bereft of reason. Like Plato, Euripides undertook to show to the world the reverse of the "unintelligent" poet; his esthetic principle that "to be beautiful everything must be known" is, as I have said, the parallel to the Socratic, "to be good everything must be known." So that we may consider Euripides as the poet of esthetic Socratism. But Socrates was that *second spectator* who did not comprehend and therefore did not esteem the Old Tragedy; in alliance with him Euripides dared to be the herald of a new art. If it was this then, that destroyed the older tragedy in general, it follows that esthetic Socratism was the fatal principle; but in so far as the struggle is directed against the *Dionysian element* in the older tragedy, we may recognize in Socrates the opponent of Dionysus. He is the new Orpheus rebelling against Dionysus, and although he is destined to be torn to pieces by the Maenads of the Athenian court, yet he puts to flight the overpowerful god himself. The latter, you will recall, fleeing from Lycurgus, the King of Edoni, sought refuge in the depths of the ocean—or, in this case, in the mystical flood of a secret cult which gradually overran the earth.

13

That Socrates was closely related to the tendency of Euripides did not escape the notice of contemporaneous antiquity. The most eloquent expression of this felicitous insight was the story current in Athens that Socrates used to help Euripides in poetizing. Whenever an occasion arose to enumerate the popular agitators of the day, the adherents of the "good old times" would mention both names in the same breath. To the influence of Socrates and Euripides they attributed the fact that the old Marathonian stalwart capacity of body and soul was being sacrificed more and more to a dubious enlightenment that involved the progressive degeneration of the physical and mental powers. It is in this tone, half indignant, half contemptuous, that Aristophanic comedy is wont to speak of both of them—to the consternation of modern men, who are quite willing to give up Euripides, but who cannot help being amazed that Socrates should appear in the comedies of Aristophanes as the first and leading *sophist*, as the mirror and epitome of all sophistical tendencies. The result of their bewilderment is that they give themselves the unique consolation of putting Aristophanes himself in the pillory, as a dissolute, lying Alcibiades of poetry. Without here defending the profound insight of Aristophanes against such attacks, I shall now continue to show, by means of the sentiments of the time, the close connection between Socrates and Euripides. With this in view, we must remember particularly that Socrates, as an opponent of tragic art, refrained from patronizing tragedy, but that he appeared among the spectators only when a new play of Euripides was to be performed. Most famous of all, however, is the juxtaposition of the two names by the Delphic oracle, which designated Socrates as the wisest of men, but at the same time decided that the second prize in the contest of wisdom belonged to Euripides.

Sophocles was named third in order of rank; he who could pride himself that, as compared with Æschylus, he did what was right, and moreover did so because he *knew* what the right was. Evidently it is merely the degree of clearness of this *knowledge* which distinguishes these three men in common as the three "knowing ones" of their time.

The most decisive word, however, for this new and unprecedented value set upon knowledge and insight was spoken by Socrates when he found that he was the only one who acknowledged to himself that he *knew nothing*; for in his critical peregrinations through Athens, he called on the greatest statesmen, orators, poets, and artists, and everywhere he discovered the conceit of knowledge. To his astonishment he perceived that all these celebrities were without a proper and sure insight, even with regard to their own professions, and that they practiced them only by instinct. "Only by instinct": with this phrase we touch upon the heart and core of the Socratic tendency. With it Socratism condemns existing art as well as existing ethics. Wherever Socratism turns its searching eyes it sees lack of insight, it sees the force of illusion; and from this lack it infers the essential perversity and objectionableness of existing conditions. From this point onwards, Socrates conceives it as his duty to correct existence; and, with an air of irreverence and superiority, as the precursor of an altogether different culture, art, and morality, he enters single-handed into a world, to touch whose very hem would give us the greatest happiness.

For an extraordinary hesitancy always seizes upon us with regard to Socrates. Again and again we are impelled to ascertain the sense and purpose of the most puzzling phenomenon of antiquity. Who is this that dares single-handed to disown the Greek genius, which, as Homer, Pindar, and Æschylus, as Phidias, as Pericles, as Pythia and Dionysus, as the deepest abyss and the highest height, compels our wondering admiration? What demonic power is this which dares spill this magic draught in the dust? What demigod is this to whom the chorus of spirits of the noblest of mankind must call out: "Weh! Weh!

Du hast sie zerstört, die schöne Welt, mit mächtiger Faust; sie
stürzt, sie zerfällt!" [12]

We are offered a key to the character of Socrates by the wonderful
phenomenon which he calls his daemon. In exceptional circumstances, when his gigantic intellect begins to fail him, he receives a
secure support in the utterances of a divine voice which manifests
itself at such moments. This voice, whenever it comes, always
dissuades. In this utterly abnormal nature instinctive wisdom only
appears in order to *hinder* here and there the progress of conscious
perception. Whereas in all productive men it is instinct that is the
creatively affirmative force, and consciousness that acts critically and
dissuasively; with Socrates it is instinct that becomes critic, and consciousness that becomes creator—a perfect monstrosity *per defectum!*
And we do indeed observe here a monstrous *defectus* of all mystical
aptitude so that Socrates might be called the typical *non-mystic*, in
whom, through a superfoetation, the logical nature is developed, to the
same excessive degree as instinctive wisdom is developed in the
mystic. Unlike his instinct, however, the logic of Socrates was absolutely prevented from turning against itself; in its unimpeded flow
it manifests a native power such as we meet with, to our awe and
surprise, only among the very greatest instinctive forces. Any one
who has experienced even a breath of the divine naïveté and security of the Socratic way of life in the Platonic writings, will also feel
that the enormous driving-wheel of logical Socratism is in motion,
as it were, *behind* Socrates, and that it must be viewed through Socrates as through a shadow. And that he himself had a premonition of
this relationship is apparent from the dignified seriousness with which
he everywhere, even before his judges, insists on his divine calling. It is
really as impossible to refute him here as to approve of his instinct-
disintegrating influence. In view of this indissoluble conflict, when
he had at last been brought before the forum of the Greek state,
there was only one kind of punishment demanded, namely, exile. He
might have been sped across the borders as something thoroughly
enigmatical, inexplicable, and impossible to characterize, and so posterity would never have been justified in charging the Athenians with

---

[12] [Woe! Woe!
  Thou hast it destroyed,
  The beautiful world;
  With powerful fist;
  In ruin 'tis hurled!
    Faust, Bayard Taylor's Trans.]

an ignominious deed. But that the sentence of death, and not mere exile, was pronounced upon him, seems to have been the work of Socrates himself, who encountered the decree with perfect awareness and without the natural fear of death. He met his death with the calmness with which, according to Plato's description, he, last of the revelers, leaves the Symposium at dawn to begin a new day; while his sleepy fellow-banqueters remain behind on the couches and the floor, to dream of Socrates, the true eroticist. *The dying Socrates* became the new ideal of the noble Greek youths,—an ideal they had never yet beheld,—and above all, the typical Hellenic youth, Plato, prostrated himself before this scene with all the burning devotion of his visionary soul.

14

Let us now imagine the one great Cyclops eye of Socrates fixed on tragedy, an eye in which the fine frenzy of artistic enthusiasm had never glowed. To this eye was denied the pleasure of gazing into the Dionysian abysses. For what was it bound to see in the "sublime and greatly lauded" tragic art, as Plato called it? A thing devoid of sense, full of causes apparently without effects, and effects apparently without causes; the whole, moreover, so motley and diversified that though it could not but be repugnant to a thoughtful mind, it was a dangerous incentive for sensitive and irritable souls. We know what was the only kind of poetry he understood: the *Æsopian fable:* and this he favored no doubt with the good-natured acquiescence with which the good honest Gellert sings the praise of poetry in the fable of the bee and the hen:—

> "Du siehst an mir, wozu sie nutzt,
> Dem, der nicht viel Verstand besitzt,
> Die Wahrheit durch ein Bild zu sagen." [13]

But it seemed to Socrates that tragic art did not even "tell the truth": not to mention the fact that it addressed itself to him who has "no great understanding." Consequently, it did not recommend itself to the philosopher: a twofold reason for shunning it. Like Plato, he reckoned it among the seductive arts which portray only the agreeable, not the useful; and hence he required of his disciples abstinence and strict separation from such unphilosophical temptations, with such success that the youthful tragic poet Plato first of all

---

[13] [Through me, you may observe how useful it is to tell the truth to those of no great understanding, by means of a parable.]

burned his poems that he might become a student of Socrates. But where unconquerable natural tendencies struggled against the Socratic maxims, their power, together with the momentum of his mighty character, was still enough to force poetry itself into new and hitherto unknown channels.

An instance of this is the aforesaid Plato, Plato who in condemning tragedy and art in general certainly did not lag behind the naïve cynicism of his master, was nevertheless by sheer artistic necessity constrained to create an art-form which is essentially related to those very forms of art which he repudiated. Plato's main objection to the old art—that it is the imitation of a phantom,[14] and hence belongs to a sphere still lower than the empiric world—could not at all be directed against the new art: and so we find Plato endeavoring to go beyond reality and to represent the idea which underlies this pseudo-reality. But Plato, the thinker, thereby arrived by a roundabout road at the very point where he had always been at home as poet, and from which Sophocles and all the older artists had solemnly protested against that objection. If tragedy had absorbed into itself all the earlier varieties of art, the same might also be said in an unusual sense of the Platonic dialogue, which, a mixture of all the then existent forms and styles, hovers midway between narrative, lyric and drama, between prose and poetry, and so has also broken loose from the older strict law of unity of linguistic form. This tendency was carried still farther by the *Cynic* writers, who in the greatest stylistic medley, oscillating between prose and metrical forms, realized also the literary picture of the "raving Socrates" whom they were wont to represent in real life. The Platonic dialogue was a sort of boat in which the shipwrecked ancient poetry was rescued with all her children: crowded into a narrow space and timidly submissive to the single pilot, Socrates, they now launched forth into a new world, which never tired of looking at the fantastic spectacle of this procession. The fact is that Plato has given to all posterity the prototype of a new art-form, the prototype of the *novel:* which may be described as an infinitely developed Æsop fable, in which poetry holds the same rank with reference to dialectic philosophy as this same philosophy held for many centuries with reference to theology: that is to say, the rank of *ancilla*. This was the new position into which Plato, under the pressure of the daemon-inspired Socrates, forced poetry.

Here *philosophic thought* overgrows art and compels it to cling

---

14 [Scheinbild.]

close to the trunk of dialectic. The *Apollonian* tendency has withdrawn into the shell of logical schematism; just as we noticed something analogous in the case of Euripides (and moreover a transformation of the *Dionysian* into the naturalistic emotion). Socrates, the dialectical hero of the Platonic drama, reminds us of the kindred nature of the Euripidean hero, who must defend his actions with arguments and counter-arguments, and who thereby so often incurs the danger of forfeiting our tragic pity; for who could mistake the *optimistic* element in the essence of dialectics, which celebrates a triumph with every conclusion, and can breathe only in cool clearness and consciousness: the optimistic element, which, having once forced its way into tragedy must gradually pass its Dionysian bounds, and necessarily impel it to self-destruction—even to the death-leap into the bourgeois drama. Let us but realize the consequences of the Socratic maxims: "Virtue is knowledge; man sins only from ignorance; he who is virtuous is happy." In these three fundamental forms of optimism lies the death of tragedy. For the virtuous hero must now be a dialectician; there must now be a necessary, visible connection between virtue and knowledge, between belief and morality. The transcendental justice of Æschylus is now degraded to the superficial and audacious principle of "poetic justice" with its customary *deus ex machina*.

In the light of this new Socratic-optimistic stage-world, what becomes of the *chorus* and, in general, of the entire Dionyso-musical substratum of tragedy? The chorus is something accidental, a readily dispensed-with vestige of the origin of tragedy; while, as a matter of fact, we have seen that the chorus can be understood only as the *cause* of tragedy, and of the tragic in general. This perplexity in regard to the chorus already manifests itself in Sophocles—an important indication that even with him the Dionysian basis of tragedy is already beginning to break down. He no longer dares to entrust to the chorus the main share of the effect, but he limits its sphere to such an extent that it now appears almost coördinate with the actors, just as if it were elevated from the orchestra into the scene: whereby of course its character is completely destroyed, notwithstanding that Aristotle countenances this very theory of the chorus. This alteration in the position of the chorus, which Sophocles at any rate recommended by his practice, and, according to tradition, even by a treatise, is the first step towards its destruction, the phases of which follow one another with alarming rapidity in Euripides, Agathon, and the New Comedy. Optimistic dialectic drives *music* out of tragedy with the scourge of its syllogisms: that is, it destroys the essence of tragedy, which can be interpreted only as a manifestation and illustration of Dionysian states, as the visible symbolizing of music, as the dream-world of Dionysian ecstasy.

If, therefore, we must assume an anti-Dionysian tendency operating even before Socrates, which merely received in him a uniquely great expression, we must not draw back before the question as to what such a phenomenon as that of Socrates indicates: whom in view of the Platonic dialogues we are certainly not entitled to regard as a purely disintegrating, negative force. And though there can be no doubt that the most immediate effect of the Socratic impulse tended to the dissolution of Dionysian tragedy, yet a profound experience in Socrates' own life impels us to ask whether there is *necessarily* only an antagonistic relation between Socratism and art, and whether the birth of an "artistic Socrates" is in general a contradiction in terms.

For that despotic logician had now and then with respect to art the feeling of a gap, a void, a feeling of misgiving, of a possibly neglected duty. As he tells his friends in prison, there often came to him one and the same dream-apparition, which kept constantly repeating to him: "Socrates, practice music." Up to his very last days he comforts himself with the statement that his philosophizing is the highest form of art; he finds it hard to believe that a deity should remind him of the "common, popular music." Finally, when in prison and in order that he may thoroughly unburden his conscience, he consents to practice also this music for which he has but little respect. And in this mood he composes a poem on Apollo and turns a few Æsopian fables into verse. It was something akin to the demonic warning voice which urged him to these practices; it was due to his Apollonian insight that, like a barbaric king, he did not understand the noble image of a god and was in danger of sinning against a deity—through his lack of understanding. The voice of the Socratic dream-vision is the only sign of doubt as to the limits of logic. "Perhaps"—thus he must have asked himself—"what is not intelligible to me is not therefore unintelligible? Perhaps there is a realm of wisdom from which the logician is shut out? Perhaps art is even a necessary correlative of, and supplement to, science?"

15

With reference to these last weighty questions we must now explain how the influence of Socrates (extending to the present moment, indeed, to all futurity) has spread over posterity like an ever-increasing shadow in the evening sun, and how this influence again and again involves a regeneration of *art*—yea, of art already in the most meta-physical, broadest and profoundest sense—and how its own eternity is also a warrant for the eternity of art.

Before this could be perceived, before the intrinsic dependence of every art on the Greeks, from Homer to Socrates, was conclusively demonstrated, we had to have the same experience with regard to these Greeks as the Athenians had with regard to Socrates. Nearly every age and stage of culture has at some time or other sought with deep irritation to free itself from the Greeks, because in their presence everything self-achieved, sincerely admired and apparently quite original, seemed suddenly to lose life and color, to shrink to an abortive copy, even to caricature. And so time after time hearty resentment breaks forth against this presumptuous little nation, which for all time dared to designate everything not native as "barbaric." Who are they, one asks, who, though they have nothing to show but an ephemeral historical splendor, ridiculously restricted institutions, a dubious excellence in their customs, and the stigma attaching to ugly vices, yet lay claim to the dignity and preëminence among peoples to which genius is entitled among the masses? What a pity we have not been fortunate enough to find the cup of hemlock with which we might very simply rid ourselves of such a character: for all the poison which envy, calumny, and rankling resentment created within themselves have not been able to destroy that self-sufficient grandeur! And so one feels ashamed and afraid in the presence of the Greeks, unless one prizes truth above all things; unless one dares acknowledge to one's self this truth, that the Greeks, as charioteers, hold the reins of our own and every other culture, but that almost always chariot and horses are of too poor material and hardly up to the glory of their guides. Unless we acknowledge this, who will deem it sport to run such a team into an abyss which they themselves could clear with the leap of Achilles?

In order to endow Socrates with the dignity of such a leading position, it is enough to recognize in him a type unheard of before him, the type of the *theoretical man*. Our next task will be to obtain an insight into the meaning and purpose of this theoretical man. Like the artist, the theorist finds an infinite satisfaction in the present, and, like the former also, this satisfaction protects him from the practical ethics of pessimism with its lynx eyes shining only in the dark. Whenever the truth is unveiled, the artist will always cling with rapt gaze to whatever still remains veiled after the unveiling; but the theoretical man gets his enjoyment and satisfaction out of the cast-off veil. He finds his highest pleasure in the process of a continuously successful unveiling effected through his own unaided efforts. There would have been no science if it had been concerned only with that *one* naked goddess and nothing else. For then its disciples would have felt like those who wished to dig a hole straight through the earth: each one of them perceives that with his utmost lifelong efforts he can excavate but a very small portion of the enormous depth, and this is filled up again before his eyes by the labors of his successor, so that a third man seems to be doing a sensible thing in selecting a new spot for his attempts at tunneling. Now suppose some one shows conclusively that the antipodal goal cannot be attained thus directly. Who will then still care to toil on in the old depths, unless in the meantime he has learned to content himself with finding precious stones or discovering natural laws? For this reason Lessing, the most honest of theoretical men, boldly said that he cared more for the search after truth than for truth itself: in saying which, he revealed the fundamental secret of science, to the astonishment, and indeed, to the anger of scientists. Well, to be sure, beside this detached perception there stands, with an air of great frankness, if not presumption, a profound *illusion* which first came to birth in the person of Socrates. This illusion consists in the imperturbable belief that, with the clue of logic, thinking can reach to the nethermost depths of being, and that thinking can not only perceive being but even modify it. This sublime metaphysical illusion is added as an instinct to science and again and again leads the latter to its limits, where it must change into *art; which is really the end to be attained by this mechanism.*

If we now look at Socrates in the light of this idea, he appears to us as the first who could not only live, but—what is far greater—also die by the guidance of this instinct of science: and hence the picture of the *dying Socrates,* as the man raised above the fear of death by knowledge and reason, is the sign above the entrance-gate of science reminding every one of its mission, namely, to make existence seem intelligible, and therefore justified: for which purpose, if arguments are not enough, *myth* also must be used, which I have just indicated as the necessary consequence, as the very goal of science.

He who once sees clearly how, after Socrates, the mystagogue of science, one philosophical school succeeds another, like wave upon wave;—how an entirely unforeseen universal development of the thirst for knowledge throughout the cultured world (together with the feeling that the acquisition of knowledge was the specific task of every one highly gifted) led science on to the high sea from which since then it has never been entirely driven. He who sees how through the universality of this movement a common net of thought was for the first time stretched over the entire globe, with prospects, moreover, of conformity to law in an entire solar system;—He who realizes all this, together with the amazingly high pyramid of our contemporary knowledge, cannot fail to see in Socrates the turning-point and vortex of so-called universal history. For if one were to imagine the whole incalculable sum of energy which has been used up by that universal tendency,—used *not* in the service of knowledge, but for the practical, *i.e.*, egotistical ends of individuals and peoples—then probably the instinctive love of life would be so much weakened in general wars of destruction and continual migrations of peoples, that, owing to the practice of suicide, the individual would perhaps feel the last remnant of a sense of duty, similar to that of the Fiji Islander who, as son, strangles his parents and, as friend, his friend: and thus a practical pessimism might even give rise to a horrible ethics of general slaughter out of pity—which, as matter of fact, exists and has existed wherever art in one form or another, especially as science and religion, has not appeared as a remedy for and preventive of that pestilential breath.

As against this practical pessimism, Socrates is the prototype of the theoretical optimist who with his belief in the explicability of the nature of things, attributes to knowledge and perception the power of a universal panacea, and in error sees evil in itself. To penetrate into the depths and to distinguish true perception from error and illusion seemed to the Socratic man the noblest and even the only truly human calling: just as from the time of Socrates onwards the mechanism of making concepts, judgments, and inferences was prized above all other activities as the highest talent and the most admirable gift of nature. Even the sublimest moral acts, the stirrings of pity, of self-sacrifice, of heroism, and that tranquillity of soul, so difficult of attainment, which the Apollonian Greek called Euphrosyne were, by Socrates, and his like-minded successors up to today, derived from the dialectic of knowledge and accordingly were designated as teachable. Any one who has experienced in himself the joy of a Socratic perception, and felt how, in constantly widening circles, it seeks to embrace the entire world of phenomena, will thenceforth find no stimulus urging him to existence more forcible than the desire to complete that conquest, to draw the net impenetrably close. To such a temper the Platonic Socrates then appears as the teacher of an entirely new form of "Greek cheerfulness" and vital happiness, which seeks to express itself in action, and will, for the most part, find that expression in maieutic and pedagogic influences on noble youths, with a view to the ultimate production of genius.

But now science, stimulated by its powerful illusion, hastens irresistibly to its limits, on which its optimism, hidden in the essence of logic, is wrecked. For the periphery of the circle of science has an infinite number of points, and while there is still no telling how this circle can ever be completely measured, yet the noble and gifted man, even before the middle of his career, inevitably comes in contact with those extreme points of the periphery where he stares into the unfathomable. When to his dismay he here sees how logic coils round itself at these limits and finally bites its own tail—then the new form of perception rises to view, namely *tragic perception*, which, in order even to be endured, requires art as protection and remedy.

With eyes strengthened and refreshed by the sight of the Greeks, let us look upon the highest spheres of the world around us. We behold the eagerness of the insatiate optimistic knowledge, of which Socrates is the typical representative, transformed into tragic resignation and the need for art: while, to be sure, this same avidity, in its lower stages, must exhibit itself as inimical to art, and must especially have an inward detestation of Dionyso-tragic art, as was exemplified in the opposition of Socratism to Æschylean tragedy.

Here then, in a mood of agitation, we knock at the gates of the present and the future: will that "transforming" lead to ever-new configurations of genius, and especially of the *music-practicing* Socrates? Will the net of art which is spread over the whole of existence, whether under the name of religion or of science, be knit ever more closely and delicately, or is it destined to be torn to shreds under the restlessly barbaric activity and whirl which calls itself "the present"? Anxious, yet not despairing, we stand apart for a brief space, like spectators who are permitted to be witnesses of these tremendous struggles and transitions. Alas! It is the magic effect of these struggles that he who beholds them must also participate in them!

Benedetto
CROCE

Croce conceives of aesthetics as a general linguistics because its
concern is with all expressive media, all forms of human symbol-
construction, the paradigm of which is language. He thus sets
the outlook of most twentieth-century philosophies of art which
replace the concept of beauty with that of expression, or identify
beauty, as Croce does, with expression.

Art, Croce maintains, is one of the major forms of the human
spirit, the work of spirit in its aesthetical aspect. Spirit manifests
itself as well in a logical and a practical synthesis, the latter
exhibiting itself in the economic and moral activities of man.
Croce refers to these various aspects of spirit as "the circle of
spiritual activity." At the foundation of all knowledge is art, for
intuitions, the stuff of art, precede concepts.

In his analysis of intuition Croce identifies it with expression
and maintains that the externalization of intuition is secondary
to its appearance in the consciousness of the artist. It is on this
ground—that expression is meaningful apart from its embodiment or projection in a work of art—that Croce has been most
severely criticized. The content of expression itself derives from

the impressions which the mind gathers from practical life, i.e., from its impulses, its desires, and its sensory awareness. The intuitions, then, which make up the artist's consciousness are the product of feeling on the one hand and images on the other. These are brought together and fused in the unity of lyrical expression. The artistic integrity of lyrical expression is due to the pervasiveness of feeling in it: because of feeling, an image can become an intuition. With this achievement art becomes a symbol of feeling.

"What gives coherence and unity to the intuition is feeling: the intuition is really such because it represents a feeling, and can only appear from and upon that. Not the idea, but the feeling, is what confers upon art the airy lightness of the symbol: an aspiration enclosed in the circle of a representation—that is art: and in it the aspiration alone stands for the representation, and the representation alone for the aspiration." Croce's position clearly contains the doctrine which has been developed by Susanne Langer: art is a symbol of feeling.

The essay included here is the article on "Aesthetics" from the fourteenth edition of the Encyclopaedia Britannica, which is Croce's most concise presentation of his position. For a fuller discussion, the reader is referred to The Breviary of Aesthetics.

AESTHETICS

FROM *Encyclopaedia Britannica*
(Fourteenth Edition)

If we examine a poem in order to determine what it is that makes us feel it to be a poem, we at once find two constant and necessary elements: a complex of *images*, and a *feeling* that animates them. Let us, for instance, recall a passage learnt at school: Virgil's lines (Aeneid, iii, 294, sqq.), in which Aeneas describes how on hearing that in the country to whose shores he had come the Trojan Helenus was reigning, with Andromache, now his wife, he was overcome with amazement and a great desire to see this surviving son of Priam and to hear of his strange adventures. Andromache, whom he meets

outside the walls of the city, by the waters of a river renamed
Simois, celebrating funeral rites before a cenotaph of green turf and
two altars to Hector and Astyanax; her astonishment on seeing him,
her hesitation, the halting words in which she questions him, uncertain whether he is a man or a ghost; Aeneas's no less agitated replies
and interrogations, and the pain and confusion with which she recalls
the past—how she lived through scenes of blood and shame, how she
was assigned by lot as slave and concubine to Pyrrhus, abandoned by
him and united to Helenus, another of his slaves, how Pyrrhus fell by
the hand of Orestes and Helenus became a free man and a king;
the entry of Aeneas and his men into the city, and their reception
by the son of Priam in this little Troy, this mimic Pergamon with its
new Xanthus, and its Scaean Gate whose threshold Aeneas greets
with a kiss—all these details, and others here omitted, are images of
persons, things, attitudes, gestures, sayings, joy and sorrow; mere
images, not history or historical criticism, for which they are neither
given nor taken. But through them all there runs a feeling, a feeling
which is our own no less than the poet's, a human feeling of bitter
memories, of shuddering horror, of melancholy, of homesickness, of
tenderness, of a kind of childish *pietas* that could prompt this vain
revival of things perished, these playthings fashioned by a religious
devotion, the *parva Troia*, the *Pergama simulata magnis*, the *aren-
tem Xanthi cognomine rivum*: something inexpressible in logical
terms, which only poetry can express in full. Moreover, these two elements may appear as two in a first abstract analysis, but they cannot
be regarded as two distinct threads, however intertwined; for, in
effect, the feeling is altogether converted into images, into this complex of images, and is thus a feeling that is contemplated and therefore resolved and transcended. Hence poetry must be called neither
feeling, nor image, nor yet the sum of the two, but "contemplation of feeling" or "lyrical intuition" or (which is the same thing)
"pure intuition"—pure, that is, of all historical and critical reference
to the reality or unreality of the images of which it is woven, and apprehending the pure throb of life in its ideality. Doubtless, other
things may be found in poetry besides these two elements or moments and the synthesis of the two; but these other things are either
present as extraneous elements in a compound (reflections, exhortations, polemics, allegories, etc.), or else they are just these image-
feelings themselves taken in abstraction from their context as so
much material, restored to the condition in which it was before the
act of poetic creation. In the former case, they are non-poetic ele-

ments merely interpolated into or attached to the poem; in the latter, they are divested of poetry, rendered unpoetical by a reader either unpoetical or not at the moment poetical, who has dispelled the poetry, either because he cannot live in its ideal realm, or for the legitimate ends of historical enquiry or other practical purposes which involve the degradation—or rather, the conversion—of the poem into a document or an instrument.

ARTISTIC QUALITIES.—What has been said of "poetry" applies to all the other "arts" commonly enumerated; painting, sculpture, architecture, music. Whenever the artistic quality of any product of the mind is discussed, the dilemma must be faced, that either it is a lyrical intuition, or it is something else, something just as respectable, but not art. If painting (as some theorists have maintained) were the imitation or reproduction of a given object, it would be, not art, but something mechanical and practical; if the task of the painter (as other theorists have held) were to combine lines and lights and colours with ingenious novelty of invention and effect, he would be, not an artist, but an inventor; if music consisted in similar combinations of notes, the paradox of Leibniz and Father Kircher would come true, and a man could write music without being a musician; or alternatively we should have to fear (as Proudhon did for poetry and John Stuart Mill for music) that the possible combinations of words or notes would one day be exhausted, and poetry or music would disappear. As in poetry, so in these other arts, it is notorious that foreign elements sometimes intrude themselves; foreign either *a parte objecti or a parte subjecti,* foreign either in fact or from the point of view of an inartistic spectator or listener. Thus the critics of these arts advise the artist to exclude, or at least not to rely upon, what they call the "literary" elements in painting, sculpture and music, just as the critic of poetry advises the writer to look for "poetry" and not be led astray by mere literature. The reader who understands poetry goes straight to this poetic heart and feels its beat upon his own; where this beat is silent, he denies that poetry is present, whatever and however many other things may take its place, united in the work, and however valuable they may be for skill and wisdom, nobility of intellect, quickness of wit and pleasantness of effect. The reader who does not understand poetry loses his way in pursuit of these other things. He is wrong not because he admires them, but because he thinks he is admiring poetry.

OTHER FORMS OF ACTIVITY AS DISTINCT FROM ART.—By defining art as lyrical or pure intuition we have implicitly distinguished it from all other forms of mental production. If such distinctions are made explicit, we obtain the following negations:

1. *Art is not philosophy*, because philosophy is the logical thinking of the universal categories of being, and art is the unreflective intuition of being. Hence, while philosophy transcends the image and uses it for its own purposes, art lives in it as in a kingdom. It is said that art cannot behave in an irrational manner and cannot ignore logic; and certainly it is neither irrational nor illogical; but its own rationality, its own logic, is a quite different thing from the dalectical logic of the concept, and it was in order to indicate this peculiar and unique character that the name "logic of sense" or "aesthetic" was invented. The not uncommon assertion that art has a logical character, involves either an equivocation between conceptual logic and aesthetic logic, or a symbolic expression of the latter in terms of the former.

2. *Art is not history*, because history implies the critical distinction between reality and unreality; the reality of the passing moment and the reality of a fancied world: the reality of fact and the reality of desire. For art, these distinctions are as yet unmade; it lives, as we have said, upon pure images. The historical existence of Helenus, Andromache and Aeneas makes no difference to the poetical quality of Virgil's poem. Here, too, an objection has been raised: namely that art is not wholly indifferent to historical criteria, because it obeys the laws of "verisimilitude"; but, here again, "verisimilitude" is only a rather clumsy metaphor for the mutual coherence of images, which without this internal coherence would fail to produce their effect as images, like Horace's *delphinus in silvis* and *aper in fluctibus*.

3. *Art is not natural science*, because natural science is historical fact classified and so made abstract; nor is it *mathematical science*, because mathematics performs operations with abstractions and does not contemplate. The analogy sometimes drawn between mathematical and poetical creation is based on merely external and generic resemblances; and the alleged necessity of a mathematical or geometrical basis for the arts is only another metaphor, a symbolic expression of the constructive, cohesive and unifying force of the poetic mind building itself a body of images.

4. *Art is not the play of fancy*, because the play of fancy passes from image to image, in search of variety, rest or diversion, seeking to

amuse itself with the likenesses of things that give pleasure or have an emotional and pathetic interest; whereas in art the fancy is so dominated by the single problem of converting chaotic feeling into clear intuition, that we recognize the propriety of ceasing to call it fancy and calling it imagination, poetic imagination or creative imagination. Fancy as such is as far removed from poetry as are the works of Mrs. Radcliffe or Dumas *père*.

5. *Art is not feeling in its immediacy.*—Andromache, on seeing Aeneas, becomes *amens, diriguit visu in medio, labitur, longo vix tempore fatur*, and when she speaks *longos cietbat incassum fletus*; but the poet does not lose his wits or grow stiff as he gazes; he does not totter or weep or cry; he expresses himself in harmonious verses, having made these various perturbations the object of which he sings. Feelings in their immediacy are "expressed" for if they were not, if they were not also sensible and bodily facts ("psycho-physical phenomena," as the positivists used to call them) they would not be concrete things, and so they would be nothing at all. Andromache expressed herself in the way described above. But "expression" in this sense, even when accompanied by consciousness, is a mere metaphor from "mental" or "aesthetic expression" which alone really expresses, that is, gives to feeling a theoretical form and converts it into words, song and outward shape. This distinction between contemplated feeling or poetry, and feeling enacted or endured, is the source of the power, ascribed to art, of "liberating us from the passions" and "calming" us (the power of *catharsis*), and of the consequent condemnation, from an aesthetic point of view, of works of art, or parts of them, in which immediate feeling has a place or finds a vent. Hence, too, arises another characteristic of poetic expression—really synonymous with the last—namely its "infinity" as opposed to the "finitude" of immediate feeling or passion; or, as it is also called, the "universal" or "cosmic" character of poetry. Feeling, not crushed but contemplated by the work of poetry, is seen to diffuse itself in widening circles over all the realm of the soul, which is the realm of the universe, echoing and re-echoing endlessly: joy and sorrow, pleasure and pain, energy and lassitude, earnestness and frivolity, and so forth, are linked to each other and lead to each other through infinite shades and gradations; so that the feeling, while preserving its individual physiognomy and its original dominating motive, is not exhausted by or restricted to this original character. A comic image, if it is poetically comic, carries with it something that is not comic, as in the case of Don Quixote or Falstaff; and the image of something

terrible is never, in poetry, without an atoning element of loftiness, goodness and love.

6. *Art is not instruction or oratory:* it is not circumscribed and limited by service to any practical purpose whatever, whether this be the inculcation of a particular philosophical, historical or scientific truth, or the advocacy of a particular way of feeling and the action corresponding to it. Oratory at once robs expression of its "infinity" and independence, and, by making it the means to an end, dissolves it in this end. Hence arises what Schiller called the "non-determining" character of art, as opposed to the "determining" character of oratory; and hence the justifiable suspicion of "political poetry"—political poetry being, proverbially, bad poetry.

7. As art is not to be confused with the form of practical action most akin to it, namely instruction and oratory, so *a fortiori*, it must not be confused with other forms directed to the production of certain effects, whether these consist in pleasure, enjoyment and utility, or in goodness and righteousness. We must exclude from art not only meretricious works, but also those inspired by a desire for goodness, as equally, though differently, inartistic and repugnant to lovers of poetry. Flaubert's remark that indecent books lacked *vérité*, is parallel to Voltaire's gibe that certain "poésies sacrées" were really "sacrées, car personne n'y touche."

ART IN ITS RELATIONS.—The "negations" here made explicit are obviously, from another point of view, "relations"; for the various distinct forms of mental activity cannot be conceived as separate each from the rest and acting in self-supporting isolation. This is not the place to set forth a complete system of the forms or categories of the mind in their order and their dialectic; confining ourselves to art, we must be content to say that the category of art, like every other category, mutually presupposes and is presupposed by all the rest: it is conditioned by them all and conditions them all. How could the aesthetic synthesis, which is poetry, arise, were it not preceded by a state of mental commotion? *Si vis me flere, dolendum est,* and so forth. And what is this state of mind which we have called feeling, but the whole mind, with its past thoughts, volitions and actions, now thinking and desiring and suffering and rejoicing, travailing within itself? Poetry is like a ray of sunlight shining upon this darkness, lending it its own light and making visible the hidden forms of things. Hence it cannot be produced by an empty and dull mind; hence those artists who embrace the creed of pure art or art for art's sake, and close their hearts to the troubles of life and the cares of thought, are found to be wholly unproductive, or at most rise to the imitation of others or to an impressionism devoid of concentration. Hence the basis of all poetry is human personality, and, since human personality finds its completion in morality, the basis of all poetry is the moral consciousness. Of course this does not mean that the artist must be a profound thinker or an acute critic; nor that he must be a pattern of virtue or a hero; but he must have a share in the world of thought and action which will enable him, either in his own person or by sympathy with others, to live the whole drama of human life. He may sin, lose the purity of his heart, and expose himself, as a practical agent, to blame; but he must have a keen sense of purity and impurity, righteousness and sin, good and evil. He may not be endowed with great practical courage; he may even betray signs of timidity and cowardice; but he must feel the dignity of courage. Many artistic inspirations are due, not to what the artist, as a man, is in practice, but to what he is not, and feels that he ought to be admiring and enjoying the qualities he lacks when he sees them in others. Many, perhaps the finest, pages of heroic and warlike poetry are by men who never had the nerve or the skill to handle a weapon. On the other hand, we are not maintaining that the possession of a moral personality is enough to make a poet or an artist. To be a *vir bonus* does not make a man even an orator, unless he is also *dicendi peritus*. The *sine qua non* of poetry is poetry, that form of theoretical synthesis which we have defined above; the spark of poetical genius without which all the rest is mere fuel, not burning because no fire is at hand to light it. But the figure of the pure poet, the pure artist, the votary of pure Beauty, aloof from contact with humanity, is no real figure but a caricature.

That poetry not only presupposes the other forms of human mental activity but is presupposed by them, is proved by the fact that without the poetic imagaination which gives contemplative form to the workings of feeling, intuitive expression to obscure impressions, and thus becomes representations and words, whether spoken or sung or painted or otherwise uttered, logical thought could not arise. Logical thought is not language, but it never exists without language, and it uses the language which poetry has created; by means of concepts, it discerns and dominates the representations of poetry, and it could not dominate them unless they, its future subjects, had first an existence of their own. Further, without the discerning and criticizing activity of thought, action would be impossible; and if action, then good action, the moral consciousness, duty. Every man, however much he may seem to be all logical thinker, critic, scientist, or all absorbed in practical interests or devoted to duty, cherishes at the bottom of his heart his own private store of imagination and poetry; even Faust's pedantic *famulus*, Wagner, confessed that he often had his "grillenhafte Stunden." Had this element been altogether denied him, he would not have been a man, and therefore not even a thinking or acting being. This extreme case is an absurdity; but in proportion as this private store is scanty, we find a certain superficialty and aridity in thought, and a certain coldness in action.

THE SCIENCE OF ART, OR AESTHETICS, AND ITS PHILOSOPHICAL CHARACTER.—The concept of art expounded above is in a sense the ordinary concept, which appears with greater or less clarity in all statements about art, and is constantly appealed to, explicitly or implicitly, as the fixed point round which all discussions on the subject gravitate: and this, not only nowadays, but at all times, as could be shown by the collection and interpretation of things said by writers, poets, artists, laymen and even the common people. But it is desirable to dispel the illusion that this concept exists as an innate idea, and to replace this by the truth, that it operates as an *a priori* concept. Now an *a priori* concept does not exist by itself, but only in the individual products which it generates. Just as the *a priori* reality called Art, Poetry or Beauty does not exist in a transcendent region where it can be perceived and admired in itself, but only in the innumerable works of poetry, of art and of beauty which it has formed and continues to form, so the logical *a priori* concept of art exists nowhere but in the particular judgments which it has formed and continues to form, the refutations which it has effected and continues to effect, the demonstrations it makes, the theories it constructs, the problems and groups of problems, which it solves and has solved. The definitions and distinctions and negations and relations expounded above have each its own history, and have been progressively worked out in the course of centuries, and in them we now possess the fruits of this complex and unremitting toil. Aesthetic, or the science of art, has not therefore the task (attributed to it by certain scholastic conceptions) of defining art once for all and deducing from this conception its various doctrines, so as to cover the whole field of aesthetic science; it is only the perpetual systematization, always renewed and always growing, of the problems arising from time to time out of reflection upon art, and is identical with the solutions of the difficulties and the criticisms of the errors which act as stimulus and material to the unceasing progress of thought. This being so, no exposition of aesthetic (especially a summary exposition such as can alone be given here) can claim to deal exhaustively with the innumerable problems which have arisen and may arise in the course of the history of aesthetics; it can only mention and discuss the chief, and among these, by preference, those which still make themselves felt and resist solution in ordinary educated thought; adding an implied "et cetera," so that the reader may pursue the subject according to the criteria set before him, either by going again over old discussions, or by entering into those of to-day, which change and multiply and assume new shapes almost daily. Another warning must not be omitted: namely that aesthetics, though a special philosophical science, having as its principle a special and distinct category of the mind, can never, just because it is philosophical, be detached from the main body of philosophy; for its problems are concerned with the relations between art and the other mental forms, and therefore imply both difference and identity. Aesthetics is really the whole of philosophy, but with special emphasis on that side of it which concerns art. Many have demanded or imagined or desired a self-contained aesthetics, devoid of any general philosophical implications, and consistent with more than one, or with any, philosophy; but the project is impossible of execution because self-contradictory. Even those who promise to expound a naturalistic, inductive, physical, physiological or psychological aesthetics —in a word, a non-philosophical aesthetics—when they pass from promise to performance surreptitiously introduce a general positivistic, naturalistic or even materialistic philosophy. And anyone who thinks that the philosophical ideas of positivism, naturalism and materialism are false and out of date, will find it an easy matter to refute the aesthetic or pseudo-aesthetic doctrines which mutually support them and are supported by them, and will not regard their problems as problems still awaiting solution or worthy of discussion —or, at least, protracted discussion. For instance, the downfall of psychological associationism (or the substitution of mechanism for *a priori* synthesis) implies the downfall not only of logical associationism but of aesthetics also, with its association of "content" and "form," or of two "representations," which (unlike Campanella's *tactus intrinsecus*, effected *cum magna suavitate*) was a *contactus extrinsecus* whose terms were no sooner united than they *discedebant*. The collapse of biological and evolutionary explanations of logical and ethical values implies the same collapse in the case of aesthetic value. The proved inability of empirical methods to yield knowledge of reality, which in fact they can only classify and reduce to types, involves the impossibility of an aesthetics arrived at by collecting aesthetic facts in classes and discovering their laws by induction.

INTUITION AND EXPRESSION.—One of the first problems to arise, when the work of art is defined as "lyrical image," concerns the relation of "intuition" to "expression" and the manner of the transition from the one to the other. At bottom this is the same problem which arises in other parts of philosophy: the problem of inner and outer, of mind and matter, of soul and body, and, in ethics, of intention and will, will and action, and so forth. Thus stated, the problem is insoluble; for once we have divided the inner from the outer, body from mind, will from action, or intuition from expression, there is no way of passing from one to the other or of reuniting them, unless we appeal for their reunion to a third term, variously represented as God or the Unknowable. Dualism leads necessarily either to transcendence or to agnosticism. But when a problem is found to be insoluble in the terms in which it is stated the only course open is to criticize these terms themselves, to inquire how they have been arrived at, and whether their genesis was logically sound. In this case, such inquiry leads to the conclusion that the terms depend not upon a philosophical principle, but upon an empirical and naturalistic classification, which has created two groups of facts called internal and external respectively (as if internal facts were not also external, and as if an external fact could exist without being also internal), or souls and bodies, or images and expressions; and everyone knows that it is hopeless to try to find a dialectical unity between terms that have been distinguished not philosophically or formally but only empirically and materially. The soul is only a soul in so far as it is a body; the will is only a will in so far as it moves arms and legs, or is action; intuition is only intuition in so far as it is, in that very act, expression. An image that does not express, that is not speech, song, drawing, painting, sculpture or architecture—speech at least murmured to oneself, song at least echoing within one's own breast, line and colour seen in imagination and colouring with its own tint the whole soul and organism—is an image that does not exist. We may assert its existence, but we cannot support our assertion; for the only thing we could adduce in support of it would be the fact that the image was embodied or expressed. This profound philosophical doctrine, the *identity of intuition and expression* is, moreover, a principle of ordinary common sense, which laughs at people who claim to have thoughts they cannot express or to have imagined a great picture which they cannot paint. *Rem tene, verba sequentur;* if there are no *verba,* there is no *res.* This identity, which applies to every sphere of the mind, has in the sphere of art a clearness and self-evidence lacking, perhaps, elsewhere. In the creation of a work of poetry, we are present, as it were, at the mystery of the creation of the world; hence the value of the contribution made by aesthetics to philosophy as a whole, or the conception of the One that is All. Aesthetics, by denying in the life of art an abstract spiritualism and the resulting dualism, prepares the way and leads the mind towards idealism or absolute spiritualism.

EXPRESSION AND COMMUNICATION.—Objections to the identity of intuition and expression generally arise from psychological illusions which lead us to believe that we possess at any given moment a profusion of concrete and lively images, when in fact we only possess signs and names for them; or else from faulty analysis of cases like that of the artist who is believed to express mere fragments of a world of images that exists in his mind in its entirety, whereas he really has in his mind only these fragments, together with—not the supposed complete world, but at most an aspiration or obscure working towards it, towards a greater and richer image which may take shape or may not. But these objections also arise from a confusion between *expression* and *communication,* the latter being really distinct from the image and its expression. Communication is the fixation of the intuition-expression upon an object metaphorically called material or physical; in reality, even here we are concerned not with material or physical things but with a mental process. The proof that the so-called physical object is unreal, and its resolution into terms of mind, is primarily of interest for our general philosophical conceptions, and only indirectly for the elucidation of aesthetic questions; hence for brevity's sake we may let the metaphor or symbol stand and speak of matter or nature. It is clear that the poem is complete as soon as the poet has expressed it in words which he repeats to himself. When he comes to repeat them aloud, for others to hear, or looks for someone to learn them by heart and repeat them to others as in a *schola cantorum,* or sets them down in writing or in printing, he has entered upon a new stage, not aesthetic but practical, whose social and cultural importance need not, of course, be insisted upon. So with the painter; he paints on his panel or canvas, but he could not paint unless at every stage in his work, from the original blur or sketch to the finishing touches, the intuited image, the line and colour painted in his imagination, preceded the brush-stroke. Indeed, when the brush-stroke outruns the image, it is cancelled and replaced by the artist's correction of his own work. The exact line that divides expression from communication is difficult to draw in the concrete case, for in the concrete case the two processes generally alternate rapidly and appear to mingle, but it is clear in idea, and it must be firmly grasped. Through overlooking it, or blurring it through insufficient attention, arise the confusions between *art* and *technique*. Technique is not an intrinsic element of art but has to do precisely with the concept of communication. In general it is a cognition or complex of cognitions disposed and directed to the furtherance of practical action; and, in the case of art, of the practical action which makes objects and instruments for the recording and communicating of works of art; *e.g.*, cognitions concerning the preparation of panels, canvases or walls to be painted, pigments, varnishes, ways of obtaining good pronunciation and declamation and so forth. Technical treatises are not aesthetic treatises, nor yet parts or chapters of them. Provided, that is, that the ideas are rigorously conceived and the words used accurately in relation to them it would not be worth while to pick a quarrel over the use of the word "technique" as a synonym for the artistic work itself, regarded as "inner technique" or the formation of intuition-expressions. The confusion between art and technique is especially beloved by impotent artists, who hope to obtain from practical things and practical devices and inventions the help which their strength does not enable them to give themselves.

ARTISTIC OBJECTS: THE THEORY OF THE SPECIAL ARTS, AND THE BEAUTY OF NATURE.—The work of communicating and conserving artistic images, with the help of technique, produces the material objects metaphorically called *"artistic objects"* or *"works of art"*: pictures, sculptures and buildings, and, in a more complicated manner, literary and musical writings, and, in our own times, gramophones and records which make it possible to reproduce voices and sounds. But neither these voices and sounds nor the symbols of writing, sculpture and architecture, are works of art; works of art exist only in the minds that create or recreate them. To remove the appearance of paradox from the truth that beautiful objects, beautiful things, do not exist, it may be opportune to recall the analogous case of economic science, which knows perfectly well that in the sphere of economics there are no naturally or physically *useful* things, but only demand and labour, from which physical things acquire, metaphorically, this epithet. A student of economics who wished to deduce the economic value of things from their physical qualities would be perpetrating a gross *ignoratio elenchi*.

Yet this same *ignoratio elenchi* has been, and still is, committed in aesthetic, by the theory of special *arts*, and the limits or peculiar aesthetic character of each. The divisions between the arts are merely technical or physical, according as the artistic objects consist of physical sounds, notes, coloured objects, carved or modelled objects, or constructed objects having no apparent correspondence with natural bodies (poetry, music, painting, sculpture, architecture, etc.). To ask what is the artistic character of each of these arts, what it can and cannot do, what kinds of images can be expressed in sounds, what in notes, what in colours, what in lines, and so forth, is like asking in economics what things are entitled by their physical qualities to have a value and what are not, and what relative values they are entitled to have; whereas it is clear that physical qualities do not enter into the question, and anything may be desired or demanded or valued more than another, or more than anything else at all, according to circumstances and needs. Even Lessing found himself slipping down the slope leading to this truth, and was forced to such strange conclusions as that actions belonged to poetry and bodies to sculpture; even Richard Wagner attempted to find a place in the list for a comprehensive art, namely Opera, including in itself by a process of aggregation the powers of all the arts. A reader with any artistic sense finds in a single solitary line from a poet at once musical and picturesque qualities, sculpturesque strength and architectural structure; and the same with a picture, which is never a mere thing of the eyes but an affair of the whole soul, and exists in the soul not only as colour but as sound and speech. But when we try to grasp these musical or picturesque or other qualities, they elude us and turn into each other, and melt into a unity, however we may be accustomed to distinguish them by different names; a practical proof that art is one and cannot be divided into arts. One, and infinitely varied; not according to the technical conceptions of the several arts, but according to the infinite variety of artistic personalities and their states of mind.

With this relation (and confusion) between artistic creations and instruments of communication or *objets d'art* must be connected the problem of *natural beauty*. We shall not discuss the question, raised by certain aestheticians, whether there are in nature other poets, other artistic beings, beside man; a question which ought to be answered in the affirmative not only out of respect for the song-birds, but, still more, out of respect for the idealistic conception of the world as life and spirituality throughout; even if (as the fairy-tale goes) we have lost the magic herb which when we put it in our mouth, gives us the power of understanding the language of animals and plants. The phrase *natural beauty* properly refers to persons, things and places whose effect is comparable to that of poetry, painting, sculpture and the other arts. There is no difficulty in allowing the existence of such "natural *objets d'art*," for the process of poetic communication may take place by means of objects naturally given as well as by means of objects artificially produced. The lover's imagination creates a woman beautiful to him, and personifies her in Laura; the pilgrim's imagination creates the charming or sublime landscape, and embodies it in the scene of a lake or a mountain; and these creations of theirs are sometimes shared by more or less wide social circles, thus becoming the "professional beauties" admired by everyone and the famous "views" before which all experience a more or less sincere rapture. No doubt, these creations are mortal; ridicule sometimes kills them, satiety may bring neglect, fashion may replace them by others; and —unlike works of art—they do not admit of authentic interpretation. The bay of Naples, seen from the height of one of the most beautiful Neapolitan villas, was after some time described by the Russian lady who owned the villa as *une cuvette bleue*, whose blue encircled by green so wearied her that she sold the villa. But even the *cuvette bleue* was a legitimate poetical creation.

LITERARY KINDS AND AESTHETIC CATEGORIES.—Effects at once greater and more detrimental upon the criticism and historical study of art and literature have been produced by a theory of similar but slightly different origin, the theory of *literary and artistic kinds*. This, like the foregoing, is based on a classification in itself justifiable and useful. The foregoing is based on a technical or physical classification of artistic objects; this is based on a classification according to the feelings which form their content or motive, into *tragic, comic, lyrical, heroic, erotic, idyllic, romantic* and so on, with divisions and subdivisions. It is useful in practice to distribute an artist's works, for purposes of publication, into these classes, putting lyrics in one volume, dramas in another, poems in a third and romances in a fourth; and it is convenient, in fact, indispensable, to refer to works and groups of works by these names in speaking and writing of them. But here again we must deny and pronounce illegitimate the transition from these classificatory concepts to the poetic laws of composition and aesthetic criteria of judgment, as when people try to decide that a tragedy must have a subject of a certain kind, characters of a certain kind, a plot of a certain kind and a certain length; and, when confronted by a work, instead of looking for and appraising its own poetry, ask whether it is a tragedy or a poem, and whether it obeys the "laws" of one or other "kind." The literary criticism of the 19th century owed its great progress largely to its abandonment of the criteria of kinds, in which the criticism of the Renaissance and the French classicists had always been entangled, as may be seen from the discussions arising out of the poems of Dante, Ariosto and Tasso, Guarini's *Pastor fido*, Corneille's *Cid*, and Lope de Vega's *comedias*. Artists have profited by this liberation less than critics; for anyone with artistic genius bursts the fetters of such servitude, or even makes them the instruments of his power; and the artist with little or no genius turns his very freedom into a new slavery.

It has been thought that the divisions of kinds could be saved by giving them a philosophical significance; or at any rate one such division, that of lyric, epic and dramatic, regarded as the three moments of a process of objectification passing from the lyric, the outpouring of the ego, to the epic, in which the ego detaches its feeling from itself by narrating it, and thence to the drama, in which it allows this feeling to create of itself its own mouthpieces, the *dramatis personae*. But the lyric is not a pouring-forth; it is not a cry or a lament; it is an objectification in which the ego sees itself on the stage, narrates itself, and dramatizes itself; and this lyrical spirit forms the poetry both of epic and of drama, which are therefore distinguished from the lyric only by external signs. A work which is altogether poetry, like *Macbeth* or *Antony and Cleopatra*, is substantially a lyric in which the various tones and successive verses are represented by characters and scenes.

In the old aesthetics, and even to-day in those which perpetuate the type, an important place is given to the so-called categories of beauty: the *sublime*, the *tragic*, the *comic*, the *graceful*, the *humorous* and so forth, which German philosophers not only claimed to treat as philosophical concepts, whereas they are really mere psychological and empirical concepts, but developed by means of that dialectic which belongs only to pure or speculative concepts, philosophical categories. Thus they arranged them in an imaginary progress culminating now in the Beautiful, now in the Tragic, now in the Humorous. Taking these concepts at their face value, we may observe their substantial correspondence with the concepts of the literary and artistic kinds; and this is the source from which, as excerpts from manuals of literature, they have found their way into philosophy. As psychological and empirical concepts, they do not belong to aesthetics; and as a whole, in their common quality, they refer merely to the world of feelings, empirically grouped and classified, which forms the permanent matter of artistic intuition.

RHETORIC, GRAMMAR AND PHILOSOPHY OF LANGUAGE.—Every error has in it an element of truth, and arises from an arbitrary combination of things which in themselves are legitimate. This principle may be confirmed by an examination of other erroneous doctrines which have been prominent in the past and are still to a less degree prominent to-day. It is perfectly legitimate, in teaching people to write, to make use of distinctions like that between simple style, ornate style and metaphorical style and its forms, and to point out that here the pupil ought to express himself literally and there metaphorically, or that here the metaphor used is incoherent or drawn out to excessive length, and that here the figure of "preterition," there "hypotyposis" or "irony," would have been suitable. But when people lose sight of the merely practical and didactic origin of these distinctions and construct a philosophical theory of form as divisible into simple form and ornate form, logical form and affective form, and so forth, they are introducing elements of rhetoric into aesthetics and vitiating the true concept of expression. For expression is never logical, but always affective, that is, lyrical and imaginative; and hence it is never metaphorical but always "proper"; it is never simple in the sense of lacking elaboration, or ornate in the sense of being loaded with extraneous elements; it is always adorned with itself, *simplex munditiis*. Even logical thought or science, so far as it is expressed, becomes feeling and imagination, which is why a philosophical or historical or scientific book can be not only true but beautiful, and must always be judged not only logically but also aesthetically. Thus we sometimes say that a book is a failure as theory, or criticism, or historical truth, but a success as a work of art, in view of the feeling animating it and expressed in it. As for the element of truth which is obscurely at work in this distinction between logical form and metaphorical form, dialectic and rhetoric, we may detect in it the need of a science of aesthetics side by side with that of logic; but it was a mistake to try to distinguish the two sciences within the sphere of expression which belongs to one of them alone.

Another element in education, namely the teaching of languages, has no less legitimately, ever since ancient times, classified expressions into periods, propositions and words, and words into various species, and each species according to the variations and combinations of roots and suffixes, syllables and letters; and hence have arisen alphabets, grammars and vocabularies, just as in another way for poetry has arisen a science of prosody, and for music and the figurative and architectural arts there have arisen musical and pictorial grammars and so forth. But here, too, the ancients did not succeed in avoiding an illegitimate transition *ab intellectu ad rem*, from abstractions to reality, from the empirical to the philosophical, such as we have already observed elsewhere; and this involved thinking of speech as an aggregation of words, and words as aggregations of syllables or of roots and suffixes; whereas the *prius* is speech itself, a continuum, resembling an organism, and words and syllables and roots are a *posterius*, an anatomical preparation, the product of the abstracting intellect, not the original or real fact. If grammar, like the rhetoric in the case above considered, is transplanted into aesthetic, the result is a distinction between expression and the means of expression, which is a mere reduplication; for the means of expression are just expression itself, broken into pieces by grammarians. This error, combined with the error of distinguishing between simple and ornate form, has prevented people from seeing that the philosophy of language is not a philosophical grammar, but is wholly devoid of grammatical elements. It does not raise grammatical classifications to a philosophical level; it ignores them, and, when they get in its way, destroys them. The philosophy of language, in a word, is identical with the philosophy of poetry and art, the science of intuition-expression, aesthetics; which embraces language in its whole extension, passing beyond the limits of phonetic and syllabic language, and in its unimpaired reality as living and completely significant expression.

CLASSICAL AND ROMANTIC.—The problems reviewed above belong to the past—a past extending through centuries—rather than to the present; of their mis-stated questions and misconceived solutions there now remain mere relics and superstitions which affect academic treatises more than they do the consciousness and culture of ordinary people. But it is necessary to watch carefully for new shoots from the old stock, which still appear from time to time, in order to cut them down. Such is, in our own time, the theory of styles applied to the history of art (Wölfflin and others) and extended to the history of poetry (Strich and others), a new irruption of rhetorical abstractions into the judgment and history of works of art. But the chief problem of our time, to be overcome by aesthetics, is connected with the crisis in art and in judgments upon art produced by the romantic period. Not that this crisis was not foreshadowed by precedents and parallels in earlier history, like Alexandrian art and that of the late Roman period, and in modern times the Baroque art and poetry which followed upon that of the Renaissance. The crisis of the romantic period, together with sources and characteristics peculiar to itself, had a magnitude all of its own. It asserted an antithesis between *naïve* and *sentimental* poetry, *classical* and *romantic* art, and thus denied the unity of art and asserted a duality of two fundamentally different arts, of which it took the side of the second, as that appropriate to the modern age, by upholding the primary importance in art of feeling, passion and fancy. In part this was a justifiable reaction against the rationalistic literature of classicism in the French manner, now satirical, now frivolous, weak in feeling and imagination and deficient in a deep poetic sense; but in part, *romanticism* was a rebellion not against *classicism* but against the classical as such: against the idea of the serenity and infinity of the artistic image, against catharsis and in favour of a turbid emotionalism that could not and would not undergo purification. This was very well understood by Goethe, the poet both of passion and of serenity, and therefore, because he was a poet, a classical poet; who opposed romantic poetry as "hospital poetry." Later, it was thought that the disease had run its course and that romanticism was a thing of the past; but though some of its contents and some of its forms were dead, its soul was not: its soul consisting in this tendency on the part of art towards an immediate expression of passions and impressions. Hence it changed its name but went on living and working. It called itself "realism," "verism," "symbolism," "artistic style," "impressionism," "sensualism," "imagism," "decadentism," and nowadays, in its extreme forms, "expressionism" and "futurism." The very conception of art is attacked by these doctrines, which tend to replace it by the conception of one or other kind of non-art; and the statement that they are fighting against art is confirmed by the hatred of the extremists of this movement for museums and libraries and all the art of the past—that is, for the idea of art which on the whole corresponds with art as it has been historically realized. The connection of this movement, in its latest modern form, with industrialism and the psychology produced and fostered by industrialism is obvious. What art is contrasted with is practical life as lived to-day; and art, for this movement, is not the expression of life and hence the transcending of life in the contemplation of the infinite and universal, but the cries and gesticulations and broken colours of life itself. The real poets and artists, on the other hand, rare at any time, naturally continue, nowadays as always, to work according to the old and only idea of what art is, expressing their feelings in harmonious forms; and the real connoisseurs (rarer, these also, than people think) continue to judge their work according to this same idea. In spite of this, the tendency to destroy the idea of art is a characteristic of our age; and this tendency is based on the *proton pseudos* which confuses mental or aesthetic expression with natural or practical expression—the expression which passes confusedly from sensation to sensation and is a mere effect of sensation, with the expression which art elaborates, as it builds, draws, colours or models, and which is its beautiful creation. The problem for aesthetics to-day is the reassertion and defence of the classical as against romanticism: the synthetic, formal theoretical element which is the *proprium* of art, as against the affective element which it is the business of art to resolve into itself, but which to-day has turned against it and threatens to displace it. Against the inexhaustible fertility of creative mind, the gates of hell shall not prevail; but the hostility which endeavours to make them prevail is disturbing, even if only in an incidental manner, the artistic taste, the artistic life and consequently the intellectual and moral life of to-day.

THE CRITICISM AND HISTORY OF ART AND LITERATURE.—Another group of questions raised in works on aesthetics, though not unsuitable to such works, properly belongs to logic and the theory of historical thought. These concern the aesthetic judgment and the history of poetry and the arts. By showing that the aesthetic activity (or art) is one of the forms of mind, a value, a category, or whatever we choose to call it, and not (as philosophers of various schools have thought) an empirical concept referable to certain orders of utilitarian or mixed facts, by establishing the *autonomy of aesthetic value*, aesthetics has also shown that it is the predicate of a special judgment, the *aesthetic judgment*, and the subject-matter of history, of a special history, the history of poetry and the arts, *artistic and literary history*.

The questions that have been raised concerning the aesthetic judgment and artistic and literary history are making allowance for the peculiar character of art, identical with the methodological questions that arise in every field of historical study. It has been asked whether the aesthetic judgment is *absolute* or *relative*; but every historical judgment (and the aesthetic judgment affirming the reality and quality of aesthetic facts is an historical judgment) is always both absolute and relative at once: absolute, in so far as the category involved in the construction possesses universal truth; relative, in so far as the object constructed by that category is historically conditioned: hence in the historical judgment the category is individualized and the individual becomes absolute. Those who in the past have denied the absoluteness of the aesthetic judgment (sensationalistic, hedonistic or utilitarian aestheticians) denied in effect the quality, reality and autonomy of art. It has been asked whether a knowledge of the history of the time—the whole history of the time in question—is necessary for the aesthetic judgment of the art of that time; it certainly is, because, as we know, poetic creation presupposes all the rest of the mind which it is converting into lyrical imagery, and the one aesthetic creation presupposes all the other creations (passions, feelings, customs, etc.) of the given historical moment. Hence may be seen the error both of those who advocate a merely historical judgment upon art (historical critics) and of those who advocate a merely aesthetic (aesthetic critics). The former would find in art all the rest of history (social conditions, biography of the artist, etc.), but would omit that part which is proper to art; the latter would judge the work of art in abstraction from history, depriving it of its real meaning and giving it an imaginary meaning or testing it by arbitrary standards. Lastly, there has appeared a kind of scepticism or pessimism as to the possibility of understanding the art of the past; a scepticism or pessimism which in that case ought to extend to every part of history (history of thought, politics, religion and morality), and refutes itself by a *reductio ad absurdum*, since what we call contemporary art and history really belong to the past as much as those of more distant ages, and must, like them, be re-created in the present, in the mind that feels them and the intellect that understands them. There are artistic works and periods that remain to us unintelligible; but this only means that we are not now in a position to enter again into their life and to understand them, and the same is true of the ideas and customs and actions of many peoples and ages. Humanity, like the individual, remembers some things and forgets many others; but it may yet, in the course of its mental development, reach a point where its memory of them revives.

A final question concerns the form proper to artistic and literary history, which, in the form that arose in the romantic period, and still prevails to-day, expounds the history of works of art as a function of the concepts and social needs of its various periods, regarding them as aesthetic expressions of these things and connecting them closely with civil history. This tends to obscure and almost to render invisible the peculiar character of the individual work of art, the character which makes it impossible to confuse one work of art with any other, and results in treating them as documents of social life. In practice no doubt this method is tempered by what may be called the "individualizing" method, which emphasizes the individual character of the works; but the mixture has the defects of all eclecticism. To escape this, there is nothing to do but consistently to develop individualizing history, and to treat works of art not in relation to social history but as each a world in itself, into which from time to time the whole of history is concentrated, transfigured and imaginatively transcended in the individuality of the poetic work, which is a creation, not a reflection, a monument, not a document. Dante is not simply a document of the middle ages, nor Shakespeare of the English Renaissance; as such, they have many equals or superiors among bad poets and nonpoets. It has been objected that this method imposed on artistic and literary history the form of a series of disconnected essays or monographs; but, obviously, the connection is provided by human history as a whole, of which the personalities of poets constitute a part, and a somewhat conspicuous part (Shakespearian poetry is an event no less important than the Reformation or the French Revolution), and, precisely because they are a part of it, they ought not to be submerged and lost in it, that is, in its other parts, but ought to retain their proper proportions and their original character.

John
DEWEY

Dewey's account of his own philosophy, contributed to the volume Contemporary American Philosophy *in 1930, was entitled "From Absolutism to Experimentalism," a phrase which sums up his philosophical development. In his student years Dewey was much taken with absolute idealism, then a strong influence in the American university. "Were it possible for me to be a devotee of any system," he writes in the essay of 1930, "I still should believe that there is greater richness and greater variety of insight in Hegel than in any other single systematic philosopher—though when I say this I exclude Plato, who still provides my favorite philosophic reading."*

But we cannot understand Dewey in terms of those influences alone, for his thought was also influenced by Darwinian biology and it is this more than any other single development which accounts for the functionalism of his mature philosophy and for his conception of experience as an interaction with, as well as a reconstruction of, the environment. In this process both self and world undergo change. Dewey's notion of reconstruction is his interpretation of the Hegelian dialectic. While Hegel saw the dia-

lectical process as a self-splitting, self-readjusting, self-unifying Absolute, Dewey sees process as the experimental adjustment of the living organism to its environment, and the reorganization of the environment by the living organism. For Hegel, Spirit comes to itself finally out of the social reality; and so too for Dewey the human spirit is not merely a biological but also a socially achieved form of being. Experimentalism is also experientialism, and Dewey thus replaces the monistic cosmic self-development of Absolute Spirit by the pluralistic experience of a finite human being.

This process of experience is the philosophical center of all Dewey's thinking, whether in metaphysics, logic, ethics, theory of education, political theory, or philosophy of law. It comes to fullest fruition in his aesthetics. He himself points out that the picture of human experience which is painted in his own aesthetics—understandably set forth under the heading Art as Experience—represents an abiding challenge to philosophy. As he says there, the philosopher must go to aesthetic experience in order to understand what experience is, the reason being that only in aesthetic experience do we come upon experience in its integrity, "freed from the forces that impede and confuse its development as experience." This conception of integrity follows from Hegel's conception of the truth as the whole, and since aesthetic experience is precisely experience in its integrity, the theory of aesthetics put forth by a philosopher is a test of the system he constructs to grasp the nature of experience itself.

It is this conception of experience in its integrity that for Dewey is the great subject matter for aesthetics as he interprets it. In this Dewey reminds us of Schelling's belief that aesthetic intuition is the organ of philosophy and aesthetics the crown of philosophy. It may be seriously argued that for Dewey, therefore, surprising as this may seem to those who think of him in terms of his pragmatism, his instrumentalism in logic, his liberalism in politics, and progressivism in education, it is art and the aesthetic in experience which ultimately constitutes the kernel of genuine philosophy.

For this reason it can be seen why Dewey thinks of art as experience, and particularly as experience in its integrity, for in art, which develops out of the generic aesthetic aspect of experience, the essence is experience brought to consummation and fulfillment. The chapter of Art as Experience called "Having an Experience" is the key to the whole book, and it will be useful for the reader to pay special attention to the highly specialized ideal of experience which Dewey sets forth in this chapter. Art for him

*is experience as a dynamic, self-forming, self-fulfilling, interaction
between man and reality. Through a rhythmic series of checks
and progressions, in which an inner meaningfulness is progressively developed, the individual reaches a consummatory conclusion which is the building up of the total meaning of that experience in terms of immanent, i.e., qualitative, meaning. In
Dewey's words, "The conception implied in the treatment of
esthetic experience . . . is, indeed, that the work of art has a
unique* quality, *but that it is that of clarifying and concentrating
meanings contained in scattered and weakened ways in the material of other experiences."*

ART AS EXPERIENCE

Chapter I

THE LIVE CREATURE

By one of the ironic perversities that often attend the course of affairs,
the existence of the works of art upon which formation of an esthetic
theory depends has become an obstruction to theory about them.
For one reason, these works are products that exist externally and
physically. In common conception, the work of art is often identified
with the building, book, painting, or statue in its existence apart
from human experience. Since the actual work of art is what the
product does with and in experience, the result is not favorable to
understanding. In addition, the very perfection of some of these
products, the prestige they possess because of a long history of un-
questioned admiration, creates conventions that get in the way of
fresh insight. When an art product once attains classic status, it somehow becomes isolated from the human conditions under which it
was brought into being and from the human consequences it engenders in actual life-experience.

When artistic objects are separated from both conditions of origin
and operation in experience, a wall is built around them that renders
almost opaque their general significance, with which esthetic theory
deals. Art is remitted to a separate realm, where it is cut off from that
association with the materials and aims of every other form of human
effort, undergoing, and achievement. A primary task is thus imposed
upon one who undertakes to write upon the philosophy of the fine

arts. This task is to restore continuity between the refined and intensified forms of experience that are works of art and the everyday events, doings, and sufferings that are universally recognized to constitute experience. Mountain peaks do not float unsupported; they do not even just rest upon the earth. They *are* the earth in one of its manifest operations. It is the business of those who are concerned with the theory of the earth, geographers and geologists, to make this fact evident in its various implications. The theorist who would deal philosophically with fine art has a like task to accomplish.

If one is willing to grant this position, even if only by way of temporary experiment, he will see that there follows a conclusion at first sight surprising. In order to understand the meaning of artistic products, we have to forget them for a time, to turn aside from them and have recourse to the ordinary forces and conditions of experience that we do not usually regard as esthetic. We must arrive at the theory of art by means of a detour. For theory is concerned with understanding, insight, not without exclamations of admiration, and stimulation of that emotional outburst often called appreciation. It is quite possible to enjoy flowers in their colored form and delicate fragrance without knowing anything about plants theoretically. But if one sets out to *understand* the flowering of plants, he is committed to finding out something about the interactions of soil, air, water and sunlight that condition the growth of plants.

By common consent, the Parthenon is a great work of art. Yet it has esthetic standing only as the work becomes an experience for a human being. And, if one is to go beyond personal enjoyment into the formation of a theory about that large republic of art of which the building is one member, one has to be willing at some point in his reflections to turn from it to the bustling, arguing, acutely sensitive Athenian citizens, with civic sense identified with a civic religion, of whose experience the temple was an expression, and who built it not as a work of art but as a civic commemoration. The turning to them is as human beings who had needs that were a demand for the building and that were carried to fulfillment in it; it is not an examination such as might be carried on by a sociologist in search for material relevant to his purpose. The one who sets out to theorize about the esthetic experience embodied in the Parthenon must realize in thought what the people into whose lives it entered had in common, as creators and as those who were satisfied with it, with people in our own homes and on our own streets.

In order to *understand* the esthetic in its ultimate and approved forms, one must begin with it in the raw; in the events and scenes that hold the attentive eye and ear of man, arousing his interest and affording him enjoyment as he looks and listens: the sights that hold the crowd—the fire-engine rushing by; the machines excavating enormous holes in the earth; the human-fly climbing the steeple-side; the men perched high in air on girders, throwing and catching red-hot bolts.

. . . . .

So extensive and subtly pervasive are the ideas that set Art upon a remote pedestal, that many a person would be repelled rather than pleased if told that he enjoyed his casual recreations, in part at least, because of their esthetic quality. The arts which today have most vitality for the average person are things he does not take to be arts: for instance, the movie, jazzed music, the comic strip, and, too frequently, newspaper accounts of love-nests, murders, and exploits of bandits. For, when what he knows as art is relegated to the museum and gallery, the unconquerable impulse towards experiences enjoyable in themselves finds such outlet as the daily environment provides. Many a person who protests against the museum conception of art, still shares the fallacy from which that conception springs. For the popular notion comes from a separation of art from the objects and scenes of ordinary experience that many theorists and critics pride themselves upon holding and even elaborating. The times when select and distinguished objects are closely connected with the products of usual vocations are the times when appreciation of the former is most rife and most keen. When, because of their remoteness, the objects acknowledged by the cultivated to be works of fine art seem anemic to the mass of people, esthetic hunger is likely to seek the cheap and the vulgar.

The factors that have glorified fine art by setting it upon a far-off pedestal did not arise within the realm of art nor is their influence confined to the arts. For many persons an aura of mingled awe and unreality encompasses the "spiritual" and the "ideal" while "matter" has become by contrast a term of depreciation, something to be explained away or apologized for. The forces at work are those that have removed religion as well as fine art from the scope of the common or community life. The forces have historically produced so many of the dislocations and divisions of modern life and thought that art could not escape their influence. We do not have to travel to the ends of the earth nor return many millennia in time to find peoples for whom everything that intensifies the sense of immediate living is an object of intense admiration. Bodily scarification, waving feathers, gaudy robes, shining ornaments of gold and silver, of emerald and jade, formed the contents of esthetic arts, and, presumably, without the vulgarity of class exhibitionism that attends their analogues today. Domestic utensils, furnishings of tent and house, rugs, mats, jars, pots, bows, spears, were wrought with such delighted care that today we hunt them out and give them places of honor in our art museums. Yet in their own time and place, such things were enhancements of the processes of everyday life. Instead of being elevated to a niche apart, they belonged to display of prowess, the manifestation of group and clan membership, worship of gods, feasting and fasting, fighting, hunting, and all the rhythmic crises that punctuate the stream of living.

Dancing and pantomime, the sources of the art of the theater, flourished as part of religious rites and celebrations. Musical art abounded in the fingering of the stretched string, the beating of the taut skin, the blowing with reeds. Even in the caves, human habitations were adorned with colored pictures that kept alive to the senses experiences with the animals that were so closely bound with the lives of humans. Structures that housed their gods and the instrumentalities that facilitated commerce with the higher powers were wrought with especial fineness. But the arts of the drama, music, painting, and architecture thus exemplified had no peculiar connection with theaters, galleries, museums. They were part of the significant life of an organized community.

The collective life that was manifested in war, worship, the forum, knew no division between what was characteristic of these places and operations, and the arts that brought color, grace, and dignity, into them. Painting and sculpture were organically one with architecture, as that was one with the social purpose that buildings served. Music and song were intimate parts of the rites and ceremonies in which the meaning of group life was consummated. Drama was a vital reënactment of the legends and history of group life. Not even in Athens can such arts be torn loose from this setting in direct experience and yet retain their significant character. Athletic sports, as well as drama, celebrated and enforced traditions of race and group, instructing the people, commemorating glories, and strengthening their civic pride.

Under such conditions, it is not surprising that the Athenian Greeks, when they came to reflect upon art, formed the idea that it is an act of reproduction, or imitation. There are many objections to this conception. But the vogue of the theory is testimony to the close connection of the fine arts with daily life; the idea would not have occurred to any one had art been remote from the interests of life. For the doctrine did not signify that art was a literal copying of objects, but that it reflected the emotions and ideas that are associated with the chief institutions of social life. Plato felt this connection so strongly that it led him to his idea of the necessity of censorship of poets, dramatists, and musicians. Perhaps he exaggerated when he said that a change from the Doric to the Lydian mode in music would be the sure precursor of civic degeneration. But no contemporary would have doubted that music was an integral part of the ethos and the institutions of the community. The idea of "art for art's sake" would not have been even understood.

There must then be historic reasons for the rise of the compartmental conception of fine art. Our present museums and galleries to which works of fine art are removed and stored illustrate some of the causes that have operated to segregate art instead of finding it an attendant of temple, forum, and other forms of associated life. An instructive history of modern art could be written in terms of the formation of the distinctively modern institutions of museum and exhibition gallery. I may point to a few outstanding facts. Most European museums are, among other things, memorials of the rise of nationalism and imperialism. Every capital must have its own museum of painting, sculpture, etc., devoted in part to exhibiting the greatness of its artistic past, and, in other part, to exhibiting the loot gathered by its monarchs in conquest of other nations; for instance, the accumulations of the spoils of Napoleon that are in the Louvre. They testify to the connection between the modern segregation of art and nationalism and militarism. Doubtless this connection has served at times a useful purpose, as in the case of Japan, who, when she was in the process of westernization, saved much of her art treasures by nationalizing the temples that contained them.

The growth of capitalism has been a powerful influence in the development of the museum as the proper home for works of art, and in the promotion of the idea that they are apart from the common life. The *nouveaux riches*, who are an important by-product of the capitalist system, have felt especially bound to surround themselves with works of fine art which, being rare, are also costly. Generally speaking, the typical collector is the typical capitalist. For evidence of good standing in the realm of higher culture, he amasses paintings, statuary, and artistic *bijoux*, as his stocks and bonds certify to his standing in the economic world.

Not merely individuals, but communities and nations, put their cultural good taste in evidence by building opera houses, galleries, and museums. These show that a community is not wholly absorbed in material wealth, because it is willing to spend its gains in patronage of art. It erects these buildings and collects their contents as it now builds a cathedral. These things reflect and establish superior cultural status, while their segregation from the common life reflects the fact that they are not part of a native and spontaneous culture. They are a kind of counterpart of a holier-than-thou attitude, exhibited not toward persons as such but toward the interests and occupations that absorb most of the community's time and energy.

. . . . .

Because of changes in industrial conditions the artist has been pushed to one side from the main streams of active interest. Industry has been mechanized and an artist cannot work mechanically for mass production. He is less integrated than formerly in the normal flow of social services. A peculiar esthetic "individualism" results. Artists find it incumbent upon them to betake themselves to their work as an isolated means of "self-expression." In order not to cater to the trend of economic forces, they often feel obliged to exaggerate their separateness to the point of eccentricity. Consequently artistic products take on to a still greater degree the air of something independent and esoteric.

Put the action of all such forces together, and the conditions that create the gulf which exists generally between producer and consumer in modern society operate to create also a chasm between ordinary and esthetic experience. Finally we have, as the record of this chasm, accepted as if it were normal, the philosophies of art that locate it in a region inhabited by no other creature, and that emphasize beyond all reason the merely contemplative character of the esthetic. Confusion of values enters in to accentuate the separation. Adventitious matters, like the pleasure of collecting, of exhibiting, of ownership and display, simulate esthetic values. Criticism is affected. There is much applause for the wonders of appreciation and the glories of the transcendent beauty of art indulged in without much regard to capacity for esthetic perception in the concrete.

My purpose, however, is not to engage in an economic interpretation of the history of the arts, much less to argue that economic conditions are either invariably or directly relevant to perception and enjoyment, or even to interpretation of individual works of art. It is to indicate that *theories* which isolate art and its appreciation by placing them in a realm of their own, disconnected from other modes of experiencing, are not inherent in the subject-matter but arise because of specifiable extraneous conditions. Embedded as they are in institutions and in habits of life, these conditions operate effectively because they work so unconsciously. Then the theorist assumes they are embedded in the nature of things. Nevertheless, the influence of these conditions is not confined to theory. As I have already indicated, it deeply affects the practice of living, driving away esthetic perceptions that are necessary ingredients of happiness, or reducing them to the level of compensating transient pleasurable excitations.

Even to readers who are adversely inclined to what has been said, the implications of the statements that have been made may be useful in defining the nature of the problem: that of recovering the continuity of esthetic experience with normal processes of living. The understanding of art and of its rôle in civilization is not furthered by setting out with eulogies of it nor by occupying ourselves exclusively at the outset with great works of art recognized as such. The comprehension which theory essays will be arrived at by a detour; by going back to experience of the common or mill run of things to discover the esthetic quality such experience possesses. Theory can start with and from acknowledged works of art only when the esthetic is already compartmentalized, or only when works of art are set in a niche apart instead of being celebrations, recognized as such, of the things of ordinary experience. Even a crude experience, if authentically an experience, is more fit to give a clue to the intrinsic nature of esthetic experience than is an object already set apart from any other mode of experience. Following this clue we can discover how the work of art develops and accentuates what is characteristically valuable in things of everyday enjoyment. The art product will then be seen to issue from the latter, when the full meaning of ordinary experience is expressed, as dyes come out of coal tar products when they receive special treatment.

· · · · ·

A conception of fine art that sets out from its connection with discovered qualities of ordinary experience will be able to indicate the factors and forces that favor the normal development of common human activities into matters of artistic value. It will also be able to point out those conditions that arrest its normal growth. Writers on esthetic theory often raise the question of whether esthetic philosophy can aid in cultivation of esthetic appreciation. The question is a branch of the general theory of criticism, which, it seems to me, fails to accomplish its full office if it does not indicate what to look for and what to find in concrete esthetic objects. But, in any case, it is safe to say that a philosophy of art is sterilized unless it makes us aware of the function of art in relation to other modes of experience, and unless it indicates why this function is so inadequately realized, and unless it suggests the conditions under which the office would be successfully performed.

The comparison of the emergence of works of art out of ordinary experiences to the refining of raw materials into valuable products may seem to some unworthy, if not an actual attempt to reduce works of art to the status of articles manufactured for commercial purposes. The point, however, is that no amount of ecstatic eulogy of finished works can of itself assist the understanding or the generation of such works. Flowers can be enjoyed without knowing about the interactions of soil, air, moisture, and seeds of which they are the result. But they cannot be *understood* without taking just these interactions into account—and theory is a matter of understanding. Theory is concerned with discovering the nature of the production of works of art and of their enjoyment in perception. How is it that the everyday making of things grows into that form of making which is genuinely artistic? How is it that our everyday enjoyment of scenes and situations develops into the peculiar satisfaction that attends the experience which is emphatically esthetic? These are the questions theory must answer. The answers cannot be found, unless we are willing to find the germs and roots in matters of experience that we do not currently regard as esthetic. Having discovered these active seeds, we may follow the course of their growth into the highest forms of finished and refined art.

. . . . .

We cannot answer these questions any more than we can trace the development of art out of everyday experience, unless we have a clear and coherent idea of what is meant when we say "normal experience." Fortunately, the road to arriving at such an idea is open and well marked. The nature of experience is determined by the essential conditions of life. While man is other than bird and beast, he shares basic vital functions with them and has to make the same basal adjustments if he is to continue the process of living. Having the same vital needs, man derives the means by which he breathes, moves, looks and listens, the very brain with which he coördinates his senses and his movements, from his animal forbears. The organs with which he maintains himself in being are not of himself alone, but by the grace of struggles and achievements of a long line of animal ancestry.

Fortunately a theory of the place of the esthetic in experience does not have to lose itself in minute details when it starts with experience in its elemental form. Broad outlines suffice. The first great consideration is that life goes on in an environment; not merely *in* it but because of it, through interaction with it. No creature lives merely under its skin; its subcutaneous organs are means of connection with what lies beyond its bodily frame, and to which, in order to live, it must adjust itself, by accommodation and defense but also by conquest. At every moment, the living creature is exposed to dangers from its surroundings, and at every moment, it must draw upon something in its surroundings to satisfy its needs. The career and destiny of a living being are bound up with its interchanges with its environment, not externally but in the most intimate way.

The growl of a dog crouching over his food, his howl in time of loss and loneliness, the wagging of his tail at the return of his human friend are expressions of the implication of a living in a natural medium which includes man along with the animal he has domesticated. Every need, say hunger for fresh air or food, is a lack that denotes at least a temporary absence of adequate adjustment with surroundings. But it is also a demand, a reaching out into the environment to make good the lack and to restore adjustment by building at least a temporary equilibrium. Life itself consists of phases in which the organism falls out of step with the march of surrounding things and then recovers unison with it—either through effort or by some happy chance. And, in a growing life, the recovery is never mere return to a prior state, for it is enriched by the state of disparity and resistance through which it has successfully passed. If the gap between organism and environment is too wide, the creature dies. If its activity is not enhanced by the temporary alienation, it merely subsists. Life grows when a temporary falling out is a transition to a more extensive balance of the energies of the organism with those of the conditions under which it lives.

These biological commonplaces are something more than that; they reach to the roots of the esthetic in experience. The world is full of things that are indifferent and even hostile to life; the very processes by which life is maintained tend to throw it out of gear with its surroundings. Nevertheless, if life continues and if in continuing it expands, there is an overcoming of factors of opposition and conflict; there is a transformation of them into differentiated aspects of a higher powered and more significant life. The marvel of organic, of vital, adaptation through expansion (instead of by contraction and passive accommodation) actually takes place. Here in germ are balance and harmony attained through rhythm. Equilibrium comes about not mechanically and inertly but out of, and because of, tension.

There is in nature, even below the level of life, something more than mere flux and change. Form is arrived at whenever a stable, even though moving, equilibrium is reached. Changes interlock and sustain one another. Wherever there is this coherence there is endurance. Order is not imposed from without but is made out of the relations of harmonious interactions that energies bear to one another. Because it is active (not anything static because foreign to what goes on) order itself develops. It comes to include within its balanced movement a greater variety of changes.

Order cannot but be admirable in a world constantly threatened with disorder—in a world where living creatures can go on living only by taking advantage of whatever order exists about them, incorporating it into themselves. In a world like ours, every living creature that attains sensibility welcomes order with a response of harmonious feeling whenever it finds a congruous order about it.

For only when an organism shares in the ordered relations of its environment does it secure the stability essential to living. And when the participation comes after a phase of disruption and conflict, it bears within itself the germs of a consummation akin to the esthetic.

The rhythm of loss of integration with environment and recovery of union not only persists in man but becomes conscious with him; its conditions are material out of which he forms purposes. Emotion is the conscious sign of a break, actual or impending. The discord is the occasion that induces reflection. Desire for restoration of the union converts mere emotion into interest in objects as conditions of realization of harmony. With the realization, material of reflection is incorporated into objects as their meaning. Since the artist cares in a peculiar way for the phase of experience in which union is achieved, he does not shun moments of resistance and tension. He rather cultivates them, not for their own sake but because of their potentialities, bringing to living consciousness an experience that is unified and total. In contrast with the person whose purpose is esthetic, the scientific man is interested in problems, in situations wherein tension between the matter of observation and of thought is marked. Of course he cares for their resolution. But he does not rest in it; he passes on to another problem using an attained solution only as a stepping stone from which to set on foot further inquiries.

The difference between the esthetic and the intellectual is thus one of the place where emphasis falls in the constant rhythm that marks the interaction of the live creature with his surroundings. The ultimate matter of both emphases in experience is the same, as is also their general form. The odd notion that an artist does not think and a scientific inquirer does nothing else is the result of converting a difference of tempo and emphasis into a difference in kind. The thinker has his esthetic moment when his ideas cease to be mere ideas and become the corporate meanings of objects. The artist has his problems and thinks as he works. But his thought is more immediately embodied in the object. Because of the comparative remoteness of his end, the scientific worker operates with symbols, words and mathematical signs. The artist does his thinking in the very qualitative media he works in, and the terms lie so close to the object that he is producing that they merge directly into it.

The live animal does not have to project emotions into the objects experienced. Nature is kind and hateful, bland and morose, irritating and comforting, long before she is mathematically qualified or even a congeries of "secondary" qualities like colors and their shapes. Even such words as long and short, solid and hollow, still carry to all, but those who are intellectually specialized, a moral and emotional connotation. The dictionary will inform any one who consults it that the early use of words like sweet and bitter was not to denote qualities of sense as such but to discriminate things as favorable and hostile. How could it be otherwise? Direct experience comes from nature and man interacting with each other. In this interaction, human energy gathers, is released, dammed up, frustrated and victorious. There are rhythmic beats of want and fulfillment, pulses of doing and being withheld from doing.

All interactions that effect stability and order in the whirling flux of change are rhythms. There is ebb and flow, systole and diastole: ordered change. The latter moves within bounds. To overpass the limits that are set is destruction and death, out of which, however, new rhythms are built up. The proportionate interception of changes establishes an order that is spatially, not merely temporally patterned: like the waves of the sea, the ripples of sand where waves have flowed back and forth, the fleecy and the black-bottomed cloud. Contrast of lack and fullness, of struggle and achievement, of adjustment after consummated irregularity, form the drama in which action, feeling, and meaning are one. The outcome is balance and counterbalance. These are not static nor mechanical. They express power that is intense because measured through overcoming resistance. Environing objects avail and counteravail.

There are two sorts of possible worlds in which esthetic experience would not occur. In a world of mere flux, change would not be cumulative; it would not move toward a close. Stability and rest would have no being. Equally is it true, however, that a world that is finished, ended, would have no traits of suspense and crisis, and would offer no opportunity for resolution. Where everything is already complete, there is no fulfillment. We envisage with pleasure Nirvana and a uniform heavenly bliss only because they are projected upon the background of our present world of stress and conflict. Because the actual world, that in which we live, is a combination of movement and culmination, of breaks and re-unions, the experience of a living creature is capable of esthetic quality. The live being recurrently loses and reëstablishes equilibrium with his surroundings. The moment of passage from disturbance into harmony is that of intensest life. In a finished world, sleep and waking could not be distinguished. In one wholly perturbed, conditions could not even be struggled with. In a world made after the pattern of ours, moments of fulfillment punctuate experience with rhythmically enjoyed intervals.

Inner harmony is attained only when, by some means, terms are made with the environment. When it occurs on any other than an "objective" basis, it is illusory—in extreme cases to the point of insanity. Fortunately for variety in experience, terms are made in many ways—ways ultimately decided by selective interest. Pleasures may come about through chance contact and stimulation; such pleasures are not to be despised in a world full of pain. But happiness and delight are a different sort of thing. They come to be through a fulfillment that reaches to the depths of our being—one that is an adjustment of our whole being with the conditions of existence. In the process of living, attainment of a period of equilibrium is at the same time the initiation of a new relation to the environment, one that brings with it potency of new adjustments to be made through struggle. The time of consummation is also one of beginning anew. Any attempt to perpetuate beyond its term the enjoyment attending the time of fulfillment and harmony constitutes withdrawal from the world. Hence it marks the lowering and loss of vitality. But, through the phases of perturbation and conflict, there abides the deep-seated memory of an underlying harmony, the sense of which haunts life like the sense of being founded on a rock.

Most mortals are conscious that a split often occurs between their present living and their past and future. Then the past hangs upon them as a burden; it invades the present with a sense of regret, of opportunities not used, and of consequences we wish undone. It rests upon the present as an oppression, instead of being a storehouse of resources by which to move confidently forward. But the live creature adopts its past; it can make friends with even its stupidities, using them as warnings that increase present wariness. Instead of trying to live upon whatever may have been achieved in the past, it uses past successes to inform the present. Every living experience owes its richness to what Santayana well calls "hushed reverberations." [1]

To the being fully alive, the future is not ominous but a promise; it surrounds the present as a halo. It consists of possibilities that are felt as a possession of what is now and here. In life that is truly life, everything overlaps and merges. But all too often we exist in apprehensions of what the future may bring, and are divided within ourselves. Even when not overanxious, we do not enjoy the present because we subordinate it to that which is absent. Because of the frequency of this abandonment of the present to the past and future, the happy periods of an experience that is now complete because it absorbs into itself memories of the past and anticipations of the future, come to constitute an esthetic ideal. Only when the past ceases to trouble and anticipations of the future are not perturbing is a being wholly united with his environment and therefore fully alive. Art celebrates with peculiar intensity the moments in which the past reënforces the present and in which the future is a quickening of what now is.

---

[1] "These familiar flowers, these well-remembered bird notes, this sky with its fitful brightness, these furrowed and grassy fields, each with a sort of personality given to it by the capricious hedge, such things as these are the mother tongue of our imagination, the language that is laden with all the subtle inextricable associations the fleeting hours of our childhood left behind them. Our delight in the sunshine on the deep-bladed grass today might be no more than the faint perception of wearied souls, if it were not for the sunshine and grass of far-off years, which still live in us and transform our perception into love." George Eliot in "The Mill on the Floss."

To grasp the sources of esthetic experience it is, therefore, necessary to have recourse to animal life below the human scale. The activities of the fox, the dog, and the thrush may at least stand as reminders and symbols of that unity of experience which we so fractionize when work is labor, and thought withdraws us from the world. The live animal is fully present, all there, in all of its actions: in its wary glances, its sharp sniffings, its abrupt cocking of ears. All senses are equally on the *qui vive*. As you watch, you see motion merging into sense and sense into motion—constituting that animal grace so hard for man to rival. What the live creature retains from the past and what it expects from the future operate as directions in the present. The dog is never pedantic nor academic; for these things arise only when the past is severed in consciousness from the present and is set up as a model to copy or a storehouse upon which to draw. The past absorbed into the present carries on; it presses forward.

There is much in the life of the savage that is sodden. But, when the savage is most alive, he is most observant of the world about him and most taut with energy. As he watches what stirs about him, he, too, is stirred. His observation is both action in preparation and foresight of the future. He is as active through his whole being when he looks and listens as when he stalks his quarry or stealthily retreats from a foe. His senses are sentinels of immediate thought and outposts of action, and not, as they so often are with us, mere pathways along which material is gathered to be stored away for a delayed and remote possibility.

It is mere ignorance that leads then to the supposition that connection of art and esthetic perception with experience signifies a lowering of their significance and dignity. Experience in the degree in which it *is* experience is heightened vitality. Instead of signifying being shut up within one's own private feelings and sensations, it signifies active and alert commerce with the world; at its height it signifies complete interpenetration of self and the world of objects and events. Instead of signifying surrender to caprice and disorder, it affords our sole demonstration of a stability that is not stagnation but is rhythmic and developing. Because experience is the fulfillment of an organism in its struggles and achievements in a world of things, it is art in germ. Even in its rudimentary forms, it contains the promise of that delightful perception which is esthetic experience.

Chapter II

THE LIVE CREATURE AND "ETHERIAL THINGS"

. . . Experience is the result, the sign, and the reward of that inter-action of organism and environment which, when it is carried to the full, is a transformation of interaction into participation and communication. Since sense-organs with their connected motor apparatus are the means of this participation, any and every derogation of them, whether practical or theoretical, is at once effect and cause of a narrowed and dulled life-experience. Oppositions of mind and body, soul and matter, spirit and flesh all have their origin, fundamentally, in fear of what life may bring forth. They are marks of contraction and withdrawal. Full recognition, therefore, of the continuity of the organs, needs and basic impulses of the human creature with his animal forebears, implies no necessary reduction of man to the level of the brutes. On the contrary, it makes possible the drawing of a ground-plan of human experience upon which is erected the superstructure of man's marvelous and distinguishing experience. What is distinctive in man makes it possible for him to sink below the level of the beasts. It also makes it possible for him to carry to new and unprecedented heights that unity of sense and impulse, of brain and eye and ear, that is exemplified in animal life, saturating it with the conscious meanings derived from communication and deliberate expression.

Man excels in complexity and minuteness of differentiations. This very fact constitutes the necessity for many more comprehensive and exact relationships among the constituents of his being. Important as are the distinctions and relations thus made possible, the story does not end here. There are more opportunities for resistance and tension, more drafts upon experimentation and invention, and therefore more novelty in action, greater range and depth of insight and increase of poignancy in feeling. As an organism increases in complexity, the rhythms of struggle and consummation in its relation to its environment are varied and prolonged, and they come to include within themselves an endless variety of sub-rhythms. The designs of living are widened and enriched. Fulfillment is more massive and more subtly shaded.

Space thus becomes something more than a void in which to roam about, dotted here and there with dangerous things and things that satisfy the appetite. It becomes a comprehensive and enclosed scene within which are ordered the multiplicity of doings and undergoings in which man engages. Time ceases to be either the endless and uniform flow or the succession of instantaneous points which some philosophers have asserted it to be. It, too, is the organized and organizing medium of the rhythmic ebb and flow of expectant impulse, forward and retracted movement, resistance and suspense, with fulfillment and consummation. It is an ordering of growth and maturations—as James said, we learn to skate in summer after having commenced in winter. Time as organization in change is growth, and growth signifies that a varied series of change enters upon intervals of pause and rest; of completions that become the initial points of new processes of development. Like the soil, mind is fertilized while it lies fallow, until a new burst of bloom ensues.

When a flash of lightning illumines a dark landscape, there is a momentary recognition of objects. But the recognition is not itself a mere point in time. It is the focal culmination of long, slow processes of maturation. It is the manifestation of the continuity of an ordered temporal experience in a sudden discrete instant of climax. It is as meaningless in isolation as would be the drama of Hamlet were it confined to a single line or word with no context. But the phrase "the rest is silence" is infinitely pregnant as the conclusion of a drama enacted through development in time; so may be the momentary perception of a natural scene. Form, as it is present in the fine arts, is the art of making clear what is involved in the organization of space and time prefigured in every course of a developing life-experience.

Moments and places, despite physical limitation and narrow localization, are charged with accumulations of long-gathering energy. A return to a scene of childhood that was left long years before floods the spot with a release of pent-up memories and hopes. To meet in a strange country one who is a casual acquaintance at home may arouse a satisfaction so acute as to bring a thrill. Mere recognitions occur only when we are occupied with something else than the object or person recognized. It marks either an interruption or else an intent to use what is recognized as a means for something else. To see, to perceive, is more than to recognize. It does not identify something present in terms of a past disconnected from it. The past is carried into the present so as to expand and deepen the content of the latter. There is illustrated the translation of bare continuity of external time into the vital order and organization of experience. Identification nods and passes on. Or it defines a passing moment in isolation, it marks a dead spot in experience that is merely filled in. The extent to which the process of living in any day or hour is reduced to labeling situations, events, and objects as "so-and-so" in mere succession marks the cessation of a life that is a conscious experience. Continuities realized in an individual, discrete, form are the essence of the latter.

Art is thus prefigured in the very processes of living. A bird builds its nest and a beaver its dam when internal organic pressures coöperate with external materials so that the former are fulfilled and the latter are transformed in a satisfying culmination. We may hesitate to apply the word "art," since we doubt the presence of directive intent. But all deliberation, all conscious intent, grows out of things once performed organically through the interplay of natural energies. Were it not so, art would be built on quaking sands, nay, on unstable air. The distinguishing contribution of man is consciousness of the relations found in nature. Through consciousness, he converts the relations of cause and effect that are found in nature into relations of means and consequence. Rather, consciousness itself is the inception of such a transformation. What was mere shock becomes an invitation; resistance becomes something to be used in changing existing arrangements of matter; smooth facilities become agencies for executing an idea. In these operations, an organic stimulation becomes the bearer of meanings, and motor responses are changed into instruments of expression and communication; no longer are they mere means of locomotion and direct reaction. Meanwhile, the organic substratum remains as the quickening and deep foundation. Apart from relations of cause and effect in nature, conception and invention could not be. Apart from the relation of processes of rhythmic conflict and fulfillment in animal life, experience would be without design and pattern. Apart from organs inherited from animal ancestry, idea and purpose would be without a mechanism of realization. The primeval arts of nature and animal life are so much the material, and, in gross outline, so much the model for the intentional achievements of man, that the theologically minded have imputed conscious intent to the structure of nature—as man, sharing many activities with the ape, is wont to think of the latter as imitating his own performances.

The existence of art is the concrete proof of what has just been stated abstractly. It is proof that man uses the materials and energies of nature with intent to expand his own life, and that he does so in accord with the structure of his organism—brain, sense-organs, and muscular system. Art is the living and concrete proof that man is capable of restoring consciously, and thus on the plane of meaning, the union of sense, need, impulse and action characteristic of the live creature. The intervention of consciousness adds regulation, power of selection, and redisposition. Thus it varies the arts in ways without end. But its intervention also leads in time to the *idea* of art as a conscious idea—the greatest intellectual achievement in the history of humanity.

· · · · ·

Chapter III

HAVING AN EXPERIENCE

Experience occurs continuously, because the interaction of live creature and environing conditions is involved in the very process of living. Under conditions of resistance and conflict, aspects and elements of the self and the world that are implicated in this interaction qualify experience with emotions and ideas so that conscious intent emerges. Oftentimes, however, the experience had is inchoate. Things are experienced but not in such a way that they are composed into *an* experience. There is distraction and dispersion; what we observe and what we think, what we desire and what we get, are at odds with each other. We put our hands to the plow and turn back; we start and then we stop, not because the experience has reached the end for the sake of which it was initiated but because of extraneous interruptions or of inner lethargy.

In contrast with such experience, we have *an* experience when the material experienced runs its course to fulfillment. Then and then only is it integrated within and demarcated in the general stream of experience from other experiences. A piece of work is finished in a way that is satisfactory; a problem receives its solution; a game is played through; a situation, whether that of eating a meal, playing a game of chess, carrying on a conversation, writing a book, or taking part in a political campaign, is so rounded out that its close is a consummation and not a cessation. Such an experience is a whole and carries with it its own individualizing quality and self-sufficiency. It is *an* experience.

Philosophers, even empirical philosophers, have spoken for the most part of experience at large. Idiomatic speech, however, refers to experiences each of which is singular, having its own beginning and end. For life is no uniform uninterrupted march or flow. It is a thing of histories, each with its own plot, its own inception and movement toward its close, each having its own particular rhythmic movement; each with its own unrepeated quality pervading it throughout. A flight of stairs, mechanical as it is, proceeds by individualized steps, not by undifferentiated progression, and an inclined plane is at least marked off from other things by abrupt discreteness.

Experience in this vital sense is defined by those situations and episodes that we spontaneously refer to as being "real experiences"; those things of which we say in recalling them, "that *was* an experience." It may have been something of tremendous importance—a quarrel with one who was once an intimate, a catastrophe finally averted by a hair's breadth. Or it may have been something that in comparison was slight—and which perhaps because of its very slightness illustrates all the better what is to be an experience. There is that meal in a Paris restaurant of which one says "that *was* an experience." It stands out as an enduring memorial of what food may be. Then there is that storm one went through in crossing the Atlantic—the storm that seemed in its fury, as it was experienced, to sum up in itself all that a storm can be, complete in itself, standing out because marked out from what went before and what came after.

In such experiences, every successive part flows freely, without seam and without unfilled blanks, into what ensues. At the same time there is no sacrifice of the self-identity of the parts. A river, as distinct from a pond, flows. But its flow gives a definiteness and interest to its successive portions greater than exist in the homogenous portions of a pond. In an experience, flow is from something to something. As one part leads into another and as one part carries on what went before, each gains distinctness in itself. The enduring whole is diversified by successive phases that are emphases of its varied colors.

Because of continuous merging, there are no holes, mechanical junctions, and dead centers when we have *an* experience. There are pauses, places of rest, but they punctuate and define the quality of movement. They sum up what has been undergone and prevent its dissipation and idle evaporation. Continued acceleration is breathless and prevents parts from gaining distinction. In a work of art, different acts, episodes, occurrences melt and fuse into unity, and yet do not disappear and lose their own character as they do so—just as in a genial conversation there is a continuous interchange and blending, and yet each speaker not only retains his own character but manifests it more clearly than is his wont.

An experience has a unity that gives it its name, *that* meal, that storm, that rupture of friendship. The existence of this unity is constituted by a single *quality* that pervades the entire experience in spite of the variation of its constituent parts. This unity is neither emotional, practical, nor intellectual, for these terms name distinctions that reflection can make within it. In discourse *about* an experience, we must make use of these adjectives of interpretation. In going over an experience in mind *after* its occurrence, we may find that one property rather than another was sufficiently dominant so that it characterizes the experience as a whole. There are absorbing inquiries and speculations which a scientific man and philosopher will recall as "experiences" in the emphatic sense. In final import they are intellectual. But in their actual occurrence they were emotional as well; they were purposive and volitional. Yet the experience was not a sum of these different characters; they were lost in it as distinctive traits. No thinker can ply his occupation save as he is lured and rewarded by total integral experiences that are intrinsically worth while. Without them he would never know what it is really to think and would be completely at a loss in distinguishing real thought from the spurious article. Thinking goes on in trains of ideas, but the ideas form a train only because they are much more than what an analytic psychology calls ideas. They are phases, emotionally and practically distinguished, of a developing underlying quality; they are its moving variations, not separate and independent like Locke's and Hume's so-called ideas and impressions, but are subtle shadings of a pervading and developing hue.

We say of an experience of thinking that we reach or draw a conclusion. Theoretical formulation of the process is often made in such terms as to conceal effectually the similarity of "conclusion" to the consummating phase of every developing integral experience. These formulations apparently take their cue from the separate propositions that are premises and the proposition that is the conclusion as they appear on the printed page. The impression is derived that there are first two independent and ready-made entities that are then manipulated so as to give rise to a third. In fact, in an experience of thinking, premises emerge only as a conclusion becomes manifest. The experience, like that of watching a storm reach its height and gradually subside, is one of continuous movement of subject-matters. Like the ocean in the storm, there are a series of waves; suggestions reaching out and being broken in a clash, or being carried onwards by a coöperative wave. If a conclusion is reached, it is that of a movement of anticipation and cumulation, one that finally comes to completion.

A "conclusion" is no separate and independent thing; it is the consummation of a movement.

Hence *an* experience of thinking has its own esthetic quality. It differs from those experiences that are acknowledged to be esthetic, but only in its materials. The material of the fine arts consists of qualities; that of experience having intellectual conclusion are signs or symbols having no intrinsic quality of their own, but standing for things that may in another experience be qualitatively experienced. The difference is enormous. It is one reason why the strictly intellectual art will never be popular as music is popular. Nevertheless, the experience itself has a satisfying emotional quality because it possesses internal integration and fulfillment reached through ordered and organized movement. This artistic structure may be immediately felt. In so far, it is esthetic. What is even more important is that not only is this quality a significant motive in undertaking intellectual inquiry and in keeping it honest, but that no intellectual activity is an integral event (is *an* experience), unless it is rounded out with this quality. Without it, thinking is inconclusive. In short, esthetic cannot be sharply marked off from intellectual experience since the latter must bear an esthetic stamp to be itself complete.

The same statement holds good of a course of action that is dominantly practical, that is, one that consists of overt doings. It is possible to be efficient in action and yet not have a conscious experience. The activity is too automatic to permit of a sense of what it is about and where it is going. It comes to an end but not to a close or consummation in consciousness. Obstacles are overcome by shrewd skill, but they do not feed experience. There are also those who are wavering in action, uncertain, and inconclusive like the shades in classic literature. Between the poles of aimlessness and mechanical efficiency, there lie those courses of action in which through successive deeds there runs a sense of growing meaning conserved and accumulating toward an end that is felt as accomplishment of a process. Successful politicians and generals who turn statesmen like Caesar and Napoleon have something of the showman about them. This of itself is not art, but it is, I think, a sign that interest is not exclusively, perhaps not mainly, held by the result taken by itself (as it is in the case of mere efficiency), but by it as the outcome of a process. There is interest in completing an experience. The experience may be one that is harmful to the world and its consummation undesirable. But it has esthetic quality.

The Greek identification of good conduct with conduct having proportion, grace, and harmony, the *kalon-agathon,* is a more obvious example of distinctive esthetic quality in moral action. One great defect in what passes as morality is its anesthetic quality. Instead of exemplifying wholehearted action, it takes the form of grudging piecemeal concessions to the demands of duty. But illustrations may only obscure the fact that any practical activity will, provided that it is integrated and moves by its own urge to fulfillment, have esthetic quality.

A generalized illustration may be had if we imagine a stone, which is rolling down hill, to have an experience. The activity is surely sufficiently "practical." The stone starts from somewhere, and moves, as consistently as conditions permit, toward a place and state where it will be at rest—toward an end. Let us add, by imagination, to these external facts, the ideas that it looks forward with desire to the final outcome; that it is interested in the things it meets on its way, conditions that accelerate and retard its movement with respect to their bearing on the end; that it acts and feels toward them according to the hindering or helping function it attributes to them; and that the final coming to rest is related to all that went before as the culmination of a continuous movement. Then the stone would have an experience, and one with esthetic quality.

If we turn from this imaginary case to our own experience, we shall find much of it is nearer to what happens to the actual stone than it is to anything that fulfills the conditions fancy just laid down. For in much of our experience we are not concerned with the connection of one incident with what went before and what comes after. There is no interest that controls attentive rejection or selection of what shall be organized into the developing experience. Things happen, but they are neither definitely included nor decisively excluded; we drift. We yield according to external pressure, or evade and compromise. There are beginnings and cessations, but no genuine initiations and concludings. One thing replaces another, but does not absorb it and carry it on. There is experience, but so slack and discursive that it is not *an* experience. Needless to say, such experiences are anesthetic.

Thus the non-esthetic lies within two limits. At one pole is the loose succession that does not begin at any particular place and that ends—in the sense of ceasing—at no particular place. At the other pole is arrest, constriction, proceeding from parts having only a mechanical connection with one another. There exists so much of one and the other of these two kinds of experience that unconsciously they come to be taken as norms of all experience. Then, when the esthetic appears, it so sharply contrasts with the picture that has been formed of experience, that it is impossible to combine its special qualities with the features of the picture and the esthetic is given an outside place and status. The account that has been given of experience dominantly intellectual and practical is intended to show that there is no such contrast involved in having an experience; that, on the contrary, no experience of whatever sort is a unity unless it has esthetic quality.

The enemies of the esthetic are neither the practical nor the intellectual. They are the humdrum; slackness of loose ends; submission to convention in practice and intellectual procedure. Rigid abstinence, coerced submission, tightness on one side and dissipation, incoherence and aimless indulgence on the other, are deviations in opposite directions from the unity of an experience. Some such considerations perhaps induced Aristotle to invoke the "mean proportional" as the proper designation of what is distinctive of both virtue and the esthetic. He was formally correct. "Mean" and "proportion" are, however, not self-explanatory, nor to be taken over in a prior mathematical sense, but are properties belonging to an experience that has a developing movement toward its own consummation.

I have emphasized the fact that every integral experience moves toward a close, an ending, since it ceases only when the energies active in it have done their proper work. This closure of a circuit of energy is the opposite of arrest, of *stasis*. Maturation and fixation are polar opposites. Struggle and conflict may be themselves enjoyed, although they are painful, when they are experienced as means of developing an experience; members in that they carry it forward, not just because they are there. There is, as will appear later, an element of undergoing, of suffering in its large sense, in every experience. Otherwise there would be no taking in of what preceded. For "taking in" in any vital experience is something more than placing something on the top of consciousness over what was previously known. It involves reconstruction which may be painful. Whether the necessary undergoing phase is by itself pleasurable or painful is a matter of particular conditions. It is indifferent to the total esthetic quality, save that there are few intense esthetic experiences that are wholly gleeful. They are certainly not to be characterized as amusing, and as they bear down upon us they involve a suffering that is none the less consistent with, indeed a part of, the complete perception that is enjoyed.

I have spoken of the esthetic quality that rounds out an experience into completeness and unity as emotional. The reference may cause difficulty. We are given to thinking of emotions as things as simple and compact as are the words by which we name them. Joy, sorrow, hope, fear, anger, curiosity, are treated as if each in itself were a sort of entity that enters full-made upon the scene, an entity that may last a long time or a short time, but whose duration, whose growth and career, is irrelevant to its nature. In fact emotions are qualities, when they are significant, of a complex experience that moves and changes. I say, when they are *significant,* for otherwise they are but the outbreaks and eruptions of a disturbed infant. All emotions are qualifications of a drama and they change as the drama develops. Persons are sometimes said to fall in love at first sight. But what they fall into is not a thing of that instant. What would love be were it compressed into a moment in which there is no room for cherishing and for solicitude? The intimate nature of emotion is manifested in the experience of one watching a play on the stage or reading a novel. It attends the development of a plot; and a plot requires a stage, a space, wherein to develop and time in which to unfold. Experience is emotional but there are no separate things called emotions in it.

By the same token, emotions are attached to events and objects in their movement. They are not, save in pathological instances, private. And even an "objectless" emotion demands something beyond itself to which to attach itself, and thus it soon generates a delusion in lack of something real. Emotion belongs of a certainty to the self. But it belongs to the self that is concerned in the movement of events toward an issue that is desired or disliked. We jump instantaneously when we are scared, as we blush on the instant when we are ashamed. But fright and shamed modesty are not in this case emotional states. Of themselves they are but automatic reflexes. In order to become emotional they must become parts of an inclusive and enduring situation that involves concern for objects and their issues. The jump of fright becomes emotional fear when there is found or thought to exist a threatening object that must be dealt with or escaped from. The blush becomes the emotion of shame when a person connects, in thought, an action he has performed with an unfavorable reaction to himself of some other person.

Physical things from far ends of the earth are physically transported and physically caused to act and react upon one another in the construction of a new object. The miracle of mind is that something similar takes place in experience without physical transport and assembling. Emotion is the moving and cementing force. It selects what is congruous and dyes what is selected with its color, thereby giving qualitative unity to materials externally disparate and dissimilar. It thus provides unity in and through the varied parts of an experience. When the unity is of the sort already described, the experience has esthetic character even though it is not, dominantly, an esthetic experience.

Two men meet; one is the applicant for a position, while the other has the disposition of the matter in his hands. The interview may be mechanical, consisting of set questions, the replies to which perfunctorily settle the matter. There is no experience in which the two men meet, nothing that is not a repetition, by way of acceptance or dismissal, of something which has happened a score of times. The situation is disposed of as if it were an exercise in bookkeeping. But an interplay may take place in which a new experience develops. Where should we look for an account of such an experience? Not to ledger-entries nor yet to a treatise on economics or sociology or personnel-psychology, but to drama or fiction. Its nature and import can be expressed only by art, because there is a unity of experience that can be expressed only as an experience. The *experience* is of material fraught with suspense and moving toward its own consummation through a connected series of varied incidents. The primary emotions on the part of the applicant may be at the beginning hope or despair, and elation or disappointment at the close. These emotions qualify the experience as a unity. But as the interview proceeds, secondary emotions are evolved as variations of the primary underlying one. It is even possible for each attitude and gesture, each sentence, almost every word, to produce more than a fluctuation in the intensity of the basic emotion; to produce, that is, a change of shade and tint in its quality. The employer sees by means of his own emotional reactions the character of the one applying. He projects him imaginatively into the work to be done and judges his fitness by the way in which the elements of the scene assemble and either clash or fit together. The presence and behavior of the applicant either harmonize with his own attitudes and desires or they conflict and jar. Such factors as these, inherently esthetic in quality, are the forces that carry the varied elements of the interview to a decisive issue. They enter into the settlement of every situation, whatever its dominant nature, in which there are uncertainty and suspense.

. . . . .

Chapter IV

THE ACT OF EXPRESSION

. . . It is this double change which converts an activity into an act of expression. Things in the environment that would otherwise be mere smooth channels or else blind obstructions become means, media. At the same time, things retained from past experience that would grow stale from routine or inert from lack of use, become coefficients in new adventures and put on a raiment of fresh meaning. Here are all the elements needed to define expression. The definition will gain force if the traits mentioned are made explicit by contrast with alternative situations. Not all outgoing activity is of the nature of expression. At one extreme, there are storms of passion that break through barriers and that sweep away whatever intervenes between a person and something he would destroy. There is activity, but not, from the standpoint of the one acting, expression. An onlooker may say "What a magnificent expression of rage!" But the enraged being is only raging, quite a different matter from *expressing* rage. Or, again, some spectator may say "How that man is expressing his own dominant character in what he is doing or saying." But the last thing the man in question is thinking of is to express his character; he is only giving way to a fit of passion. Again the cry or smile of an infant may be expressive to mother or nurse and yet not be an act of expression of the baby. To the onlooker it is an expression because it tells something about the state of the child. But the child is only engaged in doing something directly, no more expressive from his standpoint than is breathing or sneezing—activities that are also expressive to the observer of the infant's condition.

Generalization of such instances will protect us from the error—which has unfortunately invaded esthetic theory—of supposing that the mere giving way to an impulsion, native or habitual, constitutes expression. Such an act is expressive not in itself but only in reflective interpretation on the part of some observer—as the nurse may interpret a sneeze as the sign of an impending cold. As far as the act itself is concerned, it is, if purely impulsive, just a boiling over. While there is no expression, unless there is urge from within outwards, the welling up must be clarified and ordered by taking into itself the values of prior experiences before it can be an act of expression. And these values are not called into play save through objects of the environment that offer resistance to the direct discharge of emotion and impulse. Emotional discharge is a necessary but not a sufficient condition of expression.

There is no expression without excitement, without turmoil. Yet an inner agitation that is discharged at once in a laugh or cry, passes away with its utterance. To discharge is to get rid of, to dismiss; to express is to stay by, to carry forward in development, to work out to completion. A gush of tears may bring relief, a spasm of destruction may give outlet to inward rage. But where there is no administration of objective conditions, no shaping of materials in the interest of embodying the excitement, there is no expression. What is sometimes called an act of self-expression might better be termed one of self-exposure; it discloses character—or lack of character—to others. In itself, it is only a spewing forth.

The transition from an act that is expressive from the standpoint of an outside observer to one intrinsically expressive is readily illustrated by a simple case. At first a baby weeps, just as it turns its head to follow light; there is an inner urge but nothing to express. As the infant matures, he learns that particular acts effect different consequences, that, for example, he gets attention if he cries, and that smiling induces another definite response from those about him. He thus begins to be aware of the *meaning* of what he does. As he grasps the meaning of an act at first performed from sheer internal pressure, he becomes capable of acts of true expression. The transformation of sounds, babblings, lalling, and so forth, into language is a perfect illustration of the way in which acts of expression are brought into existence and also of the difference between them and mere acts of discharge.

There is suggested, if not exactly exemplified, in such cases the connection of expression with art. The child who has learned the effect his once spontaneous act has upon those around him performs "on purpose" an act that was blind. He begins to manage and order his activities in reference to their consequences. The consequences undergone because of doing are incorporated as the meaning of subsequent doings because the relation between doing and undergoing is perceived. The child may now cry for a purpose, because he wants attention or relief. He may begin to bestow his smiles as inducements or as favors. There is now art in incipiency. An activity that was "natural"—spontaneous and unintended—is transformed because it is undertaken as a means to a consciously entertained consequence. Such transformation marks every deed of art. The result of the transformation may be artful rather than esthetic. The fawning smile and conventional smirk of greeting are artifices. But the genuinely gracious act of welcome contains also a change of an attitude that was once a blind and "natural" manifestation of impulsion into an act of art, something performed in view of its place or relation in the processes of intimate human intercourse.

The difference between the artificial, the artful, and the artistic lies on the surface. In the former there is a split between what is overtly done and what is intended. The appearance is one of cordiality; the intent is that of gaining favor. Wherever this split between what is done and its purpose exists, there is insincerity, a trick, a simulation of an act that intrinsically has another effect. When the natural and the cultivated blend in one, acts of social intercourse are works of art. The animating impulsion of genial friendship and the deed performed completely coincide without intrusion of ulterior purpose. Awkwardness may prevent adequacy of expression. But the skillful counterfeit, however skilled, goes *through* the form of expression; it does not have the form of friendship and abide in it. The substance of friendship is untouched.

An act of discharge or mere exhibition lacks a medium. Instinctive crying and smiling no more require a medium than do sneezing and winking. They occur through some channel, but the means of outlet are not used as immanent means of an end. The act that *expresses* welcome uses the smile, the outreached hand, the lighting up of the face as media, not consciously but because they have become organic means of communicating delight upon meeting a valued friend. Acts that were primitively spontaneous are converted into means that make human intercourse more rich and gracious—just as a painter converts pigment into means of expressing an imaginative experience. Dance and sport are activities in which acts once performed spontaneously in separation are assembled and converted from raw, crude material into works of expressive art. Only where material is employed as media is there expresssion and art. Savage taboos that look to the outsider like mere prohibitions and inhibitions externally imposed may be to those who experience them media of expressing social status, dignity, and honor. Everything depends upon the way in which material is used when it operates as medium.

The connection between a medium and the act of expression is intrinsic. An act of expression always employs natural material, though it may be natural in the sense of habitual as well as in that of primitive or native. It becomes a medium when it is employed in view of its place and rôle, in its relations, an inclusive situation—as tones become music when ordered in a melody. The same tones might be uttered in connection with an attitude of joy, surprise, or sadness, and be natural outlets of particular feelings. They are *expressive* of one of these emotions when other tones are the medium in which one of them occurs.

Etymologically, an act of expression is a squeezing out, a pressing forth. Juice is expressed when grapes are crushed in the wine press; to use a more prosaic comparison, lard and oil are rendered when certain fats are subjected to heat and pressure. Nothing is pressed forth except from original raw or natural material. But it is equally true that the mere issuing forth or discharge of raw material is not expression. Through interaction with something external to it, the wine press, or the treading foot of man, juice results. Skin and seeds are separated and retained; only when the apparatus is defective are they discharged. Even in the most mechanical modes of expression there is interaction and a consequent transformation of the primitive material which stands as raw material for a product of art, in relation to what is actually pressed out. It takes the wine press as well as grapes to ex-press juice, and it takes environing and resisting objects as well as internal emotion and impulsion to constitute an *expression* of emotion.

Speaking of the production of poetry, Samuel Alexander remarked that "the artist's work proceeds not from a finished imaginative experience to which the work of art corresponds, but from passionate excitement about the subject matter. . . . The poet's poem is wrung from him by the subject which excites him." The passage is a text upon which we may hang four comments. One of these comments may pass for the present as a reënforcement of a point made in previous chapters. The real work of art is the building up of an integral experience out of the interaction of organic and environmental conditions and energies. Nearer to our present theme is the second point: The thing expressed is wrung from the producer by the pressure exercised by objective things upon the natural impulses and tendencies—so far is expression from being the direct and immaculate issue of the latter. The third point follows. The act of expression that constitutes a work of art is a construction in time, not an instantaneous emission. And this statement signifies a great deal more than that it takes time for the painter to transfer his imaginative conception to canvas and for the sculptor to complete his chipping of marble. It means that the expression of the self in and through a medium, constituting the work of art, is *itself* a prolonged interaction of something issuing from the self with objective conditions, a process in which both of them acquire a form and order they did not at first possess. Even the Almighty took seven days to create the heaven and the earth, and, if the record were complete, we should also learn that it was only at the end of that period that he was aware of just what He set out to do with the raw material of chaos that confronted Him. Only an emasculated subjective metaphysics has transformed the eloquent myth of Genesis into the conception of a Creator creating without any unformed matter to work upon.

The final comment is that when excitement about subject matter goes deep, it stirs up a store of attitudes and meanings derived from prior experience. As they are aroused into activity they become conscious thoughts and emotions, emotionalized images. To be set on fire by a thought or scene is to be inspired. What is kindled must either burn itself out, turning to ashes, or must press itself out in material that changes the latter from crude metal into a refined product. Many a person is unhappy, tortured within, because he has at command no art of expressive action. What under happier conditions might be used to convert objective material into material of an intense and clear experience, seethes within in unruly turmoil which finally dies down after, perhaps, a painful inner disruption.

Materials undergoing combustion because of intimate contacts and mutually exercised resistances constitute inspiration. On the side of the self, elements that issue from prior experience are stirred into action in fresh desires, impulsions and images. These proceed from the subconscious, not cold or in shapes that are identified with particulars of the past, not in chunks and lumps, but fused in the fire of internal commotion. They do not seem to come from the self, because they issue from a self not consciously known. Hence, by a just myth, the inspiration is attributed to a god, or to the muse. The inspiration, however, is initial. In itself, at the outset, it is still inchoate. Inflamed inner material must find objective fuel upon which to feed. Through the interaction of the fuel with material already afire the refined and formed product comes into existence. The act of expression is not something which supervenes upon an inspiration already complete. It is the carrying forward to completion of an inspiration by means of the objective material of perception and imagery.[1]

---

[1] In his interesting "The Theory of Poetry," Mr. Lascelles Abercrombie wavers between two views of inspiration. One of them takes what seems to me the correct interpretation. In the poem, an inspiration "completely and exquisitely defines

An impulsion cannot lead to expression save when it is thrown into commotion, turmoil. Unless there is com-pression nothing is expressed. The turmoil marks the place where inner impulse and contact with environment, in fact or in idea, meet and create a ferment. The war dance and the harvest dance of the savage do not issue from within except there be an impending hostile raid or crops that are to be gathered. To generate the indispensable excitement there must be something at stake, something momentous and uncertain— like the outcome of a battle or the prospects of a harvest. A sure thing does not arouse us emotionally. Hence it is not mere excitement that is expressed but excitement-about-something; hence, also, it is that even mere excitement, short of complete panic, will utilize channels of action that have been worn by prior activities that dealt with objects. Thus, like the movements of an actor who goes through his part automatically, it stimulates expression. Even an undefined uneasiness seeks outlet in song or pantomime, striving to become articulate.

Erroneous views of the nature of the act of expression almost all have their source in the notion that an emotion is complete in itself within, only when uttered having impact upon external material. But, in fact, an emotion is *to* or *from* or *about* something objective, whether in fact or in idea. An emotion is implicated in a situation, the issue of which is in suspense and in which the self that is moved in the emotion is vitally concerned. Situations are depressing, threatening, intolerable, triumphant. Joy in the victory won by a group with which a person is identified is not something internally complete, nor is sorrow upon the death of a friend anything that can be understood save as an interpenetration of self with objective conditions.

This latter fact is especially important in connection with the individualization of works of art. The notion that expression is a direct emission of an emotion complete in itself entails logically that individualization is specious and external. For, according to it, fear is fear, elation is elation, love is love, each being generic, and internally differentiated only by differences of intensity. Were this idea correct, works of art would necessarily fall within certain types. This

---

itself." At other times, he says the inspiration *is* the poem; "something self-contained and self-sufficient, a complete and entire whole." He says that "each inspiration is something which did not and could not originally exist as words." Doubtless such is the case; not even a trigonometric function exists merely as words. But if it is already self-sufficient and self-contained, why does it seek and find words as a medium of expression?

view has infected criticism but not so as to assist understanding of concrete works of art. Save nominally, there is no such thing as *the* emotion of fear, hate, love. The unique, unduplicated character of experienced events and situations impregnates the emotion that is evoked. Were it the function of speech to reproduce that to which it refers, we could never speak of fear, but only of fear-of-this-particular-oncoming-automobile, with all its specifications of time and place, or fear-under-specified-circumstances-of-drawing-a-wrong-conclusion from just-such-and-such-data. A lifetime would be too short to reproduce in words a single emotion. In reality, however, poet and novelist have an immense advantage over even an expert psychologist in dealing with an emotion. For the former build up a concrete situation and permit *it* to evoke emotional response. Instead of a description of an emotion in intellectual and symbolic terms, the artist "does the deed that breeds" the emotion.

That art is selective is a fact universally recognized. It is so because of the rôle of emotion in the act of expression. Any predominant mood automatically excludes all that is uncongenial with it. An emotion is more effective than any deliberate challenging sentinel could be. It reaches out tentacles for that which is cognate, for things which feed it and carry it to completion. Only when emotion dies or is broken to dispersed fragments, can material to which it is alien enter consciousness. The selective operation of materials so powerfully exercised by a developing emotion in a series of continued acts extracts matter from a multitude of objects, numerically and spatially separated, and condenses what is abstracted in an object that is an epitome of the values belonging to them all. This function creates the "universality" of a work of art.

If one examines into the reason why certain works of art offend us, one is likely to find that the cause is that there is no personally felt emotion guiding the selecting and assembling of the materials presented. We derive the impression that the artist, say the author of a novel, is trying to regulate by conscious intent the nature of the emotion aroused. We are irritated by a feeling that he is manipulating materials to secure an effect decided upon in advance. The facets of the work, the variety so indispensable to it, are held together by some external force. The movement of the parts and the conclusion disclose no logical necessity. The author, not the subject matter, is the arbiter.

In reading a novel, even one written by an expert craftsman, one may get a feeling early in the story that hero or heroine is doomed,

doomed not by anything inherent in situations and character but by the intent of the author who makes the character a puppet to set forth his own cherished idea. The painful feeling that results is resented not because it is painful but because it is foisted upon us by something that we feel comes from outside the movement of the subject matter. A work may be much more tragic and yet leave us with an emotion of fulfillment instead of irritation. We are reconciled to the conclusion because we feel it is inherent in the movement of the subject matter portrayed. The incident is tragic but the world in which such fateful things happen is not an arbitrary and imposed world. The emotion of the author and that aroused in us are occasioned by scenes in that world and they blend with subject matter. It is for similar reasons that we are repelled by the intrusion of a moral design in literature while we esthetically accept any amount of moral content if it is held together by a sincere emotion that controls the material. A white flame of pity or indignation may find material that feeds it and it may fuse everything assembled into a vital whole.

Just because emotion is essential to that act of expression which produces a work of art, it is easy for inaccurate analysis to misconceive its mode of operation and conclude that the work of art has emotion for its significant content. One may cry out with joy or even weep upon seeing a friend from whom one has been long separated. The outcome is not an expressive object—save to the onlooker. But if the emotion leads one to gather material that is affiliated to the mood which is aroused, a poem may result. In the direct outburst, an objective situation is the stimulus, the cause, of the emotion. In the poem, objective material becomes the content and matter of the emotion, not just its evocative occasion.

In the development of an expressive act, the emotion operates like a magnet drawing to itself appropriate material: appropriate because it has an experienced emotional affinity for the state of mind already moving. Selection and organization of material are at once a function and a test of the quality of the emotion experienced. In seeing a drama, beholding a picture, or reading a novel, we may feel that the parts do not hang together. Either the maker had no experience that was emotionally toned, or, although having at the outset a felt emotion, it was not sustained, and a succession of unrelated emotions dictated the work. In the latter case, attention wavered and shifted, and an assemblage of incongruous parts ensued. The sensitive observer or reader is aware of junctions and seams, of holes arbitrarily filled in. Yes, emotion must operate. But it works to effect continuity of movement, singleness of effect amid variety. It is selective of material and directive of its order and arrangement. But it is not *what* is expressed. Without emotion, there may be craftsmanship, but not art; it may be present and be intense, but if it is directly manifested the result is also not art.

There are other works that are overloaded with emotion. On the theory that manifestation of an emotion is its expression, there could be no overloading; the more intense the emotion, the more effective the "expression." In fact, a person overwhelmed by an emotion is thereby incapacitated for expressing it. There is at least that element of truth in Wordsworth's formula of "emotion recollected in tranquillity." There is, when one is mastered by an emotion, too much undergoing (in the language by which having an experience has been described) and too little active response to permit a balanced relationship to be struck. There is too much "nature" to allow of the development of art. Many of the paintings of Van Gogh, for example, have an intensity that arouses an answering chord. But with the intensity, there is an explosiveness due to absence of assertion of control. In extreme cases of emotion, it works to disorder instead of ordering material. Insufficient emotion shows itself in a coldly "correct" product. Excessive emotion obstructs the necessary elaboration and definition of parts.

The determination of the *mot juste*, of the right incident in the right place, of exquisiteness of proportion, of the precise tone, hue, and shade that helps unify the whole while it defines a part, is accomplished by emotion. Not every emotion, however, can do this work, but only one informed by material that is grasped and gathered. Emotion is informed and carried forward when it is spent indirectly in search for material and in giving it order, not when it is directly expended.

· · · · ·

. . . What most of us lack in order to be artists is not the inceptive emotion, nor yet merely technical skill in execution. It is capacity to work a vague idea and emotion over into terms of some definite medium. Were expression but a kind of decalcomania, or a conjuring of a rabbit out of the place where it lies hid, artistic expression would be a comparatively simple matter. But between conception and bringing to birth there lies a long period of gestation. During this period the inner material of emotion and idea is as much transformed through acting and being acted upon by objective material as the latter undergoes modification when it becomes a medium of expression.

It is precisely this transformation that changes the character of the original emotion, altering its quality so that it becomes distinctively esthetic in nature. In formal definition, emotion is esthetic when it adheres to an object formed by an expressive act, in the sense in which the act of expression has been defined.

In its beginning an emotion flies straight to its object. Love tends to cherish the loved object as hate tends to destroy the thing hated. Either emotion may be turned aside from its direct end. The emotion of love may seek and find material that is other than the directly loved one, but that is congenial and cognate through the emotion that draws things into affinity. This other material may be anything as long as it feeds the emotion. Consult the poets, and we find that love finds its expression in rushing torrents, still pools, in the suspense that awaits a storm, a bird poised in flight, a remote star or the fickle moon. Nor is this material metaphorical in character, if by "metaphor" is understood the result of any act of conscious comparison. Deliberate metaphor in poetry is the recourse of mind when emotion does not saturate material. Verbal expression may take the form of metaphor, but behind the words lies an act of emotional identification, not an intellectual comparison.

In all such cases, some object emotionally akin to the direct object of emotion takes the place of the latter. It acts in place of a direct caress, of hesitating approach, of trying to carry by storm. There is truth in Hulme's statement that "beauty is the marking time, the stationary vibration, the feigned ecstasy, of an arrested impulse unable to reach its natural end." * If there is anything wrong with the statement, it is the veiled intimation that the impulsion *ought* to have reached "its natural end." If the emotion of love between the sexes had not been celebrated by means of diversion into material emotionally cognate but practically irrelevant to its direct object and end, there is every reason to suppose it would still remain on the animal plane. The impulse arrested in its direct movement toward its physiologically normal end is not, in the case of poetry, arrested in an absolute sense. It is turned into indirect channels where it finds other material than that which is "naturally" appropriate to it, and as it fuses with this material it takes on new color and has new consequences. This is what happens when any natural impulse is

---

* *Speculations*, p. 266.

idealized or spiritualized. That which elevates the embrace of lovers above the animal plane is just the fact that when it occurs it has taken into itself, as its own meaning, the consequences of these indirect excursions that are imagination in action.

Expression is the clarification of turbid emotion; our appetites know themselves when they are reflected in the mirror of art, and as they know themselves they are transfigured. Emotion that is distinctively esthetic then occurs. It is not a form of sentiment that exists independently from the outset. It is an emotion induced by material that is expressive, and because it is evoked by and attached to this material it consists of natural emotions that have been transformed. Natural objects, landscapes, for example, induce it. But they do so only because when they are matter of an experience they, too, have undergone a change similar to that which the painter or poet effects in converting the immediate scene into the matter of an act that expresses the value of what is seen.

An irritated person is moved to do something. He cannot suppress his irritation by any direct act of will; at most he can only drive it by this attempt into a subterranean channel where it will work the more insidiously and destructively. He must act to get rid of it. But he can act in different ways, one direct, the other indirect, in manifestations of his state. He cannot suppress it any more than he can destroy the action of electricity by a fiat of will. But he can harness one or the other to the accomplishment of new ends that will do away with the destructive force of the natural agency. The irritable person does not have to take it out on neighbors or members of his family to get relief. He may remember that a certain amount of regulated physical activity is good medicine. He sets to work tidying his room, straightening pictures that are askew, sorting papers, clearing out drawers, putting things in order generally. He *uses* his emotion, switching it into indirect channels prepared by prior occupations and interests. But since there is something in the utilization of these channels that is emotionally akin to the means by which his irritation would find direct discharge, as he puts objects in order his emotion is ordered.

This transformation is of the very essence of the change that takes place in any and every natural or original emotional impulse when it takes the indirect road of expression instead of the direct road of discharge. Irritation may be let go like an arrow directed at a target and produce some change in the outer world. But having an outer effect is something very different from ordered use of objective conditions in order to give objective fulfillment to the emotion. The latter alone is expression and the emotion that attaches itself to, or is interpenetrated by, the resulting object is esthetic. If the person in question puts his room to rights as a matter of routine he is anesthetic. But if his original emotion of impatient irritation has been ordered and tranquillized by what he has done, the orderly room reflects back to him the change that has taken place in himself. He feels not that he has accomplished a needed chore but has done something emotionally fulfilling. His emotion as thus "objectified" is esthetic.

. . . . .

Chapter V

THE EXPRESSIVE OBJECT

Expression, like construction, signifies both an action and its result. The last chapter considered it as an act. We are now concerned with the product, the object that is expressive, that says something to us. If the two meanings are separated, the object is viewed in isolation from the operation which produced it, and therefore apart from individuality of vision, since the act proceeds from an individual live creature. Theories which seize upon "expression," as if it denoted simply the object, always insist to the uttermost that the object of art is purely representative of other objects already in existence. They ignore the individual contribution which makes the object something new. They dwell upon its "universal" character, and upon its meaning—an ambiguous term, as we shall see. On the other hand, isolation of the act of expressing from the expressiveness possessed by the object leads to the notion that expression is merely a process of discharging personal emotion—the conception criticized in the last chapter.

The juice expressed by the wine press is what it is because of a prior act, and it is something new and distinctive. It does not merely represent other things. Yet it has something in common with other objects and it is made to appeal to other persons than the one who produced it. A poem and picture present material passed through the alembic of personal experience. They have no precedents in existence or in universal being. But, nonetheless, their material came from the public world and so has qualities in common with the material of other experiences, while the product awakens in other persons new perceptions of the meanings of the common world. The oppositions of individual and universal, of subjective and objective, of freedom and order, in which philosophers have reveled, have no place in the work of art. Expression as personal act and as objective result are organically connected with each other.

It is not necessary, therefore, to go into these metaphysical questions. We may approach the matter directly. What does it mean to say that a work of art is representative, since it must be representative in some sense if it is expressive? To say in general that a work of art is or is not representative is meaningless. For the word has many meanings. An affirmation of representative quality may be false in one sense and true in another. If literal reproduction is signified by "representative" then the work of art is not of that nature, for such a view ignores the uniqueness of the work due to the personal medium through which scenes and events have passed. Matisse said that the camera was a great boon to painters, since it relieved them from any apparent necessity of copying objects. But representation may also mean that the work of art tells something to those who enjoy it about the nature of their own experience of the world: that it presents the world in a new experience which they undergo.

A similar ambiguity attends the question of meaning in a work of art. Words are symbols which represent objects and actions in the sense of standing for them; in that sense they have meaning. A signboard has meaning when it says so many miles to such and such a place, with an arrow pointing the direction. But meaning in these two cases has a purely external reference; it stands for something by pointing to it. Meaning does not belong to the word and signboard of its own intrinsic right. They have meaning in the sense in which an algebraic formula or a cipher code has it. But there are other meanings that present themselves directly as possessions of objects which are experienced. Here there is no need for a code or convention of interpretation; the meaning is as inherent in immediate experience as is that of a flower garden. Denial of meaning to a work of art thus has two radically different significations. It may signify that a work of art has not the kind of meaning that belongs to signs and symbols in mathematics—a contention that is just. Or it may signify that the work of art is without meaning as nonsense is without it. The work of art certainly does not have that which is had by flags when used to signal another ship. But it does have that possessed by flags when they are used to decorate the deck of a ship for a dance.

Since there are presumably none who intend to assert that works of art are without meaning in the sense of being senseless, it might seem as if they simply intended to exclude external meaning, meaning that resides outside the work of art itself. Unfortunately, however, the case is not so simple. The denial of meaning to art usually rests upon the assumption that the kind of value (and meaning) that a work of art possesses is so unique that it is without community or connection with the contents of other modes of experience than the esthetic. It is, in short, another way of upholding what I have called the esoteric idea of fine art. The conception implied in the treatment of esthetic experience set forth in the previous chapters is, indeed, that the work of art has a unique *quality*, but that it is that of clarifying and concentrating meanings contained in scattered and weakened ways in the material of other experiences.

The problem in hand may be approached by drawing a distinction between expression and statement. Science states meanings; art expresses them. It is possible that this remark will itself illustrate the difference I have in mind better than will any amount of explanatory comment. Yet I venture upon some degree of amplification. The instance of a signboard may help. It directs one's course to a place, say a city. It does not in any way supply experience of that city even in a vicarious way. What it does do is to set forth some of the conditions that must be fulfilled in order to procure that experience. What holds in this instance may be generalized. Statement sets forth the conditions under which an experience of an object or situation may be had. It is a good, that is, effective, statement in the degree in which these conditions are stated in such a way that they can be used as *directions* by which one may arrive at the experience. It is a bad statement, confused and false, if it sets forth these conditions in such a way that when they are used as directions, they mislead or take one to the object in a wasteful way.

"Science" signifies just that mode of statement that is most helpful as direction. To take the old standard case—which science today seems bent upon modifying—the statement that water is H_2O is primarily a statement of the conditions under which water comes into existence. But it is also for those who understand it a direction for producing pure water and for testing anything that is likely to be taken for water. It is a "better" statement than popular and pre-scientific ones just because in stating the conditions for the existence of water comprehensively and exactly, it sets them forth in a way that gives direction concerning generation of water. Such, however, is the newness of scientific statement and its present prestige (due ultimately to its directive efficacy) that scientific statement is often thought to possess more than a signboard function and to disclose or be "expressive" of the inner nature of things. If it did, it would come into competition with art, and we should have to take sides and decide which of the two promulgates the more genuine revelation.

The poetic as distinct from the prosaic, esthetic art as distinct from scientific, expression as distinct from statement, does something different from leading to an experience. It constitutes one. A traveler who follows the statement or direction of a signboard finds himself in the city that has been pointed towards. He then may *have* in his own experience some of the meaning which the city possesses. We may have it to such an extent that the city has expressed itself to him —as Tintern Abbey expressed itself to Wordsworth in and through his poem. The city might, indeed, be trying to express itself in a celebration attended with pageantry and all other resources that would render its history and spirit perceptible. Then there is, if the visitor has himself the experience that permits him to participate, an expressive object, as different from the statements of a gazetteer, however full and correct they might be, as Wordsworth's poem is different from the account of Tintern Abbey given by an antiquarian. The poem, or painting, does not operate in the dimension of correct descriptive statement but in that of experience itself. Poetry and prose, literal photograph and painting, operate in different media to distinct ends. Prose is set forth in propositions. The logic of poetry is super-propositional even when it uses what are, grammatically speaking, propositions. The latter have intent; art is an immediate realization of intent.

Van Gogh's letters to his brother are filled with accounts of things he has observed and many of which he painted. I cite one of many instances. "I have a view of the Rhone—the iron bridge at Trinquetaille, in which sky and river are the color of absinthe, the quays a shade of lilac, the figures leaning on the parapet, blackish, the iron bridge an intense blue, with a note of vivid orange in the background, and a note of intense malachite." Here is statement of a sort calculated to lead his brother to a like "view." But who, from the words alone—"I am trying to get something utterly heart-broken"—could infer the transition that Vincent himself makes to the particular *expressiveness* he desired to achieve in his picture? These words taken by themselves are not the expression; they only hint at it. The expressiveness, the esthetic meaning, is the picture itself. But the difference between the description of the scene and what he was striving for may remind us of the difference between statement and expression.

· · · · ·

Chapter VI

SUBSTANCE AND FORM

. . . The fact that form and matter are connected in a work of art does not mean they are identical. It signifies that in the work of art they do not offer themselves as two distinct things: the work is formed matter. But they are legitimately distinguished when reflection sets in, as it does in criticism and in theory. We are then compelled to inquire as to the formal structure of the work, and in order to carry on this inquiry intelligently, we must have a conception of what form is generically. We may get a key to this idea by starting from the fact that one idiomatic use of the word makes it equivalent with shape or figure. Especially in connection with pictures is form frequently identified simply with the patterns defined by linear outlines of shapes. Now shape is only an element in esthetic form; it does not constitute it. In ordinary perception we recognize and identify things by their shapes; even words and sentences have shapes, when heard as well as when seen. Consider how a misplaced accent disturbs recognition more than does any other kind of mispronunciation.

For shape in relation to recognition is not limited to geometric or spatial properties. The latter play a part only as they are subordinated to *adaptation to an end*. Shapes that are not in our minds associated with any function are hard to grasp and retain. The shapes of spoons, knives, forks, household articles, pieces of furniture, are means of identification because of their association with purpose. Up to a certain point, then, shape is allied with form in its artistic sense. In both there is organization of constituent parts. In some sense the typical shape of even a utensil and tool indicates that the meaning of the whole has entered into the parts to qualify them. This is the fact that has led some theorists, like Herbert Spencer, to identify the source of "beauty" with efficient and economical adaptation of parts to the function of a whole. In some cases fitness is indeed so exquisite as to constitute visible grace independent of the thought of any utility. But this special case indicates the way in which shape and form differ generically. For there is more to grace than just lack of clumsiness, in the sense in which "clumsy" means inefficiency of adaptation to an end. In shape as such adaptation is intrinsically limited to a particular end —like that of a spoon for carrying liquids to the mouth. The spoon that in addition has that esthetic form called grace bears no such limitation.

A good deal of intellectual effort has been expended in trying to identify efficiency for a particular end with "beauty" or esthetic quality. But these attempts are bound to fail, fortunate as it is that in some cases the two coincide and humanly desirable as it is that they should always meet. For adaptation to a particular end is often (always in the case of complicated affairs) something perceived by thought, while esthetic effect is found directly in sense-perception. A chair may serve the purpose of affording a comfortable and hygienically efficient seat, without serving at the same time the needs of the eye. If, on the contrary, it blocks rather than promotes the rôle of vision in an experience, it will be ugly no matter how well adapted to use as a seat. There is no preëstablished harmony that guarantees that what satisfies the need of one set of organs will fulfill that of all the other structures and needs that have a part in the experience, so as to bring it to completion as a complex of all elements. All we can say is that in the absence of disturbing contexts, such as production of objects for a maximum of private profit, a balance tends to be struck so that objects will be satisfactory—"useful" in the strict sense—to the self as a whole, even though some specific efficiency be sacrificed in the process. In so far there is a tendency for dynamic shape (as distinguished from bare geometric figure) to blend with artistic form.

Early in the history of philosophic thought the value of shape in making possible the definition and classification of objects was noted and was seized upon as a basis for a metaphysical theory of the nature of forms. The empirical fact of the relationship, effected by arrangement of parts to a definite end and use—like that of spoon or table or cup—was wholly neglected and even repudiated. Form was treated as something intrinsic, as the very essence of a thing in virtue of the metaphysical structure of the universe. It is easy to follow the course of reasoning that led to this result provided the relation of shape to use is once ignored. It is by form—in the sense of adapted shape—that we both identify and distinguish things in perception: chairs from tables, a maple from an oak. Since we note—or "know" them—in this way, and, since knowledge was believed to be a revelation of the true nature of things, it was concluded that things are what they are in virtue of having, intrinsically, certain forms.

Moreover, since things are rendered knowable by these forms, it was concluded that form is the rational, the intelligible, element in the objects and events of the world. Then it was set over against "matter," the latter being the irrational, the inherently chaotic and fluctuating, stuff upon which form was impressed. It was as eternal as the latter was shifting. This metaphysical distinction of matter and form was embodied in the philosophy that ruled European thought for centuries. Because of this fact it still affects the esthetic philosophy of form in relation to matter. It is the source of the bias in favor of their separation, especially when that takes the shape of assuming that form has a dignity and stability lacking to matter. Indeed, were it not for this background of tradition, it may be doubted whether it would occur to any one that there is a problem in their relation, so clear would it be that the only distinction important in art is that between matter inadequately formed and material completely and coherently formed.

Objects of industrial arts have form—that adapted to their special uses. These objects take on esthetic form, whether they are rugs, urns, or baskets, when the material is so arranged and adapted that it serves immediately the enrichment of the immediate experience of the one whose attentive perception is directed to it. No material can be adapted to an end, be it that of use as spoon or carpet, until raw material has undergone a change that shapes the parts and that arranges these parts with reference to one another with a view to the purpose of the whole. Hence the object has form in a definitive sense. When this form is liberated from limitation to a specialized end and serves also the purposes of an immediate and vital experience, the form is esthetic and not merely useful.

It is significant that the word "design" has a double meaning. It signifies purpose and it signifies arrangement, mode of composition. The design of a house is the plan upon which it is constructed to serve the purposes of those who live in it. The design of a painting or novel is the arrangement of its elements by means of which it becomes an expressive unity in direct perception. In both cases, there is an ordered relation of many constituent elements. The characteristic of artistic design is the intimacy of the relations that hold the parts together. In a house we have rooms *and* their arrangement with respect to one another. In the work of art, the relations cannot be told apart from *what* they relate except in later reflection. A work of art is poor in the degree in which they exist in separation, as in a novel wherein plot—the design—is felt to be superimposed upon incidents and characters instead of being their dynamic relations to one another. To understand the design of a complicated piece of machinery we have to know the purpose the machine is intended to serve, and how the various parts fit in to the accomplishment of that purpose. Design is, as it were, superimposed upon materials that do not actually share in it, as privates engage in a battle while they have only a passive share in the general's "design" for the battle.

Only when the constituent parts of a whole have the unique end of contributing to the consummation of a conscious experience, do design and shape lose superimposed character and become form. They cannot do this so long as they serve a specialized purpose; while they can serve the inclusive purpose of having *an* experience only when they do not stand out by themselves but are fused with all other properties of the work of art. In dealing with the significance of form in painting, Dr. Barnes has brought out the necessity for this completeness of blending, the interpenetration of "shape" and pattern with color, space, and light. Form is, as he says, "the synthesis or fusion of *all* plastic means . . . their harmonious merging." On the other hand, pattern in its limited sense, or plan and design, "is merely the skeleton upon which plastic units . . . are engrafted." [1]

This interfusion of all properties of the medium is necessary if the object in question is to serve the whole creature in his unified vitality. It therefore defines the nature of form in all the arts. With respect to a specialized utility, we can characterize design as being related to this and that end. One chair has a design fitted to give comfort; another, to hygiene; a third, to regal splendor. Only when all means are diffused through one another does the whole suffuse the parts so as to constitute an experience that is unified through inclusion instead of by exclusion. This fact confirms the position of the previous chapter as regards the union of qualities of direct sensuous vividness with other expressive qualities. As long as "meaning" is a matter of association and suggestion, it falls apart from the qualities of the sensuous medium and form is disturbed. Sense qualities are the carriers of meanings, not as vehicles carry goods but as a mother carries a baby when the baby is part of her own organism. Works of art, like words, are literally pregnant with meaning. Meanings, having their source in past experience, are means by which the particular organization that marks a given picture is effected. They are not added on by "association" but are either, and equally, the soul of which colors are the

---

[1] "The Art in Painting," pp. 85 and 87. Chapter I of Book II should be consulted. Form in the sense defined is, as is shown there, "the criterion of value."

body or the body of which colors are the soul—according as we happen to be concerned with the picture.

. . . . .

Chapter VII

THE NATURAL HISTORY OF FORM

. . . In a word, form is not found exclusively in objects labeled works of art. Wherever perception has not been blunted and perverted, there is an inevitable tendency to arrange events and objects with reference to the demands of complete and unified perception. Form is a character of every experience that is *an* experience. Art in its specific sense enacts more deliberately and fully the conditions that effect this unity. *Form may then be defined as the operation of forces that carry the experience of an event, object, scene, and situation to its own integral fulfillment.* The connection of form with substance is thus inherent, not imposed from without. It marks the matter of an experience that is carried to consummation. If the matter is of a jolly sort, the form that would be fitting to pathetic matter is impossible. If expressed in a poem, then meter, rate of movement, words chosen, the whole structure, will be different, and in a picture so will the whole scheme of color and volume relationships. In comedy, a man at work laying bricks while dressed in evening clothes is appropriate; the form fits the matter. The same subject-matter would bring the movement of another experience to disaster.

The problem of discovering the nature of form is thus identical with that of discovering the means by which are effected the carrying forward of an experience to fulfillment. When we know these means, we know what form is. While it is true that every matter has its own form, or is intimately individual, yet there are general conditions involved in the orderly development of any subject-matter to its completion, since only when these conditions are met does a unified perception take place.

Some of the conditions of form have been mentioned in passing. There can be no movement toward a consummating close unless there is a progressive massing of values, a cumulative effect. This result cannot exist without conservation of the import of what has gone before. Moreover, to secure the needed continuity, the accumulated experience must be such as to create suspense and anticipation of resolution. Accumulation is at the same time preparation, as with each phase of the growth of a living embryo. Only that is carried on which is led up to; otherwise there is arrest and a break. For this reason consummation is relative; instead of occurring once for all at a given point, it is recurrent. The final end is anticipated by rhythmic pauses, while that end is final only in an external way. For as we turn from reading a poem or novel or seeing a picture the effect presses forward in further experiences, even if only subconsciously.

Such characteristics as continuity, cumulation, conservation, tension and anticipation are thus formal conditions of esthetic form. The factor of resistance is worth especial notice at this point. Without internal tension there would be a fluid rush to a straightaway mark; there would be nothing that could be called development and fulfillment. The existence of resistance defines the place of intelligence in the production of an object of fine art. The difficulties to be overcome in bringing about the proper reciprocal adaptation of parts constitute what in intellectual work are problems. As in activity dealing with predominatingly intellectual matters, the material that constitutes a problem has to be converted into a means for its solution. It cannot be sidestepped. But in art the resistance encountered enters into the work in a more immediate way than in science. The perceiver as well as artist has to perceive, meet, and overcome problems; otherwise, appreciation is transient and overweighted with sentiment. For, in order to perceive esthetically, he must remake his past experiences so that they can enter integrally into a new pattern. He cannot dismiss his past experiences nor can he dwell among them as they have been in the past.

A rigid predetermination of an end-product whether by artist or beholder leads to the turning out of a mechanical or academic product. The processes by which the final object and perception are reached are not, in such cases, means that move forward in the construction of a consummating experience. The latter is rather of the nature of a stencil, even though the copy from which the stencil is made exists in mind and not as a physical thing. A statement that an artist does not care how his work eventuates would not be literally true. But it is true that he cares about the end-result as a completion of what goes before and not because of its conformity or lack of conformity with a ready-made antecedent scheme. He is willing to leave the outcome to the adequacy of the means from which it issues and which it sums up. Like the scientific inquirer, he permits the subject-matter of his perception in connection with the problems it presents to determine the issue, instead of insisting upon its agreement with a conclusion decided upon in advance.

The consummatory phase of experience—which is intervening as well as final—always presents something new. Admiration always includes an element of wonder. As a Renascence writer said: "There is no excellent beauty that hath not some strangeness in the proportion." The unexpected turn, something which the artist himself does not definitely foresee, is a condition of the felicitous quality of a work of art; it saves it from being mechanical. It gives the spontaneity of the unpremeditated to what would otherwise be a fruit of calculation. The painter and poet like the scientific inquirer know the delights of discovery. Those who carry on their work as a demonstration of a preconceived thesis may have the joys of egotistic success but not that of fulfillment of an experience for its own sake. In the latter they learn by their work, as they proceed, to see and feel what had not been part of their original plan and purpose.

The consummatory phase is recurrent throughout a work of art, and in the experience of a great work of art the points of its incidence shift in successive observations of it. This fact sets the insuperable barrier between mechanical production and use and esthetic creation and perception. In the former there are no ends until the final end is reached. Then work tends to be labor and production to be drudgery. But there is no final term in appreciation of a work of art. It carries on and is, therefore, instrumental as well as final. Those who deny this fact confine the significance of "instrumental" to the process of contributing to some narrow, if not base, office of efficacy. When the fact is not given a name, they acknowledge it. Santayana speaks of being "carried by contemplation of nature to a vivid faith in the ideal." This statement applies to art as to nature, and it indicates an instrumental function exercised by a work of art. We are carried to a refreshed attitude toward the circumstances and exigencies of ordinary experience. The work, in the sense of working, of an object of art does not cease when the direct act of perception stops. It continues to operate in indirect channels. Indeed, persons who draw back at the mention of "instrumental" in connection with art often glorify art for precisely the enduring serenity, refreshment, or re-education of vision that are induced by it. The real trouble is verbal. Such persons are accustomed to associate the word with instrumentalities for narrow ends—as an umbrella is instrumental to protection from rain or a mowing machine to cutting grain.

Some features, that at first sight seem extraneous, belong in fact to expressiveness. For they further the development of an experience so as to give the satisfaction peculiar to striking fulfillment. This is true, for example, of evidence of unusual skill and of economy in use of means, when these traits are integrated with the actual work. Skill is then admired not as part of the external equipment of the artist, but as an enhanced expression belonging to the object. For it facilitates the carrying on a continuous process to its own precise and definite conclusion. It belongs to the product and not merely to the producer, because it is a constituent of form; just as the grace of a greyhound marks the movements he performs rather than is a trait possessed by the animal as something outside the movements.

Costliness is, also, as Santayana has pointed out, an element in expression, a costliness that has nothing in common with vulgar display of purchasing power. Rarity counts to intensify expression whether the rarity is that of infrequent occurrence of patient labor, or because it has the glamor of a distant clime and initiates us into hardly known modes of living. Such instances of costliness are part of form because they operate as do all factors of the new and unexpected in promoting the building up of a unique experience. The familiar may also have this effect. There are others beside Charles Lamb who are peculiarly sensitive to the charm of the domestic. But they *celebrate* the familiar instead of reproducing its forms in waxy puppets. The old takes on a new guise in which the sense of the familiar is rescued from the oblivion that custom usually effects. Elegance is also a part of form for it marks a work whenever subject-matter moves to its conclusion with inevitable logic.

Some of the traits mentioned are more often referred to technique than to form. The attribution is correct whenever the qualities in question are referred to the artist rather than to his work. There is a technique that obtrudes, like the flourishes of a writing master. If skill and economy suggest their author, they take us away from the work itself. The traits of the work which suggest the skill of its producer are then *in* the work but they are not *of* it. And the reason they are not of it is precisely the negative side of the point which I am emphasizing. They do not take us anywhere in the institution of unified developing experience; they do not act as inherent forces to carry the object of which they are a professed part to consummation. Such traits are like any other superfluous or excrescent element. Technique is neither identical with form nor yet wholly independent of it. It is, properly, the skill with which the elements constituting form are managed. Otherwise it is show-off or a virtuosity separated from expression.

Significant advances in technique occur, therefore, in connection with efforts to solve problems that are not technical but that grow out of the need for new modes of experience. This statement is as true of esthetic arts as of the technological. There are improvements in technique that have to do merely with the bettering of an old-style vehicle. But they are insignificant in comparison with the change in technique from the wagon to the automobile when social needs called for a rapid transportation under personal control that was not possible even with the railway locomotive. If we take developments in the major techniques of painting during and since the Renascence we find that they were connected with efforts to solve problems that grew out of the experience expressed in painting and not out of the craftsmanship of painting itself.

There was first the problem of transition from depiction of contours in flat-like mosaics to "three-dimensional" presentations. Until experience expanded to demand expression of something more than decorative renderings of religious themes determined by ecclesiastic fiat there was nothing to motivate this change. In its own place, the convention of "flat" painting is just as good as any other convention, as Chinese rendering of perspective is as perfect in one way as that of Western painting in another. The force that brought about the change in technique was the growth of naturalism in experience outside of art. Something of the same sort applies to the next great change, mastery of means for rendering aërial perspective and light. The third great technical change was the use by the Venetians of color to effect what other schools, especially the Florentine, had accomplished by means of the sculpturesque line—a change indicative of a vast secularization of values with its demand for the glorification of the sumptuous and suave in experience.

I am not concerned, however, with the history of an art, but with indicating how technique functions in respect to expressive form. The dependence of significant technique upon the need for expressing certain distinctive modes of experience is testified to by the three stages that usually attend the appearance of a new technique. At first there is experimentation on the side of artists, with considerable exaggeration of the factor to which the new technique is adapted. This was true of the use of line to define recognition of the value of the round, as with Mantegna; it is true of the typical impressionists in respect to light-effects. On the side of the public there is general condemnation of the intent and subject-matter of these adventures in art. In the next stage, the fruits of the new procedure are absorbed; they are naturalized and effect certain modifications of the old tradition. This period establishes the new aims and hence the new technique as having "classic" validity, and is accompanied with a prestige that holds over into subsequent periods. Thirdly, there is a period when special features of the technique of the masters of the balanced period are adopted for imitation and made ends in themselves. Thus in the later seventeenth century, the treatment of dramatic movement characteristic of Titian and still more of Tintoretto, by means chiefly of light and shade, is exaggerated to the point of the theatrical. In Guercino, Caravaggio, Feti, Carracci, Ribera, the attempt to depict movement dramatically results in posed tableaux and defeats itself. In this third stage (which dogs creative work after the latter has received general recognition), technique is borrowed without relation to the urgent experience that at first evoked it. The academic and eclectic result.

I have previously stated that craftsmanship alone is not art. What is now added is the often ignored point of the thorough relativity of technique to form in art. It was not lack of dexterity that gives early Gothic sculpture its special form nor that gives Chinese paintings their special kind of perspective. The artists said what they had to say better with the techniques they used than they could have done with another. What to us is a charming naïveté was to them the simple and direct method of expressing a felt subject-matter. For this reason, while there is not continuity of repetition in any esthetic art, neither is there, of necessity, advance. Greek sculpture will never be equaled in its own terms. Thorwaldsen is no Pheidias. That which Venetian painters achieved will stand unrivaled. The modern reproduction of the architecture of the Gothic cathedral always lacks the quality of the original. What happens in the movement of art is emergence of new materials of experience demanding expression, and therefore involving in their expression new forms and techniques. Manet went back in time to achieve his brush-work, but his return involved no mere copying of an old technique.

The relativity of technique to form is nowhere better exemplified than in Shakespeare. After his reputation was established as the universal literary artist, critics thought it necessary to assume that greatness adhered to all his work. They built up theories of literary form on the basis of special techniques. They were shocked when a more accurate scholarship showed that many much lauded things were borrowed from the conventions of the Elizabethan stage. To those who have identified technique with form, the effect is to deflate Shakespeare's greatness. But his substantial form remains just what it always has been and is unaffected by his local adaptations. Allowance for some aspects of his technique should indeed but concentrate attention upon what is significant in his art.

It is hardly possible to overstate the relativity of technique. It varies with all sorts of circumstances having little relation to the work of art —perhaps a new discovery in chemistry that affects pigments. The significant changes are those which affect form itself in its esthetic sense. The relativity of technique to instruments is often overlooked. It becomes important when the new instrument is a sign of a change in culture—that is, in material to be expressed. Early pottery is largely determined by the potters' wheel. Rugs and blankets owe much of their geometric design to the nature of the instrument of weaving. Such things by themselves are like the physical constitution of an artist—as Cezanne wished he had Manet's muscles. Such things become of more than antiquarian interest only when they relate to a change in culture and experience. The technique of those who painted long ago on walls of caves and who carved bone served the purpose that conditions offered or imposed. Artists always have used and always will use all kinds of techniques.

There is, on the other side, a tendency among lay critics to confine experimentation to scientists in the laboratory. Yet one of the essential traits of the artist is that he is born an experimenter. Without this trait he becomes a poor or a good academician. The artist is compelled to be an experimenter because he has to express an intensely individualized experience through means and materials that belong to the common and public world. This problem cannot be solved once for all. It is met in every new work undertaken. Otherwise an artist repeats himself and becomes esthetically dead. Only because the artist operates experimentally does he open new fields of experience and disclose new aspects and qualities in familiar scenes and objects.

If, instead of saying "experimental" one were to say "adventurous," one would probably win general assent—so great is the power of words. Because the artist is a lover of unalloyed experience, he shuns objects that are already saturated, and he is therefore always on the growing edge of things. By the nature of the case, he is as unsatisfied with what is established as is a geographic explorer or a scientific inquirer. The "classic" when it was produced bore the marks of adventure. This fact is ignored by classicists in their protest against romantics who undertake the development of new values, often without possessing means for their creation. That which is now classic is so because of completion of adventure, not because of its absence. The one who perceives and enjoys esthetically always has the sense of adventure in reading any classic that Keats had in reading Chapman's "Homer."

. . . . .

. . . Many tangled problems, multifarious ambiguities, and historic controversies are involved in the question of the subjective and objective in art. Yet if the position that has been taken regarding form and substance is correct, there is at least one important sense in which form must be as objective as the material which it qualifies. If form emerges when raw materials are selectively arranged with reference to rendering an experience unified in movement to its intrinsic fulfillment, then surely objective conditions are controlling forces in the production of a work of art. A work of fine art, a statue, building, drama, poem, novel, when done, is as much a part of the objective world as is a locomotive or a dynamo. And, as much as the latter, its existence is causally conditioned by the coördination of materials and energies of the external world. I do not mean that this is the whole of the work of art; even the product of industrial art was made to serve a purpose and is actually, instead of potentially, a locomotive as it operates in conditions where it produces consequences beyond its bare physical being; as, namely, it transports human beings and goods. But I do mean that there can be no esthetic experience apart from an *object*, and that for an object to be the content of esthetic appreciation it must satisfy those *objective* conditions without which cumulation, conservation, reënforcement, transition into something more complete, are impossible. The general conditions of esthetic form, of which I spoke a few paragraphs ago, are objective in the sense of belonging to the world of physical materials and energies: while the latter do not suffice for an esthetic experience, they are a *sine qua non* of its existence. And the immediate artistic evidence for the truth of this statement is the interest that obsesses every artist in observing the world about him and his devoted care for the physical media with which he works.

What, then, are those formal conditions of artistic form that are rooted deep in the world itself? The implications of the question involve no material not already considered. Interaction of environment with organism is the source, direct or indirect, of all experience and from the environment come those checks, resistances, furtherances, equilibria, which, when they meet with the energies of the organism in appropriate ways, constitute form. The first characteristic of the environing world that makes possible the existence of artistic form is rhythm. There is rhythm in nature before poetry, painting, architecture and music exist. Were it not so, rhythm as an essential property of form would be merely superimposed upon material, not an operation through which material effects its own culmination in experience.

The larger rhythms of nature are so bound up with the conditions of even elementary human subsistence, that they cannot have escaped the notice of man as soon as he became conscious of his occupations and the conditions that rendered them effective. Dawn and sunset, day and night, rain and sunshine, are in their alternation factors that directly concern human beings.

The circular course of the seasons affects almost every human interest. When man became agricultural, the rhythmic march of the seasons was of necessity identified with the destiny of the community. The cycle of irregular regularities in the shape and behavior of the moon seemed fraught with mysterious import for the welfare of man, beast, and crops, and inextricably bound up with the mystery of generation. With these larger rhythms were bound up those of the ever-recurring cycles of growth from seed to a maturity that reproduced the seed; the reproduction of animals, the relation of male and female, the never-ceasing round of births and deaths.

Man's own life is affected by the rhythm of waking and sleeping, hungering and satiety, work and rest. The long rhythms of agrarian pursuits were broken into minuter and more directly perceptible cycles with the development of the crafts. With the working of wood, metal, fibers, clay, the change of raw material into consummated result, through technically controlled means, is objectively manifest. In working the matter, there are the recurrent beats of patting, chipping, molding, cutting, pounding, that mark off the work into measures. But more significant were those times of preparation for war and planting, those times of celebrating victory and harvest, when movements and speech took on cadenced form.

Thus, sooner or later, the participation of man in nature's rhythms, a partnership much more intimate than is any observation of them for purposes of knowledge, induced him to impose rhythm on changes where they did not appear. The apportioned reed, the stretched string and taut skin rendered the measures of action conscious through song and dance. Experiences of war, of hunt, of sowing and reaping, of the death and resurrection of vegetation, of stars circling over watchful shepherds, of constant return of the inconstant moon, were undergone to be reproduced in pantomime and generated the sense of life as drama. The mysterious movements of serpent, elk, boar, fell into rhythms that brought the very essence of the lives of these animals to realization as they were enacted in dance, chiseled in stone, wrought in silver, or limned on the walls of caves. The formative arts that shaped things of use were wedded to the rhythms of voice and the self-contained movements of the body, and out of the union technical arts gained the quality of fine art. Then the apprehended rhythms of nature were employed to introduce evident order into some phase of the confused observations and images of mankind. Man no longer conformed his activities of necessity to the rhythmic changes of nature's cycles, but used those which necessity forced upon him to celebrate his relations to nature as if she had conferred upon him the freedom of her realm.

The reproduction of the order of natural changes and the perception of that order were at first close together, so close that no distinction existed between art and science. They were both called *technē*. Philosophy was written in verse and, under the influence of imaginative endeavor, the world became a cosmos. Early Greek philosophy told the story of nature, and since a story has beginning, movement, and climax, the substance of the story demanded esthetic form. Within the story, minor rhythms became parts of the great rhythm of generation and destruction, of coming into being and passing out of being; of remission and concentration; of aggregation and dispersion; of consolidation and dissolution. The idea of law emerged with the idea of harmony, and conceptions that are now prosaic commonplaces emerged as parts of the art of nature as that was construed in the art of language.

. . . . .

Chapter VIII

THE ORGANIZATION OF ENERGIES

It has been repeatedly intimated that there is a difference between the art product (statue, painting or whatever), and the *work* of art. The first is physical and potential; the latter is active and experienced. It is what the product does, its working. For nothing enters experience bald and unaccompanied, whether it be a seemingly formless happening, a theme intellectually systematized, or an object elaborated with every loving care of united thought and emotion. Its very entrance is the beginning of a complex interaction; upon the nature of this interaction depends the character of the thing as finally experienced. When the structure of the object is such that its force interacts happily (but not easily) with the energies that issue from the experience itself; when their mutual affinities and antagonisms work together to bring about a substance that develops cumulatively and surely (but not too steadily) toward a fulfilling of impulsions and tensions, then indeed there is a work of art.

In the previous chapter, I emphasized the dependence of this final work upon the existence of rhythms in nature; as I pointed out, they are the conditions of form in experience and hence of expression. But an esthetic experience, the work of art in its actuality, is *perception*. Only as these rhythms, even if embodied in an outer object that is itself a product of art, become a rhythm in experience itself are they esthetic. And this rhythm in what is experienced is something quite different from intellectual recognition that there is rhythm in the external thing: as different as is the perceptual enjoyment of glowing harmonious colors from the mathematical equations that define them for a scientific inquirer.

. . . . .

The term "energy" has been used many times in this discussion. Perhaps insistence upon the idea of energy in connection with fine art seems to some minds out of place. Yet there are certain commonplaces that it is proper to utter in connection with art that cannot be intelligible unless the fact of energy be made central: its power to move and stir, to calm and tranquillize. And surely either rhythm and balance are either characters foreign to art or else art, because of their basic rôle, is only definable as organization of energies. With respect to what the work of art does to us and for us, I see but two alternatives. Either it operates because some transcendent essence (usually called "beauty") descends upon experience from without, or esthetic effect is due to art's unique transcript of the energy of the things of the world. As between these two alternatives, I do not know how mere argument can determine the choice. But it is something to know what is involved in making the choice.

Taking my stand, then, upon the connection of esthetic effect with qualities of all experience as far as any experience is unified, I would ask how art can be expressive and yet not be imitative or slavishly representative, save by selecting and ordering the energies in virtue of which things act upon us and interest us? If art is in any sense reproductive, and yet reproduces neither details nor generic features, it necessarily follows that art operates by selecting those potencies in things by which an experience—any experience—has significance and value. Elimination gets rid of forces that confuse, distract, and deaden. Order, rhythm and balance, simply means that energies significant for experience are acting at their best.

The term "ideal" has been cheapened by sentimental popular use, and by use in philosophic discourse for apologetic purposes to disguise discords and cruelties in existence. But there is a definite sense in which art is ideal—namely, the sense just indicated. Through selection and organization those features that make any experience worth having as an experience are prepared by art for commensurate perception. There must be, in spite of all indifference and hostility of nature to human interests, some congruity of nature with man or life could not exist. In art the forces that are congenial, that sustain not this or that special aim but the processes of enjoyed experience itself, are set free. That release gives them ideal quality. For what ideal can man honestly entertain save the idea of an environment in which all things conspire to the perfecting and sustaining of the values occasionally and partially experienced?

An English writer, Galsworthy I think, has somewhere defined art "as the imaginative expression of energy which, through technical concretion of feeling and perception, tends to reconcile the individual with the universal by exciting in him impersonal emotion." Energies that constitute the objects and events of the world and hence determine our experience are the "universal." "Reconciliation" is the attaining, in immediate unargumentative form, of periods of harmonious coöperation of man and the world in experiences that are complete. The resultant emotion is "impersonal" because it is attached not to personal fortune but to the object to the construction of which the self has surrendered itself in devotion. Appreciation is equally impersonal in its emotional quality because it also involves construction and organization of objective energies.

Chapter IX

THE COMMON SUBSTANCE
OF THE ARTS

. . . Every work of art has a particular medium by which, among other things, the qualitative pervasive whole is carried. In every experience we touch the world through some particular tentacle; we carry on our intercourse with it, it comes home to us, through a specialized organ. The entire organism with all its charge of the past and varied resources operates, but it operates through a particular medium, that of eye, as it interacts with eye, ear, and touch. The fine arts lay hold of this fact and push it to its maximum of significance. In any ordinary visual perception, we see by means of light; we distinguish by means of reflected and refracted colors: that is a truism. But in ordinary perceptions, this medium of color is mixed, adulterated. While we see, we also hear; we feel pressures, and heat or cold. In a painting, color renders the scene without these alloys and impurities. They are part of the dross that is squeezed out and left behind in an act of intensified expression. The medium becomes color alone, and since color alone must now carry the qualities of movement, touch, sound, etc., that are present physically on their own account in ordinary vision, the expressiveness and energy of color are enhanced.

Photographs to primitive folk have, so it is said, a fearful magical quality. It is uncanny that solid and living things should be thus presented. There is evidence that when pictures of any kind first made their appearance, magical power was imputed to them. Their power of representation could come only from a supernatural source. To one who is not rendered callous by common contact with pictorial representations there is still something miraculous in the power of a contracted, flat, uniform thing to depict the wide and diversified universe of animate and inanimate things: it is possibly for this reason that popularly "art" tends to denote painting, and "artist" one who paints. Primitive man also imputed to sounds when used as words the power to control supernaturally the acts and secrets of men and to command, provided the right word was there, the forces of nature. The power of mere sounds to express in literature all events and objects is equally marvelous.

Such facts as these seem to me to suggest the rôle and significance of media for art. At first sight, it seems a fact not worth recording that every art has a medium of its own. Why put it down in black and white that painting cannot exist without color, music without sound, architecture without stone and wood, statuary without marble and bronze, literature without words, dancing without the living body? The answer has, I believe, been indicated. In every experience, there is the pervading underlying qualitative whole that corresponds to and manifests the whole organization of activities which constitute the mysterious human frame. But in every experience, this complex, this differentiated and recording, mechanism operates through special structures that take the lead, not in dispersed diffusion through all organs at once—save in panic when, as we truly say, one has lost one's *head.* "Medium" in fine art denotes the fact that this specialization and individualization of a particular organ of experience is carried to the point wherein all its possibilities are exploited. The eye or ear that is centrally active does not lose its specific character and its special fitness as the bearer of an experience that it uniquely makes possible. In art, the seeing or hearing that is dispersed and mixed in ordinary perceptions is concentrated until the peculiar office of the special medium operates with full energy, free from distraction.

"Medium" signifies first of all an intermediary. The import of the word "means" is the same. They are the middle, the intervening, things through which something now remote is brought to pass. Yet not all means are media. There are two kinds of means. One kind is external to that which is accomplished; the other kind is taken up into the consequences produced and remains immanent in them. There are ends which are merely welcome cessations and there are ends that are fulfillments of what went before. The toil of a laborer is too often only an antecedent to the wage he receives, as consumption of gasoline is merely a means to transportation. The means cease to act when the "end" is reached; one would be glad, as a rule, to get the result without having to employ the means. They are but a scaffolding.

Such external or *mere* means, as we properly term them, are usually of such a sort that others can be substituted for them; the particular ones employed are determined by some extraneous consideration, like cheapness. But the moment we say "media," we refer to means that are incorporated in the outcome. Even bricks and mortar become a part of the house they are employed to build; they are not mere means to its erection. Colors *are* the painting; tones are the music. A picture painted with water colors has a quality different from that painted with oil. Esthetic effects belong intrinsically to their medium; when another medium is substituted, we have a stunt rather than an object of art. Even when substitution is practiced with the utmost virtuosity or for any reason outside the kind of end desired, the product is mechanical or a tawdry sham—like boards painted to resemble stone in the construction of a cathedral, for stone is integral not just physically, but to the esthetic effect.

The difference between external and intrinsic operations runs through all the affairs of life. One student studies to pass an examination, to get promotion. To another, the means, the activity of learning, is completely one with what results from it. The consequence, instruction, illumination, is one with the process. Sometimes we journey to get somewhere else because we have business at the latter point and would gladly, were it possible, cut out the traveling. At other times we journey for the delight of moving about and seeing what we see. Means and end coalesce. If we run over in mind a number of such cases we quickly see that all the cases in which means and ends are external to one another are non-esthetic. This externality may even be regarded as a definition of the non-esthetic.

Being "good" for the sake of avoiding penalty, whether it be going to jail or to hell, makes conduct unlovely. It is as anesthetic as is going to the dentist's chair so as to avoid a lasting injury. When the Greeks identified the good and beautiful in actions, they revealed, in their feeling of grace and proportion in right conduct, a perception of fusion of means and ends. The adventures of a pirate have at least a romantic attraction lacking in the painful acquisitions of him who stays within the law merely because he thinks it pays better in the end to do so. A large part of popular revulsion against utilitarianism in moral theory is because of its exaggeration of sheer calculation. "Decorum" and "propriety" which once had a favorable, because esthetic, meaning are taking on a disparaging signification because they are understood to denote a primness or smugness assumed because of desire for an external end. In all ranges of experience, externality of means defines the mechanical. Much of what is termed spiritual is also unesthetic. But the unesthetic quality is because the things denoted by the word also exemplify separation of means and end; the "ideal" is so cut off from the realities, by which alone it can be striven for, that it is vapid. The "spiritual" gets a local habitation and achieves the solidity of form required for esthetic quality only when it is embodied in a sense of actual things. Even angels have to be provided in imagination with bodies and wings.

I have referred more than once to the esthetic quality that may inhere in scientific work. To the layman the material of the scientist is usually forbidding. To the inquirer there exists a fulfilling and consummatory quality, for conclusions sum up and perfect the conditions that lead up to them. Moreover, they have at times an elegant and even austere form. It is said that Clark-Maxwell once introduced a symbol in order to make a physical equation symmetrical, and that it was only later that experimental results gave the symbol its meaning. I suppose that it is also true that if business men were the mere money-grubbers they are often supposed to be by the unsympathetic outsider, business would be much less attractive than it is. In practice, it may take on the properties of a game, and even when it is socially harmful it must have an esthetic quality to those whom it captivates.

Means are, then, media when they are not just preparatory or preliminary. As a medium, color is a go-between for the values weak and dispersed in ordinary experiences and the new concentrated perception occasioned by a painting. A phonographic disk is a vehicle of an effect and nothing more. The music which issues from it is also a vehicle but is something more; it is a vehicle which becomes one with what it carries; it coalesces with what it conveys. Physically, a brush and the movement of the hand in applying color to canvas are external to a painting. Not so artistically. Brush-strokes are an integral part of the esthetic effect of a painting when it is perceived. Some philosophers have put forth the idea that esthetic effect or beauty is a kind of ethereal essence which, in accommodation to flesh, is compelled to use external sensuous material as a vehicle. The doctrine implies that were not the soul imprisoned in the body, pictures would exist without colors, music without sounds, and literature without words. Except, however, for critics who tell us how they feel without telling or knowing in terms of media used *why* they feel as they do, and except for persons who identify gush with appreciation, media and esthetic effect are completely fused.

Sensitivity to a medium as a medium is the very heart of all artistic creation and esthetic perception. Such sensitiveness does not lug in extraneous material. When, for example, paintings are looked at as illustrations of historical scenes, of literature, of familiar scenes, they are not perceived in terms of their media. Or, when they are looked at simply with reference to the technic employed in making them what they are, they are not esthetically perceived. For here, too, means are separated from ends. Analysis of the former becomes a substitute for enjoyment of the latter. It is true that artists seem themselves often to approach a work of art from an exclusively technical standpoint—and the outcome is at least refreshing after having had a dose of what is regarded as "appreciation." But in reality, for the most part, they so feel the whole that it is not necessary to dwell upon the end, the whole, in words, and so they are freed to consider how the latter is produced.

The medium is a mediator. It is a go-between of artist and perceiver. Tolstoi in the midst of his moral preconceptions often speaks as an artist. He is celebrating this function of an artist when he makes the remarks already quoted about art as that which unites. The important thing for the theory of art is that this union is effected through the use of special material as a medium. By temperament, perhaps by inclination and aspiration, we are all artists—up to a certain point. What is lacking is that which marks the artist in execution. For the artist has the power to seize upon a special kind of material and convert it into an authentic medium of expression. The rest of us require many channels and a mass of material to give expression to what we should like to say. Then the variety of agencies employed get in the way of one another and render expression turbid, while the sheer bulk of material employed makes it confused and awkward. The artist sticks to his chosen organ and its corresponding material, and thus the idea singly and concentratedly felt in terms of the medium comes through pure and clear. He plays the game intensely, because strictly.

Something which Delacroix said of painters of his day applies to inferior artists generally. He said they used coloration rather than color. The statement signified that they applied color *to* their represented objects instead of making them out of color. This procedure signifies that colors as means and objects and scenes depicted were kept apart. They did not use color as medium with complete devotion. Their minds and experience were divided. Means and end did not coalesce. The greatest esthetic revolution in the history of painting took place when color was used structurally; then pictures ceased to be colored drawings. The true artist sees and feels in terms of his medium and the one who has learned to perceive esthetically emulates the operation. Others carry into their seeing of pictures and hearing of music preconceptions drawn from sources that obstruct and confuse perception.

Fine art is sometimes defined as power to create illusions. As far as I can see this statement is a decidedly unintelligent and misleading way of stating a truth—namely, that artists create effects by command of a single medium. In ordinary perception we depend upon contribution from a variety of sources for our understanding of the meaning of what we are undergoing. The artistic use of a medium signifies that irrelevant aids are excluded and one sense quality is concentratedly and intensely used to do the work usually done loosely with the aid of many. But to call the result an illusion is to mix matters that should be distinguished. If measure of artistic merit were ability to paint a fly on a peach so that we are moved to brush if off or grapes on a canvas so that birds come to peck at them, a scare-crow would be a work of consummate fine-art when it succeeds at keeping away the crows.

The confusion of which I have just spoken can be cleared up. There *is* something physical, in its ordinary sense of real existence.

There is the color or sound that constitutes the medium. And there is an experience having a sense of reality, quite likely a heightened one. This sense would be illusory, if it were like that which appertains to the sense of the real existence of the medium. But it is very different. On the stage the media, the actors and their voices and gestures, are really there; they exist. And the cultivated auditor has as a consequence a heightened sense (supposing the play to be genuinely artistic) of the reality of things of *ordinary* experience. Only the uncultivated theatergoer has such an illusion of the reality of what is enacted that he identifies what is done with the kind of reality manifested in the psychical presence of the actors, so that he tries to join in the action. A painting of trees or rocks may make the characteristic reality of tree or rock more poignant than it had ever been before. But that does not imply that the spectator takes a part of the picture to be an actual rock of the kind he could hammer or sit on. What makes a material a medium is that it is used to express a meaning which is other than that which it is in virtue of its bare physical existence: the meaning not of what it physically is, but of what it expresses.

In the discussion of the qualitative background of experience and of the special medium through which distinct meanings and values are projected upon it, we are in the presence of something common in the substance of the arts. Media are different in the different arts. But possession of a medium belongs to them all. Otherwise they would not be expressive, nor without this common substance could they possess form.

. . . .

Chapter XII

THE CHALLENGE TO PHILOSOPHY

Esthetic experience is imaginative. This fact, in connection with a false idea of the nature of imagination, has obscured the larger fact that all *conscious* experience has of necessity some degree of imaginative quality. For while the roots of every experience are found in the interaction of a live creature with its environment, that experience becomes conscious, a matter of perception, only when meanings enter it that are derived from prior experiences. Imagination is the only gateway through which these meanings can find their way into a present interaction; or rather, as we have just seen, the conscious adjustment of the new and the old *is* imagination. Interaction of a living being with an environment is found in vegetative and animal life. But the experience enacted is human and conscious only as that which is given here and now is extended by meanings and values drawn from what is absent in fact and present only imaginatively.[1]

There is always a gap between the here and now of direct interaction and the past interactions whose funded result constitutes the meanings with which we grasp and understand what is now occurring. Because of this gap, all conscious perception involves a risk; it is a venture into the unknown, for as it assimilates the present to the past it also brings about some reconstruction of that past. When past and present fit exactly into one another, when there is only recurrence, complete uniformity, the resulting experience is routine and mechanical; it does not come to consciousness in perception. The inertia of habit overrides adaptation of the meaning of the here and now with that of experiences, without which there is no consciousness, the imaginative phase of experience.

Mind, that is the body of organized meanings by means of which events of the present have significance for us, does not always enter into the activities and undergoings that are going on here and now. Sometimes it is baffled and arrested. Then the stream of meanings aroused into activity by the present contact remain aloof. Then it forms the matter of reverie, of dream; ideas are floating, not anchored to any existence as its property, its possession of meanings. Emotions that are equally loose and floating cling to these ideas. The pleasure they afford is the reason why they are entertained and are allowed to occupy the scene; they are attached to existence only in a way that, as long as sanity abides, is felt to be only fanciful and unreal.

In every work of art, however, these meanings are actually embodied in a material which thereby becomes the medium for their expression. This fact constitutes the peculiarity of all experience that is definitely esthetic. Its imaginative quality dominates, because meanings and values that are wider and deeper than the particular here and now in which they are anchored are realized by way of *expressions* although not by way of an object that is physically efficacious in relation to other objects. Not even a useful object is produced except by the intervention of imagination. Some existent material was perceived in the light of relations and possibilities not hitherto re-

---

[1] "Mind denotes a whole system of meanings as they are embodied in the workings of organic life. . . . Mind is a constant luminosity; consciousness is intermittent, a series of flashes of different intensities."—"Experience and Nature," p. 303.

alized when the steam engine was invented. But when the imagined possibilities were embodied in a new assemblage of natural materials, the steam engine took its place in nature as an object that has the same physical effects as those belonging to any other physical object. Steam did the physical work and produced the consequences that attend any expanding gas under definite physical conditions. The sole difference is that the conditions under which it operates have been arranged by human contrivance.

The work of art, however, unlike the machine, is not only the outcome of imagination, but operates imaginatively rather than in the realm of physical existences. What it does is to concentrate and enlarge an immediate experience. The formed matter of esthetic experience directly *expresses*, in other words, the meanings that are imaginatively evoked; it does not, like the material brought into new relations in a machine, merely provide *means* by which purposes over and beyond the existence of the object may be executed. And yet the meanings imaginatively summoned, assembled, and integrated are embodied in material existence that here and now interacts with the self. The work of art is thus a challenge to the performance of a like act of evocation and organization, through imagination, on the part of the one who experiences it. It is not just a stimulus to and means of an overt course of action.

This fact constitutes the uniqueness of esthetic experience, and this uniqueness is in turn a challenge to thought. It is particularly a challenge to that systematic thought called philosophy. For esthetic experience is experience in its integrity. Had not the term "pure" been so often abused in philosophic literature, had it not been so often employed to suggest that there is something alloyed, impure, in the very nature of experience and to denote something beyond experience, we might say that esthetic experience is pure experience. For it is experience freed from the forces that impede and confuse its development as experience; freed, that is, from factors that subordinate an experience as it is directly had to something beyond itself. To esthetic experience, then, the philosopher must go to understand what experience is.

For this reason, while the theory of esthetics put forth by a philosopher is incidentally a test of the capacity of its author to have the experience that is the subject-matter of his analysis, it is also much more than that. It is a test of the capacity of the system he puts forth to grasp the nature of experience itself. There is no test that so surely reveals the one-sidedness of a philosophy as its treatment of art and esthetic experience. Imaginative vision is the power that unifies all the constituents of the matter of a work of art, making a whole out of them in all their variety. Yet all the elements of our being that are displayed in special emphases and partial realizations in other experiences are merged in esthetic experience. And they are so completely merged in the immediate wholeness of the experience that each is submerged:— it does not present itself in consciousness as a distinct element.

. . . . .

Chapter XIV

ART AND CIVILIZATION

. . . The theories that attribute direct moral effect and intent to art fail because they do not take account of the collective civilization that is the context in which works of art are produced and enjoyed. I would not say that they tend to treat works of art as a kind of sublimated Æsop's fables. But they all tend to extract particular works, regarded as especially edifying, from their milieu and to think of the moral function of art in terms of a strictly personal relation between the selected works and a particular individual. Their whole conception of morals is so individualistic that they miss a sense of the *way* in which art exercises its humane function.

Matthew Arnold's dictum that "poetry is criticism of life" is a case in point. It suggests to the reader a moral intent on the part of the poet and a moral judgment on the part of the reader. It fails to see or at all events to state *how* poetry is a criticism of life; namely, not directly, but by disclosure, through imaginative vision addressed to imaginative experience (not to set judgment) of possibilities that contrast with actual conditions. A sense of possibilities that are unrealized and that might be realized are when they are put in contrast with actual conditions, the most penetrating "criticism" of the latter that can be made. It is by a sense of possibilities opening before us that we become aware of constrictions that hem us in and of burdens that oppress.

Mr. Garrod, a follower of Matthew Arnold in more senses than one, has wittily said that what we resent in didactic poetry is not that it teaches, but that it does not teach, its incompetency. He added words to the effect that poetry teaches as friends and life teach, by being, and not by express intent. He says in another place, "Poetical values are, after all, values in a human life. You cannot mark them off from other values, as though the nature of man were built in bulkheads." I do not think that what Keats has said in one of his letters can be surpassed as to the way in which poetry acts. He asks what would be the result if every man spun from his imaginative experience "an airy citadel" like the web the spider spins, "filling the air with a beautiful circuiting." For, he says, "man should not dispute or assert, but whisper results to his neighbor, and thus, by every germ of spirit sucking the sap from mold etherial, every human being might become great, and Humanity instead of being a wide heath of Furze and briars with here and there a remote Pine or Oak, would become a grand democracy of Forest Trees!"

It is by way of communication that art becomes the incomparable organ of instruction, but the way is so remote from that usually associated with the idea of education, it is a way that lifts art so far above what we are accustomed to think of as instruction, that we are repelled by any suggestion of teaching and learning in connection with art. But our revolt is in fact a reflection upon education that proceeds by methods so literal as to exclude the imagination and one not touching the desires and emotions of men. Shelley said, "The imagination is the great instrument of moral good, and poetry administers to the effect by acting upon the causes." Hence it is, he goes on to say, "a poet would do ill to embody his own conceptions of right and wrong, which are usually those of his own time and place, in his poetical creations. . . . By the assumption of this inferior office . . . he would resign participation in the cause"—the imagination. It is the lesser poets who "have frequently affected a moral aim, and the effect of their poetry is diminished in exact proportion as they compel us to advert to this purpose." But the power of imaginative projection is so great that he calls poets "the founders of civil society."

The problem of the relation of art and morals is too often treated as if the problem existed only on the side of art. It is virtually assumed that morals are satisfactory in idea if not in fact, and that the only question is whether and in what ways art should conform to a moral system already developed. But Shelley's statement goes to the heart of the matter. Imagination is the chief instrument of the good. It is more or less a commonplace to say that a person's ideas and treatment of his fellows are dependent upon his power to put himself imaginatively in their place. But the primacy of the imagination extends far beyond the scope of direct personal relationships. Except where "ideal" is used in conventional deference or as a name for a sentimental reverie, the ideal factors in every moral outlook and human loyalty are imaginative. The historic alliance of religion and art has its roots in this common quality. Hence it is that art is more moral than moralities. For the latter either are, or tend to become, consecrations of the *status quo*, reflections of custom, reënforcements of the established order. The moral prophets of humanity have always been poets even though they spoke in free verse or by parable. Uniformly, however, their vision of possibilities has soon been converted into a proclamation of facts that already exist and hardened into semi-political institutions. Their imaginative presentation of ideals that should command thought and desire have been treated as rules of policy. Art has been the means of keeping alive the sense of purposes that outrun evidence and of meanings that transcend indurated habit.

Morals are assigned a special compartment in theory and practice because they reflect the divisions embodied in economic and political institutions. Wherever social divisions and barriers exist, practices and ideas that correspond to them fix metes and bounds, so that liberal action is placed under restraint. Creative intelligence is looked upon with distrust; the innovations that are the essence of individuality are feared, and generous impulse is put under bonds not to disturb the peace. Were art an acknowledged power in human association and not treated as the pleasuring of an idle moment or as a means of ostentatious display, and were morals understood to be identical with every aspect of value that is shared in experience, the "problem" of the relation of art and morals would not exist.

The idea and the practice of morality are saturated with conceptions that stem from praise and blame, reward and punishment. Mankind is divided into sheep and goats, the vicious and virtuous, the law-abiding and criminal, the good and bad. To be beyond good and evil is an impossibility for man, and yet as long as the good signifies only that which is lauded and rewarded, and the evil that which is currently condemned or outlawed, the ideal factors of morality are always and everywhere beyond good and evil. Because art is wholly innocent of ideas derived from praise and blame, it is looked upon with the eye of suspicion by the guardians of custom, or only the art that is itself so old and "classic" as to receive conventional praise is grudgingly admitted, provided, as with, say, the case of Shakespeare, signs of regard for conventional morality can be ingeniously extracted from his work. Yet this indifference to praise and blame because of preoccupation with imaginative experience constitutes the heart of the moral potency of art. From it proceeds the liberating and uniting power of art.

Shelley said, "The great secret of morals is love, or *a going out of our nature* and the identification of ourselves with the beautiful which exists in thought, action, or person, not our own. A man to be greatly good must imagine intensely and comprehensively." What is true of the individual is true of the whole system of morals in thought and action. While perception of the union of the possible with the actual in a work of art is itself a great good, the good does not terminate with the immediate and particular occasion in which it is had. The union that is presented in perception persists in the remaking of impulsion and thought. The first intimations of wide and large redirections of desire and purpose are of necessity imaginative. Art is a mode of prediction not found in charts and statistics, and it insinuates possibilities of human relations not to be found in rule and precept, admonition and administration.

> "But art, wherein man speaks in no wise to man,
> Only to mankind—art may tell a truth
> Obliquely, do the deed shall breed the thought."

Martin
HEIDEGGER

According to the title of this essay its subject is the origin of the
work of art. As Heidegger points out, the work of art is dependent upon its creator but also the creator is dependent upon the
work; both derive from art itself. Thus the origin of the work of
art is art. The concept of art developed as the essay proceeds is
that of the creative preservation of truth in the work. (Preservation, for Heidegger, is the function of the work's public.) According to this view art is one way in which truth happens. In
art, truth is at work in the work; truth actively establishes itself
in the work. Truth, says Heidegger, exhibits an impulse to realize
itself in a work as an entity within the realm of entities. Art is
one among a number of ways in which truth establishes itself in
this realm. Heidegger mentions several such ways: political creation, religion, sacrifice, thinking. Thus like Hegel and others
before him, Heidegger assigns to art a supreme role in human
experience. Indeed, as he points out, art, being an origin of the
establishment of truth, is at the same time an origin in the history of a people. In revealing to them the truth of being which

it is their task to guard, it initiates and clarifies for them their own historical vocation.

Like Hegel, too, Heidegger does not mean by truth the correctness of a proposition. Truth for him is unconcealment, the revelation of the being of what is. He illustrates it in the course of a discussion of the being of equipment, such as a pair of peasant shoes. For this purpose he turns to a painting by Van Gogh and eloquently conjures up the earth and world of the peasant woman's life, a vision of which is unfolded in the painting. The shoes are what they are, and are seen to be such, in the way in which they function in and embody her life and world. Moreover, the truth that is revealed by this work is not a truth of a merely particular thing like a pair of shoes; in revealing the whole of the earth and world of the peasant woman, the painting's truth is a truth of all that is. It is because the truth Heidegger has in mind is a truth (that is, a revelation) of the being of all that is, that art can have the important function Heidegger gives it.

The work of art, in serving as the locus in which truth establishes itself, becomes a center in the midst of what is from which light streams over the whole, producing the light and shade in which what is shows itself to us. This center is the clearing, the lighting source, that opens up what Heidegger speaks of as the Open in which all that is stands. Revealing things to us, it at the same time affords us a comprehensive way of seeing them.

Heidegger generalizes the notion of earth so that it becomes equivalent to the matter of the work of art. Artistic matter such as wood, stone, color, tone, and word operates at once as that which conceals (in earlier philosophy it was the principle of potentiality) and that on the basis of which the revelation of world (that is, the meaningful contexture of the whole of what is) is possible. The unity of earth and world (or what in more traditional terms would be called the unity of matter and content) comes about only by way of a conflict between the two. World and earth do not fit together in easy harmony, but on the contrary the world-meaning is able to erect itself and the material is able to reveal itself as material only in the form of a dynamic movement or strife, the unity of which is the repose of the work as a whole within itself. This strife takes the form of what Heidegger calls the Riss. Untranslatable in any simple way, the Riss is at one and the same time a rift and a design. It is the opposition between material and content, and at the same time the design by which the content is actualized in the material. It is therefore the artistic figure or setting, the Gestalt. Thus it is in the figure, the distinctive characteristic of the work of art as contrasted with other modes of revelation of truth, that truth reveals itself in art. Heidegger's aesthetics is no mere content aesthetics, as one might at first suppose from the illustrations which he uses; in this concept of figure as the unity of earth and world we encounter a new and suggestive approach to the concrete work of art.

By its peculiar design, the work of art stands out as a created entity. Because truth establishes itself in the design, truth stands out there in a unique way. The work of art in its uniqueness is extraordinary; it throws a new and extraordinary light on things; it changes everything familiar into something unfamiliar; it opens up a new world. That is why, Heidegger thinks, art is not only the origin of works of art as individual entities, but also an origin of man's historical existence itself. Art has the fundamental historical function of revealing to man the being which is entrusted to him in the fulfillment of his human destiny as individual and as a people.

The essay, Der Ursprung des Kunstwerkes, here translated, first appeared in Holzwege, published in 1950. It was based on lectures given in 1935 and 1936 at Freiburg im Breslau, Zürich, and Frankfurt. It is one of the important works appearing early after the so-called Kehre, or reversal, in Heidegger's thought, from the stress on anxiety, nothingness, and human existence, to a stress on more affirmative moods and on the primacy of being. Its significance, therefore, extends even beyond its contribution to a philosophy of art and helps to bring out the positive content of his thought. Heidegger has long maintained that he is not to be considered an "existentialist" philosopher. The present work confirms this claim.

THE ORIGIN OF THE WORK OF ART

Origin here means that from and by which something is what it is and as it is. What something is, as it is, we call its essence or nature. The origin of something is the source of its nature. The question concerning the origin of the work of art asks about the source of its nature. On the usual view, the work arises out of and by means of the activity of the artist. But by what and whence is the artist what he is? By the work; for to say that the work does credit to the master means that it is the work that first lets the artist emerge as a master of his art. The artist is the origin of the work. The work is the origin of the artist. Neither is without the other. Nevertheless, neither is the sole support of the other. In themselves and in their interrelations artist and work *are* each of them by virtue of a third thing which is prior to both, namely that which also gives artist and work of art their names—art.

As necessarily as the artist is the origin of the work in a different way than the work is the origin of the artist, so it is equally certain that, in a still different way, art is the origin of both artist and work. But can art be an origin at all? Where and how does art occur? Art— this is nothing more than a word to which nothing real any longer corresponds. It may pass for a collective idea under which we find a place for that which alone is real in art: works and artists. Even if the word art were taken to signify more than a collective notion, what is meant by the word could exist only on the basis of the actuality of works and artists. Or is the converse the case? Do works and artists exist only because art exists as their origin?

This translation of "The Origin of the Work of Art" appears in Heidegger's *Poetry, Language, Thought* (Harper, 1971) and is reprinted with the permission of the publisher.

Whatever the decision may be, the question of the origin of the work of art becomes a question about the nature of art. Since the question whether and how art in general exists must still remain open, we shall attempt to discover the nature of art in the place where art undoubtedly prevails in a real way. Art is present in the art work. But what and how is a work of art?

What art is should be inferable from the work. What the work of art is we can come to know only from the nature of art. Anyone can easily see that we are moving in a circle. Ordinary understanding demands that this circle be avoided because it violates logic. What art is can be gathered from a comparative examination of actual art works. But how are we to be certain that we are indeed basing such an examination on art works if we do not know beforehand what art is? And the nature of art can no more be arrived at by a derivation from higher concepts than by a collection of characteristics of actual art works. For such a derivation, too, already has in view the characteristics that must suffice to establish that what we take in advance to be an art work is one in fact. But selecting works from among given objects, and deriving concepts from principles, are equally impossible here, and where these procedures are practiced they are a self-deception.

Thus we are compelled to follow the circle. This is neither a makeshift nor a defect. To enter upon this path is the strength of thought, to continue on it is the feast of thought, assuming that thinking is a craft. Not only is the main step from work to art a circle like the step form art to work, but every separate step that we attempt circles in this circle.

In order to discover the nature of the art that really prevails in the work, let us go to the actual work and ask the work what and how it is.

Works of art are familiar to everyone. Architectural and sculptural works can be seen installed in public places, in churches, and in dwellings. Art works of the most diverse periods and peoples are housed in collections and exhibitions. If we consider the works in their untouched actuality and do not deceive ourselves, the result is that the works are as naturally present as are things. The picture hangs on the wall like a rifle or a hat. A painting, e.g., the one by Van Gogh that represents a pair of peasant shoes, travels from one exhibition to another. Works of art are shipped like coal from the Ruhr and logs from the Black Forest. During the First World War Hölderlin's hymns were packed in the soldier's knapsack together with cleaning gear. Beethoven's quartets lie in the storerooms of the publishing house like potatoes in a cellar.

All works have this thingly character. What would they be without it? But perhaps this rather crude and external view of the work is objectionable to us. Shippers or charwomen in museums may operate with such conceptions of the work of art. We, however, have to take works as they are encountered by those who experience and enjoy them. But even the much-vaunted aesthetic experience cannot get around the thingly aspect of the art work. There is something stony in a work of architecture, wooden in a carving, colored in a painting, spoken in a linguistic work, sonorous in a musical composition. The thingly element is so irremovably present in the art work that we are compelled rather to say conversely that the architectural work is in stone, the carving is in wood, the painting in color, the linguistic work in speech, the musical composition in sound. "Obviously," it will be replied. No doubt. But what is this self-evident thingly element in the work of art?

Presumably it becomes superfluous and confusing to inquire into this feature, since the art work is something else over and above the thingly element. This something else in the work constitutes its artistic nature. The art work is, to be sure, a thing that is made, but it says something other than the mere thing itself is, *allo agoreuei*. The work makes public something other than itself; it manifests something other; it is an allegory. In the work of art something other is brought together with the thing that is made. To bring together is, in Greek, *sumballein*. The work is a symbol.

Allegory and symbol provide the conceptual frame within whose channel of vision the art work has for a long time been characterized. But this one element in a work that manifests another, this one element that joins with another, is the thingly feature in the art work. It seems almost as though the thingly element in the art work is like the substructure into and upon which the other, authentic element is built. And is it not this thingly feature in the work that the artist really makes by his handicraft?

Our aim is to arrive at the immediate and full reality of the work of art, for only in this way shall we discover real art also within it. Hence we must first bring to view the thingly element of the work. To this end it is necessary that we should know with sufficient clarity what a thing is. Only then can we say whether the art work is a thing, but a thing to which something else adheres; only then can we decide whether the work is at bottom something else and not a thing at all.

Thing and Work

What in truth is the thing, so far as it is a thing? When we inquire in this way, our aim is to come to know the thing-being (thingness) of the thing. The point is to discover the thingly character of the thing. To this end we have to be acquainted with the sphere to which all those entities belong which we have long called by the name of thing.

The stone in the road is a thing, as is the clod in the field. A jug is a thing, as is the well beside the road. But what about the milk in the jug and the water in the well? These too are things if the cloud in the sky and the thistle in the field, the leaf in the autumn breeze and the hawk over the wood, are rightly called by the name of thing. All these must indeed be called things, if the name is applied even to that which does not, like those just enumerated, show itself, i.e., that which does not appear. According to Kant, the whole of the world, for example, and even God himself, is a thing of this sort, a thing that does not itself appear, namely, a "thing-in-itself." In the language of philosophy both things-in-themselves and things that appear, all beings that in any way are, are called things.

Airplanes and radio sets are nowadays among the things closest to us, but when we have ultimate things in mind we think of something altogether different. Death and judgment—these are ultimate things. On the whole the word "thing" here designates whatever is not simply nothing. In this sense the work of art is also a thing, so far as it is not simply nothing. Yet this concept is of no use to us, at least immediately, in our attempt to delimit entities that have the mode of being of a thing, as against those having the mode of being of a work. And besides, we hesitate to call God a thing. In the same way we hesitate to consider the peasant in the field, the stoker at the boiler, the teacher in the school as things. A man is not a thing. It is true that we speak of a young girl who is faced with a task too difficult for her as being a young thing, still too young for it, but only because we feel that being human is in a certain way missing here and think that instead we have to do here with the factor that constitutes the thingly character of things. We hesitate even to call the deer in the forest clearing, the beetle in the grass, the blade of grass a thing. We would sooner think of a hammer as a thing, or a shoe, or an ax, or a clock. But even these are not mere things. Only a stone, a clod of earth, a piece of wood are for us such mere things. Lifeless beings of nature and objects of use. Natural things and utensils are the things commonly so called.

We thus see ourselves brought back from the widest domain, within which everything is a thing (thing = *res* = *ens* = an entity), including even the highest and last things, to the narrow precinct of mere things. "Mere" here means, first, the pure thing, which is simply a thing and nothing more; but then, at the same time, it means that which is only a thing, in an almost pejorative sense. It is mere things, excluding even use-objects, that count as things in the strict sense. What does the thingly character of these things, then, consist in? It is in reference to these that the thingness of things must be determinable. This determination enables us to characterize what it is that is thingly as such. Thus prepared, we are able to characterize the almost palpable reality of works, in which something else inheres.

Now it passes for a known fact that as far back as antiquity, no sooner was the question raised as to what entities are in general, than things in their thingness thrust themselves into prominence again and again as the standard type of beings. Consequently we are bound to meet with the definition of the thingness of things already in the traditional interpretations of beings. We thus need only to ascertain explicitly this traditional knowledge of the thing, to be relieved of the tedious labor of making our own search for the thingly character of the thing. The answers to the question "What is the thing?" are so familiar that we no longer sense anything questionable behind them.

The interpretations of the thingness of the thing which, predominant in the course of Western thought, have long become self-evident and are now in everyday use, may be reduced to three.

This block of granite, for example, is a mere thing. It is hard, heavy, extended, bulky, shapeless, rough, colored, partly dull, partly shiny. We can take note of all these features in the stone. Thus we acknowledge its characteristics. But still, the traits signify something proper to the stone itself. They are its properties. The thing has them. The thing? What are we thinking of when we now have the thing in mind? Obviously a thing is not merely an aggregate of traits, nor an accumulation of properties by which that aggregate arises. A thing, as everyone thinks he knows, is that around which the properties have assembled. We speak in this connection of the core of things. The Greeks are supposed to have called it to *hupokeimenon*. For them, this core of the thing was something lying at the ground of the thing, something always already there. The characteristics, however, are called *ta sumbebekota*, that which has always turned up already along with the given core and occurs along with it.

These designations are no arbitrary names. Something that lies beyond the purview of this essay speaks in them, the basic Greek experience of the Being of beings in the sense of presence. It is by these determinations, however, that the interpretation of the thingness of the thing is established which henceforth becomes standard, and the Western interpretation of the Being of beings stabilized. The process begins with the appropriation of Greek words by Roman-Latin thought. *Hupokeimenon* becomes *subiectum*; *hupostasis* becomes *substantia*; *sumbebekos* becomes *accidens*. However, this translation of Greek names into Latin is in no way the innocent process it is considered to this day. Beneath the seemingly literal and thus faithful translation there is concealed, rather, a *trans*lation of Greek experience into a different way of thinking. *Roman thought takes over the Greek words without a corresponding, equally authentic experience of what they say, without the Greek word.* The rootlessness of Western thought begins with this translation.

According to current opinion, this definition of the thingness of the thing as the substance with its accidents seems to correspond to our natural outlook on things. No wonder that the current attitude toward things—our way of addressing ourselves to things and speaking about them—has adapted itself to this common view of the thing. A simple propositional statement consists of the subject, which is the Latin translation, hence already a reinterpretation, of *hupokeimenon* and the predicate, in which the thing's traits are stated of it. Who would have the temerity to assail these simple fundamental relations between thing and statement, between sentence structure and thing-structure? Nevertheless we must ask: Is the structure of a simple propositional statement (the combination of subject and predicate) the mirror image of the structure of the thing (of the union of substance with accidents)? Or could it be that even the structure of the thing as thus envisaged is a projection of the framework of the sentence?

What could be more obvious than that man transposes his propositional way of understanding things into the structure of the thing itself? Yet this view, seemingly critical yet actually rash and ill-considered, would have to explain first how such a transposition of propositional structure into the thing is supposed to be possible without the thing having already become visible. The question which comes first and functions as the standard, proposition structure or thing-structure remains to this hour undecided. It even remains doubtful whether in this form the question is at all decidable.

Actually, the sentence structure does not provide the standard for the pattern of thing-structure, nor is the latter simply mirrored in the former. Both sentence and thing-structure derive, in their typical form and their possible mutual relationship, from a common and more original source. In any case this first interpretation of the thingness of the thing, the thing as bearer of its characteristic traits, despite its currency, is not as natural as it appears to be. What seems natural to us is probably just something familiar in a long tradition that has forgotten the unfamiliar source from which it arose. And yet this unfamiliar source once struck man as strange and caused him to think and to wonder.

Our reliance on the current interpretation of the thing is only seemingly well founded. But in addition this thing-concept (the thing as bearer of its characteristics) holds not only of the mere thing in its strict sense, but also of any being whatsoever. Hence it cannot be used to set apart thingly beings from non-thingly beings. Yet even before all reflection, attentive dwelling within the sphere of things already tells us that this thing-concept does not hit upon the thingly element of the thing, its independent and self-contained character. Occasionally we still have the feeling that violence has long been done to the thingly element of things and that thought has played a part in this violence, for which reason people disavow thought instead of taking pains to make it more thoughtful. But in defining the nature of the thing, what is the use of a feeling, however certain, if thought alone has the right to speak here? Perhaps however what we call feeling or mood, here and in similar instances, is more reasonable—that is, more intelligently perceptive—because more open to Being than all that reason which, having meanwhile become *ratio*, was misinterpreted as being rational. The hankering after the irrational, as abortive offspring of the unthought rational, therewith performed a curious service. To be sure, the current thing-concept always fits each thing. Nevertheless it does not lay hold of the thing as it is in its own being, but makes an assault upon it.

Can such an assault perhaps be avoided—and how? Only, certainly, by granting the thing, as it were, a free field to display its thingly character directly. Everything that might interpose itself between the thing and us in apprehending and talking about it must first be set aside. Only then do we yield ourselves to the undisguised presence of the thing. But we do not need first to call or arrange for this situation in which we let things encounter us without mediation. The situation always prevails. In what the senses of sight, hearing, and touch convey, in the sensations of color, sound, roughness, hardness, things move us bodily, in the literal meaning of the word. The thing is the *aistheton*, that which is perceptible by sensations in the senses belonging to sensibility. Hence the concept later becomes a commonplace according to which a thing is nothing but the unity of a manifold of what is given in the senses. Whether this unity is conceived as sum or as totality or as form alters nothing in the standard character of this thing-concept.

Now this interpretation of the thingness of the thing is as correct and demonstrable in every case as the previous one. This already suffices to cast doubt on its truth. If we consider moreover what we are searching for, the thingly character of the thing, then this thing-concept again leaves us at a loss. We never really first perceive a throng of sensations, e.g., tones and noises, in the appearance of things—as this thing-concept alleges; rather we hear the storm whistling in the chimney, we hear the three-motored plane, we hear the Mercedes in immediate distinction from the Volkswagen. Much closer to us than all sensations are the things themselves. We hear the door shut in the house and never hear acoustical sensations or even mere sounds. In order to hear a bare sound we have to listen away from things, divert our ear from them, i.e., listen abstractly.

In the thing-concept just mentioned there is not so much an assault upon the thing as rather an inordinate attempt to bring it into the greatest possible proximity to us. But a thing never reaches that position as long as we assign as its thingly feature what is perceived by the senses. Whereas the first interpretation keeps the thing at arm's length from us, as it were, and sets it too far off, the second makes it press too hard upon us. In both interpretations the thing vanishes. It is therefore necessary to avoid the exaggerations of both. The thing itself must be allowed to remain in its self-containment. It must be accepted in its own constancy. This the third interpretation seems to do, which is just as old as the first two.

That which gives things their constancy and pith but is also at the same time the source of their particular mode of sensuous pressure—colored, resonant, hard, massive—is the matter in things. In this analysis of the thing as matter (*hule*), form (*morphe*) is already coposited. What is constant in a thing, its consistency, lies in the fact that matter stands together with a form. The thing is formed matter. This interpretation appeals to the immediate view with which the thing solicits us by its looks (*eidos*). In this synthesis of matter and form a thing-concept has finally been found which applies equally to things of nature and to use-objects.

This concept puts us in a position to answer the question concerning the thingly element in the work of art. The thingly element is manifestly the matter of which it consists. Matter is the substrate and field for the artist's formative action. But we could have advanced this obvious and well-known definition of the thingly element at the very outset. Why do we make a detour through other current thing-concepts? Because we also mistrust this concept of the thing, which represents it as formed matter.

But is not precisely this pair of concepts, matter-form, usually employed in the domain in which we are supposed to be moving? To be sure. The distinction of matter and form is *the conceptual schema which is used, in the greatest variety of ways, quite generally for all art theory and aesthetics.* This incontestable fact, however, proves neither that the distinction of matter and form is adequately founded, nor that it belongs originally to the domain of art and the art work. Moreover, the range of application of this pair of concepts has long extended far beyond the field of aesthetics. Form and content are the most hackneyed concepts under which anything and everything may be subsumed. And if form is correlated with the rational and matter with the irrational; if the rational is taken to be the logical and the irrational the alogical; if in addition the subject-object relation is coupled with the conceptual pair form-matter; then representation has at its command a conceptual machinery that nothing is capable of withstanding.

If, however, it is thus with the distinction between matter and form, how then shall we make use of it to lay hold of the particular domain of mere things by contrast with all other entities? But perhaps this characterization in terms of matter and form would recover its defining power if only we reversed the process of expanding and emptying these concepts. Certainly, but this presupposes that we know in what sphere of beings they realize their true defining power. That this is the domain of mere things is so far only an assumption. Reference to the copious use made of this conceptual framework in aesthetics might sooner lead to the idea that matter and form are specifications stemming from the nature of the art work and were in the first place transferred from it back to the thing. Where does the matter-form structure have its origin—in the thingly character of the thing or in the workly character of the art work?

The self-contained block of granite is something material in a definite if unshapely form. Form means here the distribution and arrangement of the material parts in spatial locations, resulting in a particular shape, namely that of a block. But a jug, an ax, a shoe are also matter occurring in a form. Form as shape is not the consequence here of a prior distribution of the matter. The form, on the contrary, determines the arrangement of the matter. Even more, it prescribes in each case the kind and selection of the matter—impermeable for a jug, sufficiently hard for an ax, firm yet flexible for shoes. The interfusion of form and matter prevailing here is, moreover, controlled beforehand by the purposes served by jug, ax, shoes. Such usefulness is never assigned or added on afterward to a being of the type of a jug, ax, or pair of shoes. But neither is it something that floats somewhere above it as an end.

Usefulness is the basic feature from which this entity regards us, that is, flashes at us and thereby is present and thus is this entity. Both the formative act and the choice of material—a choice given with the act—and therewith the dominance of the conjunction of matter and form, are all grounded in such usefulness. A being that falls under usefulness is always the product of a process of making. It is made as a piece of equipment for something. As determinations of beings, accordingly, matter and form have their proper place in the essential nature of equipment. This name designates what is produced expressly for employment and use. Matter and form are in no case original determinations of the thingness of the mere thing.

A piece of equipment, a pair of shoes for instance, when finished, is also self-contained like the mere thing, but it does not have the character of having taken shape by itself like the granite boulder. On the other hand, equipment displays an affinity with the art work insofar as it is something produced by the human hand. However, by its self-sufficient presence the work of art is similar rather to the mere thing which has taken shape by itself and is self-contained. Nevertheless we do not count such works among mere things. As a rule it is the use-objects around us that are the nearest and authentic things. Thus the piece of equipment is half thing, because characterized by thingliness, and yet it is something more; at the same time it is half art work and yet something less, because lacking the self-sufficiency of the art work. Equipment has a peculiar position intermediate between thing and work, assuming that such a calculated ordering of them is permissible.

The matter-form structure, however, by which the being of a piece of equipment is first determined, readily presents itself as the immediately intelligible constitution of every entity, because here man himself as maker participates in the way in which the piece of equipment comes into being. Because equipment takes an intermediate place between mere thing and work, the suggestion is that nonequipmental beings—things and works and ultimately everything that is—are to be comprehended with the help of the being of equipment (the matter-form structure).

The inclination to treat the matter-form structure as *the* constitution of every entity receives a yet additional impulse from the fact that on the basis of a religious faith, namely, the biblical faith, the totality of all beings is represented in advance as something created, which here means made. The philosophy of this faith can of course assure us that all of God's creative work is to be thought of as different from the action of a craftsman. Nevertheless, if at the same time or even beforehand, in accordance with a presumed predetermination of Thomistic philosophy for interpreting the Bible, the *ens creatum* is conceived as a unity of *materia* and *forma*, then faith is expounded by way of a philosophy whose truth lies in an unconcealedness of beings which differs in kind from the world believed in by faith.

The idea of creation, grounded in faith, can lose its guiding power of knowledge of beings as a whole. But the theological interpretation of all beings, the view of the world in terms of matter and form borrowed from an alien philosophy, having once been instituted, can still remain a force. This happens in the transition from the Middle Ages to modern times. The metaphysics of the modern period rests on the form-matter structure devised in the medieval period, which itself merely recalls in its words the buried natures of *eidos* and *hule*. Thus the interpretation of "thing" by means of matter and form, whether it remains medieval or becomes Kantian-transcendental, has become current and self-evident. But for that reason, no less than the other interpretations mentioned of the thingness of the thing, it is an encroachment upon the thing-being of the thing.

The situation stands revealed as soon as we speak of things in the strict sense as mere things. The "mere," after all, means the removal of the character of usefulness and of being made. The mere thing is a sort of equipment, albeit equipment denuded of its equipmental being. Thing-being consists in what is then left over. But this remnant is not actually defined in its ontological character. It remains doubtful whether the thingly character comes to view at all in the process of stripping off everything equipmental. Thus the third mode of interpretation of the thing, that which follows the lead of the matter-form structure, also turns out to be an assault upon the thing.

These three modes of defining thingness conceive of the thing as a bearer of traits, as the unity of a manifold of sensations, as formed matter. In the course of the history of truth about beings, the interpretations mentioned have also entered into combinations, a matter we may now pass over. In such combination they have further strengthened their innate tendency to expand so as to apply in similar way to thing, to equipment, and to work. Thus they give rise to a mode of thought by which we think not only about thing, equipment, and work but about all beings in general. This long-familiar mode of thought preconceives all immediate experience of beings. The preconception shackles reflection on the being of any given entity. Thus it comes about that prevailing thing-concepts obstruct the way toward the thingly character of the thing as well as toward the equipmental character of equipment, and all the more toward the workly character of the work.

This fact is the reason why it is necessary to know about these thing-concepts, in order thereby to take heed of their derivation and their boundless presumption, but also of their semblance of self-evidence. This knowledge becomes all the more necessary when we risk the attempt to bring to view and express in words the thingly character of the thing, the equipmental character of equipment, and the workly character of the work. To this end, however, only one element is needful: to keep at a distance all the preconceptions and assaults of the above modes of thought, to leave the thing to rest in its own self, for instance, in its thing-being. What seems easier than to let a being be just the being that it is? Or does this turn out to be the most difficult of tasks, particularly if such an intention—to let a being be as it is—represents the opposite of the indifference that simply turns its back upon the being itself in favor of an unexamined concept of being? We ought to turn toward the being, think about it in regard to its being, but by means of this thinking at the same time let it rest upon itself in its very own being.

This exertion of thought seems to meet with its greatest resistance in defining the thingness of the thing; for where else could the cause lie of the failure of the efforts mentioned? The unpretentious thing evades thought most stubbornly. Or can it be that this self-refusal of the mere thing, this self-contained independence, belongs precisely to the nature of the thing? Must not this strange and uncommunicative feature of the nature of the thing become intimately familiar to thought that tries to think the thing? If so, then we should not force our way to its thingly character.

That the thingness of the thing is particularly difficult to express and only seldom expressible is infallibly documented by the history of its interpretation indicated above. This history coincides with the destiny in accordance with which Western thought has hitherto thought the Being of beings. However, not only do we now establish this point; at the same time we discover a clue in this history. Is it an accident that in the interpretation of the thing the view that takes matter and form as guide attains to special dominance? This definition of the thing derives from an interpretation of the equipmental being of equipment. And equipment, having come into being through human making, is particularly familiar to human thinking. At the same time, this familiar being has a peculiar intermediate position between thing and work. We shall follow this clue and search first for the equipmental character of equipment. Perhaps this will suggest something to us about the thingly character of the thing and the workly character of the work. We must only avoid making thing and work prematurely into subspecies of equipment. We are disregarding the possibility, however, that differences relating to the history of Being may yet also be present in the way equipment *is*.

But what path leads to the equipmental quality of equipment? How shall we discover what a piece of equipment truly is? The procedure necessary at present must plainly avoid any attempts that again immediately entail the encroachments of the usual interpretations. We are most easily insured against this if we simply describe some equipment without any philosophical theory.

We choose as example a common sort of equipment—a pair of peasant shoes. We do not even need to exhibit actual pieces of this sort of useful article in order to describe them. Everyone is acquainted with them. But since it is a matter here of direct description, it may be well to facilitate the visual realization of them. For this purpose a pictorial representation suffices. We shall choose a well-known painting by Van Gogh, who painted such shoes several times. But what is there to see here? Everyone knows what shoes consist of. If they are not wooden or bast shoes, there will be leather soles and uppers, joined together by thread and nails. Such gear serves to clothe the feet. Depending on the use to which the shoes are to be put, whether for work in the field or for dancing, matter and form will differ.

Such statements, no doubt correct, only explicate what we already know. The equipmental quality of equipment consists in its usefulness. But what about this usefulness itself? In conceiving it, do we already conceive along with it the equipmental character of equipment? In order to succeed in doing this, must we not look out for useful equipment in its use? The peasant woman wears her shoes in the field. Only here are they what they are. They are all the more genuinely so, the less the peasant woman thinks about the shoes while she is at work, or looks at them at all, or is even aware of them. She stands and walks in them. That is how shoes actually serve. It is in this process of the use of equipment that we must actually encounter the character of equipment.

As long as we only imagine a pair of shoes in general, or simply look at the empty, unused shoes as they merely stand there in the picture, we shall never discover what the equipmental being of the equipment in truth is. From Van Gogh's painting we cannot even tell where these shoes stand. There is nothing surrounding this pair of peasant shoes in or to which they might belong—only an undefined space.

There are not even clods of soil from the field or the field-path sticking to them, which would at least hint at their use. A pair of peasant shoes and nothing more. And yet—

From the dark opening of the worn insides of the shoes the toilsome tread of the worker stares forth. In the stiffly rugged heaviness of the shoes there is the accumulated tenacity of her slow trudge through the far-spreading and ever-uniform furrows of the field swept by a raw wind. On the leather lie the dampness and richness of the soil. Under the soles slides the loneliness of the field-path as evening falls. In the shoes vibrates the silent call of the earth, its quiet gift of the ripening grain and its unexplained self-refusal in the fallow desolation of the wintry field. This equipment is pervaded by uncomplaining anxiety as to the certainty of bread, the wordless joy of having once more withstood want, the trembling before the impending childbed and shivering at the surrounding menace of death. This equipment belongs to the *earth*, and it is protected in the *world* of the peasant woman. From out of this protected belonging the equipment itself rises to its resting-within-itself.

But perhaps it is only in the picture that we notice all this about the shoes. The peasant woman, on the other hand, simply wears them. If only this simple wearing were so simple. When she takes off her shoes late in the evening, in deep but healthy fatigue, and reaches out for them again in the still dim dawn, or passes them by on the day of rest, she knows all this without noticing or reflecting. The equipmental quality of the equipment consists indeed in its usefulness. But this usefulness itself rests in the abundance of an essential being of the equipment. We call it reliability. By virtue of this reliability the peasant woman is made privy to the silent call of the earth; by virtue of the reliability of the equipment she is sure of her world. World and earth exist for her, and for those who are with her in her mode of being, only thus—in the equipment. We say "only" and therewith fall into error; for the reliability of the equipment first gives to the simple world its security and assures to the earth the freedom of its steady thrust.

The equipmental being of equipment, reliability, keeps gathered within itself all things according to their manner and extent. The usefulness of equipment is nevertheless only the essential consequence of reliability. The former vibrates in the latter and would be nothing without it. A single piece of equipment is worn out and used up; but at the same time the use itself also falls into disuse, wears away, and becomes usual. Thus equipmentality wastes away, sinks into mere stuff. In such wasting, reliability vanishes. This dwindling, however, to which use-things owe their boringly obtrusive usualness, is only one more testimony to the original nature of equipmental being. The worn-out usualness of the equipment then obtrudes itself as the sole mode of being, apparently peculiar to it exclusively. Only blank usefulness now remains visible. It awakens the impression that the origin of equipment lies in a mere fabricating that impresses a form upon some matter. Nevertheless, in its genuinely equipmental being, equipment stems from a more distant source. Matter and form and their distinction have a deeper origin.

The repose of equipment resting within itself consists in its reliability. Only in this reliability do we discern what equipment in truth is. But we still know nothing of what we first sought: the thing's thingly character. And we know nothing at all of what we really and solely seek: the workly character of the work in the sense of the work of art.

Or have we already learned something unwittingly, in passing so to speak, about the work-being of the work?

The equipmental quality of equipment was discovered. But how? Not by a description and explanation of a pair of shoes actually present; not by a report about the process of making shoes; and also not by the observation of the actual use of shoes occurring here and there; but only by bringing ourselves before Van Gogh's painting. This painting spoke. In the vicinity of the work we were suddenly somewhere else than we usually tend to be.

The art work let us know what shoes are in truth. It would be the worst self-deception to think that our description, as a subjective action, had first depicted everything thus and then projected it into the painting. If anything is questionable here, it is rather that we experienced too little in the neighborhood of the work and that we expressed the experience too crudely and too literally. But above all, the work did not, as it might seem at first, serve merely for a better visualizing of what a piece of equipment is. Rather, the equipmentality of equipment first genuinely arrives at its appearance through the work and only in the work.

What happens here? What is at work in the work? Van Gogh's painting is the disclosure of what the equipment, the pair of peasant shoes, *is* in truth. This entity emerges into the unconcealedness of its being. The Greeks called the unconcealedness of beings *aletheia*. We say "truth" and think little enough in using this word. If there occurs in the work a disclosure of a particular being, disclosing what and how it is, then there is here an occurring, a happening of truth at work.

In the work of art the truth of an entity has set itself to work. "To set" means here: to bring to a stand. Some particular entity, a pair of peasant shoes, comes in the work to stand in the light of its being. The being of the being comes into the steadiness of its shining.

The nature of art would then be this: the truth of beings setting itself to work. But until now art presumably has had to do with the beautiful and beauty, and not with truth. The arts that produce such works are called the beautiful or fine arts, in contrast with the applied or industrial arts that manufacture equipment. In fine art the art itself is not beautiful, but is called so because it produces the beautiful. Truth, in contrast, belongs to logic. Beauty, however, is reserved for aesthetics.

But perhaps the proposition that art is truth setting itself to work intends to revive the fortunately obsolete view that art is an imitation and depiction of reality? The reproduction of what exists requires, to be sure, agreement with the actual being, adaptation to it; the Middle Ages called it *adaequatio*; Aristotle already spoke of *homoiosis*. Agreement with what *is* has long been taken to be the essence of truth. But then, is it our opinion that this painting by Van Gogh depicts a pair of actually existing peasant shoes, and is a work of art because it does so successfully? Is it our opinion that the painting draws a likeness from something actual and transposes it into a product of artistic—production? By no means.

The work, therefore, is not the reproduction of some particular entity that happens to be present at any given time; it is, on the contrary, the reproduction of the thing's general essence. But then where and how is this general essence, so that art works are able to agree with it? With what nature of what thing should a Greek temple agree? Who could maintain the impossible view that the Idea of Temple is represented in the building? And yet, truth is set to work in such a work, if it is a work. Or let us think of Hölderlin's hymn, "The Rhine." What is pregiven to the poet, and how is it given, so that it can then be regiven in the poem? And if in the case of this hymn and similar poems the idea of a copy-relation between something already actual and the art work clearly fails, the view that the work is a copy is confirmed in the best possible way by a work of the kind presented in C. F. Meyer's poem "Roman Fountain."

Roman Fountain

The jet ascends and falling fills
The marble basin circling round;
This, veiling itself over, spills
Into a second basin's ground.
The second in such plenty lives,
Its bubbling flood a third invests,
And each at once receives and gives
And streams and rests.

This is neither a poetic painting of a fountain actually present nor a reproduction of the general essence of a Roman fountain. Yet truth is put into the work. What truth is happening in the work? Can truth happen at all and thus be historical? Yet truth, people say, is something timeless and supertemporal.

We seek the reality of the art work in order to find there the art prevailing within it. The thingly substructure is what proved to be the most immediate reality in the work. But to comprehend this thingly feature the traditional thing-concepts are not adequate; for they themselves fail to grasp the nature of the thing. The currently predominant thing-concept, thing as formed matter, is not even derived from the nature of the thing but from the nature of equipment. It also turned out that equipmental being generally has long since occupied a peculiar preeminence in the interpretation of beings. This preeminence of equipmentality, which however did not actually come to mind, suggested that we pose the question of equipment anew while avoiding the current interpretations.

We allowed a work to tell us what equipment is. By this means, almost clandestinely, it came to light what is at work in the work: the disclosure of the particular being in its being, the happening of truth. If, however, the reality of the work can be defined solely by means of what is at work in the work, then what about our intention to seek out the real art work in its reality? As long as we supposed that the reality of the work lay primarily in its thingly substructure we were going astray. We are now confronted by a remarkable result of our considerations—if it still deserves to be called a result at all. Two points become clear:

First: the dominant thing-concepts are inadequate as means of grasping the thingly aspect of the work.

Second: what we tried to treat as the most immediate reality of the work, its thingly substructure, does not belong to the work in that way at all.

As soon as we look for such a thingly substructure in the work, we have unwittingly taken the work as equipment, to which we then also ascribe a superstructure supposed to contain its artistic quality. But the work is not a piece of equipment that is fitted out in addition with an aesthetic value that adheres to it. The work is no more anything of the kind than the bare thing is a piece of equipment that merely lacks the specific equipmental characteristics of usefulness and being made.

Our formulation of the question of the work has been shaken because we asked, not about the work but half about a thing and half about equipment. Still, this formulation of the question was not first developed by us. It is the formulation native to aesthetics. The way in which aesthetics views the art work from the outset is dominated by the traditional interpretation of all beings. But the shaking of this accustomed formulation is not the essential point. What matters is a first opening of our vision to the fact that what is workly in the work, equipmental in equipment, and thingly in the thing comes closer to us only when we think the Being of beings. To this end it is necessary beforehand that the barriers of our preconceptions fall away and that the current pseudo concepts be set aside. That is why we had to take this detour. But it brings us directly to a road that may lead to a determination of the thingly feature in the work. The thingly feature in the work should not be denied; but if it belongs admittedly to the work-being of the work, it must be conceived by way of the work's workly nature. If this is so, then the road toward the determination of the thingly reality of the work leads not from thing to work but from work to thing.

The art work opens up in its own way the Being of beings. This opening up, i.e., this deconcealing, i.e., the truth of beings, happens in the work. In the art work, the truth of what is has set itself to work. Art is truth setting itself to work. What is truth itself, that it sometimes comes to pass as art? What is this setting-itself-to-work?

The Work and Truth

The origin of the art work is art. But what is art? Art is real in the art work. Hence we first seek the reality of the work. In what does it consist? Art works universally display a thingly character, albeit in a wholly distinct way. The attempt to interpret this thing-character of the work with the aid of the usual thing-concepts failed—not only because these concepts do not lay hold of the thingly feature, but because, in raising the question of its thingly substructure, we force the work into a preconceived framework by which we obstruct our own access to the work-being of the work. Nothing can be discovered about the thingly aspect of the work so long as the pure self-subsistence of the work has not distinctly displayed itself.

Yet is the work ever in itself accessible? To gain access to the work, it would be necessary to remove it from all relations to something other than itself, in order to let it stand on its own for itself alone. But the artist's most peculiar intention already aims in this direction. The work is to be released by him to its pure self-subsistence. It is precisely in great art—and only such art is under consideration here—that the artist remains inconsequential as compared with the work, almost like a passageway that destroys itself in the creative process for the work to emerge.

Well, then, the works themselves stand and hang in collections and exhibitions. But are they here in themselves as the works they themselves are, or are they not rather here as objects of the art industry? Works are made available for public and private art appreciation. Official agencies assume the care and maintenance of works. Connoisseurs and critics busy themselves with them. Art dealers supply the market. Art-historical study makes the works the objects of a science. Yet in all this busy activity do we encounter the work itself?

The Aegina sculptures in the Munich collection, Sophocles' *Antigone* in the best critical edition, are, as the works they are, torn out of their own native sphere. However high their quality and power of impression, however good their state of preservation, however certain their interpretation, placing them in a collection has withdrawn them from their own world. But even when we make an effort to cancel or avoid such displacement of works—when, for instance, we visit the temple in Paestum at its own site or the Bamberg cathedral on its own square—the world of the work that stands there has perished.

World-withdrawal and world-decay can never be undone. The works are no longer the same as they once were. It is they themselves, to be sure, that we encounter there, but they themselves are gone by. As bygone works they stand over against us in the realm of tradition and conservation. Henceforth they remain merely such objects. Their standing before us is still indeed a consequence of, but no longer the same as, their former self-subsistence. This self-subsistence has fled from them. The whole art industry, even if carried to the extreme and exercised in every way for the sake of works themselves, extends only to the object-being of the works. But this does not constitute their work-being.

But does the work still remain a work if it stands outside all relations? Is it not essential for the work to stand in relations? Yes, of course—except that it remains to ask in what relations it stands.

Where does a work beolng? The work belongs, as work, uniquely within the realm that is opened up by itself. For the work-being of the work is present in, and only in, such opening up. We said that in the work there was a happening of truth at work. The reference to Van Gogh's picture tried to point to this happening. With regard to it there arose the question as to what truth is and how truth can happen.

We now ask the question of truth with a view to the work. But in order to become more familiar with what the question involves, it is necessary to make visible once more the happening of truth in the work. For this attempt let us deliberately select a work that cannot be ranked as representational art.

A building, a Greek temple, portrays nothing. It simply stands there in the middle of the rock-cleft valley. The building encloses the figure of the god, and in this concealment lets it stand out into the holy precinct through the open portico. By means of the temple, the god is present in the temple. This presence of the god is in itself the extension and delimitation of the precinct as a holy precinct. The temple and its precinct, however, do not fade away into the indefinite. It is the temple-work that first fits together and at the same time gathers around itself the unity of those paths and relations in which birth and death, disaster and blessing, victory and disgrace, endurance and decline acquire the shape of destiny for human being. The all-governing expanse of this open relational context is the world of this historical people. Only from and in this expanse does the nation first return to itself for the fulfillment of its vocation.

Standing there, the building rests on the rocky ground. This resting of the work draws up out of the rock the mystery of that rock's clumsy yet spontaneous support. Standing there, the building holds its ground against the storm raging above it and so first makes the storm itself manifest in its violence. The luster and gleam of the stone, though itself apparently glowing only by the grace of the sun, yet first brings to light the light of the day, the breadth of the sky, the darkness of the night. The temple's firm towering makes visible the invisible space of air. The steadfastness of the work contrasts with the surge of the surf, and its own repose brings out the raging of the sea. Tree and grass, eagle and bull, snake and cricket first enter into their distinctive shapes and thus come to appear as what they are. The Greeks early called this emerging and rising in itself and in all things *phusis*. It clears and illuminates, also, that on which and in which man bases his dwelling. We call this ground the *earth*. What this word says is not to be associated with the idea of a mass of matter deposited somewhere, or with the merely astronomical idea of a planet. Earth is that whence the arising brings back and shelters everything that arises without violation. In the things that arise, earth is present as the shelterng agent.

The temple-work, standing there, opens up a world and at the same time sets this world back again on earth, which itself only thus emerges as native ground. But men and animals, plants and things, are never present and familiar as unchangeable objects, only to represent incidentally also a fitting environment for the temple, which one fine day is added to what is already there. We shall get closer to what *is*, rather, if we think of all this in reverse order, assuming of course that we have, to begin with, an eye for how differently everything then faces us. Mere reversing, done for its own sake, reveals nothing.

The temple, in its standing there, first gives to things their look and to men their outlook on themselves. This view remains open as long as the work is a work, as long as the god has not fled from it. It is the same with the sculpture of the god, votive offering of the victor in the athletic games. It is not a portrait whose purpose is to make it easier to realize how the god looks; rather, it is a work that lets the god himself be present and thus *is* the god himself. The same holds for the linguistic work. In the tragedy nothing is staged or displayed theatrically, but the battle of the new gods against the old is being fought. The linguistic work, originating in the speech of the people, does not refer to this battle; it transforms the people's saying so that now every living word fights the battle and puts up for decision what is holy and what unholy, what great and what small, what brave and what cowardly, what lofty and what flighty, what master and what slave (cf. Heraclitus, Fragment 53).

In what, then, does the work-being of the work consist? Keeping steadily in view the points just crudely enough indicated, two essential features of the work may for the moment be brought out more distinctly. We set out here, from the long familiar foreground of the work's being, the thingly character which gives support to our customary attitude toward the work.

When a work is brought into a collection or placed in an exhibition we say also that it is "set up." But this setting up differs essentially from setting up in the sense of erecting a building, raising a statue, presenting a tragedy at a holy festival. Such setting up is erecting in the sense of dedication and praise. Here "setting up" no longer means a bare placing. To dedicate means to consecrate, in the sense that in setting up the work the holy is opened up as holy and the god is invoked into the openness of his presence. Praise belongs to dedication as doing honor to the dignity and splendor of the god. Dignity and splendor are not properties beside and behind which the god, too, stands as something distinct, but it is rather in the dignity, in the splendor that the god is present. In the reflected glory of this splendor there glows, i.e., there lightens itself, what we called the word. To e-rect means: to open the right in the sense of a guiding measure, a form in which what belongs to the nature of being gives guidance. But why is the setting up of a work an erecting that consecrates and praises? Because the work, in its work-being, demands it. How is it that the work comes to demand such a setting up? Because it itself, in its own work-being, is something that sets up. What does the work, as work, set up? Towering up within itself, the work opens up a *world* and keeps it abidingly in force.

To be a work means to set up a world. But what is it to be a world? The answer was hinted at when we referred to the temple. On the path we must follow here, the nature of world can only be indicated. What is more, this indication limits itself to warding off anything that might at first distort our view of the world's nature.

The world is not the mere collection of the countable or uncountable, familiar and unfamiliar things that are just there. But neither is it a merely imagined framework added by our representation to the sum of such given things. The *world worlds*, and is more fully in being than the tangible and perceptible realm in which we believe ourselves to be at home. World is never an object that stands before us and can be seen. World is the ever-nonobjective to which we are subject as long as the paths of birth and death, blessing and curse keep us transported into Being. Wherever those decisions of our history that relate to our very being are made, are taken up and abandoned by us, go unrecognized and are rediscovered by new inquiry, there the world worlds. A stone is worldless. Plant and animal likewise have no world; but they belong to the covert throng of a surrounding into which they are linked. The peasant woman, on the other hand, has a world because she dwells in the overtness of beings, of the things that are. Her equipment, in its reliability, gives to this world a necessity and nearness of its own. By the opening up of a world, all things gain their lingering and hastening, their remoteness and nearness, their scope and limits. In a world's worlding is gathered that spaciousness out of which the protective grace of the gods is granted or withheld. Even this doom of the god remaining absent is a way in which world worlds.

A work, by being a work, makes space for that spaciousness. "To make space for" means here especially to liberate the Open and to establish it in its structure. This in-stalling occurs through the erecting mentioned earlier. The work as work sets up a world. The work holds open the Open of the world. But the setting up of a world is only the first essential feature in the work-being of a work to be referred to here. Starting again from the foreground of the work, we shall attempt to make clear in the same way the second essential feature that belongs with the first.

When a work is created, brought forth out of this or that work-material—stone, wood, metal, color, language, tone—we say also that it is made, set forth out of it. But just as the work requires a setting up in the sense of a consecrating-praising erection, because the work's work-being consists in the setting up of a world, so a setting forth is needed because the work-being of the work itself has the character of setting forth. The work as work, in its presencing, is a setting forth, a making. But what does the work set forth? We come to know about this only when we explore what comes to the fore and is customarily spoken of as the making or production of works.

To work-being there belongs the setting up of a world. Thinking of it within this perspective, what is the nature of that in the work which is usually called the work material? Because it is determined by usefulness and serviceability, equipment takes into its service that of which it consists: the matter. In fabricating equipment—e.g., an ax—stone is used, and used up. It disappears into usefulness. The material is all the better and more suitable the less it resists perishing in the equipmental being of the equipment. By contrast the temple-work, in setting up a world, does not cause the material to disappear, but rather causes it to come forth for the very first time and to come into the Open of the work's world. The rock comes to bear and rest and so first becomes rock; metals come to glitter and shimmer, colors to glow, tones to sing, the word to speak. All this comes forth as the work sets itself back into the massiveness and heaviness of stone, into the firmness and pliancy of wood, into the hardness and luster of metal, into the lighting and darkening of color, into the clang of tone, and into the naming power of the word.

That into which the work sets itself back and which it causes to come forth in this setting back of itself we called the earth. Earth is that which comes forth and shelters. Earth, self-dependent, is effortless and untiring. Upon the earth and in it, historical man grounds his dwelling in the world. In setting up a world, the work sets forth the earth. This setting forth must be thought here in the strict sense of the word. The work moves the earth itself into the Open of a world and keeps it there. *The work lets the earth be an earth.*

But why must this setting forth of the earth happen in such a way that the work sets itself back into it? What is the earth that it attains to the unconcealed in just such a manner? A stone presses downward and manifests its heaviness. But while this heaviness exerts an opposing pressure upon us it denies us any penetration into it. If we attempt such a penetration by breaking open the rock, it still does not display in its fragments anything inward that has been disclosed. The stone has instantly withdrawn again into the same dull pressure and bulk of its fragments. If we try to lay hold of the stone's heaviness in another way, by placing the stone on a balance, we merely bring the heaviness into the form of a calculated weight. This perhaps very precise determination of the stone remains a number, but the weight's burden has escaped us. Color shines and wants only to shine. When we analyze it in rational terms by measuring its wavelengths, it is gone. It shows itself only when it remains undisclosed and unexplained. Earth thus shatters every attempt to penetrate into it. It causes every merely calculating importunity upon it to turn into a destruction. This destruction may herald itself under the appearance of mastery and of progress in the form of the technical-scientific objectivation of nature, but this mastery nevertheless remains an impotence of will. The earth appears openly cleared as itself only when it is perceived and preserved as that which is by nature undisclosable, that which shrinks from every disclosure and constantly keeps itself closed up. All things of earth, and the earth itself as a whole, flow together into a reciprocal accord. But this confluence is not a blurring of their outlines. Here there flows the steam, restful within itself, of the setting of bounds, which delimits everything present within its presence. Thus in each of the self-secluding things there is the same not-knowing-of-one-another. The earth is essentially self-secluding. To set forth the earth means to bring it into the Open as the self-secluding.

This setting forth of the earth is achieved by the work as it sets itself back into the earth. The self-seclusion of earth, however, is not a uniform, inflexible staying under cover, but unfolds itself in an inexhaustible variety of simple modes and shapes. To be sure, the sculptor uses stone just as the mason uses it, in his own way. But he does not use it up. That happens in a certain way only where the work miscarries. To be sure, the painter also uses pigment, but in such a way that color is not used up but rather only now comes to shine forth. To be sure, the poet also uses the word—not, however, like ordinary speakers and writers who have to use them up, but rather in such a way that the word only now becomes and remains truly a word.

Nowhere in the work is there any trace of a work-material. It even remains doubtful whether, in the essential definition of equipment, what the equipment consists of is properly described in its equipmental nature as matter.

The setting up of a world and the setting forth of earth are two essential features in the work-being of the work. They belong together, however, in the unity of work-being. This is the unity we seek when we ponder the self-subsistence of the work and try to express in words this closed, unitary repose of self-support.

But in the essential features just mentioned, if our account has any validity at all, we have indicated in the work rather a happening and in no sense a repose, for what is rest if not the opposite of motion? It is at any rate not an opposite that excludes motion from itself, but rather includes it. Only what is in motion can rest. The mode of rest varies with the kind of motion. In motion as the mere displacement of a body, rest is, to be sure, only the limiting case of motion. Where rest includes motion, there can exist a repose which is an inner concentration of motion, hence a higher state of agitation, assuming that the mode of motion requires such a rest. Now the repose of the work that rests in itself is of this sort. We shall therefore come nearer to this repose if we can succeed in grasping the state of movement of the happening in work-being in its full unity. We ask: What relation do the setting up of a world and the setting forth of the earth exhibit in the work itself?

The world is the self-disclosing openness of the broad paths of the simple and essential decisions in the destiny of an historical people. The earth is the spontaneous forthcoming of that which is continually self-secluding and to that extent sheltering and concealing. World and earth are essentially different from one another and yet are never separated. The world grounds itself on the earth, and earth juts through world. But the relation between world and earth does not wither away into the empty unity of opposites unconcerned with one another. The world, in resting upon the earth, strives to surmount it. As self-opening it cannot endure anything closed. The earth, however, as sheltering and concealing, tends always to draw the world into itself and keep it there.

The opposition of world and earth is a striving. But we would surely all too easily falsify its nature if we were to confound striving with discord and dispute, and thus see it only as disorder and destruction. In essential striving, rather, the opponents raise each other into the self-assertion of their natures. Self-assertion of nature, however, is never a rigid insistence upon some contingent state, but surrender to the concealed originality of the source of one's own being. In the struggle, each opponent carries the other beyond itself. Thus the striving becomes ever more intense as striving, and more authentically what it is. The more the struggle overdoes itself on its own part, the more inflexibly do the opponents let themselves go into the intimacy of simple belonging to one another. The earth cannot dispense with the Open of the world if it itself is to appear as earth in the liberated surge of its self-seclusion. The world, again, cannot soar out of the earth's sight if, as the governing breadth and path of all essential destiny, it is to ground itself on a resolute foundation.

In setting up a world and setting forth the earth, the work is an instigating of this striving. This does not happen so that the work should at the same time settle and put an end to the conflict in an insipid agreement, but so that the strife may remain a strife. Setting up a world and setting forth the earth, the work accomplishes this striving. The work-being of the work consists in the fighting of the battle between world and earth. It is because the struggle arrives at its high point in the simplicity of intimacy that the unity of the work comes about in the fighting of the battle. The fighting of the battle is the continually self-overreaching gathering of the work's agitation. The repose of the work that rests in itself thus has its presencing in the intimacy of striving.

From this repose of the work we can now first see what is at work in the work. Until now it was a merely provisional assertion that in an art work the truth is set to work. In what way does truth happen in the work-being of the work, i.e., now, how does truth happen in the fighting of the battle between world and earth? What is truth?

How slight and stunted our knowledge of the nature of truth is, is shown by the laxity we permit ourselves in using this basic word. By truth is usually meant this or that particular truth. That means: something true. A cognition articulated in a proposition can be of this sort. However, we call not only a proposition true, but also a thing, true gold in contrast with sham gold. True here means genuine, real gold. What does the expression "real" mean here? To us it is what is in truth. The true is what corresponds to the real, and the real is what is in truth. The circle has closed again.

What does "in truth" mean? Truth is the essence of the true. What do we have in mind when speaking of essence? Usually it is thought to be those features held in common by everything that is true. The essence is discovered in the generic and universal concept, which represents the one feature that holds indifferently for many things. This indifferent essence (essentiality in the sense of *essentia*) is, however, only the inessential essence. What does the essential essence of something consist in? Presumably it lies in what the entity *is* in truth. The true essential nature of a thing is determined by way of its true being, by way of the truth of the given being. But we are now seeking not the truth of essential nature but the essential nature of truth. There thus appears a curious tangle. Is it only a curiosity or even merely the empty sophistry of a conceptual game, or is it—an abyss?

Truth means the nature of the true. We think this nature in recollecting the Greek word *aletheia*, the unconcealedness of beings. But is this enough to define the nature of truth? Are we not passing off a mere change of word usage—unconcealedness instead of truth—as a characterization of fact? Certainly we do not get beyond an interchange of names as long as we do not come to know what must have happened in order to be compelled to tell the *nature* of truth in the word "unconcealedness."

Does this require a revival of Greek philosophy? Not at all. A revival, even if such an impossibility were possible, would be of no help to us; for the hidden history of Greek philosophy consists from its beginning in this, that it does not remain in conformity with the nature of truth that flashes out in the word *aletheia*, and has to misdirect its knowing and its speaking about the nature of truth more and more into the discussion of a derivative nature of truth. The nature of truth as *aletheia* was not thought out in the thinkng of the Greeks nor since then, and least of all in the philosophy that followed after. Unconcealedness is, for thought, the most concealed thing in Greek existence, although from early times it determines the presence of everything present.

Yet why should we not be satisfied with the nature of truth that has by now been familiar to us for centuries? Truth means today and has long meant the agreement or conformity of knowledge with fact. However, the fact must show itself to be fact if knowledge and the proposition that forms and expresses knowledge are to be able to conform to the fact; otherwise the fact cannot become binding on the proposition. How can fact show itself if it cannot itself stand forth out of concealedness, if it does not itself stand in the unconcealed? A proposition is true by conforming to the unconcealed, to what is true. Propositional truth is always, and always exclusively, this correctness. The critical concepts of truth which, since Descartes, start out from truth as certainty, are merely variations of the definition of truth as correctness. This nature of truth which is familiar to us—correctness in representation—stands and falls with truth as unconcealedness of beings.

If here and elsewhere we conceive of truth as unconcealedness, we are not merely taking refuge in a more literal translation of a Greek word. We are reminding ourselves of what, unexperienced and unthought, underlies our familiar and therefore outworn nature of truth in the sense of correctness. We do, of course, occasionally take the trouble to concede that naturally, in order to understand and verify the correctness (truth) of a proposition one really should go back to something that is already evident, and that this presupposition is indeed unavoidable. As long as we talk and believe in this way, we always understand truth merely as correctness, which of course still requires a further presupposition, that we ourselves just happen to make, heaven knows how or why.

But it is not we who presuppose the unconcealedness of beings; rather, the unconcealedness of beings (Being) puts us into such a condition of being that in our representation we always remain installed within and in attendance upon unconcealedness. Not only must that in *conformity* with which a cognition orders itself be already in some way unconcealed. The entire *realm* in which this "conforming to something" goes on must already occur as a whole in the unconcealed; and this holds equally of that *for* which the conformity of a proposition to fact becomes manifest. With all our correct representations we would get nowhere, we could not even presuppose that there already is manifest something to which we can conform ourselves, unless the unconcealedness of beings had already exposed us to, placed us in that lighted realm in which every being stands for us and from which it withdraws.

But how does this take place? How does truth happen as this unconcealedness? First, however, we must say more clearly what this unconcealedness itself is.

Things are, and human beings, gifts, and sacrifices are, animals and plants are, equipment and works are. That which is, the particular being, stands in Being. Through Being there passes a veiled destiny that is ordained between the godly and the countergodly. There is much in being that man cannot master. There is but little that comes to be known. What is known remains inexact, what is mastered insecure. What is, is never of our making or even merely the product of our minds, as it might all too easily seem. When we contemplate this whole as one, then we apprehend, so it appears, all that is—though we grasp it crudely enough.

And yet—beyond what is, not away from it but before it, there is still something else that happens. In the midst of beings as a whole an open place occurs. There is a clearing, a lighting. Thought of in reference to what is, to beings, this clearing is in a greater degree than are beings. This open center is therefore not surrounded by what is; rather, the lighting center itself encircles all that is, like the Nothing which we scarcely know.

That which is can only be, as a being, if it stands within and stands out within what is lighted in this clearing. Only this clearing grants and guarantees to us humans a passage to those beings that we ourselves are not, and access to the being that we ourselves are. Thanks to this clearing, beings are unconcealed in certain changing degrees. And yet a being can be *concealed*, too, only within the sphere of what is lighted. Each being we encounter and which encounters us keeps to this curious opposition of presence in that it always withholds itself at the same time in a concealedness. The clearing in which beings stand is in itself at the same time concealment. Concealment, however, prevails in the midst of beings in a twofold way.

Beings refuse themselves to us down to that one and seemingly least feature which we touch upon most readily when we can say no more of beings than that they are. Concealment as refusal is not simply and only the limit of knowledge in any given circumstance, but the beginning of the clearing of what is lighted. But concealment, though of another sort, to be sure, at the same time also occurs within what is lighted. One being places itself in front of another being, the one helps to hide the other, the former obscures the latter, a few obstruct many, one denies all. Here concealment is not simple refusal. Rather, a being appears, but it presents itself as other than it is.

This concealment is dissembling. If one being did not simulate another, we could not make mistakes or act mistakenly in regard to beings; we could not go astray and transgress, and especially could never overreach ourselves. That a being should be able to deceive as semblance is the condition for our being able to be deceived, not conversely.

Concealment can be a refusal or merely a dissembling. We are never fully certain whether it is the one or the other. Concealment conceals and dissembles itself. This means: the open place in the midst of beings, the clearing, is never a rigid stage with a permanently raised curtain on which the play of beings runs its course. Rather, the clearing happens only as this double concealment. The unconcealedness of beings—this is never a merely existent state, but a happening. Unconcealedness (truth) is neither an attribute of factual things in the sense of beings, nor one of propositions.

We believe we are at home in the immediate circle of beings. That which is, is familiar, reliable, ordinary. Nevertheless, the clearing is pervaded by a constant concealment in the double form of refusal and dissembling. At bottom, the ordinary is not ordinary; it is extra-ordinary, uncanny. The nature of truth, that is, of unconcealedness, is dominated throughout by a denial. Yet this denial is not a defect or a fault, as though truth were an unalloyed unconcealedness that has rid itself of everything concealed. If truth could accomplish this, it would no longer be itself. *This denial, in the form of a double concealment, belongs to the nature of truth as unconcealedness.* Truth, in its nature, is un-truth. We put the matter this way in order to serve notice, with a possibly surprising trenchancy, that denial in the manner of concealment belongs to unconcealedness as clearing. The proposition, "the nature of truth is untruth," is not, however, intended to state that truth is at bottom falsehood. Nor does it mean that truth is never itself but, viewed dialectically, is always also its opposite.

Truth occurs precisely as itself in that the concealing denial, as refusal, provides its constant source to all clearing, and yet, as dissembling, it metes out to all clearing the indefeasible severity of error. Concealing denial is intended to denote that opposition in the nature of truth which subsists between clearing, or lighting, and concealing. It is the opposition of the primal conflict. The nature of truth is, in itself, the primal conflict in which that open center is won within which what is, stands, and from which it sets itself back into itself.

This Open happens in the midst of beings. It exhibits an essential feature which we have already mentioned. To the Open there belong a world and the earth. But the world is not simply the Open that corresponds to clearing, and the earth is not simply the Closed that corresponds to concealment. Rather, the world is the clearing of the paths of the essential guiding directions with which all decision complies. Every decision, however, bases itself on something not mastered, something concealed, confusing; else it would never be a decision. The earth is not simply the Closed but rather that which rises up as self-closing. World and earth are always intrinsically and essentially in conflict, belligerent by nature. Only as such do they enter into the conflict of clearing and concealing.

Earth juts through the world and world grounds itself on the earth only so far as truth happens as the primal conflict between clearing and concealing. But how does truth happen? We answer: it happens in a few essential ways. One of these ways in which truth happens is the work-being of the work. Setting up a world and setting forth the earth, the work is the fighting of the battle in which the unconcealedness of beings as a whole, or truth, is won.

Truth happens in the temple's standing where it is. This does not mean that something is correctly represented and rendered here, but that what is as a whole is brought into unconcealedness and held therein. To hold (*halten*) originally means to tend, keep, take care (*hüten*). Truth happens in Van Gogh's painting. This does not mean that something is correctly portrayed, but rather that in the revelation of the equipmental being of the shoes, that which is as a whole—world and earth in their counterplay—attains to unconcealedness.

Thus in the work it is truth, not only something true, that is at work. The picture that shows the peasant shoes, the poem that says the Roman fountain, do not just make manifest what this isolated being as such is—if indeed they manifest anything at all; rather, they make unconcealedness as such happen in regard to what is as a whole. The more simply and authentically the shoes are engrossed in their nature, the more plainly and purely the fountain is engrossed in its nature—the more directly and engagingly do all beings attain to a greater degree of being along with them. That is how self-concealing being is illuminated. Light of this kind joins its shining to and into the work. This shining, joined in the work, is the beautiful. *Beauty is one way in which truth occurs as unconcealedness.*

We now, indeed, grasp the nature of truth more clearly in certain respects. What is at work in the work may accordingly have become more clear. But the work's now visible work-being still does not tell us anything about the work's closest and most obtrusive reality, about the thingly aspect of the work. Indeed it almost seems as though, in pursuing the exclusive aim of grasping the work's independence as purely as possible, we had completely overlooked the one thing, that a work is always a work, which means that it is something worked out, brought about, effected. If there is anything that distinguishes the work as work, it is that the work has been created. Since the work is created, and creation requires a medium out of which and in which it creates, the thingly element, too, enters into the work. This is incontestable. Still the question remains: how does being created belong to the work? This can be elucidated only if two points are cleared up:

1. What do being created and creation mean here in distinction from making and being made?

2. What is the inmost nature of the work itself, from which alone can be gauged how far createdness belongs to the work and how far it determines the work-being of the work?

Creation is here always thought of in reference to the work. To the nature of the work there belongs the happening of truth. From the outset we define the nature of creating by its relation to the nature of truth as the unconcealedness of beings. The pertinence of createdness to the work can be elucidated only by way of a more fundamental clarification of the nature of truth. The question of truth and its nature returns again.

We must raise that question once more, if the proposition that truth is at work in the work is not to remain a mere assertion.

We must now first ask in a more essential way: how does the impulse toward such a thing as a work lie in the nature of truth? Of what nature is truth, that it can be set into work, or even under certain conditions must be set into work, in order to be *as* truth? But we defined the setting-into-a-work of truth as the nature of art. Hence our last question becomes:

What is truth, that it can happen as, or even must happen as, art? How is it that art exists at all?

Truth and Art

Art is the origin of the art work and of the artist. Origin is the source of the nature in which the being of an entity is present. What is art? We seek its nature in the actual work. The actual reality of the work has been defined by that which is at work in the work, by the happening of truth. This happening we think of as the fighting of the conflict between world and earth. Repose occurs in the concentrated agitation of this conflict. The independence or self-composure of the work is grounded here.

In the work, the happening of truth is at work. But what is thus at work, is so *in* the work. This means that the actual work is here already presupposed as the bearer of this happening. At once the problem of the thingly feature of the given work confronts us again. One thing thus finally becomes clear: however zealously we inquire into the work's self-sufficiency, we shall still fail to find its actuality as long as we do not also agree to take the work as something worked, effected. To take it thus lies closest at hand, for in the word "work" we hear what is worked. The workly character of the work consists in its having been created by the artist. It may seem curious that this most obvious and all-clarifying definition of the work is mentioned only now.

The work's createdness, however, can obviously be grasped only in terms of the process of creation. Thus, constrained by the facts, we must consent after all to go into the activity of the artist in order to arrive at the origin of the work of art. The attempt to define the work-being of the work purely in terms of the work itself proves to be unfeasible.

In turning away now from the work to examine the nature of the creative process, we should like nevertheless to keep in mind what was said first of the picture of the peasant shoes and later of the Greek temple.

We think of creation as a bringing forth. But the making of equipment, too, is a bringing forth. Handicraft—a remarkable play of language—does not, to be sure, create works, not even when we contrast, as we must, the handmade with the factory product. But what is it that distinguishes bringing forth as creation from bringing forth in the mode of making? It is as difficult to track down the essential features of the creation of works and the making of equipment as it is easy to distinguish verbally between the two modes of bringing forth. Going along with first appearances we find the same procedure in the activity of potter and sculptor, of joiner and painter. The creation of a work requires craftsmanship. Great artists prize craftsmanship most highly. They are the first to call for its painstaking cultivation, based on complete mastery. They above all others constantly strive to educate themselves ever anew in thorough craftsmanship. It has often enough been pointed out that the Greeks, who knew quite a bit about works of art, use the same word *techne* for craft and art and call the craftsman and the artist by the same name: *technites*.

It thus seems advisable to define the nature of creative work in terms of its craft aspect. But reference to the linguistic usage of the Greeks, with their experience of the facts, must give us pause. However usual and convincing the reference may be to the Greek practice of naming craft and art by the same name, *techne*, it nevertheless remains oblique and superficial; for *techne* signifies neither craft nor art, and not at all the technical in our present-day sense; it never means a kind of practical performance.

The word *techne* denotes rather a mode of knowing. To know means to have seen, in the widest sense of seeing, which means to apprehend what is present, as such. For Greek thought the nature of knowing consists in *aletheia*, that is, in the uncovering of beings. It supports and guides all comportment toward beings. *Techne*, as knowledge experienced in the Greek manner, is a bringing forth of beings in that it *brings forth* present beings as such beings *out of* concealedness and specifically *into* the unconcealedness of their appearance; *techne* never signifies the action of making.

The artist is a *technites* not because he is also a craftsman, but because both the setting forth of works and the setting forth of equipment occur in a bringing forth and presenting that causes beings in the first place to come forward and be present in assuming an appearance. Yet all this happens in the midst of the being that grows out of its own accord, *phusis*. Calling art *techne* does not at all imply that the artist's action is seen in the light of craft. What looks like craft in the creation of a work is of a different sort. This doing is determined and pervaded by the nature of creation, and indeed remains contained within that creating.

What then, if not craft, is to guide our thinking about the nature of creation? What else than a view of what is to be created: the work? Although it becomes actual only as the creative act is performed, and thus depends for its reality upon this act, the nature of creation is determined by the nature of the work. Even though the work's createdness has a relation to creation, nevertheless both createdness and creation must be defined in terms of the work-being of the work. And now it can no longer seem strange that we first and at length dealt with the work alone, to bring its createdness into view only at the end. If createdness belongs to the work as essentially as the word "work" makes it sound, then we must try to understand even more essentially what so far could be defined as the work-being of the work.

In the light of the definition of the work we have reached at this point, according to which the happening of truth is at work in the work, we are able to characterize creation as follows: to create is to cause something to emerge as a thing that has been brought forth. The work's becoming a work is a way in which truth becomes and happens. It all rests on the nature of truth. But what is truth, that it has to happen in such a thing as something created? How does truth have an impulse toward a work grounded in its very nature? Is this intelligible in terms of the nature of truth as thus far elucidated?

Truth is un-truth, insofar as there belongs to it the reservoir of the not-yet-uncovered, the un-uncovered, in the sense of concealment. In unconcealedness, as truth, there occurs also the other "un-" of a double restraint or refusal. Truth occurs as such in the opposition of clearing and double concealing. Truth is the primal conflict in which, always in some particular way, the Open is won within which everything stands

and from which everything withholds itself that shows itself and withdraws itself as a being. Whenever and however this conflict breaks out
and happens, the opponents, lighting or clearing and concealing,
move apart because of it. Thus the Open of the place of conflict is won.
The openness of this Open, that is, truth, can be what it is, namely,
this openness, only if and as long as it establishes itself within its Open.
Hence there must always be some being in this Open, something that
is, in which the openness takes its stand and attains its constancy. In
takng possession thus of the Open, the openness holds open the Open
and sustains it. Setting and taking possession are here everywhere drawn
from the Greek sense of *thesis*, which means a setting up in the unconcealed.

In referring to this self-establishing of openness in the Open, thinking touches on a sphere that cannot yet be explicated here. Only this
much should be noted, that if the nature of the unconcealedness of
beings belongs in any way to Being itself (cf. *Being and Time*, § 44*),
then Being, by way of its own nature, lets the place of openness (the
lighting-clearing of the There) happen, and introduces it as a place of
the sort in which each being emerges or arises in its own way.

Truth happens only by establishing itself in the conflict and sphere
opened up by truth itself. Because truth is the opposition of clearing
and concealing, there belongs to it what is here to be called establishing. But truth does not exist in itself beforehand, somewhere among
the stars, only later to descend elsewhere among beings. This is impossible for the reason alone that it is after all only the openness of beings
that first affords the possibility of a somewhere and of a place filled by
present beings. Clearing of openness and establishment in the Open
belong together. They are the same single nature of the happening of
truth. This happening is historical in many ways.

One essential way in which truth establishes itself in the beings it has
opened up is truth setting itself into work. Another way in which truth
occurs is the act that founds a political state. Still another way in which
truth comes to shine forth is the nearness of that which is not simply a
being, but the being that is most of all. Still another way in which truth
grounds itself is the essential sacrifice. Still another way in which truth
becomes is the thinker's questioning, which, as the thinking of Being,

---

* Martin Heidegger, *Being and Time*, translated by John Macquarrie and
Edward Robinson, New York: Harper & Row, 1962.—Tʀ.

names Being in its question-worthiness. By contrast, science is not an original happening of truth, but always the cultivation of a domain of truth already opened, specifically by apprehending and confirming that which shows itself to be possibly and necessarily correct within that field. When and insofar as a science passes beyond correctness and goes on to a truth, which means that it arrives at the essential disclosure of what is as such, it is philosophy.

Because it is in the nature of truth to establish itself within that which is, in order thus first to become truth, therefore the impulse toward the work lies in the nature of truth as one of truth's distinctive possibilities by which it can itself occur as being in the midst of beings.

The establishing of truth in the work is the bringing forth of a being such as never was before and will never come to be again. The bringing forth places this being in the Open in such a way that what is to be brought forth first clears the openness of the Open into which it comes forth. Where this bringing forth expressly brings the openness of beings, or truth, that which is brought forth is a work. Creation is such a bringing forth. As such a bringing, it is rather a receiving and an incorporating of a relation to unconcealedness. What, accordingly, does the createdness consist in? It may be elucidated by two essential determinations.

Truth establishes itself in the work. Truth is present only as the conflict between lighting and concealing in the opposition of world and earth. Truth wills to be established in the work as this conflict of world and earth. The conflict is not to be resolved in a being brought forth for the purpose, nor is it to be merely housed there; the conflict, on the contrary, is started by it. This being must therefore contain within itself the essential traits of the conflict. In the strife the unity of world and earth is won. As a world opens itself, it submits to the decision of an historical humanity the question of victory and defeat, blessing and curse, mastery and slavery. The dawning world brings out what is as yet undecided and measureless, and thus discloses the hidden necessity of measure and decisiveness.

But as a world opens itself the earth comes to rise up. It stands forth as that which bears all, as that which is sheltered in its own law and always wrapped up in itself. World demands its decisiveness and its measure and lets beings attain to the Open of their paths. Earth, bearing and jutting, strives to keep itself closed and to entrust everything to its law. The conflict is not a rift (*Riss*) as a mere cleft is ripped open;

rather, it is the intimacy with which opponents belong to each other. This rift carries the opponents into the source of their unity by virtue of their common ground. It is a basic design, an outline sketch, that draws the basic features of the rise of the lighting of beings. This rift does not let the opponents break apart; it brings the opposition of measure and boundary into their common outline.

Truth establishes itself as a strife within a being that is to be brought forth only in such a way that the conflict opens up in this being, that is, this being is itself brought into the rift-design. The rift-design is the drawing together, into a unity, of sketch and basic design, breach and outline. Truth establishes itself in a being in such a way, indeed, that this being itself occupies the Open of truth. This occupying, however, can happen only if what is to be brought forth, the rift, entrusts itself to the self-secluding factor that juts up in the Open. The rift must set itself back into the heavy weight of stone, the dumb hardness of wood, the dark glow of colors. As the earth takes the rift back into itself, the rift is first set forth into the Open and thus placed, that is, set, within that which towers up into the Open as self-closing and sheltering.

The strife that is brought into the rift and thus set back into the earth and thus fixed in place is *figure, shape, Gestalt.* Createdness of the work means: truth's being fixed in place in the figure. Figure is the structure in whose shape the rift composes and submits itself. This composed rift is the fitting or joining of the shining of truth. What is here called figure, *Gestalt*, is always to be thought in terms of the particular placing (*Stellen*) and framing or framework (*Ge-stell*) as which the work occurs when it sets itself up and sets itself forth.

In the creation of a work, the conflict, as rift, must be set back into the earth, and the earth itself must be set forth and used as the self-closing factor. This use, however, does not use up or misuse the earth as matter, but rather sets it free to be nothing but itself. This use of the earth is a working with it that, to be sure, looks like the employment of matter in handicraft. Hence the appearance that artistic creation is also an activity of handicraft. It never is. But it is at all times a use of the earth in the fixing in place of truth in the figure. In contrast, the making of equipment is never directly the effecting of the happening of truth. The production of equipment is finished when a material has been so formed as to be ready for use. For equipment to be ready means that it is dismissed beyond itself, to be used up in serviceability.

Not so when a work is created. This becomes clear in the light of the second characterstic, which may be introduced here.

The readiness of equipment and the createdness of the work agree in this, that in each case something is produced. But in contrast to all other modes of production, the work is distinguished by being created so that its createdness is part of the created work. But does not this hold true for everything brought forth, indeed for anything that has in any way come to be? Everything brought forth surely has this endowment of having been brought forth, if it has any endowment at all. Certainly. But in the work, createdness is expressly created into the created being, so that it stands out from it, from the being thus brought forth, in an expressly particular way. If this is how matters stand, then we must also be able to discover and experience the createdness explicitly in the work.

The emergence of createdness from the work does not mean that the work is to give the impression of having been made by a great artist. The point is not that the created being be certified as the performance of a capable person, so that the producer is thereby brought to public notice. It is not the "N. N. fecit" that is to be made known. Rather, the simple "factum est" is to be held forth into the Open by the work: namely this, that unconcealedness of what is has happened here, and that as this happening it happens here for the first time; or that such a work *is* at all rather than is not. The thrust that the work as this work is, and the uninterruptedness of this plain thrust, constitute the steadfastness of the work's self-subsistence. Precisely where the artist and the process and the circumstances of the genesis of the work remain unknown, this thrust, this *"that* it is" of createdness, emerges into view most purely from the work.

To be sure, "that" it is made is a property also of all equipment that is available and in use. But this "that" does not become prominent in the equipment; it disappears in usefulness. The more handy a piece of equipment is, the more inconspicuous it remains that, for example, such a hammer is and the more exclusively does the equipment keep itself in its equipmentality. In general, of everything present to us, we can note that it *is*; but this also, if it is noted at all, is noted only soon to fall into oblivion, as is the wont of everything commonplace. And what is more commonplace than this, that a being is? In a work, by contrast, this fact, that it *is* as a work, is just what is unusual. The event of its being created does not simply reverberate through the work; rather, the work casts before itself the eventful fact that the work is as this work, and it has constantly this fact about itself. The more essentially the work opens itself, the more luminous becomes the uniqueness of the fact that it is rather than is not. The more essentially this thrust comes into the Open, the stronger and more solitary the work becomes. In the bringing forth of the work there lies this offering "that it be."

The question of the work's createdness ought to have brought us nearer to its workly character and therewith to its reality. Createdness revealed itself as the conflict's being fixed in place in the figure by means of the rift. Createdness here is itself expressly created into the work and stands as the silent thrust into the Open of the "that." But the work's reality does not exhaust itself even in createdness. However, this view of the nature of the work's createdness now enables us to take the step toward which everything thus far said tends.

The more solitarily the work, fixed in the figure, stands on its own and the more cleanly it seems to cut all ties to human beings, the more simply does the thrust come into the Open that such a work *is*, and the more essentially is the extraordinary thrust to the surface and the long-familiar thrust down. But this multiple thrusting is nothing violent, for the more purely the work is itself transported into the openness of beings—an openness opened by itself—the more simply does it transport us into this openness and thus at the same time transport us out of the realm of the ordinary. To submit to this displacement means: to transform our accustomed ties to world and to earth and henceforth to restrain all usual doing and prizing, knowing and looking, in order to stay within the truth that is happening in the work. Only the restraint of this staying lets what is created be the work that it is. This letting the work be a work we call the preserving of the work. It is only for such preserving that the work yields itself in its createdness as actual, i.e., now: present in the manner of a work.

Just as a work cannot be without being created but is essentially in need of creators, so what is created cannot itself come into being without those who preserve it.

However, if a work does not find preservers, does not at once find them such as respond to the truth happening in the work, this does not at all mean that the work may also be a work without preservers. Being a work, it always remains tied to preservers, even and particularly when it is still only waiting for preservers and only pleads and waits for them to enter into its truth. Even the oblivion into which the work can sink is not nothing; it is still a preservation. It feeds on the work. Preserving the work means: standing within the openness of beings that happens in the work. This "standing-within" of preservation, however, is a knowing. Yet knowing does not consist in mere information and notions about something. He who truly knows what is, knows what he wills to do in the midst of what is.

The willing here referred to, which neither merely applies knowledge nor decides beforehand, is thought of in terms of the basic experience of thinking in *Being and Time*. Knowing that remains a willing, and willing that remains a knowing, is the existing human being's entrance into and compliance with the unconcealedness of Being. The resoluteness intended in *Being and Time* is not the deliberate action of a subject, but the opening up of human being, out of its captivity in that which is, to the openness of Being.* However, in existence, man does not proceed from some inside to some outside; rather, the nature of *Existenz* is out-standing standing-within the essential sunderance of the clearing of beings. Neither in the creation mentioned before nor in the willing mentioned now do we think of the performance or act of a subject striving toward himself as his self-set goal.

Willing is the sober resolution of that existential self-transcendence which exposes itself to the openness of beings as it is set into the work. In this way, standing-within is brought under law. Preserving the work, as knowing, is a sober standing-within the extraordinary awesomeness of the truth that is happening in the work.

This knowledge, which as a willing makes its home in the work's truth and only thus remains a knowing, does not deprive the work of its independence, does not drag it into the sphere of mere experience, and does not degrade it to the role of a stimulator of experience. Preserving the work does not reduce people to their private experiences, but brings them into affiliation with the truth happening in the work. Thus it grounds being for and with one another as the historical standing-out of human existence in reference to unconcealedness. Most of all, knowledge in the manner of preserving is far removed from that merely aestheticizing connoisseurship of the work's formal aspects, its qualities and charms. Knowing as having seen is a being resolved; it

---

* The word for resoluteness, *Entschlossenheit*, if taken literally, would mean "unclosedness."—Tr.

is standing within the conflict that the work has fitted into the rift.

The proper way to preserve the work is cocreated and prescribed only and exclusively by the work. Preserving occurs at different levels of knowledge, with always differing degrees of scope, constancy, and lucidity. When works are offered for merely artistic enjoyment, this does not yet prove that they stand in preservation as works.

As soon as the thrust into the extraordinary is parried and captured by the sphere of familiarity and connoisseurship, the art business has begun. Even a painstaking handing on of works to posterity, all scientific efforts to regain them, no longer reach the work's own being, but only a recollection of it. But even this recollection may still offer to the work a place from which it joins in shaping history. The work's own peculiar reality, on the other hand, is brought to bear only where the work is preserved in the truth that happens by the work itself.

The work's reality is determined in its basic features by the nature of the work's being. We can now return to our opening question: how do matters stand with the work's thingly feature that is to guarantee its immediate reality? They stand so that now we no longer raise this question about the work's thingly element; for as long as we ask it, we take the work directly and as a foregone conclusion, as an object that is simply there. In that way we never question in terms of the work, but in our own terms. In our terms—we, who then do not let the work be a work but view it as an object that is supposed to produce this or that state of mind in us.

But what looks like the thingly element, in the sense of our usual thing-concepts, in the work taken as object, is, seen from the perspective of the work, its earthy character. The earth juts up within the work because the work exists as something in which truth is at work and because truth occurs only by installing itself within a particular being. In the earth, however, as essentially self-closing, the openness of the Open finds the greatest resistance (to the Open) and thereby the site of the Open's constant stand, where the figure must be fixed in place.

Was it then superfluous, after all, to enter into the question of the thingly character of the thing? By no means. To be sure, the work's work-character cannot be defined in terms of its thingly character, but as against that the question about the thing's thingly character can be brought into the right course by way of a knowledge of the work's work-character. This is no small matter, if we recollect that those ancient, traditional modes of thought attack the thing's thingly character and make it subject to an interpretation of what is as a whole, which remains unfit to apprehend the nature of equipment and of the work, and which makes us equally blind to the original nature of truth.

To determine the thing's thingness neither consideration of the bearer of properties is adequate, nor that of the manifold of sense data in their unity, and least of all that of the matter-form structure regarded by itself, which is derived from equipment. Anticipating a meaningful and weighty interpretation of the thingly character of things, we must aim at the thing's belonging to the earth. The nature of the earth, in its free and unhurried bearing and self-closure, reveals itself, however, only in the earth's jutting into a world, in the opposition of the two. This conflict is fixed in place in the figure of the work and becomes manifest by it. What holds true of equipment—namely that we come to know its equipmental character specifically only through the work itself —also holds of the thingly character of the thing. The fact that we never know thingness directly, and if we know it at all, then only vaguely and thus require the work—this fact proves indirectly that in the work's work-being the happening of truth, the opening up or disclosure of what is, is at work.

But, we might finally object, if the work is indeed to bring thingness cogently into the Open, must it not then itself—and indeed before its own creation and for the sake of its creation—have been brought into a relation with the things of earth, with nature? Someone who was bound to know what he was talking about, Albrecht Dürer, did after all make the well-known remark: "For in truth, art lies hidden within nature; he who can wrest it from her, has it." "Wrest" here means to draw out the rift and to draw the design with the drawing-pen on the drawing-board.* But we at once raise the counterquestion: how can the rift-design be drawn out if it is not brought into the Open by the creative sketch as a rift, which is to say, brought out beforehand as a conflict of measure and unmeasure? True, there lies hidden in nature a rift-design, a measure and a boundary and, tied to it, a capacity for bringing forth—that is, art. But it is equally certain that this art hidden in nature becomes manifest only through the work, because it lies originally in the work.

The trouble we are taking over the reality of the work is intended as spadework for discovering art and the nature of art in the actual work. The question concerning the nature of art, the way toward knowledge

---

* "Reissen heisst hier Herausholen des Risses und den Riss reissen mit der Reissfeder auf dem Reissbrett."

of it, is first to be placed on a firm ground again. The answer to the question, like every genuine answer, is only the final result of the last step in a long series of questions. Each answer remains in force as an answer only as long as it is rooted in questioning.

The reality of the work has become not only clearer for us in the light of its work-being, but also essentially richer. The preservers of a work belong to its createdness with an essentiality equal to that of the creators. But it is the work that makes the creators possible in their nature, and that by its own nature is in need of preservers. If art is the origin of the work, this means that art lets those who naturally belong together at work, the creator and the preserver, originate, each in his own nature. What, however, is art itself that we call it rightly an origin?

In the work, the happening of truth is at work and, indeed, at work according to the manner of a work. Accordingly the nature of art was defined to begin with as the setting-into-work of truth. Yet this definition is intentionally ambiguous. It says on the one hand: art is the fixing in place of a self-establishing truth in the figure. This happens in creation as the bringing forth of the unconcealedness of what is. Setting-into-work, however, also means: the bringing of work-being into movement and happening. This happens as preservation. Thus art is: the creative preserving of truth in the work. *Art then is the becoming and happening of truth.* Does truth, then, arise out of nothing? It does indeed if by nothing is meant the mere not of that which is, and if we here think of that which is as an object present in the ordinary way, which thereafter comes to light and is challenged by the existence of the work as only presumptively a true being. Truth is never gathered from objects that are present and ordinary. Rather, the opening up of the Open, and the clearing of what is, happens only as the openness is projected, sketched out, that makes its advent in thrownness.*

---

* Thrownness, *Geworfenheit*, is understood in *Being and Time* as an existential characteristic of *Dasein*, human being, its thatness, its "that it is," and it refers to the facticity of human being's being handed over to itself, its being on its own responsibility; as long as human being is what it is, it is thrown, cast, "im Wurf." Projection, *Entwurf*, on the other hand, is a second existential character of human being, referring to its driving forward toward its own possibility of being. It takes the form of understanding, which the author speaks of as the mode of being of human being in which human being *is* in its possibilities *as* possibilities. It is not the mere having of a preconceived plan, but is the projecting of possibility in human being that occurs antecedently to all plans and makes planning possible. Human being is both thrown and projected; it is thrown project, factical directedness toward possibilities of being.—Tr.

Truth, as the clearing and concealing of what is, happens in being composed, as a poet composes a poem. *All art*, as the letting happen of the advent of the truth of what is, is, as such, *essentially poetry*. The nature of art, on which both the art work and the artist depend, is the setting-itself-into-work of truth. It is due to art's poetic nature that, in the midst of what is, art breaks open an open place, in whose openness everything is other than usual. By virtue of the projected sketch set into the work of the unconcealedness of what is, which casts itself toward us, everything ordinary and hitherto existing becomes an unbeing. This unbeing has lost the capacity to give and keep being as measure. The curious fact here is that the work in no way affects hitherto existing entities by causal connections. The working of the work does not consist in the taking effect of a cause. It lies in a change, happening from out of the work, of the unconcealedness of what is, and this means, of Being.

Poetry, however, is not an aimless imagining of whimsicalities and not a flight of mere notions and fancies into the realm of the unreal. What poetry, as illuminating projection, unfolds of unconcealedness and projects ahead into the design of the figure, is the Open which poetry lets happen, and indeed in such a way that only now, in the midst of beings, the Open brings beings to shine and ring out. If we fix our vision on the nature of the work and its connection with the happening of the truth of what is, it becomes questionable whether the nature of poetry, and this means at the same time the nature of projection, can be adequately thought of in terms of the power of imagination.

The nature of poetry, which has now been ascertained very broadly —but not on that account vaguely, may here be kept firmly in mind as something worthy of questioning, something that still has to be thought through.

If all art is in essence poetry, then the arts of architecture, painting, sculpture, and music must be traced back to poesy. That is pure arbitrariness. It certainly is, as long as we mean that those arts are varieties of the art of language, if it is permissible to characterize poesy by that easily misinterpretable title. But poesy is only one mode of the lighting projection of truth, i.e., of poetic composition in this wider sense. Nevertheless, the linguistic work, the poem in the narrower sense, has a privileged position in the domain of the arts.

To see this, only the right concept of language is needed. In the current view, language is held to be a kind of communication. It serves for verbal exchange and agreement, and in general for communicating. But language is not only and not primarily an audible and written expression of what is to be communicated. It not only puts forth in words and statements what is overtly or covertly intended to be communicated; language alone brings what is, as something that is, into the Open for the first time. Where there is no language, as in the being of stone, plant, and animal, there is also no openness of what is, and consequently no openness either of that which is not and of the empty.

Language, by naming beings for the first time, first brings beings to word and to appearance. Only this naming nominates beings *to* their being *from out of* their being. Such saying is a projecting of the clearing, in which announcement is made of what it is that beings come into the Open *as*. Projecting is the release of a throw by which unconcealedness submits and infuses itself into what is as such. This projective announcement forthwith becomes a renunciation of all the dim confusion in which what is veils and withdraws itself.

Projective saying is poetry: the saying of world and earth, the saying of the arena of their conflict and thus of the place of all nearness and remoteness of the gods. Poetry is the saying of the unconcealedness of what is. Actual language at any given moment is the happening of this saying, in which a people's world historically arises for it and the earth is preserved as that which remains closed. Projective saying is saying which, in preparing the sayable, simultaneously brings the unsayable as such into a world. In such saying, the concepts of an historical people's nature, i.e., of its belonging to world history, are formed for that folk, before it.

Poetry is thought of here in so broad a sense and at the same time in such intimate unity of being with language and word, that we must leave open whether art, in all its modes from architecture to poesy, exhausts the nature of poetry.

Language itself is poetry in the essential sense. But since language is the happening in which for man beings first disclose themselves to him each time as beings, poesy—or poetry in the narrower sense—is the most original form of poetry in the essential sense. Language is not poetry because it is the primal poesy; rather, poesy takes place in language because language preserves the original nature of poetry. Building and plastic creation, on the other hand, always happen already, and happen only, in the Open of saying and naming. It is the Open that pervades and guides them. But for this very reason they remain their own ways and modes in which truth orders itself into work. They are an ever special poetizing within the clearing of what is, which has already happened unnoticed in language.

Art, as the setting-into-work of truth, is poetry. Not only the creation of the work is poetic, but equally poetic, though in its own way, is the preserving of the work; for a work is in actual effect as a work only when we remove ourselves from our commonplace routine and move into what is disclosed by the work, so as to bring our own nature itself to take a stand in the truth of what is.

The nature of art is poetry. The nature of poetry, in turn, is the founding of truth. We understand founding here in a triple sense: founding as bestowing, founding as grounding, and founding as beginning. Founding, however, is actual only in preserving. Thus to each mode of founding there corresponds a mode of preserving. We can do no more now than to present this structure of the nature of art in a few strokes, and even this only to the extent that the earlier characterization of the nature of the work offers an initial hint.

The setting-into-work of truth thrusts up the unfamiliar and extraordinary and at the same time thrusts down the ordinary and what we believe to be such. The truth that discloses itself in the work can never be proved or derived from what went before. What went before is refuted in its exclusive reality by the work. What art founds can therefore never be compensated and made up for by what is already present and available. Founding is an overflow, an endowing, a bestowal.

The poetic projection of truth that sets itself into work as figure is also never carried out in the direction of an indeterminate void. Rather, in the work, truth is thrown toward the coming preservers, that is, toward an historical group of men. What is thus cast forth is, however, never an arbitrary demand. Genuinely poetic projection is the opening up or disclosure of that into which human being as historical is already cast. This is the earth and, for an historical people, its earth, the self-closing ground on which it rests together with everything that it already is, though still hidden from itself. It is, however, its world, which prevails in virtue of the relation of human being to the unconcealedness of Being. For this reason, everything with which man is endowed must, in the projection, be drawn up from the closed ground and expressly set upon this ground. In this way the ground is first grounded as the bearing ground.

All creation, because it is such a drawing-up, is a drawing, as of water from a spring. Modern subjectivism, to be sure, immediately misinterprets creation, taking it as the self-sovereign subject's performance of genius. The founding of truth is a founding not only in the sense of free bestowal, but at the same time foundation in the sense of this ground-laying grounding. Poetic projection comes from Nothing in this respect, that it never takes its gift from the ordinary and traditional. But it never comes from Nothing in that what is projected by it is only the withheld vocation of the historical being of man itself.

Bestowing and grounding have in themselves the unmediated character of what we call a beginning. Yet this unmediated character of a beginning, the peculiarity of a leap out of the unmediable, does not exclude but rather includes the fact that the beginning prepares itself for the longest time and wholly inconspicuously. A genuine beginning, as a leap, is always a head start, in which everything to come is already leaped over, even if as something disguised. The beginning already contains the end latent within itself. A genuine beginning, however, has nothing of the neophyte character of the primitive. The primitive because it lacks the bestowing, grounding leap and head start, is always futureless. It is not capable of releasing anything more from itself because it contains nothing more than that in which it is caught.

A beginning, on the contrary, always contains the undisclosed abundance of the unfamiliar and extraordinary, which means that it also contains strife with the familiar and ordinary. Art as poetry is founding, in the third sense of instigation of the strife of truth: founding as beginning. Always when that which is as a whole demands, as what is, itself, a grounding in openness, art attains to its historical nature as foundation. This foundation happened in the West for the first time in Greece. What was in the future to be called Being was set into work, setting the standard. The realm of beings thus opened up was then transformed into a being in the sense of God's creation. This happened in the Middle Ages. This kind of being was again transformed at the beginning and in the course of the modern age. Beings became objects that could be controlled and seen through by calculation. At each time a new and essential world arose. At each time the openness of what is had to be established in beings themselves, by the fixing in place of truth in figure. At each time there happened unconcealedness of what is. Unconcealedness sets itself into work, a setting which is accomplished by art.

Whenever art happens—that is, whenever there is a beginning—a thrust enters history, history either begins or starts over again. History means here not a sequence in time of events of whatever sort, however important. History is the transporting of a people into its appointed task as entrance into that people's endowment.

Art is the setting-into-work of truth. In this proposition an essential ambiguity is hidden, in which truth is at once the subject and the object of the setting. But subject and object are unsuitable names here. They keep us from thinking precisely this ambiguous nature, a task that no longer belongs to this consideration. Art is historical, and as historical it is the creative preserving of truth in the work. Art happens as poetry. Poetry is founding in the triple sense of bestowing, grounding, and beginning. Art, as founding, is essentially historical. This means not only that art has a history in the external sense that in the course of time it, too, appears along with many other things, and in the process changes and passes away and offers changing aspects for historiology. Art is history in the essential sense that it grounds history.

Art lets truth originate. Art, founding preserving, is the spring that leaps to the truth of what is, in the work. To originate something by a leap, to bring something into being from out of the source of its nature in a founding leap—this is what the word origin (German *Ursprung*, literally, primal leap) means.

The origin of the work of art—that is, the origin of both the creators and the preservers, which is to say of a people's historical existence, is art. This is so because art is by nature an origin: a distinctive way in which truth comes into being, that is, becomes historical.

We inquire into the nature of art. Why do we inquire in this way? We inquire in this way in order to be able to ask more truly whether art is or is not an origin in our historical existence, whether and under what conditions it can and must be an origin.

Such reflection cannot force art and its coming-to-be. But this reflective knowledge is the preliminary and therefore indispensable preparation for the becoming of art. Only such knowledge prepares its space for art, their way for the creators, their location for the preservers.

In such knowledge, which can only grow slowly, the question is decided whether art can be an origin and then must be a head start, or whether it is to remain a mere appendix and then can only be carried along as a routine cultural phenomenon.

Are we in our existence historically at the origin? Do we know, which means do we give heed to, the nature of the origin? Or, in our relation to art, do we still merely make appeal to a cultivated acquaintance with the past?

For this either-or and its decision there is an infallible sign. Hölderlin, the poet—whose work still confronts the Germans as a test to be stood—named it in saying:

> Schwer verlässt
> was nahe dem Ursprung wohnet, den Ort.

> Reluctantly
> that which dwells near its origin departs.
> —"The Journey," verses 18–19

Epilogue

The foregoing reflections are concerned with the riddle of art, the riddle that art itself is. They are far from claiming to solve the riddle. The task is to see the riddle.

Almost from the time when specialized thinking about art and the artist began, this thought was called aesthetic. Aesthetics takes the work of art as an object, the object of *aisthesis*, of sensuous apprehension in the wide sense. Today we call this apprehension experience. The way in which man experiences art is supposed to give information about its nature. Experience is the source that is standard not only for art appreciation and enjoyment, but also for artistic creation. Everything is an experience. Yet perhaps experience is the element in which art dies. The dying occurs so slowly that it takes a few centuries.

To be sure, people speak of immortal works of art and of art as an eternal value. Speaking this way means using that language which does not trouble with precision in all essential matters, for fear that in the end to be precise would call for—thinking. And is there any greater fear today than that of thinking? Does this talk about immortal works and the eternal value of art have any content or substance? Or are these merely the half-baked clichés of an age when great art, together with its nature, has departed from among men?

In the most comprehensive reflection on the nature of art that the West possesses—comprehensive because it stems from metaphysics—namely Hegel's *Vorlesungen über die Ästhetik*, the following propositions occur:

> Art no longer counts for us as the highest manner in which truth obtains existence for itself.
>
> One may well hope that art will continue to advance and per-

fect itself, but its form has ceased to be the highest need of the spirit.

In all these relationships art is and remains for us, on the side of its highest vocation, something past.*

The judgment that Hegel passes in these statements cannot be evaded by pointing out that since Hegel's lectures in aesthetics were given for the last time during the winter of 1828–29 at the University of Berlin, we have seen the rise of many new art works and new art movements. Hegel never meant to deny this possibility. But the question remains: is art still an essential and necessary way in which that truth happens which is decisive for our historical existence, or is art no longer of this character? If, however, it is such no longer, then there remains the question why this is so. The truth of Hegel's judgment has not yet been decided; for behind this verdict there stands Western thought since the Greeks, which thought corresponds to a truth of beings that has already happened. Decision upon the judgment will be made, when it is made, from and about this truth of what is. Until then the judgment remains in force. But for that very reason the question is necessary whether the truth that the judgment declares is final and conclusive and what follows if it is.

Such questions, which solicit us more or less definitely, can be asked only after we have first taken into consideration the nature of art. We attempt to take a few steps by posing the question of the origin of the art work. The problem is to bring to view the work-character of the work. What the word "origin" here means is thought by way of the nature of truth.

The truth of which we have spoken does not coincide with that which is generally recognized under the name and assigned to cognition and science as a quality in order to distinguish from it the beautiful and the good, which function as names for the values of nontheoretical activities.

Truth is the unconcealedness of that which is as something that is. Truth is the truth of Being. Beauty does not occur alongside and apart from this truth. When truth sets itself into the work, it appears. Appearance—as this being of truth in the work and as work—is beauty. Thus the beautiful belongs to the advent of truth, truth's taking of its

* In the original pagination of the *Vorlesungen*, which is repeated in the Jubiläum edition edited by H. Glockner (Stuttgart, 1953), these passages occur at X, 1, 134; 135; 16. All are in vol. 12 of this edition.—TR.

place. It does not exist merely relative to pleasure and purely as its object. The beautiful does lie in form, but only because the *forma* once took its light from Being as the isness of what is. Being at that time made its advent as *eidos*. The *idea* fits itself into the *morphe*. The *sunolon*, the unitary whole of *morphe* and *hule*, namely the *ergon, is* in the manner of *energeia*. This mode of presence becomes the *actualitas* of the *ens actu*. The *actualitas* becomes reality. Reality becomes objectivity. Objectivity becomes experience. In the way in which, for the world determined by the West, that which is, is as the real, there is concealed a peculiar confluence of beauty with truth. The history of the nature of Western art corresponds to the change of the nature of truth. This is no more intelligible in terms of beauty taken for itself than it is in terms of experience, supposing that the metaphysical concept of art reaches to art's nature.

Addendum

On page 688 and 695 a real difficulty will force itself on the attentive reader: it looks as if the remarks about the "fixing in place of truth" and the "letting happen of the advent of truth" could never be brought into accord. For "fixing in place" implies a willing which blocks and thus prevents the advent of truth. In *letting*-happen on the other hand, there is manifested a compliance and thus, as it were, a nonwilling, which clears the way for the advent of truth.

The difficulty is resolved if we understand fixing in place in the sense intended throughout the entire text of the essay, above all in the key specification "setting-into-work." Also correlated with "to place" and "to set" is "to lay"; all three meanings are still intended jointly by the Latin *ponere*.

We must think of "to place" in the sense of *thesis*. Thus on page 686 the statement is made, "Setting and taking possession are here everywhere (!) drawn from the Greek sense of *thesis*, which means a setting up in the unconcealed." The Greek "setting" means placing, as for instance, letting a statue be set up. It means laying, laying down an oblation. Placing and laying have the sense of bringing *here* into the unconcealed, bringing *forth* into what is present, that is, letting or causing to lie forth. Setting and placing here never mean the modern concept of the summoning of things to be placed over against the self (the ego-subject). The standing of the statue (i.e., the presence of the radiance facing us) is different from the standing of what stands over against us in the sense of the object. "Standing"—(cf. p. 666)—is the constancy of the showing or shining. By contrast, thesis, antithesis, and synthesis in the dialectic of Kant and German idealism mean a placing or putting within the sphere of subjectivity of consciousness. Accordingly, Hegel

—correctly in terms of his position—interpreted the Greek *thesis* in the sense of the immediate positing of the object. Setting in this sense, therefore, is for him still untrue, because it is not yet mediated by antithesis and synthesis. (Cf. "Hegel und die Griechen" in the *Festschrift* for H. G. Gadamer, 1960).

But if, in the context of our essay on the work of art, we keep in mind the Greek sense of *thesis*—to let lie forth in its radiance and presence —then the "fix" in "fix in place" can never have the sense of rigid, motionless, and secure.

"Fixed" means outlined, admitted into the boundary (*peras*), brought into the outline—(cf. p. 687). The boundary in the Greek sense does not block off; rather, being itself brought forth, it first brings to its radiance what is present. Boundary sets free into the unconcealed; by its contour in the Greek light the mountain stands in its towering and repose. The boundary that fixes and consolidates is in this repose —repose in the fullness of motion—all this holds of the work in the Greek sense of *ergon*; this work's "being" is *energeia*, which gathers infinitely more movement within itself than do the modern "energies."

Thus the "fixing in place" of truth, rightly understood, can never run counter to the "letting happen." For one thing, this "letting" is nothing passive but a doing in the highest degree (cf. "Wissenschaft und Besinnung" in *Vorträge und Aufsätze*, p. 49)* in the sense of *thesis*, a "working" and "willing" which in the present essay—(p. 691 is characterized as the "existing human being's entrance into and compliance with the unconcealedness of Being." For another thing, the "happen" in the letting happen of truth is the movement that prevails in the clearing *and* concealing or more precisely in their union, that is to say, the movement of the lighting of self-concealment as such, from which again all self-lighting stems. What is more, this "movement" even requires a fixing in place in the sense of a bringing forth, where the bringing is to be understood in the sense given it on page 687, in that the creative bringing forth "is rather a receiving and an incorporating of a relation to unconcealedness."

In accordance with what has so far been explained, the meaning of

---

* The reference is to a discussion of the German *Tun*, doing, which points to the core of its meaning as a laying forth, placing here, bringing here and bringing forth—"working" in the sense either of something bringing itself forth out of itself into presence or of man performing the bringing here and bringing forth of something. Both are a way in which something that is present presences.—TR.

the noun "*Ge-stell*," frame, framing, framework, used on page 688, is thus defined: the gathering of the bringing-forth, of the letting-come-forth-here into the rift-design as bounding outline (*peras*). The Greek sense of *morphe* as figure, *Gestalt*, is made clear by "*Ge-Stell*," "framing," so understood. Now the word "Ge-Stell," frame, which we used in later writings as the explicit key expression for the nature of modern technology, was indeed conceived in reference to that sense of frame (*not* in reference to such other senses as bookshelf or montage, which it also has). That context is essential, because related to the destiny of Being. Framing, as the nature of modern technology, derives from the Greek way of experiencing letting-lie-forth, *logos*, from the Greek *poiesis* and *thesis*. In setting up the frame, the framework—which now means in commandeering everything into assured availability—there sounds the claim of the *ratio reddenda*, i.e., of the *logon didonai*, but in such a way that today this claim that is made in framing takes control of the absolute, and the process of representation—of V*or-stellen* or putting forth—takes form, on the basis of the Greek perception, as making secure, fixing in place.

When we hear the words "fix in place" and "framing" or "framework" in "The Origin of the Work of Art," we must, on the one hand, put out of mind the modern meaning of placing or framing, and yet at the same time we must not fail to note that, and in what way, the Being that defines the modern period—Being as framing, framework—stems from the Western destiny of Being and has not been thought *up* by philosophers but rather thought to thinking men (cf. V*orträge und Aufsätze*, pp. 28 and 49*).

---

* The reference to page 49 is to the conception of doing, as given in the previous note. The passage on page 28 of V*orträge und Aufsätze* appears in the essay "*Die Frage nach der Technik*." The "*-Stell*" in "*Ge-Stell*" comes from the German "stellen," a transtive verb meaning to place, put, set, stand, arrange. "*Ge-Stell*," if taken literally, would then be the collective name for all sorts of placing, putting, setting, arranging, ordering, or in general, putting in place. Heidegger pushes this collective reading further, in the light of his interpretation of early Greek language and thought, his general concept of truth and the history of Being, and his view of the work of Being in summoning and gathering men to their destiny. The gathering agent today is the call that challenges men to put everything that discloses itself into the position of stock, resource, material for technological processing. For this call, this gathering power, Heidegger makes use of this collective word which expresses the gathering of all forms of ordering things as resources—*das Ge-Stell*, the collective unity of all the putting, placing, setting, standing, arraying, arranging that goes into modern technology and the life oriented to it. The "*stellen*," the setting, placing, in the word, derives from an older mode, that of *poiesis*, which lets

It is still our burden to discuss the specifications given briefly on pages 686–87 about the "establishing" and "self-establishing of truth in that which is, in beings." Here again we must avoid understanding "establish" in the modern sense and in the manner of the lecture on technology as "organize" and "finish or complete." Rather, "establishing" recalls the "impulse of truth toward the work," mentioned on page 687, the impulse that, in the midst of beings, truth should itself be in the manner of work, should itself occur as being.

If we recollect how truth as unconcealedness of beings means nothing but the presence of beings as such, that is, *Being*—see page 695—then talk about the self-establishing of truth, that is, of Being, in all that is, touches on the problem of the ontological difference.* For this reason there is the note of caution on page 686 of "The Origin of the Work of Art": "In referring to this self-establishing of openness in the Open, thinking touches on a sphere that cannot yet be explicated here." The whole essay, "The Origin of the Work of Art," deliberately yet tacitly moves on the path of the question of the nature of Being. Reflection on what *art* may be is completely and decidedly determined only in regard to the question of *Being*. Art is considered neither an area of cultural achievement nor an appearance of spirit; it belongs to the *disclosure of appropriation* by way of which the "meaning of Being" (cf. *Being and Time*) can alone be defined. What art may be is one of the questions to which no answers are given in the essay. What gives the impression of such an answer are directions for questioning. (Cf. the first sentences of the Epilogue.)

Among these directions there are two *important hints*, on pages 694 and 699. In both places mention is made of an "ambiguity." On page 699 an "essential ambiguity" is noted in regard to the definition of art

---

what is present come forth into unconcealedness, as in the setting up of a statue in the temple precinct; yet both the modern technological setting up of things as resources and this ancient poetic setting up of them as bearing their world are modes of unconcealing, of truth as *aletheia*. They are not mere inventions of men or mere doings of men, but are phases in the history of the destiny of Being and of man in his historical situation in relation to Being. Contemporary man's technological "things" bear his technological "world" in their own distorted way—distorting man's earth, his heaven, his divinities, and, in the end, himself and his mortality. —Tr.

* Cf. *Identität und Differenz* (1957), pp. 37 ff.; English *Identity and Difference*, trans. by Joan Stambaugh (New York: Harper & Row, 1969), pp. 50 ff., 116 ff.

as "the setting-into-work of truth." In this ambiguity, truth is "subject" on the one hand and "object" on the other. *Both* descriptions remain "unsuitable." If truth is the "subject," then the definition "the setting-into-work of truth" means: "truth's setting itself into work"—compare pages 694 and 666. Art is then conceived in terms of disclosive appropriation. Being, however, is a call to man and is not without man. Accordingly, art is at the same time defined as the setting-into-work of truth, where truth *now* is "object" and art is human creating and preserving.

Within the *human* relation to art there results the second ambiguity of the setting-into-work of truth, which on page 694 was called creation and preservation. According to pages 693 and 683–84 the art *work* and the art*ist* rest "especially" in what goes on in art. In the heading "the setting-into-work of truth," in which it remains undecided but decid*able* who does the setting or in what way it occurs, there is concealed *the relation of Being and human being,* a relation which is unsuitably conceived even in this version—a distressing difficulty, which has been clear to me since *Being and Time* and has since been expressed in a variety of versions (cf. finally, "Zur Seinsfrage" and the present essay, p. 686, "Only this much should be noted, that . . . .").

The problematic context that prevails here then comes together at the proper place in the discussion, where the nature of language and of poetry is touched on, all this again only in regard to the belonging together of Being and Saying.

There is an unavoidable necessity for the reader, who naturally comes to the essay from without, to refrain at first and for a long time from perceiving and interpreting the facts of the case in terms of the reticent domain that is the source of what has to be thought. For the author himself, however, there remains the pressing need of speaking each time in the language most opportune for each of the various stations on his way.